The Complete Works of
WASHINGTON
IRVING

Richard Dilworth Rust
General Editor

A CHRONICLE OF THE
CONQUEST OF GRANADA

WASHINGTON
IRVING

A CHRONICLE OF THE CONQUEST OF GRANADA

BY FRAY ANTONIO AGAPIDA

Introduction by
Earl N. Harbert
Text Edited by
Miriam J. Shillingsburg

Twayne Publishers

Boston

1988

Published by Twayne Publishers
A Division of G.K. Hall & Co.

Copyright © 1988 by
G.K. Hall & Co.

The Complete Works of Washington Irving
Volume XIII

CENTER FOR EDITIONS OF
AMERICAN AUTHORS

AN APPROVED TEXT

MODERN LANGUAGE
ASSOCIATION OF AMERICA

Library of Congress Cataloging in Publication Data

Irving, Washington, 1783–1859.
A chronicle of the conquest of Granada / by Antonio Agapida
(Washington Irving) ; edited by Earl N. Harbert and Miriam
Shillingsburg,
p.   cm.—(The Complete works of Washington Irving ; v. 13)
Bibliography: p.
ISBN 0-8057-8513-2
1. Granada (Kingdom)—History—Spanish Conquest, 1476–1492.
I. Harbert, Earl N., 1934–   . II. Shillingsburg, Miriam Jones.
III. Title. IV. Series: Irving, Washington, 1783–1859. Works.
1969 ; v. 13.
DP122.I7 1988
946'.82'03—dc19   88-21008
                                                                            CIP

Manufactured in the United States of America

CONTENTS

APPENDIX

EDITORIAL APPENDIX

ACKNOWLEDGMENTS

Thanks is due to Mr. John Murray and Mrs. Virginia Murray of John Murray, Publishers, for the use of their manuscript of *Granada*; to the staff at the Pierpont Morgan Library for use of the holograph; to the staff at the Berg Collection, New York Public Library, for use of chapters 34–35.

Special acknowledgment is due Professors Anne King, Edward Clark, and Carmen McClendon, who assisted in manuscript collation; to Ms. Brenda Bridges and Mrs. Polly Hodges who input texts into computer-readable form; to the National Endowment for the Humanities, Mississippi State University, Tulane University, and Northeastern University's Research and Scholarship Development Fund, which provided generous financial support; to Ms. Marion Wright and Mrs. Eleanor Dudley who verified text transcriptions, to Ms. Susan Follett, Mr. Russell Kegley, and Professor Edwin Ellis who wrote the computer programs for text manipulation; to Professor Peter Shillingsburg who managed most of the computer operations and assisted in virtually all phases of text preparation; to Professor Richard D. Rust, whose encouragement and optimism inspired the completion of this volume; to Professors Edwin T. Bowden and Joseph McElrath who made suggestions for the "Textual Commentary"; and to Mr. Eric Partridge and Mr. Eric Harbert, who read earlier versions of the "Introduction."

Every serious student of Washington Irving will understand our debt to Professors Herbert L. Kleinfield and Henry A. Pochmann, who labored to make this edition a reality.

INTRODUCTION

The history of *A Chronicle of the Conquest of Granada* begins in 1826, and follows a confusing course through the next twenty-five years of Washington Irving's life. The idea of writing "a work for publication on the subject of the Conquest by Ferdinand and Isabella"[1] first came to him while he was completing his massive *A History of the Life and Voyages of Christopher Columbus* (4 vols., 1828). Among the manuscripts in the library of Obadiah Rich, pioneer American bibliographer and collector of books and papers concerned with the Americas, whose residence also provided a home for Irving in Madrid, the biographer found several engrossing accounts of the expulsion of the Moors from Spain during the fifteenth century. These documents diverted his attention for at least two months from the unfinished life of Columbus, which he had already offered as a whole book to John Murray of London, Irving's English publisher since the appearance of *The Sketch Book* in 1820.[2] Indeed, the author's enthusiasm over the materials for *Granada* led him to announce in a letter dated December 21, 1826, describing the Columbus manuscript to Murray, who had not yet seen it, that "I have also another work in hand, more in my own way, and which I could soon get ready for the press but I do not intend to publish it until after Columbus."[3]

As usual Irving's estimate proved wildly optimistic. During the next two years, while he wandered among the magnificient architectural remains of the old Moorish kingdom in Spain and immersed himself in other accounts of old Spanish history, especially those housed in the Archives of the Indies in Seville, which had been all but inaccessible to non-Spaniards, the American continued to rework the first rough outlines of *Granada*, now with a surer hand. Finally, in September, 1828, he was able to send off from Cadiz two manuscripts of his new book; one went to London, the other to America, and each contained the first half of a complete text. This preparation and transmission of duplicate manuscripts represented Irving's thoughtful method of attempting to guarantee copyright protection for both the English and American editions of his books. He hoped it would operate to safeguard his literary income from "pirates" on both sides of the Atlantic. As we shall see in the paragraphs below and in the "Textual Commentary," however, his method also presented the author with a special set of demands, the most obvious being a requirement for two copies of an authoritative text, from which printers in both London and Philadelphia could set editions of *Granada* at the same time. In the years before typewriting became common and before carbon-copy reproduction made duplication easy, Irving found his solution in the use of copyists, who attempted to reproduce by hand the author's original holograph version. Evidence of the employment of Spanish "Friars" in this task, as well as notations about attempts to correct the results of their work, can be found in the passages of Irving's Spanish diary that deal with *Granada*.[4]

A comprehensive discussion of the manuscripts themselves and some implications of Irving's practice for a modern editor appear in the "Textual Commentary." Here, it is enough to note that the English manuscript, delivered to Thomas Aspinwall in London—both the first and second parts—largely represents the product of paid copyists who had used Irving's American manuscript as their model. For whatever reasons, the writer preferred to send his own handwritten text to America, while the partially corrected copy went to London.

From the record it is clear that Irving's pragmatic arrangement caused him a number of artistic problems. A little more than two weeks after he had dispatched the first portion of the *Granada* manuscript to Aspinwall, the author followed it with a revision of the "Introduction" and a new opening paragraph for Chapter I (this time both in Irving's hand). This would prove to be only the first of many attempts to alter the form and contents of *Granada*, as we shall see; yet the real significance of such an early revision does not emerge clearly unless we understand that the writer himself could not anticipate any later opportunity to correct his work at the stage of printer's proof. Irving's continuing residence in Spain made his proofreading of *Granada* impractical; so, by sending manuscripts to England and America, Irving actually resigned from further authorial control of the 1829 printings. At the time that the revised "Introduction" was sent to Aspinwall, of course, John Murray had not yet accepted the manuscript for publication, and its author knew that particular care with the opening sections might help to effect a favorable judgment and perhaps more generous financial terms. Although the reasons are not entirely clear, it is interesting to note that neither the revised "Introduction" nor the new beginning for Chapter I became a part of the American edition of Granada.

Two packages containing duplicate second halves of the manuscript were sent off by Irving from Cadiz on October 18, 1828.[5] Just as the author intended, the House of Murray contracted for the English edition of *Granada*; while Carey, Lea, and Carey of Philadelphia agreed to print an American edition. These arrangements seemed to satisfy the writer, who tried to supply both printers. By putting two copies of the manuscript into transit, however, he had left himself without a complete version of *Granada* at hand, and this soon proved to be a cause of some embarrassment. Certainly Irving's method of insuring copyright protection by supplying both American and English publishers with manuscripts testifies to his competent grasp of business realities. In his personal arrangements, moreover, Irving went even further to guard against accidents; he instructed his London agent Aspinwall to send a set of Murray's proof sheets on to America as quickly as possible. With foresight that finally amounted to premonition, Irving wrote: "I wish, as the work is printed, you would procure a copy in sheets & foreward the sheets, peace [sic] meal, to America. I have sent a Ms. copy there, but it may miscarry."[6]

In view of such careful contingency planning, it now seems all the more surprising that Irving would have committed to the uncertainities of sea travel the only complete manuscripts in existence—a most unbusinesslike decision perhaps, yet one that would have caused no difficulty except for a related instance of human error, once again the author's own. The first indication of his mistake reached Irving during December, 1828, in a letter from Aspinwall.[7] As he composed his reply on the 20th, Irving explained the problem he was facing:

> In your letter of Decr 5 you say that several pages of my Ms. are wanting. . . . Had you sent me the Subject of the chapters missing—or a portion of the last page before & the first page after the hiatus—I should have been able to divine the purport of the passage wanting & to have Supplied it partly from my notes & partly from memory. At present I am utterly at a loss—I have no copy of the work by me—One copy was sent to London the other to America. . . . The work can go on printing, leaving a sheet vacant. The materials to fill it up can be made to fit exactly either by curtailing, or swelling out the Ms. I shall send. In the interim I shall rummage my papers over & over (I have done so twice already) and shall beat my brain to endeavor to guess at the passage wanting—Why the deuce could you not have sent me a sentence at least as a clew—something that gave a definite idea.[8]

As he attempted to separate the scribal copy from the holograph manuscript, Irving had erred. Both sets of Chapters 34 and 35 had been dispatched to America; and in consequence, Murray's manuscript remained incomplete.

Although the author did not fully comprehend what had happened, he acted quickly to supply what the printer needed. In the end Irving relied upon himself to provide new material. Before he actually began to compose these replacement chapters, however, the writer first sent off a letter with new instructions to his brother Ebenezer Irving, his agent in America: "I shall endeavor to devise some mode of getting out of the dilemma, but at all events, I wish you to have those chapters copied immediately, and forwarded by the first packet to Col. Thomas Aspinwall, American Consul, London."[9] Such a solution would require time, of course, before it could be effected; meanwhile the presses in London might be stopped, and the edition delayed, which would endanger the validity of the English copyright. Therefore, when Washington Irving, searching through his notes for *Grana-*

da, came upon "a memorandum in lead pencil stating the Contents of the two chapters," he forgot about the American copy and began to compose new pages to fill the "hiatus."[10] Within a few days, by December 24, 1828, the distraught writer had completed and sent off to Aspinwall new versions of the two missing chapters, and these new chapters took their places in the first English edition of 1829.[11] Of course the variant text of these chapters, as well as the revised "Introduction" and the opening paragraph of Chapter I (plus many other less obvious variants), made the English edition of 1829 distinctly and identifiably different from the first American edition of the same year. The considerable textual differences between them, however, seem to have caused their author very little concern.

In fact, his wisdom in providing the new materials to meet the crisis must have been gratifying to Irving when, two months later, he was informed that the second and final segment of the American manuscript apparently had probably been lost in yet another accident. The writer's irritation as he reported to Aspinwall is surely understandable: "I hope you have been punctual in forwarding the work in sheets, as fast as received, to America, as, by some unaccountable blunder, several of the last chapters of the Manuscript forwarded there have miscarried."[12]

Of course the practical American had good reason to order a transatlantic exchange of printer's proof as insurance against failure in his dual venture in publishing. And despite all these precautions, he was still experiencing the frustrations of trying to conduct two complicated business enterprises from a third, very distant location—his artistic home in Spain. Luckily, this time the report of trouble proved false. The American edition, printed from a manuscript that has survived in nearly complete form, appeared in March, 1829. Its title page was deposited for copyright on March 6.[13]

In London, meanwhile, John Murray had registered *Granada* for copyright on March 5, 1829, depositing at that time the required eleven copies of the title, and identifying Washington Irving as the author.[14] This priority of the English registration later proved important because it represented a necessary condition for valid English copyright. Yet the author himself was not informed about the progress of his book; nor did he make any attempt to correct the differences between the American and English editions at the stage of printer's proof. He simply had no access to the sheets so long as he remained in Spain. In 1827, Irving had explained his situation while making arrangements for the publication of *Columbus,* the first of his "Spanish" volumes:

> As to correction of the press, I must trust that to its fate, for I cannot leave Spain at present being up to the chin in literary researches which I hope to turn to good account. Mr [Alexander H.] Everett told me

some time since that he thought it probable Mr Lawrence, Secretary of
Legation at London, would feel a pleasure in superintending the publication of the work. . . . I know Mr Lawrence only by the many good
accounts I have had of him from others, and dare not ask him to undertake what I consider a very irksome task. If, however, he will permit
reference to be made to him in case of any point of doubt or obscurity
I shall feel greatly obliged, and will gladly submit my manuscript to any
correction that he may think advisable.[15]

Again in 1829, his continuing residence in Spain allowed Irving to excuse
himself from the "very irksome task" of correcting proof sheets, this time for
Granada. And his argument for entrusting the sheets of the American edition to the care of Ebenezer Irving made even better sense, since the haz-
ards of the long journey to and from America had already been
demonstrated.

This surrender of authorial control at the crucial stage of proof correction
helps to explain Washington Irving's later concern with correcting and revising the first printings of *Granada*, which appeared in both America and
England in 1829. But textual history aside, some understanding of the author's feelings of remoteness and near helplessness during the publication
process also offers us the background necessary for appreciating his response
when he first saw his book in print. What might otherwise appear as naive
pretense takes on the complex tones of apprehension, surprise, relief, and
hope tinged with foreboding: "I have just looked into the work. It reads
smoothly, and I trust will have good success among the literary; but I suspect
it will be heavy in the hands of mere readers for amusement."[16] Irving's
judgment was not shared by publishers in Germany, France, and Spain,
however, who acted quickly to bring out their own editions of *Granada*,
based upon the Murray text.

But another consequence of Irving's resignation from the usual authorial
duties proved to be especially unpleasant. Throughout the hectic months of
1828, the increasing likelihood of inconsistencies between the English and
American editions of *Granada* (introduced by the necessity of converting
two separate handwritten manuscripts into print, and made certain by Irving's submission of revised chapters to one publisher only) did not especially
trouble Irving. Instead, he believed that his position was protected; for he
had planned that both editions of *Granada* would be issued without any
clear identification of himself as the real author. In place of Irving's name,
the pseudonym "Fray Antonio Agapida" was to appear on the title page, so
that no direct link to Washington Irving would be established.

In fact, the American edition of 1829 exactly followed out this plan, which
must have occurred readily enough to a writer who earlier in his career had

hidden himself behind the names of other fictitious narrators, such as Geoffrey Crayon and Diedrich Knickerbocker. In February, 1829, Irving explained his object in *Granada*: "I have adopted a nom de guerre, as allowing me a freer scope in touching up and coloring the subject from my imagination."[17] Unlike the American publisher (the Philadelphia firm of Carey, Lea, and Carey) however, John Murray in London, with a shrewd regard for good business which Irving could respect if not always admire, overruled the wishes of the absent author and silently added to his discomfort. The mixture of pride and pain that surfaced in Irving's response when he finally looked into Murray's *Granada* and saw himself listed as author, tell the story of a sensitive man, but one much concerned about his own literary reputation:

> Murray has published the Chronicle in a beautiful style. I observe he has altered the title page. I had put "A Chronicle of the Conquest of Granada by Fray Antonio Agapida." He has inserted my name; I presume to make the work more immediately salable, but it is an unwarranted liberty, and makes me gravely, in my own name, tell many round untruths. I here openly make myself responsible as an author for the existence of the manuscript of Agapida, etc., etc. Literary mystifications are excusable when given anonymously or under feigned names, but are impudent deceptions when sanctioned by an author's real name.[18]

By disregarding Irving's intentions, Murray had opened an important question of propriety—the propriety of Fray Antonio Agapida's appearance in *Granada*—to which both the real author and his most vocal critics would address themselves in one form or another over the next twenty years.

Meanwhile, on May 9, 1829, almost a month after he first viewed his book, Irving addressed a complaint to Murray himself:

> I have received a copy of the Conquest of Granada and am much pleased with the style in which it is got up; but I must protest against the alteration you have made in the title page. I do not concieve [sic] that the purchase of the work gave you any right to make such alteration. I put in the title page the name of Fray Antonio Agapida as author of the chronicle. You must have percieved [sic] that this was a Nom de Guerre to enable me to assume greater freedom & latitude in the execution of the work, and to mingle a tinge of romance and satire with the grave historical details. By inserting my name in the title page as the avowed author, you make me personally responsible for the verity of the facts and the soundness of the opinions of what was intended to be given as a romantic chronicle. I presume you have done this to avail yourself of whatever attraction my name might have in drawing imme-

diate attention to the work; but this might have been effected in some other way, without meddling with the work itself, which ought never to be touched without the knowledge and consent of the author. I am sorry to make these complaints, but these matters displease and annoy me. I have been annoyed too by your forebodings of ill success to this work. When you have the spirit to give a large price for a work, why have you not the spirit to go manfully through with it, until the public voice determine its fate.[19]

Irving's indignant lecture to Murray, combined with fresh misunderstandings that characterized their relationship during the following months (principally over delays in the general sale of *Granada* and the related matter of secure copyright), offers ample evidence of pain. Certainly the American knew that he had paid a stiff price for his abnegation of the usual authorial responsibilities.[20]

Yet under the circumstances that surrounded publication of the two *Granada* editions of 1829—English and American—Washington Irving's anxiety (if not his occasional self-righteousness) about his work seems natural and unaffected. Doubtless after the crises caused by missing chapters, misdirected and miscarried manuscripts, and vacillations by his English publisher, and in view of his practical concern with establishing two valid copyrights, the physical presence of a completed book in any form must have been reassuring. After the excitement of delivery, when the volumes could be weighed and thumbed, then there would be ample time for reconsideration—for second thoughts about whether or not *Granada* would add some measure of hard-won luster to Irving's literary reputation. In 1829, however, the matter of achievement in *Granada*, as the author reminded Murray, should be left "until the public voice determine its fate." For, in preparing his manuscripts and arranging to have them published, Irving knew that he had acted as both an artist and a businessman.

In 1828, long before his quarrel with Murray, Irving made his ambivalent role in *Granada* a matter of record: "I should have preferred waiting until the whole manuscript was completely copied, that I might have given it a careful revision in its entire state, but the delays of the copiers are so intolerable that I was in danger of losing the season."[21] So the artist claimed defeat by necessity, all the while bargaining with a publisher, directing local agents on the scene, such as Thomas Aspinwall and Ebenezer Irving, keeping the presses supplied with copy, worrying about sales—these were the achievements of the businessman in Irving, who played a dominant part in the history of Granada up to 1829. After that date, the full story of this "experiment" in literature would find authorial roles reversed, as Washington Irving the literary artist took the leading part.

II

Any serious consideration of Irving's artistic achievements in *Granada* is best begun by calling attention to the chronologically central position of the book among his "Spanish" volumes. *Granada* was published just after what Irving regarded as a work of "straight" history, *A History of the Life and Voyages of Christopher Columbus* (1828), and just before the collection of romantic tales titled *The Alhambra* (1832). In all three books the American author sought to locate and make use of a satisfactory literary method for treating the non-American past, a matter which had occupied his thoughts as early as 1823, when he determined to avoid in his future writings any imitation of Sir Walter Scott.[22] About *Granada*, Irving later declared:

> The Chronicle, I am aware, is something of an experiment, and all experiments in literature as in any thing else are doubtful. It is not . . . a mere translation of an old Spanish chronicle, and of course, addressed merely to the taste of those who are curious in old literature of the kind (of which I confess myself one). But I have made a work out of the old chronicles, embellished, as well as I was able, by the imagination, and adapted to the romantic taste of the day. Something that was to be between a history and a romance.[23]

For Irving, then, the book marked a departure from any earlier approach to history or historical materials. *Granada*, as he envisioned it, would fill a special place, not only among volumes of Spanish or European history, but also in the corpus of his own writings, which he acknowledged as his unitary argument for professional status:

> A literary reputation, to hold well with the public, requires some *make weights* of the kind. Some massive materials, which form a foundation; the lighter works then become ornaments & embellishments.[24]

As a "make weight" *Granada* was designed to treat major source materials in an authoritative albeit experimental manner. In its author's view, the permanent value of the book rested chiefly upon two things: first, the authenticity or historical accuracy of the account presented; and second, the literary success of the narrative voice (Fray Antonio Agapida) in communicating an appropriate point of view as he recounted the action of the chronicle. On the first matter, there is now general agreement that Irving's treatment of his Spanish sources was neither slavishly imitative ("mere translation") nor, on the other hand, completely irresponsible.[25] His "romantic history" did not attempt to be "historical romance"; rather, it was designed to entertain the reader without losing in the process "the intrinsic truth of history," in which Irving firmly believed.[26] Difficult as the position may be to understand today, his desire to maintain a nice balance between "truth" and "coloring" largely explains the method of the *Granada* of 1829, and even more, the motives of the author when he continued both to revise and defend his volume after its initial appearance.

Concerning the propriety of Agapida, much has been written, some of it by Irving himself.[27] The author felt that, for the book to be successful with an audience, his fictitious friar must emerge as a plausible spokesman for the contents of the various individual chronicles. Together these tales reveal the historical roots of *Granada*, and Agapida had to supplement that authenticity with a consistent tone and style, thus creating artistic unity. In fact, Agapida was introduced into Irving's account as a useful literary device, to help eliminate the gap between the ancient past and the literary present; he was expected to erase the commonsense boundaries between fact and fiction, reality and romance.

In short, the Spanish monk served as a unifier, bringing closer into harmony the diverse segments of narrative (derived from many sources), the several points of observation and reflection on the fabulous events presented, and the overall tone of the composite account. Of course, in a different way, his presence offered a special advantage, as we have already noted. For the act of inserting Agapida into the book established a separation between the putative and the real authors, which should have kept Washington Irving out of public view until he had time enough to evaluate the results of his literary "experiment." But for readers in England and Europe, at least, this subterfuge did not exist. Because of Murray's alterations in the title page of the manuscript he printed, Washington Irving's authorship of *Granada* was immediately revealed; moreover, this was done without, in the author's view, providing any adequate explanation for the use of Agapida in the book.

Soon after receiving Irving's letter of protest, John Murray, in his turn, began to share something of the American's concern over the fate of *Granada*. Late in 1829, he proposed to pay Irving an additional fifty guineas for an article explaining the method of the book, written to appear in the *Quarterly Review*, which the English publisher owned and controlled. There, in the issue for May, 1830, an unsigned essay from Irving's hand put the author's views on *Granada* before the general public. Now, Irving had placed himself in the most unusual position of reviewing his own book in the pages of his publisher's journal. Eventually, questions about the propriety of Irving's conduct and about his self-defense led to a literary feud with Rufus W. Griswold, today remembered chiefly as an infamous biographer of Edgar Allan Poe.[28] By the time of the feud however, the merits and arguments of Irving's essay itself seem to have been lost in controversy. Here, it is interesting to note that the author's special opportunity to comment on his own intentions in his book—without revealing his identity—actually led Irving into another kind of dissimulation: the essay, when it considered the question of authorial intentions in *Granada*, elicited from the one man who should have known best, a curiously guarded response. Summarizing his own achievement of only two years before, Irving remarks: "His great object *appears to have been* to produce a complete and authentic body of facts relative to the war in question, but arranged in such a manner as to be attractive to the reader for mere amusement."[29] For the author, the light of intention no longer burned bright.

Concerning the role of Agapida, however, Irving now wrote more lucidly than ever before. He hoped at once to clear away the confusion about fiction and fact that surrounded his narrator, and to advance his reader's understanding of the literary necessities that had first occasioned his use of a *nom de guerre*:

> This friar is manifestly a mere fiction—a stalking-horse, from behind which the author launches his satire at the errors, the inconsistencies, and the self-delusions of the singularly medly [sic] of warriors, saints, politicians, and adventurers engaged in that holy war. Fray Antonio, however, may be considered as an incarnation of the blind bigotry and zealot extravagance of the 'good old orthodox Spanish chroniclers'; and, in fact, his exaggerated sallies of loyalty and religion are taken, almost word for word, from the works of some one or other of the monkish historians. Still, this fictitious personage has enabled the author to indulge his satirical vein at once more freely and more modestly, . . . the use of such machinery has thrown a doubt upon the absolute verity of his history; and it will take some time, before the general mass of readers become convinced that the pretended manuscript of Fray Antonio Agapida is, in truth, a faithful digest of actual documents.[30]

In this passage Irving again laid down the essential argument for his use of Agapida; at the same time, he made a case for the historical authenticity of *Granada*. A deeply-felt artistic need for adding to the bare narrative a coloring of romance, irony, and religious fanaticism—all in the name of a more complete and interesting history of events—became henceforth the bulwark in Washington Irving's defense of *Granada*, as well as a notion fixed in his mind.

This justification was later repeated in almost the same words in the "Note To The Revised Edition," added to the Putnam printing of 1850. Here, Irving's case was further strengthened by the inclusion of testimonials from two respected historians, the Spaniard Miguel Alcantara and the American William H. Prescott. Both verified the historical accuracy of the work. Before the "Note" appeared, to offer the author's final defense, however, the controversy over the original (and anonymous) *Quarterly Review* piece had already brought home accusations of ethical impropriety serious enough to cause Irving personal embarrassment and, more importantly, irritating enough to keep both Agapida and *Granada* alive in their author's mind and letters for at least twenty years after their debut.

III

The foregoing sections of this Introduction provide a brief history of the *Granada* of 1829, together with some suggestion about what the book in its earliest states meant to the author. His long-lived concern with improving the text of what he had written, beginning even before publication with the submission of a revised "Introduction" and a new opening paragraph for Chapter I, led Irving to rework *Granada* intermittently from 1828 until 1850, when the revised edition appeared as volume XIV in the *Works of Washington Irving*, issued by G. P. Putnam in New York and John Murray in London. An extended discussion of the various manuscripts and the earliest printed forms of *Granada* appears in the "Textual Commentary." Here, we shall notice only the chief features of *Granada*'s history between the date of the first publication and the appearance of the author's final revisions to his text.

The anonymous *Quarterly Review* essay of 1830, in which *Granada*'s author attempted to explain and defend his work, represents the first alteration to the original form of the book that would claim a place in the Author's Revised Edition of 1850. His earlier revisions of the manuscript "Introduction" and of Chapter I (which were incorporated into the 1829 English edition but not into the 1829 American), as well as the substitute Chapters 34 and 35, did not appear in the 1850 text, which was based instead on the American edition of 1829.

After 1829, Irving occupied himself off and on with correcting and revising *Granada,* and some of these efforts culminated in yet another manuscript, which consists of corrected pages from a printed copy of the 1829 English edition, together with authorial additions in Irving's hand. In its surviving form this manuscript contains 52 printed and 26 handwritten sections, approximately 63 pages in all. This partial text apparently reached Murray at some time, but so far as can be determined, it did not serve as the basis for any subsequent revision of the printed text. However it does provide documentary evidence of the author's continuing interest in his book of Moorish history, as well as an important source of information about Irving's usual methods and habits when he reworked materials already in print.[31] Although no physical evidence has survived, it is reasonable to suppose that, in preparing his text for the 1850 Putnam printing, Irving proceeded in much the same way—this time, however, correcting, changing, and supplementing a printed copy of the American rather than the English edition of 1829.

Among Irving's many changes in the original book, made as he prepared for the 1850 edition, was the insertion of material from his *Quarterly Review* article, including complimentary remarks by Prescott and Alcantara, now newly titled "Note To The Revised Edition" and appended to the old "Introduction."[32] Other specific textual alterations and additions are recorded elsewhere in this volume. As a matter of general interest, however, it should be noted that after the 1850 edition, which bears the imprint of both Murray and Putnam, further changes (except for minor corrections) represent unauthorized corruptions of the text—not authorial revisions. So far as we know, the first of these reprints was the unauthorized edition of H. G. Bohn (London, 1850), issued in possible violation of copyright, and set (without permission) from the Putnam-Murray text.[33]

As for the author himself, the motives governing his alterations and revisions were set forth in the important "Note To The Revised Edition" and in the footnotes he added to the 1850 *Granada*. Here, he acknowledged the critical response provoked by the fictive character of Fray Antonio Agapida, and also by the old debate about historical accuracy—these two matters obviously weighed heavily in all of Irving's thoughts concerning his book, from the time of its first appearance in public until at least the completion of his Revised Edition. As he remarked in a "Note" at the end of his "Introduction" to the 1850 text:

> Though I still retain the fiction of the monkish author Agapida, I have brought my narrative more strictly within historical bounds, have corrected and enriched it in various parts with facts recently brought to light by the researches of Alcantara and others; and have sought to render it a faithful and characteristic picture of the romantic portion of history to which it relates.[34]

For the reader who sought further explanation, Irving provided guidance to his reordering of materials for the 1850 edition in a new set of footnotes. A sample entry will suffice to show the direction of his changes:

> In the first edition of this work the author recounted a characteristic adventure of the stout Juan de Vera, as happening on the occasion of this embassy; a further consultation of historical authorities has induced him to transfer it to a second embassy of De Vera's; which the reader will find related in a subsequent chapter.[35]

In fact, the "subsequent chapter" begins some 240 pages after Irving's footnote. Even at some cost of artistry, however, the author seems determined to improve the historical accuracy of *Granada*, both in overall organization and conception, and in the myriad details that had come down to him from the various source materials. Everywhere in the Author's Revised Edition there are indications that the sensitive American author has paid careful attention to what his audience said about the 1829 versions of *Granada*. In particular, Irving was responding to what certain knowledgeable historians had written publicly and privately, as he worked to make his book more acceptable history.

IV

Since 1829, the critical reception of *Granada* has followed to a remarkable degree the divided course which Irving anticipated in his letters. On one hand there have been the reactions of those readers who looked to Irving for a work of imaginative literature; on the other, the responses of readers who expected from Irving nothing less than an accurate history of the Moors in Spain. And another division of opinion can also be discerned: that is, between a group of "literary" readers, past and present, who have registered great disappointment with the work, and the less well defined approval of the larger popular audience who have supported the sale of translations and reprintings over the years. So in every sense, *Granada*'s critical fate has been mixed. Still, the most helpful individual judgment of the book—helpful because it points to the reason behind this confusing critical history—was offered by the American scholar-critic Stanley Williams, who made an intensive study of Irving's writings. Williams found *Granada* to be "a book which no critic has ever been able to classify," and thus something of an anomaly.[36] In the absence of acceptable standards or models, then, *Granada*'s critical record, even up to the present, makes far better historical sense.

In fairness to *Granada* and to Irving, it should be noted that the most obvious decline in the reputation of the book has taken place among historians, whom the author originally managed to please with the 1829 printings, and for whose special approval he made many of the revisions for the 1850 edition. Certainly *Granada* no longer pretends to be good history. Writing in 1829, however, William H. Prescott claimed in an influential review that the book fell "within the class of narrative history," and went on to affirm, "we may honestly recommend it as substantially an authentic record."[37] No wonder that Irving was pleased. Prescott's review had a special value because of his acknowledged familiarity with Spanish source materials, and this expertise led him to praise the element of novelty in *Granada*. Irving, according to Prescott, was first in the field—the first popular writer to treat these episodes of Moorish history in the English language.

A more general interest in the subject and also in the American author, who was popular everywhere in Europe, helps to explain the rapid appearance of translations into Dutch, French, German, Spanish, and Swedish. All of these were in print by 1831, and many would be sustained, through multiple reprintings and into new editions, especially after 1850.[38] In Spain, as one might expect, *Granada* (which first appeared in Spanish in a greatly abridged edition) quickly assumed an important place in the historical and literary traditions of that country. There, ever since, the influence of this book has been deeply felt, and its classic reputation has endured.[39] Spanish culture gained new celebrity, but the real triumph belonged to the American; for in a recognizable way, Washington Irving had beaten Spanish writers to a worthwhile goal: he had been first to give the world a coherent account of a fascinating chapter in their own native history, and he was honored more than envied for his coup.

Elsewhere, the world has shown a milder appreciation for *Granada*, with a restrained although not an ungrateful reception. More than anything else, that element of romance which Irving worked hard to create, especially the romance embodied in the pathetic figure of Boabdil—the last royal Moor—has captured modern interest. Yet Irving's other concerns, such as the accurate accounting of the Moorish campaigns or the narrative usefulness of Fray Antonio Agapida (who seems to us finally much less memorable than either Diedrich Knickerbocker or Geoffrey Crayon), excite little interest today. Overall, *Granada's* readers seem to have justified Washington Irving's original "experiment" in literature, designed as he said, "to mingle a tinge of romance and satire with the grave historical details," by finding in the book largely what he thought he was putting there. Perhaps he would be pleased less or more with modern readers, but at least, a consensus in critical opinion seems now to have been reached: the world rates *Granada* as an interesting example, but certainly not as a masterpiece, of Washington Irving's art.

NOTES TO INTRODUCTION

1. Washington Irving to Alexander Everett, Oct. 21, 1828. See Washington Irving, *Letters, vol. II, 1823–1838*, ed. Ralph M. Aderman, Herbert L. Kleinfield, and Jenifer S. Banks (Boston: Twayne Publishers, 1979), p. 347. Hereafter cited as Letters.
2. The complex relationship between Washington Irving and the Murray establishment provided a rich chapter in the history of English publishing. For the full account, see *Washington Irving and the House of Murray: Geoffrey Crayon Charms The British, 1817–1856*, ed. Ben Harris McClary (Knoxville: Univ. of Tennessee Press, 1969). Hereafter cited as McClary.
3. WI to John Murray II, Letters, p. 213.
4. Washington Irving, Spanish Journal, 1828–1829, in *Journals and Notebooks*, Volume IV, ed. Wayne R. Kime and Andrew B. Myers (Boston: Twayne Publishers, 1984). Hereafter cited as Journals. On Irving's Spanish years, see also: Earl N. Harbert, "Irving's A Chronicle of The Conquest of Granada: An Essay in the History of Publication, Revision, and Critical Reception," *Bulletin of the New York Public Library* (Summer 1976), pp. 400–475.

5. See *Journals*, p. 234, and *Letters*, p. 349. A convenient summary treatment is: Earl N. Harbert, "The Manuscripts of A Chronicle of the Conquest of Granada: A Revised Census with Commentary," *Bulletin of Research in the Humanities* (Spring 1979), pp. 124–129.

6. Oct. 22, 1828, *Letters*, p. 348.

7. See *Journals*, esp. entry for Dec. 20, 1828, p. 243.

8. *Letters*, p. 365.

9. Dec. 20, 1828, *Letters*, p. 368.

10. See *Journals*, esp. entry for Dec. 22, 1828, p. 244.

11. WI to Thomas Aspinwall, Dec. 27, 1828, *Letters*, p. 369.

12. Feb. 28, 1829, *Letters*, p. 386.

13. See *Bibliography of American Literature*, compiled by Jacob Blanck (New Haven: Yale Univ. Press, 1966—), V, 37. Hereafter cited as *BAL*.

14. The earlier confusion about the history and validity of the English copyright for *Granada* has been cleared away by Professor McClary. See esp. p. 221.

15. WI to Thomas Aspinwall, Oct. 8, 1827, *Letters*, p. 252.

16. WI to Peter Irving, Apr. 10, 1829, *Letters*, p. 400.

17. *Letters*, p. 382. For a full discussion of the importance of the pseudonym, see Earl N. Harbert, "Fray Antonio Agapida and Washington Irving's Romance With History," *Tulane Studies in English* (1969), pp. 135–144. William Charvat, *Literary Publishing in America*, 1790–1850 (Philadelphia: Univ. of Pennsylvania Press, 1959), points out that in some American editions, "Irving's name was printed on the reverse of the title page as the copyrighter of the work" (p. 79).

18. WI to Peter Irving, Apr. 10, 1829, *Letters*, p. 400.

19. *Letters*, pp. 414–15.

20. For the full story of the troubles between author and publisher, see McClary. Irving's position has been treated by Earl N. Harbert, "Irving's *A Chronicle of The Conquest of Granada*: A Study in Authorial Intention and Untoward Accident," *Washington Irving Reconsidered*, ed. Ralph M. Aderman (Hartford: Transcendental Books, 1969), pp. 26–31.

21. WI to Peter Irving, Sept. 2, 1828, *Letters*, p. 333.

22. WI to Peter Irving, Sept. 4, 1823, *Letters*, p. 5.

23. WI to Thomas Aspinwall, Apr. 4, 1829, *Letters*, p. 396.

24. Irving's italics. See *Letters*, p. 396.

25. See Louise M. Hoffman, "Irving's Use of Spanish Sources in *The Conquest of Granada*," *Hispania* (1945), pp. 483–498, and *The Life of Washington Irving*, by Stanley T. Williams, 2 vols. (New York: Oxford Univ. Press, 1935). Hereafter cited as STW. The "Supplementary Studies," II, 308–314, are especially useful.

26. WI expressed himself most clearly in a letter to Thomas Aspinwall, dat-

ed Aug. 31, 1828. For the most complete discussion of Irving as a historian, see William L. Hedges, *Washington Irving: An American Study, 1802–1832* (Baltimore: Johns Hopkins Univ. Press, 1965). Hereafter cited as Hedges.

27. WI's main contribution to the debate, discussed briefly in the text, is contained in the *Quarterly Review* XLIII (1830), 55–80. See also STW and Hedges.
28. On this quarrel, see McClary, pp. 126, 186f.
29. Italics mine. *Quarterly Review* (May, 1830), p. 57.
30. *Quarterly Review* (May, 1830), pp. 57–58.
31. WI's methods of revising his printed work are also discussed in McClary, p. 146.
32. WI explained his "Note To The Revised Edition" in a footnote (p. xv): "Many of the observations in this note have already appeared in an explanatory article which, at Mr. Murray's request, the author furnished to the London Quarterly Review."
33. For a discussion of the copyright controversy with Bohn, see McClary, pp. 191–202.
34. *A Chronicle of the Conquest of Granada* (New York: G. P. Putnam, 1850), "Introduction," pp. xviii–xix.
35. Ibid, p. 28.
36. "Washington Irving," *Literary History of the United States*, ed. R. Spiller, et al., 3rd ed. rev. (New York: Macmillan, 1963), p. 249. For the most useful bibliographical summary, see James W. Tuttleton, "Washington Irving" in *Fifteen American Authors Before 1900*, ed. Earl N. Harbert and Robert A. Rees (Madison: Univ. of Wisconsin Press, 1984).
37. *North American Review* (Oct., 1829), p. 314. This long review was reprinted in *Biographical and Critical Miscellanies* (New York, 1845), pp. 88–122.
38. *The Complete Works of Washington Irving* will include a bibliographical volume. In addition to *BAL*, the most important listings of WI's works in English and in various translations may be found in: *Washington Irving, A Bibliography*, comp. William R. Langfeld and Philip C. Blackburn (New York: New York Public Library, 1933); *A Bibliography of the Writings of Washington Irving*, comp. S. T. Williams and M. E. Edge (New York: Oxford, 1936); S. T. Williams, *The Spanish Backgrounds of American Literature*, 2 vols. (New Haven: Yale Univ. Press, 1955); hereafter STW, II; John E. Englekirk, *Bibliografia de Obras Norteamericanas en Traduccion Espanola* (Mexico, D. F., 1944); *A Provisional Bibliography of United States Books Translated into Spanish*, comp. by the Hispanic Foundation in the Library of Congress (Washington: Library of Congress, 1957).
39. By itself, the history of *Granada* in Spain forms an interesting study, for

which there is no room in this volume. An interested reader should consult the sources cited in note 38, as well as the essays included in the memorial volume: *Washington Irving: 1859–1959* (Granada: Univ. de Granada, 1960). The first translation of *Granada* into Spanish, *La Cronica de las Conquista de Granada*, trans. J. W. Montgomery, 2 vols. (Madrid, 1831), was seriously incomplete.

A CHRONICLE
OF THE CONQUEST OF GRANADA

INTRODUCTION

Although the following chronicle bears the name of the venerable Fray Antonio Agapida, it is rather a superstructure reared upon the fragments which remain of his work. It may be asked who is this same Agapida, who is cited with such deference, yet whose name is not to be found in any of the catalogues of Spanish authors? The question is hard to answer: he appears to have been one of the many indefatigable authors of Spain, who have filled the libraries of convents and cathedrals with their tomes, without ever dreaming of bringing their labours to the press. He evidently was deeply and accurately informed of the particulars of the wars between his countrymen and the Moors, a tract of history but too much overgrown with the weeds of fable. His glowing zeal, also, in the cause of the Catholic faith, entitles him to be held up as a model of the good old orthodox chroniclers, who recorded, with such pious exultation, the united triumphs of the cross and the sword. It is deeply to be regretted, therefore, that his manuscripts, deposited in the libraries of various convents, have been dispersed during the late convulsions in Spain, so that nothing is now to be met of them, but disjointed fragments. These, however, are too precious to be suffered to fall into oblivion, as they contain many curious facts not to be found in any other historian. In the following work, therefore, the manuscript of the worthy Fray Antonio will be adopted wherever it exists entire, but will be filled up, extended, illustrated and corroborated by citations from various authors, both Spanish and Arabian, who have treated of the subject. Those who may wish to know how far the work is indebted to the chronicle of Fray Antonio Agapida, may readily satisfy their curiosity by referring to his manuscript fragments, which are carefully preserved in the library of the Escurial.

Before entering upon the history, it may be as well to notice the opinions of certain of the most learned and devout historiographers of former times relative to this war. Marinus Siculus, historian to Charles V, pronounces it a war to avenge the ancient injuries received by the Christians from the Moors, to recover the Kingdom of Granada and to extend the name and honour of the Christian religion.*

Estaven de Garibay, one of the most distinguished among the Spanish historians, regards the war as a special act of divine clemency towards the Moors; to the end that those barbarians and infidels who had dragged out so many centuries under the diabolical oppression of the absurd sect of Mahomet, should at length be reduced to the Christian faith.†

Padre Mariana, also, a venerable jesuit, and the most renowned historian of Spain, considers the past domination of the Moors as a scourge inflicted

---

*Lucio Marino Siculo. Cosas Memorabiles de España. lib. 20.
†Garibay, Compend. Hist. España. Lib. 18. c. 22.

on the Spanish nation for its iniquities, but the triumphant war with Granada as the reward of heaven for its great act of propitiation in establishing the glorious tribunal of the inquisition! No sooner, says the worthy father, was this holy office opened in Spain than there instantly shone forth a resplendent light. Then it was that, through divine favour, the nation encreased in power, and became competent to overthrow and trample down the domination of the Moors.*

Having thus cited high and venerable authority for considering this war in the light of one of those pious enterprizes denominated crusades, we trust we have said enough to engage the Christian reader to follow us into the field and to stand by us to the very issue of the contest.

*Mariana, Hist España. lib. 25. C. 1.

CHAPTER I

OF THE KINGDOM OF GRANADA, AND THE TRIBUTE
WHICH IT PAID TO THE CASTILIAN CROWN.

The history of those desperate and bloody wars, observes Fray Antonio Agapida, which have filled the world with rumour and astonishment, and have determined the fate of mighty empires, has ever been considered as a theme worthy of the pen of the philosopher and the study of the sage. What then must be the history of a holy war, or rather a pious crusade, waged by the most Catholic of sovereigns, for the restoration of the light of the true faith to one of the most beautiful but benighted regions of the globe. Listen then while from the solitude of my cell, I narrate the events of the conquest of Granada, where Christian knight and turbaned infidel disputed hand to hand every inch of the fair land of Andalusia, until the crescent, that symbol of heathenish abomination, was cast into the dust, and the blessed cross, the tree of our redemption, erected in its stead.

Upwards of eight hundred years were past and gone since the Arabian invaders had sealed the perdition of Spain, by the defeat of Don Roderick, the last of her Gothic Kings. Since that disastrous event, kingdom after kingdom had been gradually recovered by the Christian Princes, until the single, but powerful, territory of Granada alone remained under domination of the Moors.

This renowned kingdom was situated in the southern part of Spain, bordering on the Mediterranean Sea, and defended on the land side by lofty and rugged mountains, locking up within their embraces, deep, rich and verdant valleys, where the sterility of the surrounding heights was repaid by prodigal fertility.

The city of Granada lay in the centre of the kingdom, sheltered as it were in the lap of the Sierra Nevada, or chain of Snowy Mountains. It covered two lofty hills, and a deep valley which divides them, through which flows the river Darro. One of these hills was crowned by the royal palace and fortress of the Alhambra, capable of containing forty thousand men within its walls and towers. There is a Moorish tradition that the King who built this mighty pile was skilled in the occult sciences, and furnished himself with gold and silver for the purpose, by means of alchemy.* Certainly never was there an edifice accomplished in a superior style of barbaric magnificence, and the stranger who, even at the present day, wanders among its silent and deserted courts and ruined halls, gazes with astonishment at its gilded and fretted domes and luxurious decorations, still retaining their brilliancy and beauty in defiance of the ravages of time.

Opposite to the hill on which stood the Alhambra was its rival hill, on the summit of which was a spacious plain, covered with houses and crowded

*Zurita. Lib. 20. c. 42.

with inhabitants. It was commanded by a fortress called the Alcazaba. The declivities and skirts of these hills were covered with houses to the number of seventy thousand, separated by narrow streets and small squares according to the custom of Moorish cities. The houses had interior courts and gardens refreshed by fountains and running streams, and set out with oranges, citrons and pomegranetes, so that as the edifices of the city rose above each other on the sides of the hill, they presented a mingled appearance of city and grove, delightful to the eye. The whole was surrounded by high walls, three leagues in circuit, with twelve gates, and fortified by a thousand and thirty towers. The elevation of the city, and the neighborhood of the Sierra Nevada crowned with perpetual snows, tempered the fervid rays of summer; so that while other cities were panting with the sultry and stifling heat of the Dog Days, the most salubrious breezes played through the marble halls of Granada.

The glory of the city, however, was its vega or plain, which spread out to a circumference of thirty seven leagues, surrounded by lofty mountains. It was a vast garden of delight, refreshed by numerous fountains, and by the silver windings of the Xenel. The labour and ingenuity of the Moors, had diverted the waters of this river into thousands of rills and streams, and diffused them over the whole surface of the plain. Indeed they had wrought up this happy region to a degree of wonderful prosperity, and took a pride in decorating it, as if it had been a favourite mistress. The hills were clothed with orchards and vineyards, the valleys embroidered with gardens, and the wide plains covered with waving grain. Here were seen in profusion the orange, the citron, the fig and pomgranate, with great plantations of mulberry trees, from which was produced the finest of silk. The vine clambered from tree to tree; the grapes hung in rich clusters about the peasant's cottage, and the groves were rejoiced by the perpetual song of the nightingale. In a word, so beautiful was the earth, so pure the air and so serene the sky of this delicious region, that the Moors imagined the paradise of their prophet to be situated in that part of the heaven which overhung the kingdom of Granada.*

This rich and populous territory had been left in quiet possession of the infidels on condition of an annual tribute to the sovereign of Castile and Leon of two thousand doblas or pistoles of gold and sixteen hundred Christian captives, or in default of captives, an equal number of Moors to be surrendered as slaves; all to be delivered in the city of Cordova.†

At the era at which this chronicle commences, Ferdinand and Isabella, of glorious and happy memory, reigned over the united kingdom of Castile, Leon and Aragon, and Muley Aben Hassan sat on the throne of Granada.

*Juan Botero Benes. relaciones universales del mundo.
†Garibay. Compend. lib 4. c. 25.

This Muley Aben Hassan had succeeded to his father Ismael in 1465, while Henry IV, brother and immediate predecessor of Queen Isabella, was King of Castile and Leon. He was of the illustrious lineage of Mohammed Aben Alamar, the first Moorish King of Granada, and was the most potent of his line. He had in fact augmented in power in consequence of the fall of other Moorish kingdoms, which had been conquered by the Christians. Many cities and strong places of those kingdoms, which lay contiguous to Granada, had refused to submit to Christian vassalage, and had sheltered themselves under the protection of Muley Aben Hassan. His territories had thus encreased in wealth, extent and population beyond all former example, and contained fourteen cities and ninety seven fortified towns, besides numerous unwalled towns and villages, defended by formidable castles. The spirit of Muley Aben Hassan swelled with his possessions.

The tribute of money and captives had been regularly paid by his father Ismael, and Muley Aben Hassan had on one occasion attended personally in Cordova at the payment. He had witnessed the taunts and sneers of the haughty Castilians, and so indignant was the proud son of Afric at what he considered a degradation of his race, that his blood boiled whenever he recollected the humiliating scene.

When he came to the throne he ceased all payment of the tribute, and it was sufficient to put him in a transport of rage only to mention it. "He was a fierce and warlike infidel," says the Catholic Fray Antonio Agapida; "his bitterness against the holy Christian faith had been signalized in battle during the life time of his father, and the same diabolical spirit of hostility was apparent in his ceasing to pay this most righteous tribute."

CHAPTER II

HOW THE CATHOLIC SOVEREIGNS SENT TO DEMAND ARREARS OF TRIBUTE FROM THE MOOR AND HOW THE MOOR REPLIED.

In the year 1478: a Spanish cavalier of powerful frame and haughty demeanour arrived at the gates of Granada as ambassador from the Catholic monarchs, to demand the arrear of tribute. His name was Don Juan de Vera, a zealous and devout knight, full of ardour for the faith and loyalty for the crown. He was gallantly mounted, armed at all points, and followed by a moderate but well appointed retinue.

The Moorish inhabitants looked jealously at this small but proud array of Spanish chivalry, as it paraded with that stateliness possessed only by Spanish cavaliers, through the renowned gate of Elvira. They were struck with the stern and lofty demeanour of Don Juan de Vera, and his sinewy frame, which shewed him formed for hardy deeds of arms; and they supposed he had come in search of distinction by defying the Moorish knights in open tourney, or in the famous tilt with reeds for which they were so renowned. For it was still the custom of the knights of either nation to mingle in these courteous and chivalrous contests, during the intervals of war. When they learnt, however, that he was come to demand the tribute so abhorrent to the ears of the fiery monarch, they observed that it well required a warrior of his apparent nerve to execute such an embassy.

Muley Aben Hassan received the cavalier in state, seated on a magnificent divan, and surrounded by the officers of his court in the Hall of Ambassadors, one of the most sumptuous apartments of the Alhambra. When De Vera had delivered his message, a haughty and bitter smile curled the lip of the fierce monarch. "Tell your sovereigns," said he, "that the kings of Granada, who used to pay tribute in money to the Castilian crown, are dead. Our mint at present coins nothing but blades of scymetars and heads of lances."[*]

The defiance couched in this proud reply was heard with stern and lofty courtesy by Don Juan de Vera, for he was a bold soldier and a devout hater of the infidels, and he saw iron war in the words of the Moorish monarch. He retired from the audience chamber with stately and ceremonious gravity, being master of all points of etiquette. As he passed through the court of Lions and paused to regard its celebrated fountain, he fell into a discourse with the Moorish courtiers on certain mysteries of the Christian faith. The arguments advanced by those infidels, says Fray Antonio Agapida, awakened the pious indignation of this most Christian knight and discreet ambassador; but still he restrained himself within the limits of lofty gravity, leaning on the pommel of his sword and looking down with ineffable scorn upon the weak casuists around him. The quick and subtle Arabian witlings redoubled their light attacks upon this stately Spaniard, and thought they had completely foiled him in the contest; but the stern Juan de Vera had an argument in reserve for which they were but little prepared; for on one of them, of the race of the Abencerrages, daring to question, with a sneer, the immaculate conception of the blessed Virgin, the Catholic knight could no longer restrain his ire. Raising his voice of a sudden he told the infidel he lied, and raising his arm at the same time he smote him on the head with his sheathed sword.

In an instant the court of Lions glistened with the flash of arms, and its fountains would have been dyed with blood had not Muley Aben Hassan overheard the tumult and forbade all appeal to arms, pronouncing the per-

[*]Garibay, Compend. lib. 40. C. 29. Conde. Hist. de los Arabas. P. 4. c. 34.

son of the ambassador sacred, while within his territories. The Abencerrage treasured up the remembrance of the insult until an hour of vengeance should arrive, and the ambassador prayed our blessed lady to grant him an opportunity of proving her immaculate conception on the head of this turbaned infidel.*

Notwithstanding this occurrence Don Juan de Vera was treated with great distinction by Muley Aben Hassan, but nothing could make him unbend from his stern and stately reserve. Before his departure a scymetar was sent to him by the King; the blade of the finest Damascus steel; the hilt of agate enriched with precious stones, and the guard of gold. De Vera drew it and smiled grimly as he noticed the admirable temper of the blade. "His Majesty has given me a trenchant weapon," said he. "I trust a time will come, when I may shew him that I know how to use his royal present." The reply was considered as a compliment of course, the bystanders little knew the bitter hostility that lay couched beneath.

Don Juan de Vera and his companions, during their brief sojourn at Granada, scanned the force and situation of the Moor with the eyes of practiced warriors. They saw that he was well prepared for hostilities. His walls and towers were of vast strength, in complete repair and mounted with lombards and other heavy ordnance. His magazines were well stored with all the munitions of war: he had a mighty host of foot soldiers, together with squadrons of cavalry ready to scour the country and carry on either defensive or predatory warfare. The Christian warriors noted these things without dismay; their hearts rather glowed with emulation at the thoughts of encountering so worthy a foe. As they slowly pranced through the streets of Granada on their departure, they looked round with eagerness on its stately palaces, and sumptuous mosques: on its Alcayceria or Bazar crowded with silks and cloth of silver and gold, with jewels and precious stones and other rich merchandize, the luxuries of every clime, and they longed for the time when all this wealth should be the spoil of the soldiers of the faith, and when each tramp of their steeds might be fetlock deep in the blood and carnage of the infidels.

Don Juan de Vera and his little band pursued their way slowly through the country, to the Christian frontier. Every town was strongly fortified. The vega was studded with towers of refuge for the peasantry: every pass of the mountain had its castle of defence, every lofty height its watch tower. As the Christian cavaliers passed under the walls of the fortresses, lances and scymetars flashed from their battlements, and the turbaned centinels seemed to dart from their dark eyes glances of hatred and defiance. It was evident

---

*The curate of Los Palacios also records this anecdote but mentions it as happening on a subsequent occasion, when Don Juan de Vera was sent to negociate for certain Christian captives. There appears every reason, however, to consider Fray Antonio Agapida most correct in the period to which he refers it.

that a war with this kingdom must be one of doughty peril and valiant enterprize; a war of posts, where every step must be gained by toil and bloodshed, and maintained with the utmost difficulty. The warrior spirit of the cavaliers kindled at the thoughts, and they were impatient for hostilities; "not," says Antonio Agapida, "from any thirst for rapine and revenge, but from that pure and holy indignation which every Spanish knight entertained at beholding this beautiful dominion of his ancestors defiled by the footsteps of infidel usurpers. It was impossible," he adds, "to contemplate this delicious country, and not long to see it restored to the dominion of the true faith and the sway of the Christian monarchs."

When Don Juan de Vera returned to the Castilian court, and reported the particulars of his mission, and all that he had heard and seen in the Moorish territories, he was highly honoured and rewarded by King Ferdinand and the zeal he had shewn in vindication of the sinless conception of the blessed Virgin, was not only applauded by that most catholick of sovereigns, but gained him great favour and renown among all pious cavaliers and reverend prelates.

CHAPTER III

HOW THE MOOR DETERMINED TO STRIKE THE FIRST BLOW IN THE WAR.

The defiance thus hurled at the Castilian sovereigns by the fiery Moorish King would at once have been answered by the thunder of their artillery, but they were embroiled at that time in a war with Portugal, and in contests with their own factious nobles. The truce, therefore, which had existed for many years between the nations was suffered to continue, the wary Ferdinand reserving the refusal to pay tribute as a fair ground for war whenever the favorable moment to wage it should arrive.

In the course of three years the war with Portugal was terminated, and the factions of the Spanish nobles were for the most part quelled. The Castilian sovereigns now turned their thoughts to what, from the time of the union of their crowns, had been the great object of their ambition, the conquest of Granada, and the complete extirpation of the Moorish power from Spain. Ferdinand, whose pious zeal was quickened by motives of temporal policy, looked with a craving eye at the rich territory of the Moor, studded with innumerable towns and cities. He determined to carry on the war with cautious and persevering patience, taking town after town and fortress after fortress, and gradually plucking away all the supports, before he attempted the Moorish capital. "I will pick out the seeds one by one of this Pomegranate," said the wary Ferdinand.*

Muley Aben Hassan was aware of the hostile intentions of the Catholic monarch but felt confident in his means of resisting them. He had amassed great wealth during a tranquil reign; he had strengthened the defences of his kingdom and had drawn large bodies of auxiliary troops from Barbary, besides making arrangements with the African princes to assist him with supplies in case of emergency. His subjects were fierce of spirit, stout of heart and valiant of hand. Enured to the exercises of war they could fight skillfully on foot, but above all were dextrous horsemen, whether heavily armed and fully appointed, or lightly mounted *a la geneta*, with simply lance and target. They were patient of fatigue, hunger, thirst and nakedness, prompt for war at the first summons of their King and tenacious in defence of their towns and possessions.

Thus amply provided for war, Muley Aben Hassan determined to be beforehand with the politic Ferdinand and to be the first to strike a blow. In the truce which existed between them there was a singular clause, permitting either party to make sudden inroads and assaults upon towns and fortresses, provided they were done furtively and by stratagem, without display of banners or sound of trumpet or regular encampment, and that they did not last above three days.† This gave rise to frequent enterprizes of a hardy and adventurous character, in which castles and strong holds were taken by surprize and carried, sword in hand. A long time had elapsed, however, without any outrage of the kind, on the part of the Moors, and the Christian towns on the frontier had all, in consequence, fallen into a state of the most negligent security.

Muley Aben Hassan cast his eyes round to select his object of attack, when information was brought him that the fortress of Zahara was but feebly garrisoned and scantily supplied, and that its alcayde was careless of his charge. This important post was on the frontier between Ronda and Medina Sidonia and was built on the crest of a rocky mountain; with a strong castle perched above it, upon a cliff so high that it was said to be above the flight of birds or drift of clouds. The streets and many of the houses were mere excavations, wrought out of the living rock. The town had but one gate, opening to the west, and defended by towers and bulwarks. The only ascent to this cragged fortress was by roads cut in the rock, and so rugged as in many places to resemble broken stairs. Such was the situation of the mountain fortress of Zahara, which seemed to set all attack at defiance, insomuch that it had become so proverbial throughout Spain, that a woman of forbidding and

*Granada is the Spanish term for Pomegranate.
†Zurita. Anales de Aragon L. 20 C. 41. Mariana Hist de España L 25. C 1.

inaccessible virtue was called a Zahareña. But the strongest fortress and sternest virtue have their weak points and require unremitting vigilance to guard them; let warrior and dame take warning from the fate of Zahara.

CHAPTER IV

EXPEDITION OF MULEY ABEN HASSAN AGAINST THE FORTRESS OF ZAHARA.

It was in the year of our Lord one thousand four hundred and eighty one, and but a night or two after the festival of the most blessed Nativity, that Muley Aben Hassan made his famous attack upon Zahara. The inhabitants of the place were sunk in profound sleep; the very centinel had deserted his post, and sought shelter from a tempest which had raged for three nights in succession; for it appeared but little probable that an enemy would be abroad during such an uproar of the elements. But evil spirits work best during a storm, observes the worthy Antonio Agapida, and Muley Aben Hassan found such a season most suitable for his diabolical purposes. In the midst of the night an uproar arose within the walls of Zahara, more awful than the raging of the storm. A fearful alarm cry, "The Moor! the Moor!" resounded through the streets, mingled with the clash of arms, the shriek of anguish and the shout of victory. Muley Aben Hassan at the head of a powerful force had hurried from Granada and passed unobserved through the mountains in the obscurity of the tempest. While the storm pelted the centinel from his post and howled round tower and battlement, the Moors had planted their scaling ladders, and mounted securely into both town and castle. The garrison was unsuspicious of danger until battle and massacre burst forth within its very walls. It seemed to the affrighted inhabitants as if the fiends of the air had come upon the wings of the wind and possessed themselves of tower and turret. The war cry resounded on every side, shout answering shout, above, below, on the battlements of the castle, in the streets of the town. The foe was in all parts, wrapped in obscurity, but acting in concert by the aid of preconcerted signals. Starting from sleep the soldiers were intercepted and cut down as they rushed from their quarters, or if they escaped they knew not where to assemble or where to strike. Wherever lights appeared, the flashing scymetar was at its deadly work, and all who attempted resistance fell beneath its edge.

In a little while the struggle was at an end. Those who were not slain took refuge in the secret places of their houses, or gave themselves up as captives. The clash of arms ceased, and the storm continued its howling, mingled with the occasional shout of the Moorish soldiery, roaming in search of plunder. While the inhabitants were trembling for their fate, a trumpet resounded through the streets summoning them all to assemble unarmed, in the public square. Here they were surrounded by soldiery and strictly guarded until day break. When the day dawned it was piteous to behold this once prosperous community, who had lain down to rest in peaceful security, now crowded together without distinction of age, or rank, or sex, and almost without raiment during the severity of a wintry storm. The fierce Muley Aben Hassan turned a deaf ear to all their prayers and remonstrances, and ordered them to be conducted captives to Granada. Leaving a strong garrison in both town and castle with orders to put them in a complete state of defence, he returned flushed with victory to his capital, entering it at the head of his troops, laden with spoil, and bearing in triumph the banners and pennons taken at Zahara.

While preparations were making for jousts and other festivities in honour of this victory over the Christians, the captives of Zahara arrived; a wretched train of men, women and children, worn out with fatigue and haggard with despair and driven like cattle into the city gates by a detachment of Moorish soldiery.

Deep was the grief and indignation of the people of Granada at this cruel scene. Old men, who had experienced the calamities of warfare, anticipated coming troubles. Mothers clasped their infants to their breasts, as they beheld the hapless females of Zahara, with their children expiring in their arms. On every side the accents of pity for the sufferers were mingled with execrations of the barbarity of the King. The preparations for festivity were neglected, and the viands, which were to have feasted the conquerors, were distributed among the captives.

The nobles and alfaquis, however, repaired to the Alhambra to congratulate the King; for whatever storm may rage in the lower regions of society, rarely do any clouds, but clouds of incense, rise to the awful eminence of the throne. In this instance, however, a voice rose from the midst of the obsequious crowd, that burst like thunder upon the ears of Aben Hassan. "Woe! woe! woe! to Granada!" exclaimed the voice, "its hour of desolation approaches. The ruins of Zahara will fall upon our heads; my spirit tells me that the end of our Empire is at hand!" All shrunk back aghast, and left the denouncer of woe standing alone in the centre of the hall. He was an ancient and hoary man in the rude attire of a dervise. Age had withered his form without quenching the fire of his spirit, which glared in baleful lustre from his eyes. He was, say the Arabian historians, one of those holy men termed Santons, who pass their lives in hermitages, in fasting, meditation and prayer, until they attain to the purity of Saints and the foresight of prophets. "He was," says the indignant Fray Antonio Agapida, "a son of Belial; one of those fanatic infidels possessed of the devil, who are sometimes permitted to predict the truth to their followers; but with the proviso that their predictions shall be of no avail."

The voice of the Santon resounded through the lofty hall of the Alhambra, and struck silence and awe into the crowd of courtly sycophants. Muley Aben Hassan alone was unmoved, he eyed the hoary anchorite with scorn as he stood dauntless before him; and treated his predictions as the raving of a maniac. The Santon rushed from the royal presence, and descending into the city hurried through its streets and squares with frantic gesticulations. His voice was heard in every part in awful denunciation. "The peace is broken, the exterminating war is commenced. Woe! woe! woe! to Granada! its fall is at hand! desolation shall dwell in its palaces, its strong men shall fall beneath the sword, its children and maidens shall be led into captivity. Zahara is but a type of Granada."

Terror seized upon the populace, for they considered these ravings as the inspirations of prophecy. They hid themselves in their dwellings, as in a time of general mourning; or if they went abroad it was to gather together in knots in the streets and squares, to alarm each other with dismal forebodings, and to curse the rashness and cruelty of the fierce Aben Hassan.

The Moorish monarch heeded not their murmurs. Knowing that his exploit must draw upon him the vengeance of the Christians, he now threw off all reserve, and made attempts to surprize Castellar and Alvera, though without success. He sent alfaquis also to the Barbary powers, informing them that the sword was drawn, and inviting them to aid in maintaining the Kingdom of Granada and the religion of Mahomet against the violence of unbelievers.

CHAPTER V

EXPEDITION OF THE MARQUIS OF CADIZ AGAINST ALHAMA.

Great was the indignation of King Ferdinand when he heard of the storming of Zahara, more especially as it anticipated his intention of giving the first blow in this eventful war. He valued himself upon his deep and prudent policy, and there is nothing which politick monarchs can less forgive, than thus being forestalled by an adversary. He immediately issued orders to all the adelantados and alcaydes of the frontiers, to maintain the utmost vigilance at their several posts; and to prepare to carry fire and sword into the territories of the Moors, while he dispatched friars of different orders to stir up the chivalry of Christendom to take part in this holy crusade against the infidels.

Among the many valiant cavaliers who rallied round the throne of Ferdinand and Isabella, one of the most eminent in rank and renowned in arms was Don Roderigo Ponce de Leon, Marquis of Cadiz. As he was the distinguished champion of this holy war, and commanded in most of its enterprizes and battles, it is meet that some particular account should be given of him. He was born in 1443, of the valiant lineage of the Ponces, and from his earliest youth had rendered himself illustrious in the field. He was of the middle stature with a muscular and powerful frame, capable of great exertion and fatigue. His hair and beard were red and curled; his countenance was open and magnanimous, of a ruddy complexion and slightly marked with the small pox. He was temperate, chaste, valiant, vigilant; a just and generous master to his vassals; frank and noble in his deportment towards his equals; loving and faithful to his friends, fierce and terrible, yet magnanimous to his enemies. He was considered the mirror of chivalry of his times, and compared by contemporary historians to the immortal Cid.

The Marquis of Cadiz had vast possessions in the most fertile parts of Andalusia, including many towns and castles; and could lead forth an army into the field from his own vassals and dependents. On receiving the orders of the King he burned to signalize himself by some sudden incursion into the Kingdom of Granada that should give a brilliant commencement to the war, and should console the sovereigns for the insult they had received on the capture of Zahara. As his estates lay near to the Moorish frontiers and were subject to sudden inroads, he had always in his pay numbers of adalides or scouts and guides, many of them converted Moors. These he sent out in all directions to watch the movements of the enemy and to procure all kinds of information important to the security of the frontier. One of these spies came to him one day in his town of Marchena and informed him that the Moorish town of Alhama was slightly garrisoned and negligently guarded, and might be taken by surprize. This was a large, wealthy and populous place within a few leagues of Granada. It was situated on a rocky height, nearly surrounded by a river, and defended by a fortress to which there was no access but by a steep and cragged ascent. The strength of its situation and its being embosomed in the centre of the kingdom, had produced the careless security which now invited attack.

To ascertain fully the state of the fortress the marquis dispatched secretly a veteran soldier who was highly in his confidence. His name was Ortega de Prado, a man of great activity, shrewdness and valour, and captain of escaladores, or those employed to scale the walls of fortresses in time of attack. Ortega approached Alhama one moonless night and paced along its walls with noiseless step, laying his ear occasionally to the ground or to the wall.

Every time he distinguished the measured tread of a centinel, and now and then the challenge of the night watch going its rounds. Finding the town thus guarded he clambered to the castle. There all was silent: as he ranged its lofty battlements between him and the sky, he saw no centinel on duty. He noticed certain places where the wall might be ascended by scaling ladders, and having marked the hour of relieving guard, and made all necessary observations, he retired without being discovered.

Ortega returned to Marchena and assured the Marquis of Cadiz of the practicability of scaling the castle of Alhama and taking it by surprize. The marquis had a secret conference with Don Pedro Henriquez, Adelantado of Andalusia, Don Diego de Merlo, commander of Seville and Sancho de Avila, Alcayde of Carmona, who all agreed to aid him with their forces. On an appointed day the several commanders assembled at Marchena with their troops and retainers. None but the leaders knew the object or destination of the enterprize, but it was enough to rouse the Andalusian spirit to know that a foray was intended into the country of their old enemies the Moors. Secrecy and celerity were necessary for success. They set out promptly with three thousand Genetes or light cavalry, and four thousand infantry. They chose a route but little travelled, by the way of Antequera, passing with great labour through rugged and solitary defiles of the sierra or chain of mountains of Alzerifa, and left all their baggage on the banks of the river Yeguas to be brought after them. Their march was principally in the night; all day they remained quiet; no noise was suffered in their camp, and no fires were made, lest the smoke should betray them. On the third day they resumed their march as the evening darkened, and forcing themselves forward at as quick a pace as the rugged and dangerous mountain roads would permit, they descended towards midnight into a small deep valley, only half a league from Alhama. Here they made a halt, fatigued by this forced march during a long dark evening towards the end of February.

The Marquis of Cadiz now explained to the troops the object of the expedition. He told them it was for the glory of the most holy faith, and to avenge the wrongs of their countrymen of Zahara; and that the rich town of Alhama, full of wealthy spoil, was the place to be attacked. The troops were roused to new ardour by these words, and desired to be led forthwith to the assault. They arrived close to Alhama about two hours before day break. Here the army remained in ambush, while three hundred men were dispatched to scale the walls and take possession of the castle. They were picked men, many of them alcaydes and officers, men who preferred death to dishonour. This gallant band was guided by the escalador, Ortega de Prado, at the head of thirty men with scaling ladders. They clambered the ascent to the castle in silence, and arrived under the dark shadow of its towers without being discovered. Not a light was to be seen, not a sound to be heard; the whole place was wrapped in profound repose.

Fixing their ladders they ascended cautiously and with noiseless steps. Ortega was the first that mounted upon the battlements, followed by one Martin Galindo a youthful esquire full of spirit and eager for distinction. Moving stealthily along the parapet to the portal of the citadel, they came upon the centinel by surprize. Ortega seized him by the throat, brandished a dagger before his eyes, and ordered him to point the way to the guard room. The infidel obeyed and was instantly dispatched to prevent his giving any alarm. The guard room was a scene rather of massacre than combat. Some of the soldiery were killed while sleeping, others were cut down almost without resistance, bewildered by so unexpected an assault: all were dispatched, for the scaling party was too small to make prisoners or to spare. The alarm spread throughout the castle, but by this time the three hundred picked men had mounted the battlements. The garrison, startled from sleep, found the enemy already masters of the towers. Some of the Moors were cut down at once, others fought desperately from room to room and the whole castle resounded with the clash of arms, the cries of the combatants and the groans of the wounded. The army in ambush finding by the uproar that the castle was surprized, now rushed from their concealment and approached the walls with loud shouts, and sound of kettle drums and trumpets, to encrease the confusion and dismay of the garrison. A violent conflict took place in the court of the castle where several of the scaling party sought to throw open the gates to admit their countrymen. Here fell two valiant alcaydes, Nicholas de Roja and Sancho de Avila, but they fell honourably upon a heap of slain. At length Ortega de Prado succeeded in throwing open a postern, through which the Marquis of Cadiz, the Adelantado of Andalusia and Don Diego de Merlo entered with a host of followers, and the citadel remained in full possession of the Christians.

As the Spanish cavaliers were ranging from room to room, the Marquis of Cadiz entering an apartment of superior richness to the rest, beheld by the light of a silver lamp a beautiful Moorish female, the wife of the alcayde of the castle, whose husband was absent, attending a wedding feast at Velez Malaga. She would have fled at the sight of a Christian warrior in her apartment, but entangled in the covering of the bed, she fell at the feet of the marquis imploring mercy. The Christian cavalier, who had a soul full of honour and courtesy towards the sex, raised her from the earth and endeavoured to allay her fears; but they were encreased at the sight of her female attendants, pursued into the room by the Spanish soldiery. The marquis reproached his soldiers with their unmanly conduct, and reminded them that they made war upon men, not on defenceless women. Having soothed the terrors of the females by the promise of honourable protection, he appointed a trusty guard to watch over the security of their apartment.

The castle was now taken, but the town below it was in arms. It was broad day, and the people, recovered from their panic, were enabled to see and estimate the force of the enemy. The inhabitants were chiefly merchants and trades-people, but the Moors all possessed a knowledge of the use of weapons, and were of brave and warlike spirit. They confided in the strength of their walls, and the certainty of speedy relief from Granada, which was but about eight leagues distant. Manning the battlements and towers, they discharged showers of stones and arrows whenever the part of the Christian army without the walls, attempted to approach. They barricadoed the entrances of their streets, also, which opened towards the castle, stationing men expert at the cross bow and arquebus. These kept up a constant fire upon the gate of the castle, so that no one could sally forth without being instantly shot down. Two valiant cavaliers who attempted to lead forth a party in defiance of this fatal tempest, were shot dead at the very portal.

The Christians now found themselves in a situation of great peril. Reinforcements must soon arrive to the enemy from Granada; unless, therefore, they gained possession of the town in the course of the day, they were likely to be surrounded and beleaguered without provisions, in the castle. Some observed that, even if they took the town, they should not be able to maintain possession of it. They proposed therefore to make booty of every thing valuable, to sack the castle, set it on fire and make good their retreat to Seville.

The Marquis of Cadiz was of different counsel. "God has given the Citadel into Christian hands," said he; "he will no doubt strengthen them to maintain it. We have gained the place with difficulty and bloodshed; it would be a stain upon our honour to abandon it through fear of imaginary dangers." The adelantado and Don Diego de Merlo joined in his opinion, but, without their earnest and united remonstrances, the place would have been abandoned, so exhausted were the troops by forced marches and hard fighting, and so apprehensive of the approach of the Moors of Granada.

The strength and spirits of the party within the castle were in some degree restored by the provisions which they found. The Christian army beneath the town, being also refreshed by a morning's repast, advanced vigorously to the attack of the walls. They planted their scaling ladders and swarming up, sword in hand, fought fiercely with the Moorish soldiery upon the ramparts.

In the meantime the Marquis of Cadiz, seeing that the gate of the castle, which opened toward the city, was completely commanded by the artillery of the enemy, ordered a large breach to be made in the wall, through which he might lead his troops to the attack; animating them in this perilous moment, by assuring them that the place should be given up to plunder, and its inhabitants made captives.

The breach being made, the marquis put himself at the head of his troops and entered sword in hand. A simultaneous attack was made by the Christians in every part, by the ramparts, by the gate, by the roofs and walls which connected the castle with the town. The Moors fought valiantly in their streets, from their windows and from the tops of their houses. They were not equal to the Christians in bodily strength, for they were for the most part peaceful men, of industrious callings, and ennervated by the frequent use of the warm bath; but they were superior in number and unconquerable in spirit; old and young, strong and weak fought with the same desperation. The Moors fought for property, for liberty, for life. They fought at their thresholds and their hearths; with the shrieks of their wives and children ringing in their ears, and they fought in the hope that each moment would bring aid from Granada. They regarded neither their own wounds nor the deaths of their companions, but continued fighting until they fell, and seemed as if, when they could no longer contend, they would block up the thresholds of their beloved homes, with their mangled bodies. The Christians fought for glory, for revenge, for the holy faith, and for the spoil of these wealthy infidels. Success would place a rich town at their mercy, failure would deliver them into the hands of the tyrant of Granada.

The contest raged from morning until night, when the Moors began to yield. Retreating to a large mosque near the walls, they kept up so galling a fire from it with lances, cross bows, and arquebusses, that for some time the Christians dared not approach. Covering themselves at length, with bucklers and mantelets* to protect them from the deadly shower, they made their way to the mosque and set fire to the doors. When the smoke and flames rolled in upon them, the Moors gave all up as lost. Many rushed forth desperately upon the enemy, but were immediately slain; the rest surrendered.

The struggle was now at an end; the town remained at the mercy of the Christians; and the inhabitants, both male and female, became slaves of those who made them prisoners. Some few escaped by a mine or subterranean way which led to the river, and concealed themselves, their wives and children in caves and secret places, but in three or four days were compelled to surrender themselves through hunger.

The town was given up to plunder, and the booty was immense. There were found prodigious quantities of gold, and silver, and jewels, and rich silks and costly stuffs of all kinds, together with horses and beeves, and abundance of grain and oil, and honey, and all other productions of this fruitful kingdom; for in Alhama were collected the royal rents and tributes of the surrounding country: it was the richest town in the Moorish territory, and from its great strength and its peculiar situation was called the key to Granada.

Great waste and devastation was committed by the Spanish soldiery, for, thinking it would be impossible to keep possession of the place, they began

---

*Mantelet. A moveable parapet made of thick planks, to protect troops when advancing to sap or assault a walled place.

to destroy whatever they could not take away. Immense jars of oil were broken, costly furniture shattered to pieces, and magazines of grain broken open and their contents scattered to the winds. Many Christian captives who had been taken at Zahara were found buried in a Moorish dungeon, and were triumphantly restored to light and liberty, and a renegado Spaniard, who had often served as guide to the Moors in their incursions into the Christian territories, was hanged on the highest part of the battlements, for the edification of the army.

CHAPTER VI

HOW THE PEOPLE OF GRANADA WERE AFFECTED ON HEARING OF THE CAPTURE OF ALHAMA, AND HOW THE MOORISH KING SALLIED FORTH TO REGAIN IT.

A Moorish horseman had spurred across the vega; nor reined his panting steed until he alighted at the gate of the Alhambra. He brought tidings to Muley Aben Hassan of the attack upon Alhama. "The Christians," said he, "are in the land. They came upon us we know not whence or how; and scaled the walls of the castle in the night. There has been dreadful fighting and carnage on its towers and courts, and when I spurred my steed from the gate of Alhama the castle was in possession of the unbelievers."

Muley Aben Hassan felt for a moment as if swift retribution had come upon him for the woes he had inflicted upon Zahara. Still he flattered himself that this had only been some transient inroad of a party of marauders, intent upon plunder; and that a little succour, thrown into the town, would be sufficient to expel them from the castle and drive them from the land. He ordered out, therefore, a thousand of his chosen cavalry and sent them in all speed to the assistance of Alhama. They arrived before its walls the morning after its capture; the Christian standards floated upon the towers, and a body of cavalry poured forth from its gates and came wheeling down into the plain to receive them.

The Moorish horsemen turned the reins of their steeds and galloped back for Granada. They entered its gates in tumultuous confusion spreading terror and lamentation by their tidings. "Alhama is fallen! Alhama is fallen!" exclaimed they; "the Christians garrison its walls; the key of Granada is in the hands of the enemy!"

When the people heard these words they remembered the denunciation of the Santon. His prediction seemed still to resound in every ear, and its fulfilment to be at hand. Nothing was heard throughout the city but sighs and wailings. "Woe is me, Alhama!" was in every mouth, and this ejaculation of deep sorrow and doleful foreboding, came to be the burthen of a plaintive ballad, which remains until the present day.*

Many aged men who had taken refuge in Granada from other Moorish dominions which had fallen into the power of the Christians, now groaned in despair at the thoughts that war was to follow them into this last retreat, to lay waste this pleasant land, and to bring trouble and sorrow upon their declining years. The women were more loud and vehement in their grief, for they beheld the evils impending over their children, and what can restrain the agony of a mother's heart? Many of them made their way through the halls of the Alhambra into the presence of the King, weeping, and wailing and tearing their hair. "Accursed be the day," cried they, "that thou hast lit the flame of war in our land! May the holy Prophet bear witness before Allah that we and our children are innocent of this act. Upon thy head, and upon the heads of thy posterity, until the end of the world, rest the sin of the desolation of Zahara."†

Muley Aben Hassan remained unmoved amidst all this storm; his heart was hardened, observes Fray Antonio Agapida, like that of Pharaoh, to the end that through his blind violence and rage he might produce the deliverance of the land from its heathen bondage. "In fact, he was a bold and fearless warrior, and trusted soon to make this blow recoil upon the head of the enemy. He had ascertained that the captors of Alhama were but a handful; they were in the centre of his dominions, within a short distance of his capital. They were deficient in munitions of war, and provisions for sustaining a siege. By a rapid movement he might surround them with a powerful army, cut off all aid from their countrymen, and entrap them in the fortress they had taken."

To think was to act, with Muley Aben Hassan, but he was prone to act with too much precipitation. He immediately set forth in person, with three thousand horse and fifty thousand foot, and in his eagerness to arrive at the scene of action, would not wait to provide artillery and the various engines required in a siege. "The multitude of my forces," said he confidently, "will be sufficient to overwhelm the enemy."

The Marquis of Cadiz who thus held possession of Alhama, had a chosen friend and faithful companion in arms among the most distinguished of the Christian chivalry. This was Don Alonzo de Cordova, senior and lord of the house of Aguilar, and brother of Gonzalvo of Cordova, afterwards renowned as Grand Captain of Spain. As yet Alonzo de Aguilar was the glory of his name and race, for his brother was but young in arms. He was one of the

*The mournful little Spanish romance of *Ay de mi Alhama*! is supposed to be of Moorish origin, and to embody the grief of the people of Granada on this occasion.
†Garibay. Lib. 40. C. 29.

most hardy, valiant and enterprizing Spanish knights, and foremost in all service of a perilous and adventurous nature. He had not been at hand to accompany his friend Ponce de Leon, Marquis of Cadiz, in his inroad into the Moorish territory, but he hastily assembled a number of retainers, horse and foot, and pressed forward to join the enterprize. Arriving at the river Yeguas he found the baggage of the army still upon its banks, and took charge of it to carry it to Alhama. The Marquis of Cadiz heard of the approach of his friend, whose march was slow in consequence of being encumbered by the baggage.

He was within but a few leagues of Alhama, when scouts came hurrying into the place, with intelligence that the Moorish King was at hand with a powerful army. The Marquis of Cadiz was filled with alarm lest De Aguilar should fall into the hands of the enemy. Forgetting his own danger and thinking only of that of his friend, he dispatched a well mounted messenger to ride full speed and warn him not to approach.

The first determination of Alonzo de Aguilar, when he heard that the Moorish King was at hand, was to take a strong position in the mountains and await his coming. The madness of an attempt with his handful of men to oppose an immense army was represented to him with such force as to induce him to abandon the idea: he then thought of throwing himself into Alhama to share the fortunes of his friend; but it was now too late. The Moor would infallibly intercept him, and he should only give the marquis the additional distress of beholding him captured beneath his walls. It was even urged upon him that he had no time for delay if he would consult his own safety, which could only be ensured by an immediate retreat into the Christian territory. This last opinion was confirmed by the return of scouts who brought information that Muley Aben Hassan had received notice of his movements and was rapidly advancing in quest of him. It was with infinite reluctance that Don Alonzo de Aguilar yielded to these united and powerful reasons. Proudly and sullenly he drew off his forces, laden with the baggage of the army, and made an unwilling retreat towards Antequera. Muley Aben Hassan pursued him for some distance through the mountains, but soon gave up the chace and turned with his forces upon Alhama.

As the army approached the town they beheld the fields strown with the dead bodies of their countrymen, who had fallen in defence of the place, and had been cast forth and left unburied by the Christians. There they lay mangled and exposed to every indignity, while droves of half famished dogs were preying upon them and fighting and howling over their hideous repast.* Furious at the sight, the Moors, in the first transports of their rage, attacked those ravenous animals; their next measure was to vent their fury upon the Christians. They rushed like madmen to the walls, applied scaling

*Pulgar. Cronica.

ladders in all parts without waiting for the necessary mantelets and other protections, thinking by attacking suddenly and at various points to distract the enemy, and overcome them by the force of numbers.

The Marquis of Cadiz with his confederate commanders distributed themselves along the walls, to direct and animate their men in the defence. The Moors in their blind fury often assailed the most difficult and dangerous places. Darts, stones and all kinds of missiles were hurled down upon their defenceless heads. As fast as they mounted they were cut down, or dashed from the battlements; their ladders overturned and all who were on them precipitated headlong below.

Muley Aben Hassan stormed with passion at the sight: he sent detachment after detachment to scale the walls, but in vain; they were like waves rushing upon a rock only to dash themselves to pieces. The Moors lay in heaps beneath the wall, and among them many of the bravest cavaliers of Granada. The Christians, also, sallied frequently from the gates, and made great havoc in the irregular multitude of assailants.

On one of these occasions the party was commanded by Don Juan de Vera, the same pious and high handed knight who had borne the embassy to Muley Aben Hassan demanding tribute. As this doughty cavalier, after a career of carnage, was slowly retreating to the gate he heard a voice calling after him in furious accents. "Turn back! turn back!" cried the voice; "thou who canst insult in hall, prove that thou canst combat in the field." Don Juan de Vera turned and beheld the same Abencerrage whom he had struck with his sword in the Alhambra, for scoffing at the immaculate conception of the blessed virgin. All his holy zeal and pious indignation rekindled at the sight; he put lance in rest and spurred his steed to finish this doctrinal dispute. Don Juan de Vera was a potent and irresistible arguer with his weapon, and he was aided, says Fray Antonio Agapida, by the peculiar virtue of his cause. At the very first encounter his lance entered the mouth of the Moor and hurled him to the earth, never more to utter word or breath. Thus, continues the worthy Friar, did this scoffing infidel receive a well merited punishment through the very organ with which he had offended, and thus was the immaculate conception miraculously vindicated from his foul aspersions.

The vigorous and successful defence of the Christians now made Muley Aben Hassan sensible of his error in hurrying from Granada without the proper engines for a siege. Destitute of all means to batter the fortifications the town remained uninjured, defying the mighty army which raged and roamed before it. Incensed at being thus foiled, Muley Aben Hassan gave orders to undermine the walls. The Moors advanced with shouts to the attempt. They were received with a deadly fire from the ramparts, which drove them from their works. Repeatedly were they repulsed, and repeatedly did they return to the charge. The Christians not merely galled them from the battlements, but issued forth and cut them down in the excavations they were attempting to form. The contest lasted throughout a whole day, and by evening two thousand Moors were either killed or wounded.

Muley Aben Hassan now abandoned all hope of carrying the place by assault; and attempted to distress it into terms by turning the channel of the river which runs by its walls. On this stream the inhabitants depended for their supply of water, the place being destitute of fountains and cisterns, from which circumstance it is called Alhama *la Seca* "or the dry."

A desperate conflict ensued on the banks of the river, the Moors endeavouring to plant pallisadoes in its bed to divert the stream, and the Christians striving to prevent them. The Spanish commanders exposed themselves to the utmost danger to animate their men who were repeatedly driven back into the town. The Marquis of Cadiz was often up to his knees in the stream, fighting hand to hand with the Moors. The water ran red with blood and was encumbered with dead bodies. At length the overwhelming numbers of the Moors gave them the advantage, and they succeeded in diverting the greater part of the water. The Christians had to struggle severely to supply themselves from the feeble rill which remained. They sallied to the river by a subterraneous passage, but the Moorish cross bow men stationed themselves on the opposite bank keeping up a heavy fire upon the Christians whenever they attempted to fill their vessels from the scanty and turbid stream. One party of the Christians had, therefore, to fight while another drew water. At all hours of day and night this deadly strife was maintained, until it seemed as if every drop of water were purchased with a drop of blood.

In the mean time the sufferings in the town became intense. None but the soldiery and their horses were allowed the precious beverage so dearly earned, and even that in quantities that only tantalized their wants. The wounded who could not sally to procure it, were almost destitute; while the unhappy prisoners, shut up in the mosques, were reduced to frightful extremities. Many perished raving mad, fancying themselves swimming in boundless seas yet unable to assuage their thirst. Many of the soldiers lay parched and panting along the battlements, no longer able to draw a bow string or hurl a stone, while above five thousand Moors, stationed upon a rocky height which overlooked part of the town, kept up a galling fire into it with slings and cross bows; so that the Marquis of Cadiz was obliged to heighten the battlements by using the doors from the private dwellings.

The Christian cavaliers exposed to this extreme peril, and in imminent danger of falling into the hands of the enemy, dispatched fleet messengers to Seville and Cordova, entreating the chivalry of Andalusia to hasten to their aid. They sent likewise to implore assistance from the King and Queen, who at that time held their court in Medina del Campo. In the midst of their distress, a tank, or cistern, of water was fortunately discovered in the city, which gave temporary relief to their sufferings.

CHAPTER VII

HOW THE DUKE OF MEDINA SIDONIA AND THE CHIVALRY OF ANDALUSIA HASTENED TO THE RELIEF OF ALHAMA.

The perilous situation of the Christian cavaliers, pent up and beleaguered within the walls of Alhama, spread terror among their friends, and anxiety throughout all Andalusia. Nothing, however, could equal the anguish of the Marchioness of Cadiz, the wife of the gallant Roderigo Ponce de Leon; in her deep distress she looked round for some powerful noble, who had the means of rousing the country to the assistance of her husband. No one appeared more competent for the purpose than Don Juan de Guzman, the Duke of Medina Sidonia. He was one of the most wealthy and puissant grandees of Spain; his possessions extended over some of the most fertile parts of Andalusia, embracing towns and seaports and numerous villages. Here he reigned in feudal state like a petty sovereign, and could at any time bring into the field an immense force of vassals and retainers. The Duke of Medina Sidonia and the Marquis of Cadiz, however, were at this time deadly foes. An hereditary feud existed between them which had often arisen to bloodshed and open war; for as yet the fierce contests between the proud and puissant Spanish nobles had not been completely quelled by the power of the crown, and in this respect they exerted a right of sovereignty, in leading their vassals against each other in open field.

The Duke of Medina Sidonia would have appeared to many, the very last person to whom to apply for aid of the Marquis of Cadiz, but the marchioness judged of him by the standard of her own high and generous mind. She knew him to be a gallant and courteous knight, and had already experienced the magnanimity of his spirit, having been relieved by him when besieged by the Moors in her husband's fortress of Arcos. To the duke, therefore, she applied in this moment of sudden calamity, imploring him to furnish succour to her husband. The event shewed how well noble spirits understand each other. No sooner did the duke receive this appeal from the wife of his enemy, than he generously forgot all feeling of animosity, and determined to go in person to his succour. He immediately dispatched a courteous letter to the marchioness, assuring her that in consideration of the request of so honourable and estimable a lady; and to rescue from peril so valiant a cavalier as her husband, whose loss would be great, not only to Spain, but to all Christendom, he would forego the recollection of all past grievances, and hasten to his relief with all the forces he could raise.

The duke wrote at the same time to the alcaydes of his towns and fortresses, ordering them to join him forthwith at Seville with all the force they could spare from their garrisons. He called on all the chivalry of Andalusia to make a common cause in the rescue of those Christian cavaliers, and he offered large pay to all volunteers who would resort to him with horses, armour and provisions. Thus all who could be incited by honour, religion, patriotism or thirst of gain were induced to hasten to his standard, and he took the field with an army of five thousand horse and fifty thousand foot.* Many cavaliers of distinguished name accompanied him in this generous enterprize, among these was the redoubtable Alonzo de Aguilar, the chosen friend of the Marquis of Cadiz, and with him his younger brother Gonzalvo Fernandez de Cordova afterwards renowned as the Grand Captain. Don Rodrigo Giron, also, Master of the Order of Calatrava, together with Martin Alonzo de Montemayor, and the Marquis de Villena, esteemed the best lance in Spain. It was a gallant and splendid army comprizing the flower of Spanish chivalry, and poured forth in brilliant array from the gates of Seville, bearing the great Standard of that ancient and renowned city.

Ferdinand and Isabella were at Medina del Campo, when tidings came of the capture of Alhama. The King was at mass when he received the news and ordered *te deum* to be chaunted for this signal triumph of the holy faith. When the first flush of triumph had subsided, and the King learnt the imminent peril of the valorous Ponce de Leon and his companions, and the great danger that this strong hold might again be wrested from their grasp, he resolved to hurry in person to the scene of action. So pressing appeared to him the emergency that he barely gave himself time to take a hasty repast while horses were providing, and then departed at furious speed for Andalusia, leaving a request for the Queen to follow him.† He was attended by Don Beltran de la Cueva, Duke of Albuquerque, Don Inigo Lopez de Mendoza, Count of Tendilla, and Don Pedro Manriquez, Count of Trevino, with a few more cavaliers of prowess and distinction. He travelled by forced journeys, frequently changing his jaded horses, being eager to arrive in time to take command of the Andalusian chivalry. When he arrived within five leagues of Cordova the Duke of Albuquerque remonstrated with him upon entering with such incautious haste into the enemy's country. He represented to him that there were troops enough assembled to succour Alhama, and that it was not for him to venture his royal person in doing what could be done by his subjects; especially as he had such valiant and experienced captains to act for him. "Besides, Sire," added the duke, "your majesty should bethink you that the troops about to take the field are mere men of Andalusia, whereas your illustrious predecessors never made an inroad into the territory of the Moors without being accompanied by a powerful force of the staunch and iron warriors of old Castile."

"Duke," replied the King, "your counsel might have been good had I not departed from Medina with the avowed determination of succouring these

---

*Cronica de los Duques de Medina Sidonia por Pedro de Medina. Ms.
†Illescas. Hist. Pontifical.

cavaliers in person. I am now near the end of my journey, and it would be beneath my dignity to change my intention, before even I had met with an impediment. I shall take the troops of this country who are assembled, without waiting for those of Castile, and with the aid of God, shall prosecute my journey."*

As King Ferdinand approached Cordova the principal inhabitants came forth to receive him. Learning, however, that the Duke of Medina Sidonia was already on the march, and pressing forward into the territory of the Moors, the King was all on fire to overtake him, and to lead in person the succour to Alhama. Without entering Cordova, therefore, he exchanged his weary horses for those of the inhabitants who had come forth to meet him, and pressed forward for the army. He dispatched fleet couriers in advance, requesting the Duke of Medina Sidonia to await his coming that he might take command of the forces.

Neither the duke nor his companions in arms, however, felt inclined to pause in their generous expedition, and gratify the inclination of the King. They sent back missives representing that they were far within the enemy's frontier and it was dangerous either to pause or turn back. They had likewise received pressing entreaties from the besieged to hasten their speed, setting forth their great sufferings and their hourly peril of being overwhelmed by the enemy.

The King was at Porton del Maestre when he received these missives. So inflamed was he with zeal for the success of this enterprize, that he would have penetrated into the Kingdom of Granada with the handful of cavaliers who accompanied him, but they represented the rashness of such a journey, through the mountainous defiles of a hostile country thickly beset with towns and castles. With some difficulty, therefore, he was dissuaded from his inclination, and prevailed upon to await tidings from the army, in the frontier city of Antequera.

CHAPTER VIII

SEQUEL OF THE EVENTS AT ALHAMA.

While all Andalusia was thus in arms and pouring its chivalry through the mountain passes of the Moorish frontier, the garrison of Alhama was reduced to great extremity, and in danger of sinking under its sufferings before the promised succour could arrive. The intolerable thirst that prevailed in consequence of the scarcity of water, the incessant watch that had to be main-

*Pulgar. Cronica. P. 3. C. 3.

tained over the vast force of enemies without, and the great number of prisoners within, and the wounds which almost every soldier had received in the incessant skirmishes and assaults, had worn grievously both flesh and spirit. The noble Ponce de Leon, Marquis of Cadiz, still animated the soldiery, however, by word and example, sharing every hardship, and being foremost in every danger; exemplifying that a good commander is the vital spirit of an army.

When Muley Aben Hassan heard of the vast force that was approaching under the command of the Duke of Medina Sidonia, and that Ferdinand was coming in person with additional troops, he perceived that no time was to be lost: Alhama must be carried by one powerful attack, or abandoned entirely to the Christians.

A number of Moorish cavaliers, some of the bravest youth of Granada, knowing the wishes of the King, proposed to undertake a desperate enterprize, which, if successful, must put Alhama in his power. Early one morning, when it was scarcely the grey of the dawn, about the time of changing the watch, these cavaliers approached the town, at a place considered inaccessible, from the steepness of the rocks on which the wall was founded; which it was supposed elevated the battlements beyond the reach of the longest scaling ladders. The Moorish knights, aided by a number of the strongest and most active escaladors, mounted these rocks and applied the ladders without being discovered; for to divert attention from them, Muley Aben Hassan made a false attack upon the town in another quarter.

The scaling party mounted with difficulty and in small numbers; the centinel was killed at his post, and seventy of the Moors made their way into the streets before an alarm was given. The guards rushed to the walls to stop the hostile throng that was still pouring in. A sharp conflict, hand to hand, and man to man, took place on the battlements, and many on both sides fell. The Moors, whether wounded or slain, were thrown headlong without the walls, the scaling ladders were overturned, and those who were mounting were dashed upon the rocks, and from thence tumbled upon the plain. Thus in a little while the ramparts were cleared by Christian prowess, led on by that valiant knight Don Alonzo Ponce the uncle, and that brave Esquire Pedro Pinedo, nephew of the Marquis of Cadiz.

The walls being cleared, these two kindred cavaliers now hastened with their forces in pursuit of the seventy Moors who had gained an entrance into the town. The main part of the garrison being engaged at a distance, resisting the feigned attack of the Moorish King, this fierce band of infidels had ranged the streets, almost without opposition, and were making their way to the gates to throw them open to the army.* They were chosen men from among the Moorish forces, several of them gallant knights of the proudest

*Zurita. lib. 20. Cap 43.

families of Granada. Their footsteps through the city were in a manner printed in blood, and they were tracked by the bodies of those they had killed
and wounded. They had attained the gate, most of the guard had fallen beneath their scymetars, a moment more and Alhama would have been thrown
open to the enemy.

Just at this juncture Don Alonzo Ponce and Pedro de Pineda reached the
spot with their forces. The Moors had the enemy in front and rear; they
placed themselves back to back with their banner in the centre. In this way
they fought with desperate and deadly determination making a rampart
around them with the slain. More Christian troops arrived and hemmed
them in; but still they fought, without asking for quarter. As their numbers
decreased they serried their circle still closer, defending their banner from
assault, and the last Moor died at his post grasping the standard of the
Prophet. This standard was displayed from the walls, and the turbaned
heads of the Moors were thrown down to the besiegers.*

Muley Aben Hassan tore his beard with rage at the failure of this attempt
and at the death of so many of his chosen cavaliers. He saw that all further
effort was in vain: His scouts brought word that they had seen from the
heights the long columns and flaunting banners of the Christian army approaching through the mountains. To linger would be to place himself between two bodies of the enemy. Breaking up his camp, therefore, in all
haste, he gave up the siege of Alhama and hastened back to Granada, and
the last clash of his cymbals scarce died upon the ear from the distant hills,
before the standard of the Duke of Sidonia was seen emerging in another
direction from the defiles of the mountains.

When the Christians in Alhama beheld their enemies retreating on one
side and their friends advancing on the other, they uttered shouts of joy and
hymns of thanksgiving, for it was as a sudden relief from present death.
Harrassed by several weeks of incessant vigil, and fighting; suffering from
scarcity of provisions and almost continual thirst, they resembled skeletons
rather than living men. It was a noble and gracious sight to behold the meeting of those two ancient foes the Duke of Medina Sidonia and the Marquis
of Cadiz. When the marquis beheld his magnanimous deliverer approaching
he melted into tears: all past animosities only gave the greater poignancy to
present feelings of gratitude and admiration; they clasped each other in their
arms, and from that time forward were true and cordial friends.

While this generous scene took place between the commanders, a sordid
contest arose among their troops. The soldiers who had come to the rescue
claimed a portion of the spoils of Alhama, and so violent was the dispute,

*Pedro de Pineda received the honour of knighthood from the hand of King Ferdinand
for his valour on this occasion. (Alonzo Ponce was already knight.) See Zuñiga Annals of
Seville. Lib. 12. an. 1482.

that both parties seized their arms. The Duke of Medina Sidonia interfered and settled the question with his characteristic magnanimity. He declared that the spoil belonged to those who had captured the city. "We have taken the field," said he, "only for honour, for religion and for the rescue of our countrymen and fellow Christians; and the success of our enterprize is a sufficient and a glorious reward. If we desire booty, there are sufficient Moorish cities yet to be taken, to enrich us all." The soldiers were convinced by the frank and chivalrous reasoning of the duke; they replied to his speech by acclamations, and the transient broil was happily appeased.

The Marchioness of Cadiz, with the forethought of a loving wife, had dispatched her Major Domo with the army with a large supply of provisions. Tables were immediately spread beneath the tents, where the marquis gave a banquet to the duke and the cavaliers who had accompanied him, and nothing but hilarity prevailed in this late scene of suffering and death.

A garrison of fresh troops was left in Alhama, and the veterans who had so valiantly captured and maintained it, returned to their homes burthened with precious booty. The marquis and duke with their confederate cavaliers repaired to Antequera where they were received with great distinction by the King, who honoured the Marquis of Cadiz with signal marks of favour. The duke then accompanied his late enemy, but now most zealous and grateful friend, the Marquis of Cadiz, to his town of Marchena, where he received the reward of his generous conduct in the thanks and blessings of the marchioness. The marquis celebrated a sumptuous feast in honour of his guest; for a day and night his palace was thrown open and was the scene of continual revel and festivity; when the duke departed for his estates at S' Lucas, the marquis attended him for some distance on his journey, and when they separated it was as the parting scene of brothers. Such was the noble spectacle exhibited to the chivalry of Spain by these two illustrious rivals. Each reaped universal renown from the part he had performed in the campaign: the marquis from having surprized and captured one of the most important and formidable fortresses of the Kingdom of Granada, and the duke from having subdued his deadliest foe by a great act of magnanimity.

CHAPTER IX

EVENTS AT GRANADA AND RISE OF THE MOORISH KING BOABDIL EL CHICO.

The Moorish King Aben Hassan returned, baffled and disappointed, from before the walls of Alhama, and was received with groans and smothered execrations by the people of Granada. The prediction of the Santon was in every mouth, and appeared to be rapidly fulfilling; for the enemy was already strongly fortified in Alhama, in the very heart of the kingdom. The disaffection which broke out in murmurs among the common people fermented more secretly and dangerously among the nobles. Muley Aben Hassan was of a fierce and cruel nature, his reign had been marked with tyranny and bloodshed, and many chiefs of the family of the Abencerrages, the noblest lineage among the Moors, had fallen victims to his policy or vengeance. A deep plot was now formed to put an end to his oppressions and dispossess him of the throne. The situation of the royal household favoured the conspiracy.

Muley Aben Hassan though cruel was uxorious, that is to say, he had many wives, and was prone to be managed by them by turns. He had two queens in particular whom he had chosen from affection. One named Ayxa was a Moorish female. She was likewise termed in Arabic, La Horra or the chaste, from the spotless purity of her character. While yet in the prime of her beauty she bore a son to Aben Hassan the expected heir to his throne. The name of this prince was Mahomet Abdalla, or, as he has more generally been termed among historians, Boabdil. At his birth the astrologers, according to custom, cast his horoscope; they were seized with fear and trembling when they beheld the fatal portents revealed to their science. "Allah Achbar! God is great!" exclaimed they; "he alone controuls the fate of empires. It is written in the heavens that this prince shall sit upon the throne of Granada, but that the downfall of the kingdom shall be accomplished during his reign." From this time the prince was ever regarded with aversion by his father, and the series of persecutions which he suffered, and the dark prediction which hung over him from his infancy, procured him the surname of El Zogoybi, or "the unfortunate." He is more commonly known by the appellation of El Chico (the Younger) to distinguish him from an usurping uncle.

The other favourite Queen of Aben Hassan was named Fatima, to which the Moors added the appellation of La Zoroya, or the light of the dawn, from her effulgent beauty. She was a Christian by birth, the daughter of the commander Sancho Ximenes de Solis, and had been taken captive in her tender youth.*

The King, who was well stricken in years at the time, became enamoured of the blooming Christian maid; he made her his Sultana, and like most old men who marry in their dotage, resigned himself to her management. Zoroya became the mother of two princes and her anxiety for their advancement seemed to extinguish every other natural feeling in her breast. She was as ambitious as she was beautiful, and her ruling desire became to see one of her sons seated upon the throne of Granada.

For this purpose she made use of all her arts, and of the complete ascen-

*Cronica del Gran Cardinal C. 70.

dancy she had over the mind of her cruel husband, to undermine his other children in his affections, and to fill him with jealousies of their designs. Muley Aben Hassan was so wrought upon by her machinations that he publickly put several of his sons to death at the celebrated fountain of Lions, in the court of the Alhambra, a place signalized in Moorish history as the scene of many sanguinary deeds.

The next measure of Zoroya was against her rival Sultana, the virtuous Ayxa. She was past the bloom of her beauty and had ceased to be attractive in the eyes of her husband. He was easily persuaded to repudiate her and to confine her and her son in the tower of Comares, one of the principal towers of the Alhambra. As Boabdil increased in years, Zoroya beheld in him a formidable obstacle to the pretensions of her sons, for he was universally considered heir apparent to the throne. The jealousies, suspicions and alarms of his tyger hearted father were again excited, he was reminded too of the prediction that fixed the ruin of the kingdom during the reign of this prince. Muley Aben Hassan impiously set the stars at defiance. "The sword of the executioner," said he, "shall prove the falsehood of these lying horoscopes, and shall silence the ambition of Boabdil as it has the presumption of his brothers."

The Sultana Ayxa was secretly apprized of the cruel design of the old monarch. She was a woman of talents and courage, and by means of her female attendants concerted a plan for the escape of her son. A faithful servant was instructed to wait below the Alhambra, in the dead of the night on the banks of the river Darro, with a fleet Arabian courser. The Sultana, when the castle was in a state of deep repose, tied together the shawls and scarfs of herself and her female attendants and lowered the youthful prince from the tower of Comares.* He made his way in safety down the steep rocky hill to the banks of the Darro, and throwing himself on the Arabian courser, was thus spirited off to the city of Guadix in the Alpuxarres. Here he lay for some time concealed, until, gaining adherents, he fortified himself in the place, and set the machinations of his tyrant father at defiance. Such was the state of affairs in the royal household of Granada, when Muley Aben Hassan returned foiled from his expedition against Alhama. The faction which had secretly formed among the nobles determined to depose the old King Aben Hassan, and to elevate his son Boabdil to the throne. They concerted their measures with the latter, and an opportunity soon presented to put them in practice. Muley Aben Hassan had a royal country palace called Alexares, in the vicinity of Granada, to which he resorted occasionally to recreate his mind during this time of perplexity. He had been passing one day among its

*Salazar, Cronica del Gran Cardenal. Cap. 71.

bowers, when, on returning to the capital he found the gates closed against him, and his son Mohammed Abdalla, otherwise called Boabdil, proclaimed King. "Alla Achbar! God is great!" exclaimed old Muley Aben Hassan; "it is in vain to contend against what is written in the book of fate. It was predestined that my son should sit upon the throne, Alla forefend the rest of the prediction." The old monarch knew the inflammable nature of the Moors, and that it was useless to attempt to check any sudden blaze of popular passion. "A little while," said he, "and this rash flame will burn itself out, and the people, when cool, will listen to reason." So he turned his steed from the gate and repaired to the city of Baza, where he was received with great demonstrations of loyalty. He was not a man to give up his throne without a struggle, a large part of the kingdom still remained faithful to him; he trusted that the conspiracy in the capital was but transient and partial, and that by suddenly making his appearance in its streets at the head of a moderate force, he should awe the people again into allegiance. He took his measures with that combination of dexterity and daring which formed his character, and arrived one night under the walls of Granada, with five hundred chosen followers. Scaling the walls of the Alhambra he threw himself with sanguinary fury into its silent courts. The sleeping inmates were roused from their repose only to fall by the exterminating scymetar. The rage of Aben Hassan spared neither age nor rank, nor sex; the halls resounded with shrieks and yells, and the fountains ran red with blood. The alcayde, Aben Comixer, retreated to a strong tower with a few of the garrison and inhabitants. The furious Aben Hassan did not lose time in pursuing him, he was anxious to secure the city and to wreak his vengeance on its rebellious inhabitants. Descending with his bloody band into the streets he cut down the defenceless inhabitants as, startled from their sleep, they rushed forth to learn the cause of the alarm. The city was soon completely roused; the people flew to arms; lights blazed in every street, revealing the scanty numbers of this band that had been dealing such fatal vengeance in the dark. Muley Aben Hassan had been mistaken in his conjectures; the great mass of the people, incensed by his tyranny were zealous in favour of his son; a violent but transient conflict took place in the streets and squares; many of the followers of Aben Hassan were slain; the rest driven out of the city, and the old monarch with the remnant of his band retreated to his loyal city of Malaga.

Such was the commencement of those great internal feuds and divisions which hastened the downfall of Granada. The Moors became separated into two hostile factions headed by the father and the son, and several bloody encounters took place between them, yet they never failed to act with all their separate force against the Christians, as a common enemy, whenever an opportunity occurred.

CHAPTER X

ROYAL EXPEDITION AGAINST LOXA.

King Ferdinand held a council of war at Cordova, where it was deliberated what was to be done with Alhama. Most of the council advised that it should be demolished, inasmuch as being in the centre of the Moorish kingdom it would be at all times liable to attack, and could only be maintained by a powerful garrison and at a vast expense. Queen Isabella arrived at Cordova in the midst of these deliberations and listened to them with surprize and impatience. "What!" said she, "shall we destroy the first fruits of our victories? shall we abandon the first place we have wrested from the Moors? never let us suffer such an idea to occupy our minds. It would give new courage to the enemy, arguing fear or feebleness in our councils. You talk of the toil and expense of maintaining Alhama. Did we doubt, on undertaking this war, that it was to be a war of infinite cost, labour, and bloodshed? and shall we shrink from the cost, the moment a victory is obtained and the question is merely to guard or abandon its glorious trophy? Let us hear no more, about the destruction of Alhama; let us maintain its walls sacred as a strong hold granted us by heaven in the centre of this hostile land; and let our only consideration be how to extend our conquest and capture the surrounding cities." The language of the Queen infused a more lofty and chivalrous spirit into the royal council. Preparations were immediately made to maintain Alhama at all risk and expense, and King Ferdinand appointed as alcayde Luis Fernandcz Puertocarrero, senior of the house of Palma, supported by Diego Lopez de Ayola, Pero Ruyz de Alarcon and Alonzo Ortis, captains of four hundred lances and a body of one thousand foot; supplied with provisions for three months. Ferdinand resolved also to lay siege to Loxa, a city of great strength, at no great distance from Alhama. For this purpose he called upon all the cities and towns of Andalusia and Estramadura and the domains of the orders of Santiago, Calatrava and Alcantara and of the priory of S' Juan and the kingdom of Toledo and beyond to the cities of Salamanca, Toro, and Valladolid, to furnish according to their repartimientos or allotments, a certain quantity of bread, wine and cattle to be delivered at the royal camp before Loxa, one half at the end of June, and one half in July. These lands, also, together with Biscay and Guipiscoa, were ordered to send reinforcements of horse and foot, each town furnishing its quota, and great diligence was used in providing lombards, powder and other warlike munitions.

The Moors were no less active in their preparations, and sent missives into Africa entreating supplies, and calling upon the Barbary princes to aid them in this war of the faith. To intercept all succour the Castilian sovereigns stationed an armada of ships and galleys in the Straits of Gibraltar under the command of Martin Diaz de Mena and Carlos de Valera with orders to scour the Barbary coast and sweep every Moorish sail from the sea.

While these preparations were making, Ferdinand made an incursion at the head of his army into the Kingdom of Granada and laid waste the vega, destroying its hamlets and villages, ravaging its fields of grain, and driving away the cattle.

It was about the end of June that King Ferdinand departed from Cordova to sit down before the walls of Loxa, so confident was he of success that he left a great part of the army at Ecija and advanced with but five thousand cavalry and eight thousand infantry. The Marquis of Cadiz, a warrior as wise as he was valiant, remonstrated against employing so small a force, and indeed was opposed to the measure altogether as being undertaken precipitately and without sufficient preparation. King Ferdinand, however, was influenced by the counsel of Don Diego de Merlo, and was eager to strike a brilliant and decided blow. A vainglorious confidence prevailed about this time among the Spanish cavaliers; they overrated their own prowess, or rather they undervalued and despised their enemy. Many of them believed that the Moors would scarcely remain in their city, when they saw the Christian troops advancing to assail it. The Spanish chivalry marched therefore gallantly and fearlessly and almost carelessly over the border, scantily supplied with the things needful for a besieging army, in the heart of an enemy's country. In the same negligent and confident spirit they took up their station before Loxa. The country around was broken and hilly so that it was extremely difficult to form a combined camp. The river Xenel which runs by the town, was compressed between high banks and so deep as to be fordable with extreme difficulty, and the Moors had possession of the bridge. The King pitched his tents in a plantation of olives, on the banks of the river; the troops were distributed in different encampments on the heights, but separated from each other by deep rocky ravines, so as to be incapable of yielding each other prompt assistance, and there was no room for the operation of the cavalry. The artillery, also, was so injudiciously placed as to be almost entirely useless. Alonzo of Aragon, Duke of Villahermosa, and illegitimate brother of the King, was present at the siege and disapproved of the whole arrangement. He was one of the most able generals of his time and especially renowned for his skill in battering fortified places. He recommended that the whole disposition of the camp should be changed and that several bridges should be thrown across the river. His advice was adopted, but slowly and negligently followed, so that it was rendered of no avail. Among other oversights in this hasty and negligent expedition, the army had no supply of baked bread and in the hurry of encampment there was no time to erect furnaces. Cakes were therefore hastily made, and baked on the coals, and for two days the troops were supplied in this irregular way.

King Ferdinand felt too late the insecurity of his position, and endeavoured to provide a temporary remedy. There was a height near the city, called by the Moors Santo Albohacen which was in front of the bridge. He

ordered several of his most valiant cavaliers to take possession of this height
and to hold it as a check upon the enemy and a protection to the camp. The
cavaliers chosen for this distinguished and perilous post were the Marquis
of Cadiz, the Marquis of Villena, Don Roderigo Tellez Giron, Master of Calatrava, his brother the Count of Ureña; and Don Alonzo de Aguilar. These
valiant warriors, and tried companions in arms, led their troops with alacrity
to the height, which soon glittered with the array of arms and was graced by
several of the most redoubtable pennons of warlike Spain.

Loxa was commanded at this time by an old Moorish alcayde, whose
daughter was the favourite wife of Boabdil el Chico. The name of this Moor
was Ibraham Ali Atar, but he was generally known among the Spaniards as
Alatar; he had grown gray in border warfare, was an implacable enemy of
the Christians, and his name had long been the terror of the frontier. He
was in the ninetieth year of his age yet indomitable in spirit, fiery in his
passions, sinewy and powerful in frame, deeply versed in warlike stratagem
and accounted the best lance in all Mauritania. He had three thousand
horsemen under his command, veteran troops with whom he had often
scoured the borders, and he daily expected the old Moorish King with
reinforcements.

Old Ali Atar had watched from his fortress every movement of the Christian army, and had exulted in all the errors of its commanders. When he
beheld the flower of Spanish chivalry glittering about the height of Albohacen his eye flashed with exultation. "By the aid of Allah," said he, "I will
give those prankling cavaliers a rouse."

Ali Atar privately and by night sent forth a large body of his chosen troops
to lie in ambush near one of the skirts of Albohacen. On the fourth day of
the siege he sallied across the bridge and made a feint attack upon the
height. The cavaliers rushed impetuously forth to meet him, leaving their
encampments almost unprotected. Ali Atar wheeled and fled and was hotly
pursued. When the Christian cavaliers had been drawn a considerable distance from their encampments they heard a vast shout behind them, and
looking round, beheld their encampment assailed by the Moorish force
which had been placed in ambush, and which had ascended a different side
of the hill.

The cavaliers desisted from the pursuit and hastened to prevent the plunder of their tents. Ali Atar in his turn wheeled and pursued them; and they
were attacked in front and rear on the summit of the hill. The contest lasted
for an hour, the height of Albohacen was red with blood, many brave cavaliers fell expiring among heaps of the enemy. The fierce Ali Atar fought with
the fury of a demon until the arrival of more Christian forces compelled him
to retreat into the city. The severest loss to the Christians in this skirmish
was that of Roderigo Tellez Giron, Master of Calatrava; as he was raising his
arm to make a blow an arrow pierced him just beneath the shoulder, at the

open part of the corselet. He fell instantly from his horse, but was caught by Pedro Gasca, a cavalier of Avila, who conveyed him to his tent where he died. The King and Queen and the whole kingdom mourned his death, for he was in the freshness of his youth, being but twenty-four years of age, and had proved himself a gallant and high minded cavalier. A melancholy group collected about his corse on the bloody height of Albohacen; the Knights of Calatrava mourned him as a commander; the cavaliers, who were encamped on the height, lamented him as their companion in arms in a service of peril, while the Count of Ureña grieved over him with the tender affection of a brother.

King Ferdinand now perceived the wisdom of the opinion of the Marquis of Cadiz, and that his force was quite insufficient for the enterprize. To continue his camp in its present unfortunate position would cost him the lives of his bravest cavaliers, if not a total defeat in case of reinforcements to the enemy. He called a council of war late in the evening of Saturday, and it was determined to withdraw the army early the next morning to Rio Frio, a short distance from the city, and there wait for additional troops from Cordova.

The next morning early the cavaliers on the height of Albohacen began to strike their tents. No sooner did Ali Atar behold this than he sallied forth to attack them. Many of the Christian troops, who had not heard of the intention to change the camp, seeing the tents struck and the Moors sallying forth, supposed that the enemy had been reinforced in the night and that the army was on the point of retreating. Without stopping to ascertain the truth, or to receive orders, they fled in dismay, spreading confusion through the camp; nor did they halt until they had reached the Rock of the Lovers, about seven leagues from Loxa.*

The King and his commanders saw the imminent peril of the moment, and made face to the Moors, each commander guarding his quarter, and repelling all assaults, while the tents were struck and the artillery and ammunition conveyed away. The King with a handful of cavaliers, gallopped to a rising ground exposed to the fire of the enemy, calling upon the flying troops and endeavouring in vain to rally them. Setting upon the Moors he and his cavaliers charged them so vigorously that they put a squadron to flight, slaying many with their swords and lances, and driving others into the river where they were drowned. The Moors, however, were soon reinforced and returned in great numbers; the King was in danger of being surrounded, the Moors assailed him furiously and twice he owed his safety to the valour of Don Juan de Ribera, senior of Monte Mayor.

The Marquis of Cadiz beheld from a distance the peril of his sovereign. Summoning about seventy horsemen to follow him he gallopped to the spot, threw himself between the King and the enemy, and hurling his lance, trans-

*Pulgar Cronica.

pierced one of the most daring of the Moors. For some time he remained with no other weapon than his sword, his horse was wounded by an arrow and many of his followers were slain, but he succeeded in beating off the Moors and rescuing the King from imminent jeopardy, whom he then prevailed upon to retire to less dangerous ground.

The marquis continued throughout the day to expose himself to the repeated assaults of the enemy: he was ever found in the place of greatest danger, and through his bravery a great part of the army and the camp was preserved from destruction.*

It was a perilous day for the commanders, for in a retreat of the kind it is the noblest cavaliers who most expose themselves to save their people. The Duke of Medina Celi was struck to the ground, but rescued by his troops. The Count of Tendilla, whose tents were nearest to the city, received several wounds, and various other cavaliers of the most distinguished note were exposed to fearful jeopardy. The whole day was passed in bloody skirmishings in which the hidalgos and cavaliers of the royal household distinguished themselves by their bravery; at length the encampments being all broken up, and most of the artillery and baggage removed, the bloody height of Albohacen was abandoned and the neighborhood of Loxa evacuated. Several tents, a quantity of provisions and a few pieces of artillery were left upon the spot from the want of horses and mules to carry them off.

Ali Atar hung upon the rear of the retiring army and harrassed it until it reached Rio Frio; from thence Ferdinand returned to Cordova, deeply mortified, though greatly benefited by the severe lesson he had received, which served to render him more cautious in his campaigns and more diffident of fortune. He sent letters to all parts excusing his retreat, imputing it to the small number of his forces and the circumstance that many of them were quotas sent from various cities and not in royal pay; in the mean time to console his troops for their disappointment and to keep up their spirits he led them upon another inroad to lay waste the vega of Granada.

*Cura de los Palacios. C. 58.

CHAPTER XI

HOW MULEY ABEN HASSAN MADE A FORAY INTO THE LANDS OF MEDINA SIDONIA, AND HOW HE WAS RECEIVED.

Old Muley Aben Hassan had mustered an army and marched to the relief of Loxa, but arrived too late, the last squadron of Ferdinand had already passed over the border. "They have come and gone," said he, "like a summer cloud and all their vaunting has been mere empty thunder." He turned to make another attempt upon Alhama, the garrison of which was in the utmost consternation at the retreat of Ferdinand, and would have deserted the place had it not been for the courage and perseverance of the alcayde Luis Fernandez Puertocarrero. That brave and loyal commander cheered up the spirits of his men and kept the old Moorish King at bay until the approach of Ferdinand, on his second incursion into the vega, obliged him to make an unwilling retreat to Malaga.

Muley Aben Hassan felt that it would be in vain, with his inferior force, to oppose the powerful army of the Christian monarch, but to remain idle and see his territories laid waste would ruin him in the estimation of his people. "If we cannot parry," said he, "we can strike; if we cannot keep our own lands from being ravaged, we can ravage the lands of the enemy." He enquired and learnt that most of the chivalry of Andalusia, in their eagerness for a foray, had marched off with the King and left their own country almost defenceless. The territories of the Duke of Medina Sidonia were particularly unguarded; here were vast plains of pasturage, covered with flocks and herds; the very country for a hasty inroad. The old monarch had a bitter grudge against the duke for having foiled him at Alhama. "I'll give this cavalier a lesson," said he exultingly, "that will cure him of his love of campaigning." So he prepared in all haste for a foray into the country about Medina Sidonia.

Muley Aben Hassan sallied out of Malaga with fifteen hundred horse and six thousand foot, and took the way by the sea coast, marching through Estiponia and entering the Christian country between Gibraltar and Castellar. The only person that was likely to molest him on this route, was one Pedro de Vargas a shrewd, hardy and vigilant soldier, Alcayde of Gibraltar, and who lay ensconced in his old warrior rock as in a citadel. Muley Aben Hassan knew the watchful and daring character of the man, but had ascertained that his garrison was too small to enable him to make a sally or at least to ensure him any success; still he pursued his march with great silence and caution, sent parties in advance to explore every pass where a foe might lie in ambush, cast many an anxious eye towards the old rock of Gibraltar as its cloud capped summit was seen towering in the distance on his left, nor did he feel entirely at ease until he had passed through the broken and mountainous country of Castellar, and descended into the plains. Here he encamped on the banks of the Celemin. From hence he sent four hundred corredors or fleet horsemen, armed with lances who were to station themselves near Algeziras and to keep a strict watch across the bay, upon the opposite fortress of Gibraltar. If the alcayde attempted to sally forth, they were to waylay and attack him: being almost four times his supposed force, and were to send swift tidings to the camp at Celemin.

In the mean time two hundred corredors were sent to scour that vast plain called the Campiña de Tarifa, abounding with flocks and herds; and two hundred more were to ravage the lands about Medina Sidonia. Muley Aben Hassan remained with the main body of the army as a rallying point on the banks of the Celemin. The foraging parties scoured the country to such effect that they came driving vast flocks and herds before them, enough to supply the place of all that had been swept from the vega of Granada. The troops which had kept watch upon the rock of Gibraltar returned with word that they had not seen a Christian helmet stirring. The old King congratulated himself upon the secrecy and promptness with which he had conducted his foray, and upon having baffled the vigilance of Pedro de Vargas.

Muley Aben Hassan had not been so secret as he imagined; the watchful Pedro de Vargas had received notice of his movements. His garrison was barely sufficient for the defence of the place, and he feared to take the field and leave his fortress unguarded. Luckily, at this juncture, there arrived in the harbour of Gibraltar a squadron of the armed gallies stationed in the strait and commanded by Carlos de Valera. The alcayde immediately prevailed upon him to guard the place during his absence, and sallied forth at midnight with seventy horse. He made for the town of Castellar, which is strongly posted on a steep height, knowing that the Moorish King would have to return by this place. He ordered alarm fires to be lighted upon the mountains to give notice that the Moors were on the ravage, that the peasants might drive their flocks and herds to places of refuge; and he sent couriers, riding like mad in every direction summoning the fighting men of the neighborhood to meet him at Castellar.

Muley Aben Hassan saw by the fires blazing about the mountains that the country was rising. He struck his tents and pushed forward as rapidly as possible for the border, but he was encumbered with booty and with the vast cavalgada swept from the pastures of the Campiña de Tarifa. His scouts brought him word that there were troops in the field, but he made light of the intelligence, knowing that they could only be those of the Alcayde of Gibraltar, and that he had not more than a hundred horsemen in his garrison. He threw in advance two hundred and fifty of his bravest troops, and with them the Alcaydes of Marabella and Casares. Behind this vanguard was a great cavalgada of cattle and in the rear marched the King with the main force of his little army. It was near the middle of a sultry summer day that they approached Castellar. De Vargas was on the watch and beheld, by an immense cloud of dust, that they were descending one of the heights of that wild and broken country. The vanguard and rearguard were above half a league asunder, with the cavalgada between them, and a long and close forest hid them from each other. De Vargas saw that they could render but little assistance to each other in case of a sudden attack, and might be easily thrown in confusion. He chose fifty of his bravest horsemen and making a circuit took his post secretly in a narrow glen opening into a defile between two rocky heights, through which the Moors had to pass. It was his intention to suffer the vanguard and the cavalgada to pass and to fall upon the rear.

While thus lying perdue six Moorish scouts, well mounted and well armed, entered the glen, examining every place that might conceal an enemy. Some of the Christians advised that they should slay these six men and retreat to Gibraltar. "No," said De Vargas, "I have come out for higher game than these, and I hope by the aid of God and Santiago, to do good work this day. I know these Moors well, and doubt not but that they may readily be thrown into confusion."

By this time the six horsemen approached so near that they were on the point of discovering the Christian ambush. De Vargas gave the word and ten horsemen rushed forth upon them; in an instant four of the Moors rolled in the dust. The other two put spurs to their steeds, and fled towards their army, pursued by the ten Christians. About eighty of the Moorish vanguard came galloping to the relief of their companions; the Christians turned and fled towards their ambush. De Vargas kept his men concealed until the fugitives and their pursuers came clattering pellmell into the glen; at a signal trumpet his men sallied forth with great heat and in close array. The Moors almost rushed upon their weapons before they perceived them; forty of the infidels were overthrown. The rest turned their backs. "Forward!" cried De Vargas, "let us give the vanguard a brush before it can be joined by the rear." So saying he pursued the flying Moors down the hill, and came with such force and fury upon the advance guard as to overturn many of them at the first encounter. As he wheeled off with his men, the Moors discharged their lances; upon which he returned to the charge and made great slaughter. The Moors fought valiantly for a short time until the Alcaydes of Marabella and Casares were slain, when they gave way and fled for the rear guard. In their flight they passed through the cavalgada of cattle, threw the whole in confusion and raised such a cloud of dust, that the Christians could no longer distinguish objects. Fearing the King and the main body might be at hand, and finding that De Vargas was badly wounded, they contented themselves with despoiling the slain, and, taking above twenty eight horses, then returned to Castillar.

When the routed Moors came flying back upon the rear guard Muley Aben Hassan feared that the people of Xeres were in arms. Several of his followers advised him to abandon the cavalgada and retreat by another road. "No," said the old King, "he is no true soldier who gives up his booty without fighting." Putting spurs to his horse he galloped forward through the centre of the cavalgada driving the cattle to the right and left. When he reached the field of battle he found it strewed with the bodies of upwards of one hundred Moors, among which were those of the two alcaydes. Enraged at the sight, he summoned all his cross bow men and cavalry, pushed on to the very gates of Castillar, and set fire to two houses close to the walls. Pedro de Vargas was too severely wounded to sally forth in person, but he ordered out his troops and there was brisk skirmishing under the walls, until the King drew off and returned to the scene of the recent encounter. Here he had the bodies of the principal warriors laid across mules to be interred honourably at Malaga. The rest of the slain were buried on the field of battle. Then, gathering together the scattered cavalgada, he paraded it slowly, in an immense line, past the walls of Castellar, by way of taunting his foe.

With all his fierceness old Muley Aben Hassan had a gleam of warlike courtesy, and admired the hardy and soldierlike character of Pedro de Vargas. He summoned two Christian captives and demanded what were the revenues of the Alcayde of Gibraltar. They told him that among other things, he was entitled to one out of every drove of cattle that passed his boundaries. "Allah forbid," cried the old monarch, "that so brave a cavalier should be defrauded of his dues." He immediately chose twelve of the finest cattle from the twelve droves which formed the cavalgada. These he gave in charge to an alfaqui to deliver them to Pedro de Vargas. "Tell him," said he, "that I crave his pardon for not having sent these cattle sooner, but I have this moment learnt the nature of his rights and I hasten to satisfy them with the punctuality due to so worthy a cavalier. Tell him, at the same time, that I had no idea the Alcayde of Gibraltar was so active and vigilant in collecting his tolls."

The brave alcayde relished the stern soldierlike pleasantry of the old Moorish monarch and replied in the same tone.

He ordered a rich silken vest and a scarlet mantle to be given to the alfaqui and dismissed him with great courtesy.

"Tell his majesty," said he, "that I kiss his hands for the honour he has done me, and regret that my scanty force has not permitted me to give him a more signal reception on his coming into these parts. Had three hundred horsemen, whom I have been promised from Xeres, arrived in time I might have served up an entertainment more befitting such a monarch. I trust, however, they will arrive in the course of the night, in which case his majesty may be sure of a royal regale at the dawning."

Muley Aben Hassan shook his head when he received the reply of De Vargas. "Allah preserve us," said he, "from any visitation of these hard riders of Xeres. A handful of troops acquainted with the wild passes of these mountains, may destroy an army encumbered as ours is with booty."

It was some relief to the King, however, to learn that the hardy Alcayde of Gibraltar was too severely wounded to take the field in person. He immediately beat a retreat with all speed, hurrying with such precipitation that the cavalgada was frequently broken and scattered among the rugged defiles of the mountains, and above five thousand of the cattle turned back and were regained by the Christians. Muley Aben Hassan returned triumphantly with the residue to Malaga, glorying in the spoils of the Duke of Medina Sidonia.

King Ferdinand was mortified at finding his incursion into the vega of Granada counterbalanced by this incursion into his own dominions, and saw that there were two sides to the game of war, as to all other games. The only one who reaped real glory in this series of inroads and skirmishings was Pedro de Vargas, the stout Alcayde of Gibraltar.*

CHAPTER XII

FORAY OF SPANISH CAVALIERS AMONG THE MOUNTAINS OF MALAGA.

The foray of old Muley Aben Hassan had touched the pride of the Andalusian chivalry, and they determined on retaliation. For this purpose a number of the most distinguished cavaliers assembled at Antequera in the month of March 1483: The leaders of the enterprize were, the gallant Marquis of Cadiz, Don Pedro Henriquez, Adelantado of Andalusia, Don Juan de Silva, Count of Cifuentes and bearer of the royal standard, who commanded in Seville; Don Alonzo de Cardenas, Master of the religious and military order of Santiago, and Don Alonzo de Aguilar. Several other cavaliers of note hastened to take part in the enterprize, and in a little while about twenty seven hundred horse and several companies of foot were assembled within the old warlike city of Antequera, comprising the very flower of Andalusian chivalry. A council of war was held by the chiefs to determine in what quarter they should strike a blow. The rival Moorish kings were waging civil war with each other in the vicinity of Granada, and the whole country lay open to inroad. Various plans were proposed by the different cavaliers. The Marquis

---

*Alonzo de Palencia L 28. C. 3.

of Cadiz was desirous of scaling the walls of Zahara and regaining possession of that important fortress. The Master of Santiago, however, suggested a wider range and a still more important object. He had received information from his adalides, who were apostate Moors, that an incursion might be safely made into a mountainous region near Malaga, called the Axarquia. Here were valleys of pasture land well stocked with flocks and herds, and there were numerous villages and hamlets which would be an easy prey. The city of Malaga was too weakly garrisoned and had too few cavalry to send forth any force in opposition; nay, he added, they might even extend their ravages to its very gates, and peradventure carry that wealthy place by sudden assault. The adventurous spirits of the cavaliers were inflamed by this suggestion; in their sanguine confidence they already beheld Malaga in their power, and they were eager for the enterprize. The Marquis of Cadiz endeavoured to interpose a little cool caution, he likewise had apostate adalides, the most intelligent and experienced on the borders. Among these he placed especial reliance on one named Luis Amar, who knew all the mountains and valleys of the country. He had received from him a particular account of these mountains of the Axarquia.* Their savage and broken nature was a sufficient defence for the fierce people who inhabited them, who manning their rocks, and their tremendous passes, which were often nothing more than the deep dry beds of torrents, might set whole armies at defiance. Even if vanquished, they afforded no spoil to the victor. Their houses were little better than bare walls, and they would drive off their scanty flocks and herds to the fastnesses of the mountains. The sober council of the marquis, however, was overruled. The cavaliers accustomed to mountain warfare, considered themselves and their horses equal to any wild and rugged expedition, and were flushed with the idea of terminating their foray by a brilliant assault upon Malaga. Leaving all heavy baggage at Antequera, and all such as had horses too weak for this mountain scramble, they set forth full of spirit and confidence. Don Alonzo de Aguilar and the Adelantado of Andalusia led the squadron of advance. The Count of Cifuentes followed, with certain of the chivalry of Seville. Then came the battalion of the most valiant Roderigo Ponce de Leon, Marquis of Cadiz: he was accompanied by several of his brothers and nephews, and many cavaliers, who sought distinction under his banner, and this family band attracted universal attention and applause, as they paraded in martial state through the streets of Antequera. The rear guard was led by Don Alonzo Cardenas, Master of Santiago; and was composed of the knights of his order, and the cavaliers of Ecija with certain men at arms of the Holy Brotherhood, whom the King had placed

---

*Pulgar in his chronicle, reverses the case and makes the Marquis of Cadiz recommend the expedition to the Axarquia, but Fray Antonio Agapida is supported in his statement by that most veracious and contemporary chronicler Andres Bernaldes Curate of Los Palacios.

under his command. The army was attended by a great train of mules laden with provisions for a few days' supply, until they should be able to forage among the Moorish villages. Never did a more gallant and self-confident little army tread the earth. It was composed of men full of health and vigour, to whom war was a pastime and delight. They had spared no expense in their equipments, for never was the pomp of war carried to a higher pitch than among the proud chivalry of Spain. Cased in armour richly inlaid and embossed, decked with rich surcoats and waving plumes, and superbly mounted on Andalusian steeds, they pranced out of Antequera with banners flying, and their various devices and armorial bearings ostentatiously displayed; and in the confidence of their hopes promised the inhabitants to enrich them with the spoils of Malaga.

In the rear of this warlike pageant followed a peaceful band, intent upon profiting by the anticipated victories. They were not the customary wretches that hover about armies to plunder and strip the dead, but goodly and substantial traders from Seville, Cordova, and other cities of traffic. They rode sleek mules, and were clad in goodly raiment, with long leathern purses at their girdles, well filled with pistoles and other golden coin. They had heard of the spoils, wasted by the soldiery at the capture of Alhama, and were provided with monies to buy up the jewels and precious stones, the vessels of gold and silver, and the rich silks and cloths that should form the plunder of Malaga. The proud cavaliers eyed these sons of traffic with great disdain, but permitted them to follow, for the convenience of the troops, who might otherwise be overburthened with booty.

It had been intended to conduct this expedition with great celerity and secrecy, but the noise of their preparations had already reached the city of Malaga. The garrison it is true was weak, but it possessed a commander who was himself a host. This was Muley Abdallah commonly called El Zagal or the Valiant. He was younger brother of Muley Aben Hassan, and general of the few forces which remained faithful to the old monarch. He possessed equal fierceness of spirit with his brother, and surpassed him in craft and vigilance. His very name was a war cry among his soldiery, who had the most extravagant opinion of his prowess.

El Zagal suspected that Malaga was the object of this noisy expedition. He consulted with old Bexir a veteran Moor who governed the city. "If this army of marauders should reach Malaga," said he, "we should hardly be able to keep them without its walls. I will throw myself with a small force into the mountains; rouse the peasantry, take possession of the passes and endeavour to give these Spanish cavaliers sufficient entertainment upon the road."

It was on a Wednesday that the prankling army of high mettled warriors issued forth from the ancient gates of Antequera. They marched all day and night making their way secretly, as they supposed, through the passes of the

mountains. As the tract of country they intended to maraud, was far in the
Moorish territories, near the coast of the Mediterranean, they did not arrive
there until late in the following day. In passing through these stern and lofty
mountains, their path was often along the bottom of a barranco, or deep
rocky valley, with a scanty stream dashing along it, among the loose rocks
and stones which it had broken and rolled down in the time of its autumnal
violence. Sometimes their road was a mere rambla, or dry bed of a torrent;
cut deep into the mountains, and filled with their shattered fragments.
These barrancos and ramblas were overhung by immense cliffs and precipices; forming the lurking places of ambuscades, during the wars between the
Moors and Spaniards, as in after times they have become the favourite
haunts of robbers to waylay the unfortunate traveller.

As the sun went down, the cavaliers came to a lofty part of the mountains
commanding, to the right, a distant glimpse of a part of the fair vega of
Malaga, with the blue Mediterranean beyond, and they hailed it with exultation as a glimpse of the promised land. As the night closed in they reached
the chain of little valleys and hamlets, locked up among these rocky heights,
and known among the Moors by the name of the Axarquia. Here their vaunting hopes were destined to meet with the first disappointment. The inhabitants had heard of their approach; they had conveyed away their cattle and
effects, and, with their wives and children, had taken refuge in the towers
and fastnesses of the mountains. Enraged at their disappointment, the
troops set fire to the deserted houses, and pressed forward, hoping for better
fortune as they advanced. Don Alonzo de Aguilar and the other cavaliers in
the vanguard, spread out their forces to lay waste the country; capturing a
few lingering herds of cattle, with the Moorish peasants who were driving
them to some place of safety. While this marauding party carried fire and
sword in the advance, and lit up the mountain cliffs with the flames of the
hamlets, the Master of Santiago, who brought up the rearguard, maintained
strict order, keeping his knights together in martial array, ready for attack
or defence should an enemy appear. The men at arms of the Holy Brotherhood attempted to roam in quest of booty, but he called them back and
rebuked them severely.

At length they came to a part of the mountain completely broken up by
barrancos and ramblas of vast depth, and shagged with rocks and precipices.
It was impossible to maintain the order of march, the horses had no room
for action, and were scarcely manageable, having to scramble from rock to
rock, and up and down frightful declivities, where there was scarce footing
for a mountain goat. Passing by a burning village, the light of the flames
revealed their perplexed situation. The Moors who had taken refuge in a
watch tower on an impending height, shouted with exultation when they
looked down upon these glistening cavaliers, struggling and stumbling
among the rocks. Sallying forth from their tower, they took possession of the

cliffs which overhung the ravine, and hurled darts and stones upon the enemy. It was with the utmost grief of heart, that the good Master of Santiago beheld his brave men, falling like helpless victims around him, without the means of resistance or revenge. The confusion of his followers was encreased by the shouts of the Moors, multiplied by the echoes of every crag and cliff, as if they were surrounded by innumerable foes. Being entirely ignorant of the country, in their struggles to extricate themselves they plunged into other glens and defiles, where they were still more exposed to danger. In this extremity the Master of Santiago dispatched messengers in search of succour. The Marquis of Cadiz, like a loyal companion in arms, hastened to his aid with his cavalry. His approach checked the assaults of the enemy, and the master was at length enabled to extricate his troops from the defile. In the mean time Don Alonzo de Aguilar and his companions, in their eager advance, had likewise got entangled in deep glens, and the dry beds of torrents, where they had been severely galled by the insulting attacks of a handful of Moorish peasants, posted on the impending precipices. The proud spirit of De Aguilar was incensed at having the game of war thus turned upon him, and his gallant forces domineered over by mountain boors, whom he had thought to drive, like their own cattle, to Antequera. Hearing, however, that his friend the Marquis of Cadiz and the Master of Santiago were engaged with the enemy, he disregarded his own danger, and, calling together his troops, returned to assist them or rather to partake of their perils. Being once more assembled together, the cavaliers held a hasty council, amidst the hurling of stones and the whistling of arrows; and their resolves were quickened, by the sight, from time to time, of some gallant companion in arms laid low. They determined that there was no spoil in this part of the country to repay for the extraordinary peril; and that it was better to abandon the herds they had already taken, which only embarrassed their march, and to retreat with all speed to less dangerous ground.

The adalides or guides were ordered to lead the way out of this place of carnage. These, thinking to conduct them by the most secure route, led them by a steep and rocky pass, difficult for the foot soldiers, but almost impracticable to the cavalry. It was overhung with precipices, from whence showers of stones and arrows were poured upon them, accompanied by savage yells, which appalled the stoutest heart. In some places they could pass but one at a time, and were often transpierced, horse and rider, by the Moorish darts, impeding the progress of their comrades by their dying struggles. The surrounding precipices were lit up by a thousand alarm fires, every crag and cliff had its flame, by the light of which they beheld their foes, bounding from rock to rock, and looking more like fiends than mortal men. Either through terror and confusion, or through real ignorance of the country, their guides instead of conducting them out of the mountains, led them deeper into their fatal recesses. The morning dawned upon them in a narrow rambla, its bottom filled with broken rocks, where once had raved along the mountain torrent while above them beetled great arid cliffs, over the brows of which they beheld the turbaned heads of their fierce and exulting foes. What a different appearance did the unfortunate cavaliers present, from the gallant band that marched so vauntingly out of Antequera. Covered with dust, and blood, and wounds, and haggard with fatigue and horror, they looked like victims rather than like warriors. Many of their banners were lost and not a trumpet was heard to rally up their sinking spirits. The men turned with imploring eyes to their commanders, while the hearts of the cavaliers were ready to burst with rage and grief, at the merciless havoc made among their faithful followers.

All day they made ineffectual attempts to extricate themselves from the mountains. Columns of smoke rose from the heights where in the preceding night had blazed the alarm fires. The mountaineers assembled from every direction, they swarmed at every pass, getting in the advance of the Christians and garrisoning the cliffs like so many towers and battlements.

Night closed again upon the Christians, when they were shut up in a narrow valley traversed by a deep stream and surrounded by precipices, which seemed to reach the skies, and on which blazed and flared the alarm fires. Suddenly a new cry was heard resounding along the valley: "El Zagal! El Zagal!" echoed from cliff to cliff. "What cry is that?" said the Master of Santiago. "It is the war-cry of El Zagal, the Moorish general," said an old Castilian soldier. "He must be coming in person with the troops of Malaga."

The worthy master turned to his knights. "Let us die," said he, "making a road with our hearts since we cannot with our swords. Let us scale the mountain and sell our lives dearly instead of staying here to be tamely butchered."

So saying he turned his steed against the mountain and spurred him up its flinty side. Horse and foot followed his example, eager, if they could not escape to have at least a dying blow at the enemy. As they struggled up the height a tremendous storm of darts and stones was showered upon them by the Moors. Sometimes a fragment of rock came bounding and thundering down, ploughing its way through the centre of their host. The foot soldiers, faint with weariness and hunger, or crippled by wounds, held by the tails and manes of the horses to aid them in their ascent, while the horses, losing their footing among the loose stones, or receiving some sudden wound, tumbled down the steep declivity, steed, rider, and soldier rolling from crag to crag, until they were dashed to pieces in the valley. In this desperate struggle the alferez or standard bearer of the master with his standard was lost, as were many of his relations and his dearest friends. At length he succeeded in attaining the crest of the mountain, but it was only to be plunged in new difficulties. A wilderness of rocks and rugged dells lay before him; beset by cruel foes. Having neither banner nor trumpet by which to rally his troops, they wandered apart, each intent upon saving himself from the precipices of the mountains, and the darts of the enemy. When the pious Master of Santiago beheld the scattered fragments of his late gallant force he could not restrain his grief. "Oh God!" exclaimed he. "Great is thine anger this day against thy servants! Thou hast converted the cowardice of these infidels into desperate valour and hast made peasants and boors victorious over armed men of battle."

He would fain have kept with his foot soldiers, and, gathering them together, have made head against the enemy; but those around him entreated him to think only of his personal safety. To remain was to perish, without striking a blow; to escape was to preserve a life that might be devoted to vengeance on the Moors. The master reluctantly yielded to their advice. "Oh Lord of Hosts!" exclaimed he again, "from thy wrath do I fly; not from these infidels: they are but instruments in thy hands to chastise us for our sins:" so saying he sent the guides in the advance, and putting spurs to his horse dashed through a defile of the mountains before the Moors could intercept him. The moment the master put his horse to speed his troops scattered in all directions. Some endeavoured to follow his traces, but were confounded among the intricacies of the mountain. They fled hither and thither many perishing among the precipices, others being slain by the Moors and others taken prisoners.

The gallant Marquis of Cadiz guided by his trusty adalid Luis Amar had ascended a different part of the mountain. He was followed by his friend Don Alonzo de Aguilar, the adelantado, and the Count of Cifuentes; but in the darkness and confusion the bands of these commanders became separated from each other. When the marquis attained the summit he looked around for his companions in arms, but they were no longer following him, and there was no trumpet to summon them. It was a consolation to the marquis, however, that his brothers and several of his relations with a number of his retainers were still with him; he called his brothers by name and their replies gave comfort to his heart.

His guide now led the way into another valley where he would be less exposed to danger: when he had reached the bottom of it the marquis paused to collect his scattered followers, and to give time for his fellow commanders to rejoin him. Here he was suddenly assailed by the troops of El Zagal aided by the mountaineers from the cliffs. The Christians, exhausted and terrified, lost all presence of mind; most of them fled, and were either slain or taken captive. The marquis and his valiant brothers, with a few tried friends made a stout resistance. His horse was killed under him; his brothers Don Diego and Don Lope, with his two nephews Don Lorenzo and Don Manuel were, one by one, swept from his side; either transfixed with darts and lances by the soldiers of El Zagal, or crushed by stones from the heights. The marquis was a veteran warrior and had been in many a bloody battle, but never before had death fallen so thick and close around him. When he saw his remaining brother, Don Beltran, struck out of his saddle by a fragment of a rock, and his horse running wildly about without his rider, he gave a cry of anguish and stood bewildered and aghast. A few faithful followers surrounded him and entreated him to fly for his life. He would still have remained to have shared the fortunes of his friend Don Alonzo de Aguilar and his other companions in arms, but the forces of El Zagal were between him and them, and death was whistling by on every wind. Reluctantly therefore he consented to fly. Another horse was brought him; his faithful adalid guided him by one of the steepest paths, which lasted for four leagues; the enemy still hanging on his traces and thinning the scanty ranks of his followers. At length the marquis reached the extremity of the mountain defiles, and with a haggard remnant of his men escaped by dint of hoof to Antequera.

The Count of Cifuentes with a few of his retainers, in attempting to follow the Marquis of Cadiz wandered into a narrow pass where they were completely surrounded by the band of El Zagal. Finding all attempt at escape impossible and resistance vain, the worthy count surrendered himself prisoner as did also his brother Don Pedro de Silva and the few of his retainers who survived.

The dawn of day found Don Alonzo de Aguilar, with a handful of his followers still among the mountains. They had attempted to follow the Marquis of Cadiz, but had been obliged to pause and defend themselves against the thickening forces of the enemy. They at length traversed the mountain and reached the same valley where the marquis had made his last disastrous stand. Wearied and perplexed they sheltered themselves in a natural grotto under an overhanging rock, which kept off the darts of the enemy, while a bubbling fountain gave them the means of slaking their raging thirst and refreshing their exhausted steeds. As day broke the scene of slaughter unfolded its horrors. There lay the noble brothers and nephews of the gallant marquis, transfixed with darts or gashed and bruised with unseemly wounds; while many other gallant cavaliers lay stretched out dead and dying around, some of them partly stripped and plundered by the Moors. De Aguilar was a pious knight, but his piety was not humble and resigned, like that of the worthy Master of Santiago. He imprecated holy curses upon the infidels for having thus laid low the flower of Christian chivalry, and he vowed in his heart bitter vengeance upon the surrounding country.

By degrees the little force of De Aguilar was augmented by numbers of fugitives who issued from caves and chasms, where they had taken refuge in the night. A little band of mounted knights was gradually formed, and the Moors having abandoned the heights to collect the spoils of the slain, this gallant but forlorn squadron was enabled to retreat to Antequera.

This disastrous affair lasted from Thursday evening throughout Friday the twenty first of March, the festival of S' Benedict. It is still recorded in Spanish kalendars as the defeat of the mountains of Malaga, and the place where the greatest slaughter took place is pointed out to the present day, and is called *la Cuesta de la Matanza,* or the hill of the massacre. The principal leaders who survived returned to Antequera; many of the knights took refuge in Alhama, and other towns: many wandered about the mountains for eight days, living on roots and herbs, hiding themselves during the day, and sallying forth by night. So enfeebled and disheartened were they, that they offered no resistance if attacked. Three or four soldiers would surrender to a Moorish peasant, and even the women of Malaga sallied forth and made prisoners. Some were thrown into the dungeons of frontier towns; others led captive to Granada, but by far the greater number were conducted to Malaga, the city they had threatened to attack. Two hundred and fifty principal cavaliers, alcaydes, commanders, and hidalgos of generous blood, were confined in the Alcazaba or citadel of Malaga to await their ransom; and five hundred and seventy of the common soldiery were crowded in an enclosure or court yard of the Alcazaba, to be sold as slaves.*

Great spoils were collected of splendid armour and weapons taken from the slain, or thrown away by the cavaliers in their flight; and many horses magnificently caparisoned, together with numerous standards, all which were paraded in triumph into the Moorish towns.

The merchants also who had come with the army, intending to traffic in the spoils of the Moors, were themselves made objects of traffic. Several of them were driven like cattle before the Moorish viragos to the market of Malaga, and in spite of all their adroitness in trade, and their attempts to buy themselves off at a cheap ransom, they were unable to purchase their freedom without such draughts upon their money bags at home, as drained them to the very bottom.

CHAPTER XIII

EFFECTS OF THE DISASTERS AMONG THE MOUNTAINS OF MALAGA.

The people of Antequera had scarcely recovered from the tumult of excitement and admiration, caused by the departure of the gallant band of cavaliers upon their foray; when they beheld the scattered wrecks flying for refuge to their walls. Day after day and hour after hour brought some

*Cura de Los Palacios.

wretched fugitive, in whose battered plight and haggard, woe begone demeanour it was almost impossible to recognize the warrior, whom they had lately seen to issue so gaily and gloriously from their gates.

The arrival of the Marquis of Cadiz, almost alone, covered with dust and blood, his armour shattered and defaced, his countenance the picture of despair, filled every heart with sorrow, for he was greatly beloved by the people. The multitude asked where was the band of brothers which had rallied round him as he went forth to the field, and when they heard that they had, one by one, been slaughtered at his side, they hushed their voices, or spoke to each other only in whispers as he passed, gazing at him in silent sympathy. No one attempted to console him in so great an affliction, nor did the good marquis speak ever a word, but shutting himself up brooded in lonely anguish over his misfortune. It was only the arrival of Don Alonzo de Aguilar that gave him a gleam of consolation, for, amidst the shafts of death that had fallen so thickly among his family, he rejoiced to find that his chosen friend and brother in arms had escaped uninjured.

For several days every eye was turned in an agony of suspence towards the Moorish border, anxiously looking in every fugitive from the mountains, for the lineaments of some friend or relation, whose fate was yet a mystery. At length every hope and doubt subsided into certainty; the whole extent of this great calamity was known, spreading grief and consternation throughout the land, and laying desolate the pride and hopes of palaces. It was a sorrow that visited the marble hall and silken pillow. Stately dames mourned over the loss of their sons, the joy and glory of their age; and many a fair cheek was blanched with woe that had lately mantled with secret admiration. "All Andalusia," says a historian of the time, "was overwhelmed by a great affliction; there was no drying of the eyes which wept in her."*

Fear and trembling reigned for a time along the frontier. Their spear seemed broken; their buckler cleft in twain: Every border town dreaded an attack, and the mother caught her infant to her bosom when the watch dog howled in the night, fancying it the war cry of the Moor. All for a time seemed lost, and despondency even found its way to the royal breasts of Ferdinand and Isabella, amidst the splendours of their court.

Great, on the other hand, was the joy of the Moors when they saw whole legions of Christian warriors brought captive into their towns, by rude mountain peasantry. They thought it the work of Allah in favour of the faithful. But when they recognized among the captives thus dejected and broken down, several of the proudest of Christian chivalry; when they saw several of the banners and devices of the noblest houses of Spain, which they had been accustomed to behold in the foremost of the battle, now trailed ignominiously through their streets; when, in short, they witnessed the arrival

*Cura de Los Palacios.

of the Count of Cifuentes, the royal standard bearer of Spain, with his gallant brother Don Pedro de Silva, brought prisoners into the gates of Granada, there were no bounds to their exultation. They thought that the days of their antient glory were about to return, and that they were to renew their career of triumph over the unbelievers.

The Christian historians of the time are sorely perplexed to account for this misfortune; and why so many Christian knights, fighting in the cause of the holy faith, should thus miraculously, as it were, be given captive to a handful of infidel boors; for we are assured that all this rout and destruction was effected by five hundred foot and fifty horse; and those mere mountainiers without science or discipline.* "It was intended," observes one historiographer, "as a lesson to their confidence and vainglory: overrating their own prowess and thinking that so chosen a band of chivalry had but to appear in the land of the enemy, and conquer. It was to teach them that the race is not to the swift, nor the battle to the strong, but that God alone giveth the victory."

The worthy father Fray Antonio Agapida, however, asserts it to be a punishment for the avarice of the Spanish warriors. "They did not enter the kingdom of the infidels with the pure spirit of Christian knights, zealous, only, for the glory of the faith; but rather as greedy men of traffic, to enrich themselves by vending the spoils of the infidels. Instead of preparing themselves by confession and communion, and executing their testaments, and making donations to churches and convents, they thought only of arranging bargains and sales of their anticipated booty. Instead of taking with them holy monks to aid them with their prayers, they were followed by a train of trading men to keep alive their worldly and sordid ideas, and to turn what ought to be holy triumphs into scenes of brawling traffic." Such is the opinion of the excellent Agapida, in which he is joined by that most worthy and upright of chroniclers the Curate of Los Palacios. Agapida comforts himself, however, with the reflection, that this visitation was meant in mercy to try the Castilian heart, and to extract from its present humiliation the elements of future success, as gold is extracted from amidst the impurities of earth; and in this reflection he is supported by the venerable historian Pedro Abarca, of the Society of Jesuits.†

*Cura de Los Palacios.
†Abarca. Annales de Aragon. Rey 30: cap 2. §. 7.

CHAPTER XIV

HOW KING BOABDIL EL CHICO MARCHED
OVER THE BORDER.

The defeat of the Christian cavaliers among the mountains of Malaga, and the successful inroad of Muley Aben Hassan into the lands of Medina Sidonia, had produced a favorable effect on the fortunes of the old monarch. The inconstant populace began to shout forth his name in the streets, and to sneer at the inactivity of his son Boabdil el Chico. The latter, though in the flower of his age, and distinguished for vigour and dexterity in jousts and tournaments, had never yet fleshed his weapon in the field of battle, and it was murmured that he preferred the silken repose of the cool halls of the Alhambra, to the fatigue and danger of the foray and the hard encampments of the mountains.

The popularity of these rival Kings depended upon their success against the Christians, and Boabdil el Chico found it necessary to strike some signal blow to counterbalance the late triumph of his father. He was further incited by the fierce old Moor, his father in law, Ali Atar, Alcayde of Loxa, with whom the coals of wrath against the Christians still burned among the ashes of age, and had lately been blown into a flame by the attack made by Ferdinand on the city under his command.

Ali Atar informed Boabdil that the late discomfiture of the Christian knights had stripped Andalusia of the prime of her chivalry, and broken the spirit of the country. All the frontier of Cordova and Ecija now lay open to inroad, but he especially pointed out the city of Lucena as an object of attack, being feebly garrisoned and lying in a country rich in pasturage, abounding in cattle and grain, in oil and wine. The fiery old Moor spoke from thorough information, for he had made many an incursion into those parts, and his very name was a terror throughout the country. It had become a bye word in the garrison of Loxa to call Lucena the garden of Ali Atar, for he was accustomed to forage its fertile territories for all his supplies.

Boabdil el Chico listened to the persuasions of this veteran of the borders. He assembled a force of nine thousand foot and seven hundred horse, most of them his own adherents, but many the partizans of his father; for both factions, however they might fight among themselves, were ready to unite in any expedition against the Christians. Many of the most illustrious and valiant of the Moorish nobility assembled around his standard, magnificently arrayed in sumptuous armour and rich embroidery, as though they were going to a festival or a tilt of reeds, rather than an enterprize of iron war. Boabdil's mother, the Sultana Ayxa la Horra armed him for the field, and gave him her benediction as she girded his scymetar to his side. His favourite wife Morayma wept as she thought of the evils that might befal him. "Why dost thou weep, daughter of Ali Atar?" said the high minded Ayxa, "these tears become not the daughter of a warrior, nor the wife of a King. Believe me, there lurks more danger for a monarch within the strong walls of a palace, than within the frail curtains of a tent. It is by perils in the field that thy husband must purchase security on his throne."

But Morayma still hung upon his neck with tears and sad forebodings; and when he departed from the Alhambra she betook herself to her mirador which looks out over the vega. From thence she watched the army as it went, in shining order, along the road which leads to Loxa; and every burst of warlike melody that came swelling on the breeze was answered by a gush of sorrow.

As the royal cavalcade issued from the palace, and descended through the streets of Granada, the populace greeted their youthful sovereign with shouts, and anticipated success that should wither the laurels of his father. In passing through the gate of Elvira, however, the King accidentally broke his lance against the arch. At this, certain of his nobles turned pale, and entreated him to turn back, for they regarded it as an evil omen. Boabdil scoffed at their fears, for he considered them mere idle fancies; or rather, says Fray Antonio Agapida, he was an incredulous pagan, puffed up with confidence and vainglory. He refused to take another spear, but drew forth his scymetar and led the way, adds Agapida, in an arrogant and haughty style, as though he would set both heaven and earth at defiance. Another evil omen was sent to deter him from his enterprize; arriving at the rambla or dry ravine of Beyro, which is scarcely a bow shot from the city, a fox ran through the whole army and close by the person of the King, and though a thousand bolts were discharged at it, escaped uninjured to the mountains. The principal courtiers about Boabdil now reiterated their remonstrances against proceeding, for they considered these occurrences as mysterious portents of disasters to their army: the King, however, was not to be dismayed, but continued to march forward.*

At Loxa the royal army was reinforced by old Ali Atar, with the chosen horsemen of his garrison, and many of the bravest warriors of the border towns. The people of Loxa shouted with exultation when they beheld Ali Atar armed at all points and once more mounted on his Barbary steed, which had often borne him over the borders. The veteran warrior, with nearly a century of years upon his head, had all the fire and animation of youth at the prospect of a foray, and careered from rank to rank with the velocity of an Arab of the desert. The populace watched the army as it paraded over the bridge, and wound into the passes of the mountains, and still their eyes were fixed upon the pennon of Ali Atar, as if it bore with it an assurance of victory.

*Marmol. Rebel. de los Moros. Lib 1. C. XII fol. 14.

The Moorish army entered the Christian frontier by forced marches, hastily ravaging the country, driving off the flocks and herds and making captives of the inhabitants. They pressed on furiously and made the latter part of their march in the night, that they might elude observation and come upon Lucena by surprize. Boabdil was inexperienced in the art of war, but he had a veteran counsellor in his old father in law, for Ali Atar knew every secret of the country, and as he prowled through it his eye ranged over the land uniting in its glare the craft of the fox with the sanguinary ferocity of the wolf. He had flattered himself that their march had been so rapid as to out strip intelligence, and that Lucena would be an easy capture; when suddenly he beheld alarm fires blazing upon the mountains. "We are discovered," said he to Boabdil el Chico, "the country will be up in arms, we have nothing left but to strike boldly for Lucena; it is but slightly garrisoned, and we may carry it by assault before it can receive assistance." The King approved of his council and they marched rapidly for the gate of Lucena.

CHAPTER XV

HOW THE COUNT DE CABRA SALLIED FORTH FROM HIS CASTLE IN QUEST OF KING BOABDIL.

Don Diego de Cordova, Count of Cabra, was in the castle of Vaena, which, with the town of the same name, is situated on a lofty sunburnt hill on the frontier of the Kingdom of Cordova, and but a few leagues from Lucena. The range of mountains of Horquera lie between them. The castle of Vaena was strong and well furnished with arms, and the count had a numerous band of vassals and retainers, for it behoved the noblemen of the frontiers in those times to be well prepared with man and horse, with lance and buckler, to resist the sudden incursions of the Moors. The Count of Cabra was a hardy and experienced warrior, shrewd in council, prompt in action, rapid and fearless in the field. He was one of the bravest cavaliers for an inroad, and had been quickened and sharpened in thought and action by living on the borders.

On the night of the 20th of April 1483: the count was about to retire to rest, when the watchman from the turret brought him word that there were alarm fires on the mountains of Horquera, and that they were made on the signal tower overhanging the defile through which the road passes to Cabra and Lucena.

The count ascended the battlements and beheld five lights blazing on the tower, a sign that there was a Moorish army attacking some place on the frontier. The count instantly ordered the alarm bells to be sounded, and dispatched couriers to rouse the commanders of the neighbouring towns. He ordered all his retainers to prepare for action, and sent a trumpet through the town summoning the men to assemble at the castle gate at day break, armed and equipped for the field.

Throughout the remainder of the night the castle resounded with the din of preparation. Every house in the town was in equal bustle, for in these frontier towns every house had its warrior, and the lance and buckler were ever hanging against the wall, ready to be snatched down for instant service. Nothing was heard but the din of armourers, the shoeing of steeds and furbishing up of weapons: and all night long the alarm fires kept blazing on the mountain.

When the morning dawned, the Count of Cabra sallied forth at the head of two hundred and fifty cavaliers of the best families of Vaena, all well appointed, exercised in arms and experienced in the warfare of the borders. There were besides twelve hundred foot soldiers, all brave and well seasoned men of the same town. The count ordered them to hasten forward, whoever could make most speed, taking the road to Cabra which was three leagues distant. That they might not loiter on the road he allowed none of them to break their fast until they arrived at that place. The provident count dispatched couriers in advance, and the little army on reaching Cabra, found tables spread with food and refreshments at the gates of the town. There they were joined by Don Alonzo de Cordova, Senior of Yuheros.

Having made a hearty repast, they were on the point of resuming their march, when the count discovered that in the hurry of his departure from home he had forgotten to bring the standard of Vaena, which, for upwards of eighty years, had always been borne to battle by his family. It was now noon and there was not time to return; he took therefore the standard of Cabra, the device of which is a goat, and which had not been seen in the wars for the last half century. When about to depart a courier came galloping at full speed, bringing missives to the count from his nephew Don Diego Hernandez de Cordova, Senior of Lucena and Alcayde de los Donzeles entreating him to hasten to his aid, as his town was beset by the Moorish King Boabdil el Chico with a powerful army, who were actually setting fire to the gates.

The count put his little army instantly in movement for Lucena, which is only one league from Cabra; he was fired with the idea of having the Moorish King in person to contend with. By the time he reached Lucena the Moors had desisted from the attack and were ravaging the surrounding country. He entered the town with a few of his cavaliers, and was received with joy by his nephew, whose whole force consisted but of eighty horse and three hundred foot. Don Diego Hernandez de Cordova was a young man, yet he

was a prudent, careful and capable officer. Having learnt, the evening before, that the Moors had passed the frontiers, he had gathered within his
walls all the women and children from the environs; had armed the men,
sent couriers in all directions for succour, and had lighted alarm fires on the
mountains.

Boabdil had arrived with his army at day break, and had sent in a message
threatening to put the garrison to the sword if the place were not instantly
surrendered. The messenger was a Moor of Granada named Hamet, whom
Don Diego had formerly known; he contrived to amuse him with negociation, to gain time for succour to arrive. The fierce old Ali Atar, losing all
patience, had made an assault upon the town and stormed like a fury at the
gate, but had been repulsed. Another and more serious attack was expected
in the course of the night.

When the Count de Cabra had heard this account of the situation of affairs, he turned to his nephew with his usual alacrity of manner, and proposed that they should immediately sally forth in quest of the enemy. The
prudent Don Diego remonstrated at the rashness of attacking so great a force
with a mere handful of men. "Nephew," said the count, "I came from Vaena
with a determination to fight this Moorish King, and I will not be
disappointed."

"At any rate," replied Don Diego, "let us wait but two hours and we shall
have reinforcements which have been promised me from Rambla, Santaella,
Montilla and other places in the neighborhood." "If we await these," said
the hardy count, "the Moors will be off, and all our trouble will have been
in vain. You may await them if you please, I am resolved on fighting."

The count paused for no reply, but in his prompt and rapid manner sallied
forth to his men. The young Alcayde de los Donzeles, though more prudent
than his ardent uncle, was equally brave; he determined to stand by him in
his rash enterprize, and, summoning his little force, marched forth to join
the count, who was already on the move. They then proceeded together in
quest of the enemy.

The Moorish army had ceased ravaging the country and were not to be
seen, the neighborhood being hilly and broken with deep ravines. The count
dispatched six scouts on horseback to reconnoitre, ordering them to return
with all speed when they should have discovered the enemy, and by no
means to engage in skirmishing with stragglers. The scouts ascending a high
hill beheld the Moorish army in a valley behind it, the cavalry ranged in five
batallions keeping guard, while the foot soldiers were seated on the grass
making a repast. They returned immediately with the intelligence.

The count now ordered the troops to march in the direction of the enemy.
He and his nephew ascended the hill and saw that the five batallions of
Moorish cavalry had been formed into two, one of about nine hundred
lances, the other of about six hundred. The whole force seemed prepared to

march for the frontier. The foot soldiers were already under way with many
prisoners and a great train of mules and beasts of burden laden with booty.
At a distance was Boabdil el Chico; they could not distinguish his person,
but they knew him by his superb white charger magnificently caparisoned,
and by his being surrounded by a numerous guard, sumptuously armed and
attired. Old Ali Atar was careering about the valley with his usual impatience, hurrying the march of the loitering troops.

The eyes of the Count de Cabra glistened with eager joy as he beheld the
royal prize within his reach. The immense disparity of their forces never
entered into his mind. "By Santiago!" said he to his nephew as they hastened
down the hill, "had we waited for more forces the Moorish King and his
army would have escaped us!"

The count now harangued his men to enspirit them to this hazardous encounter. He told them not to be dismayed at the number of the Moors, for
God often permitted the few to conquer the many; and he had great confidence that through the divine aid they were that day to achieve a signal
victory which should win them both riches and renown. He commanded
that no man should hurl his lance at the enemy, but should keep it in his
hands, and strike as many blows with it as he could. He warned them, also,
never to shout except when the Moors did, for when both armies shouted
together there was no perceiving which made the most noise and was the
strongest. He desired his uncle Lope de Mendoza, and Diego Cabrera Alcayde of Menica to alight and enter on foot in the battalion of infantry to
animate them to the combat. He appointed also the Alcayde of Vaena and
Diego de Clavijo, a cavalier of his household, to remain in the rear, and not
to permit any one to lag behind, either to despoil the dead, or for any other
purpose.

Such were the orders given by this most adroit, active and intrepid cavalier to his little army, supplying by admirable sagacity and subtle management, the want of a more numerous force. His orders being given, and all
arrangements made, he threw aside his lance, drew his sword, and commanded his standard to be advanced against the enemy.

CHAPTER XVI

THE BATTLE OF LUCENA.

The Moorish King had descried the Spanish forces at a distance, although a
slight fog prevented his seeing them distinctly and ascertaining their numbers. His old father in law Ali Atar was by his side, who being a veteran
marauder was well acquainted with all the standards and armorial bearings

of the frontiers. When the King beheld the ancient and long disused banner of Cabra emerging from the mist he turned to Ali Atar and demanded whose ensign it was. The old borderer was for once at a loss, for the banner had not been displayed in battle in his time.

"Sire," replied he, after a pause, "I have been considering that standard but do not know it. It appears to be a dog, which device is borne by the towns of Baeza and Ubeda. If it be so, all Andalusia is in movement against you; for it is not probable that any single commander or community would venture to attack you. I would advise you therefore to retire."

The Count de Cabra in winding down the hill towards the Moors, found himself on much lower ground than the enemy; he ordered in all haste that his standard should be taken back, so as to gain the vantage ground. The Moors, mistaking this for a retreat, rushed impetuously towards the Christians. The latter having gained the height proposed, charged down upon them at the same moment, with the battle cry of Santiago! and dealing the first blows, laid many of the Moorish cavaliers in the dust.

The Moors, thus checked in their tumultuous assault, were thrown into confusion and began to give way; the Christians following hard upon them. Boabdil el Chico endeavoured to rally them. "Hold! hold! for shame!" cried he, "let us not fly at least until we know our enemy." The Moorish chivalry were stung by this reproof and turned to make front with the valour of men who feel that they are fighting under their monarch's eye.

At this moment Lorenzo de Porres, Alcayde of Luque, arrived with fifty horse and one hundred foot, sounding an Italian trumpet from among a copse of oak trees, which concealed his force. The quick ear of old Ali Atar caught the note. "That is an Italian trumpet," said he to the King, "the whole world seems in arms against your majesty!"

The trumpet of Lorenzo de Porres was answered by that of the Count de Cabra in another direction, and it seemed to the Moors as if they were between two armies. Don Lorenzo, sallying from among the oaks, now charged upon the enemy: the latter did not wait to ascertain the force of this new foe, the confusion, the variety of alarums, the attacks from opposite quarters, the obscurity of the fog, all conspired to deceive them as to the number of their adversaries. Broken and dismayed they retreated fighting, and nothing but the presence and remonstrances of the King prevented their retreat from becoming a headlong flight.

This skirmishing retreat lasted for about three leagues. Many were the acts of individual prowess between Christian and Moorish knights, and the way was strowed by the flower of the King's guards and of his royal household. At length they came to the rivulet of Mingonzalez, the verdant banks of which were covered with willows and tamarisks. It was swoln by recent rain, and was now a deep and turbid torrent.

Here the King made a courageous stand with a small body of cavalry, while his baggage crossed the stream. None but the choicest and most loyal of his guards stood by their monarch in this hour of extremity. The foot soldiers took to flight the moment they passed the ford; many of the horsemen partaking of the general panic gave reins to their steeds and scoured for the frontier. The little host of devoted cavaliers now serried their forces in front of their monarch to protect his retreat. They fought hand to hand with the Christian warriors, disdaining to yield or to ask for quarter. The ground was covered with the dead and dying. The King having retreated along the river banks, and gained some distance from the scene of combat, looked back and saw the loyal band at length give way. They crossed the ford, followed pell mell by the enemy, and several of them were struck down into the stream.

The King now dismounted from his white charger whose colour and rich caparison made him too conspicuous, and endeavoured to conceal himself among the thickets which fringed the river. A soldier of Lucena named Martin Hurtado discovered him and attacked him with a pike. The King defended himself with scymetar and target, until another soldier assailed him and he saw a third approaching. Perceiving that further resistance would be vain, he drew back and called upon them to desist, offering them a noble ransom. One of the soldiers rushed forward to seize him, but the King struck him to the earth with a blow of his scymetar.

Don Diego Fernandez de Cordova coming up at this moment, the men said to him, "Señor, here is a Moor that we have taken who seems to be a man of rank and offers a large ransom."

"Slaves! exclaimed King Boabdil, "you have not taken me. I surrender to this cavalier."

Don Diego received him with knightly courtesy. He perceived him to be a person of high rank, but the King concealed his quality and gave himself out as the son of Aben Aleyzer, a nobleman of the royal household.* Don Diego gave him in charge of five soldiers to conduct him to the castle of Lucena, then putting spurs to his horse he hastened to rejoin the Count de Cabra who was in hot pursuit of the enemy. He overtook him at a stream called Riancal, and they continued to press on the skirts of the flying army during the remainder of the day. The pursuit was almost as hazardous as the battle, for had the enemy at any time recovered from their panic they might, by a sudden reaction, have overwhelmed the small force of their pursuers. To guard against this peril the wary count kept his battalion always in close order, and had a body of a hundred chosen lances in the advance. The Moors kept up a Parthian retreat; several times they turned to make battle, but

*Garibay. Lib. 40. Cap. 31.

seeing this solid body of steeled warriors pressing upon them, they again took to flight.

The main retreat of the army was along the valley watered by the Xenel and opening through the mountains of Algaringo to the city of Loxa. The alarm fires of the preceding night had roused the country; every man snatched sword and buckler from the wall, and the towns and villages poured forth their warriors to harrass the retreating foe. Ali Atar kept the main force of the army together, and turned fiercely from time to time upon his pursuers, he was like a wolf hunted through the country he had often made desolate by his maraudings.

The alarm of this invasion had reached the city of Antequera, where were several of the cavaliers who had escaped from the carnage in the mountains of Malaga. Their proud minds were festering with their late disgrace, and their only prayer was for vengeance on the infidels. No sooner did they hear of the Moors being over the border than they were armed and mounted for action. Don Alonzo de Aguilar led them forth: a small body of but forty horsemen, but all cavaliers of prowess, and thirsting for revenge. They came upon the foe on the banks of the Xenel where it winds through the valleys of Cordova. The river, swelled by the late rains, was deep and turbulent, and only fordable at certain places. The main body of the army was gathered in confusion on the banks, endeavouring to ford the stream, protected by the cavalry of Ali Atar.

No sooner did the little band of Alonzo de Aguilar come in sight of the Moors than fury flashed from their eyes. "Remember the mountains of Malaga!" they cried to each other, as they rushed to combat. Their charge was desperate, but was gallantly resisted. A scrambling and bloody fight ensued, hand to hand, and sword to sword, sometimes on land, sometimes in the water; many were lanced on the banks, others throwing themselves into the river sunk with the weight of their armour and were drowned. Some grappling together fell from their horses but continued their struggle in the waves, and helm and turban rolled together down the stream. The Moors were far greater in number, and among them were many warriors of rank, but they were disheartened by defeat, while the Christians were excited even to desperation.

Ali Atar alone preserved all his fire and energy amid his reverses. He had been enraged at the defeat of the army; the loss of the King, and the ignominious flight he had been obliged to make through a country which had so often been the scene of his exploits; but to be thus impeded in his flight and harrassed and insulted by a mere handful of warriors, roused the violent passions of the old Moor to perfect frenzy.

He had marked Don Alonzo de Aguilar dealing his blows, says Agapida, with the pious vehemence of a righteous knight, who knows that in every wound inflicted upon the infidels, he is doing God service. Ali Atar spurred his steed along the bank of the river to come upon Don Alonzo by surprize. The back of that warrior was towards him, and collecting all his force, the Moor hurled his lance to transfix him on the spot. The lance was not thrown with the usual accuracy of Ali Atar. It tore away a part of the cuirass of Don Alonzo but failed to inflict a wound. The Moor rushed upon Don Alonzo with his scymetar, but the latter was on the alert and parried his blow. They fought desperately upon the borders of the river, alternately pressing each other into the stream and fighting their way again up the bank. Ali Atar was repeatedly wounded, and Don Alonzo having pity on his age would have spared his life; he called upon him to surrender, "Never!" cried Ali Atar, "to a Christian Dog!" The words were scarce out of his mouth when the sword of Don Alonzo clove his turbaned head and sank deep into the brain. He fell dead without a groan, his body rolled into the Xenel, nor was it ever found and recognized.* Thus fell Ali Atar who had long been the terror of Andalusia. As he had hated and warred upon the Christians all his life, so he died in the very act of bitter hostility.

The fall of Ali Atar put an end to the transient stand of the cavalry. Horse and foot mingled together in the desperate struggle across the Xenel, and many were trampled down and perished beneath the waves. Don Alonzo and his band continued to harrass them until they crossed the frontier, and every blow struck home to the Moors seemed to lighten the load of humiliation and sorrow which had weighed heavy on their hearts.

In this disastrous rout the Moors lost upwards of five thousand killed and made prisoners, many of whom were of the most noble lineages of Granada. Numbers fled to rocks and mountains, where they were subsequently taken. This battle was called by some the battle of Lucena, by others the battle of the Moorish King, because of the capture of Boabdil. Twenty two banners fell into the hands of the Christians and were carried to Vaena, and hung up in the church; where, says a historian of after times, they remain to this day. Once a year, on the day of S' George they are borne about in procession, by the inhabitants, who at the same time give thanks to God for this signal victory granted to their forefathers.

Great was the triumph of the Count de Cabra, when, on returning from the pursuit of the enemy, he found that the Moorish King had fallen into his hands. When the unfortunate Boabdil was brought before him, however, and he beheld him a dejected captive whom but shortly before he had seen in royal splendour surrounded by his army, the generous heart of the count was touched by sympathy. He said every thing that became a courteous and Christian knight to comfort him; observing that the same mutability of things which had suddenly destroyed his recent prosperity might cause his present

*Cura de Los Palacios.

misfortunes as rapidly to pass away; since in this world nothing is stable, and even sorrow has its allotted term.

Thus consoling him by gentle and soothing words and observing towards him the honour and reverence that his dignity and his misfortunes inspired, he conducted him a prisoner to his strong castle of Vaena.

CHAPTER XVII

LAMENTATIONS OF THE MOORS FOR THE BATTLE OF LUCENA.

The centinels looked out from the watch towers of Loxa along the valley of the Xenel which passes through the mountains of Algaringo. They looked to behold the King returning in triumph at the head of his shining host, laden with the spoil of the unbeliever. They looked to behold the standard of their warlike idol the fierce Ali Atar borne by the chivalry of Loxa, ever foremost in the wars of the border.

In the evening of the twenty first of April they descried a single horseman urging his faltering steed along the banks of the Xenel. As he drew near they perceived, by the flash of arms, that he was a warrior, and on nearer approach, by the richness of his armour and the caparison of his steed, they knew him to be a warrior of rank.

He reached Loxa faint and aghast, his Arabian courser covered with foam and dust and blood, panting and staggering with fatigue and gashed with wounds. Having brought his master in safety he sunk down and died before the gate of the city. The soldiers at the gate gathered round the cavalier, as he stood mute and melancholy by his expiring steed: They knew him to be the gallant Cidi Caleb, nephew of the chief Alfaqui of the Albaycin of Granada. When the people of Loxa beheld this noble cavalier thus alone, haggard and dejected, their hearts were filled with fearful forebodings.

"Cavalier," said they, "how fares it with the King and army?"

He cast his hand mournfully towards the land of the Christians. "There they lie!" exclaimed he. "The heavens have fallen upon them. All are lost: all dead!"*

Upon this there was a great cry of consternation among the people, and loud wailings of women, for the flower of the youth of Loxa were with the army. An old Moorish soldier, scarred in many a border battle, stood leaning

---

*Cura de Los Palacios.

on his lance by the gate way. "Where is Ali Atar?" demanded he eagerly. "If he lives the army cannot be lost."

"I saw his turban cleaved by the Christian sword," replied Cidi Caleb. "His body is floating in the Xenel."

When the soldier heard these words he smote his breast and threw dust upon his head, for he was an old follower of Ali Atar.

The noble Cidi Caleb gave himself no repose but mounting another steed hastened to carry the disastrous tidings to Granada. As he passed through the villages and hamlets he spread sorrow around for their chosen men had followed the King to the wars.

When he entered the gates of Granada and announced the loss of the King and army, a voice of horror went throughout the city. Every one thought but of his own share in the general calamity, and crowded round the bearer of ill tidings. One asked after a father, another after a brother, some after a lover and many a mother after her son. His replies were still of wounds and death. To one he replied, "I saw thy father pierced with a lance as he defended the person of the King." To another, "Thy brother fell wounded under the hoofs of the horses; but there was no time to aid him, for the Christian cavalry were upon us." To another, "I saw the horse of thy lover covered with blood and galloping without his rider." To another, "Thy son fought by my side on the banks of the Xenel; we were surrounded by the enemy and driven into the stream. I heard him cry upon Allah in the midst of the waters: when I reached the other bank he was no longer by my side."

The noble Cidi Caleb passed on, leaving all Granada in lamentation: he urged his steed up the steep avenue of trees and fountains that leads to the Alhambra nor stopped until he arrived before the gate of Justice. Ayxa the mother of Boabdil, and Morayma his beloved and tender wife had daily watched, from the tower of the Gomeres, to behold his triumphant return. Who shall describe their affliction when they heard the tidings of Cidi Caleb? The Sultana Ayxa spake not much, but sate as one entranced in woe. Every now and then a deep sigh burst forth, but she raised her eyes to heaven. "It is the will of Allah!" said she and with these words she endeavoured to repress the agonies of a mother's sorrow. The tender Morayma threw herself on the earth and gave way to the full turbulence of her feelings, bewailing her husband and her father. The high minded Ayxa rebuked the violence of her grief: "Moderate these transports my daughter," said she, "remember, magnanimity should be the attribute of princes. It becomes not them to give way to clamorous sorrow like common and vulgar minds." But Morayma could only deplore her loss with the anguish of a tender woman. She shut herself up in her mirador and gazed all day with streaming eyes upon the vega. Every object before her recalled the causes of her affliction. The river Xenel which ran shining amidst the groves and gardens was the same on whose banks had perished her father Ali Atar; before her lay the road to Loxa by which Boabdil had departed in martial state, surrounded by the chivalry of Granada. Ever and anon she would burst into an agony of grief: "Alas my father!" she would exclaim, "the river runs smiling before me that covers thy mangled remains: who will gather them to an honoured tomb in the land of the unbeliever? And thou oh Boabdil, light of my eyes; joy of my heart; life of my life! Woe the day and woe the hour that I saw thee depart from these walls. The road by which thou hast departed is solitary: never will it be gladdened by thy return! The mountain thou hast traversed lies like a cloud in the distance and all beyond it is darkness."

The royal minstrels were summoned to assuage the sorrows of the Queen, they attuned their instruments to cheerful strains but in a little while the anguish of their hearts prevailed and turned their songs to lamentations.

"Beautiful Granada!" they exclaimed, "how is thy glory faded. The Vivarrambla no longer echoes to the tramp of steed and sound of trumpet, no longer is it crowded with thy youthful nobles, eager to display their prowess in the tourney and the festive tilt of reeds. Alas, the flower of thy chivalry lies low in a foreign land! The soft note of the lute is no longer heard in thy moonlight streets, the lively castanet is silent upon thy hills, and the graceful dance of the Zambra is no more seen beneath thy bowers: Behold the Alhambra is forlorn and desolate! In vain do the orange and myrtle breathe their perfumes into its silken chambers: in vain does the nightingale sing within its groves. In vain are its marble halls refreshed by the sound of fountains and the gush of limpid rills. Alas! the countenance of the King no longer shines within those halls: the light of the Alhambra is set forever!"

Thus all Granada, say the Arabian chroniclers, gave itself up to lamentations: there was nothing but the voice of wailing from the palace to the cottage. All joined to deplore their youthful monarch, cut down in the freshness and promise of his youth: many feared that the prediction of the astrologers was about to be fulfilled, and that the downfall of the kingdom would follow the death of Boabdil; while all declared that had he survived he was the very sovereign calculated to restore the realm to its ancient prosperity and glory.

CHAPTER XVIII

HOW MULEY ABEN HASSAN PROFITED BY THE MISFORTUNES OF HIS SON BOABDIL.

An unfortunate death atones with the world for a multitude of errors: While the populace thought their youthful monarch had perished in the field, nothing could exceed their grief for his loss and their adoration of his memory;

when, however, they learnt that he was still alive, and had surrendered himself captive to the Christians, their feelings underwent an instant change. They decried his talents as a commander, his courage as a soldier. They railed at his expedition as rash and ill conducted, and they reviled him for not having dared to die on the field of battle, rather than surrender to the enemy.

The alfaquis, as usual, mingled with the populace and artfully guided their discontents. "Behold," exclaimed they, "the prediction is accomplished which was pronounced at the birth of Boabdil. He has been seated on the throne, and the kingdom has suffered downfall and disgrace by his defeat and captivity. Comfort yourselves, o Moslems! The evil day has passed by: the fates are satisfied, the sceptre which has been broken in the feeble hand of Boabdil, is destined to resume its former power and sway in the vigorous grasp of Aben Hassan."

The people were struck with the wisdom of these words; they rejoiced that the baleful prediction, which had so long hung over them, was at an end, and declared that none but Muley Aben Hassan had the valour and capacity necessary for the protection of the kingdom, in this time of trouble.

The longer the captivity of Boabdil continued, the greater grew the popularity of his father. One city after another renewed allegiance to him: for power attracts power and fortune creates fortune. At length he was enabled to return to Granada and establish himself once more in the Alhambra. At his approach his repudiated spouse the Sultana Ayxa gathered together the family and treasures of her captive son, and retired with a handful of the nobles into the Albaycin, the rival quarter of the city, the inhabitants of which still retained feelings of loyalty to Boabdil. Here she fortified herself and held the semblance of a court in the name of her son. The fierce Muley Aben Hassan would have willingly carried fire and sword into this factious quarter of the capital, but he dared not confide in his new and uncertain popularity. Many of the nobles detested him for his past cruelty, and a large portion of the soldiery besides many of the people of his own party, respected the virtues of Ayxa la Horra and pitied the misfortunes of Boabdil. Granada therefore presented the singular spectacle of two sovereignties within the same city. The old King fortified himself in the lofty towers of the Alhambra, as much against his own subjects, as against the Christians: while Ayxa, with the zeal of a mother's affection, which waxes warmer and warmer towards her offspring when in adversity, still maintained the standard of Boabdil on the rival fortress of the Alcazaba, and kept his powerful faction alive within the walls of the Albaycin.

CHAPTER XIX

CAPTIVITY OF BOABDIL EL CHICO.

The unfortunate Boabdil remained a prisoner, closely guarded in the castle of Vaena. From the towers of his prison he beheld the town below filled with armed men; and the lofty hill on which it was built girdled by massive walls and ramparts, on which a vigilant watch was maintained, night and day. The mountains around were studded with watch towers, over-looking the lonely roads which led to Granada; so that a turban could not stir over the border without the alarm being given and the whole country put on the alert. Boabdil saw that there was no hope of escape from such a fortress, and that any attempt to rescue him would be equally in vain. His heart was filled with anxiety as he thought on the confusion and ruin which his captivity must cause in his affairs, while sorrows of a softer kind overcame his fortitude as he thought on the evils it might bring upon his family.

The Count de Cabra, though he maintained the most vigilant guard over his royal prisoner, yet treated him with profound deference: he had appointed the noblest apartments in the castle for his abode, and sought in every way to cheer him during his captivity. A few days only had passed away when missives arrived from the Castilian sovereigns. Ferdinand had been transported with joy at hearing of the capture of the Moorish monarch seeing the deep and politic uses that might be made of such an event; but the magnanimous spirit of Isabella was filled with compassion for the unfortunate captive. Their messages to Boabdil, were full of sympathy and consolation, breathing that high and gentle courtesy which dwells in noble minds.

This magnanimity in his foe cheered the dejected spirit of the captive monarch. "Tell my sovereigns the King and Queen," said he to the messenger, "that I can not be unhappy, being in the power of such high and mighty princes, especially since they partake so largely of that grace and goodness which Allah bestows upon the monarchs whom he greatly loves. Tell them further, that I had long thought of submitting myself to their sway, to receive the Kingdom of Granada from their hands, in the same manner that my ancestor received it from King John II, father to the gracious Queen. My greatest sorrow in this my captivity, is, that I must appear to do that from force, which I would fain have done from inclination."

In the mean time Muley Aben Hassan, finding the faction of his son still formidable in Granada, was anxious to consolidate his power by gaining possession of the person of Boabdil. For this purpose he sent an embassy to the Catholic monarchs, offering large terms for the ransom or rather the purchase of his son; proposing, among other conditions, to release the Count of Cifuentes and nine other of his most distinguished captives, and to enter into a treaty of confederacy with the sovereigns. Neither did the implacable father make any scruple of testifying his indifference whether his son were delivered up alive or dead so that his person were placed assuredly within his power.

The humane heart of Isabella revolted at the idea of giving up the unfortunate prince into the hands of his most unnatural and inveterate enemy. A disdainful refusal was therefore returned to the old monarch, whose message had been couched in a vaunting spirit. He was informed that the Castilian sovereigns would listen to no proposals of peace from Muley Aben Hassan until he should lay down his arms and offer them in all humility. Overtures in a different spirit were made by the mother of Boabdil, the Sultana Ayxa la Horra: with the concurrence of the party which still remained faithful to him. It was thereby proposed that Mahomet Abdalla, otherwise called Boabdil, should hold his crown as vassal to the Castilian sovereigns, paying an annual tribute and releasing seventy Christian captives annually for five years. That he should moreover pay a large sum upon the spot for his ransom, and at the same time give freedom to four hundred Christians, to be chosen by the King. That he should also engage to be always ready to render military aid and should come to the Cortes or assemblage of nobles and distinguished vassals of the crown, whenever summoned. His only son and the sons of twelve distinguished Moorish houses, were to be delivered as hostages.

King Ferdinand was at Cordova when he received this proposition: Queen Isabella was absent at the time. He was anxious to consult her on so momentous an affair, or rather he was fearful of proceeding too precipitately, and not drawing from this fortunate event all the advantage of which it was susceptible. Without returning any reply, therefore, to the mission he sent missives to the castle of Vaena, where Boabdil remained in courteous durance of the brave Count de Cabra, ordering that the captive monarch should be brought to Cordova.

The Count de Cabra set out with his illustrious prisoner, but when he arrived at Cordova, King Ferdinand declined seeing the Moorish monarch.

He was still undetermined what course to pursue, whether to retain him prisoner, set him at liberty on ransom, or treat him with politic magnanimity; and each course would require a different kind of reception. Until this point should be resolved, therefore, he gave him in charge to Martin de Alarcon, Alcayde of the ancient fortress of Porcuna, with orders to guard him strictly, but to treat him with the distinction and deference due unto a prince. These commands were strictly obeyed, and, with the exception of being restrained in his liberty, the monarch was as nobly entertained as he could have been in his regal palace at Granada.

In the meantime Ferdinand availed himself of this critical moment while Granada was distracted with factions and dissensions, and before he had concluded any treaty with Boabdil, to make a puissant and ostentatious inroad into the very heart of the kingdom, at the head of his most illustrious nobles. He sacked and destroyed several towns and castles, and extended his ravages to the very gates of Granada. Old Muley Aben Hassan did not venture to oppose him. His city was filled with troops but he was uncertain of their affection. He dreaded that, should he sally forth, the gates of Granada might be closed against him by the faction of the Albaycin.

The old Moor stood on the lofty tower of the Alhambra, says Antonio Agapida, grinding his teeth and foaming like a tyger, shut up in his cage, as he beheld the glittering battalions of the Christians wheeling about the vega, and the standard of the cross shining forth from among the smoke of infidel villages and hamlets. "The most Catholic King," continues Agapida, "would gladly have continued this righteous ravage, but his munitions began to fail. Satisfied therefore with having laid waste the country of the enemy and insulted old Muley Aben Hassan in his very capital, he returned to Cordova covered with laurels, and his army laden with spoils and now bethought himself of coming to an immediate decision in regard to his royal prisoner."

CHAPTER XX

OF THE TREATMENT OF BOABDIL
BY THE CASTILIAN SOVEREIGNS.

A stately convention was held by King Ferdinand in the ancient city of Cordova, composed of several of the most reverend prelates and renowned cavaliers of the kingdom, to determine upon the fate of the unfortunate Boabdil.

Don Alonzo de Cardenas, the worthy Master of Santiago, was one of the first who gave his counsel. He was a pious and zealous knight, rigid in his devotion to the faith, and his holy zeal had been inflamed to peculiar vehemence since his disastrous crusade among the mountains of Malaga. He inveighed with ardour against any compromise or compact with the infidels: The object of this war, he observed, was not the subjection of the Moors, but their utter expulsion from the land, so that there might no longer remain a single stain of Mahometanism throughout Christian Spain. He gave it as his opinion, therefore, that the captive King ought not to be set at liberty.

Roderigo Ponce de Leon, the valiant Marquis of Cadiz, on the contrary, spoke warmly for the release of Boabdil. He pronounced it a measure of sound policy, even if done without conditions. It would tend to keep up the civil war in Granada, which was as a fire consuming the entrails of the enemy, and effecting more for the interests of Spain, without expense, than all the conquests of its arms.

The Grand Cardinal of Spain, Don Pedro Gonzalez de Mendoza, coincided in opinion with the Marquis of Cadiz. Nay, added that pious prelate and politic statesman, it would be sound wisdom to furnish the Moor with men and money and all other necessaries to promote the civil war in Granada: by this means would be produced great benefit to the service of God, since we are assured by his infallible word that "a kingdom divided against itself cannot stand."*

Ferdinand weighed these counsels in his mind but was slow in coming to a decision. He was religiously attentive to his own interests, observes Fray Antonio Agapida, knowing himself to be but an instrument of providence in this holy war, and that, therefore, in consulting his own advantage, he was promoting the interests of the Faith. The opinion of Queen Isabella relieved him from his perplexity. That high minded princess was zealous for the promotion of the faith, but not for the extermination of the infidels. The Moorish Kings had held their thrones as vassals to her progenitors; she was content at present, to accord the same privilege, and that the royal prisoner should be liberated on condition of becoming a vassal to the crown. By this means might be effected the deliverance of many Christian captives who were languishing in Moorish chains.

King Ferdinand adopted the magnanimous measure recommended by the Queen, but he accompanied it with several shrewd conditions, exacting tribute, military services, and safe passage and maintenance for Christian troops throughout the places which should adhere to Boabdil. The captive King readily submitted to these stipulations, and swore, after the manner of his faith, to observe them with exactitude. A truce was arranged for two years, during which the Castilian sovereigns engaged to maintain him on his throne, and to assist him in recovering all places which he had lost during his captivity.

When Boabdil el Chico had solemnly agreed to this arrangement in the castle of Porcuna, preparations were made to receive him in Cordova in regal style. Superb steeds, richly caparisoned and raiment of brocade, and silk, and the most costly clothes, with all other articles of sumptuous array were furnished to him and to fifty Moorish cavaliers who had come to treat for his ransom, that he might appear in state befitting the monarch of Granada and the most distinguished vassal of the Christian sovereigns. Money also was advanced to maintain him in suitable grandeur during his residence at the Castilian court, and his return to his dominions. Finally, it was ordered by the sovereigns that when he came to Cordova, all the nobles and dignitaries of the court should go forth to receive him.

A question now arose among certain of those ancient and experienced

*Salazar. Cronica del gran Cardenal p. 188.

men, who grow grey about a court in the profound study of forms and ceremonials, with whom a point of punctilio is as a vast political right, and who
contract a sublime and awful idea of the external dignity of the throne. Certain of these court sages propounded the momentous question, whether the
Moorish monarch, coming to do homage as a vassal, ought not to kneel and
kiss the hand of the King. This was immediately decided in the affirmative
by a large number of ancient cavaliers, accustomed, says Antonio Agapida,
to the lofty punctilio of our most dignified court and transcendant sovereigns. The King, therefore, was informed by those who arranged the ceremonials that when the Moorish monarch appeared in his presence, he was
expected to extend his royal hand to receive the kiss of homage.

"I should certainly do so," replied King Ferdinand, "were he at liberty
and in his own kingdom; but I certainly shall not do so, seeing that he is a
prisoner and in mine."

The courtiers loudly applauded the magnanimity of this reply; though
many condemned it in secret as savouring of too much generosity towards
an infidel; and the worthy Jesuit Fray Antonio Agapida fully concurs in their
opinion.

The Moorish King entered Cordova with his little train of faithful knights
and escorted by all the nobility and chivalry of the Castilian court. He was
conducted with great state and ceremony to the royal palace. When he came
in presence of Ferdinand he knelt and offered to kiss his hand, not merely
in homage as his subject, but in gratitude for his liberty. Ferdinand declined
the token of vassalage and raised him graciously from the earth. An interpreter began, in the name of Boabdil to laud the magnanimity of the Castilian monarch and to promise the most implicit submission. "Enough," said
King Ferdinand, interrupting the interpreter in the midst of his harangue,
"there is no need of these compliments. I trust in his integrity, that he will
do every thing becoming of a good man and a good King." With these words
he received Boabdil el Chico into his royal friendship and protection.

CHAPTER XXI

RETURN OF BOABDIL FROM CAPTIVITY.

In the month of August a noble Moor of the race of the Abencerrages arrived
with a splendid retinue at the city of Cordova, bringing with him the son of
Boabdil el Chico and other of the noble youths of Granada as hostages for
the fulfilment of the terms of ransom. When the Moorish King beheld his
son, his only child, who was to remain in his stead, a sort of captive in a
hostile land, he folded him in his arms and wept over him. "Woe the day

that I was born!" exclaimed he, "and evil the star, that presided at my birth! Well was I called El Zogoybi or the unlucky: for sorrow is heaped upon me by my father, and sorrow do I transmit to my son!"

The afflicted heart of Boabdil, however, was soothed by the kindness of the Christian sovereigns, who received the hostage prince with a tenderness suited to his age and a distinction worthy of his rank.

They delivered him in charge to the worthy Alcayde Martin de Alarcon, who had treated his father with such courtesy during his confinement in the castle of Porcuna, giving orders that after the departure of the latter his son should be entertained with great honour and princely attention in the same fortress.

On the second of September a guard of honour assembled at the gate of the mansion of Boabdil, to escort him to the frontiers of his kingdom. He pressed his child to his heart at parting, but he uttered not a word for there were many Christian eyes to behold his emotion. He mounted his steed and never turned his head to look again upon the youth; but those who were near him observed the vehement struggle that shook his frame wherein the anguish of the father had well nigh subdued the studied equanimity of the King.

Boabdil El Chico and King Ferdinand sallied forth side by side from Cordova amidst the acclamations of a prodigious multitude. When they were a short distance from the city they separated with many gracious expressions on the part of the Castilian monarch, and many thankful acknowledgements from his late captive, whose heart had been humbled by adversity. Ferdinand departed for Guadalupe and Boabdil for Granada. The latter was accompanied by a guard of honour; and the viceroys of Andalusia, and the generals on the frontier were ordered to furnish him with escorts and to shew him all possible honour on his journey. In this way he was conducted in royal state through the country he had entered to ravage, and was placed in safety in his own dominions.

He was met on the frontier by the principal nobles and cavaliers of his court, who had been secretly sent by his mother, the Sultana Ayxa, to escort him to the capital. The heart of Boabdil was lifted up for a moment when he found himself in his own territories, surrounded by Moslem knights, with his own standards waving over his head, and he began to doubt the predictions of the astrologers: he soon found cause, however, to moderate his exultation. The loyal train which had come to welcome him was but scanty in number, and he missed many of his most zealous and obsequious courtiers. He had returned indeed to his kingdom, but it was no longer the devoted kingdom he had left. The story of his vassalage to the Christian sovereigns had been made use of by his father to ruin him with the people. He had been represented as a traitor to his country, a renegado to his faith and as leagued with the enemies of both to subdue the Moslems of Spain to the yoke of Christian bondage. In this way the mind of the public had been turned from him. The greater part of the nobility had thronged round the throne of his father in the Alhambra, and his mother, the resolute Sultana Ayxa, with difficulty maintained her faction in the opposite towers of the Alcazaba.

Such was the melancholy picture of affairs given to Boabdil by the courtiers who had come forth to meet him. They even informed him that it would be an enterprize of difficulty and danger to make his way back to the capital, and regain the little court which still remained faithful to him in the heart of the city. The old tyger, Muley Aben Hassan, lay couched within the Alhambra, and the walls and gates of the city were strongly guarded by his troops. Boabdil shook his head at these tidings. He called to mind the ill omen of his breaking his lance against the gate of Elvira, when issuing forth so vaingloriously with his army, which he now saw clearly had foreboded the destruction of that army, on which he had so confidently relied. "Henceforth," said he, "let no man have the impiety to scoff at omens."

Boabdil approached his capital by stealth and in the night, prowling about its walls, like an enemy seeking to destroy, rather than a monarch returning to his throne. At length he seized upon a postern gate of the Albaycin, that part of the city which had always been in his favour. He passed rapidly through the streets before the populace were aroused from their sleep, and reached in safety the fortress of the Alcazaba. Here he was received into the embraces of his intrepid mother and his favourite wife Morayma. The transports of the latter on the safe return of her husband were mingled with tears, for she thought of her father Ali Atar, who had fallen in his cause, and of her only son who was left a hostage in the hands of the Christians.

The heart of Boabdil, softened by his misfortunes, was moved by the changes in every thing round him; but his mother called up his spirit. "This," said she, "is no time for tears and fondness; a King must think of his sceptre and his throne, and not yield to softness like common men. Thou hast done well my son in throwing thyself resolutely into Granada, it must depend upon thyself whether thou remain here a King or a captive."

The old King Muley Aben Hassan had retired to his couch that night, in one of the strongest towers of the Alhambra, but his restless anxiety kept him from repose. In the first watch of the night he heard a shout faintly rising from the quarter of the Albaycin, which is on the opposite side of the deep valley of the Darro. Shortly afterwards horsemen came galloping up the hill that leads to the main gate of the Alhambra, spreading the alarm that Boabdil had entered the city and possessed himself of the Alcazaba.

In the first transports of his rage the old King would have struck the messenger to earth. He hastily summoned his counsellers and commanders, exhorting them to stand by him in this critical moment, and during the night made every preparation to enter the Albaycin sword in hand in the morning.

In the mean time the Sultana Ayxa had taken prompt and vigorous measures to strengthen her party. The Albaycin was the part of the city filled by the lower orders. The return of Boabdil was proclaimed throughout the streets, and large sums of money were distributed among the populace. The nobles, assembled in the Alcazaba, were promised honours and rewards by Boabdil as soon as he should be firmly seated on the throne. These well timed measures had the customary effect, and by day break all the motley populace of the Albaycin were in arms.

A doleful day succeeded. All Granada was a scene of tumult and horror. Drums and trumpets resounded in every part: all business was interrupted; the shops were shut, the doors barricadoed. Armed bands paraded the streets, some shouting for Boabdil and some for Muley Aben Hassan. When they encountered each other they fought furiously and without mercy; every public square became a scene of battle. The great mass of the lower orders was in favour of Boabdil but it was a multitude without discipline or lofty spirit; part of the people was regularly armed, but the greater number had sallied forth with the implements of their trade. The troops of the old King, among whom were many cavaliers of pride and valour, soon drove the populace from the squares. They fortified themselves, however, in the streets and lanes which they barricadoed. They made fortresses of their houses, and fought desperately from the windows and the roofs, and many a warrior of the highest blood of Granada was laid low by plebeian hands and plebeian weapons in this civic brawl.

It was impossible that such violent convulsions should last long in the heart of a city. The people soon longed for repose and a return to their peaceful occupations, and the cavaliers detested these conflicts with the multitude, in which there were all the horrors of war without its laurels. By the interference of the alfaquis an armistice was at length effected. Boabdil was persuaded that there was no dependance upon the inconstant favour of the multitude, and was prevailed upon to quit a capital where he could only maintain a precarious seat upon his throne by a perpetual and bloody struggle. He fixed his court at the city of Almeria, which was entirely devoted to him, and which, at that time, vied with Granada in splendour and importance. This compromise of grandeur for tranquility, however, was sorely against the counsels of his proud spirited mother, the Sultana Ayxa. Granada appeared in her eyes the only legitimate seat of dominion, and she observed, with a smile of disdain, that he was not worthy of being called a monarch who was not master of his capital.

CHAPTER XXII

FORAY OF THE MOORISH ALCAYDES AND BATTLE OF LOPERA.

Though Muley Aben Hassan had regained undivided sway over the city of Granada, and the alfaquis by his command had denounced his son Boabdil as an apostate and as one doomed by heaven to misfortune, still the latter had many adherents among the common people. Whenever, therefore, any act of the old monarch was displeasing to the turbulent multitude, they were prone to give him a hint of the slippery nature of his standing, by shouting out the name of Boabdil el Chico. Long experience had instructed Muley Aben Hassan in the character of the inconstant people over whom he ruled. "Allah Achbar!" exclaimed he, "God is great: but a successful inroad into the country of the unbelievers will make more converts to my cause than a thousand texts of the Koran expounded by ten thousand alfaquis."

At this time King Ferdinand was absent from Andalusia on a distant expedition, with many of his troops. The moment was favorable for a foray and Muley Aben Hassan cast about his thoughts for a leader to conduct it. Ali Atar, the terror of the border, the scourge of Andalusia was dead, but there was another veteran general scarce inferior to him for predatory warfare. This was old Bexir the gray and crafty alcayde of Malaga; and the people under his command were ripe for an expedition of the kind. The signal defeat and slaughter of the Spanish knights in the neighbouring mountains had filled the people of Malaga with vanity and self conceit: they had attributed to their own valour the defeat which had been caused by the nature of the country. Many of them wore the armour and paraded in public with the horses of the unfortunate cavaliers slain on that occasion, which they vauntingly displayed as the trophies of their boasted victory. They had talked themselves into a contempt for the chivalry of Andalusia and were impatient for an opportunity to over run a country defended by such troops. This Muley Aben Hassan considered a favorable state of mind to ensure a daring inroad, and he sent orders to old Bexir to gather together his people and the choicest warriors of the borders, and to carry fire and sword into the very heart of Andalusia. The wary old Bexir immediately dispatched his emissaries among the alcaydes of the border towns calling upon them to assemble with their troops at the city of Ronda, close upon the Christian frontier.

Ronda was the most virulent nest of Moorish depredators in the whole border country. It was situated in the midst of the wild Serrania or chain of mountains of the same name, which are uncommonly lofty, broken and precipitous. It stood on an almost isolated rock, nearly encircled by a deep valley, or rather chasm, through which ran the beautiful river called Rio Verde. The Moors of this city were the most active, robust and warlike of all the mountaineers and their very children discharged the cross bow with unerring aim. They were incessantly harrassing the rich plains of Andalusia: their city abounded with Christian spoils, and their deep dungeons were crowded with Christian captives, who might sigh in vain for deliverance from this impregnable fortress. Such was Ronda in the time of the Moors, and it has ever retained something of the same character even to the present day. Its inhabitants continue to be among the boldest, fiercest and most adventurous of the Andalusian mountainiers, and the Serrania de Ronda is famous as the most dangerous resort of the bandit and the contrabandista.

Hamet Zeli, surnamed El Zegri, was the commander of this belligerent city and its fierce inhabitants. He was of the tribe of the Zegris and one of the most proud and daring of that warlike race. Besides the inhabitants of Ronda he had a legion of African Moors in his immediate service. They were of the tribe of the Gomeres, mercenary troops, whose hot African blood had not yet been tempered by the softer living of Spain, and whose whole business was to fight. These he kept always well armed and well appointed. The rich pasturage of the valley of Ronda produced a breed of horses famous for strength and speed. No cavalry therefore was better mounted than the band of Gomeres. Rapid on the march, fierce in the attack, it would sweep down upon the Andalusian plains like a sudden blast from the mountains, and pass away as suddenly, before there was time for pursuit.

There was nothing that stirred up the spirit of the Moors of the frontiers more thoroughly than the idea of a foray. The summons of Bexir was gladly obeyed by the alcaydes of the border towns, and, in a little while, there was a force of fifteen hundred horse and four thousand foot, the very pith and marrow of the surrounding country, assembled within the walls of Ronda. The people of the place anticipated with eagerness the rich spoils of Andalusia that were soon to crowd their gates; throughout the day the city resounded with the noise of kettle drum and trumpet; the high mettled steeds stamped and neighed in their stalls as if they shared the impatience for the foray, while the Christian captives sighed as the varied din of preparation reached to their rocky dungeons, denoting that a fresh ravage was preparing against their countrymen.

The infidel host sallied forth full of spirits, anticipating an easy ravage and abundant booty. They encouraged each other in a contempt for the prowess of the foe. Many of the warriors of Malaga and of some of the mountain towns had insultingly arrayed themselves in the splendid armour of the Christian knights slain or taken prisoners in the famous massacre, and some of them rode the Andalusian steeds which had been captured on that occasion.

The wary Bexir had concerted his plans so secretly and expeditiously that the Christian towns of Andalusia had not the least suspicion of the storm that had gathered beyond the mountains. The vast and rocky range of the Serrania de Ronda extended like a screen, covering all their movements from observation.

The army made its way as rapidly as the rugged nature of the mountains would permit, guided by Hamet el Zegri, the bold Alcayde of Ronda, who knew every pass and defile. Not a drum, nor the clash of a cymbal, nor the blast of a trumpet, was permitted to be heard. The mass of war rolled quietly on as the gathering cloud to the brow of the mountains, intending to burst down like the thunderbolt upon the plain.

Never let the most wary commander fancy himself secure from discovery, for rocks have eyes, and trees have ears, and the birds of the air have tongues to betray the most secret enterprize. There chanced at this time to be six Christian scouts prowling about the savage heights of the Serrania de Ronda. They were of that kind of lawless ruffians who infest the borders of belligerent countries, ready at any time to fight for pay or prowl for plunder. The wild mountain passes of Spain have ever abounded with loose rambling vagabonds of the kind, soldiers in war, robbers in peace, guides, guards, smugglers or cut throats, according to the circumstances of the case.

These six marauders, says Fray Antonio Agapida, were on this occasion, chosen instruments, sanctified by the righteousness of their cause. They were lurking among the mountains to entrap Moorish cattle or Moorish prisoners, both of which were equally saleable in the Christian market.

They had ascended one of the loftiest cliffs, and were looking out, like birds of prey, ready to pounce upon any thing that might offer in the valley, when they descried the Moorish army emerging from a mountain glen. They watched it in silence as it wound below them, remarking the standards of the various towns and the pennons of the commanders.

They hovered about it, on its march, skulking from cliff to cliff, until they saw the route by which it intended to enter the Christian country. They then dispersed, each making his way by the secret passes of the mountains, to some different alcayde, that they might spread the alarm far and wide and each get a separate reward.

One hastened to Luis Fernandez Puertocarrero, the same valiant alcayde who had repulsed Muley Aben Hassan from the walls of Alhama, and who now commanded at Ecija in the absence of the Master of Santiago. Others roused the town of Utrera and the places of that neighborhood, putting them all on the alert.

Puertocarrero was a cavalier of consummate vigour and activity. He immediately sent couriers to the alcaydes of the neighbouring fortresses, to Herman Carrello captain of a body of the Holy Brotherhood, and to certain knights of the order of Alcantara. Puertocarrero was the first to take the field. Knowing the hard and hungry service of these border scampers, he made every man take a hearty repast, and see that his horse was well shod and perfectly appointed. Then all being refreshed, and in valiant heart, he sallied forth to seek the Moors. He had but a handful of men, the retainers of his household, and troops of his captaincy, but they were well armed and mounted, and accustomed to the sudden rouses of the border; men whom the cry of "arm and out! to horse and to the field!" was sufficient at any time to put in a fever of animation.

While the northern part of Andalusia was thus on the alert one of the scouts had hastened southward to the city of Xeres, and given the alarm to the valiant Marquis of Cadiz. When the marquis heard that the Moor was over the border, and that the standard of Malaga was in the advance his heart bounded with a momentary joy, for he remembered the massacre in the mountains where his valiant brothers had been mangled before his eyes. The very authors of his calamity were now at hand, and he flattered himself that the day of vengeance had arrived.

He made a hasty levy of his retainers, and of the fighting men of Xeres, and hurried off with three hundred horse and two hundred foot, all resolute men and panting for revenge.

In the meantime the veteran Bexir had accomplished his march, as he imagined, undiscovered. From the openings of the craggy defiles he pointed out the fertile plains of Andalusia, and regaled the eyes of his soldiery with the rich country they were about to ravage. The fierce Gomeres of Ronda were flushed with joy at the sight, and even their steeds seemed to prick up their ears and snuff the breeze, as they beheld the scenes of their frequent forays.

When they came to where the mountain defile opened into the low land Bexir divided his force into three parts, one, composed of foot soldiers and of such as were weakly mounted, he left to guard the pass, being too experienced a veteran not to know the importance of securing a retreat. A second body he placed in ambush among the groves and thickets on the banks of the river Lopera. The third, consisting of light cavalry, he sent forth to ravage the Campiña or great plain of Utrera. Most of this latter force was composed of the fiery Gomeres of Ronda, mounted on the fleet steeds bred among the mountains. It was led by the bold Alcayde Hamet el Zegri, who was ever eager to be foremost in the forage.

Little suspecting that the country on both sides was on the alarm, and rushing from all directions to close upon them in rear, this fiery troop dashed forward until they came within two leagues of Utrera. Here they scattered themselves about the plain careering round the great herds of cattle and flocks of sheep and sweeping them into droves to be hurried to the mountains.

While they were thus dispersed in every direction, a troop of horse, and body of foot, from Utrera, came suddenly upon them. The Moors rallied together in small parties, and endeavoured to defend themselves, but they were without a leader, for Hamet el Zegri was at a distance, having, like a hawk, made a wide circuit in pursuit of prey. The marauders soon gave way and fled towards ambush on the banks of the Lopera, being hotly pursued by the men of Utrera.

When they reached the Lopera the Moors in ambush rushed forth with furious cries, and the fugitives, recovering courage from this reinforcement, rallied and turned upon their pursuers. The Christians stood their ground though greatly inferior in number. Their lances were soon broken and they came to sharp work with sword and scymetar. The Christians fought valiantly but were in danger of being overwhelmed. The bold Hamet had collected a handful of his scattered Gomeres, and, leaving his prey, had galloped towards the scene of action. His little troop of horsemen had reached the crest of a rising ground, at no great distance, when trumpets were heard in another direction, and Luis Fernandez Puertocarrero and his followers, came galloping into the field, and charged upon the infidels in flank.

The Moors were astounded at finding war thus breaking upon them from various quarters of what they had expected to find an unguarded country. They fought for a short time with desperation, and resisted a vehement assault from the Knights of Alcantara, and the men of arms of the Holy Brotherhood. At length the veteran Bexir was struck from his horse by Puertocarrero and taken prisoner, and the whole force gave way and fled. In their flight they separated and took two roads to the mountains, thinking, by dividing their forces, to distract the enemy. The Christians were too few to separate. Puertocarrero kept them together, pursuing one division of the enemy with great slaughter. This battle took place at the fountain of the fig tree, near to the Lopera. Six hundred Moorish cavaliers were slain, and many taken prisoners; much spoil was collected on the field, with which the Christians returned in triumph to their homes.

The larger body of the enemy had retreated along a road leading more to the south by the banks of the Guadalete. When they reached that river the sound of pursuit had died away, and they rallied to breathe and refresh themselves on the margin of the stream. Their force was reduced to about a thousand horse and a confused multitude of foot. While they were scattered and partly dismounted on the banks of the Guadalete a fresh storm of war burst upon them from an opposite direction. It was the Marquis of Cadiz, leading on his household troops, and the fighting men of Xeres. When the Christian warriors came in sight of the Moors they were roused to fury at beholding many of them arrayed in the armour of the cavaliers who had been slain among the mountains of Malaga: nay, some who had been in that defeat, beheld their own armour, which they had cast away in their flight, to enable themselves to climb the mountains. Exasperated at the sight they rushed upon the foe with the ferocity of tygers rather than the temperate courage of cavaliers. Each man felt as if he were avenging the death of a relative or wiping out his own disgrace. The good marquis himself beheld a powerful Moor bestriding the horse of his brother Beltran: giving a cry of rage and anguish at the sight, he rushed through the thickest of the enemy, attacked the Moor with resistless fury, and after a short combat hurled him breathless to the earth.

The Moors, already vanquished in spirit, could not withstand the assault of men thus madly excited: They soon gave way and fled for the defile of the Serrania de Ronda, where the body of troops had been stationed to secure a retreat. These seeing them come gallopping wildly up the defile, with Christian banners in pursuit, and the flash of weapons at their deadly work, thought all Andalusia was upon them and fled without awaiting an attack. The pursuit continued among glens and defiles, for the Christian warriors, eager for revenge, had no compassion on the foe.

When the pursuit was over the Marquis of Cadiz and his followers reposed themselves upon the banks of the Guadalete, where they divided the spoil. Among this were found many rich corselets, helmets and weapons, the Moorish trophies of the defeat in the mountains of Malaga. Several were claimed by their owners, others were known to have belonged to noble cavaliers who had been slain or taken prisoner. There were several horses also richly caparisoned, which had pranced proudly with the unfortunate warriors as they sallied out of Antequera upon that fatal expedition. Thus the exultation of the victors was dashed with melancholy, and many a knight was seen lamenting over the helmet or corselet of some loved companion in arms.

The good Marquis of Cadiz was resting under a tree on the banks of the Guadalete, when the horse which had belonged to his slaughtered brother Beltran was brought to him. He laid his hand upon the mane, and looked wistfully at the empty saddle. His bosom heaved with violent agitation and his lip quivered and was pale. "Ay de mi! mi hermano!" (woe is me my brother!) was all that he said, for the grief of a warrior has not many words. He looked round on the field strewn with the bodies of the enemy, and in the bitterness of his woe he felt consoled by the idea that his brother had not been unrevenged.*

Nota—*"En el despojo de la Batalla se ireron muchas ricas corazas è capacetes e barberas de las que se habian perdido en el Axarquia, è otras muchas armas, e algunas fueron conocidas de sus Dueños que las havian dejado para fuir, e otras fueron conocidas, que eran muy señaladas de hombres principales que havian quedado muertos e cautivos i fueron tornados muchos de los mismos cavallos con sus ricás síllas, de los que quedaron en la Axarquia é fueron conocidos cuios eran."—Cura de Los Palacios Cap. 67—

CHAPTER XXIII

RETREAT OF HAMET EL ZEGRI, ALCAYDE OF RONDA.

The bold Alcayde of Ronda Hamet el Zegri, had careered wide over the Campiña of Utrera, encompassing the flocks and herds, when he heard the burst of war at a distance. There were with him but a handful of his Gomeres. He saw the scamper and pursuit afar off, and beheld the Christian horsemen spurring madly on towards the ambuscade on the banks of the Lopera. Hamet tossed his hand triumphantly aloft for his men to follow him. "The Christian dogs are ours!" said he; as he put spurs to his horse to take the enemy in rear.

The little band which followed Hamet scarcely amounted to thirty horsemen. They spurred across the plain and reached a rising ground just as the force of Puertocarrero had charged, with sound of trumpet, upon the flank of the party in ambush. Hamet beheld the headlong rout of the army with rage and consternation. He found the country was pouring forth its legions from every quarter and perceived that there was no safety but in precipitate flight. But which way to fly? An army was between him and the mountain pass, all the forces of the neighborhood were rushing to the borders, the whole route by which he had come was by this time occupied by the foe. He checked his steed, rose in his stirrups and rolled a stern and thoughtful eye over the country, then sinking into his saddle he seemed to commune for a moment with himself. Turning quickly to his troop he singled out a renegado Christian, a traitor to his religion and his King. "Come hither," said Hamet. "Thou knowest all the secret passes of this country?" "I do," replied the renegado. "Dost thou know any circuitous route, solitary and untravelled, by which we can pass wide within these troops and reach the Serrania?" The renegado paused. "Such a route I know, but it is full of peril, for it leads through the heart of the Christian land." "Tis well," said Hamet, "the more dangerous in appearance, the less it will be suspected. Now hearken to me. Ride by my side. Thou seest this purse of gold and this scymetar. Take us by the route thou hast mentioned, safe to the pass of the Serrania, and this purse shall be thy reward, betray us, and this scymetar shall cleave thee to the saddle bow."*

The renegado obeyed trembling. They turned off from the direct road to the mountains and struck southward towards Lebrixa, passing by the most solitary roads and along those deep ramblas and ravines by which the country is intersected. It was indeed a daring course. Every now and then they heard the distant sound of trumpets, and the alarm bells of towns and villages, and found that the war was still hurrying to the borders. They hid themselves in thickets, and in the dry beds of rivers, until the danger had

*Cura de los Palacios. Ubi sup.

passed by, and then resumed their course. Hamet el Zegri rode on in silence, his hand upon his scymetar and his eye upon the renegado guide, prepared to sacrifice him on the least sign of treachery; while his band followed, gnawing their lips with rage at having thus to skulk through a country they had come to ravage.

When night fell they struck into more practicable roads, always keeping wide of the villages and hamlets lest the watch dogs should betray them. In this way they passed in deep midnight by Arcos, crossed the Guadalete, and effected their retreat to the mountains. The day dawned as they made their way up the savage defiles. Their comrades had been hunted up these very glens by the enemy. Every now and then they came to where there had been a partial fight, or a slaughter of the fugitives, and the rocks were red with blood and strewed with mangled bodies. The Alcayde of Ronda was almost frantic with rage at seeing many of his bravest warriors lying stiff and stark a prey to the hawks and vultures of the mountains. Now and then some wretched Moor would crawl out of a cave or glen whither he had fled for refuge; for in the retreat many of the horsemen had abandoned their steeds, thrown away their armour and clambered up the cliffs where they could not be pursued by the Christian cavalry.

The Moorish army had sallied forth from Ronda amidst shouts and acclamations, but wailings were heard within its walls as the alcayde and his broken band returned without banner or trumpet and haggard with famine and fatigue. The tidings of their disaster had preceded them, borne by the fugitives of the army. No one ventured to speak to the stern Hamet el Zegri as he entered the city, for they saw a dark cloud gathered upon his brow.

It seemed, says the pious Antonio Agapida, as if heaven meted out this defeat in exact retribution for the ills inflicted upon the Christian warriors in the heights of Malaga. It was equally signal and disastrous. Of the brilliant array of Moorish chivalry which had descended so confidently into Andalusia, not more than two hundred escaped. The choicest troops of the frontier were either taken or destroyed; the Moorish garrisons enfeebled, and many alcaydes and cavaliers of noble lineage carried into captivity, who were afterwards obliged to redeem themselves with heavy ransoms.

This was called the battle of Lopera, and was fought on the 17th of September 1483. Ferdinand and Isabella were at Vittoria in old Castile when they received news of the victory and the standards taken from the enemy. They celebrated the event with processions, illuminations and other festivities. Ferdinand sent to the Marquis of Cadiz the royal rayment which he had worn on that day and conferred on him, and on all those who should inherit his title, the privilege of wearing royal robes on our Lady's day in September in commemoration of this victory.

Queen Isabella was equally mindful of the great services of Don Luis Fernandez Puertocarrero. Besides many encomiums and favours, she sent to his wife the royal vestments and robe of brocade which she had worn on the same day, to be worn by her, during her life, on the anniversary of that battle.*

CHAPTER XXIV

OF THE HIGH AND CEREMONIOUS RECEPTION AT COURT OF THE COUNT DE CABRA AND THE ALCAYDE DE LOS DONZELES.

In the midst of the bustle of warlike affairs, the worthy chronicler Fray Antonio Agapida pauses to note, with curious accuracy, the distinguished reception given to the Count de Cabra and his nephew, the Alcayde de los Donzeles at the stately and ceremonious court of Castile, in reward for the capture of the Moorish King Boabdil.

The court, he observes, was held at the time in the ancient Moorish palace of the city of Cordova and the ceremonials were arranged by that venerable prelate Don Pedro Gonzalez de Mendoza, Bishop of Toledo and Grand Cardinal of Spain.

It was on Wednesday the fourteenth of October, continues the precise Antonio Agapida, that the good Count de Cabra according to arrangement, appeared at the gate of Cordova. Here he was met by the Grand Cardinal and the Duke of Villahermosa, illegitimate brother of the king, together with many of the first grandees and prelates of the kingdom. By this august train was he attended to the palace, amidst triumphant strains of martial music and the shouts of a prodigious multitude.

When the count arrived in the presence of the sovereigns, who were seated in state on a dais or raised part of the hall of audience, they both arose. The King advanced exactly five steps toward the count, who knelt and kissed his majesty's hand, but the King would not receive him as a mere vassal, but embraced him with affectionate cordiality. The Queen, also, advanced two steps and received the count with a countenance full of sweetness, and benignity; after he had kissed her hand the King and Queen returned to their thrones; and, cushions being brought, they ordered the worthy count to be seated in their presence. This last circumstance is written in large letters and followed by several notes of admiration, in the manuscript of the worthy

*Mariana. Abarca. Zurita. Pulgar &c.

Fray Antonio Agapida, who considers the extraordinary privilege of sitting in the presence of the Catholic sovereigns an honour well worth fighting for.

The good count took his seat at a short distance from the King, and near him was seated the Duke of Najera, then the Bishop of Palencia, then the Count of Aguilar, the Count Luna and Don Gutiere de Cardenas, Senior Commander of Leon.

On the side of the Queen were seated the Grand Cardinal of Spain, the Duke of Villahermosa, the Count of Monte Rey and the Bishops of Jaen and Cuenca, each in the order in which they are named. The Infanta Isabella was prevented by indisposition from attending this ceremony.

And now festive music resounded through the sumptuous hall, and behold twenty ladies of the Queen's retinue entered magnificently attired, upon which twenty youthful cavaliers very gay and galliard in their array stepped forth, and each seeking his fair partner they commenced a stately dance. The court, in the mean time, observes Fray Antonio Agapida, looked on with lofty and becoming gravity.

When the dance was concluded the King and Queen rose to retire to supper, and dismissed the count with many gracious expressions. He was then attended by all the grandees present to the palace of the Grand Cardinal, where they partook of a sumptuous banquet.

On the following Saturday the Alcayde de los Donzeles was received likewise with great honours; but the ceremonies were so arranged as to be a degree less in dignity than those shewn to his uncle, the latter being considered the principal actor in this great achievement. Thus the Grand Cardinal and the Duke of Villahermosa did not meet him at the gate of the city, but received him in the palace, and entertained him in conversation until summoned to the sovereigns. When the Alcayde de los Donzeles entered the presence chamber, the King and Queen rose from their chairs, but without advancing; they embraced him graciously and commanded him to be seated next to the Count de Cabra.

The Infanta Isabella came forth to this reception and took her seat beside the Queen. When the court were all seated the music again sounded through the hall, and the twenty ladies came forth as on the preceding occasion, richly attired, but in different rayment. They danced as before, and the Infanta Isabella, taking a young Portuguese damsel for a partner, joined in the dance. When this was concluded the King and Queen dismissed the Alcayde de los Donzeles with great courtesy, and the court broke up.

The worthy Fray Antonio Agapida here indulges in a long eulogy on the scrupulous discrimination of the Castilian court in the distribution of its honours and rewards, by which means every smile and gesture and word of the sovereigns had its certain value and conveyed its equivalent of joy to the heart of the subject. A matter well worthy the study, says he, of all monarchs, who are too apt to distribute honours with a heedless caprice that renders them of no avail.

On the following Sunday both the Count de Cabra and the Alcayde de los Donzeles were invited to sup with the sovereigns. The court that evening was attended by the highest nobility, arrayed with that cost and splendour for which the Spanish nobility of those days was renowned.

Before supper there was a stately and ceremonious dance, befitting the dignity of so august a court. The King led forth the Queen in grave and graceful measure; the Count de Cabra was honoured with the hand of the Infanta Isabella, and the Alcayde de los Donzeles danced with a daughter of the Marquis de Astorga.

The dance being concluded the royal party repaired to the supper table, which was placed on an elevated part of the saloon. Here, in full view of the court, the Count de Cabra and the Alcayde de los Donzeles supped at the same table with the King, the Queen and the Infanta. The royal family were served by the Marquis of Villena. The cup bearer to the King was his nephew Fadrique de Toledo, son to the Duke of Alva; Don Alvaro de Estuñiga had the honour of fulfilling that office for the Queen and Tello de Aguilar for the Infanta. Other cavaliers of rank and distinction waited on the count and the Alcayde de los Donzeles. At one o'clock the two distinguished guests were dismissed, with many courteous expressions, by the sovereigns.*

Such, says Fray Antonio Agapida, were the great honours payed at our most exalted and ceremonious court, to these renowned cavaliers; but the gratitude of the sovereigns did not end here. A few days afterwards they bestowed upon them large revenues for life, and others to descend to their heirs, with the privilege for them and their descendants to prefix the title of Don to their names. They gave them, moreover, as armorial bearings, a Moor's head crowned, with a golden chain round the neck, in a sanguine field, and twenty two banners round the margin of the escutcheon. Their descendants, of the houses of Cabra and Cordova, continue to bear these arms at the present day, in memorial of the victory of Lucena and the capture of Boabdil el Chico.

---

*The account given by Fray Antonio Agapida of this ceremonial, so characteristic of the old Spanish court, agrees in almost every particular with an ancient manuscript made up from the chronicles of the curate of los Palacios and other old Spanish writers.

CHAPTER XXV

HOW THE MARQUIS OF CADIZ CONCERTED TO SURPRIZE ZAHARA, AND THE RESULT OF HIS ENTERPRIZE.

The valiant Roderigo Ponce de Leon, Marquis of Cadiz, was one of the most vigilant of commanders. He kept in his pay a number of converted Moors to serve as adalides, or armed guides. These mongrel Christians were of great service in procuring information. Availing themselves of their Moorish character and tongue, they penetrated into the enemies' country, prowled about the castles and fortresses, noticed the state of the walls, the gates and towers, the strength of their garrisons, and the vigilance or negligence of their commanders. All this they reported minutely to the marquis, who thus knew the state of every fortress upon the frontier, and when it might be attacked with advantage. Besides the various towns and cities over which he held a feudal sway, he had always an armed force about him, ready for the field. A host of retainers fed in his hall, who were ready to follow him to danger and death itself, without enquiring who or why they fought. The armouries of his castles were supplied with helms and cuirasses and weapons of all kinds, ready burnished for use; and his stables were filled with hardy steeds that could stand a mountain scamper.

The marquis was aware that the late defeat of the Moors on the banks of the Lopera, had weakened their whole frontier; for many of the castles and fortresses had lost their alcaydes and their choicest troops. He sent out his war hounds, therefore, upon the range, to ascertain where a successful blow might be struck, and they soon returned with word that Zahara was weakly garrisoned and short of provisions.

This was the very fortress, which, about two years before, had been stormed by Muley Aben Hassan, and its capture had been the first blow of this eventful war. It had ever since remained a thorn in the side of Andalusia. All the Christians had been carried away captive and no civil population had been introduced in their stead. There were no women or children in the place. It was kept up as a mere military post commanding one of the most important passes of the mountains, and was a strong hold of Moorish marauders. The marquis was animated by the idea of regaining this fortress for his sovereigns, and wresting from the old Moorish King this boasted trophy of his prowess.

He sent missives, therefore, to the brave Luis Fernandez Puertocarrero, who had distinguished himself in the late victory, and to Juan Almaraz, captain of the men at arms of the Holy Brotherhood, informing them of his designs, and inviting them to meet him with their forces on the banks of the Guadalete.

It was on the day, says Fray Antonio Agapida, of the glorious apostles S'
Simon and Judas, the twenty eighth of October, in the year of grace one
thousand four hundred and eighty three, that this chosen band of Christian
soldiers assembled suddenly and secretly at the appointed place. Their
forces, when united, amounted to six hundred horse and fifteen hundred
foot. Their gathering place was at the entrance of the defile leading to Zahara. That ancient town, renowned in Moorish warfare, is situated in one of
the roughest passes of the Serrania de Ronda. It is built round the craggy
cone of a hill, on the lofty summit of which is a strong castle. The country
around is broken into deep barrancos or ravines, some of which approach its
very walls. The place had, until recently, been considered impregnable; but,
as the worthy Fray Antonio Agapida observes, the walls of impregnable fortresses, like the virtue of self confident saints, have their weak points of
attack.

The Marquis of Cadiz advanced with his little army in the dead of the
night, marching silently up the deep and dark defiles of the mountains, and
stealing up the ravines which extended to the walls of the town. Their approach was so noiseless that the Moorish centinels upon the walls heard not
a voice or a footfall. The marquis was accompanied by his old escalador Ortega de Prado, who had distinguished himself at the scaling of Alhama. This
hardy veteran was stationed, with ten men, furnished with scaling ladders,
in a cavity among the rocks, close to the walls: at a little distance seventy
men were hid in a ravine, to be at hand to second him when he should have
fixed his ladders. The rest of the troops were concealed in another ravine,
commanding a fair approach to the gate of the fortress.   A shrewd and wary
adalid, well acquainted with the place, was appointed to give signals and was
so stationed, that he could be seen by the various parties in ambush, but
was hidden from the garrison.

The remainder of the night passed away in profound quiet. The Moorish
centinels could be heard tranquilly patrolling the walls in perfect security.
The day dawned and the rising sun began to shine against the lofty peaks of
the Serrania de Ronda. The centinels looked from their battlements over a
savage but quiet mountain country, where not a human being was stirring;
they little dreamt of the mischief that lay lurking in every ravine and chasm
of the rocks around them. Apprehending no danger of surprize in broad day,
the greater part of the soldiers abandoned the walls and towers and descended into the city.

By orders of the marquis a small body of light cavalry passed along the
glen and, turning round a point of rock, shewed themselves before the town:
They skirred the fields almost to the gates, as if by way of bravado, and to
defy the garrison to a skirmish. The Moors were not slow in replying to it;
about seventy horse and a number of foot, who had guarded the walls, sallied
forth impetuously, thinking to make easy prey of these insolent marauders.

The Christian horsemen fled for the ravine, the Moors pursued them down the hill, until they heard a great shouting and tumult behind them. Looking round they beheld their town assailed, and a scaling party mounting the walls sword in hand. Wheeling about they gallopped furiously for the gate. The Marquis of Cadiz and Luis Fernandez Puertocarrero rushed forth at the same time, with their ambuscade, and endeavoured to cut them off, but the Moors succeeded in throwing themselves within the walls.

While Puertocarrero stormed at the gates the marquis put spurs to his horse and gallopped to the support of Ortega de Prado and his scaling party. He arrived at a moment of imminent peril, when the party was assailed by fifty Moors, armed with cuirasses and lances, who were on the point of thrusting them from the walls. The marquis sprang from his horse, mounted a ladder, sword in hand, followed by a number of his troops and made a vigorous attack upon the enemy.* They were soon driven from the walls, and the gates and towers remained in possession of the Christians. The Moors defended themselves for a short time in the street, but at length took refuge in the castle, the walls of which were strong, and capable of holding out until relief should arrive. The marquis had no desire to carry on a siege, and he had not provisions sufficient for many prisoners; he granted them therefore favorable terms. They were permitted, on leaving their arms behind them, to march out with as much of their effects as they could carry, and it was stipulated that they should pass over to Barbary. The marquis remained in the place until both town and castle were put in a perfect state of defence and strongly garrisoned.

Thus did Zahara return once more into possession of the Christians, to the great confusion of old Muley Aben Hassan; who, having paid the penalty of his illtimed violence, was now deprived of its vaunted fruits. The Castilian sovereigns were so gratified by this achievement of the valiant Ponce de Leon, that they authorized him thenceforth to entitle himself Duke of Cadiz and Marquis of Zahara; the warrior, however, was so proud of the original title, under which he had so often signalized himself, that he gave it the precedence, and always signed himself Marquis, Duke of Cadiz. As the reader may have acquired the same predilection we shall continue to call him by his ancient title.

*Cura de Los Palacios c. 68.

CHAPTER XXVI

OF THE FORTRESS OF ALHAMA; AND HOW WISELY IT WAS GOVERNED BY THE COUNT DE TENDILLA.

In this part of his chronicle the worthy father Fray Antonio Agapida indulges in triumphant exultation over the downfall of Zahara. Heaven sometimes speaks, says he, through the mouths of false prophets for the confusion of the wicked. By the fall of this fortress was the prediction of the Santon of Granada in some measure fulfilled, that the ruins of Zahara should fall upon the heads of the infidels.

Our zealous chronicler scoffs at the Moorish alcayde, who lost his fortress by surprize in broad day light, and contrasts the vigilance of the Christian governor of Alhama, the town taken in retaliation for the storming of Zahara.

The important post of Alhama was at this time confided by King Ferdinand to Don Diego Lopez de Mendoza, Count of Tendilla, a cavalier of noble blood, brother to the Grand Cardinal of Spain. He had been instructed by the King, not merely to maintain his post, but also to make sallies and lay waste the surrounding country. His fortress was critically situated. It was within seven leagues of Granada and at no great distance from the warlike city of Loxa. It was nestled in the lap of the mountains, commanding the high road to Malaga and a view over the extensive vega. Thus situated, in the heart of the enemies' country, surrounded by foes ready to assail him, and a rich country for him to ravage, it behoved this cavalier to be forever on the alert. He was in fact an experienced veteran, a shrewd and wary officer, and a commander amazingly prompt and fertile in expedients.

On assuming the command he found that the garrison consisted but of one thousand men, horse and foot. They were hardy troops, seasoned in rough mountain campaigning; but reckless and dissolute, as soldiers are apt to be, when accustomed to predatory warfare. They would fight hard for booty, and then gamble it heedlessly away, or squander it in licentious revelling. Alhama abounded with hawking, sharping, idle hangers on, eager to profit by the vices and follies of the garrison. The soldiers were oftener gambling and dancing beneath the walls than keeping watch upon the battlements; and nothing was heard, from morning till night, but the noisy contest of cards and dice, mingled with the sound of the bolero or fandango, the drowsy strumming of the guitar and the rattling of the castanets, while often the whole was interrupted by the loud brawl and fierce and bloody contest.

The Count of Tendilla set himself vigorously to reform these excesses; he knew that laxity of morals is generally attended by neglect of duty; and that the least breach of discipline in the exposed situation of his fortress might be fatal. "Here is but a handful of men," said he, "it is necessary that each man should be a hero."

He endeavoured to awaken a proper ambition in the minds of his soldiers, and to instil into them the high principles of chivalry. "A just war," he observed, "is often rendered wicked and disastrous by the manner in which it is conducted: for the righteousness of the cause is not sufficient to sanction the profligacy of the means; and the want of order and subordination among the troops, may bring ruin and disgrace upon the best concerted plans." But we cannot describe the character and conduct of this renowned commander in more forcible language than that of Fray Antonio Agapida, excepting that the pious father places in the foreground of his virtues his hatred of the Moors.

"The Count de Tendilla," says he, "was a mirror of Christian knighthood, watchful, abstemious, chaste, devout, and thoroughly filled with the spirit of the cause. He laboured incessantly and strenuously for the glory of the faith and the prosperity of their most Catholic majesties; and above all he hated the infidels with a pure and holy hatred. This worthy cavalier discountenanced all idleness, rioting, chambering and wantonness among his soldiery. He kept them constantly to the exercise of arms, making them adroit in the use of their weapons and management of their steeds, and prompt for the field at a moment's notice. He permitted no sound of lute or harp, or song, or other loose minstrelsy to be heard in his fortress, debauching the ear and softening the valour of the soldier; no other music was allowed but the wholesome rolling of the drums and braying of the trumpet, and such like spirit stirring instruments as fill the mind with thoughts of iron war. All wandering minstrels, sharping pedlars, sturdy trulls and other camp trumpery were ordered to pack up their baggage and were drummed out of the gates of Alhama. In place of such lewd rabble he introduced a train of holy friars to inspirit his people by exhortation, and prayer and choral chaunting; and to spur them on to fight the good fight of faith. All games of chance were prohibited except the game of war, and this he laboured by vigilance and vigour to reduce to a game of certainty. Heaven smiled upon the efforts of this righteous cavalier. His men became soldiers at all points, and terrors to the Moors. The good count never set forth on a ravage without observing the rites of confession, absolution and communion, and obliging his followers to do the same. Their banners were blessed by the holy friars whom he maintained in Alhama, and in this way success was secured to his arms and he was enabled to lay waste the land of the heathen."

The fortress of Alhama, continues Fray Antonio Agapida, overlooked from its lofty site a great part of the fertile vega, watered by the Cazin and the Xenel; from this he made frequent sallies, sweeping away the flocks and herds from the pasture, the labourer from the field, and the convoy from the road, so that it was said by the Moors, that a beetle could not crawl across the vega, without being seen by Count Tendilla. The peasantry, therefore, were fain to betake themselves to watch towers and fortified hamlets where they shut up their cattle, garnered their corn and sheltered their wives and children. Even there they were not safe; the count would storm these rustic fortresses with fire and sword; make captives of their inhabitants, carry off the corn, the oil, the silks and cattle and leave the ruins blazing and smoking within the very sight of Granada.

"It was a pleasing and refreshing sight," continues the good father, "to behold this pious knight and his followers returning from one of these crusades, leaving the rich land of the infidel in smoking desolation behind them. To behold the long line of mules and asses laden with the plunder of the gentiles, the hosts of captive Moors, men, women and children, droves of sturdy beeves, lowing kine and bleating sheep; all winding up the steep acclivity to the gates of Alhama, pricked on by the Catholic soldiery. His garrison thus thrived on the fat of the land and the spoil of the infidel: nor was he unmindful of the pious fathers, whose blessings crowned his enterprizes with success; a large portion of the spoil was always dedicated to the church, and the good friars were ever ready at the gate to hail him on his return, and receive the share allotted them. Besides these allotments, he made many votive offerings either in time of peril, or on the eve of a foray, and the chapels of Alhama were resplendant with chalices, crosses, and other precious gifts made by this Catholic cavalier."

Thus eloquently does the venerable Fray Antonio Agapida dilate in praise of the good Count de Tendilla and other historians of equal veracity, but less unction agree in pronouncing him one of the ablest of Spanish generals. So terrible in fact did he become in the land, that the Moorish peasantry could not venture a league from Granada or Loxa to labour in the fields without peril of being carried into captivity. The people of Granada clamoured against Muley Aben Hassan for suffering his lands to be thus outraged and insulted, and demanded to have this bold marauder shut up in his fortress. The old monarch was roused by their remonstrances. He sent forth powerful troops of horse to protect the country during the season that the husbandmen were abroad in the fields. These troops patrolled in formidable squadrons in the neighborhood of Alhama, keeping strict watch upon its gates, so that it was impossible for the Christians to make a sally without being seen and intercepted.

While Alhama was thus blockaded by a roving force of Moorish cavalry, the inhabitants were awakened one night by a tremendous crash, that shook the fortress to its foundations. The garrison flew to arms, supposing it some assault of the enemy. The alarm proved to have been caused by the rupture of a portion of the walls, which, undermined by heavy rains, had suddenly given way, leaving a large chasm yawning towards the plain.

The Count de Tendilla was for a time in great anxiety: should this breach be discovered by the blockading horsemen, they would arouse the country; Granada and Loxa would pour out an overwhelming force, and they would find his walls ready sapped for an assault. In this fearful emergency the count displayed his noted talent for expedients. He ordered a quantity of linen cloth to be stretched in front of the breach, painted in imitation of stone, and indented with battlements, so as, at a distance, to resemble the other parts of the walls. Behind this screen he employed workmen, day and night, in repairing the fracture; no one was permitted to leave the fortress, lest information of its defenceless plight should be carried to the Moor. Light squadrons of the enemy were seen hovering about the plain, but never approached near enough to discover the deception, and thus, in the course of a few days, the wall was rebuilt stronger than before.

There was another expedient of this shrewd veteran which greatly excites the marvel of Agapida. "It happened," he observes, "that this Catholic cavalier at one time was destitute of gold and silver wherewith to pay the wages of his troops, and the soldiers murmured greatly, seeing that they had not the means of purchasing necessaries from the people of the town. In this dilemma what does this most sagacious commander? He takes me a number of little morsels of paper on the which he inscribes various sums, large and small, according to the nature of the case, and signs me them with his own hand and name. These did he give to the soldiery in earnest of their pay. How! you will say, are soldiers to be paid with scraps of paper? Even so, I answer, and well paid too, as I will presently make manifest: for the good count issued a proclamation, ordering the inhabitants of Alhama to take these morsels of paper for the full amount thereon inscribed, promising to redeem them at a future time, with silver and gold, and threatening severe punishment to all who should refuse. The people, having full confidence in his words, and trusting that he would be as willing to perform the one promise as he certainly was able to perform the other, took those curious morsels of paper without hesitation or demur. Thus by a subtle and most miraculous kind of alchymy did this Catholic cavalier turn worthless paper into precious gold, and make his late impoverished garrison abound in money."

It is but just to add that the Count de Tendilla redeemed his promises like a loyal knight, and this miracle, as it appeared in the eyes of Fray Antonio Agapida, is the first instance on record of paper money, which has since inundated the civilized world with unbounded opulence.

CHAPTER XXVII

FORAY OF CHRISTIAN KNIGHTS INTO THE TERRITORIES OF THE MOORS.

The Spanish cavaliers who had survived the memorable massacre among the mountains of Malaga, although they had repeatedly avenged the death of their companions, yet could not forget the horror and humiliation of their defeat. Nothing would satisfy them but to undertake a second expedition, of the kind, to carry fire and sword throughout a wide part of the Moorish territories and to leave all those regions which had triumphed in their disaster a black and burning monument of their vengeance. Their wishes accorded with the policy of the King, who desired to lay waste the country and destroy the resources of the enemy; every assistance was therefore given to promote and accomplish their enterprize.

In the spring of 1484, the ancient city of Antequera again resounded with arms; numbers of the same cavaliers who had assembled there so gaily the preceding year, again came wheeling into the gates, with their steeled and shining warriors, but with a more dark and solemn brow than on that disastrous occasion; for they had the recollection of their slaughtered friends present to their minds, whose deaths they were to avenge.

In a little while there was a chosen force of six thousand horse and twelve thousand foot assembled in Antequera, many of them the very flower of Spanish chivalry, troops of the established military and religious orders, and of the Holy Brotherhood.

Every precaution had been taken to furnish this army with all things needful for its extensive and perilous inroad; numerous surgeons accompanied it, who were to attend upon all the sick and wounded, without charge, being paid for their services by the Queen. Isabella, also, in her considerate humanity provided six spacious tents, furnished with beds and all things needful for the wounded and infirm. These continued to be used in all great expeditions throughout the war, and were called the Queen's Hospital. The worthy father, Fray Antonio Agapida, vaunts this benignant provision of the Queen, as the first introduction of a regular camp hospital in campaigning service.

Thus thoroughly prepared the cavaliers issued forth from Antequera in splendid and terrible array, but with less exulting confidence and vaunting ostentation than on their former foray; and this was the order of the army.

Don Alonzo de Aguilar led the advance guard, accompanied by Don Diego Fernandez de Cordova, Alcayde de los Donzeles and Luis Fernandez Puertocarrero, Count of Palma, with their household troops. They were followed by Juan de Merlo, Juan de Almara and Carlos de Biezman, of the Holy Brotherhood, with the men at arms of their captaincies.

The second battalion was commanded by the Marquis of Cadiz and the

Master of Santiago, with the cavaliers of Santiago and the troops of the house of Ponce de Leon; with these also went the senior commander of Calatrava and the knights of that order, and various other cavaliers and their retainers.

The right wing of this second battalion was led by Gonzalvo de Cordova afterwards renowned as Grand Captain of Spain: the left wing by Diego Lopez de Avila. They were accompanied by several distinguished cavaliers and certain captains of the Holy Brotherhood with their men at arms.

The Duke of Medina Sidonia and the Count de Cabra commanded the third battalion with the troops of their respective houses. They were accompanied by other commanders of note with their forces.

The rear guard was brought up by the Senior Commander and Knights of Alcantara, followed by the Andalusian chivalry from Xerez, Ecija and Carmona. Such was the army that issued forth from the gates of Antequera on one of the most extensive *talas* or devastating inroads that ever laid waste the Kingdom of Granada.

The army entered the Moorish territory by the way of Alora, destroying all the cornfields, vineyards and orchards and plantations of olives round that city. It then proceeded through the rich vallies and fertile uplands of Coin, Cazarabonela, Almexia and Cartama, and in ten days all those fertile regions were a smoking and frightful desart. From hence it pursued its slow and destructive course, like the stream of lava of a volcano, through the regions of Pupiana and Alhendin and so on to the vega of Malaga, laying waste the groves of olives and almonds, and the fields of grain and destroying every green thing. The Moors of some of those places interceded in vain for their groves and fields, offering to deliver up their Christian captives. One part of the army blockaded the towns while the other ravaged the surrounding country. Sometimes the Moors sallied forth desperately to defend their property, but were driven back to their gates with slaughter; and their suburbs pillaged and burnt. It was an awful spectacle at night to behold the volumes of black smoke mingled with lurid flames that rose from the burning suburbs, and the women on the walls of the town wringing their hands and shrieking at the desolation of their dwellings.

The destroying army on arriving at the sea coast found vessels lying offshore laden with all kinds of provisions and munitions for its use, which had been sent from Seville and Xerez: it was thus enabled to continue its desolating career. Advancing to the neighborhood of Malaga it was bravely assailed by the Moors of that city, and there was severe skirmishing for a whole day; but while the main part of the army encountered the enemy the rest ravaged the whole vega and destroyed all the mills. As the object of the expedition was not to capture places but merely to burn, ravage and destroy, the host, satisfied with the mischief they had done in the vega, turned their backs upon Malaga and again entered the mountains. They passed by Coin and through the regions of Allazayna and Gutero and Alhaurin; all which were likewise desolated. In this way did they make the circuit of that chain of rich and verdant valleys, the glory of those mountains, and the pride and delight of the Moors. For forty days did they continue on, like a consuming fire, leaving a smoking and howling waste to mark their course, until weary with the work of destruction, and having fully sated their revenge, for the massacre of the Axarquia, they returned in triumph to the meadows of Antequera.

In the month of June King Ferdinand took command in person of this destructive army; he encreased its force, and he added to its means of mischief several lombards and other heavy artillery intended for the battering of towns, and managed by engineers from France and Germany. With these the Marquis of Cadiz assured the King he would soon be able to reduce the Moorish fortresses. They were only calculated for defence against the engines antiently used in warfare. Their walls and towers were high and thin, depending for security on their rough and rocky situations. The stone and iron balls thundering from the lombards would soon tumble them in ruins upon the heads of their defenders.

The fate of Alora speedily proved the truth of this opinion. It was strongly posted on a rock washed by a river. The artillery soon battered down two of the towers and a part of the wall. The Moors were thrown into consternation at the vehemence of the assault, and the effect of those tremendous engines upon their vaunted bulwarks. The roaring of the artillery and the tumbling of the walls terrified the women, who beset the alcayde with vociferous supplications to surrender. The place was given up on the 20th of June on condition that the inhabitants might depart with their effects. The people of Malaga, as yet unacquainted with the power of this battering ordnance, were so incensed at those of Alora for what they considered a tame surrender, that they would not admit them into their city.

A similar fate attended the town of Setenil built on a lofty rock and esteemed impregnable. Many times had it been besieged under former Christian kings, but never had it been taken. Even now, for several days, the artillery was directed against it without effect, and many of the cavaliers murmured at the Marquis of Cadiz for having counselled the King to attack this unconquerable place.*

On the same night that these reproaches were uttered the marquis directed the artillery himself. He levelled the lombards at the bottom of the walls and at the gates. In a little while the gates were battered to pieces, a great breach was effected in the walls and the Moors were fain to capitulate. Twenty four Christian captives, who had been taken in the defeat of the

*Cura de Los Palacios.

mountains of Malaga, were rescued from the dungeons of this fortress, and hailed the Marquis of Cadiz as their deliverer.

Needless is it to mention the capture of various other places, which surrendered without waiting to be attacked. The Moors had always shewn great bravery and perseverance in defending their towns; they were formidable in their sallies and skirmishes, and patient in enduring hunger and thirst when besieged: but this terrible ordnance which demolished their walls with such ease and rapidity, overwhelmed them with confusion and dismay, and rendered vain all resistance. King Ferdinand was so struck with the effect of this artillery that he ordered the number of lombards to be encreased; and these potent engines had henceforth a great influence on the fortunes of this war.

The last operation of this year, so disastrous to the Moors, was an inroad by King Ferdinand in the latter part of summer into the vega in which he ravaged the country and burnt two villages near to Granada and destroyed the mills near to the very gates of the city.

Old Muley Aben Hassan was overwhelmed with dismay at this desolation, which, during the whole year, had been raging throughout his territories, and had now reached to the walls of his capital. His fierce spirit was broken by misfortunes and infirmity, he offered to purchase a peace and to hold his crown as a tributary vassal. Ferdinand would listen to no propositions; the absolute conquest of Granada was the great object of this war, and he was resolved never to rest content without its complete fulfilment. Having supplied and strengthened the garrisons of the places he had taken in the heart of the Moorish territories, he enjoyned their commanders to render every assistance to the younger Moorish King in the civil war against his father. He then returned with his army to Cordova in great triumph, closing a series of ravaging campaigns, that had filled the kingdom of Granada with grief and consternation.

CHAPTER XXVIII

ATTEMPT OF EL ZAGAL TO SURPRIZE BOABDIL IN ALMERIA.

During this year of sorrow and disaster to the Moors, the younger King Boabdil, most truly called the unfortunate, held a diminished and feeble court in the maritime city of Almeria. He retained little more than the name of King, and was supported in even this shadow of royalty, by the countenance and treasures of the Castilian sovereigns. Still he trusted that in the fluctuation of events, the inconstant nation might once more return to his standard and replace him on the throne of the Alhambra.

His mother, the high spirited Sultana Ayxa la Horra, endeavoured to rouse him from this passive state. "It is a feeble mind," said she, "that waits for the turn of fortune's wheel; the brave mind seizes upon it and turns it to its purpose. Take the field and you may drive danger before you, remain cowering at home and it besieges you in your dwelling. By a bold enterprize you may regain your splendid throne in Granada, by passive forbearance you will forfeit even this miserable throne in Almeria."

Boabdil had not the force of soul to follow these courageous counsels, and in a little time the evils his mother had predicted fell upon him.

Old Muley Aben Hassan was almost extinguished by age and infirmity. He had nearly lost his sight and was completely bed ridden. His brother Abdallah surnamed El Zagal, or, the valiant, the same who had assisted in the massacre of the Spanish chivalry among the mountains of Malaga, was commander in chief of the Moorish armies and gradually took upon himself most of the cares of sovereignty. Among other things he was particularly zealous in espousing his brother's quarrel with his son; and he prosecuted it with such vehemence that many affirmed there was something more than mere fraternal sympathy at the bottom of his zeal.

The disasters and disgraces inflicted on the country by the Christians during this year, had wounded the national feelings of the people of Almeria, and many had felt indignant that Boabdil should remain passive at such a time, or rather, should appear to make a common cause with the enemy. His uncle Abdallah diligently fomented this feeling by his agents. The same arts were made use of that had been successful in Granada. Boabdil was secretly, but actively, denounced by the alfaquis as an apostate, leagued with the Christians against his country and his early faith; the affections of the populace and soldiery were gradually alienated from him, and a deep conspiracy concerted for his destruction. In the month of February 1485, El Zagal suddenly appeared before Almeria, at the head of a troop of horse. The alfaquis were prepared for his arrival, and the gates were thrown open to him. He entered with his band and gallopped to the citadel. The alcayde would have made resistance, but the garrison put him to death and received El Zagal with acclamations. El Zagal rushed through the apartments of the Alcazar but he sought in vain for Boabdil. He found the Sultana Ayxa la Horra in one of the saloons, with Ben Ahagete a younger brother of the monarch, a valiant Abencerrage and several attendants who rallied round them to protect them. "Where is the traytor Boabdil?" exclaimed El Zagal. "I know no traytor more perfidious than thyself," exclaimed the intrepid Sultana, "and I trust my son is in safety to take vengeance on thy treason." The rage of El Zagal was without bounds when he learnt that his intended victim had escaped. In his fury he slew the prince Ben Ahagete, and his followers fell upon and massacred the Abencerrage and attendants. As to the proud Sultana, she was borne away prisoner and loaded with revilings as having upheld her son in his rebellion, and fomented a civil war.

The unfortunate Boabdil had been apprized of his danger by a faithful soldier, just in time to make his escape. Throwing himself on one of the fleetest horses of his stables, and followed by a handful of adherents, he had gallopped in the confusion out of the gates of Almeria. Several of the cavalry of El Zagal, who were stationed without the walls, perceived his flight, and attempted to pursue him; their horses were jaded with travel and he soon left them far behind. But whither was he to fly? Every fortress and castle in the Kingdom of Granada was closed against him; he knew not whom among the Moors to trust, for they had been taught to detest him as a traytor and an apostate. He had no alternative but to seek refuge among the Christians, his hereditary enemies. With a heavy heart he turned his horse's head towards Cordova. He had to lurk, like a fugitive, through a part of his own dominions, nor did he feel himself secure until he had passed the frontier, and beheld the mountain barrier of his country towering behind him. Then it was that he became conscious of his humiliating state; a fugitive from his throne, an outcast from his nation; a king without a kingdom. He smote his breast in an agony of grief: "Evil indeed," exclaimed he, "was the day of my birth, and truly was I named El Zogoybi—the unlucky."

He entered the gates of Cordova with downcast countenance and with a train of but forty followers. The sovereigns were absent, but the cavaliers of Andalusia manifested that sympathy in the misfortunes of the monarch, that becomes men of lofty and chivalrous souls. They received him with great distinction, attended him with the utmost courtesy and he was honourably entertained by the civil and military commanders of that ancient city.

In the mean time El Zagal put a new alcayde over Almeria, to govern in the name of his brother and having strongly garrisoned the place he repaired to Malaga where an attack of the Christians was apprehended. The young monarch, being driven out of the land, and the old monarch blind and bed ridden, El Zagal at the head of the armies was virtually the sovereign of Granada. The people were pleased with having a new idol to look up to, and a new name to shout forth, and El Zagal was hailed with acclamations as the main hope of the nation.

CHAPTER XXIX

HOW KING FERDINAND COMMENCED ANOTHER CAMPAIGN AGAINST THE MOORS AND HOW HE LAID SIEGE TO COIN AND CARTAMA.

The great effect of the battering ordnance in demolishing the Moorish fortresses in the preceding year, induced King Ferdinand to procure a powerful train for the campaign of 1485, in the course of which he resolved to assault some of the most formidable holds of the enemy. An army of nine thousand cavalry and twenty thousand infantry assembled at Cordova early in the spring; and the King took the field on the 5th of April. It had been determined in secret council, to attack the city of Malaga, that ancient and important sea port, on which Granada depended for foreign aid and supplies. It was thought proper previously, however, to get possession of various towns and fortresses in the vallies of Santa Maria and Cartama, through which pass the roads to Malaga.

The first place assailed was the town of Benamaquex. It had submitted to the Catholic sovereigns in the preceding year but had since renounced its allegiance. King Ferdinand was enraged at the rebellion of the inhabitants. "I will make their punishment," said he, "a terror to others: they shall be loyal through force if not through faith." The place was carried by storm, one hundred and eight of the principal inhabitants were either put to the sword or hanged on the battlements; the rest were carried into captivity.*

The towns of Coin and Cartama were besieged on the same day; the first by a division of the army led on by the Marquis of Cadiz, the second by another division commanded by Don Alonzo de Aguilar and Luis Fernandez Puertocarrero, the brave Senior of Palma. The King with the rest of the army, remained posted between the two places, to render assistance to either division. The batteries opened upon both places at the same time, and the thunder of the lombards was mutually heard from one camp to the other. The Moors made frequent sallies, and a valiant defence, but they were confounded by the tremendous uproar of the batteries and the destruction of their walls. In the mean time the alarm fires gathered together the Moorish mountaineers of all the Serrania who assembled in great numbers in the city of Monda, about a league from Coin.

They made several attempts to enter the besieged town, but in vain; they were each time intercepted and driven back by the Christians, and were reduced to gaze at a distance in despair on the destruction of the place. While thus situated there rode one day into Monda a fierce and haughty Moorish chieftain at the head of a band of swarthy African horsemen; it was Hamet el Zegri, the fiery spirited Alcayde of Ronda, at the head of his band

*Pulgar, Garibay. Cura de Los Palacios.

of Gomeres. He had not yet recovered from the rage and mortification of his defeat on the banks of the Lopera in the disastrous foray of old Bexir, when he had been obliged to steal back furtively to his mountains with the loss of his bravest followers. He had ever since panted for revenge. He now rode among the host of warriors assembled at Monda. "Who among you," cried he, "feels pity for the women and children of Coin exposed to captivity and death. Whoever he is, let him follow me who am ready to die as a Moslem for the relief of Moslems." So saying he seized a white banner and waving it over his head rode forth from the town followed by the Gomeres. Many of the warriors, roused by his words and his example, spurred reso lutely after his banner. The people of Coin, being prepared for this attempt, sallied forth as they saw the white banner and made an attack upon the Christian camp, and in the confusion of the moment Hamet and his followers galloped into the gates. This reinforcement animated the besieged, and Hamet exhorted them to hold out obstinately in defence of life and town. As the Gomeres were veteran warriors, the more they were attacked the harder they fought.

At length a great breach was made in the walls, and Ferdinand, who was impatient of the resistance of the place, ordered the Duke of Naxera and the Count of Benavente to enter with their troops, and as these forces were not sufficient he sent word to Luis de Cerda Duke of Medina Celi, to send a part of his people to their assistance.

The feudal pride of the duke was roused at this demand. "Tell my lord the King," said the haughty grandee, "that I have come to succour him with my household troops; if my people are ordered to any place I am to go with them: but if I am to remain in the camp my people must remain with me, for troops cannot serve without their commander, nor their commander without his troops."

The reply of the high spirited grandee perplexed the cautious Ferdinand who knew the jealous pride of his powerful nobles. In the mean time the people of the camp, having made all preparations for the assault were impatient to be led forward. Upon this Pero Ruyz de Alarcon put himself at their head, and seizing their mantas, or portable bulwarks, and their other defenses, they made a gallant assault and fought their way in at the breach. The Moors were so overcome by the fury of their assault that they retreated fighting to the square of the town. Pero Ruyz de Alarcon thought the place was carried, when suddenly Hamet and his Gomeres came scouring through the streets with wild war cries and fell furiously upon the Christians. The latter were in their turn beaten back, and while attacked in front by the Gomeres, were assailed by the inhabitants with all kinds of missiles from their roofs and windows. They at length gave way and retreated through the breach. Pero Ruyz de Alarcon still maintained his ground in one of the principal streets, the few cavaliers that stood by him urged him to fly. "No," said he, "I came here to fight and not to fly." He was presently surrounded by the Gomeres; his companions fled for their lives; the last they saw of him he was covered with wounds, but still fighting desperately for the fame of a good cavalier.*

The resistance of the inhabitants, though aided by the valour of the Gomeres, was of no avail. The battering artillery of the Christians demolished their walls; combustibles were thrown into their town which set it on fire in various places, and they were at length compelled to capitulate. They were permitted to depart with their effects, and the Gomeres with their arms. Hamet el Zegri and his African band sallied forth and rode proudly through the Christian camp; nor could the Spanish cavaliers refrain from regarding with admiration that haughty warrior and his devoted and dauntless followers.

The capture of Coin was accompanied by that of Cartama; the fortifications of the latter were repaired and garrisoned, but Coin, being too extensive to be defended by a moderate force, its walls were demolished. The siege of these places struck such terror into the surrounding country that the Moors of many of the neighbouring towns abandoned their homes and fled, with such of their effects as they could carry away; upon which the King gave orders to demolish their walls and towers.

King Ferdinand now left his camp and his heavy artillery near Cartama and proceeded with his lighter troops to reconnoitre Malaga. By this time the secret plan of attack, arranged in the council of war at Cordova, was known to all the world. The vigilant warrior El Zagal had thrown himself into the place; he had put all the fortifications which were of vast strength, into a state of defence, and had sent orders to the alcaydes of the mountain towns, to hasten with their forces to his assistance.

The very day that Ferdinand appeared before the place El Zagal sallied forth to receive him at the head of a thousand cavalry, the choicest warriors of Granada. A hot skirmish took place among the gardens and olive trees near the city. Many were killed on both sides, and this gave the Christians a sharp foretaste of what they might expect if they attempted to besiege the place.

When the skirmish was over the Marquis of Cadiz had a private conference with the King. He represented the difficulty of besieging Malaga with their present force, especially as their plans had been discovered and anticipated, and the whole country was marching over the mountains to oppose them. The marquis, who had secret intelligence from all quarters, had received a letter from Juceph Xerife, a Moor of Ronda of Christian lineage, apprizing him of the situation of that important place and its garrison, which at that moment laid it open to attack; and the marquis was urgent with the

*Pulgar Part 3. Chap. 42.

King to seize upon this critical moment, and secure a place, which was one of the most powerful Moorish fortresses on the frontiers, and in the hands of Hamet el Zegri had been the scourge of Andalusia. The good marquis had another motive for his advice, becoming of a true and loyal knight. In the deep dungeons of Ronda languished several of his companions in arms, who had been captured in the defeat in the Axarquia. To break their chains and restore them to liberty and light he felt to be his peculiar duty, as one of those who had most promoted that disastrous enterprize.

King Ferdinand listened to the advice of the marquis. He knew the importance of Ronda, which was considered one of the keys to the Kingdom of Granada, and he was disposed to punish the inhabitants, for the aid they had rendered to the garrison of Coin. The siege of Malaga, therefore, was abandoned for the present, and preparations made for a rapid and secret move against the city of Ronda.

CHAPTER XXX

SIEGE OF RONDA.

The bold Hamet el Zegri, the Alcayde of Ronda, had returned sullenly to his stronghold after the surrender of Coin. He had fleshed his sword in battle with the Christians, but his thirst for vengeance was still unsatisfied. Hamet gloried in the strength of his fortress and the valour of his people. A fierce and warlike populace was at his command; his signal fires could summon all the warriors of the Serrania; his Gomeres almost subsisted on the spoils of Andalusia, and in the rock on which his fortress was built were hopeless dungeons, filled with Christian captives, who had been carried off by these war hawks of the mountains.

Ronda was considered as impregnable. It was situated in the heart of wild and rugged mountains, and perched upon an isolated rock, crested by a strong citadel, with triple walls and towers. A deep ravine, or rather a perpendicular chasm of the rocks of frightful depth surrounded three parts of the city; through this flowed the Rio Verde or Green River. There were two suburbs to the city, fortified by walls and towers, and almost inaccessible from the natural asperity of the rocks. Around this rugged city were deep rich vallies sheltered by the mountains, refreshed by constant streams, abounding with grain, and the most delicious fruits, and yielding verdant meadows in which was reared a renowned breed of horses, the best in the whole kingdom for a foray.

Hamet el Zegri had scarcely returned to Ronda when he received intelligence that the Christian army was marching to the siege of Malaga, and orders from El Zagal to send troops to his assistance. Hamet sent a part of his garrison for that purpose; in the mean time he meditated an expedition to which he was stimulated by pride and revenge. All Andalusia was now drained of its troops; there was an opportunity therefore for an inroad, by which he might wipe out the disgrace of his defeat at the battle of Lopera. Apprehending no danger to his mountain city, now that the storm of war had passed down into the vega of Malaga, he left but a remnant of his garrison to man its walls, and, putting himself at the head of his band of Gomeres, swept down suddenly into the plain of Andalusia. He careered almost without resistance, over those vast Campiñas or pasture lands which form a part of the domains of the Duke of Medina Sidonia. In vain the bells were rung and the alarm fires kindled; the band of Hamet had passed by before any force could be assembled, and was only to be traced, like a hurricane, by the devastation it had made.

Hamet regained in safety the Serrania de Ronda exulting in his successful inroad. The mountain glens were filled with long droves of cattle and flocks of sheep, from the Campiñas of Medina Sidonia. There were mules, too, laden with the plunder of the villages, and every warrior had some costly spoil of jewels for his favourite mistress.

As the Zegri drew near to Ronda he was roused from his dream of triumph by the sound of heavy ordnance bellowing through the mountain defiles. His heart misgave him, he put spurs to his horse and galloped in advance of his lagging cavalgada. As he proceeded the noise of the ordnance encreased, echoing from cliff to cliff. Spurring his horse up a craggy height, which commanded an extensive view, he beheld, to his consternation, the country about Ronda white with the tents of a besieging army. The royal standard, displayed before a proud encampment, shewed that Ferdinand himself was present, while the incessant blaze and thunder of artillery and the volumes of overhanging smoke told the work of destruction that was going on.

The royal army had succeeded in coming upon Ronda by surprize during the absence of its alcayde and most of its garrison; but its inhabitants were warlike and defended themselves bravely trusting that Hamet and his Gomeres would soon return to their assistance.

The fancied strength of their bulwarks had been of little avail against the batteries of the besiegers. In the space of four days three towers and great masses of the walls which defended the suburbs were battered down, and the suburbs taken and plundered. Lombards and other heavy ordnance were now levelled at the walls of the city, and stones and missiles of all kinds hurled into the streets. The very rock on which the city stood shook with the thunder of the artillery, and the Christian captives, deep within its dungeons, hailed the sound as the promise of deliverance.

When Hamet el Zegri beheld his city thus surrounded and assailed he called upon his men to follow him and make a desperate attempt to cut their way through to its relief. They proceeded stealthily through the mountains until they came to the nearest heights above the Christian camp. When night fell and part of the army was sunk in sleep, they descended the rocks, and rushing suddenly upon the weakest part of the camp, endeavoured to break their way through and gain the city. The camp was too strong to be forced; they were driven back to the crags of the mountains, from whence they defended themselves by showering down darts and stones upon their pursuers.

Hamet now lit alarm fires about the heights, his standard was joined by the neighbouring mountaineers and by troops from Malaga. Thus reinforced, he made repeated assaults upon the Christians, cutting off all stragglers from the camp. All his attempts, however, to force his way into the city were fruitless; many of his bravest men were slain and he was obliged to retreat into the fastnesses of the mountains.

In the mean while the distress of Ronda was hourly encreasing. The Marquis of Cadiz, having possession of the suburbs, was enabled to approach to the very foot of the perpendicular precipice rising from the river, on the summit of which the city is built. At the foot of this rock is a living fountain of limpid water, gushing into a great natural basin. A secret mine led down from within the city to this fountain by several hundred steps cut in the solid rock. From hence the city obtained its chief supply of water, and these steps were deep worn by the weary feet of Christian captives employed in this painful labour. The Marquis of Cadiz discovered this subterranean passage, and directed his pioneers to countermine in the side of the rock. They pierced to the shaft, and, stopping it up deprived the city of the benefit of this precious fountain.

While the brave Marquis of Cadiz was thus pressing the siege with zeal, and glowing with the generous thoughts of soon delivering his companions in arms from the Moorish dungeons, far other were the feelings of the Alcayde Hamet el Zegri. He smote his breast and gnashed his teeth in impotent fury, as he beheld from the mountain cliffs the destruction of the city. Every thunder of the Christian ordnance seemed to batter against his heart. He saw tower after tower tumbling by day, and at night the city blazed like a volcano. "They fired not merely stones from their ordnance," says a chronicler of the times, "but likewise great balls of iron cast in moulds, which demolished every thing they struck." They threw also balls of tow steeped in pitch and oil and gunpowder, which, when once on fire, were not to be extinguished, and which set the houses in flames.

Great was the horror of the inhabitants. They knew not where to fly for refuge: their houses were in a blaze or shattered by the ordnance, the streets were perilous from the falling ruins and the bounding balls, which dashed to pieces every thing they encountered. At night the city looked like a fiery furnace, the cries and wailings of the women were heard between the thunders of the ordnance, and reached even to the Moors on the opposite mountains, who answered them by yells of fury and despair.

All hope of external succour being at an end, the inhabitants of Ronda were compelled to capitulate. Ferdinand was easily prevailed upon to grant them favorable terms. The place was capable of longer resistance, and he feared for the safety of his camp, as the forces were daily augmenting on the mountains and making frequent assaults. The inhabitants were permitted to depart with their effects either to Barbary or elsewhere, and those who chose to reside in Spain had lands assigned them and were indulged in the practice of their religion.

No sooner did the place surrender than detachments were sent to attack the Moors who hovered about the neighbouring mountains. Hamet el Zegri, however, did not remain to make a fruitless battle. He gave up the game as lost and retreated with his Gomeres, filled with grief and rage, but trusting to fortune to give him future vengeance.

The first care of the good Marquis of Cadiz on entering Ronda was to deliver his unfortunate companions in arms from the dungeons of the fortress. What a difference in their looks from the time when, flushed with health and hope, and arrayed in military pomp, they had sallied forth upon the mountain foray. Many of them were almost naked, with irons at their ankles and beards reaching to their waists. Their meeting with the marquis was joyful, yet it had the look of grief, for their joy was mingled with many bitter recollections. There was an immense number of other captives, among whom were several young men of noble families, who, with filial piety, had surrendered themselves prisoners in place of their fathers.

The captives were all provided with mules and sent to the Queen at Cordova. The humane heart of Isabella melted at the sight of the piteous cavalcade. They were all supplied by her with food and rayment and money to pay their expenses to their homes. Their chains were hung as pious trophies against the exterior of the Church of S' Juan de los Reyes in Toledo, where the Christian traveller may regale his eyes with the sight of them at this very day.

Among the Moorish captives was a young infidel maiden of great beauty who desired to become a Christian and to remain in Spain. She had been inspired with the light of the true faith through the ministry of a young man who had been a captive in Ronda. He was anxious to complete his good work by marrying her. The Queen consented to their pious wishes, having first taken care that the young maiden should be properly purified by the holy sacrament of baptism.

"Thus this pestilent nest of warfare and infidelity the city of Ronda," says the worthy Fray Antonio Agapida, "was converted to the true faith by the thunder of our artillery. An example which was soon followed by Casanbonela, Alarbella and other towns in these parts, in so much that in the course of this expedition no less than seventy two places were rescued from the vile sect of Mahomet and placed under the benignant domination of the cross."

CHAPTER XXXI

HOW THE PEOPLE OF GRANADA INVITED EL ZAGAL TO THE THRONE, AND HOW HE MARCHED TO THE CAPITAL.

The people of Granada were a versatile, unsteady race and exceedingly given to make and unmake kings. They had for a long time, vacillated between old Muley Aben Hassan, and his son Boabdil el Chico, sometimes setting up the one, sometimes the other, and sometimes both at once, according to the pinch and pressure of external evils. They found, however, that the evils still went on encreasing, in defiance of every change, and were at their wits' end to devise some new combination or arrangement, by which an efficient government might be wrought out of two bad kings. When the tidings arrived of the fall of Ronda and the consequent ruin of the frontier a tumultuous assemblage took place in one of the public squares. As usual, the people attributed the misfortunes of the country exclusively to the faults of their rulers; for the populace never imagine that any part of their miseries can originate with themselves. A crafty alfaqui, named Alyme Mazer, who had watched the current of their discontents, rose and harangued them.

"You have been choosing and changing," said he, "between two monarchs, and who and what are they? Muley Aben Hassan, for one; a man worn out by age and infirmities, unable to sally forth against the foe, even when ravaging to the very gates of the city: and Boabdil el Chico for the other; an apostate, a traytor, a deserter from his throne, a fugitive among the enemies of his nation; a man fated to misfortune, and proverbially named 'the unlucky.'

"In a time of overwhelming war like the present he only is fit to sway a sceptre who can wield a sword; would you seek such a man?—you need not look far. Allah has sent such a one, in this time of distress, to retrieve the fortunes of Granada. You already know whom I mean. You know that it can be no other than your general, the invincible Abdalla; whose surname of El Zagal, has become a watchword in battle, rousing the courage of the faithful, and striking terror into the unbelievers."

The multitude received the words of the alfaqui with acclamations; they were delighted with the idea of a third King over Granada, and Abdalla el Zagal being of the royal family, and already in the virtual exercise of royal power, the measure had nothing in it that appeared either rash or violent. A deputation was, therefore, sent to El Zagal at Malaga, inviting him to repair to Granada to receive the crown.

El Zagal expressed great surprize and repugnance when the mission was announced to him, and nothing but his patriotic zeal for the public safety, and his fraternal eagerness to relieve the aged Aben Hassan from the cares of government prevailed upon him to accept the offer of the crown. Leaving therefore Rodovan Vanegas, one of the bravest Moorish generals, in command of Malaga, he departed for Granada, attended by three hundred trusty cavaliers.

Old Muley Aben Hassan did not wait for the arrival of his brother. Unable any longer to buffet with the storms of the times his only solicitude was to seek some safe and quiet harbour of repose. In one of the deep valleys which indent the Mediterranean coast, and which are shut up, on the land side, by stupendous mountains, stood the little city of Almunecar. The valley was watered by the river Frio and abounded with fruits, with grain and pasturage. The city was strongly fortified and the garrison and alcayde were devoted to the old monarch. This was the place chosen by Muley Aben Hassan for his asylum. His first care was to send thither all his treasures, his next care was to take refuge there himself, his third, that his Sultana Zorayna and their two sons should follow him.

In the mean time, Muley Abdalla el Zagal pursued his journey towards the capital attended by his three hundred cavaliers. The road from Malaga to Granada winds close by Alhama, and is dominated by that fortress. This had been a most perilous pass for the Moors during the time that Alhama was commanded by the Count de Tendilla; not a traveller could escape his eagle eye, and his garrison was ever ready for a sally. The Count de Tendilla, however, had been relieved from this arduous post, and it had been given in charge to Don Gutiere de Padilla, clavero or treasurer of the order of Calatrava; an easy indulgent man, who had with him three hundred gallant knights of his order besides other mercenary troops. The garrison had fallen off in discipline; the cavaliers were hardy in fight and daring in foray, but confident in themselves and negligent of proper precautions. Just before the journey of El Zagal a number of these cavaliers, with several soldiers of fortune, of the garrison, in all about one hundred and seventy men, had sallied forth to harrass the Moorish country during its present distracted state, and, having ravaged the valleys of the Sierra Nevada, or Snowy Mountains, were returning to Alhama in gay spirits and laden with booty.

As El Zagal passed through the neighborhood of Alhama, he recollected the ancient perils of the road, and sent light corredors in advance, to inspect each rock and ravine where a foe might lurk in ambush. One of these scouts overlooking a narrow valley which opened upon the road, descried a troop of horsemen on the banks of a little stream. They were dismounted and had taken the bridles from their steeds that they might crop the fresh grass on the banks of the river. The horsemen were scattered about, some reposing in the shade of rocks and trees, others gambling for the spoil they had taken. Not a centinel was posted to keep guard; every thing shewed the perfect security of men who consider themselves beyond the reach of danger.

These careless cavaliers were in fact the Knights of Calatrava with a part of their companions in arms returning from their foray. A part of their force had passed on with the cavalgada, ninety of the principal cavaliers had halted to repose and refresh themselves in this valley. El Zagal smiled with ferocious joy when he heard of their negligent security. "Here will be trophies," said he, "to grace our entrance into Granada."

Approaching the valley with cautious silence, he wheeled into it at full speed at the head of his troop, and attacked the Christians so suddenly and furiously that they had not time to put the bridles upon their horses, or even to leap into the saddles. They made a confused, but valiant defence, fighting among the rocks and in the rugged bed of the river. Their defence was useless; seventy nine were slain, the remaining eleven were taken prisoners.

A party of the Moors gallopped in pursuit of the cavalgada; they soon overtook it winding slowly up a hill. The horsemen who convoyed it perceiving the enemy at a distance made their escape, and left the spoil to be retaken by the Moors.

El Zagal gathered together his captives and his booty and proceeded, elate with success, to Granada. He paused before the gate of Elvira, for, as yet he had not been proclaimed King. This ceremony was immediately performed, for the fame of his recent exploit had preceded him, and had intoxicated the minds of the giddy populace.

He entered Granada in a sort of triumph. The eleven captive Knights of Calatrava walked in front. Next were paraded the ninety captured steeds, bearing the armour and weapons of their late owners, and led by as many mounted Moors. Then came seventy Moorish horsemen, with as many Christian heads hanging at their saddle bows. Muley Abdalla el Zagal followed, surrounded by a number of distinguished cavaliers richly attired, and the pageant was closed by a long cavalgada of the flocks and herds and other booty recovered from the Christians.*

The populace gazed with almost savage triumph at these captive cavaliers, and the gory heads of their companions, knowing them to have been part of the formidable garrison of Alhama, so long the scourge of Granada and the terror of the vega. They hailed this petty triumph as an auspicious opening

*Zurita lib 20 c. 62. Mariana Hist España Abarca Anales de Aragon.

of the reign of their new monarch; for several days the names of Muley Aben Hassan and Boabdil el Chico were never mentioned but with contempt, and the whole city resounded with the praises of El Zagal, or the Valiant.

CHAPTER XXXII

HOW THE COUNT DE CABRA ATTEMPTED TO CAPTURE ANOTHER KING, AND HOW HE FARED IN HIS ATTEMPT.

The elevation of a bold and active veteran to the throne of Granada in place of its late bedridden King made a vast difference in the aspect of the war, and called for some blow that should dash the confidence of the Moors in their new monarch, and animate the Christians to fresh exertions.

Don Diego de Cordova, the brave Count de Cabra was at this time in his castle of Vaena, where he kept a wary eye upon the frontier. It was now the latter part of August, and he grieved that the summer should pass away without an inroad into the country of the foe. He sent out his scouts on the prowl, and they brought him word that the important post of Moclin was but weakly garrisoned. This was a castellated town, strongly situated upon a high mountain, partly surrounded by thick forests, and partly girdled by a river. It defended one of the rugged and solitary passes by which the Christians were wont to make their inroads, insomuch that the Moors, in their figurative way, denominated it the shield of Granada.

The Count de Cabra sent word to the monarchs of the feeble state of the garrison and gave it as his opinion that, by a secret and rapid expedition the place might be surprised. King Ferdinand asked the advice of his councillors: some cautioned him against the sanguine temperament of the count and his heedlessness of danger; Moclin, they observed, was near to Granada, and might be promptly reinforced. The opinion of the count, however, prevailed, the King considering him almost infallible in matters of border warfare since his capture of Boabdil el Chico.

The King departed from Cordova, therefore; and took post at Alcalá la Real for the purpose of being near to Moclin. The Queen, also, proceeded to Vaena accompanied by her children, Prince Juan and the Princess Isabella, and her great counsellor in all matters public and private, spiritual and temporal, the venerable Grand Cardinal of Spain.

Nothing could exceed the pride and satisfaction of the loyal Count de Cabra when he saw this stately train winding along the dreary mountain roads, and entering the gates of Vaena. He received his royal guests with all due ceremony and lodged them in the best apartments that the warrior castle afforded; being the same that had formerly been occupied by the royal captive Boabdil.

King Ferdinand had concerted a wary plan to ensure the success of the enterprize. The Count de Cabra and Don Martin Alonzo de Montemayor, were to set forth with their troops so as to reach Moclin by a certain hour, and to intercept all who should attempt to enter or should sally from the town. The Master of Calatrava, the troops of the Grand Cardinal commanded by the Count of Buendia, and the forces of the Bishop of Jaen, led by that belligerent prelate, amounting in all to four thousand horse and six thousand foot, were to set off in time to cooperate with the Count de Cabra, so as to surround the town. The King was to follow with his whole force, and encamp before the place.

And here the worthy Padre Fray Antonio Agapida breaks forth into a triumphant eulogy of the pious prelates who thus mingled personally in these scenes of warfare. As this was a holy crusade, says he, undertaken for the advancement of the faith, and the glory of the church, so was it always countenanced and upheld by saintly men. For the victories of their most Catholic majesties were not followed, like those of mere worldly sovereigns, by erecting castles and towers and appointing alcaydes and garrisons, but by the founding of convents and cathedrals and the establishment of wealthy bishopricks. Wherefore their majesties were always surrounded, in court or camp, in the cabinet or in the field, by a crowd of ghostly advisers, enspiriting them to the prosecution of this most righteous war. Nay, the holy men of the church did not scruple, at times, to buckle on the cuirass over the cassock, to exchange the crosier for the lance, and thus, with corporal hands and temporal weapons, to fight the good fight of the faith.

But to return from this rhapsody of the worthy friar. The Count de Cabra, being instructed in the complicated arrangements of the King, marched forth at midnight to execute them punctually. He led his troops by the little river that winds below Vaena, and so up the wild defiles of the mountains, marching all night and stopping only in the heat of the following day, to repose under the shadowy cliffs of a deep barranco, calculating to arrive at Moclin exactly in time to cooperate with the other forces.

The troops had scarcely stretched themselves on the earth to take repose when a scout arrived, bringing word that El Zagal had suddenly sallied out of Granada, with a strong force, and had encamped in the vicinity of Moclin. It was plain that the wary Moor had received information of the intended attack. This, however, was not the idea that presented itself to the mind of the Count de Cabra. He had captured one King, here was a fair opportunity to secure another. What a triumph to lodge another captive monarch in his castle of Vaena! What a prisoner to deliver into the hands of his royal mistress! Fired with the thought, the good count forgot all the arrangements of the King; or rather, blinded by former success, he trusted every thing to courage and fortune, and thought that, by one bold swoop, he might again bear off the royal prize, and wear his laurels without competition.* His only fear was that the Master of Calatrava and the belligerent bishop might come up in time to share the glory of the victory, so ordering every one to horse this hot spirited cavalier pushed on for Moclin, without allowing his troops the necessary time for repose.

The evening closed as the count arrived in the neighborhood of Moclin. It was the full of the moon, and a bright and cloudless night. The count was marching through one of those deep valleys, or ravines worn in the Spanish mountains by the brief but tremendous torrents which prevail during the autumnal rains. It was walled on both sides by lofty and almost perpendicular cliffs, but great masses of moonlight were thrown into the bottom of the glen glittering on the armour of the squadrons as they silently passed through it. Suddenly the war cry of the Moors rose in various parts of the valley. "El Zagal! El Zagal!" was shouted from every cliff, accompanied by showers of missiles that struck down several of the Christian warriors. The count lifted up his eyes and beheld, by the light of the moon, every cliff glistening with Moorish soldiery. The deadly shower fell thickly round him, and the shining armour of his followers made them fair objects for the aim of the enemy. The count saw his brother Gonzalo struck dead by his side; his own horse sunk under him pierced by four Moorish lances, and he received a wound in the hand from an arquebuss. He remembered the horrible massacre of the mountains of Malaga and feared a similar catastrophe. There was no time to pause. His brother's horse, freed from his slaughtered rider, was running at large; seizing the reins he sprang into the saddle, called upon his men to follow him, and wheeling round, retreated out of the fatal valley.

The Moors, rushing down from the heights pursued the retreating Christians. The chace endured for a league, but it was a league of rough and broken ground, where the Christians had to turn and fight at almost every step. In these short, but fierce, combats, the enemy lost many cavaliers of note; but the loss of the Christians was infinitely more grievous comprising numbers of the noblest warriors of Vaena and its vicinity. Many of the Christians, disabled by wounds, or exhausted by fatigue, turned aside and endeavoured to conceal themselves among rocks and thickets, but never more rejoined their companions; being slain or captured by the Moors, or perishing in their wretched retreats.

The arrival of the troops led by the Master of Calatrava and the Bishop of Jaen, put an end to the rout. El Zagal contented himself with the laurels he

*Mariana L 25. C. 17. Abarca. Zurita &c.

had gained, and ordering the trumpets to call off his men from the pursuit, returned in great triumph to Moclin.*

Queen Isabella was at Vaena, awaiting in great anxiety, the result of the expedition. She was in a stately apartment of the castle, looking towards the road that winds through the mountains from Moclin, and regarding the watch towers that crowned the neighbouring heights, in hopes of favorable signals. The prince and princess her children were with her, and her venerable counsellor the Grand Cardinal. All shared in the anxiety of the moment. At length couriers were seen riding toward the town. They entered its gates, but, before they reached the castle the nature of their tidings was known to the Queen by the shrieks and wailings that rose from the streets below. The messengers were soon followed by wounded fugitives, hastening home to be relieved or to die among their friends and families. The whole town resounded with lamentations, for it had lost the flower of its youth and its bravest warriors. Isabella was a woman of courageous soul, but her feelings were overpowered by the spectacle of woe which presented itself on every side; her maternal heart mourned over the death of so many loyal subjects who so shortly before had rallied round her with devoted affection, and losing her usual self command she sunk into deep despondency.

In this gloomy state of mind a thousand apprehensions crowded upon her. She dreaded the confidence which this success would impart to the Moors. She feared, also, for the important fortress of Alhama, the garrison of which had not been reinforced since its foraging party had been cut off by this same El Zagal. On every side the Queen saw danger and disaster and feared that a general reverse was about to attend the Castilian arms.

The Grand Cardinal comforted her with both spiritual and worldly counsel. He told her to recollect that no country was ever conquered, without occasional reverses to the conquerors, that the Moors were a warlike people, fortified in a rough and mountainous country, where they never could be conquered by her ancestors, and that in fact her armies had already, in three years, taken more cities than those of any of her predecessors had been able to do in twelve. He concluded by offering himself, to take the field, with three thousand cavalry, his own retainers, paid and maintained by himself, and either hasten to the relief of Alhama, or undertake any other expedition her majesty might command. The discreet words of the cardinal soothed the spirit of the Queen; who always looked to him for consolation, and she soon recovered her usual equanimity.

Some of the counsellors of Isabella, of that politic class who seek to rise by the faults of others, were loud in their censures of the rashness of the count. The Queen defended him with prompt generosity. "The enterprize,"

*Zurita. lib. 20. C4. Pulgar Cronica.

said she, "was rash; but not more rash than that of Lucena, which was crowned with success, and which we have all applauded as the height of heroism. Had the Count de Cabra succeeded in capturing the uncle as he did the nephew, who is there that would not have praised him to the skies?"

The magnanimous words of the Queen put a stop to all invidious remarks in her presence, but certain of the courtiers, who had envied the count the glory gained by his former achievements, continued to magnify among themselves his present imprudence, and we are told by Fray Antonio Agapida, that they sneeringly gave the worthy cavalier the appellation of Count de Cabra, the King Catcher.

Ferdinand had reached the place on the frontier called the Fountain of the King, within three leagues of Moclin, when he heard of the late disaster. He greatly lamented the precipitation of the count, but forbore to express himself with severity, for he knew the value of that loyal and valiant cavalier.* He held a council of war to determine what course was to be pursued. Some of his cavaliers advised him to abandon the attempt upon Moclin, the place being strongly reinforced, and the enemy enspirited by his recent victory. Certain old Spanish hidalgos reminded him that he had but few Castilian troops in his army, without which staunch soldiery his predecessors never presumed to enter the Moorish territory; while others remonstrated that it would be beneath the dignity of the King to retire from an enterprize on account of the defeat of a single cavalier and his retainers. In this way the King was distracted by a multitude of counsellors, when fortunately a letter from the Queen put an end to his perplexities. Proceed we, in the next chapter, to relate what was the purport of that letter.

CHAPTER XXXIII

EXPEDITION AGAINST THE CASTLES OF CAMBIL AND ALBAHAR.

"Happy are those princes," exclaims the worthy padre Fray Antonio Agapida, "who have women and priests to advise them, for in these dwelleth the spirit of counsel." While Ferdinand and his captains were confounding each other in their deliberations at the Fountain of the King, a quiet but deep little council of war was held in the state apartment of the old castle of Vaena between Queen Isabella, the venerable Pedro Gonzalez de Mendoza Grand Cardinal of Spain, and Don Garcia Osorio the belligerent Bishop of Jaen. This last worthy prelate, who had exchanged his mitre for a helm, no sooner

*Abarca. Anales de Aragon.

beheld the defeat of the enterprize against Moclin, than he turned the reins of his sleek, stallfed steed, and hastened back to Vaena, full of a project for the employment of the army, the advancement of the faith, and the benefit of his own diocese. He knew that the actions of the King were influenced by the opinions of the Queen, and that the Queen always inclined a listening ear to the councils of saintly men, he laid his plans, therefore, with the customary wisdom of his cloth, to turn the ideas of the Queen into the proper channel; and this was the purport of the worthy bishop's suggestions.

The Bishoprick of Jaen had for a long time been harrassed by two Moorish castles, the scourge and terror of all that part of the country. They were situated on the frontiers of the Kingdom of Granada, about four leagues from Jaen, in a deep, narrow and rugged valley, surrounded by lofty mountains. Through this valley runs the Rio Frio (or Cold River) in a deep channel between high precipitous banks. On each side of the stream rise two vast rocks, nearly perpendicular, within a stone's throw of each other; blocking up the narrow gorge of the valley. On the summits of these rocks stood the two formidable castles of Cambil and Albahar, fortified with battlements and towers of great height and thickness. They were connected together by a bridge, thrown from rock to rock across the river. The road which passed through the valley traversed this bridge, and was completely commanded by these castles. They stood like two giants of romance guarding the pass and dominating the valley.

The Kings of Granada, knowing the importance of these castles, kept them always well garrisoned, and victualled to stand a siege, with fleet steeds and hard riders to forage the country of the Christians. The warlike race of the Abencerrages, the troops of the royal household, and others of the choicest chivalry of Granada made them their strong holds, from whence to sally forth on those predatory and roving enterprizes which were the delight of the Moorish cavaliers. As the wealthy bishoprick of Jaen lay immediately at hand it suffered more peculiarly from these marauders. They drove off the fat beeves and the flocks of sheep from the pastures and swept the labourers from the field; they scoured the country to the very gates of Jaen, so that the citizens could not venture from their walls without the risk of being borne off captive to the dungeons of these castles.

The worthy bishop, like a good pastor, beheld with grief of heart his fat bishoprick daily waxing leaner and leaner, and poorer and poorer, and his holy ire was kindled at the thoughts that the possessions of the church should thus be at the mercy of a crew of infidels.

It was the urgent council of the bishop, therefore, that the military force thus providentially assembled in the neighborhood, since it was apparently foiled in its attempt upon Moclin, should be turned against these insolent castles, and the country delivered from their domination. The Grand Cardinal supported the suggestion of the bishop, and declared that he had long meditated the policy of a measure of the kind. Their united opinions found favour with the Queen, and she dispatched a letter on the subject to the King. It came just in time to relieve him from the distraction of a multitude of counsellors and he immediately undertook the reduction of those castles.

The Marquis of Cadiz was, accordingly, sent in advance with two thousand horse, to keep a watch upon the garrisons and prevent all entrance or exit until the King should arrive with the main army and the battering artillery. The Queen, to be near at hand in case of need, moved her quarters to the city of Jaen, where she was received with martial honours by the belligerent bishop, who had buckled on his cuirass and girded on his sword, to fight in the cause of his diocese.

In the mean time the Marquis of Cadiz arrived in the valley and completely shut up the Moors within their walls. The castles were under the command of Mahomet Lentin Ben Usef, an Abencerrage, and one of the bravest cavaliers of Granada. In his garrisons were many troops of the fierce African tribe of Gomeres. Mahomet Lentin, confident in the strength of his fortresses, smiled as he looked down from his battlements upon the Christian cavalry, perplexed in the rough and narrow valley. He sent forth skirmishing parties to harrass them and there were many sharp combats between small parties and single knights, but the Moors were driven back to the castles and all attempts to send intelligence of their situation to Granada were intercepted by the vigilance of the Marquis of Cadiz.

At length the legions of the royal army came pouring with fluttering banner and vaunting trumpet along the defiles of the mountains. They halted before the castles but the King could not find room in the narrow and rugged valley, to form his camp; he had to divide it into three parts, which were posted on different heights, and his tents whitened the sides of the neighbouring hills. When the encampment was formed the army remained gazing idly at the castles. The artillery was upwards of four leagues in the rear and without artillery all attack would be in vain.

The alcayde, Mahomet Lentin knew the nature of the road by which the artillery had to be brought. It was merely a rugged path at times scaling almost perpendicular crags and precipices, up which it was utterly impossible for wheel carriages to pass, neither was it in the power of man or beast to draw up the lombards and other ponderous ordnance. He felt assured, therefore, that they never could be brought to the camp, and without their aid what could the Christians effect against his rock-built castles? He scoffed at them, therefore, as he saw their tents by day and their fires by night covering the surrounding heights. "Let them linger here a little while longer," said he, "and the autumnal torrents will wash them from the mountains."

While the alcayde was thus closely mewed up within his walls, and the Christians lay inactive in their camp, he noticed, one calm autumnal day,

the sound of implements of labour echoing among the mountains, and now
and then the crash of a falling tree or a thundering report, as if some rock
had been heaved from its bed and hurled into the valley. The alcayde was
on the battlements of his castle surrounded by his knights. "Methinks," said
he, "these Christians are making war upon the rocks and trees of the mountains, since they find our castles unassailable."

The sounds did not cease even during the night; every now and then the
Moorish centinel, as he paced the battlements, heard some crash echoing
among the heights. The return of day explained the mystery. Scarcely did
the sun shine against the summits of the mountains than shouts burst from
the cliffs opposite to the castles, and were answered from the camp with
joyful sound of kettle drums and trumpets.

The astonished Moors lifted up their eyes and beheld, as it were, a torrent
of war breaking out of a narrow defile. There was a multitude of men with
pick axes, spades and bars of iron clearing away every obstacle, while behind
them slowly moved along great teams of oxen, dragging heavy ordnance,
and all the munitions of battering artillery.

What cannot women and priests effect, when they unite in council! exclaims again the worthy Antonio Agapida. The Queen had held another consultation with the Grand Cardinal and the belligerent Bishop of Jaen. It was
clear that the heavy ordnance could never be conveyed to the camp by the
regular road of the country, and without battering artillery nothing could be
effected. It was suggested, however, by the zealous bishop that another road
might be opened through a more practicable part of the mountains. It would
be an undertaking extravagant and chimerical with ordinary means, and
therefore unlooked for by the enemy; but what could not kings effect who
had treasures and armies at command?

The project struck the enterprizing spirit of the Queen. Six thousand men
with pick axes, crow bars and every other necessary implement, were set to
work, day and night, to break a road through the very centre of the mountains. No time was to be lost, for it was rumoured that El Zagal was about
to march with a mighty host to the relief of the castles. The bustling bishop
of Jaen acted as pioneer to mark the route and superintend the labourers
and the Grand Cardinal took care that the work should never languish
through lack of means.*

"When kings' treasures," says Fray Antonio Agapida, "are dispensed by
priestly hands there is no stint, as the glorious annals of Spain bear witness."
Under the guidance of these ghostly men it seemed as if miracles were effected. Almost an entire mountain was levelled, valleys filled up, trees hewn
down, rocks broken and overturned, in short all the obstacles which nature
had heaped around entirely and promptly vanquished. In little more than

*Zurita Anales de Aragon L. 20 c 64 Pulgar. Part 3. C. 51.

twelve days this gigantic work was effected and the ordnance dragged to the camp to the great triumph of the Christians and confusion of the Moors.*

No sooner was the heavy artillery arrived than it was mounted in all haste upon the neighbouring heights: Francisco Ramirez de Madrid, the first engineer in Spain, superintended the batteries and soon opened a destructive fire upon the castles.

When the valiant Alcayde Mahomet Lentin found his towers tumbling about him and his bravest men dashed from the walls without the power of inflicting a wound upon the foe his haughty spirit was greatly exasperated. Of what avail, said he, is all the prowess of knighthood against these cowardly engines that murder from afar?

For a whole day a tremendous fire kept thundering upon the castle of Albahar. The lombards discharged large stones, which demolished two of the towers and all the battlements which guarded the portal. If any Moors attempted to defend the walls or repair the breaches, they were shot down by ribadoquines and other small pieces of artillery. The Christian soldiery issued forth from the camp, under cover of this fire, and, approaching the castles, discharged flights of arrows and stones through the openings made by the ordnance.

At length, to bring the siege to a conclusion, Francisco Ramirez elevated some of the heaviest artillery on a mount that rose in form of a cone or pyramid on the side of the river near to Albahar, and commanded both castles. This was an operation of great skill and excessive labour, but it was repaid by complete success; for the Moors did not dare to wait until this terrible battery should discharge its fury. Satisfied that all further resistance was vain the valiant alcayde made signal for a parley. The Articles of Capitulation were soon arranged. The alcayde and his garrisons were permitted to return in safety to the city of Granada, and the castles were delivered into the possession of King Ferdinand on the day of the festival of S' Matthew, in the month of September. They were immediately repaired, strongly garrisoned, and given in charge to the city of Jaen.

The effects of this triumph were immediately apparent. Quiet and security once more settled upon the bishoprick. The husbandmen tilled their fields in peace, the herds and flocks fattened unmolested in the pastures and the vineyards yielded corpulent skinsful of rosy wine. The good bishop enjoyed, in the gratitude of his people, the approbation of his conscience, the encrease of his revenues, and the abundance of his table a reward for all his toils and perils. "This glorious victory," exclaims Fray Antonio Agapida, "achieved by such extraordinary management and infinite labour, is a shining example of what a bishop can effect for the promotion of the faith and the good of his diocese."

*Idem.

CHAPTER XXXIV

ENTERPRIZE OF THE KNIGHTS OF CALATRAVA AGAINST ZALEA.

While these events were taking place on the northern frontier of the Kingdom of Granada, the important fortress of Alhama was neglected, and its commander Don Gutiere de Padilla, Clavero of Calatrava reduced to great perplexity. The remnant of the foraging party, which had been surprized and massacred by the fierce El Zagal, when on his way to Granada to receive the crown, had returned in confusion and dismay to the fortress. They could only speak of their own disgrace, being obliged to abandon their cavalgada and to fly pursued by a superior force. Of the flower of their party, the gallant Knights of Calatrava, who had remained behind in the valley, they knew nothing. A few days cleared up all the mystery of their fate. Tidings were brought that their bloody heads had been borne in triumph into Granada by the ferocious El Zagal. The surviving Knights of Calatrava, who formed a part of the garrison, burned to revenge the death of their comrades and to wipe out the stygma of this defeat, but the clavero had been rendered cautious by disaster and resisted all their entreaties for a foray. His garrison was weakened by the loss of so many of its bravest men; the vega was patrolled by numerous and powerful squadrons, sent forth by the warlike El Zagal; above all the movements of the garrison were watched by the warriors of Zalea, a strong town, only two leagues distant, on the road towards Loxa. This place was a continual check upon Alhama, when in its most powerful state, placing ambuscades to entrap the Christian cavaliers in the course of their salleys. Frequent and bloody skirmishes had taken place in consequence, and the troops of Alhama, when returning from their forays, had often to fight their way back through the squadrons of Zalea. Thus surrounded by dangers, Don Gutiere de Padilla restrained the eagerness of his troops for a salley, knowing that any additional disaster might be followed by the loss of Alhama.

In the mean while provisions began to grow scarce; they were unable to forage the country as usual for supplies and depended for relief upon the Castilian sovereigns. The defeat of the Count de Cabra filled the measure of their perplexities, as it interrupted the intended reinforcements and supplies. To such extremity were they reduced that they were compelled to kill some of their horses for provisions.

The worthy clavero, Don Gutiere de Padilla, was pondering one day on this gloomy state of affairs, when a Moor was brought before him who had surrendered himself at the gate of Alhama and claimed an audience. Don Gutiere was accustomed to visits of the kind from renegado Moors, who roamed the country as spies and adalides, but the countenance of this man was quite unknown to him. He had a box strapped to his shoulders, containing divers articles of traffic, and appeared to be one of those itinerant traders who often resorted to Alhama and the other garrison towns, under pretext of vending trivial merchandize, such as amulets, perfumes and trinkets, but who often produced rich shawls, golden chains and necklaces and valuable gems and jewels.

The Moor requested a private conference with the clavero: "I have a precious jewel," said he, "to dispose of."

"I want no jewels," replied Don Gutiere. "For the sake of him who died on the cross, the great prophet of your faith," said the Moor solemnly, "refuse not my request. The jewel I speak of you alone can purchase, but I can only treat about it in secret."

Don Gutiere perceived that there was something hidden under the mystic and figurative terms in which the Moors were often accustomed to talk. He motioned to his attendants to retire. When they were alone the Moor looked cautiously round the apartment, and then approaching close to the knight demanded in a low voice, "What will you give me if I deliver the fortress of Zalea into your hands?"

Don Gutiere looked with surprize at the humble individual that made such a suggestion.

"What means have you," said he, "of effecting such a proposition?"

"I have a brother in the garrison of Zalea," replied the Moor, "who, for a proper compensation would admit a body of troops into the citadel."

Don Gutiere turned a scrutinizing eye upon the Moor. "What right have I to believe," said he, "that thou wilt be truer to me than to those of thy blood and thy religion?" "I renounce all ties to them, either of blood or of religion," replied the Moor. "My Mother was a Christian captive, her country shall henceforth be my country and her faith my faith."*

The doubts of Don Gutiere were not dispelled by this profession of mongrel Christianity. "Granting the sincerity of thy conversion," said he, "art thou under no obligations of gratitude or duty to the alcayde of the fortress thou wouldst betray?"

The eyes of the Moor flashed fire at the words; he gnashed his teeth with fury. "The alcayde," cried he, "is a dog! He has deprived my brother of his just share of booty; he has robbed me of my merchandize, treated me worse than a jew when I murmured at his injustice and ordered me to be thrust forth ignominiously from his walls. May the curse of God fall upon my head if I rest content until I have full revenge."

"Enough!" said Don Gutiere, "I trust more to thy revenge than thy religion."

The good clavero called a council of his officers. The Knights of Calatrava were unanimous for the enterprize, zealous to appease the manes of their

*Cura de los Palacios.

slaughtered comrades. Don Gutiere reminded them of the state of the garrison, enfeebled by their late loss and scarcely sufficient for the defence of the walls. The cavaliers replied that there was no achievement without risk and that there would have been no great actions recorded in history had there not been daring spirits ready to peril life to gain renown.

Don Gutiere yielded to the wishes of his knights, for to have resisted any further might have drawn on him the imputation of timidity. He ascertained by trusty spies that every thing in Zalea remained in the usual state, and he made all requisite arrangements for the attack.

When the appointed night arrived all the cavaliers were anxious to engage in the enterprize, but the individuals were decided by lot. They set out under the guidance of the Moor and when they had arrived in the vicinity of Zalea, they bound his hands behind his back, and their leader pledged his knightly word to strike him dead on the first sign of treachery. He then bade him to lead the way.

It was near midnight when they reached the walls of the fortress. They passed silently along, until they found themselves below the citadel. Here their guide made a low and preconcerted signal. It was answered from above, and a cord let down from the wall. The knights attached to it a ladder, which was drawn up and fastened. Gutiere Muñoz was the first that mounted, followed by Pedro de Alvanado, both brave and hardy soldiers. A handful succeeded. They were attacked by a party of guards but held them at bay until more of their comrades ascended; with their assistance they gained possession of a tower and part of the wall. The garrison, by this time, was aroused, but before they could reach the scene of action most of the cavaliers were within the battlements. A bloody contest raged for about an hour, several of the Christians were slain, but many of the Moors; at length the whole citadel was carried and the town submitted without resistance.

Thus did the gallant Knights of Calatrava gain the strong town of Zalea with scarcely any loss, and atone for the inglorious defeat of their companions by El Zagal. They found the magazines of the place well stored with provisions, and were enabled to carry a seasonable supply to their own famishing garrison.

The tidings of this event reached the sovereigns just after the surrender of Cambil and Albahar. They were greatly rejoiced at this additional success of their arms, and immediately sent strong reinforcements and ample supplies for both Alhama and Zalea. They then dismissed the army for the winter. Ferdinand and Isabella retired to Alcalá de Henares, where the Queen, on the 16th. of December 1485 gave birth to the princess Catharine, afterwards wife to Henry VIII of England. Thus prosperously terminated the checquered campaign of this important year.

CHAPTER XXXV

DEATH OF MULEY ABEN HASSAN.

Muley Abdalla el Zagal had been received with great acclamations at Granada, on his return from defeating the Count de Cabra. He had endeavoured to turn his victory to the greatest advantage with his subjects, giving tilts and tournaments and other public festivities in which the Moors delighted. The loss of the castles of Cambil and Albahar, and of the fortress of Zalea, however, checked this sudden tide of popularity, and some of the fickle populace began to doubt whether they had not been rather precipitate in deposing his brother Muley Aben Hassan.

That superannuated monarch remained in his faithful town of Almunecar on the border of the Mediterranean, surrounded by a few adherents, together with his wife Zorayna and his children, and he had all his treasures safe in his possession. The fiery heart of the old monarch was almost burnt out, and all his powers of doing either harm or good seemed at an end.

While in this passive and helpless state his brother El Zagal manifested a sudden anxiety for his health. He had him removed with all tenderness and care, to Salobreña, another fortress on the Mediterranean coast, famous for its pure and salubrious air; and the alcayde, who was a devoted adherent to El Zagal, was charged to have especial care that nothing was wanting to the comfort and solace of his brother.

Salobreña was a small town situated on a lofty and rocky hill in the midst of a beautiful and fertile vega, shut up on three sides by mountains and opening on the fourth to the Mediterranean. It was protected by strong walls and a powerful castle, and, being deemed impregnable, was often used by the Moorish kings as a place of deposit for their treasures. They were accustomed to assign it as a residence for such of their sons and brothers as might endanger the security of their reign. Here the princes lived in luxurious repose. They had delicious gardens, perfumed baths, a harem of beauties at their command; nothing was denied them but the liberty to depart: that alone was wanting to render this abode an earthly paradise.

Such was the delightful place appointed by El Zagal for the residence of his brother; but, notwithstanding its wonderful salubrity, the old monarch had not been removed thither many days before he expired. There was nothing extraordinary in his death; life, with him, had long been glimmering in the socket, and for some time past he might rather have been numbered with the dead than with the living. The public, however, are fond of seeing things in a sinister and mysterious point of view, and there were many dark surmises as to the causes of this event. El Zagal acted in a manner to heighten these suspicions. He caused the treasures of his deceased brother to be packed on mules and brought to Granada, where he took possession of them to the exclusion of the children of Aben Hassan. The Sultana Zorayna and her two sons were lodged in the Alhambra, in the tower of the Comares.

This was a residence in a palace, but it had proved a royal prison to the Sultana Ayxa la Horra and her youthful son Boabdil. There the unhappy Zorayna had time to meditate upon the disappointment of all those ambitious schemes for herself and children, for which she had stained her conscience with so many crimes, and induced her cruel husband to imbrue his hands in the blood of his other offspring.

The corpse of old Muley Aben Hassan was also brought to Granada, not in state becoming the remains of a once powerful monarch, but transported on a mule like the corpse of the poorest peasant. It received no honour or ceremonial, and appears to have been interred obscurely, to prevent any popular sensation, and it is recorded by an ancient and faithful chronicler, that the body of the old monarch was deposited by two Christian captives, in his osario or charnel house.* Such was the end of the turbulent Muley Aben Hassan; who, after passing his life in constant contests for empire, could scarce gain quiet admission into the corner of a sepulchre.

No sooner were the populace well assured that old Muley Aben Hassan was dead and beyond recovery than they all began to extol his memory and deplore his loss. They admitted that he had been fierce and cruel, but then he had been brave; he had, to be sure, pulled this war upon their heads; but he had likewise been crushed by it. In a word, *he was dead*, and his death atoned for every fault; for a king, recently dead, is generally either a hero or a saint.

In proportion as they ceased to hate old Muley Aben Hassan they began to hate his brother El Zagal. The circumstances of the old king's death, the eagerness to appropriate his treasures, the scandalous neglect of his corpse, and the imprisonment of his sultana and children all filled the public mind with gloomy suspicions, and the epithet of Fratricide was sometimes substituted for that of El Zagal in the low murmurings of the people.

As the public must always have some object to like as well as to hate, there began once more to be an enquiry after their fugitive King Boabdil el Chico. That unfortunate monarch was still at Cordova, existing on the cool courtesy and meagre friendship of Ferdinand; which had waned exceedingly ever since Boabdil had ceased to have any influence in his late dominions. The reviving interest expressed in his fate by the Moorish public, and certain secret overtures made to him, once more aroused the sympathy of Ferdinand. He immediately advised Boabdil again to set up his standard within the frontiers of Granada, and furnished him with money and means for the purpose. Boabdil advanced but a little way into his late territories; he took up his post at Velez el Blanco, a strong town on the confines of Murcia; there he established the shadow of a court, and stood, as it were, with one foot over the border, and ready to draw that back upon the least alarm. His

*Cura de Los Palacios. Cap. 77.

presence in the kingdom, however, and his assumption of regal state, gave life to his faction in Granada. The inhabitants of the Albaycin, the poorest but most warlike part of the populace were generally in his favour; the more rich, courtly and aristocratical inhabitants of the quarter of the Alhambra, rallied round what appeared to be the most stable authority, and supported the throne of El Zagal. So it is in the admirable order of sublunary affairs: every thing seeks its kind; the rich befriend the rich; the powerful stand by the powerful the poor enjoy the patronage of the poor, and thus a universal harmony prevails.

CHAPTER XXXVI
OF THE CHRISTIAN ARMY WHICH ASSEMBLED AT THE CITY OF CORDOVA.

Great and glorious was the style with which the Catholic sovereigns opened another year's campaign of this eventful war. It was like commencing another act of a stately and heroic drama, where the curtain rises to the inspiring sound of martial melody, and the whole stage glitters with the array of warriors and the pomp of arms. The ancient city of Cordova was the place appointed by the sovereigns for the assemblage of the troops; and early in the spring of 1486 the fair valley of the Guadalquivir resounded with the shrill blast of trumpet, and the impatient neighing of the war horse. In this splendid era of Spanish chivalry there was a rivalship, among the nobles who most should distinguish himself by the splendour of his appearance, and the number and equipments of his feudal followers. Every day beheld some cavalier of note, the representative of some proud and powerful house, entering the gates of Cordova with sound of trumpet and displaying his banner and device renowned in many a contest. He would appear in sumptuous array, surrounded by pages and lacqueys no less gorgeously attired and followed by a host of vassals and retainers, horse and foot, all admirably equipped in burnished armour.

Such was the state of Don Inigo Lopez de Mendoza, Duke of Infantado; who may be cited as a picture of a warlike noble of those times. He brought with him five hundred men at arms of his household, armed and mounted *à la Gineta* and *à la Guisa*. The cavaliers who attended him were magnificently armed and dressed. The housings of fifty of his horses were of rich cloth embroidered with gold: and others were of brocade. The sumpter mules had housings of the same, with halters of silk; while the bridles, head pieces and all the harnessing glittered with silver.

The camp equipage of these noble and luxurious warriors was equally magnificent. Their tents were gay pavillions of various colours, fitted up with silken hangings and decorated with fluttering pennons. They had vessels of gold and silver for the service of their tables, as if they were about to engage in a course of stately feasts and courtly revels, instead of the stern encounters of rugged and mountainous warfare. Sometimes they passed through the streets of Cordova at night, in splendid cavalcade, with great numbers of lighted torches, the rays of which falling upon polished armour and nodding plumes, and silken scarfs and trappings of golden embroidery filled all beholders with admiration.*

But it was not the chivalry of Spain, alone, which thronged the streets of Cordova. The fame of this war had spread throughout Christendom: it was considered a kind of crusade and Catholic knights from all parts hastened to signalize themselves in so holy a cause. There were several valiant chevaliers from France, among whom the most distinguished was Gaston du Leon, Seneschal of Toulouse. With him came a gallant train, well armed and mounted, and decorated with rich surcoats and panaches of feathers. These cavaliers, it is said, eclipsed all others in the light festivities of the court, they were devoted to the fair, but not after the solemn and passionate manner of the Spanish lovers; they were gay, gallant, and joyous in their amours, and captivated by the vivacity of their attacks. They were at first held in light estimation by the grave and stately Spanish knights, until they made themselves to be respected by their wonderful prowess in the field.

The most conspicuous of the volunteers, however, who appeared in Cordova on this occasion, was an English knight of royal connexion. This was the Lord Scales, Earl of Rivers, related to the Queen of England, wife of Henry VII. He had distinguished himself in the preceding year, at the battle of Bosworth field, where Henry Tudor, then Earl of Richmond, overcame Richard III. That decisive battle having left the country at peace, the Earl of Rivers having conceived a passion for warlike scenes, repaired to the Castilian court to keep his arms in exercise, in a campaign against the Moors. He brought with him a hundred archers, all dextrous with the long bow and the cloth yard arrow; also two hundred yeomen, armed cap a pie, who fought with pike and battle axe; men robust of frame and of prodigious strength.

The worthy padre, Fray Antonio Agapida, describes this stranger knight and his followers with his accustomed accuracy and minuteness. "This cavalier," he observes, "was from the island of England and brought with him a train of his vassals; men who had been hardened in certain civil wars which had raged in their country. They were a comely race of men, but too fair and fresh for warriors, not having the sun burnt, warlike hue of our old

*Pulgar Part 3. Cap. 41. 56.

Castilian soldiery. They were huge feeders also and deep carousers and could not accommodate themselves to the sober diet of our troops, but must fain eat and drink after the manner of their own country. They were often noisy and unruly also in their wassail and their quarter of the camp was prone to be a scene of loud revel and sudden brawl. They were withal of great pride yet it was not like our inflammable Spanish pride; they stood not much upon the *pundonor* and high punctilio and rarely drew the stiletto in their disputes, but their pride was silent and contumelious. Though from a remote and somewhat barbarous island they believed themselves the most perfect men upon earth and magnified their chieftain the Lord Scales beyond the greatest of their grandees. With all this, it must be said of them, that they were marvellous good men in the field, dexterous archers and powerful with the battle axe. In their great pride and self will they always sought to press in the advance, and take the post of danger, trying to outvie our Spanish chivalry. They did not rush on fiercely to the fight, nor make a brilliant onset like the Moorish and Spanish troops, but they went into the fight deliberately and persisted obstinately, and were slow to find out when they were beaten. Withal they were much esteemed yet little liked by our soldiery, who considered them staunch companions in the field, yet coveted but little fellowship with them in the camp.

"Their commander the Lord Scales was an accomplished cavalier of gracious and noble presence, and fair speech, it was a marvel to see so much courtesy in a knight brought up so far from our Castilian court. He was much honoured by the King and Queen and found great favour with the fair dames about the court, who indeed are rather prone to be pleased with foreign cavaliers. He went always in costly state, attended by pages and esquires, and accompanied by noble young cavaliers of his country, who had enrolled themselves under his banner, to learn the gentle exercise of arms. In all pageants and festivals the eyes of the populace were attracted by the singular bearing and rich array of the English earl and his train, who prided themselves in always appearing in the garb and manner of their country, and were indeed something very magnificent, delectable and strange to behold."

The worthy chronicler is no less elaborate in his description of the Masters of Santiago, Calatrava and Alcantara, and their valiant knights; armed at all points and decorated with the badges of their orders. These, he affirms, were the flower of Christian chivalry: being constantly in service they became more steadfast and accomplished in discipline, than the irregular and temporary levies of the feudal nobles. Calm, solemn, and stately, they sat like towers upon their powerful chargers. On parades they manifested none of the shew and ostentation of the other troops, neither, in battle, did they endeavour to signalize themselves by any fiery vivacity, or desperate and vainglorious exploit; every thing with them was measured and sedate, yet it was observed that none were more warlike in their appearance in the camp, or more terrible for their achievements in the field.

The gorgeous magnificence of the Spanish nobles found but little favour in the eyes of the sovereigns. They saw that it caused a competition in expense, ruinous to cavaliers of moderate fortune, and they feared that a softness and effeminacy might thus be introduced incompatible with the stern nature of the war. They signified their disapprobation to several of the principal noblemen and recommended a more sober and soldierlike display while in actual service.

"These are rare troops for a tourney, my Lord," said Ferdinand to the Duke of Infantado, as he beheld his retainers glittering in gold and embroidery, "but gold, though gorgeous, is soft and yielding; iron is the metal for the field."

"Sire," replied the duke, "if my men parade in gold, your Majesty will find they fight with steel." The King smiled but shook his head, and the duke treasured up his speech in his heart.

It remains now to reveal the immediate object of this mighty and chivalrous preparation; which had in fact the gratification of a royal pique at bottom. The severe lesson which Ferdinand had received from the veteran Ali Atar, before the walls of Loxa; though it had been of great service in rendering him wary in his attacks upon fortified places, yet rankled sorely in his mind; and he had ever since held Loxa in peculiar odium. It was, in truth, one of the most belligerent and troublesome cities on the borders; incessantly harrassing Andalusia by its incursions. It also intervened between the Christian territories and Alhama and other important places, gained in the Kingdom of Granada. For all these reasons King Ferdinand had determined to make another grand attempt upon this warrior city, and for this purpose he had summoned to the field his most powerful chivalry.

It was in the month of May that the King sallied from Cordova at the head of his army. He had twelve thousand cavalry and forty thousand foot soldiers, armed with cross bows, lances and arquebusses. There were six thousand pioniers with hatchets, pick axes and crow bars, for levelling roads. He took with him, also a great train of lombards and other heavy artillery, with a body of Germans skilled in the service of ordnance and the art of battering walls.

It was a glorious spectacle, says Fray Antonio Agapida, to behold this pompous pageant issuing forth from Cordova, the pennons and devices of the proudest houses of Spain, with those of the gallant stranger knight, fluttering above a sea of crests and plumes; to see it slowly moving with flash of helm and cuirass and buckler, across the ancient bridge, and reflected in the waters of the Guadalquivir, while the neigh of steed and blast of trumpet vibrated in the air and resounded to the distant mountains. "But above all," concludes the good father, with his accustomed zeal, "it was triumphant to behold the standard of the faith every where displayed, and to reflect that this was no worldly minded army, intent upon some temporal scheme of ambition or revenge, but a Christian host bound on a crusade to extirpate the vile seed of Mahomet from the land, and to extend the pure dominion of the Church."

CHAPTER XXXVII

HOW FRESH COMMOTIONS BROKE OUT IN GRANADA AND HOW THE PEOPLE UNDERTOOK TO ALLAY THEM.

While perfect unity of object and harmony of operation gave power to the Christian arms, the devoted Kingdom of Granada continued a prey to internal feuds. The transient popularity of El Zagal had declined ever since the death of his brother, and the party of Boabdil el Chico was daily gaining strength. The Albaycin and the Alhambra were again arrayed against each other in deadly strife, and the streets of unhappy Granada were daily dyed in the blood of her children. In the midst of these dissensions tidings arrived of the formidable army assembling at Cordova. The rival factions paused in their infatuated brawls, and were roused to a temporary sense of the common danger. They forthwith resorted to their old expedient of new modelling their government, or rather of making and unmaking kings. The elevation of El Zagal to the throne had not produced the desired effect—what then was to be done? Recall Boabdil el Chico, and acknowledge him again as sovereign? While they were in a popular tumult of deliberation, Hamet Aben Zarrax, surnamed El Santo, arose among them. This was the same wild, melancholy man, who had predicted the woes of Granada. He issued from one of the caverns of the adjacent height which overhangs the Darro, and has since been called the holy mountain. His appearance was more haggard than ever, for the unheeded spirit of prophecy seemed to have turned inwardly and preyed upon his vitals. "Beware, oh Moslems," exclaimed he, "of men who are eager to govern yet are unable to protect. Why slaughter each other for El Chico or El Zagal? Let your kings renounce their contests, unite for the salvation of Granada or let them be deposed."

Hamet Aben Zarrax had long been revered as a saint, he was now considered an oracle. The old men and the nobles immediately consulted together how the two rival kings might be brought to accord. They had tried most expedients, it was now determined to divide the kingdom between them, giving Granada, Malaga, Velez Malaga, Almeria, Almunecar and their de-

pendencies to El Zagal and the residue to Boabdil el Chico. Among the cities
granted to the latter, Loxa was particularly specified, with a condition that
he should immediately take command of it in person; for the council thought
the favour he enjoyed with the Castilian monarchs, might avert the threatened attack.

El Zagal readily accorded to this arrangement; he had been hastily elevated to the throne by an ebullition of the people, and might be as hastily
cast down again. It secured him one half of a kingdom to which he had no
hereditary right, and he trusted to force or fraud to gain the other half hereafter. The wiley old monarch even sent a deputation to his nephew, making
a merit of offering him cheerfully the half, which he had thus been compelled to relinquish, and inviting him to enter into an amicable coalition for
the good of the country.

The heart of Boabdil shrunk from all connexion with a man who had
sought his life, and whom he regarded as the murderer of his kindred. He
accepted one half of the kingdom as an offer from the nation, not to be
rejected by a prince who scarcely held possession of the ground he stood on.
He asserted, nevertheless, his absolute right to the whole, and only submitted to the partition out of anxiety for the present good of his people. He
assembled his handful of adherents and prepared to hasten to Loxa. As he
mounted his horse to depart Hamet Aben Zarrax stood suddenly before him.
"Be true to thy country and thy faith," cried he. "Hold no further communication with these Christian dogs. Trust not the hollow hearted friendship
of the Castilian King, he is mining the earth beneath thy feet. Choose one
of two things, be a sovereign or a slave, thou canst not be both."

Boabdil ruminated on these words; he made many wise resolutions, but
he was prone always to act from the impulse of the moment, and was unfortunately given to temporize in his policy. He wrote to Ferdinand informing
him that Loxa and certain other cities had returned to their allegiance, and
that he held them as vassal to the Castilian crown, according to their convention. He conjured him, therefore, to refrain from any meditated attack,
offering free passage to the Spanish army to Malaga, or any other place under the dominion of his uncle.*

Ferdinand turned a deaf ear to the entreaty, and to all professions of
friendship and vassallage. Boabdil was nothing to him but as an instrument
for stirring up the flames of civil war. He now insisted that he had entered
into a hostile league with his uncle, and had, consequently forfeited all
claims to his indulgence; and he prosecuted with the greater earnestness,
his campaign against the city of Loxa.

"Thus," observes the worthy Fray Antonio Agapida, thus did this most

*Zurita. Lib. 20. C. 68.

sagacious sovereign act upon the text in the 11th. Chapter of the Evangelist
S' Luke that a kingdom divided against itself cannot stand. He had induced
these infidels to waste and destroy themselves by internal dissensions, and
finally cast forth the survivor; while the Moorish monarchs by their ruinous
contests made good the Old Castilian proverb in cases of civil war. "El vencido vencido y el vencidor perdido" (the conquered conquered, and the conqueror undone).*

CHAPTER XXXVIII

HOW KING FERDINAND HELD A COUNCIL OF WAR AT THE ROCK OF THE LOVERS.

The royal army on its march against Loxa, lay encamped one pleasant evening in May, in a meadow on the banks of the river Yeguas around the foot
of a lofty cliff called the Rock of the Lovers. The quarters of each nobleman
formed as it were a separate little encampment; his stately pavillion surmounted by his fluttering pennon, rising above the surrounding tents of his
vassals and retainers. A little apart from the others, as it were in proud
reserve, was the encampment of the English earl. It was sumptuous in its
furniture and complete in all its munitions. Archers, and soldiers armed with
battle axes kept guard around it: while above, the standard of England rolled
out its ample folds and flapped in the evening breeze.

The mingled sounds of various tongues and nations were heard from the
soldiery, as they watered their horses in the stream, or busied themselves
round the fires which began to glow, here and there, in the twilight: the gay
chauson of the Frenchman, singing of his amours on the pleasant banks of
the Loire or the sunny regions of the Garonne: the broad guttural tones of
the German, chaunting some doughty *Krieger-lied*, or extolling the vintage
of the Rhine: the wild romance of the Spaniard, reciting the achievements
of the Cid and many a famous passage of the Moorish wars, and the long and
melancholy ditty of the Englishman treating of some feudal hero or redoubtable outlaw of his distant island.

On a rising ground, commanding a view of the whole encampment, stood
the ample and magnificent pavillion of the King, with the banner of Castile
and Aragon and the holy standard of the cross erected before it. In this tent
were assembled the principal commanders of the army, having been summoned by Ferdinand to a council of war on receiving tidings that Boabdil
had thrown himself into Loxa with a considerable reinforcement. After some

*Garibay Lib. 40. C. 33.

consultation it was determined to invest Loxa on both sides: one part of the army should seize upon the dangerous but commanding height of Santo Albohacen in front of the city; while the remainder, making a circuit, should encamp on the opposite side.

No sooner was this resolved upon than the Marquis of Cadiz stood forth and claimed the post of danger in behalf of himself and those cavaliers, his companions in arms, who had been compelled to relinquish it by the general retreat of the army on the former siege. The enemy had exulted over them as if driven from it in disgrace. To regain that perilous height, to pitch their tents upon it and to avenge the blood of their valiant compeer, the Master of Calatrava, who had fallen upon it, was due to their fame; the marquis demanded, therefore, that they might lead the advance and secure that height, engaging to hold the enemy employed until the main army should take its position on the opposite side of the city.

King Ferdinand readily granted his permission; upon which the Count de Cabra entreated to be admitted to a share of the enterprize. He had always been accustomed to serve in the advance, and now that Boabdil was in the field, and a King was to be taken, he could not content himself with remaining in the rear. Ferdinand yielded his consent, for he was disposed to give the good count every opportunity to retrieve his late disaster.

The English earl, when he heard there was an enterprize of danger in question, was hot to be admitted to the party, but the King restrained his ardour. "These cavaliers," said he, "conceive that they have an account to settle with their pride; let them have the enterprize to themselves, my Lord; if you follow these Moorish wars long, you will find no lack of perilous service."

The Marquis of Cadiz and his companions in arms struck their tents before day break; they were five thousand horse and twelve thousand foot, and marched rapidly along the defiles of the mountains, the cavaliers being anxious to strike the blow, and get possession of the heights of Albohacen before the King with the main army should arrive to their assistance.

The city of Loxa stands on a high hill, between two mountains, on the banks of the Xenel. To attain the height of Albohacen the troops had to pass over a tract of rugged and broken country, and a deep valley intersected by those canals and water courses with which the Moors irrigated their lands. They were extremely embarrassed in this part of their march, and in imminent risk of being cut up in detail before they could reach the height.

The Count de Cabra, with his usual eagerness, endeavoured to push across this valley in defiance of every obstacle; he in consequence, soon became entangled with his cavalry among the canals, but his impatience would not permit him to retrace his steps and choose a more practicable but circuitous route. Others slowly crossed another part of the valley by the aid of pontoons, while the Marquis of Cadiz, Don Alonzo de Aguilar, and the

Count de Ureña, being more experienced in the ground from their former campaign, made a circuit round the bottom of the height, and winding up it, began to display their squadrons and elevate their banners on the redoubtable post, which, in the former siege they had been compelled so reluctantly to abandon.

CHAPTER XXXIX

HOW THE ROYAL ARMY APPEARED BEFORE THE CITY OF LOXA, AND HOW IT WAS RECEIVED AND OF THE DOUGHTY ACHIEVEMENTS OF THE ENGLISH EARL.

The advance of the Christian army upon Loxa, threw the wavering Boabdil el Chico into one of his usual dilemmas, and he was greatly perplexed between his oath of allegiance to the Spanish sovereigns, and his sense of duty to his subjects. His doubts were determined by the sight of the enemy glittering upon the height of Albohacen, and by the clamours of the people to be led forth to battle. "Allah!" exclaimed he, "thou knowest my heart; thou knowest I have been true in my faith to this Christian monarch: I have offered to hold Loxa as his vassal, but he has preferred to approach it as an enemy: on his head be the infraction of our treaty."

Boabdil was not wanting in courage, he only needed decision: when he had once made up his mind, he acted vigorously; the misfortune was, he either did not make it up at all, or he made it up too late. He who decides tardily, generally acts rashly, endeavouring to make up by hurry of action for slowness of deliberation. Boabdil hastily buckled on his armour and sallied forth, surrounded by his guards, and at the head of five hundred horse and four thousand foot, the flower of his army. Some he detached to skirmish with the Christians, who were scattered and perplexed in the valley, and to prevent their concentrating their forces, while, with his main body, he pressed forward, to drive the enemy from the height of Albohacen, before they had time to collect there in any number, or to fortify themselves, in that important position.

The worthy Count de Cabra was yet entangled with his cavalry, among the water courses of the valley, when he heard the war cries of the Moors, and saw their army rushing over the bridge: He recognized Boabdil himself by his splendid armour, the magnificent caparison of his steed, and the brilliant guard which surrounded him. The royal host swept on toward the height of Albohacen, an intervening hill hid it from his sight, but loud shouts and cries, the din of drums and trumpets, and the reports of arquebusses gave note that the battle had begun.

Here was a royal prize in the field, and the Count de Cabra unable to get into the action! The good cavalier was in an agony of impatience; every attempt to force his way across the valley, only plunged him into new difficulties; at length, after many eager but ineffectual efforts, he was obliged to order his troops to dismount, and slowly, and carefully to lead their horses back, along slippery paths, and amid plashes of mire and water, where often there was scarce a foothold. The good count groaned in spirit, and sweat with mere impatience as he went, fearing the battle might be fought and the prize won or lost, before he could reach the field. Having at length toilfully unravelled the mazes of the valley, and arrived at firmer ground, he ordered his troops, to mount and led them full gallop to the height. Part of the good count's wishes were satisfied, but the dearest were disappointed. He came in season to partake of the very hottest of the fight, but the royal prize was no longer in the field.

Boabdil had led on his men with impetuous valour, or rather with hurried rashness. Heedlessly exposing himself in the front of the battle, he received two wounds in the very first encounter. His guards rallied round him, defended him with matchless valour, and bore him bleeding out of the action. The Count de Cabra arrived just in time to see the loyal squadron crossing the bridge and slowly conveying their disabled monarch towards the gate of the city.

The departure of Boabdil made no difference in the fury of the battle. A Moorish warrior dark and terrible in aspect, mounted on a black charger, and followed by a band of savage Gomeres rushed forward to take the lead. It was Hamet el Zegri the fierce Alcayde of Ronda, with the remnant of his once redoubtable garrison. Animated by his example the Moors renewed their assaults upon the height. It was bravely defended on one side by the Marquis of Cadiz, on another by Don Alonzo de Aguilar, and as fast as the Moors ascended they were driven back and dashed down the declivities. The Count de Ureña took his stand upon the fatal spot where his brother had fallen, his followers entered with zeal into the feelings of their commander, and heaps of the enemy, sunk beneath their weapons, sacrifices to the manes of the lamented Master of Calatrava.

The battle continued with incredible obstinacy. The Moors knew the importance of the height to the safety of the city; the cavaliers felt their honours staked to maintain it. Fresh supplies of troops were poured out of the city; some battled on the height, while some attacked the Christians who were still in the valley, and among the orchards and gardens, to prevent their uniting their forces. The troops in the valley were gradually driven back, and the whole host of the Moors swept around the height of Albohacen. The situation of the Marquis de Cadiz and his companions, was perilous in the extreme; they were a mere handful, and while they were fighting hand to hand with the Moors who assailed the height, they were galled from a distance, by the cross-bows, and arquebusses, of a host that augmented each moment in number. At this critical juncture King Ferdinand emerged from the mountains with the main-body of the army, and advanced to an eminence commanding a full view of the field of action. By his side was the noble English cavalier the Earl of Rivers. This was the first time he had witnessed a scene of Moorish warfare. He looked with eager interest at the chance-medley fight before him, where there was the wild career of cavalry, the irregular and tumultuous rush of infantry, and where Christian helm and Moorish turban, were intermingled in deadly struggle. The high blood of the English knight mounted at the sight, and his soul was stirred within him by the confused war cries, the clangour of drums and trumpets, and the reports of arquebusses, that came echoing up the mountains. Seeing the King was sending a reinforcement to the field, he entreated permission to mingle in the affray and fight according to the fashion of his country. His request being granted he alighted from his steed; he was merely armed *en blanco*, that is to say, with morion, back piece and breast-plate, his sword was girded by his side, and in his hand he wielded a powerful battle axe. He was followed by a body of his yeomen, armed in like manner, and by a band of archers, with bows made of the tough English yew-tree. The earl turned to his troops and addressed them briefly and bluntly according to the manner of his country. "Remember, my merry men all," said he, "the eyes of strangers are upon you; you are in a foreign land fighting for the glory of God, and the honour of merry old England!" A loud shout was the reply. The earl waved his battle axe over his head. "S' George for England!" cried he, and to the inspiring sound of this old English war cry, he and his followers rushed down to the battle with manly and courageous hearts.*

They soon made their way into the midst of the enemy, but, when engaged in the hottest of the fight, they made no shouts or outcries. They pressed steadily forward, dealing their blows to right and left, hewing down the Moors, and cutting their way with their battle axes, like woodmen in a forest, while the archers, pressing into the opening they made, plied their bows vigorously and spread death on every side.

When the Castilian mountaineers beheld the valour of the English yeomanry, they would not be out done in hardihood; they could not vie with them in weight or bulk, but for vigour and activity they were surpassed by none. They kept pace with them, therefore, with equal heart, and rival prowess, and gave a brave support to the stout Englishmen.

The Moors were confounded by the fury of these assaults, and disheart-

*Cura de Los Palacios.

ened by the loss of Hamet el Zegri, who was carried wounded from the field. They gradually fell back upon the bridge, the Christians followed up their advantage, and drove them over it tumultuously. The Moors retreated into the suburb, and Lord Rivers and his troops entered with them pell-mell, fighting in the streets and in the houses. King Ferdinand came up to the scene of action with his royal guard, and the infidels were driven within the city walls. Thus were the suburbs gained by the hardihood of the English lord, without such an event having been premeditated.*

The Earl of Rivers, notwithstanding he had received a wound, still urged forward in the attack. He penetrated almost to the city gate, in defiance of a shower of missiles that slew many of his followers. A stone, hurled from the battlements, checked his impetuous career. It struck him in the face, dashed out two of his front teeth, and laid him senseless on the earth. He was removed to a short distance by his men; but recovering his senses, refused to permit himself to be taken from the suburb.

When the contest was over, the streets presented a piteous spectacle, so many of their inhabitants had died in the defence of their thresholds, or been slaughtered without resistance. Among the victims was a poor weaver who had been at work in his dwelling at this turbulent moment. His wife urged him to fly into the city. "Why should I fly?" said the Moor; "to be reserved for hunger and slavery? I tell you wife, I will await the foe here, for better is it to die quickly by the steel, than to perish piecemeal in chains and dungeons." He said no more, but resumed his occupation of weaving, and in the indiscriminate fury of the assault, was slaughtered at his loom.†

The Christians remained masters of the field, and proceeded to pitch three encampments for the prosecution of the siege. The King, with the great body of the army, took a position on the side of the city next to Granada; the Marquis of Cadiz and his brave companions once more pitched their tents upon the height of Sancto Albohacen, but the English earl planted his standard sturdily within the suburb he had taken.

CHAPTER XL

CONCLUSION OF THE SIEGE OF LOXA.

Having possession of the heights of Albohacen and the suburb of the city the Christians were enabled to choose the most favorable situations for their batteries. They immediately destroyed the stone bridge, by which the gar-

*Cura de Los Palacios. Ms.
†Pulgar Part 3. Cap 58.

rison had made its sallies; and they threw two wooden bridges across the river, and others over the canals and streams, so as to establish an easy communication between the different camps.

When all was arranged a heavy fire was opened upon the city from various points. They threw not only balls of stone and iron but great carcasses of fire, which burst like meteors on the houses wrapping them instantly in a blaze. The walls were shattered and the towers toppled down by tremendous discharges from the lombards. Through the openings thus made they could behold the interior of the city; houses tumbling down or in flames, men, women and children flying in terror through the streets, and slaughtered by the shower of missiles, sent through these openings from smaller artillery, and from cross bows and arquebusses.

The Moors attempted to repair the breaches, but fresh discharges from the lombards buried them beneath the ruins of the walls they were mending. In their despair many of the inhabitants rushed forth into the narrow streets of the suburbs and assailed the Christians with darts, scymetars and poniards, seeking to destroy rather than defend, and heedless of death, in the confidence that to die fighting with an unbeliever, was to be translated at once to paradise.

For two nights and a day this awful scene continued; when certain of the principal inhabitants began to reflect upon the hopelessness of the conflict. Their King was disabled; their principal captains were either killed or wounded, their fortifications little better than heaps of ruins. They had urged the unfortunate Boabdil to the conflict; they now clamoured for a capitulation. A parley was procured from the Christian monarch and the terms of surrender were soon adjusted. They were to yield up the city immediately, with all their Christian captives, and to sally forth with as much of their property as they could take with them. The Marquis of Cadiz, on whose honour and humanity they had great reliance, was to escort them to Granada, to protect them from assault or robbery; such as chose to remain in Spain were to be permitted to reside in Castile, Aragon or Valencia. As to Boabdil el Chico, he was to do homage as vassal to King Ferdinand, but no charge was to be urged against him of having violated his former pledge. If he should yield up all pretensions to Granada, the title of Duke of Guadix was to be assigned to him, and the territory thereto annexed, provided it should be recovered from El Zagal within six months.

The capitulation being arranged, they gave as hostages the alcayde of the city, and the principal officers, together with the sons of their late chieftain the veteran Ali Atar. The warriors of Loxa then issued forth, humbled and dejected at having to surrender those walls which they had so long maintained with valour and renown; and the women and children filled the air with lamentations at being exiled from their native homes.

Last came forth Boabdil, most truly called El Zogoybi, the unlucky. Accustomed, as he was, to be crowned and uncrowned, to be ransomed and treated as a matter of bargain, he had acceded of course to the capitulation. He was enfeebled by his wounds and had an air of dejection; yet it is said his conscience acquitted him of a breach of faith towards the Castilian sovereigns, and the personal valour he had displayed, had caused a sympathy for him among many of the Christian cavaliers. He knelt to Ferdinand, according to the forms of vassalage, and then departed in melancholy mood, for Priego, a town about three leagues distant.

Ferdinand immediately ordered Loxa to be repaired and strongly garrisoned. He was greatly elated at the capture of this place, in consequence of his former defeat before its walls. He passed great encomiums upon the commanders who had distinguished themselves; and historians dwell particularly upon his visit to the tent of the English earl. His majesty consoled him for the loss of his teeth, by the consideration that he might otherwise have lost them by natural decay; whereas the lack of them would now be esteemed a beauty rather than a defect, serving as a trophy of the glorious cause in which he had been engaged.

The earl replied that he gave thanks to God and to the holy virgin for being thus honoured by a visit from the most potent King in Christendom; that he accepted, with all gratitude, his gracious consolation for the loss of his teeth, though he held it little to lose two teeth in the service of God, who had given him all. "A speech," says Fray Antonio Agapida, "full of most courtly wit and Christian piety; and one only marvels that it should be made by a native of an island so far distant from Castile."

CHAPTER XLI

CAPTURE OF ILLORA.

King Ferdinand followed up his victory at Loxa by laying siege to the strong town of Illora. This redoubtable fortress was perched upon a high rock in the midst of a spacious valley. It was within four leagues of the Moorish capital, and its lofty castle keeping vigilant watch over a wide circuit of country, was termed the right eye of Granada.

The Alcayde of Illora was one of the bravest of the Moorish commanders, and made every preparation to defend his fortress to the last extremity. He sent the women and children, the aged and infirm, to the metropolis. He placed barricadoes in the suburbs, opened doors of communication from house to house, and pierced their walls with loop holes for the discharge of crossbows, arquebusses and other missiles.

King Ferdinand arrived before the place with all his forces; he stationed himself upon the hill of Encinilla, and distributed the other encampments in various situations, so as to invest the fortress. Knowing the valiant character of the alcayde and the desperate courage of the Moors, he ordered the encampments to be fortified with trenches and pallisadoes, the guards to be doubled, and centinels to be placed in all the watch towers of the adjacent heights.

When all was ready the Duke del Infantado demanded the attack; it was his first campaign, and he was anxious to disprove the royal insinuation made against the hardihood of his embroidered chivalry. King Ferdinand granted his demand, with a becoming compliment to his spirit; he ordered the Count de Cabra to make a simultaneous attack upon a different quarter. Both chiefs led forth their troops, those of the duke in fresh and brilliant armour, richly ornamented, and as yet uninjured by the service of the field. Those of the count were weather beaten veterans, whose armour was dented and hacked in many a hard fought battle. The youthful duke blushed at the contrast. "Cavaliers," cried he, "we have been reproached with the finery of our array; let us prove that a trenchant blade may rest in a gilded sheath. Forward! to the foe! and I trust in God that as we enter this affray knights well accoutered, so we shall leave it cavaliers well proved." His men responded by eager acclamations, and the duke led them forward to the assault. He advanced under a tremendous shower of stones, darts, balls and arrows, but nothing could check his career; he entered the suburb sword in hand, his men fought furiously, though with great loss, for every dwelling had been turned into a fortress. After a severe conflict, they succeeded in driving the Moors into the town, about the same time that the other suburb was carried by the Count de Cabra and his veterans. The troops of the Duke del Infantado came out of the contest thinned in number and covered with blood, and dust and wounds; they received the highest encomiums of the King, and there was never afterwards any sneer at their embroidery.

The suburbs being taken, three batteries, each furnished with eight large lombards were opened upon the fortress. The damage and havock were tremendous, for the fortifications had not been constructed to withstand such engines. The towers were over-thrown, the walls battered to pieces; the interior of the place was all exposed, houses demolished, and many people slain. The Moors were terrified by the tumbling ruins and the tremendous din. The alcayde had resolved to defend the place until the last extremity; he beheld it a heap of rubbish, there was no prospect of aid from Granada, his people had lost all spirit to fight and were vociferous for a surrender. With a reluctant heart he capitulated. The inhabitants were permitted to depart with all their effects, excepting their arms; and were escorted in safety by the Duke del Infantado and the Count de Cabra, to the Bridge of Pinos within two leagues of Granada.

King Ferdinand gave directions to repair the fortifications of Illora and to place it in a strong state of defence. He left as alcayde of the town and fortress Gonzalvo de Cordova, younger brother of Don Alonzo de Aguilar. This gallant cavalier was captain of the royal guards of Ferdinand and Isabella, and gave already proofs of that prowess which afterwards rendered him so renowned.

CHAPTER XLII

OF THE ARRIVAL OF QUEEN ISABELLA AT THE CAMP BEFORE MOCLIN, AND OF THE PLEASANT SAYINGS OF THE ENGLISH EARL.

The war of Granada, however poets may embroider it with the flowers of their fancy, was certainly one of the sternest of those iron conflicts which have been celebrated under the name of holy wars. The worthy Fray Antonio Agapida dwells with unsated delight upon the succession of rugged mountain enterprizes, bloody battles and merciless sackings and ravages which characterize it; yet we find him on one occasion pausing in the full career of victory over the infidels, to detail a stately pageant of the Catholic sovereigns.

Immediately on the capture of Loxa Ferdinand had written to Isabella soliciting her presence at the camp, that he might consult with her as to the disposition of their newly acquired territories.

It was in the early part of June that the Queen departed from Cordova, with the princess Isabella and numerous ladies of her court. She had a glorious attendance of cavaliers and pages with many guards and domestics. There were forty sumpter mules for the use of the Queen, the princess and their train.

As this courtly cavalcade approached the Rock of the Lovers on the banks of the river Yeguas, they beheld a splendid train of knights advancing to meet them. It was headed by that accomplished cavalier the Marquis Duke of Cadiz, accompanied by the Adelantado of Andalusia. He had left the camp the day after the capture of Illora and advanced thus far to receive the Queen and escort her over the borders. The Queen received the marquis with distinguished honour, for he was esteemed as the mirror of chivalry. His actions in this war had become the theme of every tongue and many hesitated not to compare him in prowess to the immortal Cid.*

*Cura de Los Palacios.

Thus gallantly attended the Queen entered the vanquished frontier of
Granada, journeying securely along the pleasant banks of the Xenel, so lately subject to the scourings of the Moors. She stopped at Loxa, where she
administered aid and consolation to the wounded, distributing money
among them for their support, according to their rank.

The King after the capture of Illora had removed his camp before the
fortress of Moclin with an intention of besieging it. Thither the Queen proceeded, still escorted through the mountain roads by the Marquis of Cadiz.
As Isabella drew near to the camp, the Duke del Infantado issued forth a
league and a half to receive her; magnificently arrayed and followed by all
his chivalry in glorious attire. With him came the standard of Seville borne
by the men at arms of that renowned city, and the prior of S' Juan with his
followers. They arranged themselves in order of battle on the left of the road
by which the Queen was to pass. The worthy Agapida is loyally minute in
his description of the state and grandeur of the Catholic sovereigns. The
Queen rode a chestnut mule, seated in a magnificent saddle chair, decorated
with silver gilt. The housings of the mule were of fine crimson cloth; the
borders embroidered with gold; the reins and headpiece were of satin, curiously embossed with needlework of silk, and wrought with golden letters.
The Queen wore a brial or royal skirt of velvet, under which were others of
brocade; a scarlet mantle ornamented in the moresco fashion, and a black
hat embroidered round the crown and brim.

The Infanta was likewise mounted on a chestnut mule richly caparisoned.
She wore a brial or skirt of black brocade, and a black mantle ornamented
like that of the Queen.

When the royal cavalcade passed by the chivalry of the Duke del Infantado which was drawn out in battle array, the Queen made a reverence to
the standard of Seville and ordered it to pass to the right hand. When she
approached the camp the multitude ran forth to meet her, with great demonstrations of joy; for she was universally beloved by her subjects. All the
battalions sallied forth in military array, bearing the various standards and
banners of the camp, which were lowered in salutation as she passed.

The King now came forth in royal state mounted on a superb chestnut
horse and attended by many grandees of Castile. He wore a jubon or close
vest of crimson cloth, with cuisses, or short skirts of yellow satin; a loose
cassock of brocade, a rich Moorish scymetar and a hat with plumes. The
grandees who attended him were arrayed with wonderful magnificence,
each according to his taste and invention.

These high and mighty princes, says Antonio Agapida, regarded each other with great deference as allied sovereigns, rather than with connubial familiarity, as mere husband and wife; when they approached each other
therefore, before embracing, they made three profound reverences, the
Queen taking off her hat, and remaining in a silk net or cawl, with her face
uncovered. The King then approached and embraced her and kissed her

respectfully on the cheek. He also embraced his daughter the princess, and, making the sign of the cross, he blessed her and kissed her on the lips.*

The good Agapida seems scarcely to have been more struck with the appearance of the sovereigns than with that of the English earl. He followed, says he, immediately after the King, with great pomp and in an extraordinary manner; taking precedence of all the rest. He was mounted *à la guisa* or with long stirrups, on a superb chestnut horse, with trappings of azure silk which reached to the ground. The housings were of mulberry powdered with stars of gold. He was armed in proof, and wore over his armour a short French mantle of black brocade; he had a white French hat with plumes, and carried on his left arm a small round buckler, banded with gold. Five pages attended him, apparelled in silk and brocade, and mounted on horses sumptuously caparisoned; he had also a train of followers, bravely attired after the fashion of his country.

He advanced in a chivalrous and courteous manner, making his reverences first to the Queen and Infanta, and afterwards to the King. Queen Isabella received him graciously, complimenting him on his courageous conduct at Loxa, and condoling with him on the loss of his teeth. The Earl, however, made light of his disfiguring wound; saying that "our blessed Lord who had built all that house, had opened a window there, that he might see more readily what passed within."†

Whereupon the worthy Fray Antonio Agapida is more than ever astonished at the pregnant wit of this island cavalier. The earl continued some little distance, by the side of the royal family, complimenting them all with courteous speeches, his horse curvetting and carricoling, but being managed with great grace and dexterity, leaving the grandees and the people at large, not more filled with admiration at the strangeness and magnificence of his state, than at the excellence of his horsemanship.‡

To testify her sense of the gallantry and services of this noble English knight who had come from so far to assist in their wars, the Queen sent him the next day presents of twelve horses, with stately tents, fine linen, two beds with coverings of gold brocade and many other articles of great value.**

---

*Cura de Los Palacios.

†Pietro Martyr Epist 61.

‡Cura de Los Palacios.

**Note. The description of this royal pageant and the particulars concerning the English earl, thus given from the manuscript of Fray Antonio Agapida, agree precisely with the chronicle of Andres Bernaldes the curate of Los Palacios. The English earl makes no further figure in this war. It appears from various histories that he returned in the course of the year to England. In the following year his passion for fighting took him to the continent at the head of four hundred adventurers, in aid of Francis Duke of Brittany, against Louis XI of France. He was killed in the same year (1488) in the battle of S' Albans, between the Bretons and the French.

Having refreshed himself, as it were, with the description of this progress of Queen Isabella to the camp, and the glorious pomp of the Catholic sovereigns, the worthy Antonio Agapida returns with renewed relish to his pious work of discomfiting the Moors.

CHAPTER XLIII

HOW KING FERDINAND ATTACKED MOCLIN; AND OF THE STRANGE EVENTS THAT ATTENDED ITS CAPTURE.

"The Catholic sovereigns," says Fray Antonio Agapida, "had by this time closely clipped the right wing of the Moorish vulture." In other words, most of the strong fortresses along the western frontier of Granada had fallen beneath the Christian artillery. The army now lay encamped before the town of Moclin on the frontier of Jaen, one of the most stubborn fortresses of the border. It stood on a high rocky hill, the base of which was nearly girdled by a river. A thick forest protected the back part of the town towards the mountain. Thus strongly situated, it domineered, with its frowning battlements and massive towers, all the mountain passes into that part of the country, and was called "the shield of Granada." It had a double arrear of blood to settle with the Christians; two hundred years before, a Master of Santiago and all his cavaliers had been lanced by the Moors before its gates. It had recently made terrible slaughter among the troops of the good Count de Cabra, in his precipitate attempt to entrap the old Moorish monarch. The pride of Ferdinand had been piqued by being obliged on that occasion to recede from his plan, and abandon his concerted attack on the place, he was now prepared to take a full revenge.

El Zagal, the old warrior King of Granada, anticipating a second attempt, had provided the place with ample munitions and provisions; had ordered trenches to be digged and additional bulwarks thrown up, and caused all the old men, the women, and the children to be removed to the capital.

Such was the strength of the fortress and the difficulties of its position that Ferdinand anticipated much trouble in reducing it, and made every preparation for a regular siege. In the centre of his camp were two great mounds, one of sacks of flour, the other of grain, which were called the royal granary. Three batteries of heavy ordnance were opened against the citadel and principal towers, while smaller artillery, engines for the discharge of missiles, arquebusses and crossbows were distributed, in various places, to keep up a fire into any breaches that might be made, and upon those of the garrison who should appear on the battlements.

The lombards soon made an impression on the works, demolishing a part of the wall and tumbling down several of those haughty towers which from their height had been impregnable before the invention of gunpowder. The Moors repaired their walls as well as they were able, and still confiding in the strength of their situation, kept up a resolute defence, firing down from their lofty battlements and towers upon the Christian camp. For two nights and a day an incessant fire was kept up, so that there was not a moment in which the roaring of ordnance was not heard, or some damage sustained by the Christians or the Moors. It was a conflict, however, more of engineers and artillerists than of gallant cavaliers; there was no sally of troops, or shock of armed men or rush and charge of cavalry. The knights stood looking on with idle weapons, waiting until they should have an opportunity of signalizing their prowess by scaling the walls or storming the breaches. As the place, however, was assailable only in one part, there was every prospect of a long and obstinate resistance.

The engineers, as usual, discharged not merely balls of stone and iron, to demolish the walls, but flaming balls of inextinguishable combustibles, designed to set fire to the houses. One of these which passed high through the air like a meteor, sending out sparks and crackling as it went, entered the window of a tower which was used as a magazine of gunpowder. The tower blew up with a tremendous explosion, the Moors who were upon its battlements were hurled into the air and fell mangled in various parts of the town, and the houses in its vicinity were rent and overthrown as with an earthquake.

The Moors, who had never witnessed an explosion of the kind, ascribed the destruction of the tower to a miracle; some who had seen the descent of the flaming ball imagined that fire had fallen from heaven to punish them for their pertinacity. The pious Agapida himself, believes that this fiery missive was conducted by divine agency, to confound the infidels, an opinion in which he is supported by other Catholic historians.*

Seeing heaven and earth as it were combined against them, the Moors lost all heart: and capitulated, and were permitted to depart with their effects leaving behind all arms and munitions of war.

The Catholic army, says Antonio Agapida, entered Moclin in solemn state, not as a licentious host, intent upon plunder and desolation, but as a band of Christian warriors, coming to purify and regenerate the land. The standard of the cross, that ensign of this holy crusade, was borne in the advance, followed by the other banners of the army. Then came the King and Queen

---

*Pulgar. Garibay. Lucio Marino Siculo. Cosas memorab. de Hispan Lib. 20.

at the head of a vast number of armed cavaliers. They were accompanied by a band of priests and friars, with the choir of the royal chapel, chaunting the canticle *Te deum laudamus*. As they were moving through the streets in this solemn manner, every sound hushed excepting the anthem of the choir, they suddenly heard, issuing as it were from under ground a chorus of voices chaunting the solemn response, *"Benedictum qui venit in nomine domine."** The procession paused in wonder. The sounds arose from Christian captives, and among them several priests, who were confined in subterraneous dungeons.

The heart of Isabella was greatly touched; she ordered the captives to be drawn forth from their cells, and was still more moved at beholding by their wan, discoloured and emaciated appearance, how much they had suffered. Their hair and beards were overgrown and shagged, they were wasted by hunger, half naked and in chains. She ordered that they should be clothed and cherished, and money furnished them to bear them to their homes.†

Several of the captives were brave cavaliers, who had been wounded and made prisoners, in the defeat of the Count de Cabra by El Zagal in the preceding year. There were also found other melancholy traces of that disastrous affair. On visiting the narrow pass where the defeat had taken place the remains of several Christian warriors were found in thickets, or hidden behind rocks, or in the clefts of the mountains. These were some who had been struck from their horses and wounded too severely to fly. They had crawled away from the scene of action and concealed themselves to avoid falling into the hands of the enemy, and had thus perished miserably and alone. The remains of those of note were known by their armour and devices, and were mourned over by their companions who had shared the disasters of that day.‡

The Queen had these remains piously collected, as the reliques of so many martyrs who had fallen in the cause of the faith. They were interred with great solemnity in the mosques of Moclin, which had been purified and consecrated to Christian worship. "There," says Antonio Agapida, "rest the bones of those truly Catholic knights, in the holy ground which in a manner had been sanctified by their blood, and all pilgrims, passing through those mountains, offer up prayers and masses for the repose of their souls."

The Queen remained for some time at Moclin, administering comfort to the wounded and the prisoners, bringing the newly acquired territory into order, and founding churches and monasteries and other pious institutions. "While the King marched in front, laying waste the land of the philistines," says the figurative Antonio Agapida, "Queen Isabella followed his traces as

*Marino Siculo.
†Illescas Hist. Pontif. lib 6. c 20. § 1.
‡Pulgar part 3 Cap 61.

the binder follows the reaper, gathering and garnering the rich harvest that has fallen beneath his sickle. In this she was greatly assisted by the councils of that cloud of bishops, friars and other saintly men, which continually surrounded her, garnering the first fruits of this infidel land into the granaries of the church." Leaving her thus piously employed the King pursued his career of conquest, determined to lay waste the vega and carry fire and sword to the very gates of Granada.

CHAPTER XLIV

HOW KING FERDINAND FORAGED THE VEGA; AND OF THE BATTLE OF THE BRIDGE OF PINOS, AND THE FATE OF THE TWO MOORISH BROTHERS.

Muley Abdalla el Zagal had been under a spell of ill fortune, ever since the suspicious death of the old King his brother. Success had deserted his standard, and with his fickle subjects, want of success was one of the greatest crimes in a sovereign. He found his popularity declining, and he lost all confidence in his people. The Christian army marched in open defiance through his territories and set down deliberately before his fortresses, yet, he dared not lead forth his legions to oppose them, lest the inhabitants of the Albaycin, ever ripe for a revolt, should rise, and shut the gates of Granada against his return.

Every few days some melancholy train entered the metropolis, the inhabitants of some captured town bearing the few effects that had been spared them, and weeping and bewailing the desolation of their homes. When the tidings arrived that Illora and Moclin had fallen, the people were seized with consternation. The "right eye of Granada" is extinguished, exclaimed they, the "shield of Granada" is broken, what shall protect us from the inroad of the foe? When the survivors of the garrisons of those towns arrived, with downcast looks, bearing the marks of battle, and destitute of arms and standards, the populace reviled them in their wrath; but they answered, "we fought as long as we had force to fight, or walls to shelter us, but the Christians laid our towers and battlements in ruins, and we looked in vain for aid from Granada."

The alcaydes of Illora and Moclin were brothers; they were alike in prowess and the bravest among the Moorish chevaliers: They had been the most distinguished in all tilts and tourneys which graced the happier days of Granada, and had distinguished themselves in the sterner conflicts of the field. Acclamation had always followed their banners, and they had long been the delight of the people. Yet now, when they returned after the capture of their fortresses, they were followed by the unsteady populace with execrations. The hearts of the alcaydes swelled with indignation; they found the ingratitude of their countrymen still more intolerable than the hostility of the Christians. Tidings came that the enemy was advancing with his triumphant legions to lay waste the country about Granada. Still El Zagal did not dare to take the field. The two alcaydes of Illora and Moclin stood before him: "We have defended your fortresses," said they, "until we were almost buried under their ruins, and for our reward we receive scoffings and revilings. Give us, Oh King, an opportunity where knightly valour may signalize itself; not shut up behind stone walls, but in the open conflict of the field. The enemy approaches to lay our country desolate, give us men to meet him in the advance, and let shame light upon our heads, if we be found wanting in the battle!"

The two brothers were sent forth with a large force of horse and foot; El Zagal intended, should they be successful, to issue forth with his whole force, and by a decisive victory repair the losses he had suffered. When the people saw the well known standards of the brothers going forth to battle, there was a feeble shout, but the alcaydes passed on with stern countenances, for they knew the same voices would curse them were they to return unfortunate. They cast a farewell look upon fair Granada, and upon the beautiful fields of their infancy, as if for these they were willing to lay down their lives, but not for an ungrateful people.

The army of Ferdinand had arrived within two leagues of Granada, at the Bridge of Pinos, a pass famous in the wars of the Moors and Christians, for many a bloody conflict. It was the pass by which the Castilian monarchs generally made their inroads, and was capable of great defense from the ruggedness of the country and the difficulty of the bridge. The King, with the main body of the army, had attained the brow of a hill, when they beheld the advance guard, under the Marquis of Cadiz and the Master of Santiago, furiously attacked by the enemy, in the vicinity of the bridge. The Moors rushed to the assault with their usual shouts, but with more than usual ferocity. There was a hard struggle at the bridge, both parties knew the importance of that pass. The King particularly noted the prowess of two Moorish cavaliers, alike in arms and devices and who by their bearing and attendance he perceived to be commanders of the enemy. They were the two brothers, the Alcaydes of Illora and Moclin. Wherever they turned they carried confusion and death into the ranks of the Christians, but they fought with desperation rather than valour. The Count de Cabra and his brother Don Martin de Cordova pressed forward with eagerness against them, but having advanced too precipitately were surrounded by the foe and in imminent danger. A young Christian knight seeing their peril hastened with his followers to their relief. The King recognized him for Don Juan de Ara-

gon, Count of Ribargoza, his own nephew, for he was illegitimate son of the
Duke of Villahermosa, illegitimate brother of King Ferdinand. The splendid
armour of Don Juan, and the sumptuous caparison of his steed, rendered
him a brilliant object of attack. He was assailed on all sides and his superb
steed slain under him, yet still he fought valiantly, bearing for a time the
brunt of the fight, and giving the exhausted forces of the Count de Cabra
time to recover breath.

Seeing the peril of these troops and the general obstinacy of the fight, the
King ordered the royal standard to be advanced, and hastened with all his
forces to the relief of the Count de Cabra. At his approach the enemy gave
way and retreated towards the bridge. The two Moorish commanders endeavoured to rally their troops and animate them to defend this pass to the
utmost. They used prayers, remonstrances, menaces, but almost in vain.
They could only collect a scanty handful of cavaliers; with these they planted
themselves at the head of the bridge, and disputed it inch by inch. The fight
was hot and obstinate, for but few could contend hand to hand, yet many
discharged cross-bows and arquebusses, from the banks. The river was covered with the floating bodies of the slain. The Moorish band of cavaliers was
almost entirely cut to pieces; the two brothers fell covered with wounds
upon the bridge they had so resolutely defended. They had given up the
battle for lost, but had determined not to return alive to ungrateful Granada.
When the people of the capital heard how devotedly they had fallen, they
lamented greatly their deaths, and extolled their memory. A column was
erected to their honour in the vicinity of the bridge which long went by the
name of "The tomb of the brothers."

The army of Ferdinand now marched on and established its camp in the
vicinity of Granada. The worthy Agapida gives many triumphant details of
the ravages committed in the vega, which was again laid waste; the grain
fruits and other productions of the earth destroyed; and that earthly paradise
rendered a dreary desert. He narrates several fierce but ineffectual salleys
and skirmishes of the Moors in defence of their favourite plain; among which
one deserves to be mentioned, as it records the achievement of one of the
saintly heroes of this war.

During one of the movements of the Christian army near the walls of
Granada, a batallion of fifteen hundred cavalry and a large force of foot,
had sallied from the city and posted themselves near some gardens which
were surrounded by a canal, and traversed by ditches for the purpose of
irrigation.

The Moors beheld the Duke del Infantado pass by with his two splendid
batallions; one of men at arms the other of light cavalry armed *á la gineta*.
In company with him, but following as a rear guard, was Don Garcia Osorio,
the belligerent Bishop of Jaen, attended by Francisco Bovadillo the corregidor of his city, and followed by two squadrons of men at arms, from Jaen,

Anduxar, Ubeda and Baeza.* The success of last year's campaign had given the good bishop an inclination for warlike affairs, and he had once more buckled on his cuirass.

The Moors were much given to stratagem in warfare. They looked wistfully at the magnificent squadrons of the Duke del Infantado; but their martial discipline precluded all attack. The good bishop promised to be a more easy prey. Suffering the duke and his troops to pass unmolested, they approached the squadrons of the bishop, and making a pretended attack, skirmished slightly, and fled in apparent confusion. The bishop considered the day his own, and seconded by his corregidor Bovadillo, followed with valourous precipitation. The Moors fled into the *Huerta del Rey,* or orchard of the King; the troops of the bishop followed hotly after them. When the Moors perceived their pursuers fairly embarrassed among the intricacies of the garden, they turned fiercely upon them, while some of their number threw open the sluices of the Xenel. In an instant the canal, which encircled, and the ditches which traversed the garden, were filled with water, and the valiant bishop and his followers found themselves overwhelmed by a deluge.† A scene of great confusion succeeded. Some of the men of Jaen, stoutest of heart and hand, fought with the Moors in the garden, while others struggled with the water, endeavouring to escape across the canal, in which attempt many horses were drowned. Fortunately, the Duke del Infantado perceived the snare into which his companions had fallen, and dispatched his light cavalry to their assistance. The Moors were compelled to flight, and driven along the road of Elvira up to the gates of Granada. Several Christian cavaliers perished in this affray; the bishop himself escaped with difficulty, having slipped from his saddle in crossing the canal, but saving himself by holding on to the tail of his charger. This perilous achievement seems to have satisfied the good bishop's belligerent propensities. He retired on his laurels, says Agapida, to his city of Jaen, where on the fruition of all good things, he gradually waxed too corpulent for his corselet, which was hung up in the Hall of his Episcopal palace; and we hear no more of his military deeds throughout the residue of the holy war of Granada.‡

King Ferdinand having completed his ravage of the vega, and kept El Zagal shut up in his capital, conducted his army back through the pass of Lope to rejoin Queen Isabella at Moclin. The fortresses lately taken being well garrisoned and supplied, he gave the command of the frontier to his

---

*Pulgar. Part 3. Cap 62.

†Pulgar.

‡Don Luis Osorio fué Obispo de Jaen des de el año de 1483, y presidió in esta Iglesia hasta el de 1496 en que murió en Handes, á donde fué acompañando á la Princesa Doña Juana, esposa del Archiduque Don Felipe.

España Sagrada. Por Fr: M. Bisco Tom. 41. Trat 77 Cap 4.

cousin Don Fadrique de Toledo, afterwards so famous in the Netherlands as the Duke of Alba. The campaign being thus completely crowned with success the sovereigns returned in triumph to the city of Cordova.

CHAPTER XLV

ATTEMPT OF EL ZAGAL UPON THE LIFE OF BOABDIL; AND HOW THE LATTER WAS ROUSED TO ACTION.

No sooner did the last squadron of Christian cavalry disappear behind the mountain of Elvira, and the note of its trumpets die away upon the ear, than the long suppressed wrath of old Muley el Zagal burst forth. He determined no longer to be half a King, reigning over a divided kingdom, in a divided capital, but to exterminate by any means, fair or foul, his nephew Boabdil and his faction. He turned furiously upon those whose factious conduct had deterred him from sallying upon the foe; some he punished by confiscations, others by banishment, others by death. Once undisputed monarch of the entire kingdom, he trusted to his military skill to retrieve his fortune and drive the Christians over the frontier.

Boabdil, however, had again retired to Velez el Blanco, on the confines of Murcia, where he could avail himself, in case of emergency of any assistance or protection afforded him by the policy of Ferdinand. His defeat had blighted his reviving fortunes, for the people considered him as inevitably doomed to misfortune. Still, while he lived, El Zagal knew he would be a rallying point for faction, and liable at any moment to be elevated into power by the capricious multitude. He had recourse, therefore, to the most perfidious means to compass his destruction. He sent embassadors to him representing the necessity of concord for the salvation of the kingdom; and even offering to resign the title of King, and to become subject to his sway on receiving some estate on which he could live in tranquil retirement. But while the embassadors bore these words of peace, they were furnished with poisoned herbs, which they were to administer secretly to Boabdil; and if they failed in this attempt, they had pledged themselves to dispatch him openly, while engaged in conversation. They were instigated to this treason by promises of great reward, and by assurances from the alfaquis that Boabdil was an apostate, whose death would be acceptable to heaven.

The young monarch was secretly apprized of the concerted treason, and refused an audience to the embassadors. He denounced his uncle as the murderer of his father and his kindred and the usurper of his throne, and vowed never to relent, in hostility to him, until he should place his head on the walls of the Alhambra.

Open war again broke out between the two monarchs, though feebly carried on, in consequence of their mutual embarrassments. Ferdinand again extended his assistance to Boabdil, ordering the commanders of his fortresses to aid him in all enterprizes against his uncle, and against such places as refused to acknowledge him as King. And Don Juan de Benavides, who commanded in Lorca, even made inroads in his name, into the territories of Almeria, Baza and Guadix, which owned allegiance to El Zagal.

The unfortunate Boabdil had three great evils to contend with; the inconstancy of his subjects, the hostility of his uncle, and the friendship of Ferdinand. The last was by far the most baneful, his fortunes withered under it. He was looked upon as the enemy of his faith and of his country. The cities shut their gates against him: the people cursed him; even the scanty band of cavaliers who had hitherto followed his ill starred banner began to desert him; for he had not wherewithal to reward, or even to support them. His spirits sank with his fortune, and he feared that in a little time he should not have a spot of earth whereon to plant his standard nor an adherent to rally under it.

In the midst of his despondency he received a message from his lion hearted mother, the Sultana Ayxa la Horra. "For shame," said she, "to linger timorously about the borders of your kingdom, when a usurper is seated in your capital. Why look abroad for perfidious aid, when you have loyal hearts beating true to you in Granada. The Albaycin is ready to throw open its gates to receive you. Strike home vigorously. A sudden blow may mend all, or make an end. A throne, or a grave!—for a King there is no honourable medium."

Boabdil was of an undecided character, but there are circumstances which bring the most wavering to a decision, and when once resolved, they are apt to act with a daring impulse, unknown to steadier judgements. The message of the sultana roused him from a dream. Granada, beautiful Granada! with its stately Alhambra, its delicious gardens, its gushing and limpid fountains, sparkling among groves of orange, citron and myrtle, rose before him. "What have I done," exclaimed he, "that I should be an exile from this paradise of my forefathers, a wanderer and fugitive in my own kingdom, while a murderous usurper sits proudly upon my throne. Surely, Allah will befriend the righteous cause; one blow, and all may be my own."

He summoned his scanty band of cavaliers. "Who is ready to follow his monarch unto the death?" said he and every one laid his hand upon his scymetar. "Enough," said he, "let each man arm himself, and prepare his steed in secret for an enterprize of toil and peril; if we succeed our reward is Empire."

CHAPTER XLVI

HOW BOABDIL RETURNED SECRETLY TO GRANADA, AND HOW HE WAS RECEIVED.

"In the hand of God," exclaims an old Arabian chronicler, "is the destiny of princes; he alone giveth empire. A single Moorish horseman, mounted on a fleet Arabian steed, was one day traversing the mountains which extend between Granada and the frontier of Murcia. He galloped swiftly through the valleys but paused and looked out cautiously from the summit of every height. A squadron of cavaliers followed warily at a distance. There were fifty lances. The richness of their armour and attire shewed them to be warriors of noble rank and their leader had a lofty and princelike demeanour." The squadron thus described by the Arabian chronicler was the Moorish King Boabdil and his devoted followers.

For two nights and a day they pursued their adventurous journey, avoiding all populous parts of the country and choosing the most solitary passes of the mountains. They suffered severe hardships and fatigues but they suffered without a murmur. They were accustomed to rugged campaigning and their steeds were of generous and unyielding spirit. It was midnight and all was dark and silent as they descended from the mountains and approached the city of Granada. They passed along quietly under the shadow of its walls until they arrived near the gate of the Albaycin. Here Boabdil ordered his followers to halt and remain concealed. Taking but four or five with him he advanced resolutely to the gate, and knocked with the hilt of his scymetar. The guards demanded who sought to enter at that unseasonable hour. "Your King," exclaimed Boabdil, "open the gate and admit him."

The guards held forth a light and recognized the person of the youthful monarch. They were struck with sudden awe and threw open the gates, and Boabdil and his followers entered unmolested. They galloped to the dwellings of the principal inhabitants of the Albaycin, thundering at their portals, and summoning them to rise and take arms for their rightful sovereign. The summons was instantly obeyed; trumpets resounded throughout the streets, the gleam of torches and the flash of arms shewed the Moors hurrying to their gathering places, and by day break the whole force of the Albaycin was rallied under the standard of Boabdil. Such was the success of this sudden and desperate act of the young monarch; for we are assured by contemporary historians that there had been no previous concert or arrangement. "As the guards opened the gates of the city to admit him," observes a pious chronicler, "so God opened the hearts of the Moors to receive him as their King."*

In the morning early the tidings of this event roused El Zagal from his slumbers in the Alhambra. The fiery old warrior assembled his guard in haste and made his way sword in hand to the Albaycin, hoping to come upon

*Pulgar.

his nephew by surprize. He was vigorously met by Boabdil and his adherents, and driven back into the quarter of the Alhambra. An encounter took place between the two Kings in the square before the principal mosque: here they fought hand to hand with implacable fury, as though it had been agreed to decide their competition for the crown by single combat. In the tumult of this chance medley affray, however, they were separated, and the party of El Zagal was ultimately driven from the square.

The battle raged for some time in the streets and places of the city, but finding their powers of mischief cramped within such narrow limits both parties sallied forth into the fields and fought beneath the walls until evening. Many fell on both sides and at night each party withdrew into its quarter, until the morning gave them light to renew the unnatural conflict. For several days the two grand divisions of the city remained like hostile powers arrayed against each other. The party of the Alhambra was more numerous than that of the Albaycin and contained most of the nobility and chivalry, but the adherents of Boabdil were men hardened and strengthened by labour, and habitually skilled in the exercise of arms.

The Albaycin underwent a kind of siege by the forces of El Zagal: they effected breaches in the walls and made repeated attempts to carry it sword in hand but were as often repulsed. The troops of Boabdil, on the other hand, made frequent sallies, and in the conflicts which took place the hatred of the combatants arose to such a pitch of fury that no quarter was given on either side.

Boabdil perceived the inferiority of his force, he dreaded also that his adherents, being for the most part tradesmen and artizans, would become impatient of this interruption of their gainful occupations, and disheartened by these continual scenes of carnage. He sent missives, therefore, in all haste to Don Fadrique de Toledo who commanded the Christian forces on the frontier, entreating his assistance.

Don Fadrique had received instructions from the politic Ferdinand, to aid the youthful monarch in all his contests with his uncle. He advanced therefore with a body of troops near to Granada, but, wary lest some treachery might be intended, he stood for some time aloof, watching the movements of the parties. The furious and sanguinary nature of the conflicts, which distracted unhappy Granada, soon convinced him that there was no collusion between the monarchs. He sent Boabdil, therefore, a reinforcement of Christian foot soldiers and arquebusiers under Fernan Alverez de Sotomayer Alcayde of Colomara. This was as a fire brand thrown in to light up anew the flames of war in the city, which remained raging between the Moorish inhabitants for the space of fifty days.

CHAPTER XLVII

HOW KING FERDINAND LAID SIEGE
TO VELEZ MALAGA.

Hitherto the events of this renowned war have been little else than a succession of brilliant, but brief exploits, such as sudden forays and wild skirmishes among the mountains; or the surprizals of castles, fortresses and frontier towns. We approach now to more important and prolonged operations, in which ancient and mighty cities, the bulwarks of Granada were invested by powerful armies, subdued by slow and regular sieges, and thus the capital left naked and alone.

The glorious triumphs of the Catholic sovereigns, says Fray Antonio Agapida, had resounded throughout the east, and filled all heathenesse with alarm. The Grand Turk Bajazet II, and his deadly foe the Grand Soldan of Egypt, suspending for a time their bloody feuds, entered into a league to protect the religion of Mahomet and the Kingdom of Granada from the hostilities of the Christians. It was concerted between them that Bajazet should send a powerful armada against the island of Sicily, then appertaining to the Spanish crown, for the purpose of distracting the attention of the Castilian sovereigns, while, at the same time, great bodies of troops should be poured into Granada from the opposite coast of Africa.

Ferdinand and Isabella received timely intelligence of these designs. They resolved at once to carry the war into the sea board of Granada, to possess themselves of its ports, and thus, as it were, to bar the gates of the kingdom against all external aid. Malaga was to be the main object of attack: it was the principal seaport of the kingdom, and almost necessary to its existence. It had long been the seat of opulent commerce, sending many ships to the coasts of Syria and Egypt. It was, also, the great channel of communication with Africa, through which were introduced supplies of money, troops, arms and steeds from Tunis, Tripoli, Fez, Tremezan and other Barbary powers. It was emphatically called, therefore, the Hand and Mouth of Granada.

Before laying siege to this redoubtable city, however, it was deemed necessary to secure the neighbouring city of Velez Malaga, and its dependent places, which might otherwise harrass the besieging army.

For this important campaign the nobles of the kingdom were again summoned to take the field with their forces in the spring of 1487. The menaced invasion of the infidel powers of the East had awakened new ardour in the bosoms of all true Christian knights, and so zealously did they respond to the summons of the sovereigns that an army of twenty thousand cavalry and fifty thousand foot, the flower of Spanish warriors, led by the bravest of Spanish cavaliers, thronged the renowned city of Cordova at the appointed time.

On the night before this mighty host set forth upon its march an earthquake shook the city. The inhabitants, awakened by the shaking of the walls and rocking of the towers, fled to the courts and squares, fearing to be overwhelmed by the ruins of their dwellings. The earthquake was most violent in the quarter of the royal residence, the site of the ancient palace of the Moorish Kings. Many looked upon this as an omen of some impending evil, but Fray Antonio Agapida, in that infallible spirit of divination which succeeds an event, plainly reads in it a presage that the empire of the Moors was about to be shaken to its centre.

It was on Saturday, the eve of the Sunday of palms, says a worthy and loyal chronicler of the time, that the most Catholic monarch departed with his army to render service to heaven and make war upon the Moors.* Heavy rains had swelled all the streams and rendered the roads deep and difficult. The King therefore divided his host into two bodies. In one he put all the artillery, guarded by a strong body of horse and commanded by the Master of Alcantara and Martin Alonzo, Senior of Montemayor. This division was to proceed by the road through the valleys, where pasturage abounded for the oxen which drew the ordnance.

The main body of the army was led by the King in person. It was divided into numerous batallions, each commanded by some distinguished cavalier. The King took the rough and perilous road of the mountains, and few mountains are more rugged and difficult than those of Andalusia. The roads are mere mule paths straggling amidst rocks and along the verge of precipices; clambering vast craggy heights or descending into frightful chasms and ravines, with scanty and uncertain foothold for either man or steed. Four thousand pioneers were sent in advance, under the Alcayde de los Donzeles, to conquer, in some degree, the asperities of the road. Some had pick axes and crowbars to break the rocks, others had implements to construct bridges over the mountain torrents, while it was the duty of others to lay stepping stones in the smaller streams. As the country was inhabited by fierce Moorish mountaineers Don Diego de Castrillo was dispatched, with a body of horse and foot, to take possession of the heights and passes. Notwithstanding every precaution the royal army suffered excessively on its march. At one time there was no place to encamp for five leagues of the most toilsome and mountainous country, and many of the beasts of burden sank down and perished on the road.

It was with the greatest joy, therefore, that the royal army emerged from these stern and frightful defiles, and came to where they looked down upon the vega of Velez Malaga. The region before them was one of the most delectable to the eye that ever was ravaged by an army. Sheltered from every rude blast by a screen of mountains, and sloping and expanding to the south,

*Pulgar. Cronica de los Reyes Catholicos.

this lovely valley was quickened by the most generous sunshine, watered by the silver meanderings of the Velez, and refreshed by cooling breezes from the Mediterranean. The sloping hills were covered with vineyards and olive trees, the distant fields waved with grain, or were verdant with pasturage while around the city were delightful gardens, the favorite retreats of the Moors, where their white pavillions gleamed among groves of oranges, citrons and pomegranites, and were surmounted by stately palms, those plants of southern growth, bespeaking a generous climate and a cloudless sky.

In the upper part of this delightful valley the city of Velez Malaga reared its warrior battlements in stern contrast to the landscape. It was built on the declivity of a steep and insulated hill, and strongly fortified by walls and towers. The crest of the hill rose high above the town into a mere crag, inaccessible on every other side, and crowned by a powerful castle, which domineered over the surrounding country. Two suburbs swept down into the valley, from the skirts of the town and were defended by bulwarks and deep ditches. The vast ranges of grey mountains often capped with clouds, which rose to the north, were inhabited by a hardy and warlike race, whose strong fortresses of Comares, Camillas, Competa and Benemarhorga frowned down from cragged heights.

At the time that the Christian host arrived in sight of this valley a squadron was hovering on the smooth sea before it, displaying the banner of Castile. This was commanded by the Count of Trevento and consisted of four armed galleys, convoying a number of caravels, laden with supplies for the army.

After surveying the ground King Ferdinand encamped on the side of a mountain which advanced close to the city, and which was the last of a rugged sierra or chain of heights that extended quite to Granada. On the summit of this mountain, and overlooking the camp, was a Moorish town, powerfully fortified, called Bentomiz, and which, from its vicinity, had been considered capable of yielding great assistance to Velez Malaga. Several of the generals remonstrated with the King for choosing a post so exposed to assaults from the mountaineers. Ferdinand replied that he should thus cut off all communication between the town and the city; and that, as to the danger, his soldiers must keep the more vigilant guard against surprize.

King Ferdinand rode forth attended by several cavaliers and a small number of cuirassiers, appointing the various stations of the camp. While a body of foot soldiers was taking possession, as an advanced guard, of an important height which overlooked the city, the King retired to a tent to take refreshment. While at table he was startled by a sudden uproar, and looking forth beheld his soldiers flying before a superior force of the enemy. The King had on no other armour but a cuirass; seizing a lance, however, he sprang upon his horse and galloped to protect the fugitives, followed by his handful of knights and cuirassiers. When the Spaniards saw the King hastening to their aid they turned upon their pursuers. Ferdinand in his eagerness, threw himself into the midst of the foe. One of his grooms was killed beside him but before the Moor who slew him could escape the King transfixed him with his lance. He then sought to draw his sword, which hung at his saddle bow, but in vain. Never had he been exposed to such peril; he was surrounded by the enemy, without a weapon wherewith to defend himself.

In this moment of awful jeopardy the Marquis of Cadiz, the Count de Cabra, the Adelantado of Murcia with two other cavaliers, named Garcilasso de la Vega and Diego de Atayde, came galloping to the scene of action, and surrounding the King, made a loyal rampart of their bodies against the assaults of the Moors. The horse of the marquis was pierced by an arrow and that worthy cavalier exposed to imminent danger, but, with the aid of his valorous companions, he quickly put the enemy to flight and pursued them with slaughter to the very gates of the city.

When those loyal warriors returned from the pursuit they remonstrated with the King for exposing his life in personal conflict, seeing that he had so many valiant captains whose business it was to fight. They reminded him that the life of a prince was the life of his people, and that many a brave army was lost by the loss of its commander. They entreated him, therefore, in future, to protect them with the force of his mind in the cabinet rather than of his arm in the field.

Ferdinand acknowledged the wisdom of their advice, but declared that he could not see his people in peril without venturing his person to assist them. A reply, say the old chroniclers, which delighted the whole army, inasmuch as they saw that he not only governed them as a good King, but protected them as a valiant captain. Ferdinand, however, was conscious of the extreme peril to which he had been exposed, and made a vow never again to venture into battle, without having his sword girt to his side.*

When this achievement of the King was related to Isabella, she trembled amidst her joy at his safety; and afterwards, in memorial of the event, she granted to Velez Malaga, as the arms of the city, the figure of the King on horseback, with a groom lying dead at his feet, and the Moors flying.†

The camp was formed but the artillery was yet on the road, advancing with infinite labour at the rate of merely a league a day; for heavy rains had converted the streams of the valleys into raging torrents, and completely broken up the roads. In the mean time King Ferdinand ordered an assault on the suburbs of the city. They were carried after a sanguinary conflict of six hours, in which many Christian cavaliers were killed and wounded, and among the latter Don Alvaro of Portugal son of the Duke of Braganza. The suburbs were then fortified towards the city, with trenches and pallisades, and garrisoned by a chosen force under Don Fadrique de Toledo. Other

*Illescus. Hist. Pontif lib. 6 C 20. Vedmar Hist Velez Malaga.
†Idem.

trenches were digged round the city, and from the suburbs to the royal camp, so as to cut off all communication with the surrounding country.

Bodies of troops were also sent to take possession of the mountain passes by which the supplies for the army had to be brought. The mountains, however, were so steep and rugged and so full of defiles and lurking places that the Moors could sally forth and retreat in perfect security, frequently swooping down upon Christian convoys, and bearing off both booty and prisoners to their strong holds. Sometimes the Moors would light fires at night, on the sides of the mountains, which would be answered by fires from the watch towers and fortresses. By these signals they would concert assaults upon the Christian camp, which in consequence was obliged to be continually on the alert and ready to fly to arms.

King Ferdinand flattered himself that the manifestation of his force had struck sufficient terror into the city, and that, by offers of clemency, it might be induced to capitulate. He wrote a letter, therefore, to the commanders, promising, in case of immediate surrender, that all the inhabitants should be permitted to depart with their effects, but threatening them with fire and sword if they persisted in defence. This letter was dispatched by a cavalier named Carvajal, who, putting it on the end of a lance, gave it to the Moors who were on the walls of the city. The commanders replied that the King was too noble and magnanimous to put such a threat in execution, and that they should not surrender, as they knew the artillery could not be brought to the camp, and they were promised succour by the King of Granada.

At the same time that he received this reply, the King learnt that at the strong town of Comares, upon a height about two leagues distant from the camp a large number of warriors had assembled from the Axarquia, the same mountains in which the Christian cavaliers had been massacred in the beginning of the war; others were daily expected, for this rugged sierra was capable of furnishing fifteen thousand fighting men.

King Ferdinand felt that his army, thus disjointed and enclosed in an enemy's country, was in a perilous situation, and that the utmost discipline and vigilance were necessary. He put the camp under the strictest regulations, forbidding all gaming, blasphemy or brawl, and expelling all loose women, and their attendant bully ruffians, the usual fomenters of riot and contention among soldiery. He ordered that none should sally forth to skirmish without permission from their commanders; that none should set fire to the woods on the neighbouring mountains, and that all word of security given to Moorish places or individuals should be inviolably observed. These regulations were enforced by severe penalties, and had such salutary effect, that, though a vast host of various people was collected together, not an opprobrious epithet was heard, nor a weapon drawn in quarrel.

In the mean time the cloud of war went on gathering about the summits of the mountains: multitudes of the fierce warriors of the sierra descended to the lower heights of Bentomiz, which overhung the camp, intending to force their way into the city. A detachment was sent against them, which, after sharp fighting, drove them to the higher cliffs of the mountain where it was impossible to pursue them.

Ten days had elapsed since the encampment of the army, yet still the artillery had not arrived. The lombards and other heavy ordnance were left, in despair, at Antequera; the rest came groaning slowly through the narrow valleys, which were filled with long trains of artillery and cars laden with munitions. At length part of the smaller ordnance arrived within half a league of the camp, and the Christians were animated with the hopes of soon being able to make a regular attack upon the fortifications of the city.

CHAPTER XLVIII

HOW KING FERDINAND AND HIS ARMY WERE EXPOSED TO IMMINENT PERIL, BEFORE VELEZ MALAGA.

While the standard of the cross waved on the hills before Velez Malaga, and every height and cliff bristled with hostile arms, the civil war between the factions of the Alhambra and the Albaycin, or rather between El Zagal and El Chico, continued to convulse the city of Granada.

The tidings of the investment of Velez Malaga at length roused the attention of the old men and the alfaquis, whose heads were not heated by the daily broils. They spread themselves through the city and endeavoured to arouse the people to a sense of their common danger.

"Why," said they, "continue these brawls between brethren and kindred? What battles are these, where even triumph is ignominious and the victor blushes and conceals his scars? Behold the Christians ravaging the land won by the valour and blood of your forefathers, dwelling in the houses they have built, sitting under the trees they have planted, while your brethren wander about, houseless and desolate. Do you wish to seek your real foe? he is encamped on the mountain of Bentomiz. Do you want a field for the display of your valour, you will find it before the walls of Velez Malaga."

When they had roused the spirit of the people they made their way to the rival kings and addressed them with like remonstrances. Hamet Aben Zarah the inspired Santon reproached El Zagal with his blind and senseless ambition. "You are striving to be King," said he bitterly, "yet suffer the kingdom to be lost."

El Zagal found himself in a perplexing dilemma. He had a double war to wage, with the enemy without and the enemy within. Should the Christians gain possession of the sea coast it would be ruinous to the kingdom; should he leave Granada to oppose them his vacant throne might be seized on by his nephew. He made a merit of necessity, and, pretending to yield to the remonstrances of the alfaquis, endeavoured to compromise with Boabdil. He expressed deep concern at the daily losses of the country, caused by the dissensions of the capital; an opportunity now presented to retrieve all by a blow. The Christians had in a manner put themselves in a tomb between the mountains, nothing remained but to throw the earth upon them. He offered to resign the title of King, to submit to the government of his nephew, and fight under his standard, all he desired was to hasten to the relief of Velez Malaga and to take full vengeance on the Christians.

Boabdil spurned his proposition as the artifice of a hypocrite and a traytor. "How shall I trust a man," said he, "who has murdered my father and my kindred by treachery and who has repeatedly sought my own life both by violence and stratagem!"

El Zagal foamed with rage and vexation but there was no time to be lost. He was beset by the alfaquis and the nobles of his court; the youthful cavaliers were hot for action, the common people loud in their complaints that the richest cities were abandoned to the enemy. The old warrior was naturally fond of fighting. He saw also that to remain inactive would endanger both crown and kingdom, whereas a successful blow would secure his popularity in Granada. He had a much more powerful force than his nephew; having lately received reinforcements from Baza, Guadix and Almeria he could march therefore with a large force, and yet leave a strong garrison in the Alhambra. He took his measures accordingly and departed suddenly in the night, at the head of one thousand horse and twenty thousand foot. He took the most unfrequented roads along the chain of mountains extending from Granada to the height of Bentomiz, and proceeded with such rapidity as to arrive there before King Ferdinand had notice of his approach.

The Christians were alarmed one evening by the sudden blazing of great fires on the mountain about the fortress of Bentomiz. By the ruddy light they beheld the flash of weapons and the array of troops, and they heard the distant sound of Moorish drums and trumpets. The fires of Bentomiz were answered by fires on the towers of Velez Malaga. The shouts of El Zagal! El Zagal! echoed along the cliffs and resounded from the city, and the Christians found that the old warrior King of Granada was on the mountain above their camp.

The spirits of the Moors were suddenly raised to a pitch of the greatest exultation while the Christians were astonished to see this storm of war ready to burst upon their heads. The Count de Cabra, with his accustomed eagerness when there was a King in the field, would fain have scaled the heights and attacked El Zagal before he had time to form his camp; but

Ferdinand, who was more cool and wary, restrained him. To attack the height would be to abandon the siege. He ordered every one, therefore, to keep vigilant watch at his post, and to stand ready to defend it to the utmost, but on no account to sally forth and attack the enemy.

All night the signal fires kept blazing along the mountains rousing and animating the whole country. The morning sun rose over the lofty summit of Bentomiz on a scene of martial splendour. As its rays glanced down the mountain they lighted up the white tents of the Christian cavaliers, cresting its lower prominencies, their pennons and ensigns fluttering in the morning breeze. The sumptuous pavillion of the King, with the holy standard of the cross and the royal banners of Castile and Aragon dominated the encampment. Beyond lay the city; its lofty castle and numerous towers glistening with arms, while above all, and just on the profile of the height, in the full blaze of the rising sun, were descried the tents of the Moor, his turbaned troops clustering about them, and his infidel banners floating against the sky. Columns of smoke rose where the night fire had blazed, and the clash of the Moorish cymbal, the bray of the trumpet and the neigh of steed were faintly heard from these airy heights. So pure and transparent is the atmosphere in this region, that every object can be distinctly seen at a great distance, and the Christians were able to behold the formidable hosts of foes that were gathering on the summits of the surrounding mountains.

One of the first measures of the Moorish King was to detach a large force under Rodovan de Vanegas, Alcayde of Granada, to fall upon the convoy of ordnance which stretched, for a great distance, through the mountain defiles. Ferdinand had anticipated this attempt and sent the Commander of Leon with a body of horse and foot, to reinforce the Master of Alcantara. El Zagal, from his mountain height, beheld the detachment issue from the camp, and immediately recalled Rodovan de Vanegas. The armies now remained quiet for a time, the Moor looking grimly down upon the Christian camp, like a tyger meditating a bound upon his prey. The Christians were in fearful jeopardy, a hostile city below them, a powerful army above them, and on every side mountains filled with implacable foes.

After El Zagal had maturely considered the situation of the Christian camp and informed himself of all the passes of the mountain, he conceived a plan to surprize the enemy which he flattered himself would ensure their ruin and perhaps the capture of King Ferdinand. He wrote a letter to the alcayde of the city, commanding him, in the dead of the night, on a signal fire being made from the mountain, to sally forth with all his troops and fall furiously upon the Christian camp. The King would, at the same time, rush down with his army from the mountain, and assail it on the opposite side, thus overwhelming it at the hour of deep repose. This letter he dispatched by a renegado Christian, who knew all the secret roads of the country, and if taken could pass himself for a Christian who had escaped from captivity.

The fierce El Zagal, confident in the success of his stratagem, looked down upon the Christians as his devoted victims. As the sun went down, and the long shadows of the mountains stretched across the vega, he pointed with exultation to the camp below, apparently unconscious of the impending danger. "Allah Achbar!" exclaimed he, "God is great! behold the unbelievers are delivered into our hands; their King and choicest chivalry will soon be at our mercy. Now is the time to shew the courage of men, and by one glorious victory retrieve all that we have lost. Happy he who falls fighting in the cause of the prophet: he will at once be transported to the paradise of the faithful and surrounded by immortal houris. Happy he who shall survive victorious; he will behold Granada, an earthly paradise! once more delivered from its foes, and restored to all its glory!" The words of El Zagal were received with acclamations by his troops, who waited impatiently for the appointed hour to pour down from their mountain hold upon the Christians.

CHAPTER XLIX

RESULT OF THE STRATAGEM OF EL ZAGAL TO SURPRIZE KING FERDINAND.

Queen Isabella and her court had remained at Cordova in great anxiety for the result of the royal expedition. Every day brought tidings of the difficulties which attended the transportation of the ordnance and munitions, and of the critical state of the army.

While in this state of anxious suspence couriers arrived with all speed from the frontiers, bringing tidings of the sudden sally of El Zagal from Granada to surprize the Christian camp. All Cordova was in consternation. The destruction of the Andalusian chivalry among the mountains of this very neighborhood was called to mind; it was feared that similar ruin was about to burst forth from rocks and precipices upon Ferdinand and his army.

Queen Isabella shared in the public alarm, but it served to rouse all the energies of her heroic mind. Instead of uttering idle apprehensions she sought only how to avert the danger. She called upon all the men of Andalusia under the age of seventy to arm and hasten to the relief of their sovereign and she prepared to set out with the first levies.

The Grand Cardinal of Spain, old Pedro Gonzalez de Mendoza, in whom the piety of the saint and the wisdom of the counsellor were mingled with the fire of the cavalier, offered high pay to all horsemen who would follow him to aid their King and the Christian cause, and, buckling on armour, prepared to lead them to the scene of danger.

The summons of the Queen roused the quick Andalusian spirit. Warriors who had long since given up fighting and had sent their sons to battle, now seized the sword and lance that were rusting on the wall, and marshalled forth their gray headed domestics, and their grand children for the field. The great dread was that all aid would arrive too late. El Zagal and his host had passed like a storm through the mountains and it was feared the tempest had already burst upon the Christian camp.

In the mean while the night had closed which had been appointed by El Zagal for the execution of his plan. He had watched the last light of day expire, and all the Spanish camp remained tranquil. As the hours wore away the camp fires were gradually extinguished. No drum or trumpet sounded from below; nothing was heard but now and then the dull heavy tread of troops or the echoing tramp of horses, the usual patroles of the camp and the changes of the guard. El Zagal restrained his own impatience, and that of his troops, until the night should be advanced and the camp sunk in that heavy sleep from which men are with difficulty awakened, and when awakened, so prone to be bewildered and dismayed.

At length the appointed hour arrived. By order of the Moorish King a bright flame sprung up from the height of Bentomiz, but El Zagal looked in vain for the responding light from the city. His impatience would brook no longer delay; he ordered the advance of the army to descend the mountain defile and attack the camp. The defile was narrow and overhung by rocks: as the troops proceeded they came suddenly, in a shadowy hollow, upon a dark mass of Christian warriors. A loud shout burst forth and the Christians rushed to assail them. The Moors surprized and disconcerted, retreated in confusion to the height. When El Zagal heard of a Christian force posted in the defile he doubted some counter plan of the enemy. He gave orders to light the mountain fires. On a signal given, bright flames sprung out on every height, from great pyres of wood prepared for the purpose. Cliff blazed out after cliff, until the whole atmosphere was in a glow of furnace light. The ruddy glare lit up the glens and passes of the mountains and fell strongly upon the Christian camp, revealing all its tents, and every post and bulwark. Wherever El Zagal turned his eyes he beheld the light of his fires flashed back from cuirass and helm, and sparkling lance; he beheld a grove of spears planted in every pass, every assailable point bristling with arms and squadrons of horse and foot in battle array, awaiting his attack.

In fact the letter of El Zagal to the Alcayde of Velez Malaga had been intercepted by the vigilant Ferdinand, and the renegado messenger hanged and secret measures taken, after the night had closed in, to give the enemy a warm reception. El Zagal saw that his plan of surprize was discovered and foiled; furious with disappointment he ordered his troops forward to the attack. They rushed down the defile with loud cries, but were again encountered by the mass of Christian warriors, being the advance guard of the army commanded by Don Hurtado de Mendoza, brother of the Grand Cardinal.

The Moors were again repulsed and retreated up the height. Don Hurtado would have followed them, but the ascent was steep and rugged and easily defended by the Moors. A sharp action was kept up through the night with cross bows, darts and arquebusses. The cliffs echoed with deafening uproar, while the fires, blazing upon the mountains, threw a lurid and uncertain light upon the scene.

When the day dawned and the Moors saw that there was no cooperation from the city, they began to slacken in their ardour: they beheld also every pass of the mountain filled with Christian troops and began to apprehend an assault in return. Just then King Ferdinand sent the Marquis of Cadiz, with horse and foot, to seize upon a height occupied by a batallion of the enemy. The marquis assailed the Moors with his usual intrepidity and soon put them to flight. The others, who were above, seeing their companions flying, were seized with a sudden alarm. They threw down their arms and retreated. One of those unaccountable panics which now and then seize upon great bodies of people, and to which the light spirited Moors were very prone, now spread through the camp. They were terrified they knew not why, or at what. They threw away swords, lances, breastplates, cross bows, every thing that could burthen or impede their flight, and spreading themselves wildly over the mountains fled headlong down the defiles. They fled without pursuers, from the glimpse of each other's arms; from the sound of each other's footsteps. Rodovan de Vanegas, the brave Alcayde of Granada, alone succeeded in collecting a body of the fugitives; he made a circuit with them through the passes of the mountains, and forcing his way across a weak part of the Christian lines, galloped towards Velez Malaga. The rest of the Moorish host was completely scattered. In vain did El Zagal and his knights attempt to rally them; they were left almost alone and had to consult their own security by flight. The Marquis of Cadiz, finding no opposition, ascended from height to height, cautiously reconnoitering, and fearful of some stratagem or ambush. All, however, was quiet. He reached, with his men, the place which the Moorish army had occupied; the heights were abandoned, and strewed with cuirasses, scymetars, cross bows and other weapons. His force was too small to pursue the enemy, but returned to the royal camp laden with the spoils.

King Ferdinand, at first, could not credit so signal and miraculous a defeat. He suspected some lurking stratagem. He ordered, therefore, that a strict watch should be maintained throughout the camp, and every one be ready for instant action. The following night a thousand cavaliers and hidalgos kept guard about the royal tent, as they had done for several preceding nights, nor did the King relax this vigilance until he received certain intelligence that the enemy was completely scattered and El Zagal flying in confusion.

The tidings of this route, and of the safety of the Christian army, arrived at Cordova just as the reinforcements were on the point of setting out. The anxiety and alarm of the Queen and the public were turned to transports of joy and gratitude. The forces were disbanded, solemn processions were made and *Te deums* chaunted in the churches for so signal a victory.

CHAPTER L

HOW THE PEOPLE OF GRANADA REWARDED THE VALOUR OF EL ZAGAL.

The daring spirit of the old warrior, Muley Abdalla el Zagal, in sallying forth to defend his territories, while he left an armed rival in his capital, had struck the people of Granada with admiration. They recalled his former exploits, and again anticipated some hardy achievement from his furious valour. Couriers from the army reported its formidable position on the height of Bentomiz. For a time there was a pause in the bloody commotions of the city; all attention was turned to the blow about to be struck at the Christian camp. The same considerations, which diffused anxiety and terror through Cordova, swelled every bosom with exulting confidence in Granada. The Moors expected to hear of another massacre, like that in the mountains of Malaga. "El Zagal has again entrapped the enemy!" was the cry. "The power of the unbelievers is about to be struck to the heart; and we shall soon see the Christian King led captive to the capital!" Thus the name of El Zagal was on every tongue. He was extolled as the saviour of the country, the only one worthy of wearing the Moorish crown. Boabdil was reviled as basely remaining passive while his country was invaded; and so violent became the clamour of the populace, that his adherents trembled for his safety.

While the people of Granada were impatiently looking for tidings of the anticipated victory, scattered horsemen came spurring across the vega. They were fugitives from the Moorish army, and brought the first incoherent account of its defeat. Every one who attempted to tell the tale of this unaccountable panic and dispersion was as if bewildered by the broken recollection of some frightful dream. He knew not how or why it came to pass. He talked of a battle in the night among rocks and precipices, by the glare of bale-fires; of multitudes of armed foes in every pass, seen by gleams and flashes; of the sudden horror that seized upon the army at daybreak, its headlong flight and total dispersion. Hour after hour the arrival of other fugitives confirmed the story of ruin and disgrace.

In proportion to their recent vaunting was the humiliation that now fell upon the people of Granada. There was a universal burst, not of grief, but indignation.

They confounded the leader with the army; the deserted with those who had abandoned him; and El Zagal, from being their idol, became the object of their execration. He had sacrificed the army; he had disgraced the nation; he had betrayed the country. He was a dastard, a traitor; he was unworthy to reign!

On a sudden, one among the multitude shouted, "Long live Boabdil el Chico!" The cry was echoed on all sides, and everyone shouted, "Long live Boabdil el Chico! long live the legitimate King of Granada! and death to all usurpers!" In the excitement of the moment they thronged to the Albaycin, and those, who had lately besieged Boabdil with arms, now surrounded his palace with acclamations. The keys of the city and of all the fortresses were laid at his feet; he was borne in state to the Alhambra, and once more seated, with all due ceremony, on the throne of his ancestors.

Boabdil had by this time become so accustomed to be crowned and uncrowned by the multitude, that he put no great faith in the duration of their loyalty. He knew, that he was surrounded by hollow hearts, and that most of the courtiers of the Alhambra were secretly devoted to his uncle. He ascended the throne as the rightful sovereign, who had been dispossessed of it by usurpation, and he ordered the heads of four of the principal nobles to be struck off, who had been most zealous in support of the usurper. Executions of this kind were matters of course on any change of Moorish government; and Boabdil was extolled for his moderation and humanity, in being content with so small a sacrifice. The factions were awed into obedience; the populace, delighted with any change, extolled Boabdil to the skies, and the name of Muley Abdalla el Zagal was for a time a by-word of scorn and opprobrium throughout the city.

Never was any commander more astonished and confounded by a sudden reverse of fortune, than El Zagal. The evening had seen him with a powerful army at his command, his enemy within his grasp, and victory about to cover him with glory, and to consolidate his power. The morning beheld him a fugitive among the mountains; his army, his prosperity, his power, all dispelled he knew not how; gone like a dream of the night. In vain had he tried to stem the headlong flight of the soldiery. He saw his squadrons breaking and dispersing among the cliffs of the mountains, until, of all his host, only a handful of cavaliers remained faithful to him. With these he made a gloomy retreat towards Granada, but with a heart full of foreboding. When he drew near to the city, he paused on the banks of the Xenel, and sent forth scouts to collect intelligence. They returned with dejected countenances. "The gates of Granada," said they, "are closed against you. The banner of Boabdil floats on the tower of the Alhambra."

El Zagal turned his steed, and departed in silence. He retreated to the town of Almuñecar, and from thence to Almeria, places which still remained faithful to him. Restless and uneasy at being so distant from the capital, he again changed his abode and repaired to the city of Guadix, within a few leagues of Granada. Here he remained, endeavouring to rally his forces, and preparing to avail himself of any change in the fluctuating politics of the metropolis.

CHAPTER LI
SURRENDER OF VELEZ MALAGA, AND OTHER PLACES.

The people of Velez Malaga had beheld the camp of Muley Abdalla el Zagal covering the summit of Bentomiz, and glittering in the last rays of the setting sun. During the night they had been alarmed and perplexed by signal fires on the mountain, and by the distant sound of battle. When the morning broke, the Moorish army had vanished as if by enchantment. While the inhabitants were lost in wonder and conjecture, a body of cavalry, the fragment of the army saved by Rodovan de Vanegas, the brave Alcayde of Granada, came galloping to the gates. The tidings of the strange discomfiture of the host filled the city with consternation; but Rodovan exhorted the people to continue their resistance. He was devoted to El Zagal, and confident in his skill and prowess; and felt assured, that he would soon collect his scattered forces, and return with fresh troops from Granada. The people were comforted by the words and encouraged by the presence of Rodovan, and they had still a lingering hope, that the heavy artillery of the Christians might be locked up in the impassable defiles of the mountains. This hope was soon at an end. The very next day they beheld long laborious lines of ordnance slowly moving into the Spanish camp; lombards, ribadoquines, catapultas, and cars laden with munitions, while the escort, under the brave Master of Alcantara, wheeled in great battalions into the camp, to augment the force of the besiegers.

The intelligence, that Granada had shut its gates against El Zagal, and that no reinforcements were to be expected, completed the despair of the inhabitants; even Rodovan himself lost confidence, and advised capitulation.

The terms were arranged between the alcayde and the noble Count de Cifuentes. The latter had been prisoner of Rodovan at Granada, who had treated him with chivalrous courtesy. They had conceived a mutual esteem for each other, and met as ancient friends.

Ferdinand granted favorable conditions; for he was eager to proceed against Malaga. The inhabitants were permitted to depart with their effects, except their arms, and to reside, if they chose it, in Spain, in any place distant from the sea. One hundred and twenty Christians of both sexes were rescued from captivity by the surrender of Velez Malaga, and were sent to

Cordova, where they were received with great tenderness by the Queen, and her daughter the Infanta Isabella, in the famous cathedral, in the midst of public rejoicings for the victory.

The capture of Velez Malaga was followed by the surrender of Bentomiz, Comares, and all the towns and fortresses of the Axarquia, which were strongly garrisoned, and discreet and valiant cavaliers appointed as their alcaydes. The inhabitants of nearly forty towns of the Alpuxarra mountains also sent deputations to the Castilian sovereigns, taking the oath of allegiance as Mudehares, or Moslem vassals.

About the same time came letters from Boabdil el Chico, announcing to the sovereigns the revolution of Granada in his favour. He solicited kindness and protection for the inhabitants who had returned to their allegiance, and for those of all other places which should renounce allegiance to his uncle. By this means, he observed, the whole kingdom of Granada would soon be induced to acknowledge his sway, and would be held by him in faithful vassalage to the Castilian crown.

The Catholic sovereigns complied with his request. Protection was immediately extended to the inhabitants of Granada, permitting them to cultivate their fields in peace, and to trade with the Christian territories in all articles excepting arms, being provided with letters of surety from some Christian captain or alcayde. The same favour was promised to all other places which within six months should renounce El Zagal, and come under allegiance to the younger King. Should they not do so within that time, the sovereigns threatened to make war upon them, and conquer them for themselves. This measure had a great effect in inducing many to return to the standard of Boabdil.

Having made every necessary arrangement for the government and security of the newly conquered territory, Ferdinand turned his attention to the great object of his campaign, the reduction of Malaga.

CHAPTER LII

OF THE CITY OF MALAGA AND ITS INHABITANTS.

The city of Malaga lies in the lap of a fertile valley, surrounded by mountains, excepting on the part which lies open to the sea. As it was one of the most important, so it was one of the strongest cities of the Moorish kingdom. It was fortified by walls of prodigious strength, studded with a great number of huge towers. On the land side it was protected by a natural barrier of mountains, and, on the other, the waves of the Mediterranean beat against the foundations of its massive bulwarks.

At one end of the city, near the sea, on a high mound, stood the Alcazaba or citadel, a fortress of great strength. Immediately above this rose a steep and rocky mount, on the top of which, in old times had been a pharos, or lighthouse, from which the height derived its name of Gibralfaro.* It was at present crowned by an immense castle, which, from its lofty and cragged situation, its vast walls and mighty towers, was deemed impregnable. It communicated with the Alcazaba by a covered way, six paces broad, leading down between two walls, along the profile or ridge of the rock. The castle of Gibralfaro commanded both citadel and city, and was capable, if both were taken, of maintaining a siege.

Two large suburbs adjoined the city: in the one towards the sea were dwelling-houses of the most opulent inhabitants, adorned with hanging gardens; the other, on the land side, was thickly peopled, and surrounded by strong walls and towers.

Malaga possessed a brave and numerous garrison, and the common people were active, hardy, and resolute; but the city was rich and commercial, and under the habitual control of numerous opulent merchants, who dreaded the ruinous consequences of a siege. They were little zealous for the warlike renown of their city, and longed rather to participate in the enviable security of property, and the lucrative privileges of safe traffic with the Christian territories, granted to all places which declared for Boabdil. At the head of these gainful citizens was Ali Dordux, a mighty merchant, of uncounted wealth, whose ships traded to every port of the Levant, and whose word was as a law in Malaga.

Ali Dordux assembled the most opulent and important of his commercial brethren, and they repaired in a body to the Alcazaba, where they were received by the alcayde, Albozen Connexa, with that deference generally shewn to men of their great local dignity and power of purse. Ali Dordux was ample and stately in his form, and fluent and emphatic in his discourse. His eloquence had an effect, therefore, upon the alcayde, as he represented the hopelessness of a defence of Malaga, the misery that must attend a siege, and the ruin that must follow a capture by force of arms. On the other hand, he set forth the grace that might be obtained from the Castilian sovereigns by an early and voluntary acknowledgement of Boabdil as King, the peaceful possession of their property, and the profitable commerce with the Christian ports that would be allowed them. He was seconded by his weighty and important coadjutors; and the alcayde, accustomed to regard them as the arbiters of the affairs of the place, yielded to their united counsels. He departed, therefore, with all speed to the Christian camp, empowered to ar-

*A corruption of Gibel-faro, the hill of the lighthouse.

range a capitulation with the Castilian monarch, and in the mean time his brother remained in command of the Alcazaba.

There was, at this time, as alcayde, in the old crag-built castle of Gibral-faro, a warlike and fiery Moor, an implacable enemy of the Christians. This was no other than Hamet Zeli, surnamed El Zegri, the once formidable Alcayde of Ronda, and the terror of its mountains. He had never forgiven the capture of his favourite fortress, and panted for vengeance on the Christians. Notwithstanding his reverses, he had retained the favour of El Zagal, who knew how to appreciate a bold warrior of the kind, and had placed him in command of this important fortress of Gibralfaro.

Hamet el Zegri had gathered round him the remnant of his band of Gomeres, with others of the same tribe. These fierce warriors were nestled, like so many war-hawks, about their lofty cliff. They looked down with martial contempt upon the commercial city of Malaga, which they were placed to protect; or rather, they esteemed it only for its military importance and its capability of defence. They held no communion with its trading, gainful inhabitants, and even considered the garrison of the Alcazaba as their inferiors. War was their pursuit and passion; they rejoiced in its turbulent and perilous scenes; and, confident in the strength of the city, and, above all, of their castle, they set at defiance the menace of Christian invasion. There were among them, also, many apostate Moors, who had once embraced Christianity, but had since recanted, and had fled from the vengeance of the Inquisition. These were desperadoes who had no mercy to expect should they again fall into the hands of the enemy.

Such were the fierce elements of the garrison of Gibralfaro; and its rage may easily be conceived at hearing that Malaga was to be given up without a blow; that they were to sink into Christian vassals, under the intermediate sway of Boabdil el Chico, and that the Alcayde of the Alcazaba had departed to arrange the terms of capitulation.

Hamet el Zegri determined to avert, by desperate means, the threatened degradation. He knew that there was a large party in the city faithful to El Zagal, being composed of warlike men, who had taken refuge from the various mountain towns which had been captured. Their feelings were desperate as their fortunes, and, like Hamet, they panted for revenge upon the Christians. With these he had a secret conference, and received assurances of their adherence to him in any measures of defence. As to the council of the peaceful inhabitants he considered it unworthy the consideration of a soldier, and he spurned at the interference of the wealthy merchant, Ali Dordux, in matters of warfare.

"Still," said Hamet el Zegri, "let us proceed regularly." So he descended with his Gomeres to the citadel, entered it suddenly, put to death the brother of the alcayde and such of the garrison as made any demur, and then summoned the principal inhabitants to deliberate on measures for the welfare of the city.*

The wealthy merchants again mounted to the citadel, excepting Ali Dordux, who refused to obey the summons. They entered with hearts filled with awe, for they found Hamet surrounded by his grim African guard, and all the stern array of military power, and they beheld the bloody traces of the recent massacre.

Hamet el Zegri rolled a dark and searching eye upon the assembly, "Who," said he, "is loyal and devoted to Muley Abdalla el Zagal?" Every one present asserted his loyalty. "Good!" said Hamet, "and who is ready to prove his devotion to his sovereign by defending this his important city to the last extremity?" Every one present expressed his readiness. "Enough," observed Hamet, "the Alcayde Albozen Connexa has proved himself a traytor to his sovereign and to you all; for he has conspired to deliver the place to the Christians. It behoves you to choose some other commander, capable of defending your city against the approaching enemy." The assembly declared unanimously that there could be none so worthy of the command as himself. So Hamet el Zegri was appointed Alcayde of Malaga, and immediately proceeded to man the forts and towers with his partizans, and to make every preparation for a desperate resistance.

Intelligence of these occurrences put an end to the negociations between King Ferdinand and the superseded Alcayde Albozen Connexa, and it was supposed there was no alternative but to lay siege to the place. The Marquis of Cadiz, however, found at Velez a Moorish cavalier of some note, native of Malaga, who offered to tamper with Hamet el Zegri for the surrender of the city, or at least of the castle of Gibralfaro. The marquis communicated this to the King: "I put this business and the key of my treasury into your hand," said Ferdinand, "act, stipulate and disburse, in my name, as you think proper."

The marquis armed the Moor with his own lance, cuirass and target, and mounted him on one of his own horses. He equipped in similar style, also, another Moor, his companion and relation. They bore secret letters to Hamet from the marquis, offering him the town of Coin in perpetual inheritance, and four thousand doblas in gold, if he would deliver up Gibralfaro; together with large sums to be distributed among his officers and soldiers: and he offered unlimited rewards for the surrender of the city.†

Hamet had a warrior's admiration for the Marquis of Cadiz and received his messengers with courtesy in his fortress of Gibralfaro. He even listened to their propositions with patience, and dismissed them in safety, though

*Cura de Los Palacios C. 82.
†Cura de Los Palacios C. 82.

with an absolute refusal. The marquis thought his reply was not so peremptory as to discourage another effort. The emissaries were despatched, therefore, a second time, with further propositions. They approached Malaga in the night but found the guards doubled, patroles abroad and the whole place on the alert. They were discovered, pursued, and only saved themselves by the fleetness of their steeds and their knowledge of the passes of the mountains.

Finding all attempts to tamper with the faith of Hamet el Zegri utterly futile, King Ferdinand publicly summoned the city to surrender, offering the most favorable terms in case of immediate compliance, but threatening captivity to all the inhabitants in case of resistance.

The message was delivered in presence of the principal inhabitants, who, however, were too much in awe of the stern alcayde to utter a word. Hamet el Zegri then rose haughtily and replied that the city of Malaga had not been confided to him to be surrendered but defended, and the King should witness how he acquitted himself of his charge.*

The messengers returned with formidable accounts of the force of the garrison, the strength of the fortifications and the determined spirit of the commander and his men. The King immediately sent orders to have the heavy artillery forwarded from Antequera, and, on the seventh of May, marched with his army towards Malaga.

CHAPTER LIII

ADVANCE OF KING FERDINAND AGAINST MALAGA.

The army of Ferdinand advanced in lengthened line glittering along the foot of the mountains which border the Mediterranean, while a fleet of vessels freighted with heavy artillery and warlike munitions, kept pace with it, at a short distance from the land, covering the sea with a thousand gleaming sails. When Hamet el Zegri saw this force approaching he set fire to the houses of the suburbs which adjoined the walls and sent forth three batallions to encounter the advance guard of the enemy.

The Christian army drew near to the city at that end where the castle and rocky height of Gibralfaro defend the seaboard. Immediately opposite to the castle and about two bowshots' distance, and between it and the high chain of mountains, was a steep and rocky hill, commanding a pass through which the Christians must march to penetrate to the vega and surround the city. Hamet el Zegri ordered the three batallions to take their stations one on this

*Pulgar. Part 3. Cap 74.

hill, another in the pass near the castle, and a third on the side of the mountain near the sea.

A body of Spanish foot soldiers of the advance guard, sturdy mountaineers of Gallicia, sprang forward to climb the side of the height next the sea, at the same time a number of cavaliers and hidalgos of the royal household attacked the Moors who guarded the pass below. The Moors defended their posts with obstinate valour. The Gallicians were repeatedly overpowered and driven down the hill, but as often rallied, and, being reinforced by the hidalgos and cavaliers, returned to the assault. This obstinate struggle lasted for six hours. The strife was of a deadly kind, not merely with cross bows and arquebusses, but hand to hand, with swords and daggers; no quarter was claimed or given on either side, they fought not to make captives, but to slay. It was but the advance guard of the Christian army that was engaged; so narrow was the pass along the coast that the army could proceed only in file. Horse and foot and beasts of burden were crowded one upon another, impeding each other and blocking up the narrow and rugged defile. The soldiers heard the uproar of the battle, the sound of trumpets and the war cries of the Moors, but tried in vain to press forward to the assistance of their companions.

At length a body of foot soldiers of the Holy Brotherhood climbed, with great difficulty, the steep side of the mountain which overhung the pass, and advanced, with seven banners displayed. The Moors, seeing this force above them, abandoned the pass in despair.

The battle was still raging on the height; the Gallicians though supported by Castilian troops, under Don Hurtado de Mendoza and Garcilasso de la Vega, were severely pressed, and roughly handled by the Moors; at length a brave standard bearer, Luys Mazedo by name, threw himself into the midst of the enemy and planted his banner on the summit. The Gallicians and Castilians, stimulated by this noble self devotion, followed him fighting desperately, and the Moors were at length driven to their castle of Gibralfaro.*

This important height being taken, the pass lay open to the army; but by this time evening was advancing and the host was too weary and exhausted to seek proper situations for the encampment. The King, attended by several grandees and cavaliers, went the rounds at night, stationing outposts towards the city and guards and patroles to give the alarm on the least movement of the enemy. All night the Christians lay upon their arms, lest there should be some attempt to sally forth and attack them.

When the morning dawned the King gazed with admiration at this city, which he hoped soon to add to his dominions. It was surrounded on one side by vineyards, gardens and orchards which covered the hills with ver-

*Pulgar Cronica.

dure; on the other side its walls were bathed by the smooth and tranquil sea. Its vast and lofty towers and prodigious castles hoary with age, yet unimpaired in strength, shewed the labours of magnanimous men, in former times, to protect their favorite abode. Hanging gardens, groves of oranges, citrons and pomgranites, with tall cedars and stately palms, were mingled with the stern battlements and towers, bespeaking the opulence and luxury that reigned within.

In the mean time the Christian army poured through the pass and throwing out its columns and extending its lines, took possession of every vantage ground around the city. King Ferdinand surveyed the ground and appointed the stations of the different commanders.

The important mount which had cost so violent a struggle, and faced the powerful fortress of Gibralfaro, was given in charge to Roderigo Ponce de Leon, Marquis of Cadiz, who, in all sieges, claimed the post of danger. He had several noble cavaliers with their retainers in his encampment, which consisted of fifteen hundred horse, and fourteen thousand foot; and extended from the summit of the mount to the margin of the sea, completely blocking up the approach to the city on that side.

From this post a line of encampments extended quite round the city to the sea board, fortified by bulwarks and deep ditches; while a fleet of armed ships and galleys stretched before the harbour, so that the place was completely invested by sea and land. The various parts of the valley now resounded with the din of preparation, and were filled with artificers preparing warlike engines and munitions; armourers and smiths with glowing forges and deafening hammers, carpenters and engineers constructing machines wherewith to assail the walls, stone cutters shaping stone balls for the ordnance and burners of charcoal preparing fuel for the furnaces and forges.

When the encampment was formed the heavy ordnance was landed from the ships and mounted in various parts of the camp. Five huge lombards were placed on the mount commanded by the Marquis of Cadiz, so as to bear upon the castle of Gibralfaro.

The Moors made strenuous efforts to impede these preparations. They kept up a heavy fire from their ordnance, upon the men employed in digging trenches or constructing batteries, so that the latter had to work principally in the night. The royal tents had been stationed conspicuously and within reach of the Moorish batteries, but were so warmly assailed that they had to be removed behind a hill.

When the works were completed the Christian batteries opened in return and kept up a tremendous cannonade, while the fleet approaching the land, assailed the city vigorously on the opposite side.

It was a glorious and delectable sight, observes Fray Antonio Agapida, to behold this infidel city thus surrounded by sea and land by a mighty Christian force. Every mound in its circuit was, as it were, a little city of tents, bearing the standard of some renowned Catholic warrior. Besides the warlike ships and galleys which lay before the place, the sea was covered with innumerable sails, passing and repassing, appearing and disappearing, being engaged in bringing supplies for the subsistence of the army. It seemed a vast spectacle contrived to recreate the eye, did not the volleying bursts of flame and smoke from the ships which seemed to lie asleep on the quiet sea, and the thunder of ordnance from camp and city, from tower and battlement, tell the deadly warfare that was waging.

At night the scene was far more direful than in the day. The cheerful light of the sun was gone; there was nothing but the flashes of artillery or the baleful gleams of combustibles thrown into the city, and the conflagration of the houses. The fire kept up from the Christian batteries was incessant; there were seven great lombards in particular, called the Seven Sisters of Ximenes, which did tremendous execution. The Moorish ordnance replied in thunder from the walls; Gibralfaro was wrapped in volumes of smoke rolling about its base, and Hamet el Zegri and his Gomeres looked out with triumph upon the tempest of war they had awakened. "Truly they were so many demons incarnate," says the pious Fray Antonio Agapida, "who were permitted by heaven to enter into and possess this infidel city for its perdition."

CHAPTER LIV

SIEGE OF MALAGA.

The attack on Malaga, by sea and land, was kept up for several days with tremendous violence, but without producing any great impression, so strong were the ancient bulwarks of the city. The Count de Cifuentes was the first to signalize himself by any noted achievement. A main tower of the suburb had been shattered by the ordnance and the battlements demolished so as to yield no shelter to its defenders. Seeing this the count assembled a gallant band of cavaliers of the royal household and advanced to take it by storm. They applied scaling ladders and mounted, sword in hand. The Moors having no longer battlements to protect them, descended to a lower floor, and made furious resistance from the windows and loop holes. They poured down boiling pitch and rosin and hurled stones and darts and arrows on the assailants. Many of the Christians were slain, their ladders were destroyed by flaming combustibles, and the count was obliged to retreat from before the tower. On the following day he renewed the attack with superior force, and, after a severe combat succeeded in planting his victorious banner on the tower.

The Moors now assailed the tower in their turn. They undermined the part towards the city, placed props of wood under the foundation and setting fire to them drew off to a distance. In a little while the props gave way, the foundation sank, the tower was rent, part of its wall fell with a tremendous noise, many of the Christians were thrown out headlong and the rest were laid open to the missiles of the enemy.

By this time, however, a breach had been made in the wall adjoining the tower, and troops poured in to the assistance of their comrades. A continued battle was kept up for two days and a night by reinforcements from camp and city. The parties fought backwards and forwards through the breach of the wall, with alternate success, and the vicinity of the tower was strewn with the dead and wounded. At length the Moors gradually gave way, disputing every inch of ground, until they were driven into the city, and the Christians remained masters of the greater part of the suburb.

This partial success; though gained with great toil and bloodshed, gave temporary animation to the Christians; they soon found, however, that the attack on the main works of the city was a much more arduous task. The garrison contained veterans who had served in many of the towns captured by the Christians. They were no longer confounded and dismayed by the battering ordnance and other strange engines of foreign invention, and had become expert in parrying their effects in repairing breaches and erecting counterworks.

The Christians accustomed of late to speedy conquests of Moorish fortresses, became impatient of the slow progress of the siege. Many were apprehensive of a scarcity of provisions, from the difficulty of subsisting so numerous a host in the heart of the enemies' country, where it was necessary to transport supplies across rugged and hostile mountains, or subjected to the uncertainties of the seas. Many were also alarmed at a pestilence which broke out in the neighbouring villages, and some were so overcome by these apprehensions as to abandon the camp and return to their homes.

Several of the loose and worthless hangers on that infest all great armies, hearing these murmurs, thought that the siege would soon be raised, and deserted to the enemy, hoping to make their fortunes. They gave exaggerated accounts of the alarms and discontents of the army and represented the troops as daily returning home in bands. Above all they declared that the gunpowder was nearly exhausted, so that the artillery would soon be useless. They assured the Moors, therefore, that, if they persisted a little longer in their defence, the King would be obliged to draw off his forces and abandon the siege.

The reports of these renegadoes gave fresh courage to the garrison; they made vigorous sallies upon the camp; harrassing it by night and day, and obliging every part to be guarded with the most painful vigilance. They fortified the weak parts of their walls with ditches and pallisadoes and gave every manifestation of a determined and unyielding spirit.

Ferdinand soon received intelligence of the reports which had been carried to the Moors; he understood that they had been informed, likewise, that the Queen was alarmed for the safety of the camp, and had written repeatedly urging him to abandon the siege. As the best means of disproving all these falsehoods and of destroying the vain hopes of the enemy, Ferdinand wrote to the Queen entreating her to come and take up her residence in the camp.

CHAPTER LV

SIEGE OF MALAGA CONTINUED. OBSTINACY OF HAMET EL ZEGRI.

Great was the enthusiasm of the army when they beheld their patriot Queen advancing in state to share the toils and dangers of her people. Isabella entered the camp attended by the dignitaries and the whole retinue of her court, to manifest that this was no temporary visit. On one side of her was her daughter the Infanta, on the other, the Grand Cardinal of Spain; Hernando de Talavera the prior of Prado confessor to the Queen followed, with a great train of prelates, courtiers, cavaliers, and ladies of distinction. The cavalcade moved in calm and stately order through the camp, softening the iron aspect of war by this array of courtly grace and female beauty.

Isabella had commanded that on her coming to the camp the horrors of war should be suspended, and fresh offers of peace made to the enemy. On her arrival, therefore, there had been a general cessation of firing throughout the camp. A messenger was at the same time, dispatched to the besieged, informing them of her being in the camp, and of the determination of the sovereigns to make it their residence, until the city should be taken. The same terms were offered, in case of immediate surrender, that had been granted to Velez Malaga, but the inhabitants were threatened with captivity and the sword should they persist in their defence.

Hamet el Zegri received this message with haughty contempt and dismissed the messenger without deigning a reply.

"The Christian sovereigns," said he, "have made this offer in consequence of their despair. The silence of their batteries proves the truth of what has been told us, that their powder is exhausted. They have no longer the means of demolishing our walls, and if they remain much longer, the autumnal rains will interrupt their convoys and fill their camp with famine and disease. The first storm will disperse their fleet which has no neighbouring port of shelter. Africa will then be open to us to procure reinforcements and supplies."

The words of Hamet el Zegri were hailed as oracular by his adherents. Many of the peaceful part of the community, however, ventured to remonstrate, and to implore him to accept the proffered mercy. The stern Hamet silenced them with a terrific threat. He declared that, whoever should talk of capitulating or should hold any communication with the Christians should be put to death. His fierce Gomeres, like true men of the sword, acted upon the menace of their chieftain as upon a written law, and, having detected several of the inhabitants in secret correspondence with the enemy they set upon and slew them, and then confiscated their effects. This struck such terror into the citizens that those who had been loudest in their murmurs became suddenly mute, and were remarked as evincing the greatest bustle and alacrity in the defence of the city.

When the messenger returned to the camp and reported the contemptuous reception of the royal message, King Ferdinand was exceedingly indignant. Finding the cessation of firing on the Queen's arrival had encouraged a belief among the enemy that there was a scarcity of powder in the camp he ordered a general discharge from every battery. The sudden burst of war from every quarter soon convinced the Moors of their error, and completed the confusion of the citizens, who knew not which most to dread, their assailants or their defenders, the Christians or the Gomeres.

That evening the sovereigns visited the encampment of the Marquis of Cadiz which commanded a view over a great part of the city and the camp. The tent of the marquis was of great magnitude, furnished with hangings of rich brocade, and French cloth of the rarest texture. It was in the oriental style, and as it crowned the height, with the surrounding tents of other cavaliers all sumptuously furnished, presented a gay and silken contrast to the opposite towers of Gibralfaro. Here a splendid collation was served up to the sovereigns, and the courtly revel that prevailed in this chivalrous encampment, the glitter of pageantry and the bursts of festive music, made more striking the gloom and silence that reigned over the dark Moorish castle.

The Marquis of Cadiz while it was yet light conducted his royal visitors to every point that commanded a view of the warlike scene below. He caused the heavy lombards also to be discharged, that the Queen and the ladies of the court might witness the effect of those tremendous engines. The fair dames were filled with awe and admiration as the mountain shook beneath their feet with the thunder of the artillery, and they beheld great fragments of the Moorish walls tumbling down the rocks and precipices.

While the good marquis was displaying these things to his royal guests he lifted up his eyes and to his astonishment beheld his own banner hanging out from the nearest tower of Gibralfaro. The blood mantled in his cheek, for it was a banner which he had lost at the time of the memorable massacre of the heights of Malaga.* To make this taunt more evident several of the Gomeres displayed themselves upon the battlements arrayed in the helmets and cuirasses of some of the cavaliers slain or captured on that occasion. The Marquis of Cadiz restrained his indignation and held his peace; but several of his cavaliers vowed loudly to revenge this cruel bravado on the ferocious garrison of Gibralfaro.

CHAPTER LVI

ATTACK OF THE MARQUIS OF CADIZ UPON GIBRALFARO.

The Marquis of Cadiz, was not a cavalier that readily forgave an injury or an insult. On the morning after the royal banquet his batteries opened a tremendous fire upon Gibralfaro. All day the encampment was wrapped in wreathes of smoke, nor did the assault cease with the day, but throughout the night, there was an incessant flashing and thundering of the lombards, and the following morning the assault rather encreased than slackened in its fury. The Moorish bulwarks were no proof against those formidable engines. In a few days the lofty tower on which the taunting banner had been displayed was shattered; a smaller tower in its vicinity reduced to ruins and a great breach made in the intervening walls.

Several of the hot spirited cavaliers were eager for storming the breach sword in hand; others, more cool and wary, pointed out the rashness of such an attempt, for the Moors working indefatigably in the night, had digged a deep ditch within the breach, and had fortified it with pallisadoes and a high breastwork. All, however, agreed that the camp might safely be advanced near to the ruined walls, and that it ought to be done so, in return for the insolent defiance of the enemy.

The Marquis of Cadiz felt the temerity of the measure but he was unwilling to dampen the zeal of those high spirited cavaliers, and, having chosen the post of danger in the camp, it did not become him to decline any service merely because it might appear perilous. He ordered his outposts, therefore, to be advanced within a stone's throw of the breach, but exhorted the soldiers to maintain the utmost vigilance.

*Diego de Valera. Cronica. Ms.

The thunder of the batteries had ceased, the troops, exhausted by two nights' fatigue and watchfulness, and apprehending no danger from the dismantled walls, were half of them asleep; the rest were scattered about in negligent security. On a sudden upwards of two thousand Moors sallied forth from the castle, led on by Abrahen Zenete, the principal captain under Hamet. They fell with fearful havoc upon the advance guard, slaying many of them in their sleep, and putting the rest to headlong flight. The Marquis was in his tent, about a bow shot distance, when he heard the tumult of the onset and beheld his men flying in confusion. He rushed forth, followed by his standard bearers. "Turn again cavaliers!" exclaimed he. "Turn again. I am here, Ponce de Leon! To the foe! to the foe!" The flying troops stopped at hearing his well known voice, rallied under his banner and turned upon the enemy. The encampment, by this time, was roused, several cavaliers from the adjoining stations had hastened to the scene of action, with a number of Gallicians and soldiers of the Holy Brotherhood. An obstinate and bloody contest ensued: the ruggedness of the place, the rocks, chasms and declivities broke it into numerous combats. Christian and Moor fought hand to hand with swords and daggers, and often, grappling and struggling, rolled together down the precipices.

The banner of the marquis was in danger of being taken; he hastened to its rescue followed by some of his bravest cavaliers. They were surrounded by the enemy and several of them cut down. Don Diego Ponce de Leon, brother to the marquis, was wounded by an arrow, and his son in law Luis Ponce was likewise wounded; they succeeded, however, in rescuing the banner and bearing it off in safety. The battle lasted for an hour, the height was covered with killed and wounded, and the blood flowed in streams down the rocks; at length, Abrahen Zenete being disabled by the thrust of a lance, the Moors gave way and retreated to the castle.

They now opened a galling fire from their battlements and towers, approaching the breaches so as to discharge their cross bows and arquebusses into the advanced guard of the encampment. The marquis was singled out; the shot fell thick about him, and one passed through his buckler and struck upon his cuirass, but without doing him any injury. Every one now saw the danger and inutility of approaching the camp thus near to the castle, and those who had counselled it were now urgent that it should be withdrawn. It was accordingly removed back to its original ground, from which the marquis had most reluctantly advanced it. Nothing but his valour and timely aid had prevented this attack on his outpost from ending in a total rout of all that part of the army.

Many cavaliers of distinction fell in this contest, but the loss of none was felt more deeply than that of Ortega de Prado, Captain of Escaladors. He was one of the bravest men in the service; the same who had devised the first successful blow of the war, the storming of Alhama, where he was the first to plant and mount the scaling ladders. He had always been high in the favour and confidence of the noble Ponce de Leon, who knew how to appreciate and avail himself of the merits of all able and valiant men.*

CHAPTER LVII

SIEGE OF MALAGA CONTINUED.
STRATAGEMS OF VARIOUS KINDS.

Great were the exertions now made both by the besiegers and the besieged to carry on this contest with the utmost vigour. Hamet el Zegri went the rounds of the walls and towers, doubling the guards and putting every thing into the best posture of defence. The garrison was divided into parties of a hundred, to each of which a captain was appointed. Some were to patrole, others to sally forth and skirmish with the enemy, and others to hold themselves ready armed and in reserve. Six albatozas or floating batteries were manned and armed with pieces of artillery to attack the fleet.

On the other hand the Castilian sovereigns kept open a communication by sea with various parts of Spain, from which they received provisions of all kinds; they ordered supplies of powder also from Valencia, Barcelona, Sicily and Portugal. They made great preparations also for storming the city. Towers of wood were constructed to move on wheels, each capable of holding one hundred men; they were furnished with ladders to be thrown from their summits to the tops of the walls; and within those ladders others were encased, to be let down for the descent of the troops into the city. There were gallipagos or tortoises also, being great wooden shields, covered with hides, to protect the assailants and those who undermined the walls.

Secret mines were commenced in various places; some were intended to reach to the foundations of the walls, which were to be propped up with wood, ready to be set on fire; others were to pass under the walls, and remain ready to be broken open, so as to give entrance to the besiegers. At these mines the army worked day and night, and during these secret preparations the ordnance kept up a fire upon the city to divert the attention of the besieged.

In the mean time Hamet el Zegri displayed wonderful vigour and ingenuity in defending the city, and in repairing or fortifying by deep ditches, the breaches made by the enemy. He noted, also, every place where the camp might be assailed with advantage, and gave the besieging army no

*Zurita. Mariana. Abarca.

repose, night or day. While his troops sallied on the land his floating batteries attacked the besiegers on the sea; so that there was incessant skirmishing. The tents called the Queen's hospital were crowded with wounded and the whole army suffered from constant watchfulness and fatigue. To guard against the sudden assaults of the Moors the trenches were deepened and palisadoes erected in front of the camp, and in that part facing Gibralfaro, where the rocky heights did not admit of such defences, a high rampart of earth was thrown up. The cavaliers Garcilasso de la Vega, Juan de Zuñiga and Diego de Atayde were appointed to go the rounds and keep vigilant watch that these fortifications were maintained in good order.

In a little while Hamet discovered the mines secretly commenced by the Christians. He immediately ordered counter mines. The soldiers mutually worked until they met and fought hand to hand in these subterranean passages. The Christians were driven out of one of their mines; fire was set to the wooden frame work and the mine destroyed. Encouraged by this success the Moors attempted a general attack upon the camp, the mines and the besieging fleet. The battle lasted for six hours, on land and water, above and below ground, on bulwark, and in trench and mine; the Moors displayed wonderful intrepidity, but were finally repulsed at all points and obliged to retire into the city, where they were closely invested without the means of receiving any assistance from abroad.

The horrors of famine were now added to the other miseries of Malaga. Hamet el Zegri, with the spirit of a man bred up to war, considered every thing as subservient to the wants of the soldier, and ordered all the grain in the city to be gathered and garnered up for the sole use of those who fought. Even this was dealt out sparingly and each soldier received four ounces of bread in the morning and two in the evening for his daily allowance.

The wealthy inhabitants and all those peacefully inclined, mourned over a resistance which brought destruction upon their houses, death into their families and which they saw must end in their ruin and captivity. Still none of them dared to speak openly of capitulation or even to manifest their grief, lest they should awaken the wrath of their fierce defenders. They surrounded their civic champion Ali Dordux, the great and opulent merchant, who had buckled on shield and cuirass and taken spear in hand for the defence of his native city, and, with a large body of the braver citizens, had charge of one of the gates and a considerable portion of the walls. Drawing Ali Dordux aside they poured forth their griefs to him in secret. "Why," said they, "should we suffer our native city to be made a mere bulwark and fighting place for foreign barbarians and desperate men? They have no families to care for, no property to lose, no love for the soil and no value for their lives. They fight to gratify a thirst for blood or a desire for revenge, and will fight on until Malaga become a ruin and its people slaves. Let us think and act for ourselves, our wives and our children. Let us make private terms with the Christians before it is too late, and so save ourselves from destruction."

The bowels of Ali Dordux yearned towards his fellow citizens; he bethought him also of the sweet security of peace, and the bloodless yet gratifying triumphs of gainful commerce. The idea also of a secret negociation or bargain with the Castilian sovereigns for the redemption of his native city was more conformable to his accustomed habits than this violent appeal to arms, for though he had for a time assumed the warrior, he had not forgotten the merchant. Ali Dordux communed, therefore, with the citizen soldiers under his command and they readily conformed to his opinion. Concerting together they wrote a proposition to the Castilian sovereigns, offering to admit the army into the part of the city entrusted to their care on receiving assurance of protection for the lives and properties of the inhabitants. This writing they delivered to a trusty emissary to take to the Christian camp, appointing the hour and place of his return, that they might be ready to admit him unperceived.

The Moor made his way in safety to the camp and was admitted to the presence of the sovereigns. Eager to gain the city without further cost of blood or treasure, they gave a written promise to grant the conditions and the Moor set out joyfully on his return. As he approached the walls where Ali Dordux and his confederates were waiting to receive him he was descried by a patroling band of Gomeres and considered a spy coming from the camp of the besiegers. They issued forth and seized him in sight of his employers, who gave themselves up for lost. The Gomeres had conducted him nearly to the gate when he escaped from their grasp and fled. They endeavoured to overtake him but were encumbered with armour; he was lightly clad and he fled for his life. One of the Gomeres paused and levelling his cross bow let fly a bolt which pierced the fugitive between the shoulders: he fell and was nearly within their grasp, but rose again: and, with a desperate effort, attained the Christian camp. The Gomeres gave over the pursuit, and the citizens returned thanks to Allah for their deliverance from this fearful peril. As to the faithful messenger he died of his wound shortly after reaching the camp consoled with the idea that he had preserved the secret and the lives of his employers.

CHAPTER LVIII

SUFFERINGS OF THE PEOPLE OF MALAGA.

The sufferings of Malaga spread sorrow and anxiety among the Moors; and they dreaded lest this beautiful city, once the bulwark of the kingdom, should fall into the hands of the unbelievers. The old warrior King Abdalla el Zagal, was still sheltered in Guadix, where he was slowly gathering together his shattered forces. When the people of Guadix heard of the danger and distress of Malaga they urged to be led to its relief, and the alfaquis admonished El Zagal not to desert so righteous and loyal a city in its extremity. His own warlike nature made him feel a sympathy for a place that made so gallant a resistance, and he despatched as powerful a reinforcement as he could spare, under conduct of a chosen captain, with orders to throw themselves into the city.

Intelligence of this reinforcement reached Boabdil el Chico in his royal palace of the Alhambra. Filled with hostility against his uncle and desirous of proving his loyalty to the Castilian sovereigns he immediately sent forth a superior force of horse and foot under an able commander to intercept the detachment. A sharp conflict ensued, the troops of El Zagal were routed with great loss and fled back in confusion to Guadix.

Boabdil, not being accustomed to victories, was flushed with this melancholy triumph. He sent tidings of it to the Castilian sovereigns, accompanied with rich silks, boxes of Arabian perfume, a cup of gold richly wrought and a female captive of Ubeda, as presents to the Queen, and four Arabian steeds, magnificently caparisoned, a sword and dagger richly mounted and several albornozes and other robes, sumptuously embroidered, for the King. He entreated them, at the same time, always to look upon him with favour as their devoted vassal.

Boabdil was fated to be unfortunate even in his victories. His defeat of the forces of his uncle destined to the relief of unhappy Malaga, shocked the feelings and cooled the loyalty of many of his best adherents. The mere men of traffic might rejoice in their golden interval of peace, but the chivalrous spirits of Granada spurned a security purchased by such sacrifices of pride and affection. The people at large having gratified their love of change, began to question whether they had acted generously by their old fighting monarch. "El Zagal," said they, "was fierce and bloody, but then he was true to his country; he was an usurper, it is true, but then he maintained the glory of the crown which he usurped. If his sceptre was a rod of iron to his subjects, it was a sword of steel against their enemies. This Boabdil sacrifices religion, friends, country, every thing to a mere shadow of royalty and is content to hold a rush for a sceptre."

These factious murmurs soon reached the ears of Boabdil, and he apprehended another of his customary reverses. He sent, in all haste, to the Castilian sovereigns, beseeching military aid to keep him on his throne.

Ferdinand graciously complied with a request so much in unison with his policy. A detachment of one thousand cavalry and two thousand infantry was sent under the command of Don Fernandez Gonzalvo of Cordova, subsequently renowned as the Grand Captain. With this succour Boabdil expelled from the city all those who were hostile to him and in favour of his uncle. He felt secure in these troops from their being distinct in manners, language and religion from his subjects, and compromised with his pride in thus exhibiting that most unnatural and humiliating of all regal spectacles, a monarch supported on his throne by foreign weapons and by soldiers hostile to his people.

Nor was Boabdil el Chico the only Moorish sovereign that sought protection from Ferdinand and Isabella. A splendid galley, with latine sails and several banks of oars, came one day into the harbour of Malaga, displaying the standard of the crescent but likewise a white flag in sign of amity. An ambassador landed from it within the Christian lines. He came from the King of Tremezan and brought presents similar to those of Boabdil consisting of Arabian coursers, with bits, stirrups and other furniture of gold, together with costly Moorish mantles: for the Queen there were sumptuous shawls, robes and silken stuffs, ornaments of gold and exquisite oriental perfumes.

The King of Tremezan had been alarmed at the rapid conquests of the Spanish arms and startled by the descent of several Spanish cruisers on the coast of Africa. He craved to be considered a vassal to the Castilian sovereigns and that they would extend such favour and security to his ships and subjects as had been shewn to other Moors who had submitted to their sway. He requested a painting of their arms that he and his subjects might recognize and respect their standard whenever they encountered it. At the same time he implored their clemency towards unhappy Malaga and that its inhabitants might experience the same favour that had been shewn towards the Moors of other captured cities.

This embassy was graciously received by the Castilian sovereigns. They granted the protection required; ordering their commanders to respect the flag of Tremezan unless it should be found rendering assistance to the enemy. They sent also to the Barbary monarch their royal arms, moulded in escutcheons of gold a hand's breadth in size.*

While thus the chances of assistance from without daily decreased, famine raged in the city. The inhabitants were compelled to eat the flesh of horses, and many died of hunger. What made the sufferings of the citizens the more intolerable was, to behold the sea covered with ships daily arriving with provisions for the besiegers. Day after day, also, they saw herds of fat cattle and flocks of sheep driven into the camp. Wheat and flour were piled in

*Cura de los Palacios C 84. Pulgar Part 3. C. 86.

huge mounds in the centre of the encampments, glaring in the sunshine and tantalizing the wretched citizens, who, while they and their children were perishing with hunger, beheld prodigal abundance reigning within a bow-shot of their walls.

CHAPTER LIX

HOW A MOORISH SANTON UNDERTOOK TO DELIVER THE CITY OF MALAGA FROM THE POWER OF ITS ENEMIES.

There lived at this time in a hamlet in the neighborhood of Guadix an ancient Moor of the name of Abrahin Algerbi; he was a native of Guerba, in the Kingdom of Tunis and had for several years led the life of a Santon or hermit. The hot sun of Africa had dried his blood and rendered him of an exalted yet melancholy temperament. He passed most of his time in meditation, prayer, and rigorous abstinence, until his body was wasted and his mind bewildered, and he fancied himself favoured with divine revelations. The Moors, who have a great reverence for all enthusiasts of the kind, looked upon him as inspired, listened to all his ravings as veritable prophecies, and denominated him *el santo* or the Saint.

The woes of the Kingdom of Granada had long exasperated the gloomy spirit of this man, and he had beheld with indignation this beautiful country wrested from the dominion of the faithful and becoming a prey to the unbelievers. He had implored the blessing of Allah on the troops which issued forth from Guadix for the relief of Malaga, but when he saw them return, routed and scattered by their own countrymen he retired to his cell shut himself up from the world and was plunged for a time in the blackest melancholy.

On a sudden he made his appearance again in the streets of Guadix, his face haggard, his form emaciated but his eye beaming with fire. He said that Allah had sent an angel to him in the solitude of his cell, revealing to him a mode of delivering Malaga from its perils, and striking horror and confusion into the camp of the unbelievers. The Moors listened with eager credulity to his words: four hundred of them offered to follow him even to the death, and to obey implicitly his commands. Of this number many were Gomeres, anxious to relieve their countrymen, who formed part of the garrison of Malaga.

They traversed the kingdom by the wild and lonely passes of the mountains, concealing themselves in the day and travelling only in the night, to elude the Christian scouts. At length they arrived at the mountains which tower above Malaga, and looking down beheld the city completely invested, a chain of encampments extending round it from shore to shore, and a line of ships blockading it by sea while the continual thunder of artillery, and the smoke rising in various parts shewed that the siege was pressed with great activity. The hermit scanned the encampments warily from his lofty height. He saw that the part of the encampment of the Marquis of Cadiz, which was at the foot of the height, and on the margin of the sea was most assailable, the rocky soil not admitting ditches or pallisadoes. Remaining concealed all day, he descended with his followers at night to the sea coast, and approached silently to the outworks. He had given them their instructions: they were to rush suddenly upon the camp, fight their way through and throw themselves into the city.

It was just at the grey of the dawning, when objects are obscurely visible, that they made this desperate attempt. Some sprang suddenly upon the centinels, others rushed into the sea and got round the works, others clambered over the breastworks. There was sharp skirmishing, a great part of the Moors were cut to pieces, but about two hundred succeeded in getting into the gates of Malaga.

The Santon took no part in the conflict nor did he endeavour to enter the city. His plans were of a different nature. Drawing apart from the battle he threw himself on his knees on a rising ground, and lifting his hands to heaven appeared to be absorbed in prayer. The Christians as they were searching for fugitives in the clefts of the rocks found him at his devotions. He stirred not at their approach, but remained fixed as a statue without changing colour or moving a muscle. Filled with surprize, not unmingled with awe, they took him to the Marquis of Cadiz. He was wrapped in a coarse albornoz or Moorish mantle; his beard was long and grizzled, and there was something wild and melancholy in his look that inspired curiosity.

On being examined he gave himself out as a saint to whom Allah had revealed the events that were to take place in that siege. The marquis demanded when and how Malaga was to be taken. He replied that he knew full well, but he was forbidden to reveal those important secrets except to the King and Queen. The good marquis was not more given to superstitious fancies than other commanders of his time, yet there seemed something singular and mysterious about this man; he might have some important intelligence to communicate, so he was persuaded to send him to the King and Queen. He was conducted to the royal tent surrounded by a curious multitude exclaiming *el Moro Santo!* for the news had spread through the camp that they had taken a Moorish prophet.

The King having dined was taking his siesta or afternoon's sleep in his tent; and the Queen though curious to see this singular man, yet, from a natural delicacy and reserve, delayed until the King should be present. He was taken therefore to an adjoining tent, in which were Doña Beatrix de Bovadilla Marchioness of Moya, and Don Alvaro of Portugal, son of the Duke of Braganza, with two or three attendants. The Moor, ignorant of the Spanish tongue, had not understood the conversation of the guards, and supposed, from the magnificence of the furniture and the silken hangings, that this was the royal tent. From the respect paid by the attendants to Don Alvaro and the marchioness, he concluded that they were the King and Queen.

He now asked for a draught of water; a jar was brought to him and the guard released his arm to enable him to drink. The marchioness perceived a sudden change in his countenance, and something sinister in the expression of his eye, and shifted her position to a more remote part of the tent. Pretending to raise the water to his lips the Moor unfolded his albornoz so as to grasp a scymetar which he wore concealed beneath; then dashing down the jar he drew his weapon and gave Don Alvaro a blow on the head that struck him to the earth and nearly deprived him of life. Turning then upon the marchioness he made a violent blow at her, but in his eagerness and agitation his scymetar caught in the drapery of the tent; the force of the blow was broken, and the weapon struck harmless upon some golden ornaments of her head dress.*

Ruy Lopez de Toledo, treasurer to the Queen, and Juan de Belalcazar, a sturdy friar, who were present grappled and struggled with the desperado and immediately the guards who had conducted him from the Marquis of Cadiz, fell upon him and cut him to pieces.†

The King and Queen, brought out of their tents by the noise, were filled with horror when they learned the imminent peril from which they had escaped. The mangled body of the Moor was taken by the people of the camp and thrown into the city from a catapult. The Gomeres gathered up the body with deep reverence as the remains of a saint; they washed and perfumed it, and buried it with great honour and loud lamentations. In revenge of his death they slew one of their principal Christian captives and having tied his body upon an ass they drove the animal forth into the camp.

From this time there was appointed an additional guard around the tents of the King and Queen, composed of twelve hundred cavaliers of rank of the Kingdoms of Castile and Aragon. No person was admitted to the royal presence armed. No Moor was allowed to enter the camp without a previous knowledge of his character and business and on no account was any Moor to be introduced into the presence of the sovereigns.

An act of treachery of such ferocious nature gave rise to a train of gloomy apprehensions. There were many cabins and sheds about the camp, con-

*Pietro Martyr. Epist. 62.
†Cura de Los Palacios.

structed of branches of trees which had become dry and combustible, and fears were entertained that they might be set on fire by the Mudexares or Moorish vassals, who visited the army. Some even dreaded that attempts might be made to poison the wells and fountains. To quiet these dismal alarms all Mudexares were ordered to leave the camp, and all loose idle loiterers who could not give a good account of themselves were taken into custody.

CHAPTER LX

HOW HAMET EL ZEGRI WAS HARDENED IN HIS OBSTINACY BY THE ARTS OF A MOORISH ASTROLOGER.

Among those followers of the santon that had effected their entrance into the city was a dark African of the tribe of the Gomeres, who was likewise a hermit or dervise, and passed among the Moors for a holy and inspired man. No sooner were the mangled remains of his predecessor buried with the honours of martyrdom, than this dervise elevated himself in his place, and professed to be gifted with the spirit of prophecy. He displayed a white banner which he assured the Moors was sacred; that he had retained it for twenty years for some signal purpose, and that Allah had revealed to him that under that banner the inhabitants of Malaga should sally forth upon the camp of the unbelievers; put it to utter rout, and banquet upon the provisions in which it abounded.* The hungry and credulous Moors were elated at this prediction, and cried out to be led forth at once to the attack; but the dervise told them the time was not yet arrived, for every event had its allotted day in the decrees of fate; they must await patiently, therefore, until the appointed time should be revealed to him by heaven. Hamet el Zegri listened to the dervise with profound reverence, and his example had great effect in encreasing the awe and deference of his followers. He took the holy man up into his strong hold of Gibralfaro, consulted him on all occasions, and hung out his white banner on the loftiest tower, as a signal of encouragement to the people of the city.

In the mean time the prime chivalry of Spain was gradually assembling before the walls of Malaga. The army which had commenced the siege had been worn out by extreme hardships, having had to construct immense works, to dig trenches and mines, to mount guard by sea and land, to patrole

*Cura de Los Palacios.

the mountains, and to sustain incessant conflicts. The sovereigns were obliged therefore to call upon various distant cities for reinforcements of horse and foot. Many nobles, also, assembled their vassals and repaired of their own accord, to the royal camp.

Every little while some stately galley or gallant caravel would stand into the harbour, displaying the well known banner of some Spanish cavalier, and thundering from its artillery a salutation to the sovereigns and a defiance to the Moors. On the land side also reinforcements would be seen, wending down from the mountains to the sound of drum and trumpet, and marching into the camp with glistening arms, as yet unsullied by the toils of war.

One morning the whole sea was whitened by the sails and vexed by the oars of ships and galleys bearing towards the port. One hundred vessels of various kinds and sizes arrived, some armed for warlike service others deep freighted with provisions. At the same time the clangour of drum and trumpet bespoke the arrival of a powerful force by land, which came pouring in lengthening columns into the camp.

This mighty reinforcement was furnished by the Duke of Medina Sidonia, who reigned like a petty monarch over his vast possessions. He came with this princely force, a volunteer to the royal standard, not having been summoned by the sovereigns, and he brought moreover a loan of twenty thousand doblas of gold.

When the camp was thus powerfully reinforced, Isabella advised that new offers of an indulgent kind should be made to the inhabitants, for she was anxious to prevent the miseries of a protracted siege, or the effusion of blood that must attend a general attack. A fresh summons was therefore sent for the city to surrender with a promise of life, liberty and property in case of immediate compliance, but denouncing all the horrors of war if the defence were obstinately continued.

Hamet el Zegri again rejected the offer with scorn. His main fortifications as yet were but little impaired and were capable of holding out much longer; he trusted to the thousand evils and accidents that beset a besieging army, and to the inclemencies of the approaching season; and it is said he, as well as his followers, had an infatuated belief in the predictions of the dervise.

The worthy Fray Antonio Agapida does not scruple to affirm that the pretended prophet of the city was an arch nigromancer, or Moorish magician "of which there be countless many," says he, "in the filthy sect of Mahomet," and that he was leagued with the prince of the powers of the air, to endeavour to work the confusion and defeat of the Christian army. The worthy father asserts also, that Hamet employed him in a high tower of the Gibralfaro, which commanded a wide view over sea and land, where he wrought spells and incantations with astrolabes and other diabolical instruments, to defeat the Christian ships and forces, whenever they were engaged with the Moors.

To the potent spells of this sorcerer he ascribes the perils and losses sustained by a party of cavaliers of the royal household in a desperate combat to gain two towers of the suburb near the gate of the city called la Puerta de Granada. The Christians led on by Ruy Lopez de Toldeo, the valiant treasurer of the Queen, took, and lost, and retook the towers which were finally set on fire by the Moors, and abandoned to the flames by both parties. To the same malignant influence he attributes the damage done to the Christian fleet, which was so vigorously assailed by the albatozas, or floating batteries of the Moors, that one ship belonging to the Duke of Medina Sidonia was sunk and the rest were obliged to retire.

"Hamet el Zegri," says Fray Antonio Agapida, "stood on the top of the high tower of Gibralfaro and beheld this injury wrought upon the Christian force and his proud heart was puffed up. And the Moorish nigromancer stood beside him. And he pointed out to him the Christian host below, encamped on every eminence around the city and covering its fertile valley, and the many ships floating upon the tranquil sea, and he bade him be strong of heart, for that in a few days all this mighty fleet would be scattered by the winds of heaven; and that he should sally forth under guidance of the sacred banner, and attack this host and utterly defeat it, and make spoil of those sumptuous tents, and Malaga should be triumphantly revenged upon her assailants. So the heart of Hamet was hardened like that of Pharaoh and he persisted in setting at defiance the Catholic sovereigns and their army of saintly warriors."

CHAPTER LXI

SIEGE OF MALAGA CONTINUED. DESTRUCTION OF A TOWER BY FRANCISCO RAMIREZ DE MADRID.

Seeing the infatuated obstinacy of the besieged, the Christians now approached their works to the walls gaining one position after another, preparatory to a general assault. Near the barrier of the city was a bridge with four arches, defended at each end by a strong and lofty tower by which a part of the army would have to pass in making a general attack. The commander in chief of the artillery Francisco Ramirez de Madrid, was ordered to take possession of this bridge. The approach to it was perilous in the extreme, from the exposed situation of the assailants and the numbers of Moors that garrisoned the towers. Francisco Ramirez, therefore, secretly excavated a mine leading beneath the first tower, and placed a piece of ordnance, with its mouth upwards, immediately under the foundation, with a train of powder to produce an explosion at the necessary moment.

When this was arranged he advanced slowly with his forces in face of the towers, erecting bulwarks at every step and gradually gaining ground until he arrived near to the bridge. He then planted several pieces of artillery in his works and began to batter the tower. The Moors replied bravely from their battlements, but in the heat of the combat the piece of ordnance under the foundation was discharged. The earth was rent open, a part of the tower overthrown and several of the Moors torn to pieces: the rest took to flight overwhelmed with terror at this thundering explosion bursting beneath their feet, and at beholding the earth vomiting flames and smoke, for never before had they witnessed such a stratagem in warfare. The Christians rushed forward and took possession of the abandoned post, and immediately commenced an attack upon the other tower at the opposite end of the bridge, to which the Moors had retired. An incessant fire of crossbows and arquebusses was kept up between the rival towers, vollies of stones were discharged and no one dared to venture upon the intermediate bridge.

Francisco de Ramirez at length renewed his former mode of approach, making bulwarks step by step, while the Moors at the other end swept the bridge with their artillery. The combat was long and bloody, furious on the part of the Moors, patient and persevering on the part of the Christians. By slow degrees they accomplished their advance across the bridge, drove the enemy before them and remained masters of this important pass.

For this valiant and skillful achievement King Ferdinand, after the surrender of the city, conferred the dignity of knighthood upon Francisco Ramirez, in the tower which he had so gloriously gained.* The worthy padre Fray Antonio Agapida indulges in more than a page of extravagant eulogy upon this invention of blowing up the foundation of the tower by a piece of ordnance, which he affirms to be the first instance on record of gunpowder being used in a mine.

CHAPTER LXII
HOW THE PEOPLE OF MALAGA EXPOSTULATED WITH HAMET EL ZEGRI.

While the dervise was deluding the garrison of Malaga with vain hopes, the famine encreased to a terrible degree. The Gomeres ranged about the city as though it had been a conquered place, taking by force whatever they found eatable in the houses of the peaceful citizens, and breaking open

*Pulgar. part 3. Cap. 91.

vaults and cellars and demolishing walls, wherever they thought provisions might be concealed.

The wretched inhabitants had no longer bread to eat; the horse flesh also now failed them and they were fain to devour skins and hides toasted at the fire, and to assuage the hunger of their children with vine leaves cut up and fried in oil. Many perished of famine or of the unwholesome food with which they endeavoured to relieve it, and many took refuge in the Christian camp, preferring captivity to the horrors which surrounded them.

At length the sufferings of the inhabitants became so great as to conquer even their fears of Hamet and his Gomeres. They assembled before the house of Ali Dordux the wealthy merchant whose stately mansion was at the foot of the hill of the Alcazaba, and they urged him to stand forth as their leader and to intercede with Hamet el Zegri for a surrender. Ali Dordux was a man of courage as well as policy; he perceived also that hunger was giving boldness to the citizens, while he trusted it was subduing the fierceness of the soldiery. He armed himself, therefore, cap a pie, and undertook this dangerous parley with the alcayde. He associated with him an alfaqui, named Abrahen Alharis and an important inhabitant named Amar Ben Amar, and they ascended to the fortress of Gibralfaro, followed by several of the trembling merchants.

They found Hamet el Zegri, not as before surrounded by ferocious guards and all the implements of war, but in a chamber of one of the lofty towers at a table of stone covered with scrolls and traced with strange characters and mystic diagrams, while instruments of singular and unknown form lay about the room. Beside Hamet el Zegri stood the prophetic dervise, who appeared to have been explaining to him the mysterious inscriptions of the scrolls. His presence filled the citizens with awe, for even Ali Dordux considered him a man inspired.

The alfaqui Abrahen Alharis whose sacred character gave him boldness to speak, now lifted up his voice and addressed Hamet el Zegri. "We implore you," said he solemnly, "in the name of the most powerful God, no longer to persist in a vain resistance, which must end in our destruction, but deliver up the city while clemency is yet to be obtained. Think how many of our warriors have fallen by the sword; do not suffer those who survive to perish by famine. Our wives and children cry to us for bread and we have none to give them. We see them expire in lingering agony before our eyes, while the enemy mocks our misery by displaying the abundance of his camp. Of what avail is our defence? Are our walls, peradventure more strong than the walls of Ronda? Are our warriors more brave than the defenders of Loxa? The walls of Ronda were thrown down, and the warriors of Loxa had to surrender. Do we hope for succour?—from whence are we to receive it. The time for hope is gone by. Granada has lost its power; it no longer possesses chivalry, commanders or a King. Boabdil sits a vassal in the degraded halls of the Alhambra; El Zagal is a fugitive shut up within the walls of Guadix. The kingdom is divided against itself; its strength is gone, its pride fallen, its very existence at an end. In the name of Allah we conjure thee who art our captain; be not our direst enemy but surrender these ruins of our once happy Malaga and deliver us from these overwhelming horrors."

Such was the supplication forced from the inhabitants by the extremity of their sufferings. Hamet el Zegri listened to the alfaqui without anger, for he respected the sanctity of his office. His heart, too, was at that moment lifted up with a vain confidence. "Yet a few days of patience," said he, "and all these evils will suddenly have an end. I have been conferring with this holy man and find that the time of our deliverance is at hand. The decrees of fate are inevitable; it is written in the book of destiny that we shall sally forth and destroy the camp of the unbelievers and banquet upon those mountains of grain which are piled up in the midst of it. So Allah hath promised by the mouth of this his prophet.   Allah Achbar! God is great. Let no man oppose the decrees of heaven!"

The citizens bowed with profound reverence, for no true Moslem pretends to struggle against whatever is written in the book of fate. Ali Dordux, who had come prepared to champion the city and to brave the ire of Hamet, humbled himself before this holy man; and gave faith to his prophecies as the revelations of Allah. So the deputies returned to the citizens and exhorted them to be of good cheer. "A few days longer," said they, "and our sufferings are to terminate. When the white banner is removed from the tower then look out for deliverance for the hour of sallying forth will have arrived." The people retired to their houses with sorrowful hearts; they tried in vain to quiet the cries of their famishing children, and day by day, and hour by hour, their anxious eyes were turned to the sacred banner which still continued to wave on the tower of Gibralfaro.

CHAPTER LXIII

HOW HAMET EL ZEGRI SALLIED FORTH WITH THE SACRED BANNER TO ATTACK THE CHRISTIAN CAMP.

"The Moorish nigromancer," observes the worthy Fray Antonio Agapida, "remained shut up in the tower of the Gibralfaro, devising devilish means to work mischief and discomfiture upon the Christians. He was daily consulted by Hamet el Zegri, who had great faith in those black and magic arts which he had brought with him from the bosom of heathen Africa."

From the account given of this dervise and his incantations by the worthy father, it would appear that he was an astrologer and was studying the stars, and endeavouring to calculate the day and hour when a successful attack might be made upon the Christian camp.

Famine had now encreased to such a degree as to distress even the garrison of Gibralfaro, although the Gomeres had seized upon all the provisions they could find in the city. Their passions were sharpened by hunger, and they became restless and turbulent and impatient for action.

Hamet el Zegri was one day in council with his captains, perplexed by the pressure of events, when the dervise entered among them. "The hour of victory," exclaimed he, "is at hand. Allah has commanded that tomorrow morning ye shall sally forth to the fight. I will bear before you the sacred banner and deliver your enemies into your hands. Remember, however, that ye are but instruments in the hands of Allah to take vengeance on the enemies of the faith. Go into battle, therefore, with pure hearts, forgiving each other all past offences, for those who are charitable towards each other, will be victorious over the foe."

The words of the dervise were received with rapture. All Gibralfaro and the Alcazaba resounded immediately with the din of arms; and Hamet sent throughout the towers and fortifications of the city and selected the choicest troops and most distinguished captains for this eventful combat.

In the morning early the rumour went throughout the city that the sacred banner had disappeared from the tower of Gibralfaro and all Malaga was roused to witness the sally that was to destroy the unbelievers. Hamet descended from his strong hold, accompanied by his principal captain Abrahen Zenete and followed by his Gomeres. The dervise led the way displaying the white banner, the sacred pledge of victory. The multitude shouted Allah Achbar! and prostrated themselves before the banner as it passed. Even the dreaded Hamet was hailed with praises, for in their hope of speedy relief, through the prowess of his arm, the populace forgot every thing but his bravery. Every bosom in Malaga was agitated by hope and fear; the old men, the women and children, and all who went not forth to battle mounted on tower, and battlement and roof, to watch a combat that was to decide their fate.

Before sallying forth from the city the dervise addressed the troops; reminding them of the holy nature of this enterprize and warning them not to forfeit the protection of the sacred banner by any unworthy act. They were not to pause to make spoil nor to take prisoners: They were to press forward, fighting valiantly and granting no quarter. The gate was then thrown open and the dervise issued forth followed by the army. They directed their assault upon the encampments of the Master of Santiago and the Master of Calatrava and came upon them so suddenly that they killed and wounded several of the guards. Abrahen Zenete made his way into one of the tents where he beheld several Christian striplings just starting from their slumber. The heart of the Moor was suddenly touched with pity for their youth, or perhaps he scorned the weakness of the foe. He smote them with the flat instead of the edge of his sword; "away imps," cried he, "away to your mothers." The fanatic dervise reproached him with his clemency. "I did not kill them," replied Zenete, "because I saw no beards!"*

The alarm was given in the camp and the Christians rushed from all quarters to defend the gates of the bulwarks. Don Pedro Puertocarrero, Senior of Moguer, and his brother Don Alonzo Pacheco planted themselves, with their followers, in the gateway of the encampment of the Master of Santiago, and bore the whole brunt of the battle until they were reinforced. The gate of the encampment of the Master of Calatrava was in like manner defended by Lorenzo Saurez de Mendoza. Hamet el Zegri was furious at being thus checked where he had expected a miraculous victory. He led his troops repeatedly to the attack, hoping to force the gates before succour should arrive. They fought with vehement ardour, but were as often repulsed, and every time they returned to the assault they found their enemies doubled in number. The Christians opened a cross fire of all kinds of missiles from their bulwarks; the Moors could effect but little damage upon a foe thus protected behind their works while they themselves were exposed from head to foot. The Christians singled out the most conspicuous cavaliers, the greater part of whom were either slain or wounded. Still the Moors, infatuated by the predictions of the prophet, fought desperately and devotedly, and they were furious to revenge the slaughter of their leaders.

They rushed upon certain death, endeavouring madly to scale the bulwarks or force the gates; and fell amidst showers of darts and lances, filling the ditches with their mangled bodies.

Hamet el Zegri raged along the front of the bulwarks seeking an opening for attack. He gnashed his teeth with fury as he saw so many of his chosen warriors slain around him. He seemed to have a charmed life, for though constantly in the hottest of the fight, amidst showers of missiles he still escaped uninjured. Blindly confiding in the prophecy of victory he continued to urge on his devoted troops. The dervise too ran like a maniac through the ranks, waving his white banner, and inciting the Moors by howlings rather than by shouts. In the midst of his frenzy a stone from a catapult struck him in the head and dashed out his bewildered brains.†

When the Moors beheld their prophet slain and his banner in the dust they were seized with despair and fled in confusion to the city. Hamet el

*Cura de Los Palacios C. 84.
†Garibay Lib. 18 C. 33.

Zegri made some effort to rally them, but was himself confounded by the fall of the dervise. He covered the flight of his broken forces, turning repeatedly upon their pursuers and slowly making his retreat into the city.

The inhabitants of Malaga witnessed from their walls, with trembling anxiety, the whole of this disastrous conflict. At the first onset, when they beheld the guards of the camp put to flight, they exclaimed, "Allah has given us the victory!" and they sent up shouts of triumph. Their exultation, however, was soon turned into doubt when they beheld their troops repulsed in repeated attacks. They could see, from time to time, some distinguished warrior laid low and others brought back bleeding to the city. When at length the sacred banner fell and the routed troops came flying to the gates pursued and cut down by the foe, horror and despair seized upon the populace.

As Hamet el Zegri entered the gates he was greeted with loud lamentations. Mothers whose sons had been slain shrieked curses after him as he passed. Some in the anguish of their hearts threw down their famishing babes before him, exclaiming, "trample on them with thy horse's feet, for we have no food to give them and we cannot endure their cries." All heaped execrations on his head as the cause of the woes of Malaga.

The warlike part of the citizens, also, and many warriors who with their wives and children had taken refuge in Malaga from the mountain fortresses now joined in the popular clamour, for their hearts were overcome by the sufferings of their families.

Hamet el Zegri found it impossible to withstand this torrent of lamentations, curses and reproaches. His military ascendancy was at an end, for most of his officers and the prime warriors of his African band had fallen in this disastrous sally. Turning his back, therefore, upon the city and abandoning it to its own counsels, he retired with the remnant of his Gomeres to his strong hold in the Gibralfaro.

CHAPTER LXIV

HOW THE CITY OF MALAGA CAPITULATED.

The people of Malaga being no longer overawed by Hamet el Zegri and his Gomeres, turned to Ali Dordux the magnanimous merchant and put the fate of the city into his hands. He had already gained the alcaydes of the castle of the Genoese and of the citadel into his party, and in the late confusion had gained the sway over those important fortresses. He now associated himself with the alfaqui Abrahen Alhariz and four of the principal inhabitants, and, forming a provisional junta they sent heralds to the Christian sovereigns, offering to surrender the city on certain terms, protecting the persons and property of the inhabitants, permitting them to reside as Mudexares or tributary vassals either in Malaga or elsewhere.

When these heralds arrived at the camp and made known their mission the anger of Ferdinand was kindled. "Return to your fellow citizens," said he, "and tell them that the day of grace is gone by. They have persisted in a fruitless defence until they are driven by necessity to capitulate; they must surrender unconditionally and abide the fate of the vanquished. Those who merit death shall suffer death; those who merit captivity shall be made captives."

This stern reply spread consternation among the people of Malaga; but Ali Dordux comforted them and undertook to go in person and pray for favorable terms. When the people beheld this great and wealthy merchant, who was so eminent in their city, departing with his associates on this mission, they plucked up heart, for they said, "surely the Christian King will not turn a deaf ear to such a man as Ali Dordux!"

Ferdinand, however, would not even admit the ambassadors to his presence. "Send them to the devil," said he in a great passion to the Commander of Leon, "I'll not see them. Let them get back to their city. They shall all surrender to my mercy as vanquished enemies."*

To give emphasis to this reply he ordered a general discharge from all the artillery and batteries, and there was a great shout throughout the camp, and all the lombards and catapults and other engines of war thundered furiously upon the city doing great damage.

Ali Dordux and his companions returned to the city with downcast countenances, and could scarce make the reply of the Christian sovereign be heard for the roaring of the artillery, the tumbling of the walls and the cries of women and children. The citizens were greatly astonished and dismayed when they found the little respect paid to their most eminent man, but the warriors who were in the city exclaimed, "What has this merchant to do with questions between men of battle. Let us not address the enemy as abject suppliants, who have no power to injure, but as valiant men who have weapons in their hands."

So they dispatched another message to the Christian sovereigns, offering to yield up the city and all their effects on condition of being secured in their personal liberty. Should this be denied they declared that they would hang from the battlements fifteen hundred Christian captives, male and female, that they would put all their old men, their women and children into the citadel, set fire to the city and sally forth sword in hand, to fight until the last gasp. "In this way," said they, "the Spanish sovereigns shall gain a bloody victory and the fall of Malaga be renowned while the world endures."

*Cura de Los Palacios Cap 84.

To this fierce and swelling message Ferdinand replied that if a single Christian captive were injured, not a Moor in Malaga but should be put to the edge of the sword.

A great conflict of counsels now arose in Malaga. The warriors were for following up their menace by some desparate act of vengeance or of self-devotion. Those who had families looked with anguish upon their wives and daughters, and thought it better to die than live to see them captives. By degrees, however, the transports of passion and despair subsided, the love of life resumed its sway, and they turned once more to Ali Dordux, as the man most prudent in council and able in negociation. By his advice fourteen of the principal inhabitants were chosen from the fourteen districts of the city and sent to the camp, bearing a long letter couched in terms of the most humble supplication.

Various debates now took place in the Christian camp. Many of the cavaliers were exasperated against Malaga for its long resistance, which had caused the death of many of their relations and favorite companions. It had long been a strong hold for Moorish depredators, and the mart where most of the warriors captured in the Axarquia had been exposed in triumph and sold to slavery. They represented, moreover, that there were many Moorish cities yet to be besieged, and that an example ought to be made of Malaga to prevent all obstinate resistance thereafter. They advised, therefore, that all the inhabitants should be put to the sword!*

The humane heart of Isabella revolted at such sanguinary counsels. She insisted that their triumph should not be disgraced by cruelty. Ferdinand, however, was inflexible in refusing to grant any preliminary terms, insisting on an unconditional surrender. The people of Malaga now abandoned themselves to paroxysms of despair; on the one side they saw famine and death, on the other slavery and chains. The mere men of the sword, who had no families to protect, were loud for signalizing their fall by some illustrious action. "Let us sacrifice our Christian captives and then destroy ourselves," cried some. "Let us put all the women and children to death, set fire to the city, fall on the Christian camp and die sword in hand," cried others.

Ali Dordux gradually made his voice be heard amidst the general clamour. He addressed himself to the principal inhabitants and to those who had children. "Let those who live by the sword die by the sword," cried he, "but let us not follow their desperate councils. Who knows what sparks of pity may be awakened in the bosoms of the Christian sovereigns when they behold our unoffending wives and daughters and our helpless little ones. The Christian Queen, they say, is full of mercy."

At these words the hearts of the unhappy people of Malaga yearned over

*Pulgar.

their families and they empowered Ali Dordux to deliver up the city to the mercy of the Castilian sovereigns.

The merchant now went to and fro and had several communications with Ferdinand and Isabella, and interested several principal cavaliers in his cause. And he sent rich presents to the King and Queen of oriental merchandize; silks and stuffs of gold, and jewels and precious stones, and spices and perfumes and many other rare and sumptuous things which he had accumulated in his great tradings with the east, and he gradually found favour in the eyes of the sovereigns.* Finding that there was nothing to be obtained for the city, he now, like a prudent man, and able merchant, began to negociate for himself and his immediate friends.

He represented that from the first they had been desirous of yielding up the city but had been prevented by warlike and highhanded men who had threatened their lives; he entreated, therefore, that mercy might be extended to them and that they might not be confounded with the guilty.

The sovereigns had accepted the presents of Ali Dordux, how could they turn a deaf ear to his petition? So they granted a pardon to him and to forty families which he named, and it was agreed that they should be protected in their lives and property and permitted to reside in Malaga as Mudexares or Moslem vassals, and to follow their customary pursuits.† All this being arranged, Ali Dordux delivered up twenty of the principal inhabitants to remain as hostages until the whole city should be placed in the possession of the Christians.

Don Gutiere de Cardenas, señior commander of Leon, now entered the city armed cap a pie, on horseback, and took possession in the name of the Castilian sovereigns. He was followed by his retainers and by the captains and cavaliers of the army, and in a little while the standards of the cross and of the blessed Santiago and of the Catholic sovereigns were elevated on the principal tower of the Alcazaba. When these standards were beheld from the camp, the Queen and the princess and the ladies of the court and all the royal retinue knelt down and gave thanks and praises to the holy virgin and to Santiago for this great triumph of the faith, and the bishops and other clergy who were present and the choristers of the royal chapel chaunted *Te Deum laudamus* and *Gloria in excelsis.*

*Ms. Chron. of Valera.
†Cura de Los Palacios.

CHAPTER LXV

FULFILMENT OF THE PROPHECY OF THE DERVISE. FATE OF HAMET EL ZEGRI.

No sooner was the city delivered up than the wretched inhabitants implored permission to purchase bread for themselves and their children from the heaps of grain which they had so often gazed at wistfully from their walls. Their prayer was granted, and they issued forth with the famished eagerness of starving men. It was piteous to behold the struggles of those unhappy people as they contended who first should have their necessities relieved.

"Thus," says the pious Fray Antonio Agapida, "thus are the predictions of false prophets sometimes permitted to be verified, but always to the confusion of those who trust in them; for the words of the Moorish nigromancer came to pass that they should eat of those heaps of bread; but they ate of them in humiliation and defeat, and with sorrow and bitterness of heart."

Dark and fierce were the feelings of Hamet el Zegri as he looked down from the castle of Gibralfaro and beheld the Christian legions pouring into the city, and the standard of the cross supplanting the crescent on the citadel. "The people of Malaga," said he, "have trusted to a man of trade and he has trafficked them away, but let us not suffer ourselves to be bound, hand and foot, and delivered up as part of his bargain. We have yet strong walls around us, and trusty weapons in our hands. Let us fight until buried beneath the last tumbling tower of Gibralfaro, or rushing down from among its ruins carry havoc among the unbelievers as they throng the streets of Malaga."

The fierceness of the Gomeres, however, was broken. They could have died in the breach had their castle been assailed, but the slow advances of famine subdued their strength without rousing their passions, and sapped the force both of soul and body. They were almost unanimous for a surrender.

It was a hard struggle for the proud spirit of Hamet to bow itself to ask for terms. Still he trusted that the valour of his defence would gain him respect in the eyes of a chivalrous foe. "Ali," said he, "has negociated like a merchant; I will capitulate as a soldier." He sent a herald, therefore, to Ferdinand offering to yield up his castle but demanding a separate treaty.* The Castilian sovereign sent a laconic and stern reply. "He shall receive no terms but such as have been granted to the community of Malaga."

For two days Hamet el Zegri remained brooding in his castle, after the city was in possession of the Christians; at length the clamours of his followers compelled him to surrender. When the broken remnant of this fierce African garrison descended from their cragged fortress they were so worn

*Cura de Los Palacios.

by watchfulness, famine and battle, yet carried such a lurking fury in their eyes, that they looked more like fiends than men. They were all condemned to slavery, excepting Abrahen Zenete. The instance of clemency which he had shewn in refraining to harm the Spanish striplings on the last sally from Malaga, won him favorable terms. It was cited as a magnanimous act by the Spanish cavaliers, and all admitted that, though a Moor in blood, he possessed the Christian heart of a Castilian hidalgo.*

As to Hamet el Zegri, on being asked what moved him to such hardened obstinacy, he replied, "when I undertook my command I pledged myself to fight in defence of my faith, my city and my sovereign until slain or made prisoner, and, depend upon it, had I had men to stand by me, I should have died fighting, instead of thus tamely surrendering myself without a weapon in my hand."

"Such," says the pious Fray Antonio Agapida, "was the diabolical hatred and stiffnecked opposition of this infidel to our holy cause. But he was justly served by our most Catholic and high minded sovereign, for his pertinacious defence of the city; for Ferdinand ordered that he should be loaded with chains and thrown into a dungeon."†

CHAPTER LXVI

HOW THE CASTILIAN SOVEREIGNS TOOK POSSESSION OF THE CITY OF MALAGA, AND HOW KING FERDINAND SIGNALIZED HIMSELF BY HIS SKILL IN BARGAINING WITH THE INHABITANTS FOR THEIR RANSOM.

One of the first cares of the conquerors on entering Malaga was to search for Christian captives. Nearly sixteen hundred, men and women, were found, and among them were persons of distinction. Some of them had been ten, fifteen and twenty years in captivity. Many had been servants to the Moors, or labourers on public works, and some had passed their time in chains and dungeons. Preparations were made to celebrate their deliverance as a Christian triumph. A tent was erected not far from the city, and furnished with an altar and all the solemn decorations of a chapel. Here the King and Queen waited to receive the Christian captives. They were assembled in the city and marshalled forth in piteous procession. Many of them had still the chains and shackles on their legs. They were wasted with fam-

*Cura de Los Palacios Cap 84.
†Pulgar. Cronica.

ine, their hair and beards overgrown and matted and their faces pale and haggard from long confinement. When they beheld themselves restored to liberty and surrounded by their countrymen, some stared wildly about as if in a dream; others gave way to frantic transports, but most of them wept for joy. All present were moved to tears by so touching a spectacle. When the procession arrived at what is called the gate of Granada it was met by a great concourse from the camp, with crosses and pennons, who turned and followed the captives, singing hymns of praise and thanksgiving. When they came in presence of the King and Queen, they threw themselves on their knees and would have kissed their feet, as their saviours and deliverers, but the sovereigns prevented such humiliation and graciously extended them their hands. They then prostrated themselves before the altar, and all present joined them in giving thanks to God for their liberation from this cruel bondage. By orders of the King and Queen their chains were then taken off, and they were clad in decent rayment, and food was set before them. After they had ate and drank and were refreshed and invigorated, they were provided with money and all things necessary for their journey and sent joyfully to their homes.

While the old chroniclers dwell with becoming enthusiasm on this pure and affecting triumph of humanity, they go on in a strain of equal eulogy, to describe a spectacle of a different nature. It so happened that there were found in the city twelve of those renegado Christians who had deserted to the Moors and conveyed false intelligence during the siege. A barbarous species of punishment was inflicted upon them, borrowed, it is said, from the Moors, and peculiar to these wars. They were tied to stakes in a public place, and horsemen exercised their skill in transpiercing them with pointed reeds, hurled at them while careering at full speed, until the miserable victims expired beneath their wounds. Several apostate Moors, also, who, having embraced Christianity, had afterwards relapsed into their early faith, and had taken refuge in Malaga from the vengeance of the Inquisition, were publicly burnt. "These," says an old jesuit historian exultingly, "these were the tilts of reeds and the illuminations most pleasing for this victorious festival, and for the Catholic piety of our sovereigns."*

When the city was cleansed from the impurities and offensive odours which had collected during the siege, the bishops and other clergy who accompanied the court, and the choir of the royal chapel, walked in procession to the principal mosque, which was consecrated and entitled Santa Maria de

*Los renegados fueron acañavareados; y los conversos quemados: y estos fueron las cañas y luminarias mas alegres por la fiesta de la vitoria, para la piedad Catholica de nuestros Reyes.
Abarca. Anales de Aragon.
Tom 2. Rey XXX. C. 3.

la Incarnacion. This done the King and Queen entered the city accompanied by the Grand Cardinal of Spain, and the principal nobles and cavaliers of the army, and heard a solemn mass. The church was then elevated into a cathedral, and Malaga was made a bishoprick, and many of the neighbouring towns were comprehended in its diocese. The Queen took up her residence in the Alcazaba, in the apartments of her valiant treasurer Ruy Lopez, from whence she had a view of the whole city; but the King established his quarters in the warrior castle of Gibralfaro.

And now came to be considered the disposition of the Moorish prisoners. All those who were strangers in the city and had either taken refuge there or had entered to defend it, were at once considered slaves. They were divided into three lots. One was set apart for the service of God in redeeming Christian captives from bondage either in the Kingdom of Granada, or in Africa; the second lot was divided among those who had aided either in field or cabinet in the present siege, according to their rank; the third was appropriated to defray, by their sale, the great expenses incurred in the reduction of the place. A hundred of the Gomeres were sent as presents to Pope Innocent VIII and were led in triumph through the streets of Rome, and afterwards converted to Christianity. Fifty Moorish maidens were sent to the Queen Joanna of Naples, sister to King Ferdinand, and thirty to the Queen of Portugal. Isabella made presents of others to the ladies of her household and of the noble families of Spain.

Among the inhabitants of Malaga were four hundred and fifty Moorish Jews, for the most part women, speaking the Arabic language, and dressed in the Moorish fashion. These were ransomed by a wealthy Jew of Castile, former general of the royal revenues derived from the Jews of Spain. He agreed to make up, within a certain time the sum of twenty thousand doblas or pistoles of gold; all money and jewels of the captives being taken in part payment. They were sent to Castile in two armed galleys.

As to the great mass of Moorish inhabitants they implored that they might not be scattered and sold into captivity, but might be permitted to ransom themselves by an amount paid within a certain time. Upon this King Ferdinand took the advice of certain of his ablest counsellors. They said to him, if you hold out a prospect of hopeless captivity the infidels will throw all their gold and jewels into wells and pits and you will lose the greater part of the spoil; but if you fix a general rate of ransom and receive their money and jewels in part payment, nothing will be destroyed. The King relished greatly this advice and it was arranged that all the inhabitants should be ransomed at the general rate of thirty doblas or pistoles in gold for each individual, male or female, large or small. That all their gold, jewels and other valuables should be received immediately in part payment of the general amount, and that the residue should be paid within eight months. That if any of the number actually living should die in the interim their ransom should nevertheless be paid. If, however, the whole of the amount were not paid at the expiration of the eight months, they should all be considered and treated as slaves.

The unfortunate Moors were eager to catch at the least hope of future liberty and consented to these hard conditions. The most rigorous precautions were taken to exact them to the uttermost. The inhabitants were numbered by houses and families and their names taken down. Their most precious effects were made up into parcels and sealed and inscribed with their names, and they were ordered to repair with them to certain large corrales or inclosures adjoining the Alcazaba, which were surrounded by high walls and overlooked by watch towers, to which places the cavalgadas of Christian captives had usually been driven to be confined until the time of sale, like cattle in a market. The Moors were obliged to leave their houses, one by one: all their money, necklaces, bracelets and anklets of gold, pearl, coral and precious stones were taken from them at the threshold, and their persons so rigorously searched that they carried off nothing concealed.

Then might be seen old men, and helpless women, and tender maidens, some of high birth and gentle condition, passing through the streets, heavily burthened, towards the Alcazaba. As they left their homes they smote their breasts, and wrung their hands, and raised their weeping eyes to heaven in anguish, and this is recorded as their plaint. "Oh Malaga! city renowned and beautiful! where now is the strength of thy castles; where the grandeur of thy towers? Of what avail have been thy mighty walls for the protection of thy children? Behold them driven from thy pleasant abodes, doomed to drag out a life of bondage in a foreign land, and to die far from the home of their infancy! What will become of thy old men and matrons, when their gray hairs shall be no longer reverenced! What will become of thy maidens, so delicately reared and tenderly cherished, when reduced to hard and menial servitude! Behold, thy once happy families are scattered asunder, never again to be united. Sons are separated from their fathers, husbands from their wives and tender children from their mothers. They will bewail each other in foreign lands, but their lamentations will be the scoff of the stranger. Oh Malaga! city of our birth! Who can behold thy desolation and not shed tears of bitterness!"*

When Malaga was completely secured a detachment was sent against two fortresses near the sea, called Mexas and Osuna, which had frequently harrassed the Christian camp. The inhabitants were threatened with the sword unless they instantly surrendered. They claimed the same terms that had been granted to Malaga, imagining them to be freedom of person and security of property. Their claim was granted. They were transported to Mal-

*Pulgar.

aga with all their riches, and on arriving there, were overwhelmed with consternation at finding themselves captives. "Ferdinand," observes Fray Antonio Agapida, "was a man of his word, they were shut up in the inclosure at the Alcazaba with the people of Malaga and shared their fate."

The unhappy captives remained thus crowded in the court yards of the Alcazaba, like sheep in a fold, until they could be sent by sea and land to Seville. They were then distributed about in city and country, each Christian family having one or more to feed and maintain as a servant, until the term fixed for the payment of the residue of the ransom should expire. The captives had obtained permission that several of their number should go about, among the Moorish towns of the Kingdom of Granada, collecting contributions to aid in the purchase of their liberties, but these towns were too much impoverished by the war and engrossed by their own distresses to lend a listening ear. So the time expired without the residue of the ransom being paid, and all the captives of Malaga to the number, as some say, of eleven, and others of fifteen thousand became slaves! "Never," exclaims the worthy Fray Antonio Agapida, in one of his usual bursts of zeal and loyalty, never has there been recorded a more adroit and sagacious arrangement than this made by the Catholic monarch, by which he not only secured all the property and half of the ransom of these infidels, but finally got possession of their persons into the bargain. This truly may be considered one of the greatest triumphs of the pious and politic Ferdinand, and as raising him above the generality of conquerors, who have merely the valour to gain victories, but lack the prudence and management necessary to turn them to account.

CHAPTER LXVII

HOW KING FERDINAND PREPARED TO CARRY THE WAR INTO A DIFFERENT PART OF THE TERRITORIES OF THE MOORS.

The western part of the Kingdom of Granada had now been conquered by the Christian arms. The sea port of Malaga was captured; the fierce and warlike inhabitants of the Serrania de Ronda, and the other mountain holds of the frontier, were all disarmed and reduced to peaceful and laborious vassalage. Their haughty fortresses, which had so long overawed the valleys of Andalusia, now displayed the standard of Castile and Aragon; the watch towers, which crowned every height and from whence the infidels had kept a vulture eye on the Christian territories were now either dismantled or garrisoned with Catholic troops. "What signalized and sanctified this great triumph," adds the worthy Fray Antonio Agapida, "were the emblems of ecclesiastical domination which every where appeared. In every direction arose stately convents and monastaries, those fortresses of the faith, garrisoned by its spiritual soldiery of monks and friars. The sacred melody of Christian bells was again heard among the mountains calling to early matins, or sounding the angeles at the solemn hour of evening."

While this part of the kingdom was thus reduced by the Christian sword, the central part round the city of Granada forming the heart of the Moorish territory, was held in vassalage of the Castilian monarch, by Boabdil surnamed el Chico. That unfortunate prince lost no occasion to propitiate the conquerors of his country by acts of homage and by professions that must have been foreign to his heart. No sooner had he heard of the capture of Malaga than he sent congratulations to the Catholic sovereigns, accompanied with presents of horses richly caparisoned for the King, and precious cloth of gold and oriental perfumes for the Queen. His congratulations and his presents were received with the utmost graciousness, and the short sighted prince, lulled by the temporary and politic forbearance of Ferdinand, flattered himself that he was securing the lasting friendship of that monarch.

The policy of Boabdil had its transient and superficial advantages. The portion of Moorish territory under his immediate sway had a respite from the calamities of war. The husbandmen cultivated their luxuriant fields in security and the vega of Granada once more blossomed like the rose. The merchants again carried on a gainful traffic, the gates of the city were thronged with beasts of burden, bringing the rich products of every clime, yet, while the people of Granada rejoiced in their teeming fields and crowded marts, they secretly despised the policy which had procured them these advantages, and held Boabdil for little better than an apostate and an unbeliever.

Muley Abdalla el Zagal was now the hope of the unconquered part of the kingdom, and every Moor, whose spirit was not quite subdued with his fortunes, lauded the valour of the old monarch and his fidelity to the faith, and wished success to his standard.

El Zagal, though he no longer sat enthroned in the Alhambra, yet reigned over more considerable domains than his nephew. His territories extended from the frontier of Jaen along the borders of Murcia to the Mediterranean and reached into the centre of the kingdom. On the north east he held the cities of Baza and Guadix, situated in the midst of fertile regions. He had the important sea port of Almeria, also, which at one time rivalled Granada itself in wealth and population. Besides these, his territories included a great part of the Alpuxarra mountains which extend across the kingdom and shoot out branches towards the sea coast. This mountainous region was a strong hold of wealth and power. Its stern and rocky heights rising to the clouds, seemed to set invasion at defiance; yet within their rugged embraces were sheltered delightful valleys, of the happiest temperature and richest fertility. The cool springs and limpid rills which gushed out in all parts of the mountains, and the abundant streams which, for a great part of the year were supplied by the Sierra Nevada, spread a perpetual verdure over the skirts and slopes of the hills, and collecting in silver rivers in the valleys wound along among plantations of mulberry trees, and groves of oranges and citrons, of almonds, figs and pomgranates. Here was produced the finest silk of Spain which gave employment to thousands of manufacturers. The sun burnt sides of the hills also, were covered with vineyards. The abundant herbage of the mountain ravines and the rich pasturage of the valleys, fed vast flocks and herds; and even the arid and rocky bosoms of the heights teemed with wealth, from the mines of various metals with which they were impregnated. In a word the Alpuxarra mountains had ever been the great source of revenue to the monarchs of Granada. Their inhabitants, also, were hardy and warlike, and a sudden summons from the Moorish King could at any time call forth fifty thousand fighting men from their rocky fortresses.

Such was the rich but rugged fragment of an empire which remained under the sway of the old warrior monarch El Zagal. The mountain barriers by which it was locked up had protected it from most of the ravages of the present war. El Zagal prepared himself by strengthening every fortress, to battle fiercely for its maintenance.

The Catholic sovereigns saw that fresh troubles and toils awaited them. The war had to be carried into a new quarter, demanding immense expenditures, and new ways and means must be devised to replenish their exhausted coffers. "As this was a holy war, however," says Fray Antonio Agapida, "and peculiarly redounded to the prosperity of the church, the clergy were full of zeal and contributed vast sums of money and large bodies of troops. A pious fund was also produced from the first fruits of that glorious institution the Inquisition."

It so happened that about this time there were many families of wealth and dignity in the Kingdoms of Aragon and Valencia and the principality of Catalonia, whose forefathers had been Jews, but had been converted to Christianity. Notwithstanding the outward piety of these families it was surmized and soon came to be strongly suspected, that many of them had a secret hankering after Judaism; and it was even whispered that some of them practiced Jewish rites in private.

The Catholic monarch, continues Agapida, had a righteous abhorrence of all kinds of heresy and a fervent zeal for the faith; he ordered, therefore, a strict investigation of the conduct of these pseudo Christians. Inquisitors were sent into these provinces for the purpose, who proceeded with their accustomed zeal. The consequence was that many families were convicted of apostacy from the Christian faith, and of the private practice of Judaism.

Some who had grace and policy sufficient to reform in time, were again received into the Christian fold, after being severely mulcted and condemned to heavy penance; others were burnt at *auto de fe's* for the edification of the public, and their property was confiscated for the good of the state.

As these Hebrews were of great wealth and had a hereditary passion for jewelry, there was found abundant store in their possession of gold and silver, of rings and necklaces, and strings of pearl and coral, and precious stones: Treasures easy of transportation, and wonderfully adapted for the emergencies of war. In this way, concludes the pious Agapida, these backsliders, by the allseeing contrivances of providence, were made to serve the righteous cause which they had so treacherously deserted; and their apostate wealth was sanctified by being devoted to the service of heaven and the crown, in this holy crusade against the infidels.

It must be added, however, that these pious financial expedients received some check from the interference of Queen Isabella. Her penetrating eyes discovered that many enormities had been committed under colour of religious zeal, and many innocent persons accused by false witnesses of apostacy, either through malice or a hope of obtaining their wealth: She caused strict investigation, therefore, into the proceedings which had been held: many of which were reversed and suborners punished in proportion to their guilt.*

CHAPTER LXVIII

HOW KING FERDINAND INVADED THE EASTERN SIDE OF THE KINGDOM OF GRANADA, AND HOW HE WAS RECEIVED BY EL ZAGAL.

"Muley Abdalla el Zagal," says the venerable Jesuit father, Pedro Abarca, "was the most venomous Mahometan in all Morisma," and the worthy Fray Antonio Agapida most devoutly echoes his opinion. "Certainly," adds the latter, "none ever opposed a more heathenish and diabolical obstinacy to the holy inroads of the cross and sword."

El Zagal felt that it was necessary to do something to quicken his popularity with the people, and that nothing was more effectual than a successful inroad. The Moors loved the stirring call to arms, and a wild foray among the mountains, and delighted more in a hasty spoil wrested with hard fight-

*Pulgar Part 3. Cap. 100.

ing from the Christians, than in all the steady and certain gains secured by peaceful traffic.

There reigned at this time a careless security along the frontier of Jaen. The alcaydes of the Christian fortresses were confident of the friendship of Boabdil el Chico, and they fancied his uncle too distant and too much engrossed by his own perplexities to think of molesting them. On a sudden El Zagal issued out of Guadix with a chosen band, passed rapidly through the mountains which extend behind Granada, and fell like a thunderbolt upon the territories in the neighborhood of Alcalá la Real.

Before the alarm could be spread and the frontier roused, he had made a wide career of destruction through the country sacking and burning villages, sweeping off flocks and herds, and carrying away captives. The warriors of the frontier assembled, but El Zagal was already far on his return through the mountains, and he reentered the gates of Guadix in triumph, his army laden with Christian spoil, and conducting an immense cavalgada. Such was one of the fierce El Zagal's preparations for the expected invasion of the Christian King, exciting the warlike spirit of his people, and gaining for himself a transient popularity.

King Ferdinand assembled his army at Murcia in the spring of 1488. He left that city on the fifth of June, with a flying camp of four thousand horse and fourteen thousand foot. The Marquis of Cadiz led the van, followed by the Adelantado of Murcia. The army entered the Moorish frontier by the sea coast spreading terror through the land; wherever it appeared the towns surrendered without a blow, so great was the dread of experiencing the woes which had desolated the opposite frontier. In this way, Vera, Velez el Rubio, Velez el Blanco and many towns of inferior note, to the number of sixty, yielded at the first summons.

It was not until it approached Almeria that the army met with resistance. This important city was commanded by the Prince Zelim, a relation of El Zagal. He led forth his Moors bravely to the encounter, and skirmished fiercely with the advance guard in the gardens near the city. King Ferdinand came up with the main body of the army, and called off his troops from the skirmish. He saw that to attack the place with his present force was fruitless; having reconnoitered the city and its environs, therefore, against a future campaign, he retired with his army and marched towards Baza.

The old warrior El Zagal was himself drawn up in the city of Baza with a powerful garrison. He felt confidence in the strength of the place, and rejoiced when he heard that the Christian King was approaching.

In the valley in front of Baza there extended a great tract of gardens, like a continued grove, and intersected by canals and water courses. In this he stationed a powerful ambuscade of arquebusiers and cross bow men. The vanguard of the Christian army came marching gaily up the valley with great sound of drum and trumpet, and led on by the Marquis of Cadiz and the

Adelantado of Murcia. As they drew near El Zagal sallied forth with horse and foot and attacked them for a time with great spirit. Gradually falling back, as if pressed by their superior valour, he drew the exulting Christians among the gardens. Suddenly the Moors in ambuscade burst from their concealment and opened such a terrible fire in flank and rear that many of the Christians were slain and the rest thrown into confusion. King Ferdinand arrived in time to see the disastrous situation of his troops and gave signal for the vanguard to retire.

El Zagal did not permit the foe to draw off unmolested. Ordering out fresh squadrons he fell upon the rear of the retreating troops with loud and triumphant shouts, driving them before him with dreadful havoc. The old war cry of El Zagal! El Zagal! was again put up by the Moors, and was echoed with transport from the walls of the city. The Christians were for a time in imminent peril of a complete rout, when fortunately the Adelantado of Murcia threw himself with a large body of horse and foot between the pursuers and the pursued, covering the retreat of the latter and giving them time to rally. The Moors were now attacked so vigorously in turn that they gave over the unequal contest, and drew back slowly into the city. Many valiant cavaliers were slain in the skirmish. Among the number of whom was Don Philip of Aragon Master of the chivalry of S' George of Montesor: he was illegitimate son of the King's illegitimate brother Don Carlos, and his death was greatly bewailed by Ferdinand. He had formerly been Archbishop of Palermo but had doffed the cassock for the cuirass, and had thus, according to Fray Antonio Agapida, gained a glorious crown of martyrdom by falling in this holy war.

The warm reception of his advance guard by the old warrior El Zagal, brought King Ferdinand to a pause. He encamped on the banks of the neighbouring river Guadalqueton and began to consider whether he had acted wisely in undertaking this campaign with his present force. His late successes had probably rendered him over confident. El Zagal had again schooled him into his characteristic caution. He saw that the old warrior was too formidably ensconced in Baza to be dislodged by any thing except a powerful army and battering artillery, and he feared that should he persist in his invasion, some disaster might befall his army, either from the enterprize of the foe, or from a pestilence which prevailed in various parts of the country.

Ferdinand retired, therefore, from before Baza, as he had on a former occasion from before Loxa, all the wiser for a wholesome lesson in warfare, but by no means grateful to those who had given it; and with a solemn determination to have his revenge upon his teachers.

He now took measures for the security of the places gained in this campaign, placing in them strong garrisons, well armed and supplied, charging their alcaydes to be vigilant on their posts and to give no rest to the enemy.

The whole of the frontier was placed under the command of the brave Luis Fernandez Puertocarrero. As it was evident from the warlike character of El Zagal that there would be abundance of active service and hard fighting, many hidalgos and young cavaliers, eager for distinction, remained with Puertocarrero.

All these dispositions being made King Ferdinand closed the dubious campaign of this year; not, as usual, by returning in triumph at the head of his army to some important city of his dominions, but by disbanding the troops and repairing to pray at the cross of Caravaca.

CHAPTER LXIX

HOW THE MOORS MADE VARIOUS ENTERPRIZES AGAINST THE CHRISTIANS.

"While the pious King Ferdinand," observes Fray Antonio Agapida, "was humbling himself before the cross, and devoutly praying for the destruction of his enemies, that fierce pagan El Zagal, depending merely on his arm of flesh, and his sword of steel, pursued his diabolical outrages upon the Christians." No sooner was the invading army disbanded than El Zagal sallied forth from his strong hold and carried fire and sword into all those parts that had submitted to the Spanish yoke. The castle of Nixar, being carelessly guarded, was taken by surprize and its garrison put to the sword. The old warrior raged with sanguinary fury about the whole frontier, attacking convoys, slaying, wounding and making prisoners, and coming by surprize upon the Christians wherever they were off their guard.

The alcayde of the fortress of Cullar, confiding in the strength of its walls, and towers, and on its difficult situation, being built on the summit of a lofty hill and surrounded by precipices, ventured to absent himself from his post. The vigilant El Zagal was suddenly before it with a powerful force, he stormed the town, sword in hand, fought the Christians from street to street and drove them, with great slaughter to the citadel. Here a veteran captain by the name of Juan de Avalos, a grey headed warrior, scarred in many a battle, assumed the command and made an obstinate defence. Neither the multitude of the enemy nor the vehemence of their attacks, though led on by the terrible El Zagal himself, had power to shake the fortitude of this doughty old soldier.

The Moors undermined the outer walls and one of the towers of the fortress, and made their way into the exterior court. The Alcayde manned the tops of his towers, pouring down melted pitch and showering darts, arrows, stones and all kinds of missiles upon the assailants. The Moors were driven out of the court, but being reinforced with fresh troops, returned repeatedly to the assault. For five days the combat was kept up, the Christians were nearly exhausted but they were sustained by the cheerings of their staunch old alcayde, and they feared death from the cruel El Zagal should they surrender. At length the approach of a powerful force under Puertocarrero relieved them from this fearful peril. El Zagal abandoned the assault, but set fire to the town in his rage and disappointment, and retired to his strong hold of Guadix.

The example of El Zagal roused his adherents to action. Two bold Moorish alcaydes, Ali Altar and Yza Altar, commanding the fortresses of Alhenden and Salobreña, laid waste the country of the subjects of Boabdil, and the places which had recently submitted to the Christians. They swept off the castle, carried off captives and harrassed the whole of the newly conquered frontier.

The Moors, also of Almeria and Tavernas and Purchena made inroads into Murcia and carried fire and sword into its most fertile regions. On the opposite frontier also, among the wild vallies and rugged recesses of the Sierra Bermeja or Red Mountains, many of the Moors who had lately submitted again flew to arms. The Marquis of Cadiz suppressed by timely vigilance the rebellion of the mountain town of Gausin, situated on a high peak almost among the clouds; but others of the Moors fortified themselves in rock built towers and castles inhabited solely by warriors, from whence they carried on a continual war of forage and depredation, sweeping suddenly down into the valley, and carrying off flocks and herds and all kinds of booty to these eagle nests, to which it was perilous and fruitless to pursue them.

The worthy father Fray Antonio Agapida closes his story of this checquered year in quite a different strain from those triumphant periods with which he is accustomed to wind up the victorious campaigns of the sovereigns. "Great and mighty," says this venerable chronicler, "were the floods and tempests which prevailed throughout the Kingdom of Castile and Aragon about this time. It seemed as though the windows of heaven were again opened, and a second deluge overwhelming the face of nature. The clouds burst as it were in cataracts upon the earth; torrents, rushed down from the mountains, overflowing the valleys. Brooks were swelled into raging rivers; houses were under mined, mills were swept away by their own streams, the affrighted shepherds saw their flocks drowned in the midst of the pasture, and were fain to take refuge for their lives in towers and high places. The Guadalquivir for a time became a roaring and tumultuous sea, inundating the immense plain of the Tablada and filling the fair city of Seville with affright.

"A vast black cloud moved over the land, accompanied by a hurricane and a trembling of the earth. Houses were unroofed, the walls and battlements of fortresses shaken, and lofty towers rocked to their foundations. Ships riding at anchor were either stranded or swallowed up. Others under sail were tossed to and fro upon mountain waves, and cast upon the land, where the whirlwind rent them in pieces and scattered their fragments in the air. Doleful was the ruin and great the terror, where this baleful cloud passed by; and it left a long track of desolation over sea and land. Some of the faint-hearted," adds Antonio Agapida, "looked upon this torrent of the elements as a prodigious event, out of the course of nature. In the weakness of their fears, they connected it with these troubles which occurred in various places, considering it a portent of some great calamity, about to be wrought by the violence of the bloody-handed El Zagal and his fierce adherents."

CHAPTER LXX

HOW KING FERDINAND PREPARED TO BESIEGE THE CITY OF BAZA, AND HOW THE CITY PREPARED FOR DEFENCE.

The stormy winter had passed away, and the spring of 1489 was advancing; yet the heavy rains had broken up the roads; the mountain brooks were swoln to raging torrents, and the late shallow and peaceful rivers were deep, turbulent and dangerous. The Christian troops had been summoned to assemble in early spring on the frontiers of Jaen, but were slow in arriving at the appointed place. They were entangled in the miry defiles of the mountains, or fretted impatiently on the banks of impassable floods. It was late in the month of May before they assembled in sufficient force to attempt the proposed invasion; when at length a valiant army of thirteen thousand horse and forty thousand foot marched merrily over the border. The Queen remained at the city of Jaen with the prince royal and the princesses her children, accompanied and supported by the venerable Cardinal of Spain, and those reverend prelates who assisted in her councils throughout this holy war.

The plan of King Ferdinand was to lay siege to the city of Baza, the key of the remaining possessions of the Moor. That important fortress taken, Guadix and Almeria must soon follow, and then the power of El Zagal would be at an end. As the Catholic King advanced he had first to secure various castles and strong holds in the vicinity of Baza, which might otherwise harrass his army. Some of these made obstinate resistance, especially the town of Cuxar. The Christians assailed the walls with various machines to sap them and batter them down. The brave alcayde, Hubec Adalgan, opposed force to force and engine to engine. He manned his towers with his bravest warriors who rained down an iron shower upon the enemy, and he linked cauldrons together by strong chains, and cast fire from them consuming the wooden engines of their assailants and those who managed them. The siege was protracted for several days. The bravery of the alcayde could not save his fortress from an overwhelming foe, but it gained him honourable terms. Ferdinand permitted the garrison and the inhabitants to repair with their effects to Baza, and the valiant Hubec Adalgan marched forth with the remnant of his force and took the way to that devoted city.

The delays which had been caused to the invading army by these various circumstances had been diligently improved by the old Moorish monarch El Zagal; who felt that he was now making his last stand for empire, and that this campaign would decide, whether he should continue a King, or sink into a vassal.

El Zagal was but a few leagues from Baza, at the city of Guadix. This last was the most important point of his remaining territories, being a kind of bulwark between them and the hostile city of Granada, the seat of his nephew's power. Though he heard of the tide of war, therefore, that was collecting and rolling towards the city of Baza, he dared not go in person to its assistance. He dreaded that, should he leave Guadix, Boabdil would attack him in rear while the Christian army was battling with him in front. El Zagal trusted in the great strength of Baza to defy any violent assault and he profited by the delays of the Christian army to supply it with all possible means of defence. He sent thither all the troops he could spare from his garrison of Guadix, and dispatched missives throughout his territories, calling upon all true Moslems to hasten to Baza to make a devoted stand in defence of their houses, their liberties and their religion. The cities of Tavernas and Purchena, and the surrounding heights and valleys responded to his orders, and sent forth their fighting men to the field. The rocky fastnesses of the Alpuxarras resounded with the din of arms. Troops of horse and bodies of foot soldiers were seen winding down the rugged cliffs and defiles of those marble mountains and hastening towards Baza. Many brave cavaliers of Granada also, spurning the quiet and security of Christian vassalage, secretly left the city and hastened to join their fighting countrymen. The great dependence of El Zagal, however, was upon the valour and loyalty of his cousin and brother in law Cidi Yahye Alnayar Aben Zelim, who was Alcayde of Almeria; a cavalier experienced in warfare and redoubtable in the field. He wrote to him to leave Almeria and repair with all speed, at the head of his troops to Baza. Cidi Yahye departed immediately with ten thousand of the bravest Moors in the kingdom. These were for the most part hardy mountainiers, tempered to sun and storm, and tried in many a combat. None equalled them for a sally or a skirmish. They were adroit in executing a thousand stratagems, ambuscadoes, and evolutions. Impetuous in their assaults, yet governed in their utmost fury by a word or sign from their commander, at the sound of a trumpet they would check themselves in the midst of their career, and wheel off and disperse, and at another sound of a trumpet they would as suddenly reassemble and return to the attack. They were upon the enemy when least expected, coming like a rushing blast, spreading havoc and consternation, and then passing away in an instant; so that when one recovered from the shock and looked around, behold nothing was to be seen or heard of this tempest of war but a cloud of dust, and the clatter of retreating troops.

When Cidi Yahye led his train of ten thousand valiant warriors into the gates of Baza the city rung with acclamations and for a time the inhabitants thought themselves secure. El Zagal also felt a glow of confidence notwithstanding his own absence from the city. "Cidi Yahye," said he, "is my cousin and my brother in law, related to me by blood and marriage, he is a second self; happy is that monarch who has his kinsmen to command his armies."

With all these reinforcements the garrison of Baza amounted to above twenty thousand men. There were at this time three principal leaders in the city: Mohammed Ben Hassan surnamed the veteran, who was military governor or alcayde, an old Moor of great experience and discretion. The second was Hamet Abu Hali, who was captain of the troops stationed in the place, and the third was Hubec Adalgan, the valiant Alcayde of Cuxar, who had repaired hither with the remains of his garrison. Over all these Cidi Yahye exercised a supreme command, in consequence of his being of the blood royal, and in the special confidence of Muley Abdalla el Zagal. He was eloquent and ardent in council, and fond of striking and splendid achievements, but he was a little prone to be carried away by the excitement of the moment, and the warmth of his imagination; the councils of war of these commanders, therefore, were more frequently controuled by the opinions of the old Alcayde Mohammed Ben Hassan, for whose shrewdness, caution, and experience Cidi Yahye himself felt the greatest deference.

The city of Baza was situated in a great valley, eight leagues in length and three in breadth, called the Hoya or basin of Baza. It was surrounded by a range of mountains called the Sierra of Xabalcohol; the streams of which, collecting themselves into two rivers watered and fertilized the country. The city was built in the plain, but one part of it was protected by the rocky precipices of the mountain, and by a powerful citadel, the other part was defended by massive walls studded with immense towers. It had suburbs towards the plain, imperfectly fortified by earthen walls. In front of these suburbs extended a tract of orchards and gardens nearly a league in length, so thickly planted as to resemble a continued forest. Here every citizen who could afford it had his little plantation, and his garden of fruits and flowers and vegetables; watered by canals and rivulets, and dominated by a small tower to serve for recreation or defence. This wilderness of groves and gardens, intersected in all parts by canals and runs of water, and studded by above a thousand small towers, formed a kind of protection to this side of the city, rendering all approach extremely difficult and perplexed, and affording covert to the defenders.

While the Christian army had been detained before the frontier posts, the city of Baza had been a scene of hurried and unremitting preparation. All the grain of the surrounding valley, though yet unripe, was hastily reaped and borne into the city, to prevent it from yielding sustenance to the enemy. The country was drained of all its supplies. Flocks and herds were driven, bleating and bellowing into the gates; long trains of beasts of burthen some laden with food, others with lances, darts and arms of all kind, kept pouring into the place. Already there were munitions collected sufficient for a siege of fifteen months, yet still the eager and hasty preparation was going on, when the army of Ferdinand came in sight. On one side might be seen scattered parties of foot and horse spurring to the gates, and muleteers hurrying forward their burthened animals, all anxious to get under shelter before the gathering storm; on the other side the cloud of war came sweeping down the valley, the roll of drum or clang of trumpet resounding occasionally from its deep bosom, or the bright glance of arms flashing forth, like vivid lightning from its columns.

King Ferdinand pitched his tents in the valley, beyond the green labyrinth of gardens. He sent his heralds to summon the city to surrender, promising the most favorable terms in case of immediate compliance and avowing in the most solemn terms, his resolution never to abandon the siege until he had possession of the place.

Upon receiving this summons the Moorish commanders held a council of war. The Prince Cidi Yahye, indignant at the menace of the King, was for retorting by a declaration that the garrison never would surrender, but would fight until buried under the ruins of the walls. "Of what avail," said the veteran Mohammed, "is a declaration of the kind, which we may falsify by our deeds? Let us threaten what we know we can perform, and let us endeavour to perform more than we threaten."

In conformity to the advice of Mohammed Ben Hassan, therefore, a laconic reply was sent to the Christian monarch, thanking him for his offer of favorable terms, but informing him that they were placed in the city to defend, not to surrender it.

CHAPTER LXXI

THE BATTLE OF THE GARDENS BEFORE BAZA.

When the reply of the Moorish commanders was brought to King Ferdinand he prepared to press the siege with the utmost rigour. Finding the camp too far from the city, and that the intervening orchards afforded shelter for the sallies of the Moors, he determined to advance it beyond the gardens, in the space between them and the suburbs, where his batteries would have full play upon the city walls. A detachment was sent in advance, to take possession of the gardens, and to keep a check upon the suburbs, opposing any sally while the encampment should be formed and fortified. The various commanders entered the orchards at different points. The young cavaliers marched fearlessly forward, but the experienced veterans foresaw infinite peril in the mazes of this verdant labyrinth. The Master of S' Iago, as he led his troops into the centre of the gardens exhorted them to keep by one another and to press forward, in defiance of all difficulty or danger; assuring them that God would give them the victory if they attacked hardily and persisted resolutely.

Scarce had they entered the verge of the orchards when a din of drums and trumpets, mingled with war cries, was heard from the suburbs, and a legion of Moorish warriors on foot poured forth. They were led on by the Prince Cidi Yahye. He saw the imminent danger of the city should the Christians gain possession of the orchards. "Soldiers," he cried, "we fight for life and liberty, for our families, our country, our religion,* nothing is left for us to depend upon but the strength of our hands, the courage of our hearts and the almighty protection of Allah." The Moors answered him with shouts of war and rushed to the encounter. The two hosts met in the midst of the gardens. A chance medley combat ensued with lances, arquebusses, cross bows and scymetars. The perplexed nature of the ground, cut up and intersected by canals and streams, the closeness of the trees, the multiplicity of towers and petty edifices, gave greater advantages to the Moors, who were on foot, than to the Christians who were on horseback. The Moors, too, knew the ground; all its alleys and passes, and were thus enabled to lurk, to sally forth, to attack and to retreat almost without injury.

The Christian commanders, seeing this, ordered many of the horsemen to dismount and fight on foot. The battle then became fierce and deadly, each disregarding his own life provided he could slay his enemy. It was not so much a general battle as a multitude of petty actions for every orchard and garden had its distinct contest. No one could see further than the little scene of fury and bloodshed around him, nor know how the general battle fared. In vain the captains exerted their voices, in vain the trumpets brayed

---

*"Illi (Mauri) pro fortunis, pro libertate, pro laribus patriis, pro vita denique certabant." Pietri Martyr. Epist 70.

forth signals and commands; all was confounded and unheard in the universal din and uproar; no one kept to his standard, but fought as his own fury
or fear dictated.

In some places the Christians had the advantage, in others the Moors.
Often a victorious party pursuing the vanquished came upon a superior and
triumphant force of the enemy, and the fugitives turned back upon them in
an overwhelming wave. Some broken remnants, in their terror and confusion, fled from their own countrymen and sought refuge among their enemies, not knowing friend from foe in the obscurity of the groves. The Moors
were more adroit in these wild skirmishings, from their flexibility, lightness
and agility and the rapidity with which they would disperse, rally and return
again to the charge.*

The hardest fighting was about the small garden towers and pavillions,
which served as so many petty fortresses. Each party by turns gained them,
defended them fiercely, and were driven out; many of the towers were set
on fire and encreased the horrors of the fight by the wreathes of smoke and
flame in which they wrapped the groves and by the shrieks of those who
were burning.

Several of the Christian cavaliers, bewildered by the uproar and confusion
and shocked at the carnage which prevailed, would have led their men out
of the action, but they were entangled in a labyrinth and knew not which
way to retreat. While in this perplexity the standard bearer of one of the
squadrons of the Grand Cardinal had his arm carried off by a cannon ball;
the standard was well nigh falling into the hands of the enemy when Roderigo de Mendoza, an intrepid youth, natural son of the Grand Cardinal,
rushed to its rescue, through a shower of balls, lances, and arrows and bearing it aloft, dashed forward with it into the hottest of the combat, followed
by his shouting soldiers. King Ferdinand who remained in the skirts of the
orchard, was in extreme anxiety. It was impossible to see much of the action
for the multiplicity of trees and towers and wreathes of smoke; and those
who were driven out defeated, or came out wounded and exhausted, gave
different accounts according to the fate of the partial conflicts in which they
had been engaged. Ferdinand exerted himself to the utmost to animate and
encourage his troops to this blind encounter, sending reinforcements of
horse and foot to those points where the battle was most sanguinary and
doubtful. Among those that were brought forth mortally wounded was Don
Juan de Luna, a youth of uncommon merit, greatly prized by the King,
beloved by the army and recently married to Donna Catalina de Urrea a
young lady of distinguished beauty.† They laid him at the foot of a tree and

*Mariana Lib 25 Cap 13.
†Mariana. P. Martyr. Zurita.

endeavoured to stanch and bind up his wounds, with a scarf which his bride had wrought for him; but his life blood flowed too profusely, and while a holy friar was yet administering to him the last sacred offices of the church he expired almost at the feet of his sovereign.

On the other hand the veteran alcayde, Mohammed Ben Hassan, surrounded by a little band of chieftains, kept an anxious eye upon the scene of combat from the walls of the city. For nearly twelve hours the battle had raged without intermission. The thickness of the foliage hid all the particulars from their sight; but they could see the flash of swords and glance of helmets among the trees, columns of smoke rose in every direction, while the clash of arms, the thundering of ribadoquines and arqucbusses, the shouts and cries of the combatants, and the groans and supplications of the wounded bespoke the deadly conflict that was waging in the bosom of the groves. They were harrassed too by the shrieks and lamentations of the Moorish women and children as their wounded relations were brought bleeding from the scene of action and were stunned by a general outcry of woe on the part of the inhabitants, as the body of Redoan Zalfarga, a renegado Christian, and one of the bravest of their generals, was borne breathless into the city.

At length the din of battle approached nearer to the skirts of the orchards. They beheld their warriors driven out from among the groves by fresh squadrons of the enemy, and after disputing the ground inch by inch, obliged to retire to a place between the orchards and the suburbs, which was fortified with pallisadoes.

The Christians immediately planted opposing pallisadoes and established strong out posts near to this retreat of the Moors, while, at the same time, King Ferdinand ordered that his encampment should be pitched within the hard won orchards.

Mohammed Ben Hassan sallied forth to the aid of the Prince Cidi Yahye and made a desperate attempt to dislodge the enemy from this formidable position; but the night had closed; and the darkness rendered it impossible to make any impression. The Moors, however, kept up constant assaults and alarms throughout the night, and the weary Christians exhausted by the toils and sufferings of the day, were not allowed a moment of repose.*

*Pulgar part 3. Cap 106-107. Cura de los Palacios Cap 92 Zurita lib 20   Cap. 81.

CHAPTER LXXII

SIEGE OF BAZA. EMBARRASSMENT OF THE ARMY.

The morning sun rose upon a piteous scene before the walls of Baza. The Christian outposts harrassed throughout the night were pale and haggard, while the multitude of slain which lay before their pallisadoes shewed the fierce attacks they had sustained and the bravery of their defence.

Beyond them lay the groves and gardens of Baza, once the favourite resorts for recreation and delight, now a scene of horror and desolation. The towers and pavillions were smoking ruins; the canals and water courses were discoloured with blood and choked with the bodies of the slain. Here and there the ground, deep dinted with the tramp of man and steed, and plashed and slippery with gore, shewed where there had been some fierce and mortal conflict; while the bodies of Moors and Christians, ghastly in death, lay half concealed among the matted and trampled shrubs and flowers and herbage.

Amidst the sanguinary scenes arose the Christian tents, which had been hastily pitched among the gardens in the preceding evening. The experience of the night, however, and the forlorn aspect of every thing in the morning, convinced King Ferdinand of the perils and hardships to which his camp must be exposed, in its present situation, and, after a consultation with his principal cavaliers he resolved to abandon the orchards.

It was a dangerous movement to extricate his army from so entangled a situation, in the face of so alert and daring an enemy; a bold front was therefore kept up towards the city; additional troops were ordered to the advanced posts, and works began as if for a settled encampment. Not a tent was struck in the gardens, but in the mean time the most active and unremitting exertions were made to remove all the baggage and furniture of the camp back to the original station.

All day the Moors beheld a formidable shew of war maintained in front of the gardens; while in the rear the tops of the Christian tents and the pennons of the different commanders were seen rising above the groves. Suddenly towards evening the tents sunk and disappeared; the out posts broke up their stations and withdrew, and the whole shadow of an encampment was fast vanishing from their eyes.

The Moors saw too late the subtle maneuvre of King Ferdinand. Cidi Yahye again sallied forth with a large force of horse and foot and pressed furiously upon the Christians. The latter, however, experienced in Moorish attack, retired in close order, sometimes turning upon the enemy and driving them to their barricadoes, and then pursuing their retreat. In this way the army was extricated without much further loss, from the perilous labyrinths of the gardens. The camp was now out of danger but it was also too distant from the city to do mischief; while the Moors could sally forth and return without hindrance. The King called a council of war to consider in what manner to proceed? The Marquis of Cadiz was for abandoning the siege for the present, the place being too strong, too well garrisoned and provided, and too extensive to be either carried by assault or invested and reduced by famine by their limited forces: while, in lingering before it, the army would be exposed to the usual maladies and sufferings of besieging armies; and when the rainy season came on would be shut up by the swelling of the rivers. He recommended, instead, that the King should throw garrisons of horse and foot into all the towns captured in the neighborhood, and leave them to keep up a predatory war upon Baza, while he should overrun and ravage all the country; so that in the following year, Almeria and Guadix, having all their subject towns and territories taken from them, might be starved into submission.

Don Gutiere de Cardenas senior commander of Loxa, on the other hand, maintained that to abandon the siege would be construed by the enemy into a sign of weakness and irresolution. It would give new spirits to the partizans of El Zagal, and would gain to his standard many of the wavering subjects of Boabdil if it did not encourage the fickle populace of Granada to open rebellion. He advised, therefore, that the siege should be prosecuted with vigour.

The pride of Ferdinand pleaded in favour of the last opinion; for it would be doubly humiliating again to return from a campaign in this part of the Moorish kingdom without effecting a blow. But when he reflected on all that his army had suffered, and on all that they must suffer, should the siege continue; especially from the difficulty of obtaining a regular supply of provisions for so numerous a host across a great extent of rugged and mountainous country, he determined to consult the safety of his people and to adopt the advice of the Marquis of Cadiz.

When the soldiery heard that the King was about to raise the siege in mere consideration of their sufferings, they were filled with generous enthusiasm, and entreated, as with one voice, that the siege might never be abandoned until the city surrendered.

Perplexed by conflicting counsels the King dispatched messengers to the Queen at Jaen, requesting her advice. Posts had been stationed between them in such manner that missives from the camp could reach the Queen within ten hours. Isabella sent instantly her reply. She left the policy of raising or continuing the siege to the decision of the King and his captains; but, should they determine to persevere, she pledged herself, with the aid of God, to forward them men, money, provisions, and all other supplies until the city should be taken.

The reply of the Queen determined Ferdinand to persevere, and when his determination was made known to the army it was hailed with as much joy as if it had been tidings of a victory.

CHAPTER LXXIII

SIEGE OF BAZA CONTINUED. HOW KING FERDINAND COMPLETELY INVESTED THE CITY.

The Moorish Prince Cidi Yahye had received tidings of the doubts and discussions in the Christian camp, and flattered himself with hopes that the besieging army would soon retire in despair; though the veteran Alcayde Mohammed shook his head with incredulity at the suggestion. A sudden movement one morning in the Christian camp, seemed to confirm the sanguine hopes of the prince. The tents were struck, the artillery and baggage were conveyed away, and bodies of soldiers began to march along the valley. The momentary gleam of triumph, was soon dispelled. The Catholic King had merely divided his host into two camps, the more effectually to distress the city. One consisting of four thousand horse, and eight thousand foot, with all the artillery and battering engines, took post on the side of the city towards the mountain. This was commanded by the valiant Marquis of Cadiz, with whom were Don Alonzo de Aguilar, Luis Fernandez Puertocarrero, and many other distinguished cavaliers.

The other camp was commanded by the King, having six thousand horse, and a great host of foot soldiers, the hardy mountainiers of Biscay, Guipuscon, Gallicia, and the Asturias. Among the cavaliers who were with the King, were the brave Count de Tendilla Don Roderigo de Mendoza, and Don Alonzo de Cardenas, Master of Santiago. The two camps were wide asunder, on opposite sides of the city, and between them lay the thick wilderness of orchards. Both camps were therefore fortified by great trenches, breast works and pallisadoes. The veteran Mohammed, as he saw these two formidable camps, glittering on each side of the city, and noted the well known pennons of renowned commanders fluttering above them, still comforted his companions. "These camps," said he, "are too far removed from each other for mutual succour and cooperation, and the forest of orchards is as a gulph between them." This consolation was but of short continuance. Scarcely were the Christian camps fortified, when the ears of the Moorish garrison were startled by the sound of innumerable axes, and the crash of falling trees. They looked with anxiety from their highest towers, and behold their favorite groves, were sinking beneath the blows of the Christian pioneers. The Moors sallied forth with fiery zeal to protect their beloved gardens, and the orchards in which they so much delighted. The Christians, however, were too well supported to be driven from their work. Day after day, the gardens became the scene of incessant and bloody skirmishings; still the devastation of the groves went on, for King Ferdinand was too well aware of the necessity of clearing away this screen of woods, not to bend all his forces to the undertaking. It was a work, however, of gigantic toil and patience; the trees were of such magnitude, and so closely set together, and spread over so wide an extent, that notwithstanding four thousand men were employed, they could scarcely clear a strip of land ten paces broad, within a day: and such were the interruptions from the incessant assaults of the Moors, that it was full forty days, before the orchards were completely levelled.

The devoted city of Baza, now lay stripped of its beautiful covering of groves and gardens, at once its ornament, its delight, and its protection. The besiegers went on slowly and surely, with almost incredible labours, to invest and isolate the city. They connected their camps by a deep trench across the plain, a league in length, into which they diverted the waters of the mountain streams. They protected this trench by pallisadoes, fortified by fifteen castles at regular distances. They dug a deep trench, also, two leagues in length, across the mountain in the rear of the city, reaching from camp to camp, and fortified it on each side, with walls, of earth, and stone, and wood. Thus the Moors were enclosed on all sides by trenches, pallisadoes, walls and castles, so that it was impossible for them to sally beyond this great line of circumvallation, nor could any force enter to their succour. Ferdinand made an attempt likewise to cut off the supply of water from the city; for water, observes the worthy Agapida, is more necessary to these infidels than bread, making use of it in repeated daily ablutions, enjoined by their damnable religion, and employing it in baths, and in a thousand other idle and extravagant modes, of which we Spaniards and Christians, make but little account.

There was a noble fountain of pure water, which gushed out at the foot of the hill Albohacen just behind the city. The Moors had almost a superstitious fondness for this fountain, and daily depended upon it for their supplies. Receiving intimation from some deserters of the plan of King Ferdinand to get possession of this precious fountain, they sallied forth at night, and threw up such powerful works upon the impending hill so as to set all attempts of the Christian assailants at defiance.

CHAPTER LXXIV

EXPLOIT OF HERNANDO VEREZ DEL PULGAR AND OTHER CAVALIERS.

The siege of Baza, while it displayed the skill and science of the Christian commanders, gave but little scope for the adventurous spirit and fiery valour of the young Spanish cavaliers. They repined at the tedious monotony and dull security of their fortified camp, and longed for some soul stirring exploit of difficulty and danger. Two of the most spirited of these youthful cavaliers were Francisco de Bazan and Antonio de Cueva, the latter of whom was son to the Duke of Albuquerque. As they were one day seated on the ramparts of the camp and venting their impatience at this life of inaction, they were overheard by a veteran adalid, one of those scouts or guides who are acquainted with all parts of the country. "Señores," said he, "if you wish for a service of peril and profit, if you are willing to pluck the fiery old Moor by the beard, I can lead you to where you may put your mettle to the proof. Hard by the city of Guadix are certain hamlets rich in booty. I can conduct you by a way in which you may come upon them by surprize, and if you are as cool in the head as you are hot in the spur, you may bear off your spoils from under the very eyes of old El Zagal."

The idea of thus making booty at the very gates of Guadix pleased the hot spirited youths. These predatory excursions were frequent about this time, and the Moors of Padul, Alhenden and other towns of the Alpuxarras had recently harrassed the Christian territories by expeditions of the kind. Francisco de Bazan and Antonio de Cueva soon found other young cavaliers of their age, eager to join in the adventure, and in a little while they had nearly three hundred horse and two hundred foot ready equipped and eager for the foray.

Keeping their destination secret, they sallied out of the camp on the edge of an evening, and guided by the adalid made their way by starlight through the most secret roads of the mountains. In this way they pressed on rapidly, day and night, until early one morning before cock crowing, they fell suddenly upon the hamlets, made prisoners of the inhabitants, sacked the houses, ravaged the fields, and sweeping through the meadows gathered together all the flocks and herds. Without giving themselves time to rest they set out upon their return making with all speed for the mountains, before the alarm should be given and the country roused.

Several of the herdsmen, however, had fled to Guadix and carried tidings of the ravage to El Zagal. The beard of old Muley trembled with rage; he immediately sent out six hundred of his choicest horse and foot with orders to recover the booty, and to bring these insolent marauders captive to Guadix.

The Christian cavaliers were urging their cavalgada of cattle and sheep up a mountain as fast as their own weariness would permit, when, looking back they beheld a great cloud of dust and presently descried the turbaned host hot upon their traces.

They saw that the Moors were superior in number; they were fresh also, both man and steed, whereas both they and their horses were fatigued by two days and two nights of hard marching. Several of the horsemen therefore gathered round the commanders and proposed that they should relinquish

their spoil and save themselves by flight. The captains Francisco de Bazan
and Antonio de Cueva spurned at such craven counsel. "What!" cried they,
"abandon our prey without striking a blow! Leave our foot soldiers too in
the lurch to be overwhelmed by the enemy? If any one gives such counsel
through fear, he mistakes the course of safety for there is less danger in
presenting a bold front to the foe than in turning a dastard back; and fewer
men are killed in a brave advance than in a cowardly retreat."

Some of the cavaliers were touched by these words and declared that they
would stand by the foot soldiers like true companions in arms; the great mass
of the party however, were volunteers, brought together by chance, who
received no pay, nor had any common tie to keep them together in time of
danger. The pleasure of the expedition being over, each thought but of his
own safety regardless of his companions. As the enemy approached the tumult of opinions encreased; and every thing was confusion. The captains to
put an end to the dispute ordered the standard bearer to advance against
the Moors, well knowing that no true cavalier would hesitate to follow and
defend his banner. The standard bearer hesitated; the troops were on the
point of taking to flight. Upon this a cavalier of the royal guards named
Hernando Perez del Pulgar, alcayde of the fortress of Salar rode to the front.
He took off a handkerchief which he wore round his head, after the Andalusian fashion, and tying it to the end of his lance elevated it in the air.
"Cavaliers," cried he, "why do ye take weapons in your hands if you depend
upon your feet for safety. This day will determine who is the brave man and
who the coward. He who is disposed to fight shall not want a standard; let
him follow this handkerchief." So saying he waved his banner, and spurred
bravely against the Moors. His example shamed some and filled others with
generous emulation; all turned with one accord, and, following the valiant
Pulgar, rushed with shouts upon the enemy.

The Moors scarcely waited to receive the shock of their encounter, seized
with a sudden panic they took to flight and were pursued for a great distance
with great slaughter. Three hundred of their dead strewed the road and
were stripped and despoiled by the conquerors: many were taken prisoners, and the Christian cavaliers returned in triumph to the camp with a
long cavalgada of sheep and cattle and mules laden with booty, and
bearing before them the singular standard which had conducted them to
victory.

When King Ferdinand was informed of the gallant action of Hernando
Perez del Pulgar, he immediately conferred on him the honour of knighthood and ordered that in memory of his achievements he should bear for
arms a lance with a handkerchief at the end of it, together with a castle and
twelve lions. This is but one of many hardy and heroic deeds done by that
brave cavalier in the wars against the Moors; by which he gained great re-

nown and the distinguished appellation of "El de las hazañas" or he of the exploits.*

CHAPTER LXXV

CONTINUATION OF THE SIEGE OF BAZA.

The old Moorish King El Zagal mounted a tower, and looked out eagerly to enjoy the sight of the Christian marauders, brought captive into the gates of Guadix, but his spirits fell when he beheld his own troops stealing back in the dusk of the evening in broken dejected parties.

The fortune of war bore hard against the old monarch. His mind was harrassed by the disastrous tidings brought each day from Baza, of the sufferings of the inhabitants, and the numbers of the garrison slain in the frequent skirmishes. He dared not go in person to the relief of the place, for his presence was necessary in Guadix to keep a check upon his nephew in Granada. He made efforts to send reinforcements and supplies, but they were intercepted, and either captured, or driven back. Still his situation was in some respects preferable to that of his nephew Boabdil. The old monarch was battling like a warrior on the last step of his throne; El Chiquito remained a kind of pensioned vassal, in the luxurious abode of the Alhambra. The chivalrous part of the inhabitants of Granada, could not but compare the generous stand made by the warriors of Baza for their country, and their faith, with their own time serving submission to the yoke of an unbeliever. Every account they received of the woes of Baza wrung their hearts with agony, every account of the exploits of its devoted defenders, brought blushes to their cheeks. Many stole forth secretly with their weapons, and hastened to join the besieged, and the partizans of El Zagal, wrought upon the patriotism and passions of the remainder, until another of those conspiracies was formed, that were continually menacing the unsteady throne of Granada. It was concerted by the conspirators to assail the Alhambra on a sudden, to slay Boabdil, to assemble all the troops, and march to Guadix, where, being reinforced by the garrison of that place, and led on by the old warrior monarch, they might fall with overwhelming power, upon the Christian army before Baza.

Fortunately for Boabdil, he discovered the conspiracy in time, and had the heads of the leaders struck off, and placed upon the walls of the Alham-

---

*Hernando del Pulgar the historian, secretary to Queen Isabella, is confounded with this cavalier by some writers. He was also present at the siege of Baza and has recounted this transaction in his chronicle of the Catholic sovereigns Ferdinand and Isabella.

bra; an act of severity unusual with this mild and wavering monarch, which struck terror into the disaffected, and produced a kind of mute tranquility throughout the city.

King Ferdinand had full information of all these movements and measures for the relief of Baza, and took timely precautions to prevent them. Bodies of horsemen held watch in the mountain passes, to prevent all supplies, and to intercept any generous volunteers from Granada, and watch-towers were erected or scouts were placed on every commanding height, to give the alarm, at the least sign of a hostile turban.

The Prince Cidi Yahye and his brave companions in arms, were thus gradually walled up, as it were, from the rest of the world. A line of towers, the battlements of which bristled with troops, girdled their city, and behind the intervening bulwarks and pallisadoes passed and repassed continual squadrons of troops. Week after week, and month after month passed away, but Ferdinand waited in vain for the garrison to be either terrified or starved into surrender. Every day, they sallied forth with the spirit and alacrity of troops high fed, and flushed with confidence. "The Christian monarch," said the veteran Mohammed Ben Hassan, "builds his hopes upon our growing faint and desponding; we must manifest unusual cheerfulness and vigour. What would be rashness in other service, becomes prudence with us." The Prince Cidi Yahye, agreed with him in opinion, and sallied forth with his troops upon all kinds of hare-brained exploits. They laid ambushes, concerted surprizes, and made the most desperate assaults; the great extent of the Christian works rendered them weak in many parts. Against these the Moors directed their attacks, suddenly breaking into them, making a hasty ravage, and bearing off their booty in triumph to the city. Sometimes they would sally forth by the passes and clefts of the mountain, in the rear of the city, which it was difficult to guard, and hurrying down into the plain, would sweep off all cattle and sheep that were grazing near the suburbs, and all stragglers from the camp.

These partizan sallies brought on many sharp and bloody encounters, in some of which Don Alonzo de Aguilar, and the Alcayde de los Donzeles distinguished themselves greatly. During one of these hot skirmishes which happened on the skirts of the mountain, about twilight, a valiant cavalier named Martin Galindo, beheld a powerful Moor dealing deadly blows about him, and making great havoc among the Christians. Galindo pressed forward, and challenged him to single combat. The Moor, who was of the valiant tribe of the Abencerrages, was not slow in answering the call. Couching their lances, they rushed furiously upon each other. At the first shock the Moor was wounded in the face, and borne out of his saddle. Before Galindo could check his steed, and turn from his career, the Moor sprang upon his feet, recovered his lance, and rushing upon him, wounded him in the head and the arm. Though Galindo was on horse back and the Moor on foot, yet such was the prowess and address of the latter, that the Christian knight being disabled in the arm, was in the utmost peril, when his comrades hastened to his assistance. At their approach, the valiant pagan retreated slowly up the rocks, keeping them at bay until he found himself among his companions.

Several of the young Spanish cavaliers stung by the triumph of this Moslem knight, would have challenged others of the Moors to single combat, but King Ferdinand prohibited all vaunting encounters of the kind. He forbade his troops, also, to provoke skirmishes, well knowing that the Moors were more dextrous than most people in this irregular mode of fighting, and were better acquainted with the ground.

CHAPTER LXXVI

HOW TWO FRIARS ARRIVED AT THE CAMP, AND HOW THEY CAME FROM THE HOLY LAND.

While the holy Christian army, says Fray Antonio Agapida, was thus beleaguering this infidel city of Baza, there rode into the camp one day two reverend friars of the order of Saint Francis. One was of portly person, and authoritative air, he bestrode a goodly steed, well conditioned, and well caparisoned, while his companion rode beside him upon a humble hack, poorly accoutred, and as he rode, he scarcely raised his eyes, from the ground but maintained a meek and lowly air.

The arrival of two friars in the camp was not a matter of much note, for in these holy wars the Church Militant continually mingled in the affray, and helmet and cowl were always seen together; but it was soon discovered, that these worthy saints errant, were from a far country, and on a mission of great import. They were in truth just arrived from the Holy Land, being two of the saintly men who kept vigil over the sepulchre of our blessed Lord, at Jerusalem. He of the tall and portly form, and commanding presence, was Fray Antonio Millan, prior of the Franciscan convent in the holy city. He had a full and florid countenance, a sonorous voice, and was round and swelling and copious in his periods, like one accustomed to harangue and to be listened to with deference. His companion was small and spare in form, pale of visage, and soft, and silken, and almost whispering in speech. "He had a humble and lowly way," says Agapida, "ever more bowing the head; as became one of his calling," yet he was one of the most active, zealous and effective brothers of the convent; and when he raised his small black eye from the earth, there was a keen glance out of the corner, which shewed that though harmless as a dove, he was nevertheless as wise as a serpent.

These holy men had come on a momentous embassy from the Grand Soldan of Egypt, or as Agapida terms him in the language of the day the Soldan of Babylon. The league which had been made between that potentate and his arch-foe the Grand Turk Bayjazet II. to unite in arms for the salvation of Granada, as has been mentioned in a previous chapter of this chronicle, had come to nought. The infidel princes had again taken up arms against each other, and had relapsed into their ancient hostility. Still the Grand Soldan, as head of the whole Moslem sect, considered himself bound to preserve the Kingdom of Granada from the grasp of unbelievers. He dispatched, therefore, these two holy friars with letters to the Castilian sovereigns, as well as to the Pope, and to the King of Naples, remonstrating against the evils done to the Moors of the Kingdom of Granada, who were of his faith and kindred, whereas it was well known that great numbers of Christians were indulged and protected in the full enjoyment of their property, their liberty and their faith in his dominions. He insisted, therefore, that this war should cease, that the Moors of Granada should be reinstated in the territory of which they had been dispossessed; otherwise he threatened to put to death all the Christians beneath his sway, to demolish their convents and temples, and to destroy the holy sepulchre.

This fearful menace, had spread consternation among the Christians of Palestine; and when the intrepid Fray Antonio Millan and his lowly companion departed on their mission, they were accompanied far from the gates of Jerusalem by an anxious throng of brethren and disciples, who remained watching them with tearful eyes, as they journeyed over the plains of Judea.

These holy ambassadors were received with great distinction by King Ferdinand; for men of their cloth, had ever high honour and consideration in his court. He had long and frequent conversations with them, about the holy land; the state of the Christian church in the dominions of the Grand Soldan, and of the policy and conduct of that arch infidel towards it. The portly prior of the Franciscan convent, was full and round and oratorical in his replies, and the King expressed himself much pleased with the eloquence of his periods; but the politic monarch, was observed to lend a close and attentive ear to the whispering voice of the lowly companion, "whose discourse," adds Agapida, "though modest and low, was clear and fluent, and full of subtle wisdom."

These holy friars had visited Rome in their journeying, where they had delivered the letter of the Soldan to the sovereign Pontif. His holiness had written by them to the Castilian sovereigns, requesting to know what reply they had to offer to this demand of the oriental potentate.

The King of Naples also wrote to them on the subject, but in wary terms.

He inquired into the cause of this war with the Moors of Granada, and expressed great marvel at its events, as if, says Agapida, both were not notorious throughout all the Christian world. "Nay," adds the worthy friar with becoming indignation; "he uttered opinions savouring of little better than damnable heresy, for he observed that although the Moors were of a different sect, they ought not to be maltreated without just cause, and hinted that if the Castilian sovereigns did not suffer any crying injury from the Moors, it would be improper to do any thing which might draw great damage upon the Christians. As if, when once the sword of the faith was drawn, it ought ever to be sheathed, until this scum of heathendom were utterly destroyed, or driven from the land. But this monarch," he continues, "was more kindly disposed towards the infidels, than was honest and lawful in a Christian prince, and was at that very time in league with the Soldan, against their common enemy the Grand Turk."

These pious sentiments of the truly Catholic Agapida, are echoed by Padre Mariana in his history;* but the worthy chronicler Pedro Abarca attributes the interference of the King of Naples, not to lack of orthodoxy in religion; but to an excess of worldly policy; he being apprehensive that, should Ferdinand conquer the Moors of Granada, he might have time and means, to assert a claim of the house of Aragon, to the crown of Naples.

"King Ferdinand," continues the worthy father Pedro Abarca, "was no less master of dissimulation than his cousin of Naples, so he replied to him with the utmost suavity of manner, going into a minute and patient vindication of the war, and taking great apparent pains, to inform him, of those things, which all the world knew, but of which the other pretended to be ignorant."† At the same time he soothed his solicitude about the fate of the Christians in the empire of the Grand Soldan, assuring him, that the great revenue extorted from them in rents and tributes, would be a certain protection against the threatened violence.

To the Pope, he made the usual vindication of the war; that it was for the recovery of ancient territory usurped by the Moors; for the punishment of wars and violences inflicted upon the Christians, and finally, that it was a holy crusade for the glory and advancement of the church.

It was a truly edifying sight, says Agapida, "to behold these Friars, after they had had their audience of the King, moving about the camp, always surrounded by nobles and cavaliers of high and martial renown. These were insatiable in their questions about the holy land, the state of the sepulchre of our Lord, and the sufferings of the devoted brethren who guarded it, and the pious pilgrims who resorted there to pay their vows. The portly prior, of the convent, would stand with lofty and shining countenance in the midst

*Mariana Lib 25. Cap 15.
†Abarca. Anales de Aragon Rey XXX Cap 3.

of these iron warriors and declaim with resounding eloquence on the history of the sepulchre, but the humble brother, would ever and anon, sigh deeply, and in low tones, utter some tale of suffering and outrage, at which his steel clad hearers, would grasp the hilts of their swords, and mutter between their clinched teeth, prayers for another crusade."

The pious friars, having finished their mission to the King, and been treated with all due distinction, took their leave, and wended their way to Jaen, to visit the most Catholic of Queens. Isabella, whose heart was the seat of piety, received them as sacred men, invested with more than human dignity. During their residence at Jaen, they were continually in the royal presence; the respectable prior of the convent, moved and melted the ladies of the court by his florid rhetoric, but his lowly companion was observed to have continual access to the royal ear. That saintly and soft spoken messenger, says Agapida, received the reward of his humility; for the Queen moved by his frequent representations, made in all modesty and lowliness of spirit, granted a yearly sum in perpetuity of one thousand ducats in gold for the support of the Monks of the convent of the holy sepulchre.*

Moreover on the departure of these holy Ambassadors, the excellent and most Catholic Queen, delivered to them a veil devoutly embroidered with her own royal hands, to be placed over the holy sepulchre. A precious and inestimable present, which called forth a most eloquent tribute of thanks from the portly prior, but which brought tears into the eyes of his lowly companion.†

---

*La Reyna dió à los Frailes mil ducados de renta cada año para el sustento de los religiosos del Santo Sepulcro, que es la mejor limosna y sustento que hasta nuestros dias ha quedado à estos religiosos de Jerusalem: para donde les dió la Reyna un velo labrado por sus manos, para poner encima de la Santa Sepultura del Señor. Garibay Comp: Hist: Lib 1 8. Cap 36.

†*Note.* It is proper to mention the result of this mission of the two Friars, and which the worthy Agapida has neglected to record. At a subsequent period the Catholic sovereigns sent the distinguished historian Pietro Martyr of Angleria as ambassador to the Grand Soldan. That able man, made such representations as were perfectly satisfactory to the oriental potentate. He also obtained from him the remission of many exactions and extortions heretofore practiced upon Christian pilgrims visiting the holy sepulchre; which it is presumed had been gently but cogently detailed to the monarch by the lowly friar. Pietro Martyr wrote an account of his embassy to the Grand Soldan, a work greatly esteemed by the learned and containing much curious information. It is entitled, *De Legatione Babilonica.*

CHAPTER LXXVII

HOW QUEEN ISABELLA DEVISED MEANS TO SUPPLY THE ARMY WITH PROVISIONS.

It has been the custom to laud the conduct and address of King Ferdinand in this most arduous and protracted war; but the sage Agapida is more disposed to give credit to the counsels and measures of the Queen who, he observes, though less ostensible in action, was in truth the very soul, the vital principle of this great enterprize. While King Ferdinand was bustling in his camp, and making a glittering display with his gallant chivalry, she, surrounded by her saintly counsellors, in the Episcopal palace of Jaen, was devising ways, and means to keep the King and his army in existence. She had pledged herself to keep up a supply of men, and money and provisions, until the city should be taken. The hardships of the siege caused a fearful waste of life, but the supply of men was the least difficult part of her undertaking. So beloved was the Queen by the chivalry of Spain, that on her calling on them for assistance, not a grandee or cavalier that yet lingered at home, but either repaired in person, or sent forces to the camp; the ancient and warlike families vied with each other, in marshalling forth their vassals, and thus the besieged Moors beheld each day fresh troops arriving before their city and new ensigns and pennons displayed, emblazoned with arms well known to the veteran warriors.

But the most arduous task was to keep up a regular supply of provisions. It was not the army alone that had to be supported, but also the captured towns and their garrisons; for the whole country around them had been ravaged and the conquerors were in danger of starving in the midst of the land they had desolated. To transport the daily supplies for such immense numbers was a gigantic undertaking in a country where there was neither water conveyance, nor roads for carriages. Everything had to be borne by beasts of burthen over rugged and broken paths of the mountains, and through dangerous defiles exposed to the attacks and plunderings of the Moors.

The wary and calculating merchants accustomed to supply the army, shrunk from engaging at their own risk in so hazardous an undertaking. The Queen therefore hired fourteen thousand beasts of burden, and ordered all the wheat and barley to be bought up in Andalusia and in the domains of the knights of Santiago and Calatrava. She distributed the administration of these supplies among able and confidential persons. Some were employed to collect the grain, others to take it to the mills, others to superintend the grinding and delivery, and others to convey it to the camp. To every two hundred animals a muleteer was allotted to take charge of them on the route. Thus great lines of convoys were in constant movement, traversing to and fro, guarded by large bodies of troops, to defend them from hovering parties of the Moors. Not a single day's intermission was allowed, for the army depended upon the constant arrival of these supplies for daily food. The grain when brought into the camp was deposited in an immense granary, and sold to the army at a fixed price which was never either raised or lowered.

Incredible were the expenses incurred in these supplies, but the Queen had ghostly advisers thoroughly versed in the art of getting at the resources of the country. Many worthy prelates opened the deep purses of the church, and furnished loans from the revenues of their dioceses and convents, and their pious contributions were eventually rewarded by providence an hundred fold. Merchants and other wealthy individuals, confident of the punctual faith of the Queen, advanced large sums on the security of her word; many noble families lent their plate without waiting to be asked. The Queen, also, sold certain annual rents in inheritance, at great sacrifices, assigning the revenues of towns and cities for the payment. Finding all this insufficient to satisfy the enormous expenditure, she sent her gold and plate and all her jewels to the cities of Valencia and Barcelona, where they were pledged for a great amount of money; which was immediately appropriated to keep up the supplies of the army.

Thus, through the wonderful activity, judgement and enterprize of this heroic and magnanimous woman, a great host, encamped in the heart of a warlike country, accessible only over mountain roads, was maintained in continual abundance: nor was it supplied merely with the necessaries and comforts of life. The powerful escorts drew merchants and artificers from all parts, to repair as if in caravans to this great military market. In a little while the camp abounded with tradesmen and artists of all kinds to administer to the luxury and ostentation of the youthful chivalry. Here might be seen cunning artificers in steel, and accomplished armourers, achieving those rare and sumptuous helmets and cuirasses richly gilt, inlaid and embossed in which the Spanish cavaliers delighted. Saddlers and harness makers, and horse milliners also, whose tents glittered with gorgeous housings and caparisons. The merchants spread forth their sumptuous silks, cloths, brocades, fine linen and tapestry. The tents of the nobility were prodigally decorated with all kinds of the richest stuffs, and dazzled the eye with their magnificence: nor could the grave looks and grave speeches of King Ferdinand prevent his youthful cavaliers from vying with each other in the splendour of their dresses and caparisons on all occasions of parade and ceremony.

CHAPTER LXXVIII

OF THE DISASTERS WHICH BEFELL THE CAMP.

While the Christian camp, thus gay and gorgeous, spread itself out like a holyday pageant before the walls of Baza; while a long line of beasts of burthen laden with provisions and luxuries were seen descending the valley from morning till night, and pouring into the camp a continued stream of abundance, the unfortunate garrison found their resources rapidly wasting away, and famine already began to pinch the peaceful part of the community.

Cidi Yahye had acted with great spirit and valour as long as there was any prospect of success, but he began to lose his usual fire and animation, and was observed to pace the walls of Baza, with a pensive air, casting many a wistful look towards the Christian camp, and sinking into profound reveries and cogitations. The veteran Alcayde Mohammed Ben-Hassan, noticed these desponding moods, and endeavoured to rally the spirits of the prince. "The rainy season is at hand:" would he cry; "the floods will soon pour down from the mountains; the rivers will overflow their banks, and inundate the valleys. The Christian King already begins to waver, he dare not linger and encounter such a season in a plain cut up by canals and rivulets. A single wintry storm from our mountains, would wash away his canvas city, and sweep off those gay pavilions like wreaths of snow before the blast."

The Prince Cidi Yahye took heart at these words, and counted the days as they passed until the stormy season should commence. As he watched the Christian camp, he beheld it one morning in universal commotion. There was an unusual sound of hammers in every part; as if some new engines of war were constructing. At length to his astonishment the walls and roofs of houses began to appear above the bulwarks; in a little while there were above a thousand edifices of wood and plaister erected, covered with tiles taken from the demolished towers of the orchards, and bearing the pennons of various commanders and cavaliers, while the common soldiery constructed huts of clay and branches of trees, thatched with straw. Thus, to the dismay of the Moors, within four days, the light tents and gay pavilions, which had whitened their hills and plains passed away like summer clouds, and the unsubstantial camp assumed the solid appearance of a city laid out into streets and squares. In the centre rose a large edifice which overlooked the whole, and the royal standard of Aragon and Castile, proudly floating above it, shewed it to be the palace of the King.*

Ferdinand had taken the sudden resolution thus to turn his camp into a city, partly to provide against the approaching season, and partly to convince the Moors of his fixed determination to continue the siege. In their haste to erect their dwellings, however, the Spanish cavaliers had not properly considered the nature of the climate. For the greater part of the year, there

*Cura de Los Palacios. Pulgar etc.

scarcely falls a drop of rain on the thirsty soil of Andalusia: The ramblas or dry channels of the torrents remain deep and arid gashes and clefts, in the sides of the mountains. The perennial streams shrink up to mere threads of water, which tinkling down the bottoms of the deep barrancos or ravines, scarce feed and keep alive the rivers of the valleys. The rivers almost lost in their wide and naked beds, seem like thirsty rills, winding in serpentine mazes through deserts of sand, and stones, and so shallow and tranquil in their course, as to be forded in safety in almost every part. One autumnal tempest of rain, however, changes the whole face of nature. The clouds break in deluges among the vast congregation of mountains. The ramblas are suddenly filled with raging floods, the tinkling rivulets swell to thundering torrents that come roaring down from the mountains, tumbling great masses of rocks in their career. The late meandering river spreads over its once naked bed; lashes its surges against the banks, and rushes like a wide and foaming inundation through the valley.

Scarcely had the Christians finished their slightly built edifices, when an autumnal tempest of the kind came scouring from the mountains. The camp was immediately overflowed. Many of the houses undermined by the floods or beaten by the rain crumbled away and fell to the earth, burying man and beast beneath their ruins. Several valuable lives were lost, and great numbers of horses and other animals perished. To add to the distress and confusion of the camp, the daily supply of provisions suddenly ceased; for the rain had broken up the roads, and rendered the rivers impassable. A panic seized upon the army, for the cessation of a single day's supply produced a scarcity of bread and provender. Fortunately the rain was but transient. The torrents rushed by, and ceased; the rivers shrunk back again, to their narrow channels, and the convoys that had been detained upon their banks, arrived safely in the camp.

No sooner did Queen Isabella hear of this interruption of her supplies, than with her usual vigilance and activity, she provided against its recurrence. She dispatched six thousand foot soldiers, under the command of experienced officers to repair the roads, and to make causeways and bridges for the distance of seven Spanish leagues. The troops, also, who had been stationed in the mountains by the King, to guard the defiles, made two paths, one for the convoys going to the camp, and the other for those returning, that they might not meet and impede each other. The edifices which had been demolished by the late floods were rebuilt, in a firmer manner, and precautions were taken to protect the camp from future inundations.

CHAPTER LXXIX

ENCOUNTER BETWEEN THE CHRISTIANS AND MOORS BEFORE BAZA; AND THE DEVOTION OF THE INHABITANTS TO THE DEFENCE OF THE CITY.

When King Ferdinand beheld the ravage and confusion produced by a single autumnal storm, and bethought him of all the maladies to which a besieging camp is exposed, in inclement seasons, he began to feel his compassion kindling for the suffering people of Baza, and an inclination to grant them more favorable terms. He sent, therefore, several messages to the Alcayde Mohammed Ben Hassan offering liberty of person and security of property for the inhabitants, and large rewards for himself, if he would surrender the city. The veteran Mohammed was not to be dazzled by the splendid offers of the monarch. He had received exaggerated accounts of the damage done to the Christian camp by the late storm, and of the sufferings and discontents of the army in consequence of the transient interruption of supplies. He considered the overtures of Ferdinand as proofs of the desperate state of his affairs. "A little more patience, a little more patience," said the shrewd old warrior, "and we shall see this cloud of Christian locusts driven away before the winter storms. When they once turn their backs it will be our turn to strike, and, with the help of Allah, the blow shall be decisive." He sent a firm though courteous refusal to the Castilian monarch, and in the mean time animated his companions to sally forth with more spirit than ever to attack the Spanish outposts and those labouring in the trenches. The consequence was a daily occurrence of the most daring and bloody skirmishes that cost the lives of many of the bravest and most adventurous cavaliers of either army.

In one of these sallies nearly three hundred horse and two thousand foot mounted the heights behind the city to capture the Christians who were employed upon the works. They came by surprize upon a body of guards, Esquires of the Count de Ureña, killed some, put the rest to flight, and pursued them down the mountain until they came in sight of a small force under the count de Tendilla and Gonzalvo of Cordova. The Moors came rushing down with such fury, that many of the men of the Count de Tendilla betook themselves to flight. The brave count considered it less dangerous to fight than to fly. Bracing his buckler therefore and grasping his trusty weapon he stood his ground with his accustomed prowess. Gonzalvo of Cordova ranged himself by his side, and, marshalling the troops which remained with them they made a valiant front to the Moors.

The infidels, pressed them hard and were gaining the advantage when Alonzo de Aguilar, hearing of the danger of his brother Gonzalvo, flew to his assistance accompanied by the Count of Ureña and a body of their troops. A hot fight ensued from cliff to cliff, and glen to glen. The Moors were fewer in number but they excelled in the dexterity and lightness requisite for these scrambling skirmishes; they were at length driven from their vantage ground and pursued by Alonzo de Aguilar and his brother Gonzalvo, to the very suburbs of the city, leaving many of the bravest of their men upon the field.

Such was one of innumerable rough encounters which were daily taking place, in which many brave cavaliers were slain without any apparent benefit to either party. The Moors notwithstanding repeated defeats and losses, continued to sally forth daily with astonishing spirit and vigour, and the obstinacy of their defence seemed to encrease with their sufferings.

The Prince Cidi Yahye was ever foremost in these sallies, but he grew daily more despairing of success. All the money in the military chest was expended and there was no longer wherewithall to pay the hired troops. Still the veteran Mohammed Ben Hassan undertook to provide for this emergency. Summoning the principal inhabitants, he represented the necessity of some exertion and sacrifice on their part to maintain the defence of the city "The enemy," said he, "dreads the approach of winter and our perseverance drives him to despair. A little longer and he will leave you in quiet enjoyment of your homes and families. But our troops must be paid to keep them in good heart. Our money is exhausted and all our supplies are cut off. It is impossible to continue our defence without your aid."

Upon this the citizens consulted together, and they collected all their vessels of gold and silver and brought them to Mohammed Ben Hassan. Take these, said they and coin them or sell them or pledge them for money wherewith to pay the troops. The women of Baza also were seized with generous emulation. "Shall we deck ourselves with gorgeous apparel," said they, "when our country is desolate and its defenders in want of bread?" So they took their collars and bracelets and anklets, and other ornaments of gold, and all their jewels, and put them in the hands of the veteran alcayde. "Take these spoils of our vanity," said they, "and let them contribute to the defence of our homes and families. If Baza be delivered we need no jewels to grace our rejoicing, and if Baza falls of what avail are ornaments to the captive!"

By these contributions was Mohammed enabled to pay the soldiery, and to carry on the defence of the city with unabated spirit. Tidings were speedily conveyed to King Ferdinand of this generous devotion on the part of the people of Baza, and the hopes which the Moorish commanders gave them that the Christian army would soon abandon the siege in despair. "They shall have a convincing proof of the fallacy of such hopes," said the politic monarch; so he wrote forthwith to Queen Isabella, praying her to come to the camp in state, with all her train and retinue, and publicly to take up her residence there for the winter. By this means the Moors would be convinced

of the settled determination of the sovereigns to persist in the siege until
the city should surrender, and he trusted they would be brought to speedy
capitulation.

CHAPTER LXXX

HOW QUEEN ISABELLA ARRIVED AT THE CAMP, AND THE CONSEQUENCES OF HER ARRIVAL.

Mohammed Ben Hassan still encouraged his companions, with hopes that
the royal army would soon relinquish the siege, when they heard one day
shouts of joy from the Christian camp, and thundering salvo's of artillery.
Word was brought at the same time, from the centinels on the watch towers
that a Christian army was approaching down the valley. Mohammed and his
fellow commanders ascended one of the highest towers of the walls, and
beheld in truth a numerous force, in shining array, descending the hills, and
heard the distant clangour of the trumpet and the faint swell of triumphant
music. As the host drew nearer they descried a stately dame magnificently
attired, whom they soon discovered to be the Queen. She was riding on a
mule, the sumptuous trappings of which were resplendent with gold and
reached to the ground. On her right hand rode her daughter, the Princess
Isabella, equally splendid in her array, on her left the venerable Grand Cardinal of Spain. A noble train of ladies and cavaliers followed her, together
with pages and esquires, and a numerous guard of hidalgos of high rank
arrayed in superb armour. When the veteran Mohammed Ben Hassan beheld that this was the Queen Isabella, arriving in state to take up her residence in the camp his heart failed him. He shook his head mournfully, and,
turning to his captains, "Cavaliers," said he, "the fate of Baza is decided!"

The Moorish commanders remained gazing with a mingled feeling of grief
and admiration at this magnificent pageant, which foreboded the fall of their
city. Some of the troops would have sallied forth on one of their desperate
skirmishes to attack the royal guard, but the Prince Cidi Yahye forbade
them: nor would he allow any artillery to be discharged, or any molestation
or insult to be offered; for the character of Isabella was venerated even by
the Moors; and most of the commanders possessed that high and chivalrous
courtesy which belongs to heroic spirits; for they were among the noblest
and bravest cavaliers of the Moorish nation.

The inhabitants of Baza, when they learnt that the Christian Queen was
approaching the camp, eagerly sought every eminence that could command
a view of the plain, and every battlement, and tower and mosque was cov-

ered with turbaned heads gazing at the glorious spectacle. They beheld King Ferdinand issue forth in royal state attended by the Marquis of Cadiz, the Master of Santiago, the Duke of Alva, the Admiral of Castile, and many other nobles of renown, while the whole chivalry of the camp, sumptuously arrayed followed in his train and the populace rent the air with acclamations at the sight of the patriot Queen.

When the sovereigns had met and embraced each other the two hosts mingled together, and entered the camp in martial pomp, and the eyes of the infidel beholders were dazzled by the flash of armour the splendour of golden caparisons, the gorgeous display of silks and brocades and velvets, of tossing plumes and fluttering banners. There was at the same time a triumphant sound of drums and trumpets, clarions and sackbuts, mingled with the sweet melody of the dulcimer, which came swelling in bursts of harmony that seemed to rise up to the heavens.*

On the arrival of the Queen, says the historian Hernando del Pulgar who was present at the time; it was marvellous to behold how all at once the rigour and turbulence of war was softened, and the storm of passion sunk into a calm. The sword was sheathed, the crossbow no longer launched its deadly shaft, and the artillery, which had hitherto kept up an incessant up-roar, now ceased its thundering. On both sides there was still a vigilant guard kept up, the centinels bristled the walls of Baza with their lances, and the guards patrolled the Christian camp; but there was no sallying forth to skirmish nor any wanton violence or carnage.

Prince Cidi Yahye saw by the arrival of the Queen that the Christians were determined to continue the siege, and he knew that the city would have to capitulate. He had been prodigal of the lives of his soldiers as long as he thought a military good was to be gained by the sacrifice; but he was sparing of their blood in a hopeless cause, and wary of exasperating the enemy by an obstinate yet hopeless defence.

At the request of Prince Cidi Yahye a parley was granted and the Master Commander of Leon Don Gutiere de Cardenas was appointed to confer with the veteran alcayde Mohammed. They met at an appointed place within view of both camp and city, honourably attended by cavaliers of either army. Their meeting was highly courteous, for they had learnt, from rough en-counters in the field, to admire each other's prowess. The Commander of Leon, in an earnest speech, pointed out the hopelessness of any further defence, and warned Mohammed of the ills which Malaga had incurred by its obstinacy. "I promise in the name of my sovereigns," said he, "that if you surrender immediately, the inhabitants shall be treated as subjects and pro-tected in property, liberty and religion. If you refuse, you who are now

*Cura de Los Palacios

renowned as an able and judicious commander will be chargeable with the confiscations, captivities and deaths which may be suffered by the people of Baza."

The commander ceased, and Mohammed returned to the city to consult with his companions. It was evident that all further resistance was hopeless, but the Moorish commanders felt that a cloud might rest upon their names should they, of their own discretion, surrender so important a place, without its having sustained an assault. Prince Cidi Yahye requested permission, therefore, to send an envoy to Guadix, with a letter to the old monarch El Zagal treating of the surrender; the request was granted, a safe conduct assured to the envoy and the veteran Alcayde Mohammed Ben Hassan departed upon this momentous mission.

CHAPTER LXXXI
SURRENDER OF BAZA.

The old warrior King was seated in an inner chamber of the castle of Guadix, much cast down in spirit and ruminating on his gloomy fortunes, when an envoy from Baza was announced, and the veteran Alcayde Mohammed stood before him. El Zagal saw disastrous tidings written in his countenance; How fares it with Baza? said he summoning up his spirits to the question. "Let this inform thee," replied Mohammed, and he delivered into his hands the letter from the Prince Cidi Yahye. This letter spoke of the desperate situation of Baza the impossibility of holding out longer without assistance from El Zagal, and the favorable terms held out by the Castilian sovereigns. Had it been written by any other person El Zagal might have received it with distrust, and indignation; but he confided in Cidi Yahye as in a second self, and the words of his letter sank deep in his heart. When he had finished reading it he sighed deeply and remained for some time lost in thought, with his head drooping upon his bosom. Recovering himself at length, he called together the alfaquis and the old men of Guadix, and, communicating the tidings from Baza solicited their advice. It was a sign of sore trouble of mind and dejection of heart, when El Zagal sought the advice of others, but his fierce courage was tamed, for he saw the end of his power approaching. The alfaquis and the old men did but encrease the distraction of his mind by a variety of counsel, none of which appeared of any avail; for, unless Baza were succoured, it was impossible that it should hold out, and every attempt to succour it had proved ineffectual.

El Zagal dismissed his council in despair, and summoned the veteran Mohammed before him, "Allah Achbar!" exclaimed he. "God is great, there is but one God and Mahomet is his prophet, return to my cousin Cidi Yahye; tell him it is out of my power to aid him, he must do as seems to him for the best. The people of Baza have performed deeds worthy of immortal fame, I cannot ask them to encounter further ills and perils in maintaining a hopeless defence."

The reply of El Zagal determined the fate of the city. Cidi Yahye and his fellow commanders immediately capitulated, and were granted the most favorable terms. The cavaliers and soldiers who had come from other parts to the defence of the place, were permitted to depart freely with their arms, horses and effects. The inhabitants had their choice, either to depart with their property, or to dwell in the suburbs, in the enjoyment of their religion and laws, taking an oath of fealty to the sovereigns, and paying the same tribute they had paid to the Moorish Kings. The city and citadel were to be delivered up in six days, within which period the inhabitants were to remove all their effects, and in the mean time, they were to place, as hostages, fifteen Moorish youths, sons of the principal inhabitants, in the hands of the Commander of Leon. When Cidi Yahye and the Alcayde Mohammed came to deliver up the hostages, among whom were the sons of the latter, they paid homage to the King and Queen, who received them with the utmost courtesy and kindness, and ordered magnificent presents to be given to them and likewise to the other Moorish cavaliers; consisting of money robes, horses, and other things of great value.

The Prince Cidi Yahye was so captivated by the grace, the dignity and generosity of Isabella, and the princely courtesy of Ferdinand that he vowed never again to draw his sword against such magnanimous sovereigns!

The Queen charmed with his gallant bearing and his animated professions of devotion, assured him that having him on her side, she already considered the war terminated, which had desolated the Kingdom of Granada.

Mighty and irresistible are words of praise from the lips of sovereigns. Cidi Yahye was entirely subdued by this fair speech from the illustrious Isabella. His heart burned with a sudden flame of loyalty towards the sovereigns. He begged to be enrolled amongst the most devoted of their subjects, and, in the fervour of his sudden zeal engaged, not merely to dedicate his sword to their service, but to exert all his influence, which was great, in persuading his cousin Muley Abdalla el Zagal to surrender the cities of Guadix and Almeria, and to give up all further hostilities. Nay so powerful was the effect produced upon his mind by his conversations with the sovereigns, that it extended even to his religion; for he became immediately enlightened as to the heathenish abominations of the vile sect, of Mahomet, and struck with the truths of Christianity as illustrated by such powerful monarchs. He consented therefore to be baptised and to be gathered into the fold of the church. The pious Agapida indulges in a triumphant strain of exultation on the sudden and surprizing conversion of this princely infidel. He considers it one of the greatest achievements of the Catholic sovereign and indeed one of the marvellous occurrences of this holy war; "but it is given to saints and pious monarchs," says he, "to work miracles in the cause of the faith; and such did the most Catholic Ferdinand in the conversion of the Prince Cidi Yahye."

Some of the Arabian writers have sought to lessen the wonder of this miracle by alluding to great revenues granted to the prince and his heirs by the Castilian monarchs, together with a territory in Marchena with towns, lands and vassals; but in this, says Agapida, we only see a wise precaution of King Ferdinand to clinch and secure the conversion of his proselyte. The policy of the Catholic monarch was at all times equal to his piety. Instead also of vaunting of this great conversion, and making a public parade of the entry of the prince into the church, King Ferdinand ordered that the baptism should be performed in private and kept a profound secret. He feared that Cidi Yahye might otherwise be denounced as an apostate, and abhorred and abandoned by the Moors, and thus his influence destroyed in bringing the war to a speedy termination.*

The veteran Mohammed Ben Hassan was likewise won by the magnanimity and munificence of the Castilian sovereigns, and entreated to be received into their service, and his example was followed by many other Moorish cavaliers, whose services were graciously accepted and magnificently rewarded.

Thus after a siege of six months and twenty days, the city of Baza surrendered on the 4th of December 1489, the festival of the glorious Santa Barbara, who is said, in the Catholic calendar, to preside over thunder and lightning, fire and gunpowder, and all kinds of combustious explosions. The King and Queen made their solemn and triumphal entry on the following day, and the public joy was heightened by the sight of upwards of five hundred Christian captives, men, women and children, delivered from the Moorish dungeons.

The loss of the Christians in this siege amounted to twenty thousand men, of whom seventeen thousand died of disease, and not a few of mere cold; a kind of death, says the historian Mariana peculiarly uncomfortable; but, adds the venerable Jesuit, as these latter were chiefly people of ignoble rank, baggage carriers and such like, the loss was not of great importance.

The surrender of Baza was followed by that of Almuñecar, Tavernas, and most of the fortresses of the Alpuxarra mountains. The inhabitants hoped, by prompt and voluntary submission, to secure equally favorable terms with those granted to the captured city; and the alcaydes to receive similar rewards to those lavished on its commanders; nor was either of them disappointed. The inhabitants were permitted to remain as Mudexares in the

*Conde. Tom 3. Cap 40.

quiet enjoyment of their property and religion, and as to the alcaydes, when they came to the camp to render up their charges, they were received by Ferdinand with distinguished favour, and rewarded with presents of money in proportion to the importance of the places they had commanded. Care was taken, by the politic monarch, however, not to wound their pride, or shock their delicacy; so these sums were paid under colour of arrears due to them for their services to the former government. Ferdinand had conquered by dint of sword in the earlier part of the war, but he found gold as potent as steel in this campaign of Baza.

With several of these mercenary chieftains came one named Ali Aben Fahar, a seasoned warrior who had held many important commands. He was a Moor of a lofty, stern and melancholy aspect, and stood silent and apart, while his companions surrendered their several fortresses and retired laden with treasure. When it came to his turn to speak he addressed the sovereigns with the frankness of a soldier, but with a tone of dejection and despair. "I am a Moor," said he, "and of Moorish lineage, and am Alcayde of the fair towns and castles of Purchena and Paterna. These were intrusted to me to defend, but those who should have stood by me have lost all strength and courage and seek only for security. These fortresses, therefore, most potent sovereigns are yours, whenever you will send to take possession of them."

Large sums of money in gold were immediately ordered by Ferdinand, to be delivered to the alcayde, as a recompense for so important a surrender. The Moor, however, put back the gift with a firm and haughty demeanour. "I come not," said he, "to sell what is not mine, but to yield what fortune has made yours; and your majesties may rest assured, that had I been properly seconded, death would have been the price at which I would have sold my fortresses, and not the gold you offer me."

The Castilian monarchs were struck with the lofty and loyal spirit of the Moor and desired to engage a man of such fidelity in their service; but the proud Moslem could not be induced to serve the enemies of his nation and his faith.

"Is there nothing then," said Queen Isabella, "that we can do to gratify thee, and to prove to thee our regard?" "Yes," replied the Moor. "I have left behind me, in the towns and valleys which I have surrendered, many of my unhappy countrymen with their wives and children, who cannot tear themselves from their native abodes; give me your royal word that they shall be protected in the peaceable enjoyment of their religion and their homes." "We promise it," said Isabella; "they shall dwell in peace and security. But for thyself; what dost thou ask for thyself?" "Nothing," replied Ali, "but permission to pass unmolested with my horses and effects into Africa."

The Castilian monarchs would fain have forced upon him gold and silver and superb horses richly caparisoned, not as rewards, but as marks of personal esteem, but Ali Aben Faher declined all presents and distinctions, as if he thought it criminal to flourish individually during a time of public distress, and disdained all prosperity, that seemed to grow out of the ruins of his country.

Having received a royal passport, he gathered together his horses and servants, his armour and weapons, and all his warlike effects, bade adieu to his weeping countrymen with a brow stamped with anguish but without shedding a tear; and mounting his Barbary steed turned his back upon the delightful valleys of his conquered country, departing on his lonely way to seek a soldier's fortune amidst the burning sands of Africa.*

CHAPTER LXXXII

SUBMISSION OF EL ZAGAL TO THE CASTILIAN SOVEREIGNS.

Evil tidings never fail by the way through lack of messengers; they are wafted on the wings of the wind, and it is as if the very birds of the air would bear them to the ear of the unfortunate. The old King El Zagal buried himself in the recesses of his castle to hide himself from the light of day, which no longer shone prosperously upon him, but every hour brought missives thundering at the gate with the tale of some new disaster. Fortress after fortress had laid its keys at the feet of the Christian sovereigns. Strip by strip of warrior mountain and green fruitful valley was torn from his domains, and added to the territories of the conquerors. Scarcely a remnant remained to him except a tract of the Alpuxarras and the noble cities of Guadix and Almeria. No one any longer stood in awe of the fierce old monarch; the terror of his frown had declined with his power. He had arrived at that stage of adversity when a man's friends feel emboldened to tell him hard truths and to give him unpalatable advice, and when his spirit is bowed down to listen quietly if not meekly.

El Zagal was seated on his divan, his whole spirit absorbed in rumination on the transitory nature of human glory, when his kinsman and brother in law the Prince Cidi Yahye was announced. That illustrious convert to the true faith and the interests of the conquerors of his country had hastened to Guadix with all the fervour of a new proselyte, eager to prove his zeal in the service of heaven and the Castilian sovereigns; by persuading the old monarch to abjure his faith and surrender his possessions.

Cidi Yahye still bore the guise of a Moslem, for his conversion was as yet a secret. The stern heart of El Zagal softened at beholding the face of a

*Pulgar. Garibay lib 40. Cap 40. Cura de Los Palacios.

kinsman in this hour of adversity. He folded his cousin to his bosom and gave thanks to Allah that amidst all his troubles he had still a friend and counsellor on whom he might rely. Cidi Yahye soon entered upon the real purpose of his mission. He represented to El Zagal the desperate state of affairs and the irretrievable decline of Moorish power in the Kingdom of Granada. Fate, said he, is against our arms; our ruin is written in the heavens; remember the prediction of the astrologers at the birth of your nephew Boabdil. We had hoped that their prediction was accomplished by his capture at Lucena; but it is now evident that the stars portended not a temporary and passing reverse of the kingdom but a final overthrow. The constant succession of disasters which have attended our efforts shew that the sceptre of Granada is doomed to pass into the hands of the Christian monarchs, such, concluded the prince emphatically, and with a profound and pious reverence, "such is the almighty will of God!"

El Zagal listened to these words in mute attention, without so much as moving a muscle of his face or winking an eye lid. When the prince had concluded he remained for a long time silent and pensive; at length heaving a profound sigh from the very bottom of his heart. "Alahuma, subahana hu!" exclaimed he, "the will of God be done! Yes my cousin it is but too evident that such is the will of Allah, and what he wills, he fails not to accomplish. Had he not decreed the fall of Granada this arm and this scymetar would have maintained it."*

"What then remains," said Cidi Yahye, "but to draw the most advantage from the wreck of empire that is left you. To persist in a war is to bring complete desolation upon the land and ruin and death upon its faithful inhabitants. Are you disposed to yield up your remaining towns to your nephew El Chiquito, that they may augment his power and derive protection from his alliance with the Christian sovereigns?"

The eye of El Zagal flashed fire at this suggestion. He grasped the hilt of his scymetar and gnashed his teeth in fury. "Never," cried he, "will I make terms with that recreant and slave; sooner would I see the banners of the Christian monarchs floating above my walls, than they should add to the possessions of the vassal Boabdil!"

Cidi Yahye immediately seized upon this idea and urged El Zagal to make a frank and entire surrender. "Trust," said he, "to the magnanimity of the Castilian sovereigns; they will doubtless grant you high and honourable terms; it is better to yield to them as friends, what they must infallibly and before long wrest from you as enemies; for such my cousin is the almighty will of God!"

"Alahuma, Subahana hu!" repeated El Zagal, "the will of God be done!" So the old monarch bowed his haughty neck and agreed to surrender his

*Conde, L 3. C. 40.

territories to the enemies of his faith, rather than suffer them to augment the Moslem power under the sway of his nephew.

Cidi Yahye now returned to Baza empowered by El Zagal to treat on his behalf with the Christian sovereigns. The prince felt a species of exultation as he expatiated on the rich reliques of empire which he was authorized to cede. There was a great part of that line of mountains which extends from the metropolis to the Mediterranean Sea, with their series of beautiful green valleys, like precious emralds set in a golden chain. Above all there were Guadix and Almeria, two of the most inestimable jewels in the crown of Granada.

In return for these possessions and for the claim of El Zagal to the rest of the kingdom the sovereigns received him into their friendship and alliance, and gave him in perpetual inheritance the territory of Andarax and the valley of Alhaurin in the Alpuxarras, with half of the Salinas or salt pits of Malcha. He was to enjoy the title of King of Andarax with two thousand Mudexares or conquered Moors for subjects; and his revenues were to be made up to the sum of four millions of maravedies.* All these he was to hold as a vassal of the Castilian crown.

These arrangements being made Cidi Yahye returned with them to Muley Abdalla, and it was concerted that the ceremony of surrender and homage should take place at the city of Almeria.

On the 17th of December King Ferdinand departed from Baza with a part of his army, and the Queen soon followed with the remainder. Ferdinand passed in triumph by several of the newly acquired towns, exulting in these trophies of his policy rather than his valour. As he drew near to Almeria the Moorish King came forth to meet him, accompanied by the Prince Cidi Yahye and a number of the principal inhabitants on horseback. The fierce brow of El Zagal was clouded with a kind of forced humility, but there was an impatient curl of the lip with now and then a swelling of the bosom and an indignant breathing from the distended nostril. It was evident he considered himself conquered, not by the power of man, but by the hand of heaven, and while he bowed to the decrees of fate it galled his proud spirit to have to humble himself before its mortal agent. As he approached the Christian King he alighted from his horse and advanced to kiss his hand in token of homage. Ferdinand, however, respected the royal title which the Moor had held; and would not permit the ceremony, but, bending from his saddle graciously embraced him and requested him to remount his steed.† Several courteous speeches passed between them, and the fortress and city of Almeria and all the remaining territories of El Zagal, were delivered up in form; when all was accomplished, the old warrior Moor retired to the moun-

*Cura de Los Palacios Cap 94.
†Cura de Los Palacios Cap 93.

tains with a handful of adherents, to seek his petty territory of Andarax, to bury his humiliation from the world, and to console himself with the shadowy title of a King.*

CHAPTER LXXXIII

EVENTS AT GRANADA SUBSEQUENT TO THE SUBMISSION OF EL ZAGAL.

Who can tell when to rejoice in this fluctuating world? Every wave of prosperity has its reacting surge, and we are often overwhelmed by the very billow on which we thought to be wafted into the haven of our hopes. When Jusef Aben Commixa the vizier of Boabdil surnamed El Chico, entered the royal saloon of the Alhambra and announced the capitulation of El Zagal, the heart of the youthful monarch leaped for joy. His great wish was accomplished; his uncle was defeated and dethroned and he reigned without a rival, sole monarch of Granada. At length he was about to enjoy the fruits of his humiliation and vassalage. He beheld his throne fortified by the friendship and alliance of the Castilian monarchs; there could be no question therefore of its stability. "Allah Achbar," exclaimed he, "God is great! Rejoice with me, oh Jusef, the stars have ceased their persecution. Hence forth let no man call me El Zogoybi."

In the first moment of his exultation Boabdil would have ordered public rejoicings, but the shrewd Jusef shook his head. "The tempest has ceased," said he, "from one point of the heavens but it may begin to rage from another; a troubled sea is beneath us and we are surrounded by rocks and quicksands. Let my lord the King defer rejoicings until all has settled into a calm." El Chico, however, could not remain tranquil in this day of exultation. He ordered his steed to be sumptuously caparisoned and issuing out of the gate of the Alhambra, descended with a glittering retinue along the avenue of trees and fountains into the city to receive the acclamations of the populace. As he entered the great square of the Vivarrambla he beheld crowds of people in violent agitation, but as he approached, what was his surprize to hear groans and murmurs and bursts of execration. The tidings had spread through Granada that Muley Abdalla el Zagal had been driven to capitulate, and that all his territories had fallen into the hands of the Christians. No one had enquired into the particulars, but all Granada had been thrown into a ferment of grief and indignation. In the heat of the moment old Muley was extolled to the skies as a patriot prince who had fought to the last for the

*Pulgar, Garibay, etc. etc.

salvation of his country; as a mirror of monarchs, scorning to compromise the dignity of his crown by any act of vassalage. Boabdil on the contrary, had looked on exultingly, at the hopeless yet heroic struggle of his uncle; he had rejoiced in the defeat of the faithful and the triumph of unbelievers. He had aided in the dismemberment and downfall of the empire. When they beheld him riding forth in gorgeous state in what they considered a day of humiliation for all true Moslems, they could not contain their rage, and amidst the clamours that met his ears, Boabdil more than once heard his name coupled with the epithets of traytor and renegado.

Shocked and discomfited the youthful monarch returned in confusion to the Alhambra. He shut himself up within its innermost courts, and remained a kind of voluntary prisoner until the first burst of popular feeling should subside. He trusted that it would soon pass away, that the people would be too sensible of the sweets of peace to repine at the price at which it was obtained; at any rate he trusted to the strong friendship of the Christian sovereigns to secure him even against the factions of his subjects.

The first missives from the politic Ferdinand shewed Boabdil the value of his friendship.

The Catholic monarch reminded him of a treaty which he had made when captured in the city of Loxa. By this he had engaged that in case the Catholic sovereigns should capture the cities of Guadix, Baza and Almeria, he would surrender Granada into their hands within a limited time, and accept in exchange certain Moorish towns, to be held by him as their vassal. Ferdinand now informed him that Guadix, Baza and Almeria had fallen; he called upon him therefore to fulfil his engagement. If the unfortunate Boabdil had possessed the will, he had not the power to comply with this demand. He was shut up in the Alhambra while a tempest of popular fury raged without. Granada was thronged by refugees from the captured towns, many of them disbanded soldiers; others broken down citizens, rendered fierce and desperate by ruin; all railed at Boabdil as the real cause of their misfortunes. How was he to venture forth in such a storm? above all, how was he to talk to such men of surrender? In his reply to Ferdinand he represented the difficulties of his situation, and that, so far from having controul over his subjects, his very life was in danger from their turbulence. He entreated the King, therefore, to rest satisfied for the present, with his recent conquests; promising him that should he be able to regain full empire over his capital, and its inhabitants, it would but be to rule over them as vassal to the Castilian crown.

Ferdinand was not to be satisfied with such a reply. The time was come to bring his game of policy to a close, and to consummate his conquest, by seating himself on the throne of the Alhambra. Professing to consider Boabdil as a faithless ally, who had broken his plighted word, he discarded him from his friendship and addressed a second letter, not to that monarch, but to the commanders and council of the city. He demanded a complete surrender of the place, with all the arms in the possession either of the citizens, or of others who had recently taken refuge within its walls. If the inhabitants should comply with this summons he promised them the indulgent terms which had been granted to Baza Guadix, and Almeria, if they should refuse he threatened them with the fate of Malaga.*

The message of the Catholic monarch produced the greatest commotion in the city. The inhabitants of the Alcaiceria, that busy hive of traffic, and all others who had tasted the sweets of gainful commerce during the late cessation of hostilities, were for securing their golden advantages by timely submission; others, who had wives and children, looked on them with tenderness and solicitude, and dreaded by resistance to bring upon them the horrors of slavery. But on the other hand Granada was crowded with men from all parts, ruined by the war, exasperated by their sufferings, and eager only for revenge; with others who had been reared amidst hostilities, who had lived by the sword, and whom a return of peace would leave without home or hope. Besides these there were others no less fiery and warlike in disposition, but animated by a loftier spirit. These were valiant and haughty cavaliers, of the old chivalrous lineages, who had inherited a deadly hatred to the Christians from a long line of warrior ancestors, and to whom the idea was worse than death that Granada, illustrious Granada! for ages the seat of Moorish grandeur and delight, should become the abode of unbelievers. Among these cavaliers the most eminent was Muza Ben Abil Gazan. He was of royal lineage, of a proud and generous nature and a form combining manly strength and beauty; none could excel him in the management of the horse, and dexterous use of all kinds of weapons. His gracefulness and skill in the tourney was the theme of praise among the Moorish dames, and his prowess in the field had made him the terror of the enemy. He had long repined at the timid policy of Boabdil, and had endeavoured to counteract its enervating effects, and to keep alive the martial spirit of Granada. For this reason he had promoted jousts and tiltings with the reed, and all those other public games which bear the semblance of war. He endeavoured also to inculcate into his companions in arms those high chivalrous sentiments which lead to valiant and magnanimous deeds, but which are apt to decline with the independence of a nation. The generous efforts of Muza had been in a great measure successful; he was the idol of the youthful cavaliers, they regarded him as a mirror of chivalry and endeavoured to imitate his lofty and heroic virtues.

When Muza heard the demand of Ferdinand that they should deliver up their arms his eye flashed fire. "Does the Christian King think that we are old men," said he, "and that staffs will suffice us? or that we are women and

*Cura de Los Palacios Cap. 96.

can be contented with distaffs? Let him know that a Moor is born to the
spear and scymetar; to career the steed, bend the bow and launch the jav-
elin; deprive him of these and you deprive him of his nature. If the Christian
King desires our arms let him come and win them; but let him win them
dearly. For my part sweeter were a grave beneath the walls of Granada, on
the spot I had died to defend, than the richest couch within her palaces
earned by submission to the unbeliever."

The words of Muza were received with enthusiastic shouts by the warlike
part of the populace. Granada once more awoke as a warrior shaking off a
disgraceful lethargy. The commanders and council partook of the public excitement, and dispatched a reply to the Christian sovereigns, declaring that
they would suffer death rather than surrender their city.

CHAPTER LXXXIV

HOW KING FERDINAND TURNED HIS HOSTILITIES AGAINST THE CITY OF GRANADA.

When King Ferdinand received the defiance of the Moors he made preparations for bitter hostilities. The winter season did not admit of an immediate
campaign, he contented himself, therefore, with throwing strong garrisons
into all his towns and fortresses in the neighborhood of Granada, and gave
the command of all the frontier of Jaen to Inigo Lopez de Mendoza, Count
of Tendilla, who had shewn such consummate vigilance and address in maintaining the dangerous post of Alhama. This renowned veteran established
his head quarters in the mountain city of Alcalá la Real, within eight leagues
of the city of Granada and commanding the most important passes of that
rugged frontier.

In the mean time the city of Granada resounded with the stir of war.
The chivalry of the nation had again controul of its councils, and the populace, having once more resumed their weapons, were anxious to wipe
out the disgrace of their late passive submission by signal and daring
exploits.

Muza Ben Abil Gazan was the soul of action. He commanded the cavalry,
which he had disciplined with uncommon skill; he was surrounded by the
noblest youth of Granada, who had caught his own generous and martial
fire, and panted for the field, while the common soldiers, devoted to his
person, were ready to follow him in the most desperate enterprizes. He did
not allow their courage to cool for want of action. The gates of Granada once
more poured forth legions of light scouring cavalry, which skirred the coun-

try up to the very gates of the Christian fortresses, sweeping off flocks and herds. The name of Muza became formidable throughout the frontier; he had many encounters with the enemy in the rough passes of the mountains, in which the superior lightness and dexterity of his cavalry gave him the advantage. The sight of his glistening legion returning across the vega with long cavalgadas of booty, was hailed by the Moors as a revival of their ancient triumphs; but when they beheld Christian banners borne into their gates as trophies, the exultation of the light minded populace was beyond all bounds. The winter passed away, the spring advanced, yet Ferdinand delayed to take the field. He knew the city of Granada to be too strong and populous to be taken by assault, and too full of provisions to be speedily reduced by siege. "We must have patience and perseverance," said the politic monarch, "by ravaging the country this year we shall produce a scarcity the next, and then the city may be invested with effect."

An interval of peace aided by the quick vegetation of a prolific soil and happy climate had restored the vega to all its luxuriance and beauty. The green pastures on the borders of the Xenel were covered with flocks and herds, the blooming orchards gave promise of abundant fruit and the open plain was waving with ripening corn. The time was at hand to put in the sickle and reap the golden harvest when suddenly a torrent of war came sweeping down from the mountains, and Ferdinand with an army of five thousand horse and twenty thousand foot appeared before the walls of Granada. He had left the Queen and princess at the fortress of Moclin, and came attended by the Duke of Medina Sidonia, the Marquis of Cadiz, the Marquis de Villena, The Counts of Ureña and Cabra, Don Alonzo de Aguilar and other renowned cavaliers. On this occasion King Ferdinand, for the first time, led his son Prince Juan into the field, and bestowed upon him the dignity of knighthood. As if to stimulate him to grand achievements, the ceremony took place on the banks of the grand canal almost beneath the embattled walls of that warlike city, the object of such daring enter- prizes; and in the midst of that famous vega which had been the field of so many chivalrous exploits. High above them shone resplendent the red tow- ers of the Alhambra, rising from amidst delicious groves, with the standard of Mahomet waving defiance to the Christian arms.

The Duke of Medina Sidonia and the valiant Roderigo Ponce de Leon, Marquis of Cadiz, were sponsors and all the chivalry of the camp was assem- bled on the occasion. The prince after he was knighted, bestowed the same honour on several youthful cavaliers of high rank, just entering like himself on the career of arms.

Ferdinand did not loiter in carrying his desolating plans into execution. He detached parties in every direction to lay waste the country; villages were sacked, burnt and destroyed, and the lovely vega once more laid waste

with fire and sword. The ravage was carried so close to Granada that the city
was wrapped in the smoke of its hamlets and gardens. The dismal cloud
rolled up the hill and hung about the towers of the Alhambra, where the
unfortunate Boabdil still remained shut up from the indignation of his subjects. The hapless monarch smote his breast as he looked down from his
mountain palace on the desolation effected by his late ally. He dare not even
shew himself in arms among the populace, for they cursed him as the cause
of the miseries once more brought to their doors. The Moors, however, did
not suffer the Christians to carry on their ravages as unmolested as in former
years. Muza incited them to incessant sallies. He divided his cavalry into
small squadrons, each led by a daring commander. They were taught to
hover round the Christian camp; to harrass it from various and opposite
quarters, cutting off convoys and straggling detachments; to way lay the
army in its ravaging expeditions, lurking among rocks and passes of the
mountains, or in hollows and thickets of the plain, and practicing a thousand
stratagems and surprizes.

The Christian army had one day spread itself out rather unguardedly in
its foraging about the vega. As the troops commanded by the Marquis de
Villena approached the skirts of the mountains they beheld a number of
Moorish peasants hastily driving a herd of cattle into a narrow glen. The
soldiers eager for booty, pressed in pursuit of them. Scarcely had they entered the glen when shouts arose from every side and they were furiously
attacked by an ambuscade of horse and foot. Some of the Christians took to
flight, others stood their ground and fought valiantly. The Moors had the
vantage ground; some showered darts and arrows from the clefts of the
rocks, others fought hand to hand on the plain while their cavalry, rapid as
lightning in their movements, carried havoc and confusion into the midst of
the Christian forces. The Marquis de Villena with his brother Don Alonzo
de Pacheco at the first onset of the Moors, spurred into the hottest of the
fight. They had scarce entered when Don Alonzo was struck lifeless from his
horse before the eyes of his brother. Estevan de Luzon a gallant captain fell
fighting bravely by the side of the marquis, who remained with his chamberlain Solier and a handful of knights surrounded by the enemy. Several
cavaliers from other parts of the army hastened to their assistance, when
King Ferdinand, seeing that the Moors had the vantage ground and that the
Christians were suffering severely, gave signal for retreat. The marquis
obeyed slowly and reluctantly, for his heart was full of grief and rage at the
death of his brother. As he was retiring he beheld his faithful chamberlain
Solier defending himself valiantly against six Moors. The marquis turned
and rushed to his rescue; he killed two of the enemy with his own hand and
put the rest to flight. One of the Moors, however, in retreating rose in his

stirrups and hurling his lance at the marquis wounded him in the right arm and crippled him for life.*

Such was one of the many ambuscados concerted by Muza; nor did he hesitate, at times, to present a bold front to the Christian forces, and to defy them in the open field. King Ferdinand soon perceived, however, that the Moors seldom provoked a battle without having the advantage of the ground; and that though the Christians generally appeared to have the victory, they suffered the greatest loss; for retreating was a part of the Moorish system, by which they would draw their pursuers into confusion and then turn upon them with a more violent and fatal attack. He commanded his captains, therefore, to decline all challenges to skirmish, and to pursue a secure system of destruction, ravaging the country and doing all possible injury to the enemy with slight risk to themselves.

CHAPTER LXXXV
THE FATE OF THE CASTLE OF ROMA.

About two leagues from Granada, on an eminence commanding an extensive view of the vega stood the strong Moorish castle of Roma; a great place of refuge and security. Hither the neigboring peasantry drove their flocks and herds, and hurried with their most precious effects on the irruption of a Christian force; and any foraging or skirmishing party from Granada on being intercepted in their return, threw themselves into Roma, manned its embattled towers and set the enemy at defiance. The garrison were accustomed to these sudden claims upon their protection; to have parties of Moors clattering up to their gates so hotly pursued that there was barely time to throw open the portal, receive them within and shut out their pursuers, while the Christian cavaliers had many a time reined in their panting steeds at the very entrance of the barbican, and retired, cursing the strong walls of Roma, that robbed them of their prey.

---

*In consequence of this wound the marquis was ever after obliged to write his signature with his left hand, though capable of managing his lance with his right. The Queen one day demanded of him why he had adventured his life for that of a domestic. "Does not your majesty think," replied he, "that I ought to risk one life for him, who would have adventured three for me had he possessed them?" The Queen was charmed with the magnanimity of the reply and often quoted the marquis as setting an heroic example to the chivalry of the age. Mariana, L. 25. c. 15.

The late ravages of Ferdinand and the continual skirmishings in the vega, had roused the vigilance of the castle. One morning early, as the centinels kept watch upon the battlements, they beheld a cloud of dust advancing rapidly from a distance; turbans and Moorish weapons soon caught their eyes, and as the whole approached they descried a drove of cattle urged on in great haste and conveyed by one hundred and fifty Moors, who led with them two Christian captives in chains.

When the cavalgada had arrived near to the castle a Moorish cavalier of noble and commanding mein and splendid attire rode up to the foot of the tower and entreated admittance. He stated that they were returning with rich booty from a foray into the lands of the Christians, but that the enemy was on their traces, and they feared to be overtaken before they could reach Granada. The centinels decended in all haste and flung open the gates. The long cavalgada defiled into the courts of the castle, which were soon filled with lowing and bleating flocks and herds, with neighing and stamping steeds, and with fierce looking Moors from the mountains. The cavalier who had asked admission was the chief of the party; he was somewhat advanced in life, of a lofty and gallant bearing and had with him a son, a young man of great fire and spirit. Close by them followed the two Christian captives, with looks cast down and disconsolate.

The soldiers of the garrison had roused themselves from their sleep, and were busily occupied attending to the cattle which crowded the courts, while the foraging party distributed themselves about the castle to seek refreshment or repose. Suddenly a shout arose that was echoed from courtyard and hall and battlement. The garrison astonished and bewildered would have rushed to their arms, but found themselves almost before they could make resistance, completely in the power of an enemy.

The pretended foraging party consisted of Mudexares, or Moors tributary to the Christians, and the commanders were the Prince Cidi Yahye and his son Alnayer. They had hastened from the mountains with this small force to aid the Catholic sovereigns, during the summer's campaign, and they had concerted to surprize this important castle, and present it to King Ferdinand, as a gauge of their faith and the first fruits of their devotion.

The politic monarch overwhelmed his new converts and allies with favours and distinctions in return for this important acquisition, but he took care to dispatch a strong force of veterans and genuine Christian troops to man the fortress.

As to the Moors who had composed the garrison, Cidi Yahye remembered that they were his countrymen, and could not prevail upon himself to deliver them into Christian bondage. He set them at liberty and permitted them to repair to Granada, a proof says the pious Agapida, that his conversion was not entirely consummated, but that there were still some lingerings of the infidel in his heart. His lenity was far from procuring him indulgence in the opinions of his countrymen; on the contrary, the inhabitants of Granada, when they learnt from the liberated garrison the stratagem by which Roma had been captured, cursed Cidi Yahye for a traytor, and the garrison joined in the malediction.

But the indignation of the people of Granada was destined to be aroused to tenfold violence. The old warrior Muley Abdalla el Zagal had retired to his little mountain territory and for a short time endeavoured to console himself with his petty title of King of Andarax. He soon grew impatient, however, of the quiet and inaction of his mimic kingdom. His fierce spirit was exasperated by being shut up within such narrow limits, and his hatred rose to downright fury against Boabdil, whom he considered as the cause of his downfall; when tidings were brought him that King Ferdinand was laying waste the vega he took a sudden resolution. Assembling the whole disposable force of his kingdom, which amounted but to two hundred men, he descended from the Alpuxarras and sought the Christian camp, content to serve as a vassal the enemy of his faith and his nation, so that he might see Granada, wrested from the sway of his nephew.

In his blind passion the old wrathful monarch injured his cause, and strengthened the cause of his adversary. The Moors of Granada had been clamorous in his praise, extolling him as a victim to his patriotism and had refused to believe all reports of his treaty with the Christians; but when they beheld from the walls of the city his banner mingling with the banners of the unbelievers, and arrayed against his late people and the capital he had commanded, they broke forth into curses and revilings and heaped all kind of stigmas upon his name.

Their next emotion of course was in favour of Boabdil. They gathered under the walls of the Alhambra, and hailed him as their only hope, as the sole dependence of the country. Boabdil could scarcely believe his senses when he heard his name mingled with praises and greeted with acclamations. Encouraged by this unexpected gleam of popularity he ventured forth from his retreat and was received with rapture. All his past errors were attributed to the hardship, of his fortune and the usurpation of his tyrant uncle, and whatever breath the populace could spare from uttering curses on El Zagal was expended in shouts in honour of El Chico.

CHAPTER LXXXVI

HOW BOABDIL EL CHICO TOOK THE FIELD;
AND HIS EXPEDITION AGAINST ALHENDIN.

For thirty days had the vega been overrun by the Christian forces, and that vast plain, late so luxuriant and beautiful, was one wide scene of desolation. The destroying army having accomplished its task, passed over the bridge of Pinos and wound up into the mountains, on the way to Cordova, bearing away the spoils of towns and villages and driving off flocks and herds in long dusty columns. The sound of the last Christian trumpet died away along the side of the mountain of Elvira, and not a hostile squadron was seen glistening on the mournful fields of the vega.

The eyes of Boabdil el Chico were at length opened to the real policy of King Ferdinand, and he saw that he had no longer any thing to depend upon, than the valour of his arm. No time was to be lost in hastening to counteract the effect of the late Christian ravage, and in opening the channel for distant supplies to Granada.

Scarcely had the retiring squadrons of Ferdinand disappeared among the mountains, than Boabdil buckled on his armour, sallied forth from the Alhambra and prepared to take the field. When the populace beheld him actually in arms against his late ally, both parties thronged with zeal to his standard. The hardy inhabitants also of the Sierra Nevada, or chain of snow capped mountains which rise above Granada, descended from their heights, and hastened into the city gates to proffer their devotion to their youthful King. The great square of the Vivarrambla shone with the proud array of legions of cavalry decked with the colours and devices of the most ancient Moorish families, and marshalled forth by the patriot Muza to follow the King to battle.

It was on the 15th of June that Boabdil once more issued forth from the gates of Granada on martial enterprize. A few leagues from the city, within full view of it and at the entrance of the Alpuxarra mountains stood the powerful castle of Alhendin. It was built on an eminence, rising from the midst of a small town, and commanding a great part of the vega, and the main road to the rich valleys of the Alpuxarras. The castle was commanded by a valiant Christian cavalier named Mendo de Quexada, and garrisoned by two hundred and fifty men, all seasoned and experienced warriors. It was a continual thorn in the side of Granada. The labourers of the vega were swept off from their fields, by its hardy soldiers, convoys were cut off in the passes of the mountains, and as the garrison commanded a full view of the gates of the city, no band of merchants could venture forth on their needful journeys, without being swooped up by the warhawks of Alhendin.

It was against this important fortress that Boabdil first led his troops. For six days and nights the fortress was closely besieged. The alcayde and his veteran garrison defended themselves valiantly but they were exhausted by fatigue and constant watchfulness; for the Moors being continually relieved by fresh troops from Granada, kept up an unremitted and vigorous attack. Twice the barbican was forced, and twice the assailants were driven forth headlong with excessive loss. The garrison, however, was diminished in number by the killed and wounded, there were no longer soldiers sufficient to man the walls and gateway, the brave alcayde was compelled to retire with his surviving force to the keep of the castle, in which he continued to make a desperate resistance.

The Moors now approached the foot of the tower under shelter of wooden screens covered with wet hides, to ward off missiles and combustibles. They went to work vigorously to undermine the tower, placing props of wood under the foundations, to be afterwards set on fire, so as to give the besiegers time to escape before the edifice should fall. Some of the Moors plied their cross-bows and arquebusses to defend the workmen and to drive the Christians from the wall, while the latter showered down stones and darts and melted pitch and flaming combustibles on the miners.

The brave Mendo de Quexada had cast many an anxious eye across the vega, in hopes of seeing some Christian force hastening to his assistance. Not a gleam of spear or helm was to be descried, for no one had dreamt of this sudden irruption of the Moors. The alcayde beheld his bravest men dead or wounded around him, while the remainder were sinking with watchfulness and fatigue. In defiance of all opposition the Moors had accomplished their mine; the fire was brought before the walls that was to be applied to the stancheons in case the garrison persisted in defence. In a little while the tower would crumble beneath him and be rent and hurled a ruin to the plain. At the very last moment the brave alcayde made the signal of surrender. He marched forth with the remnant of his veteran garrison who were all made prisoners. Boabdil immediately ordered the walls of the fortress to be razed and fire to be applied to the stancheons, that the place might never again become a strong hold to the Christians, and a scourge to Granada. The alcayde and his fellow captives were led in dejected convoy across the vega, when they heard a tremendous crash behind them. They turned to look upon their late fortress, but beheld nothing but a heap of tumbling ruins and a vast column of smoke and dust, where once had stood the lofty tower of Alhendin.

CHAPTER LXXXVII

EXPLOIT OF THE COUNT DE TENDILLA.

Boabdil el Chico followed up his success by capturing the two fortresses of Marchena and Bulduy; he sent his alfaquis in every direction to proclaim a holy war and to summon all true Moslems of town or castle, mountain or valley to saddle steed and buckle on armour, and hasten to the standard of the faith. The tidings spread far and wide that Boabdil el Chico was once more in the field and was victorious. The Moors of various places, dazzled by this gleam of success, hastened to throw off their sworn allegiance to the Castilian crown and to elevate the standard of Boabdil, and the youthful monarch flattered himself that the whole kingdom was on the point of returning to its allegiance.

The fiery cavaliers of Granada, were eager to renew those forays into the Christian lands, in which they had formerly delighted. A number of them therefore concerted an irruption to the north, into the territory of Jaen to harrass the country about Quexada. They had heard of a rich convoy of merchants and wealthy travellers on the way to the city of Baeza, and they anticipated a glorious conclusion to their foray, in capturing this convoy.

Assembling a number of horsemen, lightly armed and fleetly mounted, and one hundred foot soldiers, these hardy cavaliers issued forth by night from Granada, made their way in silence through the defiles of the mountains, crossed the frontier without opposition, and suddenly appeared as if fallen from the clouds, in the very heart of the Christian country.

The mountainous frontier which separates Granada from Jaen, was at this time under the command of the Count de Tendilla, the same veteran who had distinguished himself by his vigilance and sagacity, when commanding the fortress of Alhama. He held his head quarters at the city of Alcalá la Real, in its impregnable fortress perched high among the mountains, about six leagues from Granada, and dominating all the frontier. From this cloud capt hold among the rocks, he kept an eagle eye upon Granada, and had his scouts and spies in all directions so that a crow could not fly over the border without his knowledge.

His fortress was a place of refuge for the Christian captives who escaped by night from the Moorish dungeons of Granada. Often, however, they missed their way in the defiles of the mountains, and wandering about bewildered, either repaired by mistake to some Moorish town, or were discovered and retaken at day light by the enemy. To prevent these accidents, the count had a tower built at his own expense, on the top of one of the heights near Alcalá which commanded a view of the vega, and the surrounding country. Here he kept a light blazing throughout the night, as a beacon for all Christian fugitives, to guide them to a place of safety.

The count was aroused one night from his repose, by shouts and cries, which came up from the town and approached the castle walls. "To arms! to arms! the Moor is over the border!" was the cry. A Christian soldier pale and emaciated and who still bore traces of the Moorish chains, was brought before the count. He had been taken as guide by the Moorish cavaliers who had sallied from Granada, but had escaped from them among the mountains, and after much wandering had found his way to Alcalá by the signal fire.

Notwithstanding the bustle and agitation of the moment, the Count de Tendilla listened calmly and attentively to the account of the fugitive, and questioned him minutely as to the time of departure of the Moors, and the rapidity and direction of their march. He saw that it was too late to prevent their incursion and ravage, but he determined to await them and give them a warm reception on their return. His soldiers were always on the alert, and ready to take the field at a moment's warning. Choosing one hundred and fifty lances, hardy and valiant men, well disciplined and well seasoned as indeed were all his troops, he issued forth quietly before break of day, and descending through the defiles of the mountains, stationed his little force in ambush in a deep barranco, or dry channel of a torrent near Barzino, but three leagues from Granada, on the road by which the marauders would have to return. In the mean time he sent out scouts to post themselves upon different heights and look out for the approach of the enemy.

All day they remained concealed in the ravine, and for a great part of the following night; not a turban, however, was to be seen, excepting now and then a peasant returning from his labour, or a solitary muleteer hastening towards Granada. The cavaliers of the count began to grow restless and impatient; they feared that the enemy might have taken some other route, or might have received intelligence of their ambuscade. They urged the Count to abandon the enterprize and return to Alcalá. "We are here," said they; "almost at the gates of the Moorish capital, our movements may have been descried, and before we are aware, Granada may pour forth its legions of swift cavalry, and crush us, with an overwhelming force." The Count de Tendilla, however, persisted in remaining until his scouts should come in. About two hours, before daybreak, there were signal fires on certain Moorish watch-towers of the mountains. While they were regarding these with anxiety the scouts came hurrying into the ravine. "The Moors are approaching," said they; "we have reconnoitered them near at hand. They are between one and two hundred strong, but encumbered with many prisoners, and much booty." The Christian cavaliers laid their ears to the ground, and heard the distant tramp of horses, and the tread of foot soldiers. They mounted their horses, braced their shields, couched their lances, and drew near to the entrance of the ravine where it opened upon the road.

The Moors had succeeded in waylaying and surprizing the Christian convoy on its way to Baeza. They had captured a great number of prisoners, male and female, with great store of gold and jewels, and sumpter mules, laden with rich merchandize. With these they had made a forced march over the dangerous parts of the mountains; but now finding themselves so near to Granada, they fancied themselves in perfect security. They loitered along the road, therefore, irregularly and slowly, some singing, others laughing and exulting at having eluded the boasted vigilance of the Count de Tendilla: while ever and anon, was heard the plaint of some female captive bewailing the jeopardy of her honour, and the heavy sighing of the merchant, at beholding his property in the grasp of ruthless spoilers.

The Count de Tendilla waited until some of the escort had passed the ravine, then giving the signal for assault, his cavaliers set up great shouts and cries, and charged furiously into the centre of the foe. The obscurity of the place, and the hour, added to the terrors of the surprize. The Moors were thrown into confusion; some rallied, fought desperately, and fell covered with wounds; thirty six were killed, and fifty five were made prisoners, the rest under cover of the darkness, made their escape to the rocks and defiles of the mountains. The good count unbound the prisoners, gladdening the hearts of the merchants, by restoring to them their merchandize; to the female captives, also, he restored the jewels of which they had been despoiled, excepting such as had been lost beyond recovery. Forty five saddle horses of the choice Barbary breed, remained as captured spoils of the Moors, together with costly armour, and booty of various kinds. Having collected every thing in haste, and arranged his cavalgada, the count urged his way with all speed for Alcalá la Real, lest he should be pursued and overtaken by the Moors of Granada. As he wound up the steep ascent to his mountain city, the inhabitants poured forth to meet him with shouts of joy; this triumph was doubly enhanced by being received at the gates of the city by his wife, the daughter of the Marquis of Villena, a lady of distinguished merit, whom he had not seen for two years that he had been separated from his home, by the arduous duties of these iron wars.

CHAPTER LXXXVIII

EXPEDITION OF BOABDIL EL CHICO AGAINST SALOBREÑA, EXPLOIT OF HERNANDO PEREZ DEL PULGAR.

King Boabdil found that his diminished territory was too closely dominated by Christian fortresses like Alcalá la Real, and too strictly watched by vigilant alcaydes like the Count of Tendilla, to be able to maintain itself by internal resources. His foraging expeditions were liable to be intercepted and defeated, while the ravage of the vega, had swept off every thing on which the city depended for future sustenance. He felt the want of a sea port through which, as formerly, he might keep open a communication with Africa, and obtain reinforcements and supplies from beyond the seas. All the ports and harbours were in the hands of the Christians, and Granada and its remnant of dependant territory were completely land locked.

In this emergency the attention of Boabdil was called by circumstances to the sea port of Salobreña. This redoubtable town has already been mentioned in this chronicle, as a place deemed impregnable by the Moors; insomuch that their Kings were accustomed in time of peril to keep their treasures in its citadel. It was situated on a high rocky hill, dividing one of those rich little vegas or plains which lie open to the Mediterranean, but run like deep green bays, into the stern bosoms of the mountains. The vega was covered with beautiful vegetation, with rice and cotton, with groves of oranges, citrons, figs and mulberries, and with gardens inclosed by hedges of reeds, of aloes and the Indian fig. Running streams of cool water from the springs and snows of the Sierra Nevada, kept this delightful valley continually fresh and verdant, while it was almost locked up by mountain barriers and lofty promontories that stretched far into the sea.

Through the centre of this rich vega the rock of Salobreña reared its rugged back nearly dividing the plain, and advancing to the margin of the sea, with just a strip of sandy beach at its foot laved by the blue waves of the Mediterranean.

The town covered the ridge and sides of the rocky hill, and was fortified by strong walls and towers; while on the highest and most precipitous part stood the citadel, a huge castle that seemed to form a part of the living rock; the massive ruins of which at the present day attract the gaze of the traveller, as he winds his way far below, along the road which passes through the vega.

This important fortress had been entrusted to the command of Don Francisco Ramirez, de Madrid, captain general of the artillery and the most scientific of all the Spanish leaders. That experienced veteran, however, was with the King at Cordova having left a valiant cavalier as alcayde of the place.

Boabdil el Chico had full information of the state of the garrison and the absence of its commander; putting himself at the head of a powerful force, therefore, he departed from Granada and made a rapid march through the mountains, hoping by this sudden move to seize upon Salobreña before King Ferdinand could come to its assistance.

The inhabitants of Salobreña were Mudexares, or Moors who had sworn allegiance to the Christians. Still when they heard the sound of the Moorish drums and trumpets and beheld the squadrons of their countrymen, advancing across the vega, their hearts yearned towards the standard of their nation and their faith. A tumult arose in the place, the populace shouted the name of Boabdil el Chico and throwing open the gates admitted him within the walls.

The Christian garrison was too few in number to contend for the possession of the town. They retreated to the citadel and shut themselves within its massive walls which were considered impregnable. Here they maintained a desperate defence, hoping to hold out until succour should arrive from the neighbouring fortresses.

The tidings that Salobreña was invested by the Moorish King, spread along the sea coast and filled the Christians with alarm. Don Francisco Enriquez, uncle of the King, commanded the city of Velez Malaga, about twelve leagues distant, but separated by ranges of those vast rocky mountains which are piled along the Mediterranean, and tower in steep promontories and precipices above its waves.

Don Francisco summoned the alcaydes of his district to hasten with him to the relief of this important fortress. A number of cavaliers and their retainers answered to his call, among whom was Hernando Perez del Pulgar, surnamed "El de las Hazañas" (he of the exploits) the same who had signalized himself in a foray by elevating a handkerchief on a lance for a banner, and leading on his disheartened comrades to victory. As soon as Don Francisco beheld a little band collected round him he set out with all speed for Salobreña. The march was rugged and severe, climbing and descending immense mountains, and sometimes winding along the edge of giddy precipices with the surges of the sea raging far below. When Don Francisco arrived with his followers at the lofty promontory that stretches along one side of the little vega of Salobreña, he looked down with sorrow and anxiety upon a Moorish army of great force encamped at the foot of the fortress; while Moorish banners, on various parts of the walls, shewed that the town was already in possession of the infidels. A solitary Christian standard alone floated on the top of the castle keep shewing that the brave garrison were hemmed up in their rock built citadel.

Don Francisco found it impossible, with his small force, to make any impression on the camp of the Moors, or to get to the relief of the castle. He stationed his little band upon a rocky height near the sea, where they were safe from the assaults of the enemy. The sight of his friendly banner waving in their neighborhood cheered the heart of the garrison, and he conveyed to them assurance of speedy succour from the King. In the mean time Hernando Perez del Pulgar, who always burned to distinguish himself by bold and striking exploits, in the course of a prowling expedition along the borders of the Moorish camp, remarked a postern gate of the castle opening upon the steep part of the rocky hill which looked towards the mountains. A sudden thought flashed upon the daring mind of Pulgar; "who will follow my banner," said he, "and make a dash for yonder postern?" A bold proposition in time of warfare never wants for bold spirits to accept it. Seventy resolute men immediately stepped forward. Pulgar put himself at their head; they cut their way suddenly through a weak part of the camp, fought their way up to the gate, which was eagerly thrown open to receive them, and succeeded in making their way into the fortress, before the alarm of their attempt had spread through the Moorish army.

The garrison was roused to new spirit by this unlooked for reinforcement, and were enabled to make a more vigorous resistance. The Moors had intelligence however, that there was a great scarcity of water in the castle and they exulted in the idea that this additional number of warriors, would soon exhaust the cisterns and compel them to surrender. When Pulgar heard of this hope entertained by the enemy he caused a bucket of water to be lowered from the battlements and threw a silver cup in bravado to the Moors.

The situation of the garrison, however, was daily growing more and more critical; they suffered greatly from thirst, while to tantalize them in their sufferings they beheld limpid streams winding in abundance through the green plain below them. They began to fear that all succour would arrive too late, when one day they beheld a little squadron of vessels far at sea, but standing towards the shore. There was some doubt at first whether it might not be a hostile armament from Africa but as it approached they descried to their great joy the banner of Castile.

It was a reinforcement brought in all haste by the governor of the fortress, Don Francisco Ramirez. The squadron anchored at a steep rocky island, which rises from the very margin of the smooth sandy beach, directly in front of the rock of Salobreña, and stretches out into the sea. On this island Ramirez landed his men and was as strongly posted as if in a fortress. His force was too scanty to attempt a battle, but he assisted to harrass and distract the besiegers. Whenever King Boabdil made an attack upon the fortress, his camp was assailed on one side by the troops of Ramirez who landed from their island; and on another by those of Don Francisco Enriquez who swept down from their rock, while Hernando del Pulgar kept up a fierce defence from every tower and battlement of the castle. The attention of the Moorish King was diverted also, for a time, by an ineffectual attempt to relieve the little port of Adra, which had recently declared in his favour, but which had been recaptured for the Christians by Cidi Yahye and his son Alnayar. Thus the unlucky Boabdil bewildered on every hand, lost all the advantage that he had gained by his rapid march from Granada. While he was yet besieging the obstinate citadel, tidings were brought him that King Ferdinand was in full march with a powerful host to its assistance. There was no time for farther delay. He made a furious attack with all his forces upon the castle but was again repulsed by Pulgar and his coadjutors when, abandoning the siege in despair, he retreated with his army, lest King Ferdinand should get between him and his capital. On his way back to Granada, however, he in some sort consoled himself for his late disappointment, by overrunning a part of the territories and possessions lately assigned to his uncle El Zagal and to Cidi Yahye. He defeated their alcaydes, destroyed

several of their fortresses, burnt their villages and leaving the country behind him reeking and smoking with his vengeance, returned with considerable booty to repose himself within the walls of the Alhambra.

CHAPTER LXXXIX

HOW KING FERDINAND TREATED THE PEOPLE OF GUADIX, AND HOW EL ZAGAL FINISHED HIS REGAL CAREER.

Scarcely had Boabdil ensconced himself in his capital when King Ferdinand,
at the head of seven thousand horse and twenty thousand foot again appeared in the vega. He had set out in all haste from Cordova to the relief of
Salobreña, but hearing on his march that the siege was raised, he turned
with his army to make a second ravage round the walls of devoted Granada.
His present forage lasted fifteen days, in the course of which every thing
that had escaped his former desolating visit was destroyed and scarce a green
thing or a living animal was left on the face of the land. The Moors sallied
frequently and fought desperately in defence of their fields, but the work of
destruction was accomplished, and Granada, once the Queen of gardens,
was left surrounded by a desert.

From hence Ferdinand marched to crush a conspiracy which had lately
manifested itself in the cities of Guadix, Baza and Almeria. These recently
conquered places had entered into secret correspondence with King Boabdil, inviting him to march to their gates, promising to rise upon the Christian
garrisons, seize upon the citadels and surrender themselves into his power.
The Marquis of Villena had received notice of the conspiracy and had suddenly thrown himself, with a large force, into Guadix. Under pretence of
making a review of the inhabitants he made them sally forth into the fields
before the city. When the whole Moorish population capable of bearing arms
was thus without the walls, he ordered the gates to be closed. He then
permitted them to enter two by two and three by three, and to take forth
their wives, children and effects. The houseless Moors were fain to make
themselves temporary hovels in the gardens and orchards about the city.
They were clamorous in their complaints at being thus excluded from their
homes; but were told they must wait with patience until the charges against
them could be investigated and the pleasure of the King be known.[*]

When Ferdinand arrived at Guadix he found the unhappy Moors in their

---

*Zurita L 20. C. 85. Cura de Los Palacios C 97.

cabins among the orchards. They complained bitterly of the deception that had been practiced upon them, and implored permission to return into the city, and live peaceably in their dwellings, as had been promised them in their articles of capitulation.

King Ferdinand listened graciously to their complaints. "My friends," said he in reply, "I am informed that there has been a conspiracy among you to kill my alcayde and garrison and to make pact with my enemy the King of Granada. I shall make a thorough investigation of this conspiracy. Those among you who shall be proved innocent shall be restored to their dwellings, but the guilty shall incur the penalty of their offences. As I wish, however, to proceed with mercy as well as justice I now give you your choice, either to depart at once without further question, going wherever you please, and taking with you your families and effects, under an assurance of safety, or to deliver up those who are guilty; not one of whom, I give you my royal word, shall escape punishment."

When the people of Guadix heard these words they communed among themselves, and as most of them, says the worthy Agapida, were either culpable or feared to be considered so, they accepted the alternative, and departed sorrowfully, they and their wives and their little ones. "Thus," in the words of that excellent and contemporary historian, Andres Bernaldes commonly called the Curate of los Palacios. "Thus did the King deliver Guadix from the hands of the enemies of our holy faith, after seven hundred and seventy years that it had been in their possession even since the time of Roderick the Goth; and this was one of the mysteries of our Lord, who would not consent that the city should remain longer in power of the Moors." A pious and sage remark which is quoted with peculiar approbation by the worthy Agapida.

King Ferdinand offered similar alternatives to the Moors of Baza, Almeria and other cities accused of participation in this conspiracy; who generally preferred to abandon their homes rather than incur the risk of an investigation. Most of them relinquished Spain as a country where they could no longer live in security and independence and departed with their families for Africa; such as remained were suffered to live in villages and hamlets and other unwalled places.*

While Ferdinand was thus occupied at Guadix, dispensing justice and mercy, and receiving cities in exchange, the old monarch Muley Abdallah, surnamed El Zagal, appeared before him. He was haggard with care and almost crazed with passion. He had found his little territory of Andarax and his two thousand subjects as difficult to govern as had been the distracted Kingdom of Granada. The charm which had bound the Moors to him was broken when he appeared in arms under the banner of Ferdinand. He had

*Garibay lib 13. Cap 39. Pulgar L 3. C 132.

returned from his inglorious campaign with his petty army of two hundred men followed by the execrations of the people of Granada, and the secret repining of those he had led into the field. No sooner had his subjects heard of the successes of Boabdil el Chico than they had seized their arms, assembled tumultuously, declared for the young monarch and threatened the life of El Zagal.* The unfortunate old King had with difficulty evaded their fury; and this last lesson seemed entirely, to have cured him of his passion for sovereignty. He now entreated Ferdinand to purchase the towns and castles and other possessions which had been granted to him; offering them at a low rate, and begging safe passage for himself and his followers to Africa. King Ferdinand graciously complied with his wishes. He purchased of him three and twenty towns and villages in the valleys of Andarax and Alhauren, for which he gave him five millions of maravedies. El Zagal relinquished his right to one half of the salinas or salt-pits of Malcha in favour of his brother in law Cidi Yahye. Having thus disposed of his petty empire and possessions, he packed up all his treasure, of which he had a great amount, and, followed by many Moorish families, passed over to Africa.†

And here let us cast an eye beyond the present period of our chronicle and trace the remaining career of El Zagal. His short and turbulent reign and disastrous end would afford a wholesome lesson to unprincipled ambition, were not all ambition of the kind fated to be blind to precept and example. When he arrived in Africa, instead of meeting with kindness and sympathy, he was seized and thrown in prison by the King of Fez, as though he had been his vassal. He was accused of being the cause of the dissensions and downfall of the Kingdom of Granada, and the accusation being proved to the satisfaction of the King of Fez, he condemned the unhappy El Zagal to perpetual darkness. A basin of glowing copper was passed before his eyes, which effectually destroyed his sight. His wealth, which had probably been the secret cause of these cruel measures, was confiscated, and seized upon by his oppressor, and El Zagal was thrust forth, blind, helpless and destitute upon the world. In this wretched condition the late Moorish monarch groped his way through the regions of Tingetania until he reached the city of Velez de Gomera. The King of Velez had formerly been his ally and felt some movement of compassion at his present altered and abject state. He gave him food and raiment, and suffered him to remain unmolested in his dominions. Death, which so often hurries off the prosperous and happy from the midst of untasted pleasures, spares, on the other hand, the miserable to drain the last drop of his cup of bitterness. El Zagal dragged out a wretched existence of many years in the city of Velez. He wandered about blind and disconsolate an object of mingled scorn and pity; and bearing above his rai-

*Cura de los Palacios C 97.
†Conde Part 4 Cap 41.

ment a parchment on which was written in Arabic "this is the unfortunate King of Andalusia."*

PREPARATIONS OF GRANADA FOR A DESPERATE DEFENCE.

"How is thy strength departed, oh Granada! how is thy beauty withered and despoiled, oh city of groves and fountains! The commerce that once thronged thy streets is at an end; the merchant no longer hastens to thy gates with the luxuries of foreign lands. The cities which once paid thee tribute are wrested from thy sway, the chivalry which filled thy Vivarrambla with the sumptuous pageantry of war, have fallen in many battles. The Alhambra still rears its ruddy towers from the midst of groves, but melancholy reigns in its marble halls, and the monarch looks down from his lofty balconies upon a naked waste, where once had extended the blooming glories of the vega."

Such is the lament of the Moorish writers over the lamentable state of Granada, which now remained a mere phantom of its former greatness. The two ravages of the vega, following so closely upon each other, had swept off all the produce of the year, and the husbandman had no longer the heart to till the field seeing that the ripening harvest only brought the spoiler to his door.

During the winter season King Ferdinand made diligent preparations for the last campaign that was to decide the fate of Granada. As this war was waged purely for the promotion of the Christian faith he thought it meet that its enemies should bear the expenses. He levied, therefore, a general contribution upon all the jews throughout his kingdom, by synagogues and districts, and obliged them to render in the proceeds at the city of Seville.†

On the 11th of April Ferdinand and Isabella departed for the Moorish frontier with the solemn determination to lay close siege to Granada, and never to quit its walls until they had planted the standard of the faith on the towers of the Alhambra. Many of the nobles of the kingdom, particularly those from the parts remote from the scene of action, wearied by the toils of war and foreseeing that this would be a tedious siege, requiring patience and vigilance rather than hardy deeds of arms, contented themselves with

---

*Marmol de Rebelione Maur: lib 1 cap 16, Pedraza Hisp: Granat: P. 3. C. 4—Suarez Hist de Obispados de Guadiz y Baza C. 10.

†Garibay. lib. 18. C. 39.

sending their vassals, while they staid at home, to attend to their domains. Many cities furnished soldiers at their cost, and the King took the field with an army of forty thousand infantry and ten thousand horse. The principal captains who followed the King in this campaign were Roderigo Ponce de Leon, the marquis of Cadiz, the Master of Santiago, the Marquis of Villena, the Counts of Tendilla, Cifuentes, Cabra and Ureña and Don Alonzo de Aguilar.

Queen Isabella accompanied by her son, the Prince Juan, and by the Princesses Juana, Maria, and Cathalina her daughters, proceeded to Alcalá la Real, the mountain fortress and strong hold of the Count de Tendilla. Here she remained to forward supplies to the army and to be ready to repair to the camp whenever her presence might be required.

The army of Ferdinand poured into the vega by various defiles of the mountains, and on the 23d. of April the royal tent was pitched at a village called Los Ojos de Huescar, about a league and a half from Granada. At the approach of this formidable force, the harrassed inhabitants turned pale and even many of the warriors trembled; for they felt that the last desperate struggle was at hand.

Boabdil el Chico assembled his council in the Alhambra, from the windows of which they could behold the Christian squadrons glistening through clouds of dust as they poured along the vega. The utmost confusion and consternation reigned in the council. Many of the members, terrified with the horrors impending over their families, advised Boabdil to throw himself upon the generosity of the Christian monarch; even several of the bravest suggested the possibility of obtaining honourable terms.

The wazir of the city Abul Casim Abdelmelic, was called upon to report the state of the public means for sustenance and defiance. There were sufficient provisions, he said, for a few months' supply, independent of what might exist in the possession of merchants and other rich inhabitants. But of what avail, said he, is a supply for a few months, against the sieges of the Castilian monarch which are interminable?

He produced also the lists of men capable of bearing arms. The number, said he, is great, but what can be expected from mere citizen soldiers? They vaunt and menace in time of safety, none are so arrogant when the enemy is at a distance; but when the din of war thunders at their gates, they hide themselves in terror.

When Muza heard these words he rose with generous warmth. "What reason have we," said he, "to despair? The blood of those illustrious Moors the ancient conquerors of Spain, still flows in our veins. Let us be true to ourselves and fortune will again be with us. We have a veteran force, both horse and foot the flower of our chivalry, seazoned in war and scarred in a thousand battles. As to the multitude of our citizens, spoken of so slightly, why should we doubt their valour? There are twenty thousand young men in the fire of youth, for whom I will engage that in the defence of their homes, they will rival the most valiant veterans. Do we want provisions? Our horses are fleet and our horsemen daring in the foray. Let them scour and scourge the country of those apostate Moslems who have surrendered to the Christians. Let them make inroads into the lands of our enemies. We shall soon see them returning, with calvagadas to our gates; and to a soldier there is no morsel so sweet as that wrested with hard fighting from the foe."

Boabdil el Chico, though he wanted firm and durable courage, was readily excited to sudden emotions of bravery. He caught a glow of resolution from the noble ardour of Muza. "Do what is needful," said he to his commanders, "into your hands I confide the common safety. You are the protectors of the kingdom, and, with the aid of Allah, will revenge the insults of our religion, the deaths of our friends and relations and the sorrows and sufferings heaped upon our land."*

To every one was now assigned his separate duty. The wazir had charge of the arms and provisions, and the enrolling of the people. Muza was to command the cavalry, to defend the gates and to take the lead in all sallies and skirmishings. Naim Reduan and Muhamed Aben Zayde were his adjutants, Abdel Kerim Zegri and the other captains were to guard the walls, and the alcaydes of the Alcazaba and of the Red Towers had command of the fortresses.

Nothing now was heard but the din of arms and the bustle of preparation. The Moorish spirit quick to catch fire was immediately in a flame, and the populace, in the excitement of the moment, set at naught the power of the Christians. Muza was in all parts of the city, infusing his own generous zeal into the bosoms of the soldiery. The young cavaliers rallied round him as their model; the veteran warriors regarded him with a soldier's admiration, the vulgar throng followed him with shouts and the helpless part of the inhabitants the old men and the women hailed him with blessings as their protector.

On the first appearance of the Christian army the principal gates of the city had been closed and secured with bars and bolts and heavy chains; Muza now ordered them to be thrown open. "To me and my cavaliers," said he, "is entrusted the defence of the gates; our bodies shall be their barriers." He stationed at each gate a strong guard, chosen from his bravest men. His horsemen were always completely armed and ready to mount at a moment's warning. Their steeds stood saddled and caparisoned in the stables with lance and buckler beside them. On the least approach of the enemy a squadron of horse gathered within the gate ready to launch forth like the bolt from the thundercloud. Muza made no empty bravado nor haughty threat: he was more terrible in deeds than in words, and executed daring exploits, beyond

*Conde.

even the vaunt of the vainglorious. Such was the present champion of the Moors; had they possessed many such warriors, or had Muza risen to power at an earlier period of the war, the fate of Granada might have been deferred and the Moor, for a long time, have maintained his throne within the walls of the Alhambra.

HOW KING FERDINAND CONDUCTED THE SIEGE CAUTIOUSLY, AND HOW QUEEN ISABELLA ARRIVED AT THE CAMP.

Though Granada was shorn of its glories and nearly cut off from all external aid, still its mighty castles and massive bulwarks seemed to set all attack at defiance. Being the last retreat of Moorish power it had assembled within its walls the remnants of the armies that had contended, step by step, with the invaders, in their gradual conquest of the land. All that remained of high born and high bred chivalry was here. All that was loyal and patriotic was roused to activity by the common danger; and Granada that had so long been lulled into inaction by vain hopes of security, now assumed a formidable aspect in the hour of its despair.

Ferdinand saw that any attempt to subdue the city by main force would be perilous and bloody. Cautious in his policy and fond of conquests gained by art rather than by valour, he resorted to the plan which had been so successful with Baza and determined to reduce the place by famine. For this purpose his armies penetrated into the very heart of the Alpuxarras and ravaged the valleys and sacked and burnt the towns upon which the city depended for its supplies. Scouting parties, also, ranged the mountains behind Granada, and captured every casual convoy of provisions. The Moors became more daring as their situation became more hopeless. Never had Ferdinand experienced such vigorous sallies and assaults. Muza, at the head of his cavalry, harrassed the borders of the camp, and even penetrated into the interior, making sudden spoil and ravage, and leaving his course to be traced by the slain and wounded. To protect his camp from these assaults Ferdinand fortified it with deep trenches and strong bulwarks. It was of a quadrangular form, divided into streets, like a city, the troops being quartered in tents, and in booths constructed of bushes and branches of trees. When it was completed Queen Isabella came in state, with all her court, and the prince and princesses, to be present at the siege. This was intended, as on former occasions, to reduce the besieged to despair by shewing the determination of the sovereigns to reside in the camp until the city should surrender. Immediately after her arrival the Queen rode forth to survey the camp and its environs. Wherever she went she was attended by a splendid retinue, and all the commanders vied with each other in the pomp and ceremony with which they received her. Nothing was heard from morning until night but shouts and acclamations and bursts of martial music so that it appeared to the Moors as if a continual festival and triumph reigned in the Christian camp.

The arrival of the Queen, however, and the menaced obstinacy of the siege, had no effect in damping the fire of the Moorish chivalry. Muza inspired the youthful warriors with the most devoted heroism. "We have nothing left to fight for," said he, "but the ground we stand on; when this is lost we cease to have a country and a name."

Finding the Christian King forbore to make an attack, Muza incited his cavaliers to challenge the youthful chivalry of the Christian army to single combat, or partial skirmishes. Scarce a day passed without gallant conflicts of the kind in sight of the city and the camp. The combatants rivalled each other in the splendour of their armour and array, as well as in the prowess of their deeds. Their contests were more like the stately ceremonials of tilts and tournaments than the rude conflicts of the field. Ferdinand soon perceived that they animated the fiery Moors with fresh zeal and courage, while they cost the lives of many of his bravest cavaliers; he again, therefore, forbade the acceptance of any individual challenges, and ordered that all partial encounters should be avoided. The cool and stern policy of the Catholic sovereign bore hard upon the generous spirits of either army but roused the indignation of the Moors, when they found they were to be subdued in this inglorious manner. "Of what avail," said they, "is chivalry and heroic valour, the crafty monarch of the Christians has no magnanimity in warfare; he seeks to subdue us through the weakness of our bodies, but shuns to encounter the courage of our souls!"

CHAPTER XCII

OF THE INSOLENT DEFIANCE OF TARFE THE MOOR, AND THE DARING EXPLOIT OF HERNANDO PEREZ DEL PULGAR.

When the Moorish knights beheld that all courteous challenges were unavailing they sought various means to provoke the Christian warriors to the field. Sometimes a body of them, fleetly mounted, would gallop up to the skirts of the camp and try who should hurl his lance farthest within the barriers, having his name inscribed on it or a label affixed to it containing some taunting defiance. These bravadoes caused great irritation but still the Spanish warriors were restrained by the prohibition of the King.

Among the Moorish cavaliers was one named Tarfe, renowned for his great strength and daring spirit; but whose courage partook of fierce audacity rather than chivalric heroism. In one of these sallies, when they were skirting the Christian camp, this arrogant Moor outstripped his companions, overleaped the barriers and galloping close to the royal quarters launched his lance so far within, that it remained quivering in the earth, close by the pavilions of the sovereigns. The royal guards rushed forth in pursuit, but the Moorish horsemen were already beyond the camp, and scouring in a cloud of dust for the city. Upon wresting the lance from the earth a label was found upon it, importing that it was intended for the Queen.

Nothing could equal the indignation of the Christian warriors at the insolence of the bravado and the discourteous insult offered to the Queen. Hernando Perez del Pulgar, surnamed "he of the exploits," was present, and resolved not to be outbraved by this daring infidel. "Who will stand by me," said he, "in an enterprize of desperate peril?" The Christian cavaliers well knew the harebrained valour of Hernando del Pulgar, yet not one hesitated to step forward. He chose fifteen companions, all men of powerful arm and dauntless heart. In the dead of the night he led them forth from the camp, and approached the city cautiously until he arrived at a postern gate, which opened upon the Darro and was guarded by foot soldiers. The guards, little thinking of such an unwonted and partial attack, were for the most part asleep. The gate was forced and a confused and chance medley skirmish ensued. Hernando del Pulgar stopped not to take part in the affray. Putting spurs to his horse he galloped furiously through the streets, striking fire out of the stones at every bound. Arrived at the principal mosque he sprang from his horse and kneeling at the portal took possession of the edifice as a Christian chapel, dedicating it to the blessed virgin. In testimonial of the ceremony he took a tablet which he had brought with him, on which was inscribed in large letters, AVE MARIA, and nailed it to the door of the mosque with his dagger. This done, he remounted his steed and galloped back to the gate. The alarm had been given, the city was in an uproar, soldiers were gathering from every direction. They were astonished at seeing a Christian warrior galloping from the interior of the city. Hernando del Pulgar overturned some, cut down others, rejoined his companions, who still maintained possession of the gate by dint of hard fighting and all made good their retreat to the camp. The Moors were at a loss to conjecture the meaning of this wild and apparently fruitless assault; but great was their exasperation when on the following day they discovered the trophy of hardihood and prowess, the AVE MARIA, thus elevated in the very centre of the city. The mosque thus boldly sanctified by Hernando del Pulgar, was eventually consecrated into a cathedral after the capture of Granada.*

CHAPTER XCIII

HOW QUEEN ISABELLA TOOK A VIEW OF THE CITY OF GRANADA, AND HOW HER CURIOSITY COST THE LIVES OF MANY CHRISTIANS AND MOORS.

The royal encampment lay at such a distance from Granada that the general aspect of the city only could be seen, as it rose gracefully from the vega, covering the sides of the hills with palaces and towers. Queen Isabella had expressed an earnest desire to behold, nearer at hand, a city, whose beauty was so renowned throughout the world; and the Marquis of Cadiz, with his accustomed courtesy, prepared a great military escort and guard, to protect the Queen and the ladies of the court, while they enjoyed this perilous gratification.

It was on the morning after the event recorded in the preceding chapter, that a magnificent and powerful train issued forth from the Christian camp. The advanced guard was composed of legions of cavalry heavily armed, that looked like moving masses of polished steel. Then came the King and Queen with the prince and princess and the ladies of the court, surrounded by the royal body guard, sumptuously arrayed, composed of the sons of the most illustrious houses of Spain. After these was the rear guard composed of a powerful force of horse and foot; for the flower of the army sallied forth that day. The Moors gazed with fearful admiration at this glorious pageant, wherein the pomp of the court was mingled with the terrors of the camp. It moved along in a radiant line across the vega to the melodious thunders of martial music, while banner, and plume, and silken scarf and rich brocade, gave a gay and gorgeous relief to the grim visage of iron war that lurked beneath.

---

*In commemoration of this daring feat the Emperor Charles V in after years, conferred on Pulgar and his descendants the right of Sepulture in that church, and the privilege of sitting in the choir during high mass. This Hernando Perez del Pulgar was a man of letters, as well as arms, and inscribed to Charles V a summary of the achievements of Gonzalvo of Cordova, surnamed the great captain, who had been one of his comrades in arms. He is often confounded with Hernando del Pulgar, historian and secretary to Queen Isabella. See note to Pulgar's chron. of the Catholic sovereigns Part 3. C. 3. Edit Valencia 1780.

The army moved towards the hamlet of Zubia, built on the skirts of the mountains, to the left of Granada, and commanding a view of the Alhambra, and the most beautiful quarter of the city. As they approached the hamlet the Marquis of Villena, the Count Ureña and Don Alonzo de Aguilar filed off with their battalions and were soon seen glittering along the side of the mountain above the village. In the mean time the Marquis of Cadiz, the Count de Tendilla, the Count de Cabra and Don Alonzo Fernandez, Senior of Alcandrete and Montemayor, drew up their forces in battle array on the plain below the hamlet, presenting a living barrier of loyal chivalry between the sovereigns and the city. Thus securely guarded, the royal party alighted and entering one of the houses of the hamlet, which had been prepared for their reception, enjoyed a full view of the city from its terraced roof. The ladies of the court gazed with delight at the red towers of the Alhambra rising from amidst shady groves anticipating the time when the Catholic sovereigns should be enthroned within its walls, and its courts shine with the splendour of Spanish chivalry. "The reverend prelates and holy friars, who always surrounded the Queen, looked with serene satisfaction," says Fray Antonio Agapida, "at this modern Babylon, enjoying the triumph that awaited them when those mosques and minarets should be converted into churches, and goodly priests and bishops should succeed to the infidel alfaquis."

When the Moors beheld the Christians thus drawn forth in full array in the plain, they supposed it was to offer them battle; and they hesitated not to accept it. In a little while the Queen beheld a body of Moorish cavalry pouring into the vega, the riders managing their fleet and fiery steeds with admirable address. They were richly armed and clothed in the most brilliant colours, and the caparisons of their steeds flamed with gold and embroidery. This was the favourite squadron of Muza composed of the flower of the youthful cavaliers of Granada; others succeeded; some heavily armed, some *a la ginete* with lance and buckler; and lastly came the legions of foot soldiers with arquebus, and cross bow and spear and scymetar.

When the Queen saw this army issuing from the city, she sent to the Marquis of Cadiz and forbade any attack upon the enemy or the acceptance of any challenge to a skirmish; for she was loth that her curiosity should cost the life of a single human being.

The marquis promised to obey though sorely against his will, and it grieved the spirit of the Spanish cavaliers to be obliged to remain with sheathed swords while bearded by the foe. The Moors could not comprehend the meaning of this inaction of the Christians after having apparently invited a battle. They sallied several times from their ranks and approached near enough to discharge their arrows, but the Christians were immovable. Many of the Moorish horsemen gallopped close to the Christian ranks, brandishing their lances and scymetars, and defying various cavaliers to single combat; but King Ferdinand had rigorously prohibited all duels of the kind, and they dared not transgress his orders under his very eye.

While this grim and reluctant tranquility prevailed along the Christian line there rose a mingled shout and sound of laughter near the gate of the city. A Moorish horseman, armed at all points, issued forth, followed by a rabble, who drew back as he approached the scene of danger. The Moor was more robust and brawny than was common with his countrymen. His visor was closed; he bore a huge buckler and ponderous lance, his scymetar was of a Damascus blade, and his richly ornamented dagger was wrought by an artificer of Fez. He was known by his device to be Tarfe, the most insolent, yet valiant, of the Moslem warriors; the same who had hurled into the royal camp his lance inscribed to the Queen. As he rode slowly along in front of the army his very steed, prancing with fiery eye and distended nostril, seemed to breathe defiance to the Christians. But what were the feelings of the Spanish cavaliers when they beheld, tied to the tail of his steed, and dragged in the dust, the very inscription, *Ave Maria* which Hernando Perez del Pulgar had affixed to the door of the mosque! A burst of horror and indignation broke forth from the army. Hernando del Pulgar was not at hand to maintain his previous achievement, but one of his young companions in arms, Garcilasso de la Vega by name, putting spurs to his horse gallopped to the hamlet of Zubia, threw himself on his knees before the King and besought permission to accept the defiance of this insolent infidel, and to revenge the insult offered to our blessed Lady. The request was too pious to be refused: Garcilasso remounted his steed, he closed his helmet, graced by four sable plumes, grasped his buckler of Flemish workmanship, and his lance of matchless temper, and defied the haughty Moor in the midst of his career. A combat took place in view of the two armies and of the Castilian court. The Moor was powerful in wielding his weapons, and dexterous in managing his steed. He was of larger frame than Garcilasso and more completely armed; and the Christians trembled for their champion. The shock of their encounter was dreadful; their lances were shivered and sent up splinters in the air. Garcilasso was thrown back in his saddle, his horse made a wide career before he could recover, gather up the reins and return to the conflict. They now encountered each other with swords. The Moor circled round his opponent as a hawk circles when about to make a swoop, his arabian steed obeyed his rider with matchless quickness; at every attack of the infidel it seemed as if the Christian knight must sink beneath his flashing scymetar. But if Garcilasso were inferior to him in power he was superior in agility; many of his blows he parried, others he received upon his Flemish shield, which was proof against the Damascus blade. The blood streamed from numerous wounds received by either warrior. The Moor, seeing his antagonist exhausted, availed himself of his superior force, and, grappling, endeavoured to wrest him from his saddle. They both fell to earth, the Moor placed his knee upon the breast of his victim and brandishing his dagger aimed a blow at his throat; a cry of despair was uttered by the Christian warriors when suddenly they beheld the Moor rolling lifeless in the dust. Garcilasso had shortened his sword, and, as his adversary raised his arm to strike, had pierced him to the heart. It was a singular and miraculous victory, says Fray Antonio Agapida, "but the Christian knight was armed by the sacred nature of his cause, and the holy virgin gave him strength, like another David, to slay this gigantic champion of the Gentiles."

The laws of chivalry were observed throughout the combat; no one interfered on either side. Garcilasso now despoiled his adversary; then, rescuing the holy inscription of AVE MARIA from its degrading situation, he elevated it on the point of his sword and bore it off as a signal of triumph amidst the rapturous shouts of the Christian army.

The sun had now reached the meridian, and the hot blood of the Moors was inflamed by its rays, and by the sight of the defeat of their champion. Muza ordered two pieces of ordnance to open a fire upon the Christians. A confusion was produced in one part of their ranks. Muza called to the chiefs of the army, "Let us waste no more time in empty challenges, let us charge upon the enemy, he who assaults has always an advantage in the combat." So saying he rushed forward, followed by a large body of horse and foot, and charged so furiously upon the advance guard of the Christians that he drove it in, upon the battalion of the Marquis of Cadiz.

The gallant marquis now considered himself absolved from all further obedience to the Queen's commands. He gave the signal to attack. Santiago! was shouted along the line and he pressed forward to the encounter with his battalion of twelve hundred lances. The other cavaliers followed his example, and the battle instantly became general.

When the King and Queen beheld the armies thus rushing to the combat, they threw themselves on their knees and implored the holy virgin to protect her faithful warriors. The prince and princess, the ladies of the court, and the prelates and friar who were present, did the same, and the effect of the prayers of these illustrious and saintly persons was immediately apparent. The fierceness with which the Moors had rushed to the attack was suddenly cooled; they were bold and adroit for a skirmish, but unequal to the veteran Spaniards in the open field. A panic seized upon the foot soldiers, they turned and took to flight. Muza and his cavaliers in vain endeavoured to rally them. Some took refuge in the mountains, but the greater part fled to the city, in such confusion, that they overturned and trampled upon each other. The Christians pursued them to the very gates. Upwards of two thousand were either killed, wounded or taken prisoner, and the two pieces of ordnance were brought off as trophies of the victory. Not a Christian lance but was bathed that day in the blood of an infidel.*

Such was the brief but bloody action which was known among the Christian warriors by the name of the Queen's Skirmish, for when the Marquis of Cadiz waited upon her majesty to apologize for breaking her commands, he attributed the victory entirely to her presence. The Queen, however, insisted that it was all owing to her troops being led on by so valiant a commander. Her majesty had not yet recovered from her agitation at beholding so terrible a scene of bloodshed; though certain veterans present, pronounced it as gay and gentle a skirmish as they had ever witnessed.

To commemorate this victory the Queen afterwards erected a monastery in this village of Zubia, dedicated to S' Francisco, which still exists, and in its garden is a laurel planted by the hands of her majesty.†

CHAPTER XCIV

CONFLAGRATION OF THE CHRISTIAN CAMP.

The ravages of war had as yet spared a little portion of the vega of Granada. A green belt of gardens and orchards still flourished round the city, extending along the banks of the Xenel and the Darro. They had been the solace and delight of the inhabitants in their happier days, and contributed to their sustenance in this time of scarcity. Ferdinand determined to make a final and exterminating ravage to the very walls of the city, so that there should not remain a single green thing for the sustenance of man or beast. The evening of a hot July day shone splendidly upon the Christian camp, which was in a bustle of preparation for the next day's service, for desperate resistance was expected from the Moors. The camp made a glorious appearance in the setting sun. The various tents of the royal family and the attendant nobles were adorned with rich hangings and sumptuous devices, and costly furniture, forming as it were a little city of silk and brocade, where the pinnacles of pavillions of various gay colours, surmounted with waving stan-

*Cura de Los Palacios.

†The house from whence the King and Queen contemplated the battle is likewise to be seen at the present day. It is in the first street, to the right on entering the village from the vega and the royal arms are painted on the ceilings. It is inhabited by a worthy farmer, Francisco Garcia, who in shewing the house refuses all compensation, with true Spanish pride; offering on the contrary the hospitalities of his mansion to the stranger. His children are versed in the old Spanish ballads about the exploits of Hernando Perez del Pulgar and Garcilasso de la Vega.

dards and fluttering pennons, might vie with the domes and minarets of the capital they were besieging.

In the midst of this little gaudy metropolis the lofty tent of the Queen domineered over the rest like a stately palace. The Marquis of Cadiz had courteously surrendered his own tent to the Queen. It was the most complete and sumptuous in Christendom, and had been carried about with him throughout the war. In the centre rose a stately alfaneque or pavillion in oriental taste, the rich hangings being supported by columns of lances, ornamented with martial devices. This centre pavillion or silken tower, was surrounded by other compartments, some of painted linen lined with silk, and all separated from each other by curtains. It was one of those camp palaces which are raised and demolished in an instant, like the city of canvas that surrounds them.

As the evening advanced the bustle in the camp subsided. Every one sought repose, preparatory to the next day's toil. The King retired early that he might be up with the crowing of the cock, to head the destroying army in person. All stir of military preparation was hushed in the royal quarters; the very sound of minstrelsy was mute, and not the tinkling of a guitar was to be heard from the tents of the fair ladies of the court.

The Queen had retired to the innermost part of her pavillion, where she was performing her orizons before a private altar; perhaps the peril to which the King might be exposed in the next day's foray inspired her with more than usual devotion. While thus at her prayers she was suddenly aroused by a glare of light, and wreaths of suffocating smoke. In an instant the whole tent was in a blaze: there was a high gusty wind which whirled the light flames from tent to tent and wrapped the whole in one conflagration.

Isabella had barely time to save herself by instant flight. Her first thought on being extricated from her tent was for the safety of the King. She rushed to his tent, but the vigilant Ferdinand was already at the entrance of it. Starting from bed on the first alarm, and fancying it an assault of the enemy he had seized his sword and buckler, and sallied forth undressed, with his cuirass upon his arm.

The late gorgeous camp was now a scene of wild confusion. The flames kept spreading from one pavillion to another, glaring upon the rich armour and golden and silver vessels, which seemed melting in the fervent heat. Many of the soldiery had erected booths and bowers of branches, which being dry, crackled and blazed and added to the rapid conflagration. The ladies of the court fled shrieking and half-dressed from their tents. There was an alarm of drum and trumpet and a distracted hurry about the camp of men half armed.

The Prince Juan had been snatched out of bed by an attendant and conveyed to the quarters of the Count de Cabra, which were at the entrance of the camp. The loyal count immediately summoned his people and those of his cousin Don Alonzo de Montemayor, and formed a guard round the tent in which the prince was sheltered.

The idea that this was a stratagem of the Moors soon subsided, but it was feared that they might take advantage of it to assault the camp. The Marquis of Cadiz, therefore, sallied forth with three thousand horse to check any advance from the city. As they passed along, the whole camp was a scene of hurry and consternation, some hastening to their posts at the call of drum and trumpet, some attempting to save rich effects and glittering armour from the tents; others dragging along terrified and restive horses.

When they emerged from the camp they found the whole firmament illumined. The flames whirled up in long light spires, and the air was filled with sparks and cinders.   A bright glare was thrown upon the city revealing every battlement and tower. Turbaned heads were seen gazing from every roof and armour gleamed along the walls, yet not a single warrior sallied from the gates. The Moors suspected some stratagem on the part of the Christians, and kept quietly within their walls. By degrees the flames expired; the city faded from sight, all again became dark and quiet, and the Marquis of Cadiz returned with his cavalry to the camp.

CHAPTER XCV

THE LAST RAVAGE BEFORE GRANADA.

When the day dawned on the Christian camp, nothing remained of that beautiful assemblage of stately pavillions, but heaps of smouldering rubbish, with helms and corselets and other furniture of war, and masses of melted gold and silver glittering among the ashes. The wardrobe of the Queen was entirely destroyed, and there was an immense loss in plate, jewels, costly stuffs and sumptuous armour of the luxurious nobles. The fire at first had been attributed to treachery but on investigation it proved to be entirely accidental. The Queen on retiring to her prayers, had ordered her lady in attendance to remove a light burning near her couch lest it should prevent her sleeping. Through heedlessness the taper was placed in another part of the tent near the hangings, which being blown against it, by a gust of wind, immediately took fire.

The wary Ferdinand knew the sanguine temperament of the Moors, and hastened to prevent their deriving confidence from the night's disaster. At break of day the drums and trumpets sounded to arms, and the Christian army issued from among the smoking ruins of their camp in shining squadrons, with flaunting banners and bursts of martial melody, as though the preceding night had been a time of high festivity instead of terror.

The Moors had beheld the conflagration with wonder and perplexity. When the day broke and they looked towards the Christian camp they saw nothing but a dark smoking mass. Their scouts came in with the joyful intelligence that the whole camp was a scene of ruin. Scarce had the tidings spread throughout the city, than they beheld the Christian army advancing towards their walls. They considered it a feint to cover their desperate situation and prepare for a retreat. Boabdil el Chico had one of his impulses of valour; he determined to take the field in person, and to follow up this signal blow which Allah had inflicted on the enemy.

The Christian army approached close to the city and were laying waste the gardens and orchards, when Boabdil sallied forth surrounded by all that was left of the flower and chivalry of Granada. There is one place where even the coward becomes brave, that sacred spot called home. What then must have been the valour of the Moors, a people always of fiery spirit, when the war was thus brought to their thresholds? They fought among the scenes of their loves and pleasures; the scenes of their infancy and the haunts of their domestic life. They fought under the eyes of their wives and children, their old men and their maidens, of all that was helpless and all that was dear to them, for all Granada crowded on tower and battlement, watching with trembling heart the fate of this eventful day.

There was not so much one battle as a variety of battles; every garden and orchard became a scene of deadly contest; every inch of ground was disputed with an agony of grief and valour, by the Moors; every inch of ground that the Christians advanced they valiantly maintained, but never did they advance with severer fighting, or greater loss of blood.

The cavalry of Muza was in every part of the field; wherever it came it gave fresh ardour to the fight. The Moorish soldier fainting with heat, fatigue and wounds was roused to new life at the approach of Muza; and even he who lay gasping in the agonies of death turned his face towards him, and faintly uttered cheers and blessings as he passed.

The Christians had by this time gained possession of various towers near the city, from whence they had been annoyed by crossbows and arquebusses. The Moors, scattered in various actions, were severely pressed. Boabdil at the head of the cavaliers of his guard displayed the utmost valour, mingling in the fight in various parts of the field, and endeavouring to enspirit the foot soldiers to the combat. But the Moorish infantry was never to be depended upon. In the heat of the action a panic seized upon them; they fled leaving their sovereign exposed with his handful of cavaliers, to an overwhelming force. Boabdil was on the point of falling into the hands of the Christians, when, wheeling round, with his followers, they threw the reins on the necks of their fleet steeds, and took refuge by dint of hoof within the walls of the city.*

Muza endeavoured to retrieve the fortune of the field. He threw himself before the retreating infantry calling upon them to turn and fight for their homes, their families, for every thing that was sacred and dear to them. It was all in vain. They were totally broken and dismayed and fled tumultuously for the gates. Muza would fain have kept the field with his cavalry; but this devoted band, having stood the brunt of war throughout this desperate campaign, was fearfully reduced in number, and many of the survivors were crippled and enfeebled by their wounds. Slowly and reluctantly Muza retreated to the city, his bosom swelling with indignation and despair. When he entered the gates he ordered them to be closed and secured with bolts and bars, for he refused to place any further confidence in the archers and arquebusiers, who were stationed to defend them; and he vowed never more to sally forth with foot soldiers to the field.

In the mean time the artillery thundered from the walls and checked all further advances of the Christians. King Ferdinand, therefore, called off his troops, and returned in triumph to the ruins of his camp, leaving the beautiful city of Granada, wrapped in the smoke of her fields and gardens, and surrounded by the bodies of her slaughtered children.

Such was the last sally made by the Moors in defence of their favourite city. The French ambassador who witnessed it, was filled with wonder at the prowess, the dexterity and daring of the Moslems. In truth this whole war was an instance, memorable in history, of the most persevering resolution. For nearly ten years had the war endured an almost uninterrupted series of disasters to the Moorish arms. Their towns had been taken, one after another, and their brethren slain or led into captivity. Yet they disputed every city and town and fortress and castle, nay every rock itself, as if they had been enspirited by victories. Wherever they could plant foot to fight, or find wall or cliff from whence to launch an arrow, they disputed their beloved country, and now, when their capital was cut off from all relief and had a whole nation thundering at its gates, they still maintained defence, as if they hoped some miracle to interpose in their behalf. Their obstinate resistance, says an ancient chronicler, shews the grief with which the Moors yielded up the vega, which was to them a paradise and heaven. Exerting all the strength of their arms they embraced, as it were, that most beloved soil, from which neither wounds, nor defeats, nor death itself could part them. They stood firm battling for it with the united force of love and grief, never drawing back the foot while they had hands to fight or fortune to befriend them.†

*Zurita Lib 20 C. 88.
†Abarca Reyes de Aragon R 30 C. 3.

BUILDING OF THE CITY OF SANTA FE:
DESPAIR OF THE MOORS.

The Moors now shut themselves up gloomily within their walls; there were no longer any daring sallies from their gates; and even the martial clangour of the drum and trumpet which had continually resounded within that warrior city, was now seldom heard from its battlements. For a time they flattered themselves with hopes that the late conflagration of the camp would discourage the besiegers; that, as in former years, their invasion would end with the summer, and that they would again withdraw before the autumnal rains. The measures of Ferdinand and Isabella soon crushed these hopes. They gave orders to build a regular city upon the site of their camp, to convince the Moors that the siege was to endure until the surrender of Granada. Nine of the principal cities of Spain were charged with this stupendous undertaking, and they emulated each other with a zeal worthy of the cause. "It verily seemed," says Fray Antonio Agapida, "as though some miracle operated to aid this pious work, so rapidly did arise a formidable city with solid edifices and powerful walls, and mighty towers, where lately had been seen nothing but tents and light pavilions. The city was traversed by two principal streets in form of a cross, terminating in four gates, facing the four winds; and in the centre was a vast square, where the whole army might be assembled. To this city it was proposed to give the name of Isabella, so dear to the army and the nation, but that pious princess," adds Antonio Agapida, "calling to mind the holy cause in which it was erected, gave it the name of Santa Fé, (or the city of the Holy Faith), and it remains to this day, a monument of the piety and glory of the Catholic sovereigns."

Hither the merchants soon resorted from all points; long trains of mules were seen every day, entering and departing from its gates, the streets were crowded with magazines filled with all kinds of costly and luxurious merchandize; a scene of bustling commerce and prosperity took place, while unhappy Granada remained shut up, and desolate.

In the meantime the besieged city, began to suffer the distress of famine. Its supplies were all cut off. A cavalgada of flocks and herds, and mules laden with money, coming to the relief of the city from the mountains of the Alpuxarras, was taken by the Marquis of Cadiz, and led in triumph to the camp, in sight of the suffering Moors. Autumn arrived; but the harvests had been swept from the face of the country; a rigorous winter was approaching and the city was almost destitute of provisions. The people sank into deep despondency. They called to mind all that had been predicted by astrologers at the birth of their illstarred sovereign, and all that had been foretold of the fate of Granada at the time of the capture of Zahara.

Boabdil was alarmed by the gathering dangers from without and by the clamours of his starving people. He summoned a council composed of the principal officers of the army, the alcaydes of the fortresses, the xequis or sages of the city, and the alfaquis or doctors of the faith. They assembled in the great Hall of Audience of the Alhambra, and despair was painted in their countenances. Boabdil demanded of them what was to be done, in their present extremity; and their answer was "surrender." The venerable Abul Casim Abdelmelic, governor of the city, represented its unhappy state. "Our granaries are nearly exhausted, and no further supplies are to be expected. The provender for the war horses is required as sustenance for the soldiery; the very horses themselves, are killed for food. Of seven thousand steeds which once could be sent into the field, three hundred only remain. Our city contains two hundred thousand inhabitants, old and young, with each a mouth that calls piteously for bread."

The xequis and principal citizens, declared that the people could no longer sustain the labours and sufferings of a defence; "and of what avail is our defence," said they, "when the enemy is determined to persist in the siege. What alternative remains but to surrender, or to die?"

The heart of Boabdil was touched by this appeal, and he maintained a gloomy silence. He had cherished some faint hope of relief from the Soldan of Egypt or the Barbary powers; but it was now at an end, even if such assistance were to be sent, he had no longer a sea-port where it might debark. The counsellors saw that the resolution of the King was shaken, and they united their voices in urging him to capitulate.

The valiant Muza alone arose in opposition. "It is yet too early," said he, "to talk of a surrender. Our means are not exhausted; we have yet one source of strength remaining, terrible in its effects, and which often has achieved the most signal victories. It is our despair. Let us rouse the mass of the people, let us put weapons in their hands, let us fight the enemy to the very utmost, until we rush upon the points of their lances. I am ready to lead the way into the thickest of their squadrons, and much rather would I be numbered among those who fell in the defence of Granada, than of those who survived to capitulate for her surrender."

The words of Muza were without effect, for they were addressed to broken spirited and heartless men, or men perhaps to whom sad experience had taught discretion. They were arrived at that state of public depression when heroes and heroism are no longer regarded, and when old men and their councils rise into importance. Boabdil el Chico yielded to the general voice, it was determined to capitulate with the Christian sovereigns and the venerable Abul Casim Abdelmelic was sent forth to the camp empowered to treat for terms.

CAPITULATION OF GRANADA.

The old governor Abul Casim Abdelmelic was received with great distinction by Ferdinand and Isabella, who appointed Gonzalvo of Cordova and Fernando de Zafra secretary to the King to confer with him. All Granada awaited in trembling anxiety the result of his negociations. After repeated conferences he at length returned with the ultimate terms of the Catholic sovereigns. They agreed to suspend all attack for seventy days, at the end of which time, if no succour had arrived to the Moorish King, the city of Granada should be surrendered.

All Christian captives should be liberated without ransom.

Boabdil and his principal cavaliers should take an oath of fealty to the Castilian crown and certain valuable territories in the Alpuxarra mountains should be assigned to the Moorish monarch for his maintenance.

The Moors of Granada should become subjects of the Spanish sovereigns, retaining their possessions, their arms, and horses, and yielding up nothing but their artillery. They should be protected in the exercise of their religion and governed by their own laws administered by cadis of their own faith, under governors appointed by the sovereigns. They should be exempted from tribute for three years, after which term they should pay the same that they had been accustomed to render to their native monarchs.

Those who chose to depart for Africa, within three years, should be provided with a passage for themselves and their effects, free of charge, from whatever port they should prefer.

For the fulfilment of these articles four hundred hostages from the principal families were required previous to the surrender, to be subsequently restored. The son of the King of Granada and all other hostages in possession of the Castilian sovereigns, were to be restored at the same time.

Such were the conditions that the wazir Abul Casim laid before the council of Granada, as the best that could be obtained from the besieging foe.

When the members of the council found that the awful moment had arrived when they were to sign and seal the perdition of their empire, and blot themselves out as a nation, all firmness deserted them, and many gave way to tears. Muza alone retained an unaltered mien. "Leave Seniors," cried he, "this idle lamentation to helpless women and children. We are men, we have hearts, not to shed tender tears, but drops of blood. I see the spirit of the people so cast down, that it is impossible to save the kingdom. Yet, there still remains an alternative for noble minds—a glorious death! Let us die defending our liberty and avenging the woes of Granada. Our mother earth will receive her children into her bosom, safe from the chains and oppressions of the conqueror; or should any fail a sepulchre to hide his remains, he will not want a sky to cover him. Allah forbid it should be said the nobles of Granada feared to die in her defence!"

Muza ceased to speak and a dead silence reigned in the assembly. Boabdil el Chico looked anxiously round, and scanned every face; but he read in them all the anxiety of care worn men, in whose hearts enthusiasm was dead, and who had grown callous to every chivalrous appeal. "Allah Achbar!"—God is great! exclaimed he. "There is no god but God, and Mahomet is his prophet! It is in vain to struggle against the will of heaven. Too surely was it written in the book of fate that I should be unfortunate, and the kingdom expire under my rule."

"Allah Achbar! God is great!" echoed the viziers and alfaquis. "The will of God be done!" So they all accorded with the King that these evils were preordained, that it was hopeless to contend with them; and that the terms offered by the Castilian monarchs were as favorable as could be expected.

When Muza saw that they were about to sign the treaty of surrender he rose in violent indignation. "Do not deceive yourselves," cried he, "nor think the Christians will be faithful to their promises, or their King as magnanimous in conquest as he has been victorious in war. Death is the least we have to fear: It is the plundering and sacking of our city; the profanation of our mosques, the ruin of our homes, the violation of our wives and daughters—cruel oppression, bigoted intolerance, whips and chains; the dungeon, the faggot and the stake; such are the miseries and indignities we shall see and suffer; at least those grovelling souls will see them who now shrink from an honourable death. For my part, by Allah, I will never witness them!"

With these words he left the council chamber and strode gloomily through the Court of Lions, and the outer halls of the Alhambra, without deigning to speak to the obsequious courtiers who attended in them. He repaired to his dwelling, armed himself at all points, mounted his favourite war horse; and issuing forth from the city by the gate of Elvira was never seen or heard of more.*

Such is the account given by Arabian historians of the exit of Muza Ben Abil Gazan, but the venerable Fray Antonio Agapida, endeavours to clear up the mystery of his fate. That very evening a party of Andalusian cavaliers, somewhat more than half a score of lances, were riding along the banks of the Xenel, where it winds through the vega. They beheld in the twilight a Moorish warrior approaching closely locked up from head to foot in proof. His visor was closed, his lance in rest, his powerful charger barbed, like himself, in steel. The Christians were lightly armed, with corselet, helm and target, for, during the truce, they apprehended no attack. Seeing, however, the unknown warrior approach in this hostile guise, they challenged him to stand and declare himself.

The Moslem answered not, but, charging into the midst of them, transfixed one knight with his lance and bore him out of his saddle to the earth.

*Conde part 4.

Wheeling round he attacked the others with his scymetar. His blows were furious and deadly; he seemed regardless what wounds he received, so he could but slay. He was evidently fighting, not for glory, but revenge; eager to inflict death, but careless of surviving to enjoy victory. Near one half of the cavaliers fell beneath his sword, before he received a dangerous wound so completely was he cased in armour of proof: at length he was desperately wounded, and his steed being pierced by a lance, sank to the ground. The Christians, admiring the valour of the Moor, would have spared his life, but he continued to fight upon his knees, brandishing a keen dagger of Fez. Finding at length he could no longer battle, and determined not to be taken prisoner, he threw himself, with an expiring exertion, into the Xenel, and his armour sank him to the bottom of the stream.

This unknown warrior the venerable Agapida pronounces to have been Muza Ben Abil Gazan, and says his horse was recognized by certain converted Moors of the Christian camp; the fact, however, has always remained in doubt.

CHAPTER XCVIII

COMMOTIONS IN GRANADA.

The capitulation for the surrender of Granada, was signed on the 25 of November 1481 and produced a sudden cessation of those hostilities which had raged for so many years. Christian and Moor might now be seen mingling courteously on the banks of the Xenel and the Darro, where to have met a few days previous, would have produced a scene of sanguinary contest. Still as the Moors might be suddenly aroused to defence, if, within the allotted term of seventy days, succours should arrive from abroad; and as they were at all times a rash, inflammable people, the wary Ferdinand, maintained a vigilant watch upon the city; and permitted no supplies of any kind to enter. His garrisons in the sea ports and his cruisers in the Straits of Gibraltar were ordered likewise to guard against any relief from the Grand Soldan of Egypt or the princes of Barbary.

There was no need of such precautions. Those powers were either too much engrossed by their own wars, or too much daunted by the success of the Spanish arms, to interfere in a desperate cause, and the unfortunate Moors of Granada, were abandoned to their fate.

The month of December had nearly passed away; the famine became extreme, and there was no hope of any favorable event, within the term specified in the capitulation. Boabdil saw that to hold out to the end of the allotted time, would but be to protract the miseries of his people. With the consent of his council, he determined to surrender the city on the sixth of January. On the 30th of December he sent his grand vizier Jusef Aben Comixa, with the four hundred hostages to King Ferdinand, to make known his intention, bearing him at the same time a present of a magnificent scymetar and two Arabian steeds superbly caparisoned.

The unfortunate Boabdil was doomed to meet with trouble to the end of his career. The very next day the Santon or dervise Hamet Aben Zarah, the same who had uttered prophecies and excited commotions on former occasions, suddenly made his appearance. Whence he came, no one knew, it was rumoured that he had been in the mountains of the Alpuxarras, and on the coast of Barbary, endeavouring to rouse the Moslems to the relief of Granada. He was reduced to a skeleton. His eyes glowed like coals in their sockets and his speech was little better than frantic raving. He harangued the populace in the streets and squares, inveighed against the capitulation, denounced the King and nobles as Moslems only in name, and called upon the people to sally forth against the unbelievers for that Allah had decreed them a signal victory.

Upwards of twenty thousand of the populace seized their arms and paraded the streets with shouts and outcries. The shops and houses were shut up; the King himself did not dare to venture forth, but remained a kind of prisoner in the Alhambra.

The turbulent multitude continued roaming and shouting and howling about the city, during the day and a part of the night. Hunger and a wintry tempest tamed their frenzy, and when morning came the enthusiast who had led them on had disappeared. Whether he had been disposed of by the emissaries of the King, or by the leading men of the city is not known; his disappearance remains a mystery.*

The Moorish King now issued from the Alhambra, attended by his principal nobles and harangued the populace. He set forth the necessity of complying with the capitulation from the famine that reigned in the city, the futility of defence, and from the hostages having already been delivered into the hands of the besiegers.

In the dejection of his spirits the unfortunate Boabdil attributed to himself the miseries of the country. "It was my crime in ascending the throne in rebellion against my father," said he mournfully, "which has brought these woes upon the kingdom; but Allah has grievously visited my sins upon my head. For your sake my people I have now made this treaty to protect you from the sword; your little ones from famine, your wives and daughters from the outrages of war, and to secure you in the enjoyment of your properties, your liberties, your laws and your religion, under a sovereign of happier destinies than the illstarred Boabdil." The versatile populace were touched

*Mariana.

by the humility of their sovereign; they agreed to adhere to the capitulation, there was even a faint shout of long live Boabdil the unfortunate, and they all returned to their homes, in perfect tranquility.

Boabdil immediately sent missives to King Ferdinand apprizing him of these events, and of his fears lest further delay should produce new tumults. He proposed, therefore, to surrender the city on the following day. The Castilian sovereigns assented with great satisfaction, and preparations were made in city and camp, for this great event that was to seal the fate of Granada.

It was a night of doleful lamentings within the walls of the Alhambra, for the household of Boabdil were preparing to take a last farewell of that delightful abode. All the royal treasures and the most precious effects of the Alhambra were hastily packed upon mules, the beautiful apartments were despoiled with tears and wailings by their own inhabitants. Before the dawn of day a mournful cavalcade moved obscurely out of a postern gate, of the Alhambra, and departed through one of the most retired quarters of the city. It was composed of the family of the unfortunate Boabdil, which he sent off thus privately, that they might not be exposed to the eyes of scoffers or the exultation of the enemy. The mother of Boabdil, the Sultana Ayxa la Horra rode on in silence with dejected, yet dignified demeanour; but his wife Zorayma, and all the females of his household, gave way to loud lamentations, as they looked back upon their favorite abode, now a mass of gloomy towers behind them. They were attended by the ancient domestics of the household and by a small guard of veteran Moors, loyally attached to the fallen monarch, and who would have sold their lives dearly in defence of his family. The city was yet buried in sleep as they passed through its silent streets. The guards at the gate shed tears as they opened it for their departure. They paused not, but proceeded along the banks of the Xenel on the road that leads to the Alpuxarras, until they arrived at a hamlet at some distance from the city, where they halted and waited until they should be joined by King Boabdil.

CHAPTER XCVIX

SURRENDER OF GRANADA.

The sun had scarcely begun to shed his beams upon the summits of the snowy mountains, which rise above Granada, when the Christian camp was in motion. A detachment of horse and foot, led by distinguished cavaliers, and accompanied by Hernando de Talavera, Bishop of Avila proceeded to take possession of the Alhambra and the towers. It had been stipulated in the capitulation that the detachment sent for this purpose, should not enter by the streets of the city; a road had therefore been opened outside of the walls, leading by the Puerta de los Molinos (or the Gate of the Mills) to the summit of the hill of Martyrs, and across the hill to a postern gate of the Alhambra.

When the detachment arrived at the summit of the hill, the Moorish King came forth from the gate, attended by a handful of cavaliers, leaving his vizier Jusef Aben Comixa to deliver up the palace. "Go Senior," said he to the commander of the detachment; "go and take possession of those fortresses which Allah has bestowed upon your powerful sovereigns in punishment of the sins of the Moors." He said no more, but passed mournfully on, along the same road by which the Spanish cavaliers had come; descending to the vega, to meet the Catholic sovereigns. The troops entered the Alhambra, the gates of which were wide open, and all its splendid courts and halls, silent and deserted. In the mean time the Christian court and army poured out of the city of Santa Fé and advanced across the vega. The King and Queen with the prince and princess and the dignitaries and ladies of the court took the lead, accompanied by the different orders of monks and friars, and surrounded by the royal guards, splendidly arrayed. The procession moved slowly forward; and paused at the village of Armilla at the distance of half a league from the city.

The sovereigns waited here with impatience, their eyes fixed on the lofty tower of the Alhambra, watching for the appointed signal of possession. The time that had elapsed since the departure of the detachment, seemed to them more than necessary for the purpose; and the anxious mind of Ferdinand began to entertain doubts of some commotion in the city. At length, they saw the silver cross, the great standard of this crusade, elevated on the Torre de la Vela, or great watch tower and sparkling in the sunbeams. This was done by Hernando de Talavera, Bishop of Avila. Beside it was planted the pennon of the glorious apostle S' James, and a great shout of Santiago! Santiago! rose throughout the army. Lastly was reared the royal standard by the King of Arms, with the shout of "Castile! Castile! For King Ferdinand and Queen Isabella!" The words were echoed by the whole army with acclamations that resounded across the vega. At sight of these signals of possession the sovereigns sank upon their knees, giving thanks to God for this great triumph; the whole assembled host followed their example, and the choristers of the royal chapel broke forth into the solemn anthem of *Te Deum laudamus.*

The procession now resumed its march, with joyful alacrity to the sound of triumphant music, until they came to a small mosque, near the banks of the Xenel, and not far from the foot of the Hill of Martyrs, which edifice remains to the present day, consecrated as the hermitage of S' Sebastian. Here the sovereigns were met by the unfortunate Boabdil, accompanied by about fifty cavaliers and domestics. As he drew near he would have dismounted in token of homage, but Ferdinand prevented him. He then proffered to kiss the King's hand, but this sign of vassalage was likewise declined, whereupon, not to be outdone in magnanimity, he leaned forward, and kissed the right arm of Ferdinand. Queen Isabella also refused to receive this ceremonial of homage, and to console him under his adversity, delivered to him his son, who had remained as hostage ever since Boabdil's liberation from captivity. The Moorish monarch pressed his child to his bosom with tender emotion, and they seemed mutually endeared to each other by their misfortunes.*

He then delivered the keys of the city to King Ferdinand, with an air of mingled melancholy and resignation. "These keys," said he, "are the last reliques of the Arabian empire in Spain; thine, oh King, are our trophies, our kingdom, and our person. Such is the will of God! Receive them with the clemency thou hast promised, and which we look for at thy hands."†

King Ferdinand restrained his exultation into an air of serene magnanimity. "Doubt not our promises," replied he; "nor that thou shalt regain from our friendship the prosperity of which the fortune of war has deprived thee."

On receiving the keys, King Ferdinand handed them to the Queen, she in her turn presented them to her son Prince Juan, who delivered them to the Count de Tendilla, that brave and loyal cavalier being appointed alcayde of the city, and Captain General of the Kingdom of Granada.

Having surrendered the last symbol of power, the unfortunate Boabdil continued on towards the Alpuxarras, that he might not behold the entrance of the Christians into his capital. His devoted band of cavaliers followed him in gloomy silence; but heavy sighs burst from their bosoms, as shouts of joy and strains of triumphant music were borne on the breeze from the victorious army.

Having rejoined his family, Boabdil set forward with a heavy heart for his allotted residence, in the valley of Porchena. At two leagues' distance the cavalcade winding into the skirts of the Alpuxarras, ascended an eminence commanding the last view of Granada. As they arrived at this spot the Moors paused involuntarily to take a farewell gaze at their beloved city, which a few steps more, would shut from their sight forever. Never had it appeared so lovely in their eyes. The sunshine, so bright in that transparent climate, lit up each tower and minaret, and rested gloriously upon the crowning battlements of the Alhambra; while the vega spread its enamelled bosom of verdure below, glistening with the silver windings of the Xenel. The Moorish cavaliers gazed with a silent agony of tenderness and grief, upon that delicious abode, the scene of their loves and pleasures. While they yet

*Zurita. Anales de Aragon.
†Abarca. Anales de Aragon Rey: 30. C. 3.

looked, a light cloud of smoke burst forth from the citadel; and presently a peal of artillery, faintly heard, told that the city was taken possession of, and the throne of the Moslem Kings was lost for ever. The heart of Boabdil, softened by misfortunes and overcharged with grief, could no longer contain itself. "Allah Achbar! God is great" said he, but the words of resignation died upon his lips, and he burst into a flood of tears.

His mother, the intrepid Sultana Ayxa la Horra, was indignant at his weakness. "You do well," said she, "to weep like a woman, for what you failed to defend like a man!"

The Vizier Aben Comixa endeavoured to console his royal master. "Consider Sire," said he, "that the most signal misfortunes often render men as renowned as the most prosperous achievements, provided they sustain them with magnanimity."

The unhappy monarch, however, was not to be consoled, his tears continued to flow. "Allah Achbar!" exclaimed he. "When did misfortunes ever equal mine!"

From this circumstance the hill which is not far from Padul took the name of Feg Allah Achbar; but the point of view commanding the last prospect of Granada, is known among Spaniards by the name of *el ultimo suspiro del Moro*, or "the last sigh of the Moor."

CHAPTER C

HOW THE CASTILIAN SOVEREIGNS TOOK POSSESSION OF GRANADA.

When the Castilian sovereigns had received the keys of Granada from the hands of Boabdil el Chico, the royal army resumed its triumphant march. As it approached the gates of the city in all the pomp of courtly and chivalrous array, a procession of a different kind, came forth to meet it. This was composed of more than five hundred Christian captives, many of whom had languished for years, in Moorish dungeons. Pale and emaciated they came clanking their chains in triumph and shedding tears of joy. They were received with tenderness by the sovereigns. The King hailed them as good Spaniards; as men loyal and brave; as martyrs to the holy cause. The Queen distributed liberal relief among them with her own hands, and they passed on before the squadrons of the army, singing hymns of jubilee.*

The sovereigns did not enter the city on this day of its surrender; but

---

*Abarca. lib. sup, Zurita &c.

waited until it should be fully occupied by their troops and public tranquility ensured. The Marquis de Villena and the Count de Tendilla, with three thousand cavalry and as many infantry, marched in, and took possession accompanied by the proselyte Prince Cidi Yahye, now known by the Christian appellation of Don Pedro de Granada, who was appointed chief Alguazil of the city, and had charge of the Moorish inhabitants, and by his son the late Prince Alnager, now Don Alonzo de Granada, who was appointed admiral of the fleets. In a little while every battlement glistened with Christian helms and lances, the standard of the faith and of the realm floated from every tower, and the thundering salvos of the ordnance told that the subjugation of the city was complete.

The grandees and cavaliers now knelt, and kissed the hands of the King and Queen, and the Prince Juan, and congratulated them on the acquisition of so great a kingdom, after which the royal procession returned in state to Santa Fé.

It was on the sixth of January, the day of Kings and festival of the Epiphany that the sovereigns made their triumphal entry. The King and Queen, says the worthy Fray Antonio Agapida, looked on this occasion as more than mortal. The venerable ecclesiastics, to whose advice and zeal this glorious conquest ought in a great measure to be attributed, moved along with hearts swelling with holy exultation, but with chastened and downcast looks of edifying humility; while the hardy warriors in tossing plumes, and shining steel, seemed elevated with a stern joy, at finding themselves in possession of this object of so many toils and perils. As the streets resounded with the tramp of steed and swelling peals of music, the Moors buried themselves in the deepest recesses of their dwellings. There they bewailed in secret the fallen glory of their race, but suppressed their groans, lest they should be heard by their enemies and encrease their triumph.

The royal procession advanced to the principal mosque which had been consecrated as a cathedral. Here the sovercigns offered up prayers, and thanksgivings and the choir of the royal chapel, chanted a triumphant anthem, in which they were joined by all the courtiers and cavaliers. Nothing says Fray Antonio Agapida could exceed the thankfulness to God of the pious King Ferdinand for having enabled him to eradicate from Spain the empire and name of that accursed heathen race, and for the elevation of the cross in that city, wherein the impious doctrines of Mahomet had so long been cherished. In the fervour of his spirit he supplicated from heaven a continuance of its grace, and that this glorious triumph might be perpetuated.* The prayer of the pious monarch, was responded by the people, and even his enemies were for once convinced of his sincerity.

---

*The words of Fray Antonio Agapida, are little more than an echo of those of the worthy Jesuit father Mariana. (L: 25 C: 18.)

When the religious ceremonies were concluded the court ascended to the stately palace of the Alhambra and entered by the great gate of justice. The halls lately occupied by turbaned infidels now rustled with stately dames and Christian courtiers, who wandered with eager curiosity over this far famed palace, admiring its verdant courts and gushing fountains, its halls decorated with elegant arabesques, and storied with inscriptions, and the splendour of its gilded and brilliantly painted ceilings.

It had been a last request of the unfortunate Boabdil, and one which shewed how deeply he felt the transition of his fate, that no person might be permitted to enter or depart by the gate of the Alhambra through which he had sallied forth to surrender his capital. His request was granted; the portal was closed up, and remains so to the present day, a mute memorial of that event.* The existence of this gateway and the story connected with it, are perhaps known to few, but were identified in the researches made to verify this history. The gateway is at the bottom of a great tower at some distance from the main body of the Alhambra. The tower has been rent and ruined by gunpowder at the time when the fortress was evacuated by the French. Great masses lie around, half covered by vines and fig trees. A poor man by the name of Matteo Ximenes who lives in one of the hovels among the ruins of the Alhambra, where his family has lived for many generations, pointed out the gateway, still closed up with stones. He remembered to have heard his father and grand-father say that it had always been stopped up, and that out of it King Boabdil had gone, when he surrendered Granada. The route of the unfortunate King may be traced from thence across the garden of the convent of Los Martyres and down a ravine beyond, through a street of gipsey caves and hovels by the gate of Los Molinos, and so on to the Hermitage of S' Sebastian. None but an antiquarian, however, will be able to trace it unless aided by the humble historian of the place, Matteo Ximenes.

The Spanish sovereigns fixed their throne, in the presence chamber of the palace, so long the seat of Moorish royalty. Hither the principal inhabitants of Granada repaired to pay them homage, and kiss their hands, in token of vassallage, and their example was followed by deputies from all the towns and fortresses of the Alpuxarras, which had not hitherto submitted.

Thus terminated the war of Granada, after ten years of incessant fighting, equalling, says Fray Antonio Agapida, the far famed siege of Troy in duration, and ending like that in the capture of the city. Thus ended also, the dominion of the Moors in Spain, having endured seven hundred and seventy eight years, from the memorable defeat of Roderick the last of the Goths on the banks of the Guadalete. The authentic Agapida is uncommonly particular in fixing the epoch of this event. This great triumph of our holy Catholic

*Garibay Compend Hist. L. 40. C. 42.

faith; according to his computation took place in the beginning of January, in the year of our Lord 1492, being 3655 years from the population of Spain by the patriarch Tubal; 3797 from the general deluge; 5453 from the creation of the world according to Hebrew calculation; and in the month Rabic, in the eight hundred and ninety seventh year of the Hegira or flight of Mahomet, whom may God confound! saith the pious Agapida.

APPENDIX
FATE OF BOABDIL EL CHICO.

The chronicle of the conquest of Granada, is finished, but the reader may be desirous of knowing the subsequent fortunes of some of the principal personages. The unfortunate Boabdil retired to the valley of Porchena, where a small, but fertile, territory had been allotted him, comprising several towns, with all their rights and revenues. Great estates had likewise been bestowed on his vizier Jusef Aben Comixa and his valiant relation and friend Josef Venegas both of whom resided near him. Were it in the heart of man, in the enjoyment of present competence, to forget past splendour, Boabdil might at length have been happy. Dwelling in the bosom of a delightful valley, surrounded by obedient vassals, devoted friends, and a loving family, he might have looked back upon his past career as upon a troubled and terrific dream; and might have thanked his stars that he had at length awaked to sweet and tranquil security. But the dethroned prince could never forget that he had once been a monarch, and the remembrance of the regal splendours of Granada, made all present comforts, contemptible in his eyes. No exertions were spared by Ferdinand and Isabella, to induce him to embrace the Catholic religion, but he remained true to the faith of his fathers, and it added not a little to his humiliation to live a vassal under Christian sovereigns.

It is probable that his residence in the kingdom was equally irksome to the politic Ferdinand, who could not feel perfectly secure in his newly conquered territories, while there was one within their bounds, who might revive pretensions to the throne. A private bargain, was therefore made in the year 1496, between Ferdinand, and Jusef Aben Comixa, in which the latter as vizier of Boabdil, undertook to dispose of his master's scanty territory for eighty thousand ducats of gold. This, it is affirmed, was done without the consent or knowledge of Boabdil; but the vizier probably thought he was acting for the best. The shrewd Ferdinand does not appear to have made any question about the right of the vizier to make the sale, but paid the money with secret exultation. Jusef Aben Comixa loaded the treasure upon mules, and departed joyfully for the Alpuxarras. He spread the money in triumph before Boabdil. "Senior," said he, "I have observed that as long as you live here, you are exposed to constant peril. The Moors are rash and irritable; they may make some sudden insurrection, elevate your standard as a pretext, and thus overwhelm you and your friends, with utter ruin. I have observed, also, that you pine away with grief, being continually reminded in this country, that you were once its sovereign, but never more must hope to reign. I have put an end to these evils; your territory is sold: behold the price of it. With this gold, you may buy far greater possessions in Africa, where you may live in honour and security."

When Boabdil heard these words, he burst into a sudden transport of rage, and drawing his scymetar, would have sacrificed the officious Jusef on the spot, had not the attendants interfered, and hurried the vizier from his presence.

Boabdil was not of a vindictive spirit and his anger soon passed away. He saw that the evil was done, and he knew the spirit of the politic Ferdinand too well to hope, that he would retract the bargain. Gathering together the money, therefore, and all his jewels and precious effects, he departed with his family and household for a port where a vessel had been carefully provided by the Castilian King to transport them to Africa.

A crowd of his former subjects witnessed his embarcation. As the sails were unfurled and swelled to the breeze, and the vessel parted from the land, the spectators would fain have given him a parting cheering; but the humbled state of their once proud sovereign forced itself upon their minds, and the ominous surname of his youth rose involuntarily to their tongues. "Farewell Boabdil! Allah preserve thee *El Zogoybi!*" burst spontaneously from their lips. The unlucky appellation sank into the heart of the expatriated monarch, and tears dimmed his eyes, as the snowy summits of the mountains of Granada, gradually faded from his view.

He was received with welcome at the court of his relation Muley Ahmed, King of Fez, and resided for many years in his territories. How he passed his life, whether repining or resigned, history does not mention. The last we find recorded of him, is in the year 1536, forty four years after the surrender of Granada, when he followed the King of Fez to the field, to quell the rebellion of two brothers named Xerifes. The armies came in sight of each other on the banks of the Guadiswed at the ford of Bacuba. The river was deep, the banks were high, and broken; for three days the armies remained firing at each other across the stream, neither venturing to attempt the dangerous ford.

At length the King of Fez divided his army, into three batallions; the first

led on by his son and by Boabdil el Chico. They boldly dashed across the
ford, scrambled up the opposite bank, and attempted to keep the enemy
employed, until the other batallions should have time to cross. The rebel
army, however, attacked them with such fury that the son of the King of Fez
and several of the bravest alcaydes were slain upon the spot, multitudes
were driven back into the river, which was already crowded with passing
troops. A dreadful confusion took place; the horse trampled upon the foot;
the enemy pressed on them with fearful slaughter; those who escaped the
sword perished by the stream, the river was choked by the dead bodies of
men and horses, and by the scattered baggage of the army. In this scene of
horrible carnage, fell Boabdil, truly called el Zogoybi or the unlucky. "An
instance," says the ancient chronicler, "of the scornful caprice of fortune,
dying in defence of the kingdom of another, after wanting spirit to die in
defence of his own."*

DEATH OF THE MARQUIS OF CADIZ.

The renowned Roderigo Ponce de Leon, Marquis, Duke of Cadiz, was un-
questionably the most distinguished among the cavaliers of Spain, for his
zeal, enterprize and heroism in the great crusade of Granada. He began the
war by the capture of Alhama; he was engaged in almost every inroad and
siege of importance during its continuance, and he was present at the surrender of the capital which was the closing scene of the conquest. The renown he thus acquired was sealed by his death, which happened in the forty
eighth year of his age, almost immediately at the close of his triumphs, and
before a leaf of his laurels had time to wither. He died at his palace, in the
city of Seville, on the twenty seventh day of August 1492, but a few months
after the surrender of Granada, and of an illness caused by the exposure and
fatigues he had undergone in this memorable war. That honest chronicler,
Andrés Bernaldes, the Curate of Los Palacios, who was a contemporary of
the marquis, draws his portrait from actual knowledge and observation: He

---

*Marmol Descrip de Africa, P: 1. L: 2. C: 40 Idem Hist: reb: de los Moros, L: 1. C: 21.
Note: A portrait of Boabdil el Chico, is to be seen in the picture gallery of the Generalife.
He is represented with a mild handsome face, a fair complexion and yellow hair. His dress
is of yellow brocade, relieved with black velvet, and he has a black velvet cap, surmounted
with a crown. In the armoury of Madrid are two suits of armour said to have belonged to
him; one of solid steel with very little ornament; the helmet closed. From the proportions
of these suits of armour he must have been of full stature and vigorous form.

was universally cited, says he, as the most perfect model of chivalrous virtue of the age. He was temperate, chaste, and rigidly devout; a benignant commander, a valiant defender of his vassals, a great lover of justice, and an enemy to all flatterers, liars, robbers, traytors and poltroons. His ambition was of a lofty kind; he sought to distinguish himself and his family by heroic and resounding deeds, and to encrease the patrimony of his ancestors by the acquisition of castles, domains, vassals and other princely possessions. His recreations were all of a warlike nature, he delighted in geometry, as applied to fortifications, and spent much time and treasure in erecting and repairing fortresses. He relished music, but of a military kind; the sound of clarions and sackbuts, of drums and trumpets. Like a true cavalier he was a protector of the sex on all occasions, and an injured woman never applied to him in vain for redress. His prowess was so well known, and his courtesy to the fair, that the ladies of the court, when they accompanied the Queen to the wars, rejoiced to find themselves under his protection; for wherever his banner was displayed, the Moors dreaded to adventure. He was a faithful and devoted friend, but a formidable enemy, for he was slow to forgive and his vengeance was persevering and terrible.

The death of this good cavalier spread grief and lamentation throughout all ranks, for he was universally honoured and beloved. His relations, dependents, and companions in arms put on mourning for his loss, and so numerous were they, that half of Seville was clad in black. None, however, deplored his death more deeply and sincerely than his friend and chosen companion Don Alonzo de Aguilar.

The funereal ceremonies, were of the most solemn and sumptuous kind. The body of the marquis was arrayed in a costly shirt, a doublet of brocade, a sayo or long robe of black velvet, a marlota or Moorish tunic of brocade, that reached to the feet and scarlet stockings. His sword, superbly gilt, was girded to his side, as he used to wear it when in the field. Thus magnificently attired, the body was inclosed in a coffin which was covered with black velvet, and decorated with a cross of white damask. It was then placed on a sumptuous bier in the centre of the great hall of the palace.

Here the Duchess made great lamentation over the body of her lord, in which she was joined by her train of damsels and attendants, as well as by the pages and esquires and innumerable vassals of the marquis.

In the close of the evening just before the Ave Maria, the funeral train issued from the palace. Ten banners were borne around the bier, the particular trophies of the marquis, won from the Moors by his valour in individual enterprizes, before King Ferdinand had commenced the war of Granada. The procession was swelled by an immense train of bishops, priests and friars of different orders, together with the civil and military authorities, and all the chivalry of Seville; headed by the count of Cifuentes, at that time Intendente or commander of the city. It moved slowly and solemnly through the streets, stopping occasionally, and chanting litanies and responses. Two hundred and forty waxen tapers shed a light like the day about the bier. The balconies and windows were crowded with ladies who shed tears, as the funeral train passed by, while the women of the lower classes were loud in their lamentations, as if bewailing the loss of a father or a brother. On approaching the Convent of S' Augustine, the monks came forth with the cross and tapers, and eight censers, and conducted the body into the church where it lay in state, until all the vigils were performed, by the different orders, after which it was deposited in the family tomb of the Ponces in the same church, and the ten banners were suspended over the sepulchre.*

The tomb of the valiant Roderigo Ponce de Leon, with his banners mouldering above it, remained for ages an object of veneration, with all who had read or heard of his virtues and achievements. In the year 1810, however, the chapel was sacked by the French, its altars overturned, and the sepulchres of the family of the Ponces shattered to pieces. The present Duchess of Benavente, the worthy descendant of this illustrious and heroic line, has since piously collected the ashes of her ancestors, restored the altar and repaired the chapel; the sepulchres however, were utterly destroyed; an inscription in gold letters on the wall of the chapel, to the right of the altar, is all that denotes the place of sepulture of the brave Roderigo Ponce de Leon.

THE LEGEND OF THE DEATH OF
DON ALONZO DE AGUILAR.

To such as feel an interest in the fortunes of the valiant Don Alonzo de Aguilar, the chosen friend and companion in arms of Ponce de Leon, Marquis of Cadiz, and one of the most distinguished heroes of the war of Granada, a few particulars of his remarkable fate will not be unacceptable. They are found among the manuscripts of the worthy Padre Fray Antonio Agapida and appear to have been appended to his chronicle.

For several years after the conquest of Granada, the country remained feverish and unquiet. The zealous efforts of the Catholic clergy to effect the conversion of the infidels, and the pious coercion used for that purpose by government, exasperated the stubborn Moors of the mountains. Several zealous missionaries were maltreated and in the town of Dayrin two of them

*Cura de Los Palacios C: 104.

were seized and exhorted, with many menaces, to embrace the Moslem faith; on their resolutely refusing, they were killed with staffs and stones, by the Moorish women and children, and their bodies burnt to ashes.*

Upon this event a body of Christian cavaliers assembled in Andalusia, to the number of eight hundred, and, without waiting for orders from the King, revenged the death of these martyrs, by plundering and laying waste the Moorish towns and villages. The Moors fled to the mountains, and their cause was espoused by many of their nation, who inhabited those rugged regions. The storm of rebellion began to gather and mutter its thunders in the Alpuxarras. They were echoed from the Serrania of Ronda, ever ready for rebellion; but the strongest hold of the insurgents was in the Sierra Vermeja, or chain of Red Mountains, which lie near the sea, and whose savage rocks and precipices may be seen from Gibraltar.

When King Ferdinand heard of these tumults, he issued a proclamation ordering all the Moors of the insurgent regions to leave them within ten days, and repair to Castile; giving secret instructions, however, that those who should voluntarily embrace the Christian faith might be permitted to remain. At the same time, he ordered Don Alonzo de Aguilar, and the Counts of Ureña and Cifuentes to march against the rebels.

Don Alonzo de Aguilar was at Cordova when he received the commands of the King. "What force is allotted us for this expedition?" said he. On being told, he perceived that the number of troops was far from adequate. "When a man is dead," said he, "we send four men into his house to bring forth the body. We are now sent to chastise these Moors who are alive, vigorous, in open rebellion, and ensconced in their castles; yet they do not give us man to man." These words of the brave Alonzo de Aguilar were afterwards frequently repeated; but, though he saw the desperate nature of the enterprize, he did not hesitate to undertake it.

Don Alonzo was at that time in the fifty first year of his age. He was a veteran warrior, in whom the fire of youth was yet unquenched, though tempered by experience. The greater part of his life had been passed in the camp and in the field until danger was as his natural element. His muscular frame had acquired the firmness of iron without the rigidity of age. His armour and weapons seemed to have become a part of his nature, and he sat like a man of steel on his powerful war horse.

He took with him, on this expedition, his son Don Pedro de Cordova, a youth of bold and generous spirit, in the freshness of his days, and armed and arrayed with all the bravery of a young Spanish cavalier. When the populace of Cordova beheld the veteran father, the warrior of a thousand battles, leading forth his youthful son to the field, they bethought themselves of the

*Cura de Los Palacios C. 165.

family appellation. "Behold," cried they, "the Eagle teaching his young to fly! Long live the valiant line of Aguilar!"*

The prowess of Don Alonzo and of his companions in arms, was renowned throughout the Moorish towns; at their approach, therefore, numbers of the Moors submitted and hastened to Ronda to embrace Christianity. Among the mountaineers, however, there were many of the Gandules, a fierce tribe from Africa, too proud of spirit to bend their necks to the yoke. At their head was a Moor named El Feri of Ben Estepar, renowned for strength and courage. At his instigations his followers gathered together their families and most precious effects, placed them on mules, and driving before them their flocks and herds, abandoned their valleys and retired up the craggy passes of the Sierra Vermeja. On the summit was a fertile plain, surrounded by rocks and precipices, which formed a natural fortress. Here El Feri placed all the women and children and all the property. By his orders his followers piled great stones on the rocks and cliffs which commanded the defiles and the steep sides of the mountain, and prepared to defend every pass that led to his place of refuge.

The Christian commanders arrived and pitched their camp before the town of Monarda, a strong place, curiously fortified, and situated at the foot of the highest part of the Sierra Vermeja. Here they remained for several days, unable to compel a surrender. They were separated from the skirt of the mountain by a deep barranco or ravine, at the bottom of which flowed a small stream. The Moors, commanded by El Feri, drew down from their mountain height and remained on the opposite side of the brook to defend a pass which led up to their strong hold.

One afternoon a number of Christian soldiers, in mere bravado, seized a banner, crossed the brook and scrambling up the opposite bank, attacked the Moors. They were followed by numbers of their companions, some in aid, some in emulation, but most in hope of booty. A sharp action ensued on the mountain side. The Moors were greatly superior in number and had the vantage ground. When the counts of Ureña and Cifuentes beheld this skirmish, they asked Don Alonzo de Aguilar his opinion. "My opinion," said he, "was given at Cordova and remains the same; this is a desperate enterprize; however, the Moors are at hand, and if they suspect weakness in us, it will encrease their courage and our peril. Forward then to the attack, and I trust in God we shall gain a victory." So saying he led his troops into the battle.†

On the skirts of the mountain were several level places like terraces; here the Christians pressed valiantly upon the Moors and had the advantage; but the latter retreated to the steep and craggy heights, from whence they hurled darts and overturned rocks upon their assailants. They defended

*Aguilar. The Spanish for Eagle.
†Bleda L 5. C 26.

their passes and defiles with ferocious valour, but were driven from height to height, until they reached the plain on the summit of the mountain, where their wives and children were sheltered. Here they would have made a stand; but Alonzo de Aguilar with his son Don Pedro charged upon them at the head of three hundred men and put them to flight with dreadful carnage. While they were pursuing the flying enemy, the rest of the army, thinking the victory achieved, dispersed themselves over the little plain in search of plunder. They pursued the shrieking females, tearing off their necklaces, bracelets and anklets of gold, and they found so much treasure of various kinds collected in this spot, that they threw by their armour and weapons to load themselves with booty.

Evening was closing: the Christians, intent upon spoil, had ceased to pursue the Moors, and the latter were arrested in their flight by the cries of their wives & children. Their fierce leader El Feri threw himself before them. "Friends. Soldiers," cried he. "Whither do you fly? whither can you seek refuge, where the enemy cannot follow you? Your wives, your children are behind you, turn and defend them; you have no chance for safety but from the weapons in your hands."

The Moors turned at his words. They beheld the Christians scattered about the plain many of them without armour and all encumbered with spoil. "Now is the time," shouted El Feri, "charge upon them while laden with your plunder. I will open a path for you!" He rushed to the attack, followed by his Moors with shouts and cries that echoed through the mountains. The scattered Christians were seized with panic and throwing down their booty began to fly in all directions. Don Alonzo de Aguilar advanced his banner and endeavoured to rally them. Finding his horse of no avail in these rocky heights, he dismounted and caused his men to do the same; he had a small band of tried followers with which he opposed a bold front to the Moors, calling on the scattered troops to rally in the rear.

Night had completely closed. It prevented the Moors from seeing the smallness of the force with which they were contending, and Don Alonzo and his cavaliers dealt their blows so vigorously that aided by the darkness they seemed multiplied to ten times their number. Unfortunately a small cask of gun powder blew up near to the scene of action. It shed a momentary, but brilliant light over all the plain and on every rock and cliff. The Moors beheld, with surprize, that they were opposed by a mere handful of men and that the greater part of the Christians were flying from the field. They put up loud shouts of triumph. While some continued the conflict with redoubled ardour, others pursued the fugitives, hurling after them stones and darts and discharging showers of arrows. Many of the Christians in their terror, and their ignorance of the mountains, rushed headlong from the brinks of precipices and were dashed in pieces.

Don Alonzo de Aguilar still maintained his ground; but while some of the

Moors assailed him in front, others galled him with all kinds of missiles from the impending cliffs. Some of the cavaliers, seeing the hopeless nature of the conflict, proposed that they should abandon the height and retreat down the mountain. "No," said Don Alonzo proudly, "never did the banner of the house of Aguilar retreat one foot in the field of battle." He had scarcely uttered these words when his son Don Pedro was stretched at his feet. A stone hurled from a cliff had struck out two of his teeth and a lance passed quivering through his thigh. The youth attempted to rise, and, with one knee on the ground, to fight by the side of his father. Don Alonzo, finding him wounded urged him to quit the field. "Fly my son," said he. "Let us not put every thing at venture upon one hazard; conduct thyself as a good Christian and live to comfort and honour thy mother."

Don Pedro still refused to leave his side, whereupon Don Alonzo ordered several of his followers to bear him off by force. His friend Don Francisco Alvarez of Cordova, taking him in his arms, conveyed him to the quarters of the Count of Ureña; who had halted on the height, at some distance from the scene of battle, for the purpose of rallying and succouring the fugitives. Almost at the same moment the count beheld his own son, Don Pedro Giron, brought in grievously wounded.

In the mean time Don Alonzo, with two hundred cavaliers, maintained the unequal contest. Surrounded by foes, they fell, one after another, like so many noble stags encircled by the hunters. Don Alonzo was the last survivor. He was without horse and almost without armour; his corselet unlaced and his bosom gashed with wounds. Still he kept a brave front towards the enemy, and, retiring between two rocks, defended himself with such valour that the slain lay in a heap before him.

He was assailed in this retreat by a Moor of surpassing strength and fierceness. The contest was for some time doubtful; but Don Alonzo received a wound in the head and another in the breast that made him stagger. Closing and grappling with his foe they had a desperate struggle, until the Christian cavalier, exhausted by his wounds fell upon his back. He still retained his grasp upon his enemy. "Think not," cried he, "thou hast an easy prize; know that I am Don Alonzo, he of Aguilar!"—"If thou art Don Alonzo," replied the Moor, "know that I am El Feri of Ben Estepar." They continued their deadly struggle and both drew their daggers; but Don Alonzo was exhausted by seven ghastly wounds; while he was yet struggling, his heroic soul departed from his body, and he expired in the grasp of the Moor.

Thus fell Alonzo de Aguilar the mirror of Andalusian chivalry; one of the most powerful grandees of Spain for person, blood, estate and office. For forty years he had waged successful wars upon the Moors: In childhood by his household and retainers, in manhood by the prowess of his arm, and the wisdom and valour of his spirit. His pennon had always been foremost in danger; he had been general of armies, vice roy of Andalusia, and the author

of glorious enterprizes, in which Kings were vanquished and mighty alcaydes and warriors laid low. He had slain many Moslem chiefs with his own
arm, and among others the renowned Ali Atar of Loxa, fighting foot to foot,
on the banks of the Xenel. His judgement, discretion, magnanimity and
justice vied with his prowess. He was the fifth lord of his warlike house that
fell in battle with the Moors. His soul, observes the worthy Padre Abarca,
"it is believed ascended to heaven to receive the reward of so Christian a
captain; for that very day he had armed himself with the sacraments of
confession and communion."*

The Moors, elated with their success, pursued the fugitive Christians
down the defiles and sides of the mountains. It was with the utmost difficulty
that the Count de Ureña could bring off a remnant of his forces from that
disastrous height. Fortunately on the lower slope of the mountain, they
found the rear guard of the army, led by the Count de Cifuentes who had
crossed the brook and the ravine to come to their assistance. As the fugitives
came flying in headlong terror down the mountain it was with difficulty the
count kept his own troops from giving way in panic, and retreating in confusion across the brook. He succeeded, however, in maintaining order; in
rallying the fugitives, and checking the fury of the Moors. Then taking his
station on a rocky eminence he maintained his post until morning; sometimes sustaining violent attacks, at other times rushing forth and making
assaults upon the enemy. When morning dawned the Moors ceased to combat and drew up to the summit of the mountain.

It was then that the Christians had time to breathe and to ascertain the
dreadful loss they had sustained. Among the many valiant cavaliers who had
fallen was Don Francisco Ramirez of Madrid, who had been captain general
of artillery throughout the war of Granada, and had contributed greatly by
his valour and ingenuity to that renowned conquest. But all other griefs and
cares were forgotten in anxiety for the fate of Don Alonzo de Aguilar. His
son Don Pedro de Cordova, had been brought off with great difficulty from
the battle, and afterwards lived to be Marquis of Priego; but of Don Alonzo
nothing was known, except that he was left with a handful of cavaliers, fighting valiantly against an overwhelming force. As the rising sun lighted up the
red cliffs of the mountains, the soldiers watched with anxious eyes, if per
chance his pennon might be descried, fluttering from any precipice or defile,
but nothing of the kind was to be seen. The trumpet call was repeatedly
sounded, but empty echoes alone replied. A silence reigned about the
mountain summit, which shewed that the deadly strife was over. Now and
then a wounded warrior came dragging his feeble steps from among the
clefts and rocks; but, on being questioned, he shook his head mournfully,
and could tell nothing of the fate of his commander.

*Abarca Anales de Aragon Rey XXX Cap II.

The tidings of this disastrous defeat, and of the perilous situation of the survivors, reached King Ferdinand at Granada. He immediately marched at the head of all the chivalry of his court, to the mountains of Ronda. His presence, with a powerful force, soon put an end to the rebellion. A part of the Moors were suffered to ransom themselves, and to embark for Africa; others were made to embrace Christianity; and those of the town where the Christian missionaries had been massacred, were sold as slaves. From the conquered Moors the mournful but heroic end of Don Alonzo de Aguilar was ascertained. On the morning after the battle when the Moors came to strip and bury the dead, the body of Don Alonzo was found among those of more than two hundred of his followers, many of them alcaydes and cavaliers of distinction. Though the person of Don Alonzo was well known to the Moors, being so distinguished among them, both in peace and war, yet it was so covered and disfigured with wounds, that it could with difficulty be recognized. They preserved it with great care, and, on making their submission, delivered it up to King Ferdinand. It was conveyed with great state to Cordova, amidst the tears and lamentations of all Andalusia. When the funeral train entered Cordova, and the inhabitants saw the coffin, containing the remains of their favorite hero, and the war horse, led in mournful trappings, on which they had so lately seen him sally forth from their gates, there was a general burst of grief throughout the city. The body was interred with great pomp and solemnity in the church of S' Hypolito. Many years afterwards his grand daughter Doña Catalina of Aguilar and Cordova, Marchioness of Priego, caused his tomb to be altered. On examining the body, the head of a lance was found among the bones, received, without doubt, among the wounds of his last mortal combat. The name of this accomplished and Christian cavalier, has ever remained a popular theme of the chronicler and poet; and is endeared to the public memory by many of the historical ballads and songs of his country. For a long time the people of Cordova were indignant at the brave Count de Ureña, who they thought had abandoned Don Alonzo in his extremity; but the Castilian monarch acquitted him of all charge of the kind, and continued him in honour and office. It was proved that neither he nor his people could succour Don Alonzo, or even know of his peril, from the darkness of the night. There is a mournful little Spanish ballad or romance, which breathes the public grief on this occasion, and the populace on the return of the count de Ureña to Cordova, assailed him with one of its plaintive and reproachful verses

Count Ureña! Count Ureña!
Tell us, where is Don Alonzo!
(Decid Conde de Ureña
Don Alonzo donde queda?*)

*Bleda L 5. C 26—

EDITORIAL APPENDIX

Textual Commentary,
Discussions, and Lists by
Miriam J. Shillingsburg

TEXTUAL COMMENTARY

As detailed in the "Introduction" by Earl N. Harbert above, securing copyright protection in both England and America made it necessary for Irving to provide two copies of his manuscript, one for his American publisher and one for his English publisher.[1] Consequently, the English and American first editions (1829) were printed independently of each other from these two surviving manuscripts, which provide some 2,200 pages of holograph/scribal text. Furthermore, there are an Author's Revised Edition (ARE) published in 1850, a host of reprints of both the first American edition and the ARE, and continental editions derived from the English.

MANUSCRIPTS

The more than 1,025 pages of the American manuscript are housed at the Pierpont Morgan Library in New York City, while the nearly 1,200-page English manuscript resides in the original publisher's archive at 50 Albemarle Street, London. In addition, 16 leaves belong to the Irving Papers in the Berg collection of the New York Public Library, and the Barrett Collection at the University of Virginia houses some 63 pages of manuscript and marked sheets of the London 1829 edition. No other sheets, drafts, or notes are known to exist for this work.[2]

All known manuscripts have been examined by the present editor; four other scholars aided in collating and checking transcriptions of those texts. Apparently no proof sheets have survived, although collation of each manuscript with its respective printed version indicates that alterations, including substantives, were made, apparently in proof stage. Since Irving himself remained in Spain, he did not proofread either the Philadelphia or the London edition.[3] Therefore, both those texts have been judged non-authorial, although collation shows that occasional corrections needed in the manuscript were first made by editors or proofreaders of these printed versions.

The Morgan manuscript is made up of about 1025 leaves bound by stitching into five volumes and preserved in the Morgan Library. Generally, the Morgan sheets comprise the earliest extant form of the work; many of its pages resemble a first draft although portions of this manuscript are "cleaner"—that is, less revised—than corresponding portions of the English manuscript. Whether there was a draft prior to this Morgan manuscript is unknown, but, from the evidence of the sheets themselves, it seems doubtful that a previous form existed for very much of the work. This manuscript is entirely in Irving's handwriting, except for notations infrequently made and sometimes initialed by his brother Ebenezer Irving, who acted as his American agent and editor, or others at the Philadelphia printing house of Carey, Lea, and Carey. Such notations are clearly in a different hand from Irving's and usually only clarify some spelling or other detail of form. For example, a string of letters which looks like "indomptible" is clarified between the lines by an editor to read "indomitable"—as good a reading as can be determined. Likewise, the editor correctly interlined "Roderigo" over "Rodrigez" and made many similar clarifications. However, the same hand also altered Irving's spellings and punctuation as discussed below, and several times inserted or changed a word apparently for clarification, as "Fearing ↑ that ↓ the king", "marched <up> ↑ into ↓ the . . . defile", or "deep ↑ ly ↓ ".

Ebenezer Irving is the source of the following correction—for someone with the initials E.I. pencilled the correct "Guadix" into the Morgan text, with the notation: "Should not this be Guadix?" In ink, then, an editor interlined "Guadix;" and lined through "Baza," which Washington Irving had erroneously written and which the Spanish scribe producing the second manuscript had already copied. Besides such evidence and an occasional pencilled "copied" in Irving's handwriting, the degree and extent of authorial revision occurring in this draft testifies to an author at work, not just a scrivener, in the writing of those pages.

The Murray manuscript, maintained by the house of John Murray, Irving's London publisher, was copied from the Morgan manuscript by Washington Irving himself and at least six other scribes, apparently Spanish-speaking, some of whom seem to have known little English. Examination of this manuscript confirms that Irving himself read carefully and marked all scribal pages with the possible exception of Chapters 34–35, and some twenty pages scattered throughout the book. Irving may have read those sheets also, but if he did, he made no corrections or clarifications in his own handwriting.

In general, the Murray manuscript is a very readable copy (though there are scribal errors in it) and is extremely reliable in all accidentals except certain spellings. In the language of classical textual criticism, the Murray manuscript is "sincere," not "sophisticated"; its errors are naive and therefore readily identifiable. After the Murray manuscript was copied from it, the Morgan manuscript underwent a "sophistication" by the publisher's editor that makes recovery of authorial accidentals virtually impossible.

The Morgan (American) manuscript represents the author's working draft, his "foul" papers, a still amorphous and fluid version of the work. Evidence of his moving chapters and pages within chapters is abundant: deletions, additions, strikeovers, substitutions, false starts and a host of other blemishes are readily seen. Multiple layers of pagination—as many as four in some instances—indicate that Irving kept moving around portions which he had composed. Sometimes he must have been writing, not on the level of the entire work, but on the level of the chapter, deciding later where it should be placed in the book. This is particularly apparent in Chapters 42, 43, 66–71, and 75–82. In dozens of places Irving literally "cut out" a portion which he was writing, moved it to another place, and pasted it in, often making a sheet of roughly legal size in a packet of letter-size pages. Other portions show the opposite evidence, passages prematurely shortened by the author's folding and ripping the sheet in two.

The Murray manuscript shows almost no evidence of the processes of composition. By the time the amanuensis was given the papers to copy, Irving was nearly finished with them. Not quite, in some instances, for he sometimes changed his mind, struck out a short portion, and rewrote it. Such revisions occur most often, not surprisingly, when Irving himself is the copyist. There he is examining his work one last time, making corrections, additions, and deletions, perhaps changing the earlier draft to coincide. Examples of such changes abound throughout the work such as one place in which Irving paid special attention to the voice of his verbs. The Morgan draft uses the active voice while the copy has the passive: "They kept up a heavy fire from their ordnance" in the Morgan version is "A heavy fire was kept up from their ordnance" in the Murray. However, it seems that he may have originally used the passive voice, transcribed it into the English copy, and *then* changed to the active—for the American draft used a pasted-on revision of a dozen lines at that point. (Morgan 551, Murray 659) Similarly, Irving transposed two adverbial expressions: the first version reads "they persisted a little longer in their defence. . ." and the copied portion says "they persisted in their defence a little longer . . ." In another instance, Irving first wrote: "several banks of oars, displaying the standard of the crescent, but likewise a white flag in sign of amity came one day into the harbour." When he copied it over, he wrote: "several banks of oars, came one day into the harbour of Malaga, displaying the standard of the crescent but likewise a white flag the sign of amity." (Morgan 585, Murray 694)

In some instances the same reading is deleted from both manuscripts, making the method of revision rather explicit. For example, at Murray 446 and Morgan 344 Irving had written: "A large part of their force" and he copied the same words into the Murray. Rethinking, he deleted "large" in both copies and proceeded. About a dozen lines later he wrote: "and attacked the Christians with sword and lance, so suddenly". In the Murray he copied as far as "with", then evidently struck it out, returned to the first draft and deleted the entire phrase "with sword and lance," leaving "and attacked so suddenly" which was then completed in the Murray copy. Sometimes he forgot to go back and change the original version, as when the Morgan's "entrance to Granada" erroneously became the "entrance to Alhama" in the Murray.

In this same chapter (31) where Irving is his own secretary, he evidently

decided that several long passages should be completely revised. He therefore began to rewrite in the Murray version, and the passages show the
evidence of compositional changes not usual in that text. Apparently he discarded the sheets from the Morgan version, substituting in their place three
pages (338-340) for what had previously been four; he then salvaged the
(former) fifth and sixth pages, substituted the seventh, and continued. This
evidence is clear, not only from the amount of revision in the Murray copy
and the lack of revision in the Morgan, but from the obvious renumbering
of sheets and the squeezing-in of lines at the bottom of page 340 and top of
341 in the Morgan draft. Other obvious extensive revision in the Murray
occurs in chapters 32 and 33, in chapters 68–70, and especially in chapter
23, where Irving ripped off the bottom of Morgan 257, substituting a series
numbered 1,2, with the notation that it was to be inserted in chapter 23.
And in a few places Irving inserted material in margins while he proofed the
scribal copy. Often this material was not added to the author's draft.

Examination of the Morgan manuscript also reveals editorial or perhaps
publisher's preference; for example, Irving's characteristic so-called British
spellings are changed to the "American" form as in *neighbour, favour, succour, saviour*, etc. These become *neighbor, favor, succor, savior*, etc. by a
vertical editorial "delete" mark through the "u". Irving's use of *horror, terror, error*, and *warrior* are, however, left consistently after the "American"
fashion. Likewise, Irving's idiosyncratic spelling of *harrass, gallopping, pavillion*, and other words, is emended by the same editorial stroke through
the second occurrence of the doubled letter to produce *harass, galloping,
and pavilion*. The author is, however, changeable in some spellings: *pomegranate, pomegranite, battalion*, and *batallion*, to name only a few. But his
nearly consistent use of *sovreign, disasterous, scymetar*, and *caparaisoned*,
along with his perversely consistent misspelling of *council* for *counsel* are
also corrected in the manuscript by an editor or compositor.

Preliminary sight collation of the existing copy edited Morgan manuscript
with the Murray manuscript also revealed extensive changes in punctuation
made in the Morgan manuscript, apparently after the Murray was copied
from it. These changes represent thousands of added (and superfluous) commas, the altering of Irving's commas to semicolons or dashes, the addition
of hundreds of quotation marks including proper corrections as well as the
improper alteration of Irving's correct ones, and the almost consistent raising
of the author's commas to parentheses around the parenthetical expression,
"says Fray Antonio Agapida." From the beginning these changes were suspected of being the work of the American publisher's editor or Ebenezer
Irving because in thousands of instances the pen tip or ink color differed
slightly from Irving's; yet they might have been his own corrections made
during re-reading. The suspicion that the changes represent another hand

proved a certainty with the discovery of the sixteen leaves in the Berg Collection.

Apparently, the Berg fragment was intended to belong with the manuscript copy to be sent to John Murray in London. However, it must have been inadvertently included along with the American text; thus, Ebenezer Irving received two copies of chapters 34 and 35 while Colonel Aspinwall, Irving's London agent, received no copy of those chapters. Frantic letter-writing between the Colonel and the author occurred, with Irving requesting a summary of events to that point, then reconstructing the missing chapters from memory and—evidently—from a few notes, by dictating to his scribe.[4] Meanwhile, Ebenezer Irving must have laid aside the duplicate chapters, remarkably clean and in Irving's own hand. They subsequently disappeared, resurfacing in 1940 when they became a part of a larger purchase by the Berg Collection.

The Berg manuscript containing all but one leaf of the missing chapters 34 and 35 confirmed early suspicions about the unreliability of the accidentals in the presently existing Morgan holograph. Several categories of possibly editorial changes in the Morgan had to be reconsidered, for the fragment is apparently untouched by any reader/editor save Washington Irving acting as his own copyist. To be specific, in the Morgan manuscript it appeared that Irving had revised two sentences into a single compound sentence by changing the period to either a colon or semicolon and lowering the following capital letter. On Morgan p. 378 the text shows "their fate: <T> ↑ t ↓ idings" and on p. 381 a series of revisions had left the ambiguous reading "my request; The jewel". Yet in both these instances and many more the holograph Berg fragment was perfectly clear: a period preceded the beginning of a new sentence. The clear-cut Irving accidentals in these instances cast considerable doubt on the authority of the thousands of similar changes formerly believed to be his. Could a scholar "restore" Irving's simpler sentence structures throughout a thousand pages on the basis of sixteen leaves? Separating with any certainty Irving's own corrections from his editor's interventions, even with the new evidence of the Berg pages, was literally impossible. It is difficult to overemphasize the importance of the Berg fragment. Its pristine condition presents an eloquent contrast to the editorial tamperings in the Morgan manuscript.

Irving "proofread" the scribal copy, making the kinds of corrections outlined below. Apparently he wrote the Morgan manuscript without chapter titles, giving it piecemeal to a copyist when he considered the portions finished. Although sometimes Irving entitled the Murray chapters first, it was usually the Morgan first (but both were entitled late), for in the first sixty-five chapters all but seven Murray titles are in Irving's writing even when the text itself was copied by a clerk. Titles provide a synopsis or argument of the chapter which would more easily have been made immediately after re-reading than during composition; furthermore, several titles and chapter numbers are obviously squeezed into a narrow top margin in the Morgan manuscript, as if an afterthought.

Pagination in both manuscripts is in Irving's hand, and both manuscripts show several layers of re-pagination, as well as of re-chaptering in the Morgan especially from Chapter 70 to the end. The eighteen pages of Chapters 49–51 (pages 629–647) are missing from the Murray. Page 16 (between pages numbered 15 and 17) and about a dozen lines between consecutively numbered 23 and 24 are missing not only from the English manuscript but also from the London book set from it. About a dozen lines are missing from between the consecutively-numbered pages 737 and 738 and between first pages 793 and 794 of the English manuscript (although they appear in the London book). The manuscript contains leaves numbered 1–15, 17–628, 646–799, 780–1122. Duplicate numbers 780–799 indicate the probable late addition of material occurring in Chapters 68–70 (corresponding with the first-numbered pages 786–799) after the copyist had written and numbered the sheets of the second pages 780–799. Authorial substitution of two lines and the dozen lines missing between the consecutively numbered first pages 793 and 794 in the Murray, as well as the Morgan manuscript's noticeable change of paper, several re-paginations and re-chapterings, beginning with chapter 66 and extending through chapter 79 attest to the fact that although the author had given the matter to his scribe, he continued to shuffle pages. After Chapter 80 he often composed in two-chapter units, lettering the units a–h. The Morgan contains pages 1–195, 197–284, [5], 285–393, 395–720, [721 misnumbered 5], [722 misnumbered 721], [723 missing], 724–801, [1–12], 805–824, [1–2], 825–827, [1], 828–971, [1], 972–1014. Only pages 196 (the last paragraph of Chapter 16, also missing from the Philadelphia), 396 (the last page in packet two), and page 723 (eight lines at the end of chapter 72) are actually missing. It has two sheets numbered 114, 216, 266, 421, and page 734 is bound out of order.[5] The evidence of the paper itself and the kinds of revisions suggest that chapters 42–43 were among the earliest-written portions; chapters 66–71, also on especially small paper with wide margins, might have been very early writings, inserted at a later moment more appropriate for the siege and fall of Baza.

Washington Irving's personal examination of what his scribes had written resulted in three general categories of notations in the Murray manuscript, giving the author's approval to the manuscript for whose printed version he did not—apparently—read proof. 1) He traced or corrected letters or punctuation which seemed ambiguous, or added a few marks—notably quotations. 2) He occasionally filled in words left blank by a scribe who could not read his writing or whose English was not sufficient to determine readings from context; this he apparently did without recourse to the Morgan draft, for variant words are sometimes introduced at these points. 3) Occasionally, he decided to rewrite a passage, usually revising the corresponding portion in the Morgan manuscript; several times, however, the rewriting was so extensive that he had to go back and insert by paste-up several pages into the Morgan manuscript. In several other portions he apparently re-wrote in the Murray and re-copied into the Morgan although the evidence is usually not so clear as in chapters 23, 32, 33, and 52–54, discussed above.

The use of Spanish scribes was particularly fortunate for sorting out details of form. Their work produced an extremely faithful—though occasionally ludicrously nonsensical—copy with almost no "improvements" of the kind the Philadelphia editor made in the Morgan manuscript. The scribes simply did not change Washington Irving's spellings or punctuation of English. Of the six copyists besides Irving, only one shows any fluency in English. One, it appears, went over the work of a junior, or apprentice, scribe in chapter 44, but so also did the author. Another scribe seems to have previously copied German, for he superfluously capitalizes nouns, and at one place he wrote *angst* which Washington Irving restored to *anger*. Scribal idiosyncrasies often correspond with handwriting changes and include changes in -our spellings, dashes to fill out short lines, and erratic capital letters. When Irving uses Spanish names, one scribe is likely to correct the spelling; when he quotes an old Spanish historian, this scribe apparently corrects or modernizes the spellings, changing *Alpuxarra* to *Alpujarra* or *Cordova* to *Cordoba*. In contrast, the Americans edited little in the Spanish portions.

These two manuscripts represent the setting copy of the two first editions of *Granada*: the Carey, Lea, and Carey (Philadelphia, 1829) and the J. Murray (London, 1829). However, since Irving had no hand in proofreading either edition, and since collation between the books and their respective setting copy shows that both are heavily edited (the Philadelphia on the manuscript itself, and the London apparently in the type-setting or type-correction stage), both are considered without authority.

The manuscript existing at the University of Virginia seems to be an early revision of the London 1829 text probably intended for publication at some future time. However, the twenty-six handwritten changes and additions were never incorporated into the 1850 ARE, nor was the English edition used as setting copy for that edition. The evidence of those sheets, fifty-two printed passages interspersed with twenty-six handwritten sections, comprising about 44 pages, sheds light on what must have been the working method for the revision of the ARE. The other three holograph sheets at Virginia are the revised introduction and two initial paragraphs for the London edition. Unlike the Morgan manuscript, but like the Berg fragment, they are unedited.

THE PHILADELPHIA EDITION

In general the Philadelphia edition is a faithful reproduction—house-styled and corrected to be sure—of the copy edited Morgan manuscript. Some substantive changes occurred, perhaps in proofreading, the evidence of which is now lost. But the house of Carey did only what nineteenth-century authors seem to have expected printers to do with manuscripts. The footnotes to historical sources, used throughout the text, are heavily styled, apparently in the typesetting process, since they are seldom actually marked on the manuscript with discernible copy editor's symbols. Similarly Irving's confusion of "ie" and "ei" is corrected in the printed version. As the compositor entered Volume II, he had learned what he was expected to do with "-our", certain doubled letters, "en-" prefixes, and "-ize" suffixes. The editor ceased to mark them in the copy; yet the printer maintained the consistency established earlier. Collation shows that the printers were accurate in deciphering Irving's words and, in general, the punctuation existing in the manuscript. However, there are numbers of places in which there was silent editorial tampering other than "correction" and simple house styling.

For example, the Philadelphia book shows *greeted* while both manuscripts and the London edition show *embraced*; Philadelphia reads "arrayed" where the other three read "arranged". Philadelphia correctly uses *whom* when the other three use *who*; and Philadelphia has *frustrated* for *intercepted* in all other versions. Philadelphia incorrectly uses *vanished* where the others read *vanquished,* and *the* for *these, while above, there beetled* for *while above them beetled, sunk* for *sank* and so forth. Some of these variants may be attributed to printer's oversight, others to a proofreader, but positive evidence of copy editing word changes occurs also. For instance, the editor revised "be made" into "have been made", "the mystic . . . terms" to "these mystic . . . terms", "all hours of day" into "all hours of the day", and other changes which are printed in the Philadelphia edition but which do not appear in either the London manuscript or book. Since there is no evidence to suggest that these Philadelphia readings have any authority, there is no need to cite further examples of the American editor's preferences.

THE LONDON EDITION

Although compositors' stints marked on the pages prove it was setting copy, the Murray manuscript shows only the most insignificant evidence of possible editorial tampering (occurring when a hand in addition to Irving's marked chapters 44–45). Occasionally another hand offered an alternative word (interlined in pencil) without cancelling Irving's reading, and these suggested changes were usually employed in print. Obvious orthographic errors (such as the restoration to British -our spellings from some scribes'

-or's) are corrected sometime between manuscript and print. Minor expressions are emended apparently in proofreading for no changes appear on the manuscript itself. "Since that disasterous" becomes "From the period of that disastrous"; "most correct" becomes "correct"; "careful of his brother" becomes "watchful over the health of his brother"; "the attentions" changes to "the assiduous attentions"; "had not been removed here" becomes "had not been here", and on and on. The breadth of emendation almost makes one believe Irving must have read proofs. But his continued residence in Spain and the complete absence of external evidence precludes this inference. Moreover, though Irving complimented the book's appearance, he was also furious that his name was attached to the title page of a work which he intended to assign to the worthy Fray Antonio Agapida, the cross between an experiment in historical fiction and a practical joke.[6] This edition is without authority in substantives although its accidentals are less emended than the Morgan manuscript's.

The Murray edition was the source of another European edition in two issues without permission. The Galignani 1829 *Granada* was set from the London in a line-for-line (but not page-for-page) resetting of type. The Baudry (1829) is from the same typesetting (except for title pages) including the same misnumbering of pages.[7]

AUTHOR'S REVISED EDITION

Only one printed text of the work has independent authority: the Author's Revised Edition (ARE) (New York: G. P. Putnam, 1850), which was also issued without change in the same year by J. Murray in London, and for the rest of Irving's life by Putnam in America. For once, Murray apparently did not publish a separate London impression but simply sold Putnam's American impression. The revised edition is composed, apparently, of a combination of new material, revised paste-up, marginal amendment, and simple resetting of the Philadelphia (1829) edition. The ARE is authoritative in most substantives, but the author was indifferent to the formal matters of punctuation, allowing that which had been used in the heavily-styled American first edition to stand for his revised work. Although extensive revision occurred in the addition of the "Note To The Revised Edition," in the "Introduction," and in some portions of the text itself, collation shows indisputably that Irving tired of such revision after chapter 3, reverting to cosmetic changes, adding material at the ends of paragraphs or chapters, and refining footnote references until the last five chapters. Large changes occur in the addition of two incidents—the second embassy of Juan de Vera and Pulgar's nailing up the *Ave Maria*. The last ravage of the Moors and the burning of the Christian camp are reversed, probably to increase suspense; but other-

wise major revision results from a serious interest in historical detail. A list
of substantive variants between the Twayne and the Author's Revised editions appears in the editorial apparatus.

Two motivations seem to have actuated the revision for the ARE. First,
access to works not available in 1829 now provided Irving with sources used
primarily in expanded footnotes and historical information added to paragraphs and at chapter ends of the first edition. Second, the fact that major
revision falls in the first six and last seven chapters suggests a possible commercial interest primarily designed to encourage even first edition owners
of *Granada* to purchase the new, revised, and expanded edition.

Collation of the ARE and the Philadelphia text from which it was set reveals that portions are so extensively revised that the computer simply
"dumps" huge chunks of half a dozen paragraphs in each text as being un-
collatable. Visual collation confirms that, although some information is similar in both texts, the language varies almost in alternate words. Such
significant substantive changes can, however, be described as consisting of
three major kinds.

First, Irving has sought to tighten up his prose by deleting and condens-
ing descriptive elements appearing in the 1829 edition. This loose description of such revision might be illustrated by the following three examples.
The "mass of christian warriors. A loud shout burst forth, and the christians
rushed" becomes "mass of warriors, who, with a loud shout, rushed" in the
ARE. Or "The situation of the garrison, however, was daily growing more
and more critical; they suffered greatly" is condensed to "The garrison, in
truth, suffered intensely" (Philadelphia, II, 239). Simpler changes reduce
"the valiant Roderigo" to "Roderigo"; the relative clause "which had been
the field" becomes a simple appositive, "the field". If this were the only kind
of change in the ARE, the book would be considerably shortened.

However, the second type of revision generally lengthens the work, for in
the light of new historical research, Irving added material, especially in
chapters 46 (3 pp.), 66 (½ p.), 82 (3½ p.), 87 (2 pp.), 88 (½ p.), 93 (2 pp.),
97 (1 p.), 100 (½ p.). In addition, long explanatory footnotes are added in
chapters 52, 66, and 70, as well as numerous short notes throughout the
book. These extensive additions tend to occur at the end of chapters or paragraphs; they are additions, not substitutions for material already in the Philadelphia version.

The third kind of major revision occurs when the author neither adds nor
deletes bulk to the text; rather, he substitutes language and sometimes information for matter already appearing in the 1829 text. These revisions usually range in length from a single word to two lines and are seen most
obviously at the beginning and end of the book where they might be most
visible to the casual observer.

Besides the major revisions described above—scattered deletions from

1829 to 1850, extensive additions in 1850, and thorough-going substitutions in about a dozen chapters—there are an estimated 3200 variants between the Philadelphia edition and the ARE; approximately 70 percent involve word changes, that is, substantives. The other 30 percent include a few changes in punctuation, capitalizing (mainly of *Christian*), restoring Irving's "z" to words like *recognize*, and altering name spellings (especially *Cidi Yahye* to *Cid Hiaya*, *Rodovan* to *Reduan*, and *Muley Aben Hassan* to *Muley Abul Hassan*). Other variants occur through altered word-divisions, typographical mistakes and corrections, and the use of alternate spellings (such as *visitor* for *visiter*).

COLLATION OF TEXTS

The text presented herein could scarcely have been produced without computer technology. A text—possibly a good one—could have been established, but it would not have rested on the extensive detail, completeness, and even trivia which lies behind this Twayne text.

MANUSCRIPT COLLATION

The difficulty and unreliability of using a microfilm of one manuscript (the Murray) and a Xerox of the other (the Morgan) with an ocean between the two originals was complicated by the sheer bulk of pages—over 1000 in the Morgan and nearly 1200 in the Murray—and the expense of such evaluation in both money and time. Furthermore, not only did the two manuscripts require collation and notation of their "fair" versions from which their respective printers derived the Philadelphia and London editions, but also the very excisions and obviously authorial emendations were so interesting that they needed careful examination.

Under funding from the National Endowment for the Humanities, sophisticated computer programs were developed at Mississippi State University for an edition of the Works of William Makepeace Thackeray. These programs not only collate unlike texts of a work, but also manipulate revisions in manuscripts, producing on command the complete diplomatic transcription, a "fair" copy, alterations in the manuscripts, tables of variants or emendations, historical collations, punctuation-only variants, and other editorial data. Both setting-copy manuscripts and the partial Berg manuscript were transcribed into computer-readable form, including coded deletions, insertions (the two together forming substitutions), authorial and (in so far as possible) editorial emendations, repaginations, and whatever other changes could be discerned. Those transcriptions have been verified by computer collation with other manuscript forms, both first editions, and the

1850 Putnam edition. A printout of the diplomatic transcription of the Murray manuscript was taken to London in June, 1981, verified by sight collation with the original, and then corrected.[8]

After the first computer collation of the tentative copytext, the Murray manuscript, with the most distant "first" printed version, the Philadelphia edition, both the microfilm and the computer-readable transcription were re-examined for input errors reported as variants, and corrections were made in the transcription. This process was repeated with the other printed texts, and finally with the Morgan manuscript transcription. Only a few additional transcription errors were found; these were corrected.

PRINTED TEXT COLLATION

The late Professor Henry Pochmann performed and directed machine collations of multiple copies of three editions. Conclusions about the various issues of the printed texts rely on Professor Pochmann's and Professor Edwin Bowden's findings.

Machine collation of copies of the Carey, Lea, and Carey, 1829 edition proved them identical except for damaged type. The same was true with an 1831 Carey, Lea, and Carey. Collation reveals that Carey, Lea, and Blanchard brought out the same plates in 1835, 1836, and 1837. The Carey, Lea, and Blanchard 1838 "new edition" was also identical except for rather extensive type damage, especially at line-ends. Of course, the title page was revised calling this issue "A NEW EDITION"; but only that page and its verso actually were new.[9] The sole variation between copies of the J. Murray edition (1829) was in type jostle; broken letters and typographical errors appeared the same in both copies.[10]

Within the 1850 printing of the Putnam ARE, machine collation reveals only minor type damage (including a comma, period, and hyphen completely missing in some copies). Machine collation of the Putnam against the Putnam and Murray (London, 1850) showed that they are the same typesetting.[11]

Beginning with the 1851 reprinting of the ARE, plate damage becomes apparent although there is also evidence of repair but not of either correction or revision; particularly vulnerable, as might be expected, are end-of-line characters on both margins. By 1853 not only are characters broken, but also letters, hyphens, and other punctuation marks are often completely missing. In a few cases such damage results in a word change: *the* become *he*; *time* is *tim*; and *they* is *hey*. On the other hand, in several places printing seems better-inked than the 1851 example used for collation, and plate repair has occurred in half a dozen instances. No incorrect repairs were observed and no revisions or corrections are evident.

Putnam's 1859 *Granada,* issued from the same plates as all other 1850's ARE's, displays considerable attention to plate repair. However, obvious errors are introduced into the text during the correction process: *Alhama* changes to *Alhams.*; *let* to *lat*; and *martial* to *marital.* Scores of hyphens are accurately restored in 1859 although additional ones are broken off, and hundreds of other figures are replaced, including *the, time,* and *they* missing from the 1853 printing. But in general, in addition to three obvious new errors, this last lifetime issue shows considerably more damage than the 1853 printing to which it was compared.[12]

CHOICE OF COPYTEXT

There are only three authoritative forms of *A Chronicle of the Conquest of Granada*: The holograph at the Pierpont Morgan Library; the holograph/scribal copy derived from it at the John Murray archive; and the Author's Revised Edition (ARE) (New York: G. P. Putnam, 1850). The Statement of Editorial Principles and Procedures of the MLA indicates that sometimes the texts of a work differ so extensively "as to constitute, in effect, two different works, each with its own copy-text." Opinions differ on whether the ARE is sufficiently variant from the Philadelphia text to constitute a new work. The ARE differs from the 1829 Philadelphia edition by the complete revision of a dozen chapters, the addition of about 25 pages, the deletion of about 200 scattered lines including footnotes, and the appearance of some 2500 smaller substantive variants. Yet one need not hold this to be sufficient to consider the revised edition a new work, for the book contains one hundred chapters—about 170,000 words conservatively estimated in addition to prefaces and appendices. However, the locally concentrated revisions in chapters 1–6, 93, and 96–100 are so extensive that it would be difficult, if not absolutely impossible, to attempt to produce a traditionally eclectic text.

In the absence of the now-lost paste-up which apparently intervened for some portions, most substantive revisions in the ARE can be considered authoritative; but the accidentals, following the editorial style of the Philadelphia edition, must be rejected because of positive evidence that the manuscript which lay behind that version was highly copy edited. Moreover, certain word changes like "from whence" to "whence" seem to reflect the work of a copy editor rather than the author. Whether *The Conquest of Granada* is two works or one, it certainly had two separate versions which this editor thinks should remain distinct. The editor's first decision, then, must be whether to present a reading text of the 1829 or the 1850 *Granada.* Either choice seems legitimate. Although there may be good reason to produce an eclectic text, or even to choose the ARE as copytext, the Twayne edition presents, not the "best" text of Irving's "final" intentions (ARE), but rather the "best" text of the author's "first" intentions (1829). The choice of copytext, then, has not been between the ARE and a manuscript, but between the American holograph and the scribal copy.

Standard editorial procedure would incline toward the Morgan manuscript as the appropriate choice for copytext. Accidentals (punctuation, spelling, paragraphing, and other matters of form) are usually more subject to corruption than are wordings, and therefore the version closest to the author's own hand should normally be the most reliable in demonstrating the author's "intention." However, the Morgan manuscript, as it presently exists, obscures such authorial intention by extensive copy editing, probably done by an editor at Carey, Lea & Carey. The extent of editorial intervention which that copy bears (especially in punctuation, paragraphing, capitalization, and spelling) would require extensive restoration of Irving's own intentions—at best a risky enterprise, for sorting the author's marks from the editor's is probably impossible beyond about 80 percent accuracy.

It becomes imperative, then, to entertain the somewhat heretical notion that the Murray manuscript, about seventy percent written by several scribes, should be copytext for a new authoritative edition even though a virtually complete holograph exists. The Murray manuscript's advantage is that it was copied from the Morgan manuscript before the Philadelphia copyeditor did his work. But the choice of the Murray manuscript as copytext is not based entirely on how bad the Morgan manuscript has become. The selection of the scribal manuscript over the American holograph rests on several important findings. As detailed above, the scribes were faithful, if naive, copyists; Irving proofread thoroughly; and he revised as he proofread. The Morgan manuscript is a first draft; but because it is exclusively in Irving's handwriting, it has been used extensively to mend errors in matters of spelling and occasionally in language in the scribal portions of the Murray manuscript, the primary copytext for the Twayne edition. But ultimately it is on the basis of the greater reliability of the accidentals that the Murray manuscript is chosen as copytext.

The Murray manuscript is missing in parts and was occasionally superseded by Irving during the final stages of proofreading the two manuscipts and preparing them for publication. Where the Murray is missing, or it has been consciously replaced by Washington Irving in the portion reconstructed from memory to fill in a lost portion, other forms have been used as copytext for the Twayne edition. Three sheets of the Virginia manuscript, chapters 49–50 and part of chapter 51 of the London edition, chapters 34–35 from the Berg fragment, and parts of pages 13–14, 19–20, 631, and 681 of the Morgan manuscript supplement the main copytext. (See Segments Used as Copytext.)

TREATMENT OF SUBSTANTIVES

All departures in the Twayne edition from the copytext substantives have been recorded in the editorial apparatus. When apparent error in scribal accidentals arises, the holograph has been consulted for amendment. Irving's own substantives have been restored from the holograph, unless it was determined that he was revising as he copied into the Murray manuscript. All copy editor substantives have been rejected except when they correct manifest errors. Chapters 49–51 (in which the unauthoritative London edition is used as copytext) occur in a portion which Irving himself was copying. Collation shows that the London text agrees with the Murray substantives more closely than with the Morgan manuscript. It is conjectured that Washington Irving was writing in the missing pages, revising as he went. Therefore, substantives have generally been rejected from the Morgan manuscript in this portion and are listed in the editorial apparatus with the ARE variants. Conflicting substantives have been restored from the Morgan manuscript.

TREATMENT OF ACCIDENTALS

"Accidentals" is too general a term to be useful in establishing textual cruxes in *Granada*, for there are three distinct problems presented by the two manuscripts: paragraphing and punctuation, spelling, and capitalization.

The first question—punctuation and paragraphing—bears most specifically on choice of copytext. In the Murray text with a very few, very obvious, exceptions, all changes in and additions to punctuation are by Irving himself; but in the Morgan, these myriad alterations are almost never Irving's. On this basis the Murray has been chosen for the primary copytext, and deviations in punctuation from it in the Twayne edition are noted according to the following plan. Quotation marks, like parentheses, come in pairs; yet, Irving often forgot to close a quotation which has a very clear opening mark (or vice versa). The Philadelphia edition tends to over-quote; the London deletes unpaired quotation marks. Moreover, when Irving did close quotation marks, he placed them haphazardly in relation to periods, commas, and other points. Additions of quotation marks are listed in the table of emendations, but regularizing of the American printer's convention that periods and commas belong within the quotation and footnotation references (*) without (when the quote mark is present) is not noted.

Hyphenation and apostrophes are punctuation marks which can change the spellings or even meanings of words. Hyphenation presents a minor problem in the copytext, although it would be a great problem if only the Morgan text had survived. In general, Irving syllabicated a word at the end of a line by using either a hyphen or an "equal" mark, coupled with a hyphen at the beginning of the next line, as *enter-/-ed* or *command-/-er.* There is little ambiguity in this practice; it meant "make this a single word." Irving habitually lifted his pen between syllables as in *illus trious,* and *sudd enly,* or alternatively, he ran words together like *ofGranada* or *tobe.* In simple words this quirk is unobtrusive, but in possibly compound words, such as *foot soldier, cross bow,* or *hot spirited,* his intention is often difficult to resolve. The two witnesses—the American copy editor and the Spanish scribe—often differed in what they thought was the author's wish. Many words in the American manuscript are obviously ligatured by a copy editor to become a single word, such as *day light* or *day break.* Others are hyphenated, such as *cross-bow-men* or *foot-soldiers.* Others, like *saddle bow* or *Puerto carrero* were interpreted in print as two words. Moreover, the practice of the American editor was inconsistent, and the second volume shows far less change in the manuscript than does the first, although the typesetter or proofreader attempted to make consistent the practice established in the first volume, whether the hyphen or ligature actually appears in the manuscript or not. On the other hand, the Spanish scribes tended to exaggerate the spaces between words, and because Irving obviously examined nearly every page of that manuscript, the inconsistencies of copytext have generally been maintained and ambiguities resolved in light of the holograph.

Irving simply did not use apostrophes in the possessive case. The boldly editorial appearance of the apostrophes in the American manuscript, and the absence of that mark in possessives in the scribal copy prove this true, although Irving and his scribes use apostrophes in some contractions and plurals. In the Twayne edition all apostrophes in the abbreviation for *Saint* are restored from the holograph; all other apostrophes are emendations in Washington Irving's work and are listed in the emendations table.

The second problem arises from spellings: because the Morgan is a holograph and the Murray mostly the work of paid copyists, the author's correct orthography has been followed whenever there is an error in the copy. Because the American copy editor's spelling "corrections" can almost always be detected, and because scribes do miscopy, the author's "intention," or at least his practice, in spellings can be discovered with a higher percentage of accuracy than in pointing. Therefore, the copytext has been restored to Irving's original spellings whenever feasible. He constantly misspelled some words, and others he spelled inconsistently. If Irving's variant spellings were acceptable in the nineteenth century they are preserved. The Twayne edition regularizes the spellings of -our endings based on the extremely consistent practice in Irving's handwriting.[13] Likewise, Irving's clear preference for "z" over "s" in "-ize" verbs,[14] scribal corruptions of Irving's usually correct spellings,[15] and a few purely formal matters[16] have been silently regularized from the holograph practice, despite scribal errors. The Twayne edition also regularizes the spelling of proper names in accord with Irving's usual orthography,[17] and a few words which Irving nearly always misspelled have been silently corrected.[18]

The policy governing emendation of punctuation and spelling is very conservative except for regularizing proper name spellings and restoring Irving's usual practice in certain prefixes and suffixes. But Irving's use of capital letters requires a more liberal plan. Here the editor has chosen to "read" the Murray manuscript in a consistent fashion. Just as little benefit results from transcribing both *Boabdel* and *Boabdil* only to require either preserving the inconsistency or noting the emendations, little is gained from transcribing both *Hassan* and *hassan*. Similarly, no conceivable purpose exists for preserving as a lower case any letter following a sentence end; yet many such characters *look* like small letters. Washington Irving's handwriting is remarkably clear except for initial letters in which the capital differs from the lower case only in size, such as a, c, g, k, m, s, u, v, w. This idiosyncrasy is particularly troublesome in words like *aben, alcayde, christian, count, king, marquis, moor, valley, vega,* and *woe.* Rather than attempt to decipher whether Irving "intended" to have *Christian Cavaliers* or *christian cavaliers* and *Moors* or *moors* on a case by case basis depending on the size of the character, this new edition interprets such ambiguities consistently, based, not on the scribe's, but on the present editor's interpretation of Irving's handwriting in the Morgan manuscript, and on their context. Furthermore, Irving's own or the author-examined scribal copy sometimes employs a "capital" letter for a perfectly ordinary common noun, adjective, or even conjunction, like *brother, every, delivered,* or *inhabitants.* These simple handwriting idiosyncrasies are interpreted contextually, leaning toward the simplest possible reading. The most significant effect of this policy occurs in the Twayne edition where both the English 1829 and the ARE capitalize *Christian,* the American 1829 uses lower case, and the manuscripts are ambiguous and inconsistent.

Because the capitalization of the words listed below is ambiguous in the manuscripts, the Twayne text regularizes it as indicated. Titles such as *Alcayde, Adelantado, Count, Duke, Marquis, and Sultana,* are made capital only in expressions like the "Count de Tendilla," the "Marquis of Cadiz," or "Sultana Ayxa la Horra." If Irving refers to "the good count," "the worthy alcayde," or "the duke," lower case has been used. *King* has always been capitalized, but *kingdom* normally begins with a lower case letter. Only a construction like the "Kingdom of" Granada or Castile is capitalized. This seems to be the intention most nearly discernible from the documentary evidence left in the Morgan manuscript.[19]

Chapter titles have been capitalized by Twayne Publishers; final periods have been silently supplied when omitted from the manuscript.

NOTES

1. Earl N. Harbert, "Irving's *A Chronicle of the Conquest of Granada*: An Essay in the History of Publication, Revision, and Critical Reception," *Bulletin of the New York Public Library*, 79 (1976), 400–415.
2. Earl N. Harbert, "The Manuscripts of *A Chronicle of the Conquest of Granada*: A Revised Census with Commentary," *Bulletin of Research in the Humanities*," 82 (1979), 124–129.
3. Harbert, "An Essay in the History . . . ."
4. See Harbert, "An Essay in the History . . . ."
5. This description corrects points of pagination in Harbert, "The Manuscripts of . . . ."
6. Earl N. Harbert, "Washington Irving's *Conquest of Granada*: A Spanish Experiment that Failed," *Clio: An Interdisciplinary Journal of Literature, History, and the Philosophy of History*," 3 (1974), 305–313.
7. Correspondence from Professor Edwin T. Bowden to Professor Earl N. Harbert, July, 1972.
8. Miriam J. Shillingsburg, "Computer Assistance to Scholarly Editing," *Bulletin of Research in the Humanities*, 81 (1978), 448–463.
9. Copies used for collation are: (1829) University of Iowa DP/122/I7/ 1829a, University of Wisconsin Y/Ir8/G/1829/ Cutter (Vol.I), University of Wisconsin Rare Books CA1917, personal copy of Miriam J. Shillingsburg; (1831) University of Texas Rare Books Aw/Ir86/1829cb; (1838) University of Wisconsin DP/I723/1838; also checked were Carey & Lea (1833), and Carey, Lea, & Blanchard (1835, 1836, 1837, 1840, 1841).
10. Copies used for collation are: University of Wisconsin DP/122/I723/2, University of Wisconsin Rare Books CA9236, and Mississippi State University Special Collections copy.
11. Copies used for collation are: University of Texas Ir/8cw/1850; University of California DP/122/I7; personal copy of Ralph M. Aderman; personal copy of Earl N. Harbert.
12. Copies used for collation are: (1851) University of Texas Ir/8cw/1851, personal copy of Miriam J. Shillingsburg; (1853) Allegheny College 946/ Ir/c.3; (1859) Case Western Reserve 946.03/I72; other copies checked were G. P. Putnam, 1852, 1854, 1856, 1857, and a second 1859.
13. To be specific, the -our ending of the scribes' hand has been regularized to Irving's usual practice. Except for *armorial, laborious(ly), rigorous(ly), timorous(ly), valorous(ly), vigorous(ly)*, the author seems to have preferred the -our spelling. He was inconsistent in *favourite* and

neighbouring but leans toward those spellings which the Twayne text has adopted.

14. These stems and their inflected forms follow Irving's preference which is highly regular: apprize, authorize, comprize, enterprize, merchandize, recognize, signalize, surmize, surprize, and surprizal.

15. Irving consistently spelled correctly the following words which were reproduced by various scribes in several different ways, including correctly: *centinel, despair, destroy, destruction, display, encreased, expense*, the suffix *-ful* in lieu of *-full, jewel, marquis* (although Irving rather often used the correct *marques*), *practice, resource, S'* (for *Saint*), *scymetar, separated, until, valiant, vigilance, vigilant, warrior*.

16. Regularization of ampersands to *and*, placement of periods and quotation marks in relationship to footnote markers, the removal of scribal dashes used to fill out short lines, restoration of holograph *S'* for scribal *St.*, and the styling of Irving's highly irregular footnotes appear in the Twayne. Commas and periods expected by the interrupter "he said" in quotations, and commas expected with *however* and *therefore* have been regularized to accord with other volumes of the Twayne edition; each instance has been noted, however.

17. Ben Abil Gazan, Abrahen, Abul Casim, Albohacen, Alcalá, Alhambra, Allah, Alonzo, Alpuxarra, Antequera, Aragon, Bexir, Boabdil, Castellar, Castilian, Cidi Yahye, Gonzalvo, Granada, Hernando Perez, Hubec Aldagan, Jusef Aben Comixa, Mohammed, Puertocarrero, Roderigo, Ruyz, Salobreña, Valencia, Xenel, Zarah.

18. Twayne reading is on the left of the bracket, Irving's spelling is on the right: *brethren*] *bretheren, brethern; caparison*] *caparaison; career*] *carreer, carier; counsel*] *council; disastrous*] *disasterous; discipline*] *dicipline; siege*] *seige; seize*] *sieze; sovereign*] *sovreign*.

19. Regularization to lower case occurs in: adalid(es), adelantado (but Adelantado of [name]), albatoza, albornoz, alcayde (but Alcayde of [name]), alfaqui, altar, army(ies), arms, bishop, camp, capital, captain (but Captain of [name]), captive, castle, cavalry, cavalier, cavalgada, chivalry, chronicle(r)(s), city(ies), commander (but Commander of [name]), companion, count (but Count of [name]), country, countrymen, court, cross, crown, dervise, duke (but Duke of [name]), earl (but Earl of [name]), el (between names, but El if first of two), empire, enemy, father, garden, garrison, gate(s), guide, heaven, hermit, host, infidel, key, kingdom (but Kingdom of [name]), knight (but Knights of [name]), lady, marquis (but Marquis of [name]), master (but Master of [name]), men, monarch, mosque, mountain(s)(eer)(eirs), orchard, oriental, prince and princess (but Prince [name] and Princess [name]), queens (but Queen in reference to Isabella), saint, scout, soldier(y)(s), sovereign, square, standard, street, valley, vassal, vega, and wall.

Regularization to upper case occurs in: Aben, African, Albaycin, Alcazaba, Arabian, Ben, Catholic, Chico, Christian, Christendom, Damascus, Flemish, French, Gomeres, Grand Cardinal, Grand Soldan, Grand Turk, Holy Brotherhood, Infanta, King, Moor(s)(ish), Moslem, Mudexares, and Order of [name].

LIST OF EMENDATIONS

With the exception of the silent emendations discussed in the Textual Commentary, this list reports all changes which the Twayne edition has made in the copytext. The numbers on the left refer to the page and line in the present text. The reading to the left of the semicolon is the Twayne reading; to the right of the semicolon is the rejected copy-text reading. If a substantive emendation rests on the authority of the Morgan manuscript, the abbreviation MORG will appear to the left of the semicolon; if an emendation was made in the copytext which differs from the Morgan manuscript, that rejected Morgan variant will appear with the substantives rejected from the ARE. Because of extensive editorial tampering with the Morgan manuscript, it has not been possible to use it for authority in punctuation emendations.

A wavy dash ~ has been used to indicate an invariant word which may be necessary to locate an emendation. These emendations almost always concern punctuation, and a caret ∧ has been used to represent the absence of a mark of punctuation or other sign. A hyphen slash -/ represents the hyphenation of a possibly compound word at the end of a line in the copytext.

3.12	zeal, ; ~∧
3.15	regretted, ; ~∧
3.15	manuscripts, ; ~∧
3.20	work, ; ~∧
3.21	abomination, ; ~∧
3.26	fragments, ; ~∧
3.27	history, ; ~∧
3.29	V, ; ~∧
3.31	Moors, ; ~;
3.31	Granada ; ~,
3.35	infidels ; ~,
3.36–37	Mahomet, ; ~∧
3.38	Mariana, ; ~∧
3.38	jesuit, ; ~∧
4.9	crusades, ; ~;
5.6	considered as ; considered
5.11	cell, ; ~∧
5.41	summit] MORG ; submit
6.16	circumference ; circumferance
6.27	peasant's ; peasants
6.29	air ; ~,
6.29	sky ; ~,

6.36	default] MORG ; defect
7.9	Hassan. His territories ; ~, ~ ~,
7.10	example, ; ~∧
7.22	infidel," ; ~∧"
7.22	Agapida; ; ~,
7.25	tribute." ; ~∧"
8.9	well required] MORG ; required
8.15	sovereigns," ; ~∧"
8.16	crown,] MORG ; crowns,
8.26	infidels, ; ~∧
8.36	lied, ; ~∧
9.16	their] MORG ; his
10.4	at] MORG ; with
10.5	"not," ; "~∧"
10.5	Agapida, ; ~∧
10.8	usurpers. It was impossible," he adds, ; ~." "~ ~ ~∧" ~ ~∧
11.1–2	Pomegranate," ; ~∧"
11.40	Pomegranate. ; Pomegranate ~∧
12.17	Moor! the Moor!" ; ~"! ~ ~"!"
12.21	While] MORG ; When
12.29	town. The ; ~, the
13.5	piteous ; pitious
13.5–6	prosperous ; properous
13.6	lain ; laid
13.25	preparations ; preparation
13.33	voice, ; ~.
13.41	foresight ; forsight
15.24	near to] MORG ; near
16.38	preferred ; prefcred
16.39	escalador, ; ecalador;
16.42	seen, ; ~∧
17.5	the throat,] MORG ; throat,
17.16	combatants ; combatients
18.22	he; ; ~,
18.23	bloodshed; ; ~,
18.31	morning's] MORG ; morning
19.35	were ; was
20.30	they; ; ~,
21.1	me, Alhama!" ; ~∧ ~!∧
21.2	foreboding, ; forebiding,
21.16	Zahara."† ; ~∧†
21.26	army, ; ~;

21.27	taken." ; ~.∧
21.38	Grand] MORG ; the Grand
22.3	Cadiz, ; ~∧
22.23	distress, ; ~∧
23.17	¶On ; On
23.21	back!" ; ~!∧
23.21	voice; ; ~,
23.27	Juan de Vera] MORG ; Juan
23.30	Thus, ; ~∧
23.36	siege. ; ~∧
24.1	lasted throughout] MORG ; lasted
24.40	implore ; emplore
25.16	immense ; inmense
25.18	which] MORG ; that
25.22	against ; agaist
25.28	husband's ; husbands
25.37	recollection ; reccollection
26.1	horses, ; ~∧
26.11	flower] MORG ; power
26.30	enemy's ; enemies
26.32	venture] MORG ; adventure
27.17–18	enemy's frontier] MORG ; enemies frontiers
27.18	turn] MORG ; to turn
27.22	missives.] MORG ; missions.
27.27	dissuaded ; dessuaded
27.36	water, ; ~∧
28.1	without,] MORG ; thithout,
28.19	beyond ; beyound
28.23	Hassan ; Hassand
29.40	Pedro de Pineda] MORG ; Pedro Pineda
30.18–19	with great distinction by the King,] MORG ; by the King with great distinction,
31.5	tyranny ; tyrany
31.20	Allah ; Alla
31.21	great!" exclaimed they; ; ~" ~ ~,
31.39	became] MORG ; was
32.12	pretensions ; pretentions
32.17	executioner,"] executinor,"
32.17	"shall] ∧~
32.33	had] MORG ; had been
33.3	∧God ; "~
33.3	great!" ; ~∧"
33.3	Hassan; ; Hassan

33.32	tyranny ; tyrrany
33.34	the followers] MORG ; followers
34.7	a vast expense.] MORG ; vast expence.
34.8	listened ; listined
34.8	surprize ; surprise
34.12	feebleness ; feebliness
34.23	Palma, ; ~∧
34.24	Ruyz ; Ruiz
34.24	Ortis, ; Ortis
34.27	Loxa, ; ~∧
34.33	Loxa, ; ~∧
35.1	preparations ; preperations
35.1	making, ; ~∧
35.17	chivalry ; chavalry
35.18	almost ; almostly
35.19	enemy's ; enemie's'
35.29	artillery, ; ~∧
35.35	river. His] MORG ; the river, This
36.14	indomitable ; indomptible
36.19	reinforcements. ; reinforcemnts.
36.23	flashed] MORG ; flushed
36.23	exultation. ; ~∧
36.23	Allah," said he, ; ~∧" "~ ~∧
36.27	feint] MORG ; faint
36.29	hotly] MORG ; hastily
37.5	group ; groupe
37.20	the Christian] MORG ; Christian
37.35	Moors, ; Moors
38.21	and mules] MORG ; or mules
39.7	gone," said he, ; ~∧" ~ ~∧
39.13	his men] MORG ; the men
39.19	parry," ; ~∧"
39.19	if ; If
39.27	exultingly, ; ~∧
39.35	ensconced ; ensconsed
39.37	ensure] MORG ; assure
39.38	success; ; sucess;
40.6	him: ; ~;
40.30	their] MORG ; the
40.33	¶Muley] MORG ; Muley
40.36	de Tarifa. ; of Tarifa.
40.38	only be ; only

41.8	in]MORG ; into
41.15	"No," ; ∧~∧"
41.24	relief ; releif
41.26	glen; ; ~,
41.41	then ; and then
42.1	upon] MORG ; on
42.14	interred] MORG ; enterred
42.15	on] MORG ; in
42.16	Then, gathering] MORG ; Gathering
42.24	dues."] MORG ; right."
42.32	relished ; releshed
42.33–36	tone. ¶He ordered a rich silken vest and a scarlet mantle to be given to the alfaqui and dismissed him with great courtesy. ¶"Tell] MORG ; tone. "Tell
42.42–43.1	dawning." ¶Muley] MORG ; dawning." ¶He then ordered that a rich silken vest and scarlet mantle should be given to the alfaqui and dismissed him with great courtesy. ¶Muley
43.2	Allah ; Alla
43.3–4	destroy ; distroy
43.11	Sidonia. ; ~∧
43.24	Henriquez, ; ~∧
43.28	while] MORG ; time
44.5	safely made] MORG ; made with safety
44.9	added,] MORG ; added that
44.9	even extend] MORG ; extend
44.14	interpose] MORG ; enterpose
44.21	beds] MORG ; bed
44.24–25	marquis, however,] MORG ; marquis∧
44.27	idea of terminating their foray by] MORG ; idea of
44.42	Bernaldes ; Bernalds
45.2	days' ; days
45.3	self-confident ; selfconfident
45.17	goodly] MORG ; fair
45.26	secrecy,] MORG ; secresy,
45.27–28	it possessed a commander who was himself] MORG ; the commander himself was
45.40	road." ; ~:"
46.5	rocky ; rockey
46.7	violence. ; voilence.
46.14	the] MORG ; their
46.15	Mediterranean ; meditarranian

46.15	hailed ; hailded
47.14	the dry] MORG ; dry
47.20	Hearing, however, ; ~∧ ~∧
47.20	his friend] MORG ; *omitted*
47.24	the whistling] MORG ; whistling
48.14	fires. ; fire.
48.20	valley:] MORG ; ~∧
48.24	die," ; ~∧∧
48.24	"making ; ∧~
49.5	he. ; ~∧
49.30	however, ; ~∧
49.31	he ; He
49.34	when ; When
50.31	nephews of ; nephews of of
50.43	forlorn ; folorn
51.7	other towns: many] MORG ; others
52.6	greatly ; greately
52.7–8	had rallied] MORG ; rallied
52.9	had, ; ~∧
52.15	to find] MORG ; *omitted*
52.24	sons, ; ~∧
52.29	twain: ; ~;
52.40	foremost ; formost
53.10–11	mountainiers ; mountaniers
53.18	"They ; ∧~
53.26	worldly ; wordly
53.29	comforts ; conforts
54.24	especially] MORG ; specially
54.38	Boabdil's ; Boabdils
55.5	forebodings; ;] MORG ; forebidings;
55.23	scarcely ; scacely
55.35	of youth] MORG ; of a youth
56.6	counsellor ; councillor
56.13	strike ; strick
56.19	Cabra, ; ~∧
56.31	the 20th] MORG ; 20.th
57.17	ordered ; orderded
58.23	await these," ; wait there,"
58.24	count, ; ~∧
58.30	on] MORG ; of
58.34	reconnoitre, ; recconnoitre,
59.3	Chico; ; ~,
59.10	Santiago∧!" ; ~,"!

59.23	battalion] MORG ; batallion
59.24	Alcayde ; Alcalde
60.10	de] MORG ; of
60.11	enemy; ; ~,
60.19	them. ; ~∧
60.22	monarch's ; monarchs
60.39	King's ; Kings
61.15	conspicuous, ; conspcuous,
61.23	moment, ; ~∧
63.36	whom ; who
63.39	comfort ; confort
64.28	"Cavalier," said they, ; ∧~." ~ ~∧
64.29	Christians. ; Christian's∧
64.30	he. ; ~,
65.1	Ali Atar?" ; Ali-atar?
65.3	sword," ; ~∧"
65.5	soldier ; soldiers
65.16	replied, ; ~∧
65.19	another, ; ~∧
65.24	all Granada] MORG ; Granada
65.33	mother's ; mothers
65.36	daughter," ; ~∧"
66.4	exclaim, ; ~∧
66.9	will it] MORG ; it will
66.9	gladdened ; gladened
66.14	exclaimed, ; ~∧
66.16	crowded ; croweded
66.19	moonlight] MORG ; mournful
66.20–21	Alhambra ; Alambra
66.22	perfumes] MORG ; parfumes
66.24	limpid ; limped
66.29	promise ; promisse
66.29	prediction ; prodicttion
67.3	commander, ; commander
67.8	they, ; ~∧
67.11	Comfort ; Confort
67.12	in] MORG ; on
67.19	continued, ; ~∧
67.31	besides ; beside
67.36	mother's ; mothers
68.4	with ; withe
68.13	affairs, ; ~∧
68.13	overcame ; overcome

68.17   apartments ; appartments
68.22   with] MORG ; the
68.26   Queen,"] MORG ; the Queen,"
68.32   II., father to] MORG ; II.$_\wedge$ ~ of
68.38   ransom] MORG ; ransome
69.11–12   Boabdil, ; ~$_\wedge$
69.16   chosen ; chusen
69.28   Cordova. ; Cordoba.
70.11   "The ; $_\wedge$The
70.11   King," continues Agapida, "would ; ~." ~ ~, $_\wedge$~
70.12–13   fail. Satisfied ; ~, satisfied
70.15   laden] MORG ; loaded
70.16   prisoner." ; ~.$_\wedge$
70.20–21   Cordova, ; Cordoba,
70.27   observed, ; ~$_\wedge$
70.30   therefore, ; ~$_\wedge$
71.2   Cadiz. Nay, ; ~, nay,
71.15   progenitors; ; ~,
71.21   Queen, ; ~;
71.22   maintenance ; maintainance
71.38   Cordova, ; Cordoba,
72.6   affirmative ; afirmative
72.7   Agapida, ; ~$_\wedge$
72.9   therefore, ; therefore
72.13–14   a prisoner] MORG ; prisoner
72.22   Ferdinand] MORG ; King Ferdinand
73.34   knights, ; ~$_\wedge$
73.36   the astrologers:] MORG ; astrologers.
73.36   cause, ; ~$_\wedge$
73.36–37   exultation.] MORG ; exaltation.
73.41   the people.] MORG ; his people.
73.42   country,] MORG ; ~$_\wedge$
74.14   had foreboded] MORG ; and forboded
74.16   he, ; ~$_\wedge$
74.28   "This," ; "~$_{\wedge\wedge}$
74.29   fondness; ; ~,"
74.30   softness ; softeness
74.42   moment, ; ~$_\wedge$
75.10   business ; bussiness
75.19   fortified ; ~,
75.23   civic] MORG ; civil
75.36   legitimate ; legimate
75.37   disdain, ; desdain,

76.6	misfortune, ; ~∧
76.7	Whenever, therefore, ; ~∧ ~∧
76.11–12	ruled. "Allah Achbar!" ; ~∧ "~ ~"!
76.12	"God ; ∧~
76.14	alfaquis." ; ~∧"
76.18	dead, ; ~∧
76.42	mountaineers ; mountaneers
77.4	the time ; time
77.7	mountainiers, ; mountaniers,
77.10	Zegris ; Zegries
77.11	Besides ; Beside
77.28	trumpet; ; ~,
77.42	screen, ; ~∧
78.5	burst ; burt
78.29	separate ; reparate
78.35	consummate ; consumate
78.36	couriers ; courriers
79.1	captaincy, ; ~∧
79.2	whom] MORG ; with whom
79.4	put in] MORG ; put them in
79.27	thickets ; thickuts
79.32	forage. ; ~∧
80.2	ambush] MORG ; the ambush
81.15	corselets, ; ~∧
81.21	exultation] MORG ; exaltation
81.25	Guadalete, ; ~;
81.25	had] MORG ; has
81.30	round] MORG ; around
81.33	*"En ; *∧En
81.37	mismos ; missmos
82.24	do," ; ~∧"
82.28	land." ; ~∧"
83.13	bodies. ; ~∧
83.22	returned ; ~,
83.29	had descended] MORG ; descended
83.37–38	festivities. ; festivities ∧
83.40	Lady's ; Ladys
84.1	Besides ; Beside
84.25	the presence] MORG ; presence
84.28	majesty's ; majesties
84.32	ordered] MORG ; desired
85.5	Aguilar, ; ~∧
85.5	Cardenas, ; ~∧

85.8	Monte Rey] MORG ; Monterey
85.12	Queen's ; Queens
85.28	chamber, ; ~∧
85.32	music] MORG ; musick
85.41	value ; ~,
86.20	o'clock ; oclock
86.28	Moor's ; Moors
86.34	court, ; ~∧
87.9	enemies' ; enemies
87.26	provisions. ; provissions.
87.31	women ; woman
88.10	barrancos] MORG ; barranco's
88.11	recently, ; ~∧
88.11	impregnable; ; ~∧
88.18	centinels] MORG ; centinel;
88.25	shrewd ; shrewed
89.8	gates ; gate
89.17	castle, ; castle;
89.32	Marquis,] MORG ; ~∧
90.4	father Fray] MORG ; Fray
90.7	this] MORG ; the
90.9	heads] MORG ; hands
90.14	cavalier ; ~,
90.21	enemies' ; enemies
90.27	dissolute, ; disolute,
90.28	predatory ; predatary
91.1	instil] MORG ; instill
91.5	plans." ; ~.∧
91.15	wantonness] MORG ; wantoness
91.16	soldicry.] MORG ; soldiers.
91.18	moment's ; moments
91.20	softening ; softning
91.23	minstrels,] MORG ; minstrells,
91.25	lewd rabble] MORG ;] rabble
91.35	heathen." ; ~.∧
91.41	peasantry, ; ~∧
91.43	cattle, ; ~∧
92.3	oil, ; ~∧
92.4	smoking] MORG ; smoaking
92.5	sight," ; ~∧"
92.5	father, ; Father∧
92.11	acclivity ; aclivity

92.15	gate] MORG ; gates
92.33	intercepted.] MORG ; interrupted.
93.12	linen ; linnen
93.7	never] MORG ; none
93.11	happened," ; ~ᴧ"
93.16	the which] MORG ; which
93.19	say, are ; ~ᴧ "~
93.20	as ; ~,
93.23	threatening ; threatning
93.26	those] MORG ; these
93.27	Thus] MORG ; ¶Thus
93.29	impoverished ; impovrished
94.15	arms; ; ~,
94.24	furnish] MORG ; provide
94.28–29	needful] MORG ; requisite
94.29–30	Queen's ; Queens
94.34	thoroughly ; throughly
94.38	Luis ; Luiz
95.2	de Leon; ; Leon;
95.3	retainers. ; ~ᴧ
95.5	Spain: the] MORG ; Spain. The
95.6	distinguished cavaliers] MORG ; cavaliers
95.12	Xerez, ; Xeriz
95.27	Sometimes ; ~,
95.43	through] MORG ; thro'
96.9	encreased] MORG ; inreased
96.14	antiently] MORG ; anciently
96.15	depending for security] MORG ; depending
96.16	thundering ; thundered
97.8	overwhelmed ; overwhelmned
97.16	near] MORG ; close
98.4	she, ; ~ᴧ
98.5	fortune's ; fortunes
98.18	brother's ; Brothers
98.20	mere fraternal] MORG ; fraternal
99.7	of adherents,] MORG ; Adherents,
99.12	Kingdom of Granada] MORG ; kingdom
99.15	horse's ; horses
99.21	indeed," exclaimed he, ; ~ᴧ" ~ ~ᴧ
100.19	punishment," ; ~ᴧ"
100.22	captivity.* ; ~:*
100.33	all the] MORG ; the

100.35   vain; ; ~,
100.40   Zegri, ; ~∧
101.5   Monda. ; ~∧
101.5–6   you," cried he, ; ~∧" ~ ~∧
101.20   these] MORG ; their
101.25   troops; ; ~,
101.37   came ; ~∧
102.13   followers.] MORG ; adherents.
102.25   place; ; ~,
103.10   keys to] MORG ; keys of
103.12   of Coin.] MORG ; at Coin.
103.29   the rocks] MORG ; rocks
104.2   purpose; ; ~,
104.4   troops; ; ~,
105.7   from whence] MORG ; whence
105.10   now] MORG ; soon
105.13   attempts, ; ~∧
105.14   fruitless; ; ~,
105.16   encreasing. ; increasing.
105.25   countermine in the side] MORG ; counter-/mine it through
                   the solid body
105.25   rock. ; ~∧
105.29   thoughts] MORG ; thought
105.30   were ; was
105.35   ordnance," ; ~∧"
106.12   practice] MORG ; exercise
106.14   Zegri, ; ~∧
106.15   make] MORG ; try
106.42   Ronda," ; ~∧"
107.11   vacillated ; vaccilated
107.15   wits' ; wits
107.29–30   'the unlucky.' ¶"In ; "the unlucky." ¶∧In
107.34   know that] MORG ; know
107.35   invincible ; invin-/able
107.37   unbelievers." ; ~∧"
108.27   dominated] MORG ; commanded
108.34   besides ; beside
108.38   garrison, ; ~;
108.38   about one] MORG ; one
108.42   recollected ; reccollected
108.43   corredors ; corradors
109.14   he, "to ; ~∧ ∧~
109.14   Granada." ¶Approaching] MORG ; Alhama." ∧~

109.30	triumph. ; ~∧
111.3	Boabdil. ; ~∧
111.21	the founding] MORG ; founding
111.28	rhapsody] MORG ; raphsody
111.31	that] MORG ; which
112.25	brother's ; brothers
112.26	rider, ; ~∧
112.40	rout. ; route.
113.4	expedition. ; ~∧
113.27	recollect ; reccollect
113.28	conquerors, that ; ~. That
113.32	offering himself,] MORG ; offering
114.4	skies?" ; ~?∧
114.11	Fountain ; fountain
114.32	Fountain ; fountain
115.9	bishop's ; bishops
115.16	stone's ; stones
116.37	rock-built ; rock-/built
116.41	mountains." ; ~.∧
117.36	kings' ; kings
118.3	mounted] MORG ; disposed
118.10	avail, said he, ; ~∧ ~ ~∧
118.11	afar? ; ~?"
118.29	Matthew, ; Mathew,
119.6	commander ; ~,
119.6	Calatrava ; ~,
119.8	Zagal, ; ~∧
119.11	fly ; ~,
119.11	force. Of ; force: of
119.13	all the] MORG ; the
119.40	renegado ; renagado
120.3	amulets, ; alumets,
120.7	he, ; ~∧
120.8	jewels," ; ~∧"
120.21	Zalea," ; ~∧"
120.24	believe," ; ~∧"
121.23	comrades ; comerades
121.27	Moors; ; ~,
121.28	resistance. ; ~∧
121.33	garrison. ; ~∧
122.24	Mediterranean. ; ~∧
122.35	death; ; ~,
123.24	king's ; kings

124.14	year's ; years
124.22	splendour ; spendour
124.27	lacqueys ; laqueys
125.37	"was ; ∧~
126.9	believed] MORG ; yet
126.11	their] MORG ; our
126.21	"Their ; ∧This
126.34	Santiago, ; ~∧
126.42	vainglorious ; vain glorious
127.6	effeminacy might thus] MORG ; effeminancy might this
127.14	"Sire," ; "~∧"
127.15	steel." ; ~∧"
127.19	Ali ; Aly
127.31	armed with] MORG ; with
127.36	spectacle, ; ~∧
127.38	the gallant ; gallant
127.41	blast] MORG ; the blast
128.6	Church." ; ~.∧
128.15	dyed ; died
128.30	he, ; ~∧
129.21	him. ; ~∧
129.22	thy ; they
129.22	faith,"] MORG ; ~."
129.36	war.] MORG ; discord.
129.40	"Thus," ; "~∧"
129.40	Agapida, ; ~∧
129.40	thus ; "~
130.7	undone).* ; undone)∧*
130.12	May, ; ~;
130.17	all its] MORG ; its
130.25	guttural ; gutteral
131.6	in behalf] MORG ; on ~
131.12	that] MORG ; the
131.17	Boabdil ; Boadel
131.23	cavaliers," said he, "conceive ; ~∧" ~ ~∧ ∧~
131.28	and] MORG ; and they
131.34	rugged and broken country,] MORG ; country rugged and broken,
131.38	¶The] MORG ; The
132.18	treaty." ; Treaty.∧
133.2	begun.] MORG ; began.
133.14	count's ; Counts
133.17	had] MORG ; has

134.14	cries, ; crys,
134.19	breast-plate, ; breast-/plate,
135.21	await the foe] MORG ; await
135.22	piecemeal ; peacemeal
136.39	Ali ; Aly
136.42	homes.] MORG ; houses.
137.12	encomiums] MORG ; enumiums
137.23	speech," ; ~∧"
137.23	Agapida, ; ~∧
137.38	crossbows, ; crossbows∧
138.13	troops, those ; ~. Those
138.17	"Cavaliers," ; "~∧"
138.17	array;] MORG ; arms,
138.18	trenchant ; tranchant
138.34	over-thrown, ; over-/thrown,
139.25	sumpter mules] MORG ; mules
139.27	Rock ; rock
139.29–30	of Cadiz, ; de Cadiz,
139.35	immortal ; inmortal
140.9	del Infantado ; de Infantado
140.23	chestnut] MORG ; chesnut
140.26	del] MORG ; de
140.31	battalions ; battallions
140.33	chestnut ; chesnut
140.42	reverences, ; ~∧
141.2	kissed her] MORG ; kissed
141.4	followed, ; ~∧
141.7	chestnut] MORG ; chesnut
141.13	bravely attired] MORG ; attired
141.15	advanced] MORG ; advance
141.29	her] MORG ; his
141.37	[holograph footnote appears in copytext without designator; placement is as in MORG]
142.9	"The ; ∧~
142.31	Ferdinand∧ ; ~,
143.1	crossbows ; cross-/bows
143.2	breaches] MORG ; breach
143.6	impregnable ; inpregnable
143.17	was assailable] MORG ; assailable
143.19	engineers,] MORG ; engines,
143.19	merely] MORG ; only
143.28	an ; and
143.28	the] MORG ; this

143.37	army, ; ~∧
144.12	discoloured ; discouloured
144.18	melancholy ; melancoly
144.38	philistines,"] MORG ; phillistines,"
145.3	other] MORG ; clergymen and other
145.5	church." ; ~.∧
145.10	THE BATTLE OF THE BRIDGE OF PINOS, AND] MORG ; *omitted*
145.27	arrived, ; ~;
145.29	answered, ; ~·∧
145.32	Granada." ; ~.∧
145.34	chevaliers:] MORG ; cavaliers:
146.1	Yet now,] MORG ; Now,
146.8	fortresses," ; ~∧"
146.10	us, Oh King, ; ~∧ ~ ~∧
146.21	farewell ; fare-/well
146.37	brothers, the Alcaydes∧ ; ~∧ ~ ~,
146.40	Don] MORG ; Dn.
147.03	Don] MORG ; Dn.
147.42	Bishop ; bishop
148.1	year's ; years
148.13	embarrassed ; embarrased
148.27	on to] MORG ; on
148.28	bishop's ; bishops
148.29	laurels, says Agapida, ; ~∧ ~ ~∧
149.12	those∧ ; ~,
149.13	him∧ ; ~,
149.15	skill∧ ; ~,
149.15	fortune∧ ; ~,
149.18	emergency∧ ; ~,
149.22	liable∧ ; ~,
149.22	moment∧ ; ~,
149.25	concord∧ ; ~,
149.27	estate∧ ; ~,
149.28	furnished∧ ; ~,
149.29	and∧ ; ~,
149.32	alfaquis∧ ; ~,
150.15	feared∧ ; ~,
150.15	time∧ ; ~,
150.20	timorously about] MORG ; about
150.28	impulse, ; impluse,
150.31	and myrtle,] MORG ; myrtle,

150.38	scymetar. ; ~∧
150.38	"Enough," said he, ; "~∧" ~ ~∧
151.16	murmur. ; ~∧
151.37	King," ; ~∧"
151.26	threw ; thew
151.37	chronicler, ; ~∧
151.37	King." ; King.∧
152.13	grand divisions] MORG ; divisions
152.22	combatants ; combattants
152.30	instructions] MORG ; orders
152.35	Granada, ; ~∧
152.36	therefore, ; ~∧
152.39	flames] MORG ; flame
153.6	castles, ; ~∧
153.11–12	Agapida, ; ~∧
153.22	board ; bord
153.25–26	existence. ; existance.
155.35	cuirassiers, ; curiassiers,
155.36	was ; were
155.42	cuirassiers. ; curiassers.
156.07	Cabra, ; ~∧
156.18	him, ; ~∧
156.31	flying.†] MORG ; ~.∧
157.4–5	mountains, however, ; ~∧ ~∧
157.14	clemency, ; ~∧
157.30–31	enemy's ; enemies
158.17	war] MORG ; wars
158.23	danger. ; ~∧
158.35	King," ; ~∧"
159.12	Christians. ; ~∧
159.21	He ; he
159.23	nephew; ; ~,
159.32	By] MORG ; by
160.2	siege. ; ~∧
160.34	conceived ; concieved
160.43	captivity. ; ~∧
161.4–5	danger. ; ~
161.5	"God ; ∧~
161.37	danger. ; ~:
162.11	dull heavy] MORG ; heavy
163.1	height.] MORG ; heights
163.2	followed] MORG ; pursued

163.4   arquebusses. The] MORG ; ~, the
163.21   other's ; others
163.21   other's ; others
163.41   enemy] MORG ; army
164.18   "The ; ¶"The
165.6   shouted,] MORG ; cried out,
165.37   near to] MORG ; near
166.31   Cifuentes.] MORG ; Cipientes.
167.9   Mudehares,] MORG ; Mudchares,
167.22   which] MORG ; that
168.24   was as] MORG ; was
168.28   shewn ; shown
168.40   Gibel-faro,] MORG ; Gibel-fano,
169.26   conceived ; concieved
170.6   stern array] MORG ; array
170.10   his] MORG ; is
170.27   hand," ; ~∧"
170.37   warrior's ; warriors
171.1   refusal. ; ~∧
171.32   seaboard.] MORG ; seabord.
171.33   bowshots' ; bowshots
172.17   battle, ; ~∧
172.23   despair. ; ~∧
172.24   height; ; ~∧
172.31   Gibralfaro.* ; ~∧*
173.14   Leon, ; Leon∧ the
173.15   in] MORG ; on
173.18   side. ; ~∧
173.20   board,] MORG ; bord,
173.33–34   They kept up a heavy fire] MORG ; A heavy fire was kept
                up
174.2   Besides ; Beside] MORG
175.10   comrades.] MORG ; comerades.
175.39   Moors, ; ~∧
175.39–40   a little longer in their defence,] MORG ; in their defence a
                little longer
175.42   garrison; ; ~∧
176.8   abandon] MORG ; aband
176.19   Infanta, ; ~∧
176.19   the other, the] MORG ; the
176.21   courtiers, ; ~∧
176.26   a general] MORG ; a
176.36   despair. ; ~∧

177.8	terrific ; terriffic
177.18	message, ; ~∧
177.19	Queen's ; Queens
178.5	Malaga.* *footnote*] MORG ; ~.∧*footnote omitted*
178.7	occasion.∧ *footnote omitted*] MORG ; ~.*footnote*
178.26	night, ; ~;
178.35	stone's ; stones
179.2	nights' ; nights
179.6	havoc ; havock
179.24	wounded; ; ~,
179.30	discharge ; descharge
179.36	accordingly ; accordngly
179.38	rout ; route
180.22	descent ; decent
181.3	Queen's ; Queens
181.16	camp, the mines] MORG ; mines
181.42	fight on] MORG ; fight
183.17	foot under an able commander] MORG ; foot
183.30	adherents. ; ~∧
183.35	"El Zagal," ; ∧~ ~,∧
183.35	"was ; ∧~
184.2	was] MORG ; were
184.17	bits, ; ~∧
184.22	Africa. ; ~∧
184.34	hand's ; hands
185.35	Malaga. ; ~:
186.8	was] MORG ; was the
186.26	unmingled] MORG ; unmixed
186.41	afternoon's ; afternoons
188.13	the Gomeres, ; Gomeres,
188.25	await ; wait
188.34	worn out] MORG ; wornout
189.8–9	wending ; winding] MORG
189.15	pouring ; pourring
189.36	"of ; ∧~
189.36	many," ; ~∧"
189.36	he, "in ; ~∧ ∧~
189.36	Mahomet," ; ~."
190.9	belonging to] MORG ; of
190.11	Zegri," ; ~∧"
192.31	you," ; ~∧"
194.11	victory," ; ~∧"
194.17	foe." ; ~.∧

194.21   combat. ; ~∧
194.38   were not to pause to make spoil nor to take prisoners: They
              were to] MORG ; were to
195.5   imps," ; ~∧"
195.7   "because ; ∧~
195.30   attack. ; ~∧
196.17   horse's ; horses
196.29   Gibralfaro. ; ~∧
197.13   great and wealthy] MORG ; great
197.15   said, ; ~∧
197.19   "I'll ; "Ill
197.23   engines of war] MORG ; engines
197.30   "What ; ∧~
197.41   endures." ; ~.∧
198.1   message∧ Ferdinand replied∧ ; ~, ~ ~,
198.8   degrees, however, ; ~∧ ~∧
198.10   advice ; ~,
198.12   city ; ~,
198.12   letter ; ~,
198.13   supplication. ; ~∧
198.25   preliminary ; preleminary
198.26   surrender. ; ~∧
198.31   some. ; ~∧
198.32   hand," ; ~∧"
198.35   sword," ; ~;"
199.20   pursuits.† ; ~∧†
199.33   choristers ; choiristers
200.10   "Thus ; ∧thus
200.18   "have ; ∧~
200.32   "Ali," ; "~∧"
200.42   *Cura de los Palacios.] MORG ; *omitted*
201.9   "when ; ∧~
201.10   faith, ; ~∧
201.14   "was ; ∧~
201.18   dungeon."† ; ~."∧
201.31   chapel. ; ~∧
202.4   dream; ; ~∧
204.32   stranger. ; ~∧
205.3–4   the inclosure at the Alcazaba ; the Alcazaba
205.23   victories, ; victorys,
206.1   triumph," ; ~∧"
206.1   Agapida, "were ; de ~, ∧~
206.9   Boabdil ; Boaddil

206.18	flattered ; flatered
206.22	luxuriant ; luxarant
206.28	Boabdil ; Boaddil
206.36	Mediterranean ; Meditterranean
207.5	skirts ; skerts
207.20–21	the present] MORG ; present
207.21	strengthening ; strenghtning
207.26	war, however," says ; ~∧ ~∧" ~,
207.27	Agapida, ; ~∧
207.30	Inquisition." ; inquisition.∧
207.39	ordered, ; ~∧
208.9	adapted ; addapted
208.21	punished] MORG ; furnished
208.32	venomous ; venemous
209.16	Zagal's ; Zagals
209.24	blow, ; ~∧
209.34	reconnoitered] MORG ; reconoitered
210.8	for] MORG ; to
210.9	Ordering∧ ; ~,
210.12	put up] MORG ; put up again
210.14	complete ; compleat
210.21	King's ; Kings
210.23	cassock ; cassak
210.34–35	enterprize ; emterprize
210.37	retired, ; ~∧
211.11	ENTERPRIZES ; ENTREPRIZES
211.24	Cullar, ; Callar,
211.32	enemy nor] MORG ; enemy,
211.37	darts, ; darts
212.3	exhausted ; exausted
212.18	Red Mountains, ; red mountains,
212.26	father Fray] MORG ; Fray
212.29	floods ; flowds
212.41	"A ; ∧~
213.7	nature. ; ~∧
213.10	bloody-handed ; bloody-/handed
213.10	adherents." ; ~.∧
214.10–11	monarch El Zagal;] MORG ; El Zagal;
214.21–22	profited ; proffited
214.24	missives ; messives
214.40	mountainiers, ; mountaniers,
215.11	also ; ~,
215.17	city: ; ~∧

215.22	exercised ; excercised
215.28	Mohammed ; Mohammud
215.28	shrewdness, ; shewdness,
215.40	fruits ; fruit
216.9	trains ; train
216.20–21	labyrinth ; labarynth
216.21–22	promising ; promissing
216.28	walls. "Of ; walls, "of
216.28	avail," ; ~∧"
216.29	Mohammed, ; Mohammud∧
217.13	labyrinth. ; labarynth.
217.13	Iago,] MORG ; Jago,
217.19	was ; were
217.22	fight ; figth
217.23	families, ; ~∧
217.25	midst] MORG ; middle
217.33	to retreat] MORG ; retreat
217.41	"Illi ; "~"
217.41	patriis, ; patruis,
217.41	certabant." ; ~.∧
218.10	lightness ; lightress
218.11	disperse, ; ~∧
218.15	fiercely, ; ~;
218.17	shrieks ; shreeks
218.17	night, ; night∧
218.21	labyrinth ; labarynth
218.28	skirts ; skerts
218.35	most] MORG ; more
218.36	Don ; Dn
218.37	Luna,] MORG ; Lara∧
219.11	arquebusses, ; ~∧
219.12	combatants, ; ~:
219.17	inhabitants,] MORG ; combattants,
219.17	Zalfarga, ; ~∧
219.18	generals, ; ~∧
219.24	pallisadoes. ; ~∧
220.9	smoking ; smoaking
220.16	scenes ; ~;
220.21	principal] MORG ; principle
220.25	encampment. ; emcampment.
220.33	shadow ; shaddow
220.40–41	labyrinths ; labarynths
220.42	Moors ; ~,

221.2–3	garrisoned and provided, and too ; ~, ~ ~∧ ~ two
221.5	armies;] MORG ; enemies;
221.6	shut] MORG ; shot
221.7	rivers.] MORG ; two rivers.
221.18	therefore, ; ~∧
221.20–21	would be] MORG ; would
221.24–25	provisions for so] MORG ; provissions for the
222.22	Don ; Dn
222.28	camps," ; ~∧"
222.36	Christians, ; ~∧
222.38	skirmishings; ; ~∧
222.41	work, however, ; ~∧ ~∧
223.19	water, ; ~∧
223.19	Agapida, ; ~∧
224.16	Christian ; Christians
224.18	join] MORG ; join them
224.28	making ; makeing
224.30	however, ; ~∧
224.36	fast as] MORG ; fast
224.39	They] MORG ; The
225.22	ye] MORG ; you
225.40	handkerchief at the end of it,] MORG ; handkerchief,
226.7	Guadix, ; Baza,
226.27	was ; were
226.34–227.1	Alhambra; ; Alhamra;
226.36	has recounted] MORG ; recounted
227.8	every] MORG ; any
227.18	Ben Hassan,] MORG ; Ban-Hassan
227.21	Yahye,] MORG ; Yahge,
228.35	Millan, ; ~∧
228.40	way," ; ~∧"
228.34	Agapida, "ever ; ~∧ "even
230.1	inquired] MORG ; enquired
230.3	"Nay," ; "~∧"
230.11	monarch," ; ~,∧
230.11	"was ; ∧~
230.14	Turk." ; ~.∧
230.16	Abarca ; ~,
230.26	ignorant."† ; ~.∧†
230.34	"to ; ~∧
231.1	iron] MORG ; Iron
231.7	wended] MORG ; winded
231.8	Queens. ; ~∧

231.12   rhetoric, ; rethoric,
231.17   convent ; convents
231.23   companion.† ; ~.∧
231.31   representations] MORG ; represantations
232.29   rugged] MORG ; ragged
232.41   traversing] MORG ; traversing the mountains
233.1   day's ; days
233.3   granary,] MORG ; granery,
233.5   expenses] MORG ; expences
233.14   assigning] MORG ; assignning
233.19   activity, ; ~∧
233.21   accessible ; accesible
233.31–32   brocades, ; ~∧
233.36   on] MORG ; in
234.2   BEFELL ; BEFEL
234.15   rainy season] MORG ; rainy-/season
234.15   cry; ; ~∧
234.34   squares. ; ~;
235.1   ramblas ; Ramblas
235.9   rain, ; ~∧
235.24   day's ; days
235.27   convoys] MORG ; conveys
236.4   DEFENCE ; DEFFENCE
236.13   exaggerated] MORG ; exaggereted
236.17   patience, a little more patience,"] MORG ; patience∧"
236.17   shrewd] MORG ; shrewed
236.21   Castilian] MORG ; Christian
236.27   nearly] MORG ; near
236.35   fly.] MORG ; flight.
236.35   grasping] MORG ; grassping
236.36   Gonzalvo] MORG ; Gozalvo
237.3   skirmishes;] MORG ; ~,
237.13   there ; their] MORG
237.17   winter ; ~"
237.19   homes] MORG ; towers
237.20   heart.] MORG ; health.
237.21   defence] MORG ; deffence
237.21   aid." ; ~.∧
237.26   apparel," ; ~,∧
237.27   "when ; ∧~
237.30   vanity," said they, ; ~∧" ~ ~∧
237.41   publicly] MORG ; publickly

237.42	this] MORG ; these
238.14	trumpet] MORG ; trumpets
238.17	resplendent ; resplendant
238.18	ground. ; ~;
238.20	Spain. A] MORG ; Spain, a
238.25	"Cavaliers," ; "~∧"
239.17	softened,] MORG ; softned,
239.17	passion] MORG ; passions
239.29	yet hopeless] MORG ; hopeless
239.31	Don Gutiere ; Dn. Gutierre
239.32	veteran alcayde] MORG ; valiant alcaide
239.35	other's ; others
239.38	sovereigns," ; ~∧"
239.40	property, ; ~∧
240.8	permission, ; ~∧
240.19	question. ; ~,
240.26	sank ; sunk] MORG
240.26	heart.] MORG ; hearth.
240.29	alfaquis ; alfaques
240.29	communicating ; comunicating
240.33	alfaquis ; alfaques
240.36	ineffectual. ; innefectual.
241.4	maintaining] MORG ; mainting
241.26	professions] MORG ; profession
241.29	irresistible] MORG ; irresisible
241.43	infidel. ; ~;
242.15	apostate,] MORG ; apostata,
242.29	men, ; ~∧
242.41	Mudexares ; Mudexarras
243.16	Moor," ; ~∧"
243.17	intrusted ; entrusted
243.18	who] MORG ; that
243.25	majesties ; majesty's
243.29	engage ; engaged
243.32	Isabella, ; ~∧
243.33	"Yes," ; "~∧"
243.33	replied∧ ; ~"
243.36	abodes; ; ~,
243.37	peaceable ; peaceble
243.38	Isabella; "they ; ~∧ ∧~
243.39	thyself?" ; ~?∧
243.39	"Nothing," ; "~∧"

243.40   my horses] MORG ; horses
244.9   seek a soldier's] MORG ; see a soldiers
244.25   man's ; mans
244.28   divan, ; ~∧
244.31   faith ; ~;
244.31   interests] MORG ; interest
245.6   Fate, said he, ; ~∧ ~ ~∧
245.13   profound and pious] MORG ; pious
245.19   done! ; ~!"
245.23   remains," ; ~∧"
245.26   inhabitants. ; ~,
245.26   disposed] MORG ; dispose
245.28   sovereigns?" ; ~?∧
245.30   he, ; ~∧
245.39   God!" ; ~!∧
245.40   done!" ; done!∧
246.9   jewels ; jewells
246.13–14   Andarax and the valley of Alhaurin] MORG ; Alhaurin
246.17   maravedies.* ; ~;*
247.1   Andarax, ; Andaraxa,
247.37   King.* *footnote* ; King.∧ *omitted*
247.11   Alhambra ; Alhamba
247.17   great! ; ~!"
247.18   me, ; ~∧
247.21   ccased," ; ~∧"
247.23–24   quicksands. ; quiksands.
247.25   Chico, ; ~∧
247.30   approached, ; ~∧
247.31   groans] MORG ; growns
248.4   unbelievers. ; ~;
248.5   dismemberment ; desmemberment
248.10   discomfited ; descomfited
248.17   missives] MORG ; missions
248.27   Alhambra] MORG ; Alxambra
248.36   promising ; promissing
249.25   excel ; excell
250.27   councils, ; ~∧
250.35   in the most] MORG ; on the most
251.11   provisions ; provissions
251.17   Xenel ; Zenil
251.37   was] MORG ; had been
252.8   Moors, however, ; ~∧ ~∧
252.27   havoc and confusion] MORG ; havoc

252.28	forces. ; ~∧
252.39	valiantly] MORG ; bravely
253.2	life.* ; ~.∧
253.3	ambuscadoes] MORG ; ambuscades
253.5	perceived, however, ; ~∧ ~∧
253.9	would ; woul
253.26	Christian] MORG ; Christians
253.29	*In] MORG ; ∧~
253.30–31	one day demanded ; demanded one day
253.35	age. Mariana, L. 25. c. 15. ; age∧
254.18	son, ; ~∧
254.25	battlement.] MORG ; battlements.
254.28	or Moors] MORG ; Moors
254.31	summer's ; summers
254.32	this] MORG ; that
254.33	gauge ; guage
254.41	Agapida, ; ~;
254.42	consummated, ; consumated,
255.13	downfall; ; ~∧
255.14	disposable ; disposeable
255.17	a vassal] MORG ; vassal to
255.23	the banners] MORG ; banners
255.27	of course] MORG ; of
255.28	the Alhambra,] MORG ; Alhambra,
256.17	squadrons] MORG ; squadron
256.37	in] MORG ; on
257.4	barbican ; barbacan
257.5	garrison, however, ; ~∧ ~∧
257.15	cross-bows] MORG ; cross-/bows
257.26	tower] MORG ; town
257.26	ruin] MORG ; ruins
257.30	stancheons,] MORG ; stauncheons,
258.16	Quexada. ; Quezada.
258.34	Often, however, ; ~∧ ~∧
259.12	moment's ; moments
259.21	turban, however, ; ~∧ ~∧
259.26	here," ; ~∧"
259.30	Tendilla, ; ~∧
259.33–34	approaching," ; ~∧"
259.38	shields, ; ~∧
260.8	escort ; ~,
260.34	Real, ; real,
261.2	formerly, ; ~∧

261.13	vegetation, ; vegation,
261.13	cotton, ; ∼∧
261.14	mulberries, ; mulberies,
261.18	promontories ; promonteries
261.24	precipitous ; precepitous
261.30	veteran, ; ∼∧
261.33	commander; ; ∼,
262.2	within] MORG ; up within
262.3	maintained ; mantained
262.22	promontory ; promontary
262.40	banner," ; ∼∧"
262.42	head; ; ∼.
263.19	fortress, ; ∼.
263.30	ineffectual ; inefectual
263.37	farther] MORG ; further
264.2	reeking and smoking] MORG ; reaking and smoaking
264.6	REGAL] MORG ; ROYAL
264.24	and had] MORG ; and
264.30	wives, ; wives∧ and
265.2	practiced ; practiced,
265.3	in their] MORG ; on their
265.5	friends," ; ∼∧"
265.10	wish, however, ; ∼∧ ∼∧
265.14	royal word,] MORG ; word,
265.18	feared ; feard
265.20	contemporary historian, ∧Andres ; cotemporary ∼, "∼
266.2	execrations ; excrations
266.7	entirely, ; intirely,
267.2	Andalusia."* ; ∼.∧*
267.6	"How ; ∧∼
267.17	now remained] MORG ; remained
267.17	phantom ; phamton
267.19	husbandman] MORG ; husbandmen
267.25	that its ; its
267.26	Jews ; jews
268.4	campaign ; campain
268.6	Don ; Dn.
268.28	months' supply, independent ; months ∼, independant
268.38	"to ; ∧∼
269.3	the foray. Let] MORG ; foray, let
269.6	calvagados ; calvagades
269.11	"into ; ∧into
269.16	provisions, ; provissions,

269.18	skirmishings.] MORG ; skirmishes.
269.18	Muhamed Aben Zayde ; Muhammed ~ Zayda
269.27	soldier's ; soldiers
269.33–34	cavaliers," said he, "is ; ~∧∧ ~ ~∧∧~
270.5	Alhambra. ; ~∧
271.24	avoided. ; ~∧
272.17	exploits," ; ~,∧
272.38	others, rejoined ; ~ ∧ ~,
273.3	Granada.* ;~∧*
273.17	magnificent ; magnificient
273.20	princess] MORG ; princesses
273.26	melodious ; melodius
273.34	comrades ; comerades
273.36	Pulgar's ; Pulgars
274.17	satisfaction," ; ~∧"
274.21	alfaquis." ; ~∧"
274.41	immovable. ; inmoveable.
275.9	huge] MORG ; large
275.39	to him] MORG ; him
275.40	upon] MORG ; on
275.41	shield,] MORG ; buckler
276.3	upon] MORG ; on
276.8	"but ; ∧~
276.19	to the] MORG ; the
276.26	Queen's ; Queens
276.36	cooled; ; ~∧
276.42	either killed,] MORG ; killed,
276.42	prisoner,] MORG ; prisoners,
277.4	Queen's ; Queens
277.6	attributed ; attributted
277.7	it was all] MORG ; all was
277.24	day's ; days
277.26	various] MORG ; warriors
278.3	little gaudy] MORG ; gaudy
278.4	domineered ; domineeried
278.15	day's ; days
278.17	preparation] MORG ; preparations
278.21	altar; ; ~,
278.22	day's ; days
279.17	within] MORG ; with
279.26	plate, ; ~∧
279.31	heedlessness] MORG ; heedleness
279.35	night's ; nights

280.1   melody,] MORG ; melodys,
280.9   their] MORG ; the
280.22   them, ; ~.
281.3   himself] MORG ; themselves
281.9   survivors] MORG ; survivers
281.14   defend ; deffend
281.24   persevering] MORG ; persueing
281.25   uninterrupted ; unimterrupted
281.36   beloved∧ ; ~,
282.23   princess," ; ~,∧
282.24   "calling ; ∧~
282.33   cavalgada ; cavalgade
282.38   sank ; sunk
282.40   foretold ; fortold
283.24   early," ; ~∧"
284.8   attack ; attacks
284.14   maintenance. ; maintainance.
285.5   "There ; ∧~
285.9   "Allah ; ∧Allah
285.9   viziers and alfaquis. ; Viziers and alfaquies;
285.22   part, by Allah, ; ~∧ ~ ~∧
285.22   them!" ; ~!∧
285.32   were ; where
286.37   end ; ehd
287.14–15   denounced ; denonced
287.22   roaming] MORG ; running
287.35   mournfully, ; ~∧
287.36   grievously ; grieviously
288.13   apartments ; appartments
288.14   inhabitants. ; ~:
288.22   upon] MORG ; to
288.34   begun] MORG ; began
289.8   Senior," ; ~∧"
289.27   crusade, ; cruzade,
289.36–37   choristers ; choiristers
290.3   King's ; Kings
290.7   Boabdil's ; Boabdils
290.8   bosom ; bossom
290.15   hands."† ; ~."∧
290.30   leagues' ; leagues
291.8   she, ; ~;
291.11   Sire," ; ~∧"
291.14   monarch, ; ~∧

291.34	squadrons ; squadroons
292.35	accursed] MORG ; accused
293.3	turbaned] MORG ; turban
293.7	ceilings. ; cielings.
293.13–29	The existence . . . . Ximenes [appears as footnote in MORG]
293.21	with] MORG ; the
293.27	antiquarian, however, ; ~∧ ~∧
293.36	Agapida, ; ~∧
294.21	terrific ; terriffic
294.32	pretensions ; pretentions
294.34	master's ; masters
295.4	"Senior," ; "~∧"
295.27	involuntarily ; involuntaraly
295.28	spontaneously ; spontaniously
295.35	forty ; thirty] MORG
296.12	instance," ; ~,∧
296.12	chronicler, "of ; ~∧ ∧~
296.19	crusade ; cruzade
296.23	death, which happened] MORG ; death∧
296.24	age, almost] MORG ; age, which happened almost
297.16	None, ; ~∧
297.42	helmet ; morion
298.19	in] MORG ; of
299.2	resolutely] MORG ; resolute
299.10	Alpuxarras. ; ~;
299.18	time, ; ~∧
299.23	dead," ; ~∧"
300.1	appellation. ; appellaion.
300.1	they, ; ~∧
300.4	throughout ; througout
300.4	towns; ; towens;
300.4	approach, ; ~∧
300.16	sides ; side
300.32	he, ; ~:
300.37	mountain ; mountains
300.37	terraces; ; ~,
300.40	overturned rocks ; rocks
301.15	he. ; ~∧
301.16	wives, ; ~∧
301.21	time," ; ~∧"
302.4	"No," said Don Alonzo proudly, ; ∧~," ~ Dn ~ ~ ~∧
302.6	stretched ; streched

302.10   "Let ; ∧~
302.16   height, ; heights,
302.19   grievously ; greviously
302.32   "thou ; ∧~
302.32   prize; ; ~;"
303.4   discretion, ; ~∧
303.6–9   His soul . . . communion ; [separate paragraph in MORG]
303.6   the worthy Padre] MORG ; Padre
303.9   communion."* ; ~.∧*
303.18   succeeded, however, ; ~∧ ~∧
303.27   had contributed] MORG ; contributed
303.40   clefts] MORG ; clifts

LIST OF REJECTED SUBSTANTIVES

This list records substantive variants which appear in the Author's Revised Edition [ARE] (New York: George P. Putnam, 1850). When the only variant is in spelling, including the spelling of names, the entry has been omitted from this list; however, if an entry is given because of other variants, the spellings of the respective editions have been retained.

The numbers on the left refer to the page and line number of the Twayne *Granada*. The reading on the left of the spaced semicolon is the Twayne reading; the reading on the right is from the ARE. When a substantive from the Morgan manuscript is rejected, it is identified by the abbreviation MORG. A reading in the ARE which agrees with the Twayne edition but differs from the MORG will be designated ARE to the left of the spaced semicolon.

The variants at the beginning and end of the ARE are so great that the pertinent texts have been reprinted in their entirety in the Appendix.

4.6–7	domination of the Moors.* ; Moorish domination.*
4.11	contest. ; encounter.
7.28	TRIBUTE FROM] ARE ; TRIBUTE OF] MORG
7.29	¶It was in ; ¶In
12.7–8	that Muley Aben Hassan made his famous attack upon Zahara. The ; the
12.14–15	storm, . . . In ; storm. In
13.6	lain ; laid
13.32	that burst ; and burst
14.1	possessed of ; possessed by
14.12	shall dwell ; will dwell
14.12–13	shall fall ; will fall
14.13	shall be led ; will be led
14.16	They ; Some
14.17	mourning; . . . gather ; morning: while some gathered
14.18	to alarm ; alarm
14.19	to curse ; cursing
14.19	fierce Aben Hassan. ; king.
14.24	them to aid ; the African princes to aid him with men and supplies
14.26	unbelievers. [end of chapter] ; unbelievers. ¶While discontent exhaled itself in murmurs among the common people, however, it fomented in dangerous conspiracies

among the nobles, and Muley Abul Hassan was startled by information of a design to depose him and place his son Boabdil upon the throne. His first measure was to confine the prince and his mother in the tower of Comares; then, calling to mind the prediction of the astrologers, that the youth would one day set [sic] on the throne of Granada, he impiously set the stars at defiance. "The sword of the executioner," said he, "shall prove the fallacy of those lying horoscopes, and shall silence the ambition of Boabdil." ¶The Sultana Ayxa, apprised of the imminent danger of her son, concerted a plan for his escape. At the dead of the night she gained access to his prison, and tying together the shawls and scarfs of herself and her female attendants, lowered him down from a balcony of the Alhambra, to the steep rocky hill-side which sweeps down to the Darro. Here some of her devoted adherents were waiting to receive him, who, mounting him on a swift horse, spirited him away to the city of Guadix, in the Alpuxaras. [end of chapter]

14.31–34   of Zahara, ... He immediately ; of Zahara, though the outrage of the Moor happened most opportunely. The war between Castile and Portugal had come to a close; the factions of the Spanish nobles were for the most part quelled. The Castilian monarchs had now, therefore, turned their thoughts to the cherished object of their ambition, the conquest of Granada. The pious heart of Isabella yearned to behold the entire peninsula redeemed from the domination of the Infidel; while Ferdinand, in whom religious zeal was mingled with temporal policy, looked with a craving eye to the rich territory of the Moor, studded with wealthy towns and cities. Muley Abul Hassan had rashly or unwarily thrown the brand that was to produce the wide conflagration. Ferdinand was not the one to quench the flames. He immediately

14.37–15.2   Moors, ... ¶Among ; Moors. ¶Among
15.23   on ; in
16.11   and Sancho ; Sancho
16.12   who ; and others, who
16.22   Their ; This
16.32   of Zahara; ; at Zahara;
16.32   rich town ; town
16.37   take possession ; get possession
17.34   The ; That

17.35	earth ; floor
17.38	their unmanly ; unmanly
19.21	they ; the latter
19.24	surrendered. ; surrendered themselves captives.
19.26	slaves ; the slaves
19.39	was ; were
20.19	on ; in
20.27	the ; its
22.1	Spanish ; of the Spanish
23.17–35	assailants. . . . sensible of ; assailants. ¶Muley Abul Hassan now became sensible of
24.22	day ; the day
24.25	in ; of
24.40	likewise to implore ; likewise, imploring
28.37	main part ; main party
29.24	Sidonia ; Medina Sidonia
29.31–32	gracious sight to behold the ; gracious spectacle–the
29.32	those two ancient foes ; those hitherto inveterate foes
29.33	Cadiz. When the marquis beheld his ; Cadiz. At sight of his
29.33	deliverer approaching he melted ; deliverer the marques melted
29.35	admiration; they ; admiration. The late deadly rivals
31.2–33.15	the kingdom. . . . He took ; the kingdom. At the same time the nobles who had secretly conspired to depose the old king and elevate his son Boabdil to the throne, had matured their plans, in concert with the prince, who had been joined in Guadix by hosts of adherents. An opportunity soon presented to carry their plans into operation. ¶Muley Abul Hassan had a royal country palace, with gardens and fountains, called the Alixares, situated on the Cerro del Sol, or Mountain of the Sun; a height, the ascent to which leads up from the Alhambra, but which towers far above that fortress, and looks down as from the clouds upon it, and upon the subjacent city of Granada. It was a favorite retreat of the Moorish kings, to inhale the pure mountain breezes, and leave far below the din and turmoil of the city. Muley Abul Hassan had passed a day among its bowers, in company with his favorite wife, Zoraya, when, towards evening, he heard a strange sound rising from the city, like the gathering of a storm, or the sullen roar of the ocean. Apprehensive of evil, he ordered the officers of his guard to descend with all speed to the city, and reconnoitre. The intelligence brought back was as-

tounding. A civil war was raging in the city. Boabdil had
been brought from Guadix by the conspirators, the foremost of whom were the gallant race of the Abencerrages.
He had entered the Albaycin in triumph, and been hailed
with rapture, and proclaimed king in that populous quarter of the city. Abul Cacim Vanegas, the vizier, at the head
of the royal guards, had attacked the rebels; and the noise
which had alarmed the king, was the din of fighting in the
streets and squares.

¶Muley Abul Hassan hastened to descend to the Alhambra,
confident that, ensconced in that formidable fortress, he
could soon put an end to the rash commotion. To his surprise and dismay he found the battlements lined with hostile troops; Aben Comixa, the alcayde, had declared in
favor of Boabdil, and elevated his standard on the towers;
thus, cut off from his stronghold, the old monarch was fain
to return to the Alixares.

¶The conflict lasted throughout the night with carnage on
both sides. In the morning Abul Cacim, driven out of the
city, appeared before the old king with his broken squadrons, and told him there was no safety but in flight. "Allah
Achbar, (God is great!)" exclaimed old Muley, "it is in vain
to contend against what is written in the book of fate. It
was predestined that my son should sit upon the throne—
Allah forfend the rest of the prediction." So saying he
made a hasty retreat, escorted by Abul Cacim Vanegas and
his troops, who conducted him to the castle of Mondujar,
in the valley of Locrin. Here he was joined by many powerful cavaliers, relatives of Abul Cacim and partisans of
Zoraya; among whom were Cid Hiaya, Aben Jamy, and
Reduan Vanegas, men who had alcaydes, vassals at their
command, and possessed great influence in Almeria and
Baza. He was joined, also, by his brother Abdallah, commonly called El Zagal, or the Valiant; who was popular in
many parts of the kingdom. All these offered to aid him
with their swords in suppressing the rebellion.

¶Thus reinforced, Muley Abul Hassan determined on a sudden blow for the recovery of his throne and the punishment of the rebels. He took

33.39   son, and several bloody ; son, the latter of whom was called
              by the Spaniards *El Rey Chico*, or the Young King; but
              though bloody

33.40   yet they ; they

34.9   she, "shall we ; she,
34.10   shall we abandon ; Abandon
34.11–12   would give new courage to the enemy, arguing fear or fee-
                  bleness in our councils. You ; would argue fear or feeble-
                  ness, and give new courage to the enemy. You
34.14   a war ; one
34.21   were immediately ; were
34.27   Loxa, ; Loxa, or Loja,
34.27–28   Alhama. For this purpose he called ; Alhama, and all impor-
                  tant to its protection. It was in fact a military point, situ-
                  ated in a pass of the mountains between the kingdoms of
                  Granada and Castile, and commanded a main entrance to
                  the vega. The Xenil flowed by its walls, and it had a strong
                  castle or citadel built on a rock. In preparing for the siege
                  of this formidable place, Ferdinand called
35.17   chivalry marched therefore ; chivalry, therefore, marched
35.28   assistance, and there ; assistance. There
36.10   Boabdil el Chico. ; Boabdil.
36.13–14   frontier. He was in ; frontier. Lord of Zagra, and in the re-
                  ceipt of rich revenues, he expended them all in paying
                  scouts and spies, and maintaining a small but chosen
                  force, with which to foray into the Christian territories;
                  and so straitened was he at times by these warlike ex-
                  penses, that when his daughter married Boabdil, her brid-
                  al dress and jewels had to be borrowed. He was now in
36.42   Giron, Master of Calatrava; as ; Giron, grand master of Cal-
                  atrava, whose burnished armor, emlazoned with the red
                  cross of his order, made him a mark for the missiles of the
                  enemy. As
37.1   He fell instantly from his horse, but ; The lance and bridle
                  fell from his hands, he faltered in his saddle, and would
                  have fallen to the ground, but
37.37   surrounded, the Moors assailed him furiously and twice he
                  owed ; surrounded, and twice owed
38.3   were slain,] ARE ; slain,] MORG
38.7   greatest ; the greatest
38.8   the camp ; camp
38.23   from thence Ferdinand returned ; Ferdinand returned
                  thence
40.2   Celemin. From hence he sent ; Celemin, and sent
40.3   lances who were ; lances
40.4   to keep ; keep
40.19   ¶Muley Aben Hassan ; ¶He

40.19   secret ; secret, however,
40.20   Pedro de Vargas ; alcayde of Gibraltar
40.20   movements. His ; movements; but his
40.21–29   of the place, . . . notice that ; of his post. Luckily there ar-
               rived at this juncture a squadron of the armed galleys, un-
               der Carlos de Valera, recently stationed in the Straits.
               Pedro de Vargas prevailed upon him to take charge of Gi-
               braltar during his temporary absence, and forthwith sal-
               lied out at midnight, at the head of seventy chosen
               horsemen. By his command alarm fires were lighted on
               the mountains, signals that
40.29–30   that the peasants might drive ; at sight of which the peasants
               were accustomed to drive
40.30–31   of refuge; and he sent couriers, riding like mad in ; of refuge.
               He sent couriers also spurring in
40.31–32   summoning the fighting men of the neighborhood to ; sum-
               moning all capable of bearing arms to
40.32–33   Castellar. ¶Muley Aben Hassan ; Castellar. This was a town
               strongly posted on a steep height, by which the Moorish
               king would have to return. ¶Muley Abul Hassan
40.33   about ; on
40.41   vanguard was ; van-guard followed
41.1   that they ; when they
41.8   thrown in ; thrown into
41.21   rushed forth ; rushed
41.31   the hill, ; hill,
41.39   Fearing ; Fearing that
41.41–42   returned ; retreated
42.26   deliver them ; deliver
42.33   monarch and replied in the same tone. ¶He ; monarch. He
42.42   at ; in
43.7   speed, hurrying ; speed, before the close of day, hurrying
43.13   incursion into his own ; inroad into his
45.9   they pranced] ARE ; pranced] MORG
45.41   prankling ; pranking
47.22   partake of ; partake
47.23   assembled together, ; together,
48.1   filled with ; formed of
48.2   above them ; above, there
48.5   from ; from that of
48.36   footing ; foothold
49.13   their ; the
50.18–21   Zagal. Finding . . . . survived. [end of paragraph] ; Zagal.

The count, himself, was assailed by six of the enemy, against whom he was defending himself with desperation, when their leader, struck with the inequality of the fight, ordered the others to desist, and continued the combat alone. The count, already exhausted, was soon compelled to surrender; his brother, Don Pedro de Silva, and the few of his retainers who survived, were likewise taken prisoners. The Moorish cavalier who had manifested such a chivalrous spirit in encountering the count singly, was Raduan Vanegas, brother of the former vizier of Muley Abul Hassan, and one of the leaders of the faction of the sultana Zoraya. [end of paragraph]

51.3	place ; spot
51.4	place is pointed out to the present day, and is ; place, is [*sic*]
51.9	by ; at
51.22	into ; in
52.2–3	warrior, whom they had lately seen to issue so ; warrior who had lately issued so
52.7	asked ; asked of his companions,
52.8–9	when . . . been ; when told that one by one they had been
52.10	spoke ; spake
52.14	consolation, for, ; consolation, rejoicing to find that
52.15	that ; which
52.15	family, . . . his ; family, his
52.17	turned in an agony of suspence towards ; turned, in fearful suspense, toward
52.19	relation, ; relative,
52.25	that ; which
52.38	several ; some
53.23	donations ; donations and bequests
54.17	by the fierce old Moor, his ; by his
54.27	those ; these
54.36	around ; round
54.37–38	though they were going to a ; though for a
54.38	reeds, ; canes,
55.7	which looks out over the vega. From thence ; overlooking the vega, whence
55.8	which leads ; leading
55.13	and anticipated success that should ; anticipating deeds of prowess that would
55.13–14	father. In passing ; father. The appearance of Boabdil was well calculated to captivate the public eye, if we may judge from the description given by the abbot of Rute, in

his manuscript history of the House of Cordoba. He was mounted on a superb white charger, magnificently caparisoned. His corselets were of polished steel, richly ornamented; studded with gold nails, and lined with crimson velvet. He wore a steel casque, exquisitely chiselled and embossed; his scimetar and dagger of Damascus were of highest temper; he had a round buckler at his shoulder, and bore a ponderous lance. In passing

55.14	the King ; he
55.17–19	fears, for he considered them mere idle fancies; or rather, says Fray Antonio Agapida, he was an incredulous pagan, puffed up with confidence and vainglory. He ; fears as idle fancies. He
55.26	courtiers about Boabdil ; courtiers
55.27–28	proceeding, . . . the King, ; proceeding; the king,
55.28–29	dismayed, but ; dismayed by these portents, but
55.30	royal army ; army
55.33	once more mounted ; mounted
56.4	that they might elude ; to elude
56.5	the art of war, but he ; warfare, but
56.12	Boabdil el Chico, ; Boabdil;
56.28	cavaliers ; of cavaliers
57.8	were ; was
57.10	steeds ; studs,
57.16	all brave ; brave
57.22	There ; Here
57.32	Donzeles ; Donzeles,* [footnote: *The Donzeles were young cavaliers who had been pages in the royal household, but now formed an élite corps in the army.]
58.35	when they should have discovered ; on discovering
59.4	superb white ; superb black and white
59.22–23	Deigo Cabrera Alcayde of Menica ; Diego de Cabrera, alcayde of Doña Mencia,
60.5	¶"Sire," ; "In truth,"
60.6	but ; for some time, but I confess, I
60.6	It appears ; It cannot be the ensign of any single commander or community, for none would venture single-handed to attack you. It appears
60.8–9	you; for it is not probable that any single commander or community would venture to attack you. I ; you, and I
60.9	you therefore ; you
60.1	charged down ; charged

60.27   majesty!" ; highness!"

60.36–61.32   flight. . . . spurs to ; flight. If Boabdil had displayed little of
               the talents of a general in the outset of his enterprise, he
               manifested courage and presence of mind amid the disas-
               ters of its close. Seconded by a small body of cavalry, the
               choicest and most loyal of his guards, he made repeated
               stand against the press of the foe, in a skirmishing retreat
               of about three leagues; and the way was strown with the
               flower of his chivalry. At length, they came to the brook
               of Martin Gonzales, or Mingozales, as it is called by the
               Moorish chroniclers; which swollen by recent rain was
               now a deep and turbid torrent. Here a scene of confusion
               ensued. Horse and foot precipitated themselves into the
               stream. Some of the horses stuck fast in the mire and
               blocked up the ford; others trampled down the foot sol-
               diers; many were drowned and more carried down the
               stream. Such of the foot-soldiers as gained the opposite
               side, immediately took to flight; the horsemen, too, who
               had struggled through the stream, gave reins to their
               steeds and scoured for the frontier. ¶The little band of de-
               voted cavaliers about the king serried their forces, to keep
               the enemy in check, fighting with them hand to hand, un-
               til he should have time to cross. In the tumult, his horse
               was shot down, and he became environed in the throng of
               foot-soldiers, struggling forward to the ford, and in peril
               from the lances of their pursuers. Conscious that his rich
               array made him a conspicuous object, he retreated along
               the bank of the river, and endeavored to conceal himself
               in a thicket of willows and tamarisks. Thence, looking
               back, he beheld his loyal band at length give way, suppos-
               ing, no doubt, he had effected his escape. They crossed
               the ford, followd pell-mell by the enemy, and several of
               them were struck down in the stream. ¶While Boabdil was
               meditating to throw himself into the water, and endeavor
               to swim across, he was discovered by Martin Hurtado,
               regidor of Lucena, a brave cavalier, who had been captive
               in the prisons of Granada, and exchanged for a Christian
               knight. Hurtado attacked the king with a pike, but was
               kept at bay; until seeing other soldiers approaching, Boab-
               dil cried for quarters; proclaiming himself a person of high
               rank, who would pay a noble ransom. At this moment
               came up several men of Vaena, of the troop of the count

de Cabra. Hearing the talk of ransom, and noticing the splendid attire of the Moor, they endeavored to secure for themselves so rich a prize. One of them seized hold of Boabdil, but the latter resented the indignity, by striking him to the earth with a blow of his poniard. Others of Hurtado's townsmen coming up, a contest arose between the men of Lucena and Vaena, as to who had a right to the prisoner. The noise brought Don Diego Fernandez de Cordova to the spot, who, by his authority, put an end to the altercation. Boabdil, finding himself unknown by all present, concealed his quality, giving himself out as the son of Aben Alnayer, a cavalier of the royal household.*
[*footnote:* *Garibay, Lib. 40, cap. 31.] Don Diego treated him with great courtesy; put a red band round his neck in sign of his being a captive, and sent him under an escort to the castle of Lucena, where his quality would be ascertained, his ransom arranged, and the question settled as to who had made him prisoner. ¶This done, the count put spurs to

61.32	horse he ; horse, and
61.34	continued to ; continued together to
61.39	lances ; lancers
62.25	they cried ; cried they
62.29	sunk ; sank
62.36	army; the loss of the King, and ; army, and
63.2	that ; the
63.25–64.30	subsequently taken. . . . George they ; subsequently taken.

¶Boabdil remained a prisoner in the state tower of the citadel of Lucena, under the vigilance of Alonzo de Rueda, esquire of the alcayde of the Donzeles; his quality was still unknown, until the 24th of April, three days after the battle. On that day some prisoners, natives of Granada, just brought in, caught a sight of the unfortunate Boabdil, despoiled of his royal robes. Throwing themselves at his feet, they broke forth in loud lamentations; apostrophizing him as their lord and king.

Great was the astonishment and triumph of the count de Cabra and Don Diego Fernandez de Cordova on learning the rank of the supposed cavalier. They both ascended to the castle to see that he was lodged in a style befitting his quality. When the good count beheld, in the dejected captive before him, the monarch who had so recently appeared in royal splendor, surrounded by an army, his generous heart was touched by sympathy. He said every thing to comfort him that became a courteous and Christian knight, observing that the same mutability of things which had suddenly brought him low, might as rapidly restore him to prosperity, since in this world nothing is stable, and sorrow, like joy, has its allotted term. ¶The action here recorded was called by some the battle of Lucena, by others the battle of the Moorish king, because of the capture of Boabdil. Twenty-two banners, taken on the occasion, were borne in triumph into Vaena on the 23d of April, St. George's day, and hung up in the church. There they remain (says a historian of after times) to this day. Once a year, on the festival of St. George, they

63.32–64.2   their forefathers. . . . allotted term. ; their forefathers.*
[*footnote:* *Several circumstances relative to the capture of Boabdil vary in this from the first edition, in consequence of later light thrown on the subject by Don Miguel Lafuente Alcantara in his history of Granada. He has availed himself much of various ancient documents relative to the battle, especially the History of the House of Cordova, by the Abbot of Rute, a descendant of that family; a rare manuscript, of which few copies exist. ¶The question as to the person entitled to the honor and reward for having captured the king, long continued a matter of dispute between the people of Lucena and Vaena. On the 20th of October, 1520, about thirty-seven years after the event, an examination of several witnesses to the fact took place before the Chief Justice of the fortress of Lucena, at the instance on Bartolomy Hurtado, the son of Martin, when the claim of his father was established by Doña Leonora Hernandez, lady in attendant on the mother of the alcayde of los Donzeles, who testified being present when Boabdil signalized Martin Hurtado as his captor. ¶The chief honor of the day, and of course of the defeat and capture of the Moorish Monarch, was given by the sovereign to the count de Cabra; the second to his nephew, Don Diego Fernandez de Cordova. ¶Among the curious papers cited by Alcantara, is one existing in the archives of the House of Medina Celi, giving the account of the treasurer of Don Diego Fernandez, as to the sums expended by his lord in the capture of the king; the reward given to some soldiers for a standard of the king's which they had taken; to others for the wounds they had re-

ceived, &c. ¶Another paper speaks of an auction at Lucena on the 28th of April, of horses and mules taken in the battle. Another paper states the gratuities of the alcayde of los Donzeles to the soldiery—four fanegas, or about four hundred weight of wheat, and a lance to each horseman, two fanegas of wheat and a lance to each foot soldier.]

64.3–5	Thus . . . Vaena. [sheet missing in MORG; not in PHIL or ARE]
64.20	his Arabian courser ; his courser
64.24	stood mute and melancholy by ; stood by
64.25	the gallant Cidi ; Cidi
64.25–27	the Albaycin . . . . their hearts ; the mosque in the Albaycin, and their hearts
64.35	Cura de los Palacios. ; Bernaldez (Cura de los Palacios) Hist. de los reyes Catol., MS. cap. 61.
65.3	his turban cleaved by ; his helm cleft by
65.3–4	sword," replied Cidi Caleb. "His body ; sword; his body
65.7	¶The noble Cidi ; ¶Cidi
65.8	hastened to carry the disastrous tidings to ; hastened towards
65.15	were still ; all spoke
65.24	¶The noble Cidi ; ¶Cidi
65.28	the Gomeres, ; Gomeres,
65.30	entranced in woe. ; entranced.
65.32	she endeavoured ; endeavored
65.41	object before her ; object
65.42	the groves ; groves
66.10	beyond it ; beyond
66.11	the sorrows of the Queen, ; her sorrows:
66.14	they exclaimed, ; exclaimed they,
66.14–15	faded. . . . echoes to ; faded! The flower of thy chivalry lies low in the land of the stranger; no longer does the Vivarrambla echo to
66.16–17	nobles, ... soft ; nobles, gloriously arrayed for the tilt and tourney. Beautiful Granada! the soft
66.17–18	lute . . . the ; lute no longer floats through thy moonlit streets; the serenade is no more heard beneath thy balconies; the
66.19	thy hills, and the ; hills; the
66.20–21	bowers: Behold the Alhambra is forlorn ; bowers! Beautiful Granada! why is the Alhambra so lorn
66.21	In vain do the orange ; The orange
66.21–22	breathe ; still breathe

66.22   chambers: in vain does the nightingale sing ; chambers; the nightingale still sings

66.23   groves. In vain are its ; groves; its

66.23   refreshed by the sound ; are still refreshed with the plash

66.24   Alas! ; Alas! alas!

67.11–12   by: the fates are satisfied, the ; by; the prophecy is fulfilled: the

67.13   power and sway ; sway

68.3   guarded in ; guarded, but treated with great deference and respect, in

68.4   Vaena. From ; Lucena, where the noblest apartments were appointed for his abode. From

68.15–18   family. . . . ; family. ¶A few

69.20–22   hostages. . . . Queen Isabella ; hostages. ¶An embassy, composed of the alcayde Aben Comixa, Muley, the royal standard-bearer, and other distinguished cavaliers, bore this proposition to the Spanish Court at Cordova, where they were received by King Ferdinand. Queen Isabella

69.22   on ; in

69.25–30   he sent . . . . declined ; he ordered that the captive monarch should be brought to Cordova. ¶The alcayde of the Donzeles was the bearer of this mandate, and summoned all the hidalgos of Lucena and of his own estates, to form an honorable escort for the illustrious prisoner. In this style he conducted him to the capital. The cavaliers and authorities of Cordova came forth to receive the captive king with all due ceremony; and especial care was taken to prevent any taunt or insult from the multitude, or any thing that might remind him of his humiliation. In this way he entered the once proud capital of the Abda'rahmans, and was lodged in the house of the king's major-domo. Ferdinand, however, declined

69.37   obeyed, and, ; obeyed; he was escorted, as before, in royal state, to the fortress which was to form his prison; and,

69.38   the monarch was ; was

69.38   entertained ; entertained there

70.3   Old Muley Aben ; Muley Abul

70.14   old Muley Aben ; Muley Abul

70.32   the valiant Marquis ; marques

71.32   clothes, ; cloths,

71.35   Christian ; Castilian

72.29   of a ; a

73.34	in ; on
73.35	standards ; banners
73.37	loyal ; royal
75.16	was ; were
75.25	longed ; long
75.27	there were ; were
76.12	ruled. "Allah Achbar!" exclaimed he, God is great: but a successful ; ruled. "A successful
76.13	unbelievers will ; unbelievers," said he, "will
76.24	which had been caused ; caused
76.26–27	occasion, which they vauntingly displayed as the ; occasion, vauntingly displaying them as
76.30	to ensure a ; for a
76.31	he sent ; sent
76.31	together his people and the ; together the
76.32	and to ; and
76.33	The wary old Bexir ; Bexir
76.35	Ronda, close upon the Christian frontier. ; Ronda.
77.2–3	Christian spoils, and their deep dungeons were crowded with Christian captives, ; Christian captives,
77.11	Besides ; Beside
77.12	Ronda he ; Ronda and some of his own tribe, he
77.13	Gomeres, mercenary troops, ; Gomeres, so called from their native mountains, mercenary troops,
77.26–27	Andalusia that were soon ; Andalusia, soon
77.31	fresh ravage was preparing against ; fresh expedition against
77.38	steeds which had been captured ; Andalusian steeds captured
77.39	Bexir had ; Bexir
77.40–41	storm that had gathered beyond ; storm gathering beyond
78.23	it in silence ; it
78.34	alert. ; alert.* [footnote: *Pulgar, p. 3, c. 24. Cura de los Palacios, cap. 67.]
79.30	the fiery Gomeres ; the Gomeres
79.31	the bold Alcayde Hamet ; Hamet
79.31–32	Zegri, who was ever ; Zegri, ever
79.34	in rear, ; in the rear,
79.39	¶While . . . troop ; ¶While thus dispersed, a troop
80.2	towards ambush ; towards the ambush
80.9	Hamet had ; Hamet
80.10	Gomeres, . . . galloped ; Gomeres, left his prey, and galloped
81.28	mi! mi hermano!" ; mi! hermano!"

81.31	he felt ; felt
82.7	madly on ; madly
82.20	his stirrups ; the stirrups,
82.24	for a moment ; a moment
82.24	this country?" ; the country."
82.40	the dry beds ; dry beds
83.24	Hamet el Zegri ; Hamet,
83.25	cloud gathered upon ; cloud upon
83.41–42	and on all ; and all
83.41	victory. ¶Queen Isabella ; victory.* [*footnote:* *Mariana, Abarca, Zurita, Pulgar, &c.] ¶Queen Isabella]
84.4	battle.* [*footnote:* *Mariana. Abarca. Zurita. Pulgar &c.]
84.6	HIGH AND CEREMONIOUS RECEPTION ; RECEPTION
84.12	Castile, ; the Castilian sovereigns,
84.23	triumphant strains ; strains
84.27–28	his majesty's hand, but the ; his royal hand, however, the
84.32	worthy count ; count de Cabra
85.2	the presence ; presence
85.10	this ceremony ; the ceremony.
85.11	sumptuous hall, ; hall,
85.11	behold twenty ; twenty
85.29	embraced ; greeted
86.6	was renowned. ; were renowned.
86.21	sovereigns.* [*footnote:* *The account . . . writers.] ¶Such, says ; vereigns. [footnote not cited here] ¶Such says
86.32	Chico. [end of chapter] ; Chico.* [footnote as cited at 86.21] [end of chapter]
87.14	Besides ; Beside
87.14–15	a feudal sway, ; feudal sway,
88.16	up the deep ; into
88.26	signals and was so ; signals, and
88.28	but was hidden from the ; but not by the
88.34	that lay lurking ; lurking
89.3	round they ; round towards the town, they
89.3	beheld their town assailed, and a ; beheld a
89.4	gallopped furiously for ; galloped for
89.25	more into possession ; more in possession
89.16	Besides ; Beside ;
94.3	TERRITORIES ; TERRITORY
94.6	yet could not ; could not
94.7	but to undertake a second ; but a second
94.9	to leave all those regions ; leave the region
94.11–12	the King, . . . destroy ; the king, to destroy

94.13   to promote and accomplish their ; to their
94.16   year, again came ; year, came
94.24   ¶Every precaution ; ¶Precautions
94.25   its extensive and perilous ; its perilous
94.26   upon all the sick ; upon the sick
94.37   the advance] ARE ; led advance] MORG
94.38   Alcayde de ; the alcayde de
95.2   Ponce de Leon; ; Ponce Leon;
95.20   From hence ; Hence
95.30   that rose ; rising
95.34–45   munitions for its use, which had been sent ; munitions sent
95.35   it was thus ; and was thus
96.1   that chain of ; a chain of
96.9   and he added ; and added
96.13   fortresses. They ; fortresses, which
96.16   thundering ; thundered
96.31   had it been taken. ; taken.
97.8   with confusion and dismay, ; with dismay,
97.14   King Ferdinand ; Ferdinand,
97.15   country and ; country,
97.16   near to the ; near the
97.17   this desolation, ; the desolation,
97.18   been raging ; raged
97.19   to the ; the
97.24   places he had taken ; places taken
98.12   infirmity. ; paralysis.
98.23   had felt ; felt
98.35   acclamations. El Zagal ; acclamations. The latter
98.37   Ben Ahagete ; Aben Haxig,
98.38   monarch, . . . who ; monarch, and several Abencerrages,
               who
99.1   Ben Ahagete, ; Aben Haxig,
99.2   Abencerrage and attendants. ; Abencerrages.
99.6–7   of the fleetest horses of his stables, and ; his fleetest horses,
               and
99.7–8   he had gallopped ; galloped
99.9   El Zagal who were ; El Zagal,
99.25   monarch, that ; monarch which
99.30   place he ; place,
99.34   Granada. The people ; Granada. He was supported by the
               brave and powerful family of the Alnayans and Venegas;
               the people
100.5   great effect ; recent effect

100.6	in the preceding year, induced ; induced
100.7	in the course of which he resolved ; intending
100.16	Benamaquex. ; Benamexi or Bonameji.
101.4	of his bravest followers. ; of his bravest of his followers. [follows an error in MORG]
101.20	these forces ; their forces
101.26–27	me, for ; me. For the
102.7	were thrown ; thrown
102.7	town which set ; town, set
102.10	band sallied forth and ; band
102.25	place; he had put ; place, put
102.26	and had ; and
102.30	hot ; sharp
102.32	sharp foretaste ; foretaste
102.37	marching over the mountains ; marching
103.24	captives, who had been ; captives,
104.10	form ; formed
105.1	make a desperate attempt to ; cut
105.7	from whence ; whence
105.13	attempts, however, ; attempts,
105.16	was hourly encreasing. ; increased hourly.
105.22	From hence ; Hence
105.23	deep ; deeply
105.24	subterranean ; subterraneous
105.28	brave Marquis of Cadiz ; marques
105.28–29	with zeal, and glowing with the ; with the
105.34	at night ; various parts of
105.34–35	city blazed like a volcano. ; city in a blaze at night.
106.2	women were heard ; women
106.3	and reached ; reached even
106.10	Barbary or elsewhere, ; Barbary, Granada, or else where;
106.34	day. ; day.* [footnote: *Seen by the author in 1826.]
107.20	country exclusively ; country
108.10	offer of the crown. ; offer.
108.14	Old Muley Aben ; Muley Abul
108.19	river Frio ; limpid river Frio,
108.27	fortress. ; lofty
109.9–10	Calatrava . . . returning ; Calatrava, returning
109.12	repose and refresh ; refresh
109.16–17	so suddenly and furiously ; so suddenly,
109.20	slain, ; slain, and
109.22	convoyed it ; conveyed it,
109.28	and had ; and

109.34	Abdalla el Zagal ; Abdallah
109.35	richly ; splendidly
110.9	a vast ; an important
110.30	from Cordova, therefore, ; therefore, from Cordova,
111.1–4	castle . . . . \King Ferdinand ; castle afforded. \King Ferdinand
111.22	bishopricks. ; bishoprics.
111.31	up ; up to
111.41–42	What a triumph . . . . prisoner ; What a prisoner
112.12	both sides ; each side
112.14	squadrons ; shining squadrons,
112.31	ground, ; road,
113.3	in ; with
113.6	watch towers that crowned ; watchtowers on
113.11	wailings that rose ; wailings
113.16	by . . . on every ; by spectacles of woe on every
113.18	so shortly ; shortly
113.24	the Queen ; she
113.32	himself, to take the field ; to take the field himself
115.14–15	channel between ; channel, worn between
115.17	narrow gorge ; gorge
115.18	castles of ; castles,
115.28	strong holds, from whence ; strongholds, or posts of arms, whence
115.29–30	which . . . cavaliers. As ; in which they delighted. As
116.21	the castles ; their castles,
116.22	intercepted ; frustrated
116.23–24	fluttering banner and vaunting trumpet ; vaunting trumpet and fluttering banner,
116.25	rugged ; narrow and rugged
116.43	lay ; remained
117.39	filled up, ; were filled up,
117.41	vanquished. ; vanished.
118.7	the valiant ; the
118.10	he, ; he, bitterly,
118.17	issued forth ; issued
118.31	given ; delivered
119.8	the fierce El Zagal, ; El Zagal
119.11	to fly ; fly,
119.14–15	Granada by the ferocious El Zagal. ; Granada.
119.20–21	the warlike El Zagal; ; El Zagal;
120.12	that there ; there
120.12	the mystic ; these mystic

120.15	round ; around
120.25	or of ; or
121.9	all ; all the
121.27–28	whole citadel ; citadel
122.14	monarch ; king
122.27	accustomed ; accustomed also
122.43	the Comares. ; Comares.
123.5–6	crimes, . . . offspring. ; crimes.
123.7	Muley Aben Hassan ; Muley
123.8	monarch, ; sovereign,
123.9–10	ceremonial, ; ceremonial from El Zagal,
123.11	chronicler, ; chronicler of the time,
123.13–14	Muley Aben Hassan ; Muley,
123.24	brother El Zagal. ; brother.
123.36	He immediately ; he
124.1	regal ; royal
125.26	related to ; brother
125.37	island ; far island
125.39	had raged ; raged
126.7	and high ; the high
127.28	he had ; had
128.13	Boabdil el Chico ; Boabdil
129.6	accorded ; agreed
132.4	the former ; their former
132.29	to collect] ARE ; collect] MORG
134.2	they were fighting ; fighting
134.3	they were ; were
134.11–12	Christian helm and Moorish turban, ; Christian and Moor
134.15	arquebusses, . . . the King ; arquebusses. Seeing that the king
136.9	tumbling down ; tumbling
136.11	these ; the
137.24	be ; have been
137.36	barricadoes ; barricades
138.31	large ; huge
138.35	demolished, ; were demolished,
139.21	characterize ; characterized
139.30	sumpter mules ; mules,
139.38	esteemed as ; esteemed
139.40	prowess to ; prowess with
140.13	arranged ; ranged
140.20	royal ; regal
140.24	or skirt of] ARE ; of or skirt] MORG

141.37–44   **Note. The description . . . . the French. ; [in text] The
               description . . . . the French.
142.4   Moors. ; Moors. [paragraph containing same material as in
               footnote in Twayne 141.37–44.]
142.27   munitions ; ammunitions
143.13   or shock ; nor shock
143.14   or rush ; nor rush
143.35   and capitulated, ; they capitulated,
144.6   chaunting the ; chanting in
145.17   set ; sat
145.22   that had been spared ; spared
145.31   towers ; town
145.34   chevaliers: ; cavaliers.
145.35   all ; those
149.9   old Muley el ; Muley El
150.14   or even ; nor even
150.19   Horra. "For ; Horra. It was brought by the steadfast adher-
               ent to their fortunes, Aben Comixa. "For
150.37–38   he . . . . "let each ; he; "let each
151.2   RECEIVED. ; RECEIVED. SECOND EMBASSY OF
               DON JUAN DE VERA, AND HIS PERILS IN THE
               ALHAMBRA.
151.5   A single Moorish ; A Moorish
151.16   fatigues but they ; fatigues, but
151.33   and by ; by
151.34   Boabdil. Such ; Boabdil, and Aben Comixa was made al-
               cayde of the fortress. Such
152.31–32   advanced therefore with ; advanced with
152.32–33   Granada, . . . of the ; Granada. The moment Boabdil dis-
               cerned, from the towers of the
152.34   the parties. . . . nature of the ; the Albaycin, the Christian
               banners and lances winding round the base of the
152.34–35   the conflicts, . . . that there ; the mountain of Elvira, he sal-
               lied forth to meet them, escorted by asquadron of Aben-
               cerrages under Aben Comixa. El Zagal, who was equally
               on the alert, and apprised that the Christian troops came
               in aid of his nephew, likewise sallied forth and drew up
               his troops in battle array. Don Fadrique, wary lest some
               treachery should be intended, halted among some plan-
               tatiohs of olives, retained Boabdil by his side, and signi-
               fied his wish that Aben Comixa would advance with his
               squadron and offer battle to the old king. The provocation
               was given, but El Zagal maintained his position. He threw

out some light parties, however, which skirmished with the Abencerrages of Aben Comixa, after which he caused his trumpets to sound a recall, and retired into the city; mortified, it is said, that the Christian cavaliers should witness these fratricidal discords between true believers. ¶Don Fadrique, still distrustful, drew off to a distance, and encamped for the night near the bridge of Cabillas. ¶Early in the morning, a Moorish cavalier with an escort, approached the advance guard, and his trumpets sounded a parley. He craved an audience, as an envoy from El Zagal, and was admitted to the tent of Don Fadrique. El Zagal had learnt that the Christian troops had come to aid his nephew, and now offered to enter into an alliance with them on terms still more advantageous than those of Boabdil. The wary Don Fadrique listened to the Moor with apparent complacency, but determined to send one of his most intrepid and discreet cavaliers, under the protection of a flag, to hold a conference with the old king within the very walls of the Alhambra. The officer chosen for this important mission was Don Juan de Vera, the same stanch and devout cavalier, who in times preceding the war had borne the message from the Castilian sovereigns, to old Muley Abul Hassan, demanding arrears of tribute. Don Juan was received with great ceremony by the king. No records remain of his diplomatic negotiations, but they extended into the night, and it being too late to return to camp, he was sumptuously lodged in an apartment of the Alhambra. In the morning, one of the courtiers about the palace, somewhat given to jest and raillery, invited Don Juan to a ceremony which some of the alfaquis were about to celebrate in the mosque of the palace. The religious punctilio of this most discreet cavalier immediately took umbrage at what he conceived a banter. "The servants of queen Isabella of Castile," replied he stiffly and sternly, "who bear on their armor the cross of St. Jago, never enter the temples of Mahomet, but to level them to the earth, and trample on them." ¶The Moslem courtier retired somewhat disconcerted by this Catholic, but not very courteous reply, and reported it to a renegado of Antiquera. The latter, eager, like all renegadoes, to show devotion to his newly adopted creed, volunteered to return with the courtier and have a tilt of words with the testy diplomatist. They found Don Juan playing a game of chess with the alcaydeof the Alhambra, and took occasion to indulge in sportive commentson some of the mysteries of the Christian religion. Theire of this devout knight and discreet ambassador began tokindle; but he restrained it within the limits of lofty gravity. "You would do well," said he, "to cease talking about what you do not understand." This only provoked light attacks of the witlings; until one of them dared to make some degrading and obscene comparison between the Blessed Virgin and Amina, the mother of Mahomet. In an instant Don Juan sprang to his feet, dashed chess-board and chess-men aside, and drawing his sword, dealt, says the curate of los Palacios, such a *fermosa cachillada* (such a handsome slash) across the head of the blaspheming Moor, as felled him to the earth. The renegado, seeing his comrade fall, fled for his life, making the halls and galleries ring with his outcries. Guards, pages and attendants rushed in, but Don Juan kept them at bay, until the appearance of the king restored order. On inquiring into the cause of the affray, he acted with proper discrimination. Don Juan was held sacred as an ambassador, and the renegado was severely punished for having compromised the hospitality of the royal palace.

¶The tumult in the Alhambra, however, soon caused a more dangerous tumult in the city. It was rumored that Christians had been introduced into the palace with some treasonable design. The populace caught up arms, and ascended in throngs to the gate of Justice, demanding the death of all Christian spies and those who had introduced them. This was no time to reason with an infuriate mob, when the noise of their clamors might bring the garrison of the Albaycin to back them. Nothing was left for El Zagal but to furnish Don Juan with a disguise, a swift horse, and an escort, and to let him out of the Alhambra by a private gate. It was a sore grievance to the stately cavalier to have to submit to these expedients, but there was no alternative. In Moorish disguise he passed through crowds that were clamoring for his head; and once out of the gate of the city, gave reins to his horse, nor ceased spurring until he found himself safe under the banners of Don Fadrique.

¶Thus ended the second embassy of Don Juan de Vera, less stately, but more perilous than the first. Don Fadrique extolled his prowess, whatever he may have thought of his discretion; and rewarded him with a superb horse, while at the same time he wrote a letter to El Zagal, thanking him for the courtesy and protection he had observed to his ambassador. Queen Isabella also was particularly delighted with the piety of Don Juan, and his promptness in vindicating the immaculate character of the Blessed Virgin, and, beside conferring on him various honorable distinctions, made him a royal present of three hundred thousand maravadils.* [*footnote:* *Alcántara, Hist. Granad. vol. 3, c. 17, apud De Harro Nobiliario Genealogico, lib. 5, cap. 15.] ¶The report brought by this cavalier of affairs in Granada, together with the preceding skirmishings between the Moorish factions before the walls, convinced Don Fadrique that there

152.36–37	monarchs. . . . a reinforcement ; monarchs; on returning to his frontier post, therefore, he sent Boabdil a reinforcement
153.5	forays and ; forays,
153.6	or ; and
155.5	around ; round
155.20	¶At the time that ; ¶When
155.23	convoying ; conveying
155.25	and which was ; and was
155.28–29	Bentomiz, . . . considered ; Bentomiz, considered
155.31	mountaineers. Ferdinand ; mountaineers; but he
155.32	the town ; Bentomiz
155.34	forth ; about,
155.35	While ; Having directed
155.36	foot soldiers was taking possession, ; foot-soldiers to possess themselves,
155.37	the King ; he
155.42	Spaniards ; soldiers
156.9	loyal rampart ; rampart
156.25	Ferdinand, ; He,
156.29	she granted ; granted
156.42	†Idem. ¶The ; *Illescas, Hist. Pontif. lib. 6, c. 20. Vedmar, Hist. Velez Malaga. ¶The
157.12	alert and ready to fly to arms. ; alert.
157.14	gave ; reached
157.20	Moors who were on ; Moors on
157.20	The commanders replied ; Abul Cacim, Vanegas, son of Reduan and alcayde of the fortress, replied,

157.20–21	that they should ; that he should
157.21	as they knew ; as he knew
157.23	they were promised succour ; he was promised succor
157.28	war; others ; war, and that others
157.42	went on gathering ; continued to gather
157.43	mountains: ; mountains, and
158.2	into ; to
158.3	cliffs of the mountain ; cliffs,
158.24	broils. They spread themselves through the city and endeavoured ; broils, and they endeavored
158.27	have built, ; built,
158.28	have planted, ; planted,
159.15	who has ; has
159.17	foamed ; boiled
159.20	the enemy. ; the mercy of the enemy.
159.22	would ; might
159.25	march therefore ; march
159.25	force, and ; force, therefore, to the relief of Velez Malaga, and
159.27–28	foot. He took the most ; foot, and urged his way rapidly by the most
159.29–30	the height . . . . ¶The Christians ; the heights above Velez Malaga. ¶The Christians
160.1	Ferdinand, who was ; Ferdinand,
160.3	and to stand ; and stand
160.14	turbaned troops ; troops
160.17	the trumpet ; trumpet,
160.18	these ; the
160.20	that were gathering ; gathering
160.28	Rodovan de Vanegas. ; Reduan.
160.43	had escaped] ARE ; escaped] MORG
160.43	¶The fierce El Zagal, ; ¶El Zagal,
161.01	the success of his ; his
161.4–5	danger. "Allah . . . unbelievers ; danger. "Behold," said he, "the unbelievers
161.28	the Christian camp. ; the camp.
162.2	lance that were rusting lance, rusting
162.7	while ; time,
162.23–24	of Christian . . . . rushed warriors, who, with a loud shout, rushed
163.17	or at what. They threw ; nor at what, and throwing
163.19	burthen or impede ; impede
163.19	their flight, and spreading ; their motions, scattered

163.19–20	over the mountains . . . . They ; in every direction. They
163.24	mountains,] ARE ; mountain,] MORG
163.34	the spoils. ; spoils.
163.35	defeat. He ; defeat, but
164.1	as the ; as
164.8	of the old warrior, Muley Abdalla el Zagal, ; of Muley Abdallah El Zagal,
164.9	had struck ; struck
164.11	furious valour. ; valor.
164.19	heart; and we ; heart. We
164.20	Thus ; Thus was
164.20	was on ; on
164.25	looking ; looking out
165.2	became ; became suddenly
165.20	this ; the
165.21	of ; in
165.22	extolled ; lauded
165.33	soldiery. ; army.
165.35	faithful to him. ; faithful.
165.36	When ; As
162.24	them. The Moors surprized ; them. Surprised
162.24	retreated ; they
162.25	force posted in ; force in
162.27	sprung out ; sprang up
162.28	great pyres ; pyres
162.36	fact the letter of El Zagal ; fact, his letter
162.37	and the ; the
162.38	after the night had closed in, to ; after nightfall, to
162.38	enemy ; Moors
162.41	defile with loud cries, ; defile,
163.2	defended by the Moors. ; defended.
163.7	began to slacken ; slackened
163.13	their companions flying, ... threw ; their comrades flying, . . . threw] MORG their comrades fly, threw
163.16	very prone, ; prone,
163.17	through ; throughout
165.42	from thence ; thence
165.42	places which ; which places
166.3	any change ; any sudden change
166.6	Abdalla el Zagal ; Abdallah,
166.9	distant sound of ; sound of distant
166.28–31	capitulation. . . . ¶Ferdinand ; capitulation. ¶Ferdinand
167.4	surrender of Velez Malaga, ; surrender,

167.13	allegiance ; adherence
167.30	INHABITANTS. ; INHABITANTS.——MISSION OF HERNANDO DEL PULGAR.
168.22	wealth, whose ; wealth, connected, it is said, with the royal family of Granada, whose
168.23	port ; part
168.27	Albozen Connexa, ; Aben Comixa,
169.12	tribe. ; tribe, recently arrived from Morocco.
169.22	had fled ; fled
169.22	Inquisition. ; Inquisition.* [*footnote:* *Zurita, lib. 30, cap. 71.]
169.29	¶Hamet el Zegri ; ¶Hamet
170.1	inhabitants ; inhabitants of Malaga,
170.7	¶Hamet el Zegri ; ¶Hamet
170.12	expressed ; declared
170.17	there could be none ; there was no one] MORG ; no one was] ARE
170.18	Hamet el Zegri ; Hamet
170.24	native ; a native
170.27	hand," ; hands,"
170.32	relation. ; relative.
170.35	with large ; with a farm and two thousand doblas for his lieutenant Ibrahim Zenete, and large
170.36	City.* [footnote]; City.* [footnote]
170.37	admiration for ; admiration of
171.6	mountains. ; mountains.* [*footnote:* *Cura de los Palacios, MS., c. 82.]
174.17	Hamet el Zegri ; Hamet
171.11–12	¶The message . . . . in awe of ; ¶It required a man of nerve to undertake the delivery of such a summons in the present heated and turbulent state of the Moorish community. Such a one stepped forward in the person of a cavalier of
171.31	opposite to the castle and about ; opposite, at about
171.32	bowshots' distance, ; bow-shots distance, stood the castle;
171.33	hill, commanding ; hill, at present called the hill of St. Christobal, commanding
171.35	Hamet el Zegri ; Hamet
172.3	advance guard ; advance
173.12	mount which ; mount of St. Christobal, which
174.2	Besides ; Beside
174.17	Hamet el Zegri ; Hamet
174.18	awakened. ; awaked.
174.19	says ; concludes

174.26	tower of the ; tower, protecting what is at present called
174.26	suburb had ; suburb of Santa Ana, had
175.6	sank, ; sunk, and
175.9	wall adjoining ; wall of the suburb adjoining
175.14	wall, with ; wall, and in the narrow and winding streets adjacent, with
175.30	the seas. Many were also ; the sea. Many also were
176.9	and of ; and
176.9	Ferdinand ; he
176.28	residence, ; settled residence
176.33	reply. ¶"The Christian ; reply, and accompanied by an escort to prevent his holding any communication with the inhabitants in the streets. "The Christian
176.34	said he, ; said Hamet to those about him,
177.10	His fierce Gomeres, ; The Gomeres,
177.12	enemy they ; enemy,
177.13	and then ; and
177.21	every battery. ; all the batteries.
177.26	city and the camp. ; city, the camp, and the sea with its flotillas.
177.34	dark Moorish ; Moorish
177.38	the ladies ; ladies
178.19	its fury. ; fury.
178.26	working ; had worked
178.26	night, ; night; they
179.6	advance ; advanced
179.10	he. "Turn again. I ; he; "I
180.8	Hamet el Zegri ; Hamet
180.10	into ; in
180.13	ready ; armed
180.32	Hamet el Zegri ; Hamet
181.23	Hamet el Zegri, ; Hamet,
182.3	and so ; and
182.6	commerce. ; traffic.
182.35	employers. ; employers.* [*footnote:* *Pulgar. Cronica, p. 3, c. 80.]
183.35	true ; faithful
184.13	oars, came one day into the harbour of Malaga, displaying ; oars, displaying the
184.14–15	of amity. An ambassador ; of amity, came one day into the harbor. An Ambassador
184.30	¶This ; ¶The
184.30	Castilian ; Christian

185.10   Abrahin Algerbi; he ; Ibrahim el Guerbi. He
185.10   Guerba, ; the island of Guerbes,
185.13   in meditation, ; in caves of the mountains, in meditation,
185.15   revelations. The ; revelations, and visited by angels, sent by
                    Mahomet. The
185.16–17   kind, looked upon him as inspired, ; kind, believed in his
                    being inspired,
185.22   blessing]ARE ; blessings]MORG
187.23   Marquis of Cadiz,]ARE ; Marquis de Cadiz,]MORG
187.27   people of ; people to
187.34   twelve hundred ; four hundred
187.42   Palacios. ; Palacios, cap. 84.
188.25   await ; wait
189.8   wending ; winding
189.29   ¶Hamet el Zegri ; ¶Hamet
189.32   he, ; that he,
190.30   a general attack. ; an attack.
191.7   torn ; were torn
191.27   which he affirms to ; which, in fact, is said to
192.6   or of the]ARE ; or the]MORG
192.13   Hamet el Zegri ; Hamet
192.23   and traced ; traced
192.25   Hamet el Zegri ; Hamet
192.31   you" ; thee,"
193.8   Hamet el Zegri ; Hamet
193.26   houses ; homes,
193.34   the tower ; a tower
193.36   Hamet el Zegri, ; Hamet,
194.42   Calatrava ; Alcantara,
195.12   the ; battle ; battle
195.14   Hamet el Zegri ; Hamet
195.36   shouts. In ; shouts. "Fear not! the victory is ours! for so it is
                    written!" cried he. In
196.14   ¶As Hamet el Zegri ; ¶As Hamet
196.14   he was greeted with loud ; he heard nothing but loud
196.35   the Genoese]ARE ; Genoese]MORG
197.4   these heralds ; the herald
197.5   mission the anger of Ferdinand was ; mission to king Ferdi-
                    nand, his anger was
197.36   that they ; they
198.16   relations ; relatives
198.17   strong hold ; stronghold also
199.1

199.7	rare and sumptuous things ; sumptuous things,
199.16–17	they turn ; they then turn
199.19	lives and property ; liberties and property,
200.13	that they ; that the people of Malaga
200.14	ate of them ; ate
200.35	sent ; made
200.39	broken remnant ; remnant
200.41	Palacios. ; Palacios, cap. 84.
201.18	dungeon."† ; dungeon." He was subsequently retained in rigorous confinement at Carmona.†
201.36	Pulgar. Cronica. ; Pulgar, part 3, cap. 93. Pietro Martyr, lib. 1, cap. 69. Alcantara, Hist. Granada, vol. 4, c. 18.
202.2	beheld ; found
202.11	extended ; extended to
202.17	sent] ARE ; were sent joyfully] MORG
202.21	different ; far different
203.7–8	from whence ; when
203.25	Moorish ; Moresco
203.28	all money ; all the money
203.29–30	galleys. ¶As to ; galleys. As to Ali Dordux, such favors and honors were heaped upon him by the Spanish sovereigns for his considerate mediation in the surrender, that the disinterestedness of his conduct has often been called in question. He was appointed chief justice and alcayde of the Mudaxares or Moorish subjects, and was presented with twenty houses, one public bakery, and several orchards, vineyards, and tracts of open country. He retired to Antiquera, where he died several years afterwards, leaving his estate and name to his son Mohamed Dordux. The latter embraced the Christian faith, as did his wife, the daughter of a Moorish noble. On being baptized he received the name of Don Fernando de Malaga, his wife that of Isabella, after the queen. They were incorporated with the nobility of Castile, and their descendants still bear the name of Malaga.* [*footnote:* *Conversaciones Malagueñas, 26, as cited by Alcantara in his History of Granada, vol. 4, c. 18.] ¶As to]
204.1	the amount] ARE ; this amount] MORG
204.21	renowned ; so renowned
204.29–30	are separated ; separated
205.8	as a servant, ; as servants,
205.24	account. ; account."* [*footnote:* *The detestable policy of Ferdinand in regard to the Moorish captives of Malaga, is

recorded at length by the curate of los Palacios, (c. 87,) a cotemporary [*sic*], a zealous admirer of the king, and one of the most honest of chroniclers; who really thought he was recording a notable instance of sagacious piety.]

205.35   and from whence ; whence

205.36   eye on ; eye over

206.6   evening." ; evening."* [*footnote:* *The worthy curate of los Palacios intimates in his chronicle, that this melody, so grateful to the ears of pious Christians, was a source of perpetual torment to the ears of infidels.]

206.40   Besides ; Beside

208.6   a hereditary ; an hereditary

209.16   the fierce El Zagal's ; El Zagal's

209.16   preparations ; preparatives

209.40   and intersected ; intersected

209.41   a powerful ambuscade ; an ambuscade

210.5   terrible fire ; fire

210.10   loud and triumphant ; triumphant

210.12   was echoed ; echoed

210.13   were for a time ; were

210.18   unequal contest, ; contest,

210.19   the skirmish. Among ; this skirmish; among

210.19   number of whom ; number

210.23   and had thus, according ; and, according

210.24   gained ; had gained

210.26   guard by the old warrior El Zagal, brought King ; guard, brought king

210.36–37 country. ¶Ferdinand retired ; country. He retired,

211.1   the brave Luis Fernandez ; Luiz Fernandez

211.15   his arm ; arm

211.16   flesh, and his sword ; flesh and sword

211.17   than El Zagal ; than he ;

211.19   that ; which

211.24   ¶The alcayde ; ¶Carlos de Biedma, alcayde

211.25   on ; in

211.26–28 post. The . . . he stormed ; post. He was engaged to be married to a fair and noble lady of Baeza, and repaired to that city to celebrate his nuptials, escorted by a brilliant array of the best horsemen of his garrison. Apprised of his absence, the vigilant El Zagal suddenly appeared before Cullar with a powerful force, stormed

212.3   exhausted but they were ; exhausted, but were

212.4   and they feared death ; and the fear of death
212.5   the cruel El Zagal ; El Zagal,
212.5   Puertocarrero ; Don Luis Puerto Carrero
212.22   warriors, from whence ; warriors; whence
212.22   sweeping suddenly ; sweeping
212.26   story ; history
213.3   their ; them in
213.6   torrent ; torment] ARE tumult] LONDON [in absence of
               Mur-ms]
213.8   these ; those
213.10   adherents." ; adherents."* [footnote: *See Cura de los Pa-
               lacios, cap. 91. Palencia, De Bello Granad., lib. 8.]
213.17   swoln ; swollen
213.36   Hubec Adalgan ; Hubec
214.9   delays which had been caused ; delays caused
214.10   the old Moorish monarch El Zagal; ; El Zagal;
214.14   vassal. ¶El Zagal ; vassal. He
214.17   that was collecting ; collecting
214.21   assault and he ; assault, and
214.25   upon all] ARE ; upon] MORG
214.25   to make ; and make
214.26   houses, ; homes,
214.35   Cidi Yahye Alnayar Aben Zelim, who was ; Cid Hiaya Alna-
               yar,* [footnote: *This name has generally been written
               Cidi Yahye. The present mode is adopted on the authority
               of Alcantara in his history of Granada; who appears to have
               derived it from Arabic manuscripts, existing in the ar-
               chives of the marques de Corvera, descendant of Cid
               Hiaya. The latter (Cid Hiaya) was son of Aben Zalim, a
               deceased prince of Almeria, and was a lineal descendant
               from the celebrated Aben Had, surnamed the Just. The
               wife of Cid Hiaya was sister of the two Moorish generals,
               Abul Cacim and Reduan Vanegas, and like them the fruit
               of the union of a Christian knight, Don Pedro Vanegas,
               with Cetimerien, a Moorish princess.] who was
215.2   their career, and wheel off ; their career, wheel off
215.8   retreating troops. ; retreating hoofs.* [footnote: *Pulgar,
               part 3, c. 106.]
215.14   kinsmen ; kindred
215.20   Hubec . . . who ; Hubec Abdilbar, late alcayde of Zujar, who
215.23   special] ARE ; especial] MORG
215.34   but ; one

215.35   other part was defended ; other by
216.3   perplexed, and affording covert to the defenders. ;
                perplexed
216.11   there were ; were
216.12   yet still ; still
216.32   advice . . . therefore, ; advice . . . therefore,
217.9   and to keep ; and keep
217.32   all its ; with all its
217.33   forth, to attack and to retreat ; forth, attack and retreat
218.22   perplexity ; perplexity, Juan Pereo,
218.28   soldiers. ; soldiery.
218.36   those that ; those who
219.8   had raged ; raged
219.13   that was waging ; waging
219.15   relations ; relatives
220.7   once the ; once
220.12   there had ; had
220.16   ¶Amidst the ; ¶Amidst these
220.16   which had been hastily ; hastily
221.3–4   too extensive . . . while, ; too extensive, for their limited
                forces either to carry it by assault, or invest and reduce it
                by famine; while,
221.13   Loxa, ; Leon,
222.6   Alcayde Mohammed ; Mohammed
222.7   incredulity at the suggestion. ; incredulity.
222.15   valiant Marquis ; marques
222.34   groves, were sinking ; groves sinking
223.26   daily ; chiefly
223.34   hill so ; hill,
224.34   these ; those
225.14   was confusion. ; was in confusion.
225.19   guards named Hernando Perez ; guards rode to the front. It
                was Hernan Perez
225.19   Salar rode ; Salar: the same dauntless ambassador who once
                bore
225.19–20   the front. He took ; the turbulent people of Malaga the king's
                summons to surrender. Taking
225.21   fashion, and tying it ; fashion, he tied it
225.21   of his lance elevated ; of a lance and elevated
225.24   the valiant Pulgar, ; Pulgar,
225.30   a sudden panic ; a panic,
225.30   great distance ; considerable distance,

225.32   ¶When King Ferdinand was informed of the gallant ; ¶King
              Ferdinand was so pleased with the gallant
225.33   del Pulgar, he ; del Pulgar that he
225.38-40   knighthood . . . a lance ; knighthood; using in the ceremony
              the sword of Diego de Aguero, the captain of the royal
              guards; the duke of Esculona girded one of his own gilt
              spurs upon his heel, and the grand master of Santiago, the
              count de Cabra, and Gonsalvo of Cordova officiated as wit-
              nesses. Furthermore, to perpetuate in his family the
              memory of his achievement, the sovereigns authorized
              him to emblazon on his escutcheon a golden lion in an
              azure field, bearing a lance
225.40–41   of it, ... is but ; of it. Round the border of the escutcheon
              were depicted the eleven alcaydes vanquished in the bat-
              tle.* [footnote: *Alcantara, Hist. de Granada, tomo iv.,
              cap. 18. Pulgar, Cron., part iii.] The foregoing is but
225.42   that brave cavalier ; this brave cavalier,
226.35   *Hernando del Pulgar ; *Hernan or Hernando del Pulgar
226.5   ¶The old Moorish King ; ¶The Moorish king
226.8   broken ; broken and
226.10   by the disastrous ; by disastrous
226.14   He made efforts to send ; He sent
226.16   Boabdil. The old monarch was ; Boabdil. He was
226.17   El Chiquito ; El Chico
226.29   to slay ; slay
226.29   to assemble all ; assemble
226.34   and had the heads of the leaders struck ; and the heads of
              the leaders were struck
227.4   ¶King Ferdinand ; ¶Ferdinand
227.4   these movements ; the movements
227.5   took timely precautions ; took precautions
227.6   prevent all supplies, ; prevent supplies,
227.7   to intercept ; intercept
227.8   scouts were placed ; scouts placed
227.12   troops, girdled their city, ; troops, girded their city;
227.27   by the passes ; by passes
227.27   would sweep off ; sweep off
227.34   a valiant cavalier ; a cavalier,
227.37–38   Moor, . . . was not ; Moor was not
228.12   FRIARS ARRIVED AT THE CAMP, AND HOW THEY
              CAME FROM THE HOLY LAND. ; FRIARS FROM
              THE HOLY LAND ARRIVED AT THE CAMP.

229.10	sect, ; religion,
229.26	they journeyed over the plains of Judea. ; long as they were in sight.
231.2	humble brother, ; humbler brother
232.36	distributed ; intrusted
232.37	among ; to
232.37	to collect ; collect
233.30	whose ; were there, whose
235.9	tempest of rain ; tempest,
235/27	that ; which
236.2	ENCOUNTER ; ENCOUNTERS
236.4	THE ; THEIR
236.12	city. The veteran Mohammed ; city. ¶The veteran
236.24	the most daring ; daring
236.34	betook themselves ; took
236.34–35	brave count . . . . his ; count braced his buckler, grasped his
236.36	weapon he stood ; weapon, and stood
237.1	hot fight ; fight
237.2	they excelled ; excelled
237.2	these scrambling ; scrambling
237.5	the bravest of their ; their bravest
237.6	which were daily ; daily
237.7	any apparent ; apparent
237.11	he grew ; grew
237.14	Mohammed Ben Hassan ; Mohammed
237.22	they collected ; collected
237.23	Mohammed Ben Hassan. ; Mohammed:
237.24	coin them ; coin,
237.24	sell them ; sell,
237.34	to carry ; carry
238.5	ARRIVES ; ARRIVED
238.20	followed her, ; followed,
238.22–23	Mohammed Ben Hassan beheld that this was the Queen-Isabella, arriving ; Mohammed beheld the queen thus arriving
238.24	camp his heart failed him. He shook ; camp, he
238.31	to be offered; ; offered;
238.34	bravest cavaliers ; bravest
238.25	nation. ; cavaliers.
238.35–36	Baza, when they learnt that the Christian Queen was approaching the camp, eagerly ; Baza eagerly
239.7	embraced each other ; embraced,
239.17	was ; were

239.23	carnage. ¶Prince Cidi ; carnage.* [*footnote:* *Many particu-lars of the scenes and occurrences at the siege of Baza, are also furnished in the letters of the learned Peter Martyr, who was present, and an admiring eye-witness.] ¶Prince Cid
239.28	wary ; weary
239.30	Prince Cidi Yahye ; the prince,
239.33	honourably attended ; attended
240.10	treating of ; treating
240.11	the veteran Alcayde Mohammed Ben Hassan ; Hassan
240.24	and, communicating the tidings from Baza solicited ; and solicited
240.38	him, "Allah Achbar!" exclaimed he. "God is great, there is ; him. "God is great," exclaimed he, "there is
241.7	fellow commanders immediately ; fellow-commanders
241.9	depart freely ; depart
241.11	to dwell ; dwell
241.21	graciously ; generously
242.27	triumphal ; triumphant
242.41	nor was [passage not in ARE] ; nor were] MORG
243.6	pride, or ; pride nor
243.15	a ; the
243.21	money in gold ; gold
243.24	haughty demeanour. "I come not," ; haughty demeanour. "I came not,"] MORG dignified demeanor: "I came not,"] ARE
244.24	stage ; state
245.8	had hoped ; hoped
245.24	that is left you. ; left to you?
245.27	Chiquito, ; Chico,
246.6	which extends ; extending
246.14	half ; the fourth part
246.41	maravedies.* ; marevedies. [footnote deleted in ARE]
246.22–24	departed . . . . newly ; departed for that city. Cid Hiaya and his principal officers, incorporated with a division com-manded by the count de Tendilla, marched in the van-guard. The king was with the centre of the army, and the queen with the rear-guard. In this martial state Ferdinand
246.25–247.3	than his valor . . . [replaced to end of chapter] ; than his valor. In traversing the mountainous region, which ex-tends towards the Mediterranean, the army suffered ex-ceedingly from raging vandavales, or southwest gales,

accompanied by snow-storms. Several of the soldiers, and many horses and beasts of burden, perished with the cold. One of the divisions under the marques of Cadiz, found it impossible to traverse in one day the frozen summits of Filabres, and had to pass the night in those inclement regions. The marques caused two immense fires to be kindled in the vicinity of his encampment to guide and enlighten those lost and wandering among the defiles, and to warm those who were benumbed and almost frozen.

¶The king halted at Tabernas, to collect his scattered troops and give them time to breathe after the hardships of the mountains. The queen was travelling a day's march in the rear.

¶On the 21st of December, the king arrived and encamped in the vicinity of Almeria. Understanding that El Zagal was sallying forth to pay him homage, according to appointment, he mounted on horseback and rode forth to receive him, attended by Don Alonzo de Cardenas, master of Santiago, on his right hand, and the marques of Cadiz on his left, and dispatched in the advance Don Gutierrez de Cardenas, commander of Leon, and other cavaliers to meet and form an honorable escort to the Moorish monarch. With this escort went that curious eyewitness, Peter Martyr, from whom we have many of these particulars.

¶El Zagal was accompanied by twelve cavaliers on horseback, among whom was his cousin, the prince Cid Hiaya (who had no doubt joined him from the Spanish camp) and the brave Reduan Vanegas. Peter Martyr declares that the appearance of El Zagal touched him with compassion, for though a "lawless barbarian, he was a king and had given signal proofs of heroism." The historian Palencia gives us a particular description of his appearance. He was, says he, of elevated stature and well proportioned, neither robust nor meagre; the natural fairness of his countenance was increased by an extreme paleness which gave it a melancholy expression. His aspect was grave; his movements were quiet, noble, and dignified. He was modestly attired in a garb of mourning, a sayo, or loose surcoat, of dark cloth, a simple albornoz or Moorish mantle, and a turban of dazzling whiteness.

¶On being met by the commander, Gutierrez de Cardenas, El Zagal saluted him courteously, as well as the cavaliers who accompanied him, and rode on, conversing with him through the medium of interpreters. Beholding king Ferdinand and his splendid train at a distance, he alighted and advanced towards him on foot. The punctilious Ferdinand, supposing this voluntary act of humiliation had been imposed by Don Gutierrez, told that cavalier, with some asperity, that it was an act of great discourtesy to cause a vanquished king to alight before another king who was victorious. At the same time he made him signs to remount his horse and place himself by his side. El Zagal, persisting in his act of homage, offered to kiss the king's hand; but being prevented by that monarch, he kissed his own hand, as the Moorish cavaliers were accustomed to do in presence of their sovereigns; and accompanied the gesture by a few words expressive of obedience and fealty. Ferdinand replied in a gracious and amiable manner; and causing him to remount and place himself on his left hand, they proceeded, followed by the whole train to the royal pavilion, pitched in the most conspicuous part of the camp.

¶There a banquet was served up to the two kings, according to the rigorous style and etiquette of the Spanish court. They were seated in two chairs of state under the same canopy, El Zagal on the left hand of Ferdinand. The cavaliers and courtiers admitted to the royal pavilion remained standing. The count de Tendilla served the viands to king Ferdinand in golden dishes, and the count Cifuentes gave him to drink out of cups of the same precious metal; Don Alvaro Bazan and Garcilaso de la Vega performed the same offices in similar style and with vessels of equal richness, to the Moorish monarch.

¶The banquet ended, El Zagal took courteous leave of Ferdinand, and sallied from the pavilion attended by the cavaliers who had been present. Each of these now made himself known to the old monarch by his name, title, or dignity, and each received and affable gesture in reply. They would all have escorted the old king back to the gates of Almeria, but he insisted on their remaining in the camp, and with difficulty could be persuaded upon to accept the honorable attendance of the marques of Villena, the commander, Don Gutierrez de Cardenas, the count de Cifuentes, and Don Luis Puertocarrero.

¶On the following morning (22d December), the troops were

all drawn out in splendid array in front of the camp, awaiting the signal of the formal surrender of the city. This was
given at mid-day, when the gates were thrown open and
a corps marched in, led by Don Gutierrez de Cardenas,
who had been appointed governor. In a little while the
gleam of Christian warriors was seen on the walls and bulwarks; the blessed cross was planted in place of the standard of Mahomet, and the banner of the sovereigns floated
triumphantly above the Alcazar. At the same time a numerous deputation of alfaquis and the noblest and weal-
thiest inhabitants of the place sallied forth to pay homage
to king Ferdinand.

¶On the 23d of December, the king himself entered the city
with grand military and religious pomp, and repaired to
the mosque of the castle, which had previously been purified and sanctified and converted into a Christian tem-
ple; here grand mass was performed in solemn celebration
of this great triumph of the faith.

¶These ceremonies were scarcely completed, when joyful
notice was given of the approach of the queen Isabella,
with the rear-guard of the army. She came accompanied
by the princess Isabella, and attended by her ghostly
counsellor the cardinal Mendoza, and her confessor Talavera. The king sallied forth to meet her, accompanied by
El Zagal, and it is said the reception of the latter by the
queen was characterized by that deference and considerate delicacy which belonged to her magnanimous nature.

The surrender of Almeria was followed by that of Almuñecar,
Salobriña, and other fortified places of the coast and the
interior, and detachments of Christian troops took quiet
possession of the Alpuxarra mountains and their secluded
and fertile valleys.* [footnote: *Cura de los Palacios, cap.
93, 94. Pulgar, Cron., part 3, cap. 124. Garibay, comp.
Hist., lib. 18, cap. 37, &c., &c.]

247.17   Achbar," exclaimed he, "God ; Achbar! God
247.17   Rejoice with me oh Jusef, ; exclaimed he;
247.21   ceased," said he, "from ; ceased, from
247.22   heavens but ; heavens," said he, "but
247.27   descended with a glittering retinue ; descended, with glit-
          tering retinue
248.6   state in ; state, on
248.11   Alhambra. He shut ; Alhambra; shut
248.19   Catholic ; Christian

248.23–24	Ferdinand now informed him that Guadix, Baza and Almeria had fallen; he called ; Guadix, Baza, and Almeria, had now fallen; Ferdinand called
248.29	soldiers; others ; soldiers, and others
248.30	Boabdil ; him,
248.36	him that ; that
248.37	but be ; be but
248.43	that monarch, ; him,
249.5	which had been granted ; granted
249.7	¶The message of the Catholic monarch ; ¶This message
249.13	slavery. But on ; slavery. ¶On
249.27	was ; were
249.29	had endeavoured ; endeavored
249.30	to keep ; keep
250.26	the city of Granada ; Granada
251.10	to be too ; too
251.26	King Ferdinand, ; he
251.31	vega which had been ; vega,
251.32	High above ; Above
251.35	the valiant Roderigo ; Roderigo
251.42	once more ; was once more
252.2	hamlets and gardens. ; gardens and hamlets.
252.6	dare ; dared
252.9	as unmolested ; unmolested
252.26–27	cavalry, rapid as lightning in their movements, ; cavalry
252.31	de Luzon ; Luzon,
253.4	to ; defy ; defy
253.5	King Ferdinand ; Ferdinand
253.11	to pursue ; pursue
253.17	Roma; a great place of refuge and security. ; Roma.
253.23	to these sudden claims upon their protection; to have ; to have
253.26	in ; up
254.6	conveyed ; convoyed
254.8	had arrived near to ; arrived near
254.15	lowing and bleating ; bleating and lowing
254.19	fire and spirit. ; spirit and fire.
254.31	they had ; had
254.36	veterans ; veteran
255.5	malediction. ; malediction.* [*footnote: *Pulgar, Cron. part 3, cap. 130. Cura de los Palacios, cap. 90.*]
255.6	aroused ; roused
255.25	curses and revilings ; revilings,

255.26	heaped all kind of stigmas ; heaped curses
256.14	upon, than the valour ; upon but the valor
256.18	than Boabdil ; when Boabdil
256.24	with the proud array of legions ; with legions
256.41	troops. For ; troops, and for
256.42	the fortress ; it
257.1	they were ; were
257.7	gateway, ; gateway; and
257.15	and to drive ; and drive
258.4	Bulduy; he ; Albolodny, belonging to Cid Hiaya; he also
258.13	were eager ; eager
258.14	delighted. A number of them therefore concerted ; delight-ed, concerted
258.17	Baeza, and they ; Baza; and
258.20	these hardy cavaliers ; they
258.29–30	hold among the rocks, he ; hold, he
259.2	emaciated and ; emaciated,
259.2	the Moorish ; Moorish
259.21	turban, ; Moor,
259.24	they feared ; fearing
259.29–30	Count de Tendilla, ; count,
260.2	they fancied ; fancied
260.6	honour, and ; honor, or
260.8	¶The Count de Tendilla ; ¶The count
260.10	charged furiously ; charged
260.24	joy; this ; joy. His
260.27	years that ; years, during which
260.28	iron wars. [end of chapter] ; iron wars. ¶We have yet another act to relate of this good count de Tendilla, who was in truth a mirror of knightly virtue. One day, a Christian soldier, just escaped from captivity in Granada, brought word to the count, that an illustrious damsel named Fatima, niece of the alcayde Aben Comixa, was to leave the city on a certain day, escorted by a numerous party of relatives and friends of distinguished rank, on a journey to Almuñecar, there to embark for the African coast, to celebrate her nuptials with the alcayde of Tetuan. This was too brilliant a prize to be neglected. The count accordingly sallied forth with a light company of cavalry, and descending the defiles of the mountains, stationed himself behind the rocky sierra of Elvira, not far from the eventful bridge of Pinos, within a few short miles of Granada. Hence he

detached Alonzo de Cardenas Ulloa, with fifty light horsemen, to post himself in ambush by the road the bridal
party had to travel. After a time, the latter came in sight,
proving less numerous than had been expected; for the
damsel was escorted merely by four armed domestics, and
accompanied by a few relatives and two female attendants.
The whole party was surrounded and captured almost
without resistance, and carried off to the count at the
bridge of Pinos. The good count conveyed his beautiful
captive to his stronghold at Alcala, where he treated her
and her companions with all the delicacy and respect due
to their rank and to his own character as a courteous
cavalier.

¶The tidings of the capture of his niece gave poignant affliction to the vizier Aben Comixa. His royal master Boabdil,
of whom he was the prime favorite and confidential advis-
er, sympathized in his distress. With his own hand he
wrote a letter to the count, offering in exchange for the
fair Fatima one hundred Christian captives, to be chosen
from those detained in Granada. This royal letter was sent
by Don Francisco de Zuniga, an Aragonese cavalier, who
[sic] Aben Comixa held in captivity, and who was set at
liberty for the purpose.

¶On receiving the letter of Boabdil, the count de Tendilla at
once gave freedom to the Moorish maid, making her a
magnificent present of jewels, and sending her and her
companions under honorable escort to the very gates of
Granada. ¶Boabdil, exceeding his promises, immediately
set free twenty captive priests, one hundred and thirty
Castilian and Aragonian cavaliers, and a number of peasant women. His favorite and vizier, Aben Comixa, was so
rejoiced at the liberation of his niece, and so struck with
the chivalrous conduct of her captor, that he maintained
from that day a constant and amicable correspondence
with the count de Tendilla; and became, in the hands of
the latter, one of the most efficacious agents in bringing
the war of Granada to a triumphant close.* [footnote:
*This interesting anecdote of the count de Tendilla, which
is a key to the subsequent conduct of the vizier Aben Comixa, and had a singular influence on the fortunes of Boabdil and his kingdom, is originally given in a manuscript
history of the counts of Tendilla, written about the middle

of the sixteenth century, by Gabriel Rodriguez de Ardila, a Grenadine clergyman. It has been brought to light recently by the researches of Alcantara, for his History of Granada. (Vol. 4, cap. 18.)] [end of chapter]

261.18   that stretched ; stretching

261.24   precipitous ; precipitate

261.27   road which passes ; road

261.32   ¶Boabdil el Chico ; ¶Boabdil

261.35   hoping by this sudden move to ; hoping to

262.29   shewed ; proved

262.28   citadel. ¶Don Francisco ; They were in fact reduced to great extremity, through want of water and provisions. ¶Don Francisco

262.33–34   he conveyed to ; gave

262.34   King. In ; king; while the hostile menaces of Don Francisco, served to check the attacks of the Moors upon the citadel. ¶In

262.36–39   exploits, ... "who will ; exploits, had discovered in the course of his prowlings, a postern gate of the castle opening upon the steep part of the rocky hill looking towards the mountains. The thought occurred to him, that by a bold dash at a favorable moment, this postern might be attained, and succor thrown into the castle. He pointed the place out to his comrades. "Who will

262.42   immediately stepped ; men stepped

262.42–43   Pulgar put . . . through ; Pulgar chose the early daybreak for his enterprise, when the Moors, just aroused from sleep, were changing guard, and making the various arrangements of the morning. Favored by these movements, and the drowsiness of the hour, Pulgar approached the Moorish line silently and steadily, most of his followers armed with cross-bows and espingardas, or muskets. Then suddenly making an onset, they broke through

262.43–263.5   camp, . . . enabled ; camp, before the alarm had spread through the army, and succeeded in fighting their way up to the gate, which was eagerly thrown open to receive them. ¶The garrison, roused to new spirit by this unlooked-for reinforcement, was enabled

263.5   The Moors had intelligence however, that there ; The Moors, however, who knew there was

263.6–7   castle and they ; castle,

263.8–9   compel . . . . caused ; compel a surrender. Pulgar, hearing of this hope, caused

263.11   ¶The . . . thirst, ; ¶The garrison, in truth, suffered intensely
                from thirst,
263.28–29   fierce defence ; brave defence,
264.3   Alhambra. [no footnote] ; Alhambra.* [*footnote:* *Pulgar,
                Cron. p. 3, c. 131. Cura de los Palacios, cap. 97.]
264.10–11   turned with his army ; turned
264.12   every thing ; almost every thing
264.18   ¶From hence Ferdinand marched ; ¶Ferdinand next
                hastened
264.18–19   conspiracy which had lately manifested itself in ; conspiracy
                in
264.20   King Boabdil, ; Boabdil,
264.22   themselves ; them
264.23   and had ; and
264.24–25   of making a ; of a
264.28   to take ; take
265.1–2   deception that had been practiced, ; deception practised
265.6   "I am informed ; "I have been informed
265.7   make pact ; take part
265.23   even since ; ever since
265.25   in power ; in the power
266.23   in prison ; into prison
266.23   King of Fez, as ; caliph of Fez, Benimerin, as
266.33   de Gomera. ; de la Gomera.
266.33   King ; emir
267.11   with . . . have ; with sumptuous pageantry, have
267.14   once had ; once
267.17   which now remained ; now
267.17   of its former ; of former
267.20   seeing that ; seeing
267.22   King Ferdinand ; Ferdinand
267.23   last campaign ; campaign,
267.26   all the ; the
267.30   to quit ; quit
267.32   the parts ; parts
268.2   the King ; him
268.8–9   by the Princesses ; the princesses
268.27   defiance. ; defence.
268.35   their ; the
268.38   Moors the ancient ; Moors, the
269.1   for whom ; whom
269.8   ¶Boabdil el Chico, ; ¶Boabdil,
270.13   that ; which

270.16   Granada that had ; Granada,
270.17   been lulled ; lulled
270.21   by valour, ; valor,
270.21   plan which had been ; plan
271.26   found ; found that
271.27   is chivalry ; "are chivalry
272.2   on it ; upon it,
272.2   affixed to it ; affixed,
272.3   irritation but ; irritation;
272.5–6   for his great strength ; for strength
272.7   when they were skirting ; when skirting
272.21   all men ; all
272.22   heart. In ; heart. ¶His project was to penetrate Granada in
272.22–40   the night . . . . to the camp. ; the night, by a secret pass,
                made known to him by a Moorish renegade of the city,
                whom he had christened Pedro Pulgar, and who was to act
                as guide. They were to set fire to the Alcaiceria and other
                principal edifices, and then effect their retreat as best they
                might. At the hour appointed, the adventurous troop set
                forth provided with combustibles. The renegade led them
                silently to a drain or channel of the river Darro, up which
                they proceeded cautiously, single file, until they halted
                under a bridge near the royal gate.

           ¶Here dismounting, Pulgar stationed six of his companions
                to remain silent and motionless and keep guard, while fol-
                lowed by the rest, and still guided by the renegade, he
                continued up the drain or channel of the Darro, which
                passes under a part of the city, and was thus enabled to
                make his way undiscovered into the streets. All was dark
                and silent. At the command of Pulgar, the renegade led
                him to the principal mosque. Here the cavalier, pious as
                brave, threw himself on his knees, and drawing forth a
                parchment scroll on which was inscribed in large letters
                AVE MARIA, nailed it to the door of the mosque, thus con-
                verting the heathen edifice into a Christian chapel and
                dedicating it to the blessed Virgin. This done, he hastened
                to the Alcaiceria to set it in a blaze.

           ¶The combustibles were all placed, but Tristan de Monte-
                mayor, who had charge of the firebrand, had carelessly left
                it at the door of the mosque. It was too late to return
                there.

           ¶Pulgar was endeavoring to strike fire with flint and steel
                into the ravelled end of a cord, when he was startled by

the approach of the Moorish guard going the rounds. His hand was on his sword in an instant. Seconded by his brave companions, he assailed the astonished Moors and put them to flight. In a little while the whole city resounded with alarms, soldiers were hurrying through the streets in every direction; but Pulgar, guided by the renegade, made good his retreat by the channel of the Darro, to his companions at the bridge, and all mounting their horses, spurred back to the camp.

272.33	letters, ; characters] MORG [passage not in ARE]
272.40	conjecture ; imagine
272.42	exasperation when on the following day they discovered the ; exasperation, on the following day, when the trophy
273.1	thus elevated in the ; was discovered thus elevated in bravado in the
273.2	eventually ; actually
273.30	*In commemoration ; *The account here given of the exploit of Hernan del Pulgar, differs from that given in the first edition, and is conformable to the record of the fact in a manuscript called *"The House of Salar,"* existing in the library of Salazar, and cited by Alcantara in his History of Granada. ¶In commemoration
273.30	feat the Emperor ; feat of Pulgar, the emperor
273.30–32	conferred on . . . Perez del ; conferred on that cavalier, and on his descendants the marquesses of Salar, the privilege of sitting in the choir during high mass, and assigned as the place of sepulture of Pulgar himself, the identical spot where he kneeled to affix the sacred scroll; and his tomb is still held in great veneration. This Hernan Perez del
273.8	lay at such a distance from ; lay so distant from
273.14	protect the Queen ; protect her
273.16–17	gratification. . . . a magnificent ; gratification. ¶On the morning of June the 18th, a magnificent
273.17	issued forth from ; issued from
273.18	armed, that looked like ; armed, looking like
273.22	rear . . . powerful ; rear-guard, a powerful
273.26	in a radiant ; in radiant
274.14	amidst ; amid
274.23	offer them battle; and they hesitated ; offer battle; and hesitated
274.30	armed, some *a la ginete* ; armed, others *à la gineta*
275.2	King Ferdinand ; Ferdinand
275.3	¶While this ; ¶Here, however, the worthy Fray Antonio

Agapida, in his enthusiasm for the triumphs of the faith, records the following incident, which we fear is not sustained by any grave chronicler of the times, but rests merely on tradition, or the authority of certain poets and dramatic writers, who have perpetuated the tradition in their works. While this

275.6   line there ; line, says Agapida, there
275.9   and ponderous ; and a ponderous
275.19   Hernando del Pulgar ; Hernan
275.25   steed, he ; steed;
275.36   when about ; whereabout
275.36–37 his arabian steed ; his steed
275.39   if Garcilasso were ; if Garcilasso was
276.15   army. ¶The sun ; army.* [*footnote:* *The above incident has been commemorated in old Spanish ballads, and made the subject of a scene in an old Spanish drama, ascribed by some to Lope de Vega.] ¶The sun
277.30   los Palacios. ; los Palacios, cap. 101. Zurita, lib. 20, c. 88.
277.10–11 witnessed. ¶To commemorate this victory the Queen afterwards ; witnessed. ¶The gayety of this gentle pass at arms, however, was somewhat marred by a rough reverse in the evening. Certain of the Christian cavaliers, among whom were the count de Ureña, Don Alonzo Aguilar, his brother Gonsalvo of Cordova, Diego Castrillo commander of Calatrava, and others to the number of fifty, remained in ambush near Armilla, expecting the Moors would sally forth at night to visit the scene of battle and to bury their dead. They were discovered by a Moor, who had climbed an elm-tree to reconnoitre, and hastened into the city to give notice of their ambush. Scarce had night fallen when the cavaliers found themselves surrounded by a host which in the darkness seemed innumerable. The Moors attacked them with sanguinary fury, to revenge the disgrace of the morning. The cavaliers fought to every disadvantage, overwhelmed by numbers, ignorant of the ground, perplexed by thickets and by the water-courses of the gardens, the sluices of which were all thrown open. Even retreat was difficult. The count de Ureña was surrounded and in imminent peril, from which he was saved by two of his faithful followers at the sacrifice of their lives. Several cavaliers lost their horses, and were themselves put to death in the water-courses. Gonsalvo of Cordova came near having his own illustrious career cut short in this ob-

scure skirmish. He had fallen into a water-course, whence he extricated himself, covered with mud, and so encumbered with his armor, that he could not retreat. Inigo de Mendoza, a relative of his brother Alonzo, seeing his peril, offered him his horse: "Take it Señor," said he, "for you cannot save yourself on foot, and I can: but should I fall, take care of my wife and daughters."

¶Gonsalvo accepted the devoted offer; mounted the horse, and had made but few paces, when a lamentable cry caused him to turn his head, and he beheld the faithful Mendoza transfixed by Moorish lances. The four principal cavaliers already named, with several of the followers, effected their retreat and reached the camp in safety; but this nocturnal reverse obscured the morning's triumph. Gonsalvo remembered the last words of the devoted Mendoza, and bestowed a pension on his widow and marriage portions on his daughters.* [*footnote:* *The account of this nocturnal affair, is from Peter Martyr, lib. 4, Epist. 90, and Pulgar Hazañas del Gran. Capitan, page 188, as cited by Alcantara, hist. Granada, tom. 4, cap. 18.] ¶To commemorate the victory of which she had been an eye-witness, queen Isabella afterwards

277.13	by the hands of her majesty. ; by her hands.
277.31	house from whence ; house whence
277.34	house refuses all ; house to the writer, refused all
277.35	mansion to the stranger. His mansion.
277.15	CONFLAGRATION OF THE CHRISTIAN CAMP. ; THE LAST RAVAGE BEFORE GRANADA.
277.21–22	beast. The evening of a hot July day shone ; beast. [The account of the "Last Ravage before Granada" is moved to this point in the ARE from the next chapter in the original edition. The variants are reported in the order of accounts as found in the manuscript. Hence ARE readings for 500.11–503.28 are given below at 280.7–13.] ¶The setting sun of a hot summer's day, on the 10th of July, shone
277.23	service, for desperate resistance was expected from the Moors. The ; service, when an attack was meditated on the city. The
277.24–25	appearance in the setting sun. The ; appearance. The
278.8–9	lances, ornamented ; lances, and ornamented
278.9	This centre ; This central
278.12	that ; which
278.15	toil. ; trial.

278.36   soldiery ; soldiers
279.5   feared that ; feared
279.11   illumined. ; illuminated.
279.19–22   camp. THE LAST RAVAGE BEFORE GRANADA. ¶When
                the ; camp. ¶When the
279.37   issued ; issued forth
280.7–13   ruin. . . .¶The Christian ; [replaced by a bridge passage
                printed below when the account of the "last ravage" was
                moved ahead of the "conflagration" in the ARE.] ; ruin.
                [The account of the "last ravage" was moved from here to
                the previous chapter with the following bridge passage
                added. It follows "man or beast" at ARE 500.11:] The
                eighth of July was the day appointed for this act of deso-
                lation. Boabdil was informed by his spies of the intention
                of the Christian king, and prepared to make a desperate
                defence. Hernando de Baeza, a Christian, who resided
                with the royal family in the Alhambra as interpreter, gives
                in a manuscript memoir an account of the parting of Boab-
                dil from his family as he went forth to battle. At an early
                hour of the appointed day, the eighth of July, he bathed
                and perfumed himself as the Moors of high rank were ac-
                customed to do when they went forth to peril their lives.
                Arrayed in complete armor he took leave of his mother,
                his wife and his sister, in the ante-chamber of the tower of
                Comares. Ayxa la Horra, with her usual dignity, bestowed
                on him her benediction, and gave him her hand to kiss. It
                was a harder parting with his son and his daughter; who
                hung round him with sobs and tears; the dueñas and don-
                cellas too of the royal household made the halls of the Al-
                hambra resound with their lamentations. He then
                mounted his horse and put himself in front of his squad-
                rons.* [footnote: *Hernando de Baeza as cited by Alcan-
                tara, Hist. Granada, t. 4, c. 18.] ¶The Christian
280.17   fiery spirit, ; chivalrous spirit,
280.22   watching ; watched
280.35   from whence ; whence
280.37   guard displayed the utmost valour, mingling ; guard
                mingling
280.38   and endeavouring ; endeavoured
280.43   round, with his followers, they threw ; round, he and his
                followers threw
281.1   fleet steeds, ; steeds,
281.5   that was sacred ; sacred

281.5–6	them. It was all in vain. They were ; them. All in vain: totally
281.6	and fled ; fled
281.9	in number,] ARE ; in numbers,] MORG
281.10	Muza retreated ; therefore he retreated
281.11–12	When he entered ; Entering
281.14	who were stationed ; stationed
281.14	he vowed ; vowed
281.15	sally forth ; sally
281.21	sally made by ; sally of
281.30	from whence ; whence
281.31–32	and had ; and
281.32	thundering ; thundered
281.34	the Moors ; they
282.1–2	BUILDING OF THE CITY OF SANTA FE: DESPAIR OF THE MOORS. ¶The Moors ; CONFLAGRATION OF THE CHRISTIAN CAMP. BUILDING OF SANTA FE. ¶The Moors
282.7–9	battlements. . . . would discourage ; battlements. In the midst of this deep despondency, a signal disaster in the Christian camp, for a moment lit up a ray of hope in the bosom of the Moors. [Here ends the portion moved ahead in the ARE.] In the exultation of the moment, they flattered themselves with hopes that the catastrophe would discourage
282.10	summer, and that they ; summer and they
282.10	again withdraw ; withdraw
282.16	seemed," ; seems,"
282.31–32	desolate. ¶In the meantime the besieged ; desolate. FAMINE AND DISCORD IN THE CITY. ¶The besieged
283.5	their present ; the present
283.6–7	Casim Abdelmelic, ; Cazim,
283.24	¶The valiant Muza ; ¶Muza
283.29	Casim Abdelmelic ; Cazim
284.3	Casim Abdelmelic ; Cazim
284.3	distinction ; courtesy
284.4–10	Isabella, who . . . . ¶All Christian ; Isabella, who (being informed of the purport of his embassy, granted the besieged a truce of sixty days from the 5th of October, and appointed Gonsalvo of Cordova, and Fernando de Zafra, the secretary of the king, to treat about the terms of surrender with such commissioners as might be named by Boabdil. The latter on his part named Abul Cazim, Aben Comixa the vizier, and the grand cadi. As a pledge of good

faith, Boabdil gave his son in hostage, who was taken to Moclin, where he was treated with the greatest respect and attention by the good count de Tendilla, as general of the frontier. ¶The commissioners on both parts, held repeated conferences in secret in the dead of the night, at the village of Churriana; those who first arrived at the place of meeting giving notice to the others by signal-fires, or by means of spies. After many debates and much difficulty, the capitulation was signed on the 25th of November. According to this, the city was to be delivered up, with all its gates, towers and fortresses, within sixty days. ; ¶All Christian

284.12   should take ; should perform the act of homage, and take

284.13–15   Castilian . . . . ¶The Moors ; Castilian crown. ¶The Moors

284.25   four hundred ; five hundred

284.26   surrender to be subsequently ; surrender, who should be treated with great respect and distinction by the Christians, and subsequently

284.29   ¶Such . . . . laid before ; ¶Such are the main articles affecting the public weal, which were agreed upon after much discussion, by the mixed commission. There were other articles, however, secretly arranged, which concerned the royal family. These secured to Boabdil, to his wife Morayma, his mother Ayxa, his brothers, and to Zoraya, the widow of Muley Abul Hassan, all the landed possessions, houses, mills, baths, and other hereditaments which formed the royal patrimony, with the power of selling them, personally or by agent, at any and all times. To Boabdil was secured, moreover, his wealthy estates, both in and out of Granada, and to him and his descendants in perpetuity, the lordships of various towns and lands and fertile valleys in the Alpuxarras, forming a petty sovereignty. In addition to all which it was stipulated, that, on the day of surrender, he should receive thirty thousand castellanos of gold.* [footnote: *Alcantara, t. 4, c. 18.] ¶The conditions of surrender being finally agreed upon by the commissioners, Abul Cazim proceded to the royal camp at Santa Fé, where they were signed by Ferdinand and Isabella; he then returned to Granada, accompanied by Fernando de Zafra, the royal secretary, to have the same ratified also by the Moorish king. Boabdil assembled his council, and with a dejected countenance laid before

284.29–30	the council of Granada, as ; before it the articles of capitulation as
284.31	found that ; found
284.31	had arrived ; arrived
285.1–2	Boabdil el Chico ; Boabdil
285.3	them all ; all
285.?	God is great! exclaimed ; exclaimed
285.6	prophet! It ; prophet! We have no longer forces in the city and the kingdom to resist our powerful enemies. It
285.9	God is great!" echoed ; echoed
285.10	all accorded ; all agreed
285.13	Muza saw that they were about to sign ; Muza heard them assent to
285.21	see them who ; see and suffer them, who
285.23	and strode gloomily ; and passed gloomily
285.27	issuing forth from ; issuing from
285.29– 286.16	more.* ¶Such . . . . in doubt. ; [these three paragraphs deleted]
286.1	the others ; [passage not in ARE] the rest] MORG
286.25	seventy ; sixty
287.1	January. On the 30th of December he sent ; January. He accordingly sent
287.3	Comixa, with the four hundred hostages to King ; Comixa, to king
287.28	¶The Moorish King now ; ¶Boabdil now
287.38	from the outrages of war, and ; from outrage; and
287.41	populace ; population
288.2	there was ; and there was
288.6	tumults. [For ARE text from 288.6–296.15 see Appendix]
296.15	[Begin collation again at the Marquis of Cadiz]
296.20	and he was ; and was
296.21	capital which was the ; capital the
296.26	the exposure ; exposures
296.27	he had undergone ; undergone
297.13	good cavalier ; good and well-beloved cavalier
297.14	ranks, for he was universally honoured and beloved. ; ranks.
297.14	brocade, that reached ; brocade reaching
297.29	vassals of the marquis. ; vassals.
298.14	overturned, ; were overturned,
298.20	Roderigo Ponce ; Ponce
298.27–30	unacceptable. . . . For several ; unacceptable. ¶For several
298.32	the pious coercion ; the coercion

299.12	and whose savage rocks ; the savage rocks
299.13	precipices may ; precipices of which may
299.29–30	age. He was a veteran warrior, ; age: a warrior,
299.31–32	in the camp and in the field ; in camp and field,
299.32	natural ; habitual
299.38	with all ; with
299.40	youthful son ; son
300.6	there were ; were
300.6	fierce tribe ; tribe
300.29	in emulation,] ARE ; emulation,] MORG
300.39	from whence ; whence
300.40	overturned rocks ; rocks
301.1	ferocious valour, ; valor,
301.5–6	dreadful carnage. ; great carnage.
301.14	Their fierce leader ; Their leader,
301.43	Alonzo de Aguilar ; Alonzo
302.3	proposed that they should ; proposed to
302.6	Don Pedro ; Pedro
302.22	noble stags ; stags
302.23–24	survivor. He was without ; survivor, without
302.24	towards the enemy, ; to the enemy,
302.29	breast that ; breast, which
302.40	had waged successful wars ; had made successful war
302.42	and the wisdom ; and in the wisdom
303.25	the dreadful loss ; the sad loss
303.27	had contributed ; contributed
304.5	to embark ; embark
304.8	Don Alonzo ; Alonzo

APPENDIX A
UNCOLLATABLE PORTIONS REJECTED FROM THE ARE

NOTE TO THE REVISED EDITION

THE foregoing introduction, prefixed to the former editions of this work, has been somewhat of a detriment to it. Fray Antonio Agapida was found to be an imaginary personage; and this threw a doubt over the credibility of his chronicle; which was increased by a vein of irony, indulged here and there, and by the occasional heightening of some of the incidents, and the romantic coloring of some of the scenes. A word or two explanatory may therefore be of service.*

The idea of the work was suggested while I was occupied at Madrid in writing the life of Columbus. In searching for traces of his early life, I was led among the scenes of the war of Granada; he having followed the Spanish sovereigns in some of their campaigns, and been present at the surrender of the Moorish capital. I actually wove some of these scenes into the biography; but found they occupied an undue space, and stood out in romantic relief, not in unison with the general course of the narrative. My mind, however, had become so excited by the stirring events and romantic achievements of this war, that I could not return with composure to the sober biography I had in hand. The idea then occurred, as a means of allaying this excitement, to throw off a rough draught of the history of this war, to be revised and completed at future leisure. It appeared to me that its true course and character had never been fully illustrated. The world had received a strangely perverted idea of it through Florian's romance of Gonsalvo of Cordova, or through the legend, equally fabulous, entitled "The Civil Wars of Granada," by Ginez Perez de la Hita; the pretended work of an Arabian contemporary, but in reality a Spanish fabrication. It had been woven over with love tales and scenes of sentimental gallantry totally opposite to its real character; for it was, in truth, one of the sternest of those iron conflicts, sanctified by the title of "Holy Wars." In fact, the genuine nature of the war placed it far above the need of any amatory embellishments. It possessed sufficient interest in the striking contrast presented by the combatants, of Oriental and European creeds, costumes, and manners; and in the hardy and harebrained enterprises, the romantic adventures, the picturesque forays through mountain regions; the daring assaults and surprisals of cliff-built castles and cragged fortresses, which succeeded each other with a variety and brilliancy beyond the scope of mere invention.

---

*Many of the observations in this note have already appeared in an explanatory article, which, at Mr. Murray's request, the author furnished to the London Quarterly Review.

The time of the contest, also, contributed to heighten the interest. It was not long after the invention of gunpowder; when firearms and artillery mingled the flash, and smoke, and thunder of modern warfare, with the steely splendor of ancient chivalry, and gave an awful magnificence and terrible sublimity to battle; and when the old Moorish towers and castles, that for ages had frowned defiance to the battering-rams and catapults of classic tactics, were toppled down by the lombards of the Spanish engineers. It was one of the cases in which history rises superior to fiction.

The more I thought about the subject the more I was tempted to undertake it, and the facilities at hand at length determined me. In the libraries of Madrid, and in the private library of the American consul, Mr. Rich, I had access to various chronicles and other works, both printed and in manuscript, written at the time by eye-witnesses, and in some instances by persons who had actually mingled in the scenes recorded, and gave descriptions of them from different points of view, and with different details. These works were often diffuse and tedious, and occasionally discolored by the bigotry, superstition, and fierce intolerance of the age; but their pages were illumined at times with scenes of high emprise, of romantic generosity, and heroic valor, which flashed upon the reader with additional splendor from the surrounding darkness. I collated these various works, some of which have never appeared in print, drew from each facts relative to the different enterprises, arranged them in as clear and lucid order as I could command, and endeavored to give them somewhat of a graphic effect, by connecting them with the manners and customs of the age in which they occurred. The rough draught being completed, I laid the manuscript aside, and proceeded with the Life of Columbus. After this was finished and sent to the press, I made a tour in Andalusia, visited the ruins of the Moorish towns, fortresses, and castles, and the wild mountain passes and defiles, which had been the scenes of the most remarkable events of the war, and passed some time in the ancient palace of the Alhambra, the once favorite abode of the Moorish monarchs. Every where I took notes, from the most advantageous points of view, of whatever could serve to give local verity and graphic effect to the scenes described. Having taken up my abode for a time at Seville, I there resumed my manuscript and rewrote it, benefited by my travelling notes and the fresh and vivid impressions of my recent tour. In constructing my chronicle, I adopted the fiction of a Spanish monk as the chronicler. Fray Antonio Agapida was intended as a personification of the monkish zealots, who hovered about the sovereigns in their campaigns, marring the chivalry of the camp by the bigotry of the cloister, and chronicling in rapturous strains every act of intolerance towards the Moors. In fact, scarce a sally of the pretended friar, when he bursts forth in rapturous eulogy of some great stroke of selfish policy on the part of Ferdinand, or exults over some overwhelming disaster of the gallant and devoted Moslems, but is taken almost

word for word from one or other of the orthodox chroniclers of
Spain.

The ironical vein also was provoked by the mixture of kingcraft and
priestcraft, discernible throughout this great enterprise, and the mistaken
zeal and self-delusion of many of its most gallant and generous champions.
The romantic coloring seemed to belong to the nature of the subject, and
was in harmony with what I had seen in my tour through the poetical and
romantic regions in which the events had taken place. With all these deduc-
tions the work, in all its essential points, was faithful to historical fact, and
built upon substantial documents. It was a great satisfaction to me, therefore, after the doubts that had been expressed of the authenticity of my
chronicle, to find it repeatedly and largely used by Don Miguel Lafuente
Alcántara, of Granada, in his recent learned and elaborate history of his
native city; he having had ample opportunity, in his varied and indefatigable
researches, of judging how far it accorded with documentary authority.

I have still more satisfaction in citing the following testimonial of Mr. Prescott, whose researches for his admirable history of Ferdinand and Isabella
took him over the same ground I had trodden. His testimonial is written in
the liberal and courteous spirit characteristic of him; but with a degree of
eulogium which would make me shrink from quoting it, did I not feel the
importance of his voucher for the substantial accuracy of my work.

"Mr. Irving's late publication, the 'Chronicle of the Conquest of Granada,'
has superseded all further necessity for poetry, and, unfortunately for me,
for history. He has fully availed himself of all the picturesque and animating
movement of this romantic era; and the reader who will take the trouble to
compare his chronicle with the present more prosaic and literal narrative,
will see how little he has been seduced from historic accuracy by the poetical
aspect of his subject. The fictitious and romantic dress of his work has enabled him to make it the medium of reflecting more vividly the floating
opinions and chimerical fancies of the age, while he has illuminated the picture with the dramatic brilliancy of coloring denied to sober history."*

In the present edition I have endeavored to render the work more worthy
of the generous encomium of Mr. Prescott. Though I still retain the fiction
of the monkish author Agapida, I have brought my narrative more strictly
within historical bounds, have corrected and enriched it in various parts
with facts recently brought to light by the researches of Alcántara and others;
and have sought to render it a faithful and characteristic picture of the romantic portion of history to which it relates.

W. I.

Sunnyside, 1850

*Prescott's Ferdinand and Isabella, vol. ii. c. 15.

A CHRONICLE OF THE CONQUEST OF GRANADA.

CHAPTER I.
OF THE KINGDOM OF GRANADA, AND THE TRIBUTE WHICH IT PAID TO THE CASTILIAN CROWN.

THE history of those bloody and disastrous wars, which have caused the downfall of mighty empires, (observes Fray Antonio Agapida,) has ever been considered a study highly delectable, and full of precious edification. What then must be the history of a pious crusade, waged by the most Catholic of sovereigns, to rescue from the power of the Infidels one of the most beautiful but benighted regions of the globe? Listen then, while, from the solitude of my cell, I relate the events of the conquest of Granada, where Christian knight and turbaned Infidel disputed, inch by inch, the fair land of Andalusia, until the crescent, that symbol of heathenish abomination, was cast down, and the blessed cross, the tree of our redemption, erected in its stead.

Nearly eight hundred years were past and gone, since the Arabian invaders had sealed the perdition of Spain, by the defeat of Don Roderick, the last of her Gothic kings. Since that disastrous event, one portion after another of the peninsula had been gradually recovered by the Christian princes, until the single, but powerful and warlike territory of Granada, alone remained under the domination of the Moors.

This renowned kingdom, situated in the southern part of Spain, and washed on one side by the Mediterranean sea, was traversed in every direction by Sierras or chains of lofty and rugged mountains, naked, rocky, and precipitous, rendering it almost impregnable, but locking up within their sterile embraces deep, rich, and verdant valleys of prodigal fertility.

In the centre of the kingdom lay its capital, the beautiful city of Granada, sheltered, as it were, in the lap of the Sierra Nevada, or Snowy Mountains. Its houses, seventy thousand in number, covered two lofty hills with their declivities, and a deep valley between them, through which flowed the Darro. The streets were narrow, as is usual in Moorish and Arab cities, but there were occasionally small squares and open places. The houses had gardens and interior courts, set out with orange, citron, and pomegranate trees, and refreshed by fountains, so that as the edifices ranged above each other up the sides of the hills, they presented a delightful appearance of mingled grove and city. One of the hills was surmounted by the Alcazaba, a strong fortress, commanding all that part of the city; the other by the Alhambra, a royal palace and warrior castle, capable of containing within its alcazar and towers a garrison of forty thousand men; but possessing also its harem, the voluptuous abode of the Moorish monarchs, laid out with courts and gardens, fountains and baths, and stately halls, decorated in the most costly

style of oriental luxury. According to Moorish tradition, the king who built
this mighty and magnificent pile, was skilled in the occult sciences, and
furnished himself with the necessary funds by means of alchemy.* Such was
its lavish splendor that even at the present day, the stranger, wandering
through its silent courts and deserted halls, gazes with astonishment at gilded ceilings and fretted domes, the brilliancy and beauty of which have survived the vicissitudes of war and the silent dilapidation of ages.

The city was surrounded by high walls, three leagues in circuit, furnished
with twelve gates, and a thousand and thirty towers. Its elevation above the
sea, and the neighborhood of the Sierra Nevada crowned with perpetual
snows, tempered the fervid rays of summer; so that, while other cities were
panting with the sultry and stifling heat of the dogdays, the most salubrious
breezes played through the marble halls of Granada.

The glory of the city, however, was its vega or plain, which spread out to
a circumference of thirty-seven leagues, surrounded by lofty mountains, and
was proudly compared to the famous plain of Damascus. It was a vast garden
of delight, refreshed by numerous fountains, and by the silver windings of
the Xenil. The labor and ingenuity of the Moors had diverted the waters of
this river into thousands of rills and streams, and diffused them over the
whole surface of the plain. Indeed, they had wrought up this happy region
to a degree of wonderful prosperity, and took a pride in decorating it, as if
it had been a favorite mistress. The hills were clothed with orchards and
vineyards, the valleys embroidered with gardens, and the wide plains covered with waving grain. Here were seen in profusion the orange, the citron,
the fig, and pomegranate, with great plantations of mulberry trees, from
which was produced the finest silk. The vine clambered from tree to tree;
the grapes hung in rich clusters about the peasant's cottage, and the groves
were rejoiced by the perpetual song of the nightingale. In a word, so beautiful was the earth, so pure the air, and so serene the sky, of this delicious
region, that the Moors imagined the paradise of their Prophet to be situated
in that part of the heaven which overhung the kingdom of Granada.

Within this favored realm, so prodigally endowed and strongly fortified
by nature, the Moslem wealth, valor, and intelligence, which had once shed
such a lustre over Spain, had gradually retired, and here they made their
final stand. Granada had risen to splendor on the ruin of other Moslem kingdoms; but in so doing had become the sole object of Christian hostility, and
had to maintain its very existence by the sword. The Moorish capital accordingly presented a singular scene of Asiatic luxury and refinement, mingled with the glitter and the din of arms. Letters were still cultivated,
philosophy and poetry had their schools and disciples, and the language

*Zurita, lib. 20, c. 42.

spoken was said to be the most elegant Arabic. A passion for dress and ornament pervaded all ranks. That of the princesses and ladies of high rank,
says Al Kattib, one of their own writers, was carried to a height of luxury
and magnificence that bordered on delirium. They wore girdles and bracelets and anklets of gold and silver, wrought with exquisite art and delicacy,
and studded with jacinths, chrysolites, emeralds, and other precious stones.
They were fond of braiding and decorating their beautiful long tresses, or
confining them in knots sparkling with jewels. They were finely formed,
excessively fair, graceful in their manners, and fascinating in their conversation; when they smiled, says Al Kattib, they displayed teeth of dazzling
whiteness, and their breath was as the perfume of flowers.

The Moorish cavaliers, when not in armor, delighted in dressing themselves in Persian style, in garments of wool, of silk, or cotton, of the finest
texture, beautifully wrought with stripes of various colors. In winter they
wore, as an outer garment, the African cloak or Tunisian albornoz; but in the
heat of summer, they arrayed themselves in linen of spotless whiteness. The
same luxury prevailed in their military equipments. Their armor was inlaid
and chased with gold and silver. The sheaths of their scimetars were richly
labored and enamelled, the blades were of Damascus bearing texts from the
Koran, or martial and amorous mottoes; the belts were of golden filigree,
studded with gems, their poniards of Fez, were wrought in the arabesque
fashion; their lances bore gay bandaroles; their horses were sumptuously
caparisoned with housings of green and crimson velvet; wrought with silk
and enamelled with gold and silver. All this warlike luxury of the youthful
chivalry was encouraged by the Moorish kings, who ordained that no tax
should be imposed on the gold and silver employed in these embellishments; and the same exception was extended to the bracelets and other ornaments worn by the fair dames of Granada.

Of the chivalrous gallantry which prevailed between the sexes in this romantic period of Moorish history, we have traces in the thousand ballads
which have come down to our day, and which have given a tone and coloring
to Spanish amatory literature, and to every thing in Spain connected with
the tender passion.

War was the normal state of Granada, and its inhabitants; the common
people were subject at any moment to be summoned to the field, and all
the upper class was a brilliant chivalry. The Christian princes, so successful
in regaining the rest of the peninsula, found their triumphs checked at the
mountain boundaries of this kingdom. Every peak had its atalaya or watch-
tower, ready to make its fire by night or to send up its column of smoke by
day, a signal of invasion, at which the whole country was on the alert. To
penetrate the defiles of this perilous country; to surprise a frontier fortress;
or to make a foray into the vega and a hasty ravage within sight of the very

capital, were among the most favorite and daring exploits of the Castilian chivalry. But they never pretended to hold the region thus ravaged; it was sack, burn, plunder, and away! and these desolating inroads were retaliated in kind by the Moorish cavaliers, whose greatest delight was a *tala*, or predatory incursion into the Christian territories beyond the mountains.

A partisan warfare of this kind had long existed between Granada and its most formidable antagonists, the kingdoms of Castile and Leon. It was one which called out the keen yet generous rivalry of Christian and Moslem cavaliers, and gave rise to individual acts of chivalrous gallantry and daring prowess; but it was one which was gradually exhausting the resources and sapping the strength of Granada. One of the latest of its kings, therefore, Aben Ismael by name, disheartened by a foray which had laid waste the vega, and conscious that the balance of warfare was against his kingdom, made a truce in 1457 with Henry IV., king of Castile and Leon, stipulating to pay him an annual tribute of twelve thousand doblas or pistoles of gold, and to liberate annually six hundred Christian captives, or in default of captives, to give an equal number of Moors as hostages; all to be delivered at the city of Cordova.*

The truce, however, was of a partial nature, with singular reservations. It did not include the Moorish frontier towards Jaen, which was to remain open for the warlike enterprises of either nation; neither did it prohibit sudden attacks upon towns and castles, provided they were mere forays, conducted furtively, without sound of trumpet or display of banners; or pitching of camps, or regular investment, and that they did not last above three days.†

Aben Ismael was faithful in observing the conditions of the truce, but they were regarded with impatience by his eldest son, Muley Abul Hassan, a prince of a fiery and belligerent spirit, and fond of casing himself in armor and mounting his war horse. He had been present at Cordova at one of the payments of tribute, and had witnessed the scoffs and taunts of the Christians, and his blood boiled whenever he recalled the humiliating scene. When he came to the throne in 1465, on the death of his father, he ceased the payment of the tribute altogether, and it was sufficient to put him into a tempest of rage only to mention it.

"He was a fierce and warlike infidel," says the pious Fray Antonio Agapida; "his bitterness against the holy Christian faith had been signalized in battle during the lifetime of his father, and the same diabolical spirit of hostility was apparent in his ceasing to pay this most righteous tribute."

---

*Garibay, Compend., L. 17, c. 3.

†Zurita Anales de Aragon, L. 20, c. 42. Mariana Hist. de España, L. 25, c. 1. Bleda Coron de los Moros, L. 5, c. 3.

CHAPTER II.
OF THE EMBASSY OF DON JUAN DE VERA TO DEMAND ARREARS OF TRIBUTE
FROM THE MOORISH MONARCH.

THE flagrant want of faith of Muley Abul Hassan in fulfilling treaty stipulations, passed unresented during the residue of the reign of Henry the Impotent, and the truce was tacitly continued without the enforcement of
tribute, during the first three years of the reign of his successors, Ferdinand
and Isabella, of glorious and happy memory, who were too much engrossed
by civil commotions in their own dominions, and by a war of succession
waged with them by the king of Portugal, to risk an additional conflict with
the Moorish sovereign. When, however, at the expiration of the term of
truce, Muley Abul Hassan sought a renewal of it, the pride and piety of the
Castilian sovereigns were awakened to the flagrant defalcation of the Infidel
king, and they felt themselves called upon, by their dignity as monarchs,
and their religious obligations as champions of the faith, to make a formal
demand for the payment of arrearages.

In the year of grace 1478, therefore, Don Juan de Vera, a zealous and
devout knight, full of ardor for the faith and loyalty to the crown, was sent
as ambassador for the purpose. He was armed at all points, gallantly mounted, and followed by a moderate but well-appointed retinue; in this way he
crossed the Moorish frontier, and passed slowly through the country, looking
round him with the eyes of a practised warrior, and carefully noting its military points and capabilities. He saw that the Moor was well prepared for
possible hostilities. Every town was strongly fortified. The vega was studded
with towers of refuge for the peasantry: every pass of the mountain had its
castle of defence, every lofty height its watchtower. As the Christian cavaliers passed under the walls of the fortresses, lances and scimetars flashed
from their battlements, and the Moorish sentinels darted from their dark
eyes glances of hatred and defiance. It was evident that a war with this kingdom must be a war of posts, full of doughty peril and valiant enterprise,
where every step must be gained by toil and bloodshed, and maintained
with the utmost difficulty. The warrior spirit of the cavaliers kindled at the
thoughts, and they were impatient for hostilities; "not," says Antonio Agapida, "from any thirst for rapine and revenge, but from that pure and holy
indignation which every Spanish knight entertained at beholding this beautiful dominion of his ancestors defiled by the footsteps of Infidel usurpers.
It was impossible," he adds, "to contemplate this delicious country, and not
long to see it restored to the dominion of the true faith and the sway of the
Christian monarchs."

Arrived at the gates of Granada, Don Juan de Vera and his companions
saw the same vigilant preparations on the part of the Moorish king. His
walls and towers were of vast strength, in complete repair, and mounted

with lombards and other heavy ordnance. His magazines were well stored with the munitions of war: he had a mighty host of foot-soldiers, together with squadrons of cavalry, ready to scour the country and carry on either defensive or predatory warfare. The Christian warriors noted these things without dismay; their hearts rather glowed with emulation, at the thoughts of encountering so worthy a foe. As they slowly pranced through the streets of Granada, they looked round with eagerness on its stately palaces, and sumptuous mosques; on its alcayceria or bazar, crowded with silks and cloth of silver and gold, with jewels and precious stones, and other rich merchandise, the luxuries of every clime; and they longed for the time when all this wealth should be the spoil of the soldiers of the faith, and when each tramp of their steeds might be fetlock deep in the blood and carnage of the Infidels.

The Moorish inhabitants looked jealously at this small but proud array of Spanish chivalry, as it paraded, with that stateliness possessed only by Spanish cavaliers, through the renowned gate of Elvira. They were struck with the stern and lofty demeanor of Don Juan de Vera, and his sinewy frame, which showed him formed for hardy deeds of arms; and they supposed he had come in search of distinction, by defying the Moorish knights in open tourney, or in the famous tilt with reeds, for which they were so renowned: for it was still the custom of the knights of either nation to mingle in these courteous and chivalrous contests, during the intervals of war. When they learnt, however, that he was come to demand the tribute so abhorrent to the ears of the fiery monarch, they observed that it well required a warrior of his apparent nerve, to execute such an embassy.

Muley Abul Hassan received the cavalier in state, seated on a magnificent divan, and surrounded by the officers of his court, in the hall of ambassadors, one of the most sumptuous apartments of the Alhambra. When De Vera had delivered his message, a haughty and bitter smile curled the lip of the fierce monarch. "Tell your sovereigns," said he, "that the kings of Granada, who used to pay tribute in money to the Castilian crown, are dead. Our mint at present coins nothing but blades of scimetars and heads of lances."*

The defiance couched in this proud reply was heard with secret satisfaction by Don Juan de Vera, for he was a bold soldier and a devout hater of the Infidels; and he saw iron war in the words of the Moorish monarch. Being master, however, of all points of etiquette, he retained an inflexible demeanor, and retired from the apartment with stately and ceremonious gravity. His treatment was suited to his rank and dignity; a magnificent apartment in the Alhambra was assigned to him; and before his departure, a scimetar was sent to him by the king; the blade of the finest Damascus steel, the hilt of agate enriched with precious stones, and the guard of gold.

*Garibay, L. 40, c. 29. Conde, Hist. Arab. p. 4, c. 34.

De Vera drew it, and smiled grimly as he noticed the admirable temper of the blade. "His majesty has given me a trenchant weapon," said he: "I trust a time will come when I may show him that I know how to use his royal present." The reply was considered a compliment, of course; the bystanders little knew the bitter hostility that lay couched beneath.

On his return to Cordova, Don Juan de Vera delivered the reply of the Moor, but at the same time reported the state of his territories. These had been strengthened and augmented during the weak reign of Henry IV., and the recent troubles of Castile. Many cities and strong places contiguous to Granada, but heretofore conquered by the Christians, had renewed their allegiance to Muley Abul Hassan, so that his kingdom now contained fourteen cities, ninety-seven fortified places, besides numerous unwalled towns and villages defended by formidable castles, while Granada towered in the centre as the citadel.

The wary Ferdinand, as he listened to the military report of Don Juan de Vera, saw that the present was no time for hostilities with a warrior kingdom, so bristled over with means of defence. The internal discords of Castile still continued, as did the war with Portugal; under these circumstances he forbore to insist upon the payment of tribute, and tacitly permitted the truce to continue; but the defiance contained in the reply of Muley Abul Hassan remained rankling in his bosom as a future ground of war; and De Vera's description of Granada as the centre of a system of strongholds and rock-built castles, suggested to him his plan of conquest; by taking town after town, and fortress after fortress, and gradually plucking away all the supports before he attempted the capital. He expressed his resolution in a memorable pun, or play upon the name of Granada, which signifies a pomegranate. "I will pick out the seeds of this pomegranate one by one," said the cool and crafty Ferdinand.

NOTE.—In the first edition of this work the author recounted a characteristic adventure of the stout Juan de Vera, as happening on the occasion of this embassy; a further consultation of historical authorities has induced him to transfer it to a second embassy of De Vera's; which the reader will find related in a subsequent chapter.

CHAPTER III.
DOMESTIC FEUDS IN THE ALHAMBRA—RIVAL SULTANAS—PREDICTIONS
CONCERNING BOABDIL THE HEIR TO THE THRONE—HOW FERDINAND
MEDITATES WAR AGAINST GRANADA, AND HOW HE IS ANTICIPATED.

THOUGH Muley Abul Hassan was at peace in his external relations, a civil war raged in his harem, which it is proper to notice, as it had a fatal effect upon the fortunes of the kingdom. Though cruel by nature, he was uxorious, and somewhat prone to be managed by his wives. Early in life he had married his kinswoman, Ayxa, (or Ayesha,) daughter of his great uncle, the Sultan Mohammed VII., surnamed El Hayzari, or the left-handed. She was a woman of almost masculine spirit and energy, and of such immaculate and inaccessible virtue, that she was generally called La Horra, or, The Chaste. By her he had a son, Abu Abdallah; or, as he is commonly named by historians, Boabdil. The court astrologers, according to custom, cast the horoscope of the infant, but were seized with fear and trembling as they regarded it. "Allah Achbar! God is great!" exclaimed they, "He alone controls the fate of empires. It is written in the book of fate that this child will one day sit upon the throne, but that the downfall of the kingdom will be accomplished during his reign." From that time the prince had been regarded with aversion by his father; and the prediction which hung over him, and the persecutions to which he became subjected, procured him the surname of El Zogoybi, or, The Unfortunate. He grew up, however, under the protection of his valiant-hearted mother, who, by the energy of her character, long maintained an undisputed sway in the harem, until, as her youth passed away and her beauty declined, a formidable rival arose.

In one of the forays of the Moorish chivalry into the Christian territories, they had surprised a frontier fortress, commanded by Sancho Ximenes de Solis, a noble and valiant cavalier, who fell in bravely defending it. Among the captives was his daughter Isabella, then almost in her infancy; who was brought to Granada; delicately raised, and educated in the Moslem faith.* Her Moorish captors gave her the name of Fatima, but as she grew up her surpassing beauty gained her the surname of Zoraya, or, the Morning Star, by which she has become known in history. Her charms at length attracted the notice of Muley Abul Hassan, and she soon became a member of his harem. Some have spoken of her as a Christian slave, whom he had made his concubine; but others, with more truth, represent her as one of his wives, and ultimately his favorite Sultana; and indeed it was often the case that female captives of rank and beauty, when converted to the faith of Islam, became united to the proudest and loftiest of their captors.

Zoraya soon acquired complete ascendency over the mind of Muley Abul Hassan. She was as ambitious as she was beautiful, and, having become the mother of two sons, looked forward to the possibility of one of them sitting on the throne of Granada. These ambitious views were encouraged, if not suggested, by a faction which gathered round her, inspired by kindred sympathies. The king's vizier, Abul Cacem Vanegas, who had great influence over him, was, like Zoraya, of Christian descent, being of the noble house

*Cronica del Gran. Cardinal, cap. 71.

of Luque. His father, one of the Vanegas of Cordova, had been captured in infancy and brought up as a Moslem.* From him sprang the vizier, Abul Cacem Vanegas, and his brother Reduan Vanegas, likewise high in rank in the court of Muley Abul Hassan; and they had about them numerous and powerful connections, all basking in court favor. Though Moslems in faith, they were all drawn to Zoraya by the tie of foreign and Christian descent, and sought to elevate her and her children to the disparagement of Ayxa la Horra and her son Boabdil. The latter, on the other hand, were supported by the noble and once potent family of the Abencerrages, and by Aben Co-mixer, alcayde of the Alhambra; and between these two factions, headed by rival sultanas, the harem of Muley Abul Hassan became the scene of inveterate jealousies and intrigues, which in time, as will be shown, led to popular commotions and civil wars.†

While these female feuds were threatening Muley Abul Hassan with trouble and disaster at home, his evil genius prompted him to an enterprise which involved him in tenfold danger from abroad. The reader has already been apprised of a singular clause in the truce existing between the Christians and the Moors, permitting hasty dashes into each others' territories, and assaults of towns and fortresses, provided they were carried on as mere forays, and without the parade of regular warfare. A long time had elapsed, however, without any incursion of the kind on the part of the Moors, and the Christian towns on the frontiers had, in consesquence, fallen into a state of the most negligent security. In an unlucky moment, Muley Abul Hassan was tempted to one of these forays by learning that the fortress of Zahara, on the frontier between Ronda and Medina Sidonia, was but feebly garrisoned and scantily supplied, and that its alcayde was careless of his charge. This important post was built on the crest of a rocky mountain, with a strong castle perched above it, upon a cliff, so high that it was said to be above the flight of birds or drift of clouds. The streets and many of the houses were mere excavations, wrought out of the living rock. The town had but one gate, opening to the west, and defended by towers and bulwarks. The only ascent to this cragged fortress was by roads cut in the rock, so rugged in many places as to resemble broken stairs. In a word, the impregnable security of Zahara had become so proverbial throughout Spain, that a woman of forbidding and inaccessible virtue was called a Zahareña. But the strongest fortress and sternest virtue have weak points, and require unremitting vigilance to guard them: let warrior and dame take warning from the fate of Zahara.

*Cura de los Palacios, Hist. de los Reyes Catol, cap. 56.
†It is to be noted that several historians have erroneously represented Zoraya as the mother of Boabdil, instead of Ayxa la Horra; and the Abencerrages as the opponents of Boabdil, instead of his strenuous adherenta.[sic] The statement in the text is according to the most reliable authorities.

288.6–296.15 tumults. ; tumults. The vizier Yusef Aben Comixa was again the agent between the monarchs. He was received with unusual courtesy and attention by Ferdinand and Isabella, and it was arranged between them that the surrender should take place on the second day of January instead of the sixth. A new difficulty now arose in regard to the ceremonial of surrender. The haughty Ayxa la Horra, whose pride rose with the decline of her fortunes, declared that, as sultana mother, she would never consent that her son should stoop to the humiliation of kissing the hand of his conquerors, and, unless this part of the ceremonial were modified, she would find means to resist a surrender accompanied by such indignities.

Aben Comixa was sorely troubled by this opposition. He knew the high spirit of the indomitable Ayxa, and her influence over her less heroic son, and wrote an urgent letter on the subject to his friend, the count de Tendilla. The latter imparted the circumstance to the Christian sovereigns; a council was called on the matter. Spanish pride and etiquette were obliged to bend in some degree to the haughty spirit of a woman. It was agreed that Boabdil should sally forth on horseback, that on approaching the Spanish sovereigns he should make a slight movement as if about to draw his foot from the stirrup and dismount, but would be prevented from doing so by Ferdinand, who should treat him with a respect due to his dignity and elevated birth. The count de Tendilla dispatched a messenger with this arrangement; and the haughty scruples of Ayxa la Horra were satisfied.*

CHAPTER XCIX.
SURRENDER OF GRANADA

THE night preceding the surrender was a night of doleful lamentings, within the walls of the Alhambra; for the household of Boabdil were preparing to take a last farewell of that delightful abode. All the royal treasures, and most precious effects, were hastily packed upon mules; the beautiful apartments were despoiled, with tears and wailings, by their own inhabitants. Before the dawn of day, a mournful cavalcade moved obscurely out of a postern-gate of the Alhambra, and departed through one of the most retired quarters of the city. It was composed of the family of the unfortunate Boabdil, which he sent off thus privately, that they might not be exposed to the eyes of scoffers, or the exultation of the enemy. The mother of Boabdil, the sultana Ayxa la Horra, rode on in silence, with dejected yet dignified demeanor; but his wife Zorayma, and all the females of his household, gave way to loud lamentations, as they looked back upon their favorite abode, now a mass of gloomy towers behind them. They were attended by the ancient domestics

*Salazar de Mendoza. Chron. del Gran. Cardinal, lib. 1. c. 69, p. 1. Mondajar His. MS. as cited by Alcantara, t. 4, c. 18.

of the household, and by a small guard of veteran Moors, loyally attached to the fallen monarch, and who would have sold their lives dearly in defence of his family. The city was yet buried in sleep, as they passed through its silent streets. The guards at the gate shed tears, as they opened it for their departure. They paused not, but proceeded along the banks of the Xenel on the road that leads to the Alpuxarras, until they arrived at a hamlet at some distance from the city, where they halted, and waited until they should be joined by king Boabdil.

The night which had passed so gloomily in the sumptuous halls of the Alhambra, had been one of joyful anticipation in the Christian camp. In the evening proclamation had been made that Granada was to be surrendered on the following day, and the troops were all ordered to assemble at an early hour under their several banners. The cavaliers, pages, and esquires were all charged to array themselves in their richest and most splendid style, for the occasion; and even the royal family determined to lay by the mourning they had recently assumed for the sudden death of the prince of Portugal, the husband of the princess Isabella. In a clause of the capitulation it had been stipulated that the troops destined to take possession, should not traverse the city, but should ascend to the Alhambra by a road opened for the purpose outside of the walls. This was to spare the feelings of the afflicted inhabitants, and to prevent any angry collision between them and their conquerors. So rigorous was Ferdinand in enforcing this precaution, that the soldiers were prohibited under pain of death from leaving the ranks to enter into the city.

The rising sun had scarce shed his rosy beams upon the snowy summits of the Sierra Nevada, when three signal guns boomed heavily from the lofty fortress of the Alhambra. It was the concerted sign that all was ready for the surrender. The Christian army forthwith poured out of the city, or rather camp of Santa Fé, and advanced across the vega. The king and queen, with the prince and princess, the dignitaries and ladies of the court, took the lead, accompanied by the different orders of monks and friars, and surrounded by the royal guards splendidly arrayed. The procession moved slowly forward, and paused at the village of Armilla, at the distance of half a league from the city.

In the mean time, the grand cardinal of Spain, Don Pedro Gonzalez de Mendoza, escorted by three thousand foot and a troop of cavalry, and accompanied by the commander Don Gutierrez de Cardenas, and a number of prelates and hidalgos, crossed the Xenel and proceeded in the advance, to ascend to the Alhambra and take possession of that royal palace and fortress. The road which had been opened for the purpose led by the Puerta de los Molinos, or gate of mills, up a defile to the esplanade on the summit of the Hill of Martyrs. At the approach of this detachment, the Moorish king sallied forth from a postern gate of the Alhambra, having left his vizier Yusef Aben

Comixa to deliver up the palace. The gate by which he sallied passed through a lofty tower of the outer wall, called the tower of the seven floors (de los siete suelos). He was accompanied by fifty cavaliers, and approached the grand cardinal on foot. The latter immediately alighted, and advanced to meet him with the utmost respect. They stepped aside a few paces, and held a brief conversation in an under tone, when Boabdil, raising his voice, exclaimed, "Go, Senor, and take possession of those fortresses in the name of the powerful sovereigns, to whom God has been pleased to deliver them in reward of their great merits, and in punishment of the sins of the Moors." The grand cardinal sought to console him in his reverses, and offered him the use of his own tent during any time he might sojourn in the camp. Boabdil thanked him for the courteous offer, adding some words of melancholy import, and then taking leave of him gracefully, passed mournfully on to meet the Catholic sovereigns, descending to the vega by the same road by which the cardinal had come. The latter, with the prelates and cavaliers who attended him, entered the Alhambra, the gates of which were thrown wide open by the alcayde Aben Comixa. At the same time the Moorish guards yielded up their arms, and the towers and battlements were taken possession of by the Christian troops.

While these transactions were passing in the Alhambra and its vicnity, the sovereigns remained with their retinue and guards near the village of Armilla, their eyes fixed on the towers of the royal fortress, watching for the appointed signal of possession. The time that had elapsed since the departure of the detachment seemed to them more than necessary for the purpose, and the anxious mind of Ferdinand began to entertain doubts of some commotion in the city. At length they saw the silver cross, the great standard of this crusade, elevated on the Torre de la Vela, or Great Watch-Tower, and sparkling in the sunbeams. This was done by Hernando de Talavera, bishop of Avila. Beside it was planted the pennon of the glorious apostle St. James, and a great shout of "Santiago! Santiago!" rose throughout the army. Lastly was reared the royal standard by the king of arms, with the shout of "Castile! Castile! For king Ferdinand and queen Isabella!" The words were echoed by the whole army, with acclamations that resounded across the vega. At sight of these signals of possession, the sovereigns sank upon their knees, giving thanks to God for this great triumph; the whole assembled host followed their example, and the choristers of the royal chapel broke forth into the solemn anthem of "Te Deum laudamus."

The king now advanced with a splendid escort of cavalry and the sound of trumpets, until he came to a small mosque near the banks of the Xenel, and not far from the foot of the Hill of Martyrs, which edifice remains to the present day consecrated as the hermitage of St. Sebastian. Here he beheld the unfortunate king of Granada approaching on horseback, at the head of his slender retinue. Boabdil, as he drew near made a movement to dismount, but, as had previously been concerted, Ferdinand prevented him. He then offered to kiss the king's hand, which according to arrangement was likewise declined, whereupon he leaned forward and kissed the king's right arm; at the same time he delivered the keys of the city with an air of mingled melancholy and resignation: "These keys," said he, "are the last relics of the Arabian empire in Spain: thine, oh king, are our trophies, our kingdom, and our person. Such is the will of God! Receive them with the clemency thou hast promised, and which we look for at thy hands."*

King Ferdinand restrained his exultation into an air of serene magnanimity. "Doubt not our promises," replied he, "nor that thou shalt regain from our friendship the prosperity of which the fortune of war has deprived thee."

Being informed that Don Inigo Lopez de Mendoza, the good count of Tendilla, was to be governor of the city, Boabdil drew from his finger a gold ring set with a precious stone, and presented it to the count. "With this ring," said he, "Granada has been governed; take it and govern with it, and God make you more fortunate than I."†

He then proceeded to the village of Armilla, where the queen Isabella remained with her escort and attendants. The queen, like her husband, declined all act of homage, and received him with her accustomed grace and benignity. She at the same time delivered to him his son, who had been held as a hostage for the fulfilment of the capitulation. Boabdil pressed his child to his bosom with tender emotion, and they seemed mutually endeared to each other by their misfortunes.‡

Having rejoined his family, the unfortunate Boabdil continued on towards the Alpuxarras, that he might not behold the entrance of the Christians into his capital. His devoted band of cavaliers followed him in gloomy silence; but heavy sighs burst from their bosoms, as shouts of joy and strains of triumphant music were borne on the breeze from the victorious army.

Having rejoined his family, Boabdil set forward with a heavy heart for his allotted residence in the valley of Purchena. At two leagues' distance, the cavalcade, winding into the skirts of the Alpuxarras, ascended an eminence commanding the last view of Granada. As they arrived at this spot, the Moors paused involuntarily, to take a farewell gaze at their beloved city, which a few steps more would shut from their sight for ever. Never had it appeared so lovely in their eyes. The sunshine, so bright in that transparent climate, lit up each tower and minaret, and rested gloriously upon the

---

*Abarca, Anales de Aragon, Rey 30, c. 3

†This ring remained in the possession of the descendants of the count until the death of the marques Don Inigo, the last male heir, who died in Malaga without children, in 1656. The ring was then lost through inadvertence and ignorance of its value, Dona Maria, the sister of the marques, being absent in Madrid. Alcantara, l. 4, c. 18.

‡Zurita, Anales de Aragon, lib. 20, cap. 92.

crowning battlements of the Alhambra; while the vega spread its enamelled bosom of verdure below, glistening with the silver windings of the Xenel. The Moorish cavaliers gazed with a silent agony of tenderness and grief upon that delicious abode, the scene of their loves and pleasures. While they yet looked, a light cloud of smoke burst forth from the citadel, and presently a peal of artillery, faintly heard, told that the city was taken possession of, and the throne of the Moslem kings was lost for ever. The heart of Boabdil, softened by misfortunes and overcharged with grief, could no longer contain itself: "Allah Achbar! God is great!" said he; but the words of resignation died upon his lips, and he burst into tears.

His mother, the intrepid Ayxa, was indignant at his weakness: "You do well," said she, "to weep like a woman, for what you failed to defend like a man!"

The vizier Aben Comixa endeavored to console his royal master. "Consider, Senor," said he, "that the most signal misfortunes often render men as renowned as the most prosperous achievements, provided they sustain them with magnanimity."

The unhappy monarch, however, was not to be consoled; his tears continued to flow. "Allah Achbar!" exclaimed he; "when did misfortunes ever equal mine?"

From this circumstance, the hill, which is not far from Padul, took the name of Feg Allah Achbar: but the point of view commanding the last prospect of Granada, is known among Spaniards by the name of *El ultimo suspiro del Moro;* or, "The last sigh of the Moor."

CHAPTER C.
HOW THE CASTILIAN SOVEREIGNS TOOK POSSESSION OF GRANADA.

QUEEN ISABELLA having joined the king, the royal pair, followed by a triumphant host, passed up the road by the Hill of Martyrs, and thence to the main entrance of the Alhambra. The grand cardinal awaited them under the lofty arch of the great gate of justice, accompanied by Don Gutierrez de Cardenas and Aben Comixa. Here king Ferdinand gave the keys which had been delivered up to him into the hands of the queen; they were passed successively into the hands of the prince Juan, the grand cardinal, and finally into those of the count de Tendilla, in whose custody they remained, that brave cavalier having been named alcayde of the Alhambra, and captain-general of Granada.

The sovereigns did not remain long in the Alhambra on this first visit, but leaving a strong garrison there under the count de Tendilla, to maintain tranquillity in the palace and the subjacent city, returned to the camp at Santa Fé.

We must not omit to mention a circumstance attending the surrender of the city, which spoke eloquently to the hearts of the victors. As the royal army had advanced in all the pomp of courtly and chivalrous array, a procession of a different kind came forth to meet it. This was composed of more than five hundred Christian captives, many of whom had languished for years in Moorish dungeons. Pale and emaciated, they came clanking their chains in triumph, and shedding tears of joy. They were received with tenderness by the sovereigns. The king hailed them as good Spaniards, as men loyal and brave, as martyrs to the holy cause; the queen distributed liberal relief among them with her own hands, and they passed on before the squadrons of the army, singing hymns of jubilee.*

The sovereigns forbore to enter the city until it should be fully occupied by their troops, and public tranquillity insured. All this was done under the vigilant superintendence of the count de Tendilla, assisted by the marques of Villena; and the glistening of Christian helms and lances along the walls and bulwarks, and the standards of the faith and of the realm flaunting from the towers, told that the subjugation of the city was complete. The proselyte prince, Cid Hiaya, now known by the Christian appellation of Don Pedro de Granada Vanegas,† was appointed chief alguazil of the city, and had charge of the Moorish inhabitants; and his son, lately the prince Alnayer, now Alonzo de Granada Vanegas, was appointed admiral of the fleets.

It was on the sixth of January, the day of kings and festival of the Epiphany, that the sovereigns made their triumphal entry with grand military parade. First advanced, we are told, a splendid escort of cavaliers in burnished armor, and superbly mounted. Then followed the prince Juan, glittering with jewels and diamonds; on each side of him, mounted on mules, rode the grand cardinal, clothed in purple, Fray Hernando de Talavero, bishop of Airla, and the archbishop elect of Granada. To these succeeded the queen and her ladies, and the king, managing in galliard style, say the Spanish chroniclers, a proud and mettlesome steed (un caballo arrogante). Then followed the army in shining columns, with flaunting banners and the inspiring clamor of military music. The king and queen (says the worthy Fray Antonio Agapida) looked, on this occasion, as more than mortal: the venerable ecclesiastics, to whose advice and zeal this glorious conquest ought in a great measure to be attributed, moved along with hearts swelling with holy exultation, but with chastened and downcast looks of edifying humility; while the hardy warriors, in tossing plumes and shining steel, seemed elevated with a stern joy, at finding themselves in possession of this object of so many toils and perils. As the streets resounded with the tramp of steeds and swell-

---

*Abarca, lib. sup. Zurita, &c.

†Cid Hiaya was made cavalier of the order of Santiago. He and his son intermarried with the Spanish nobility, and the marqueses of Compotejar are among their descendants. Their portraits, and the portraits of their grandsons, are to be seen in one of the rooms of the Generalife at Granada.

ing peals of music, the Moors buried themselves in the deepest recesses of their dwellings. There they bewailed in secret the fallen glory of their race, but suppressed their groans, lest they should be heard by their enemies and increase their triumph.

The royal procession advanced to the principal mosque, which had been consecrated as a cathedral. Here the sovereigns offered up prayers and thanksgivings, and the choir of the royal chapel chanted a triumphant anthem, in which they were joined by all the courtiers and cavaliers. Nothing (says Fray Antonio Agapida) could exceed the thankfulness to God of the pious king Ferdinand, for having enabled him to eradicate from Spain the empire and name of that accursed heathen race, and for the elevation of the cross in that city wherein the impious doctrines of Mahomet had so long been cherished. In the fervor of his spirit, he supplicated from Heaven a continuance of its grace, and that this glorious triumph might be perpetuated.* The prayer of the pious monarch was responded by the people, and even his enemies were for once convinced of his sincerity.

When the religious ceremonies were concluded, the court ascended to the stately palace of the Alhambra, and entered by the great gate of justice. The halls lately occupied by turbaned infidels now rustled with stately dames and Christian courtiers, who wandered with eager curiosity over this far-famed palace, admiring its verdant courts and gushing fountains, its halls decorated with elegant arabesques, and storied with inscriptions, and the splendor of its gilded and brilliantly painted ceilings.

It had been a last request of the unfortunate Boabdil, and one which showed how deeply he felt the transition of his fate, that no person might be permitted to enter or depart by the gate of the Alhambra, through which he had sallied forth to surrender his capital. His request was granted; the portal was closed up, and remains so to the present day—a mute memorial of that event.†

*The words of Fray Antonio Agapida are little more than an echo of those of the worthy Jesuit father Mariana. (L. 25, c. 18.)

†Garibay, Compend. Hist. lib. 40, c. 42. The existence of this gateway, and the story connected with it, are perhaps known to few; but were identified, in the researches made to verify this history. The gateway is at the bottom of a tower, at some distance from the main body of the Alhambra. The tower has been rent and ruined by gunpowder, at the time when the fortress was evacuated by the French. Great masses lie around half covered by vines and fig-trees. A poor man, by the name of Matteo Ximenes, who lives in one of the halls among the ruins of the Alhambra, where his family has resided for many generations, pointed out to the author the gateway, still closed up with stones. He remembered to have heard his father and grandfather say, that it had always been stopped up, and that out of it king Boabdil had gone when he surrendered Granada. The route of the unfortunate king may be traced thence across the garden of the convent of Los Martyros, and down a ravine beyond, through a street of Gipsy caves and hovels, by the gate of Los Molinos, and so on to the Hermitage of St. Sebastian. None but an antiquarian, however, will be able to trace it, unless aided by the humble historian of the place, Matteo Ximenes.

The Spanish sovereigns fixed their throne in the presence-chamber of the palace, so long the seat of Moorish royalty. Hither the principal inhabitants of Granada repaired, to pay them homage and kiss their hands in token of vassalage; and their example was followed by deputies from all the towns and fortresses of the Alpuxarras, which had not hitherto submitted.

Thus terminated the war of Granada, after ten years of incessant fighting; equalling (says Fray Antonio Agapida) the far-famed siege of Troy in duration, and ending, like that, in the capture of the city. Thus ended also the dominion of the Moors in Spain, having endured seven hundred and seventy-eight years, from the memorable defeat of Roderick, the last of the Goths, on the banks of the Guadalete. The authentic Agapida is uncommonly particular in fixing the epoch of this event. This great triumph of our holy Catholic faith, according to his computation, took place in the beginning of January, in the year of our Lord 1492, being 3655 years from the population of Spain by the patriarch Tubal; 3797 from the general deluge; 5453 from the creation of the world, according to Hebrew calculation; and in the month Rabic, in the eight hundred and ninety-seventh year of the Hegira, or flight of Mahomet; whom may God confound! saith the pious Agapida!

APPENDIX.

THE Chronicle of the Conquest of Granada is finished, but the reader may be desirous of knowing the subsequent fortunes of some of the principal personages.

The unfortunate Boabdil retired with his mother, his wife, his son, his sister, his vizier and bosom counsellor Aben Comixa, and many other relatives and friends to the valley of Purchena, where a small, but fertile territory, had been allotted him, comprising several towns of the Alpuxarras, with all their rights and revenues. Here, surrounded by obedient vassals, devoted friends, and a loving family, and possessed of wealth sufficient to enable him to indulge in his habitual luxury and magnificence, he for a time led a tranquil life, and may have looked back upon his regal career as a troubled dream, from which he had happily awaked. Still he appears to have pleased himself with a shadow of royalty, making occasionally, progresses about his little domains, visiting the different towns, receiving the homage of the inhabitants, and bestowing largesses with a princely hand. His great delight, however, was in sylvan sports and exercises, with horses, hawks, and hounds, being passionately fond of hunting and falconry, so as to pass weeks together in sporting campaigns among the mountains. The jealous suspicions of Ferdinand, followed him into his retreat. No exertions were spared by the politically pious monarch, to induce him to embrace the Christian religion, as a means of severing him in feelings and sympathies from his late subjects; but he remained true to the faith of his fathers; and it must have added not a little to his humiliation to live a vassal under Christian sovereigns.

His obstinacy, in this respect, aggravated the distrust of Ferdinand, who, looking back upon the past inconstancy of the Moors, could not feel perfectly secure in his newly conquered territories, while there was one within their bounds who might revive pretensions to the throne, and rear the standard of an opposite faith in their behalf. He caused therefore a vigilant watch to be kept upon the dethroned monarch in his retirement, and beset him with spies, who were to report all his words and actions. The reader will probably be surprised to learn, that the foremost of these spies was Aben Comixa! Ever since the capture and release of the niece of the vizier by the count de Tendilla, Aben Comixa had kept up a friendly correspondence with that nobleman, and through this channel had gradually been brought over to the views of Ferdinand. Documents which have gradually come to light, leave little doubt that the vizier had been corrupted by the bribes and promises of the Spanish king, and had greatly promoted his views in the capitulation of Granada. It is certain that he subsequently received great estates from the Christian sovereigns. While residing in confidential friendship with Boabdil in his retirement, Aben Comixa communicated secretly with Hernando de Zafra, the secretary of Ferdinand, who resided at Granada, giving him information of all Boabdil's movements; which the secretary reported by letter to the king. Some of the letters of the secretary still exist in the archives of Samancas, and have been recently published in the collection of unedited documents.*

The jealous doubts of Ferdinand were quickened by the letters of his spies. He saw in the hunting campaigns and royal progresses of the ex-king a mode of keeping up a military spirit, and a concerted intelligence among the Moors of the Alpuxarras, that might prepare them for future rebellion. By degrees, the very residence of Boabdil within the kingdom became incompatible with Ferdinand's ideas of security. He gave his agents, therefore, secret instructions to work upon the mind of the deposed monarch, and induce him, like El Zagal, to relinquish his Spanish estates for valuable considerations, and retire to Africa. Boabdil, however, was not to be persuaded; to the urgent suggestions of these perfidious counsellors, he replied, that he had given up a kingdom to live in peace; and had no idea of going to a foreign land to encounter new troubles, and to be under the control of alarabes.†

Ferdinand persisted in his endeavors, and found means more effectual of operating on the mind of Boabdil and gradually disposing him to enter into

---

*El rey Muley Babdali (Boabdil) y sus criados andan continuamente á caza con glagos y azores, y alla esta agora en al campo de Dalias y en Verja, aunque su casa tiene en Andaraxa y dican que estará por todo este mes.–*Carta Secret a de Hernando de Zafra. Decembre,* 1492.

†Letter of Hernando de Zafra to the sovereigns, Dec 9, 1493.

negotiations. It would appear that Aben Comixa was secretly active in this matter, in the interests of the Spanish monarch, and was with him at Barcelona, as the vizier and agent of Boabdil. The latter, however, finding that his residence in the Alpuxarras was a cause of suspicion and uneasiness to Ferdinand, determined to go himself to Barcelona, have a conference with the sovereigns, and conduct all his negotiations with them in person. Zafra, the secretary of Ferdinand, who was ever on the alert, wrote a letter from Granada, apprising the king of Boabdil's intention, and that he was making preparations for the jonrney. He received a letter in reply, charging him by subtle management to prevent, or at least delay, the coming of Boabdil to court.* The crafty monarch trusted to effect through Aben Comixa as vizier and agent of Boabdil, an arrangement which might be impossible to obtain from Boabdil himself. The politic plan was carried into effect. Boabdil was detained at Andarax by the management of Zafra. In the mean time, a scandalous bargain was made on the 17th March, 1493, between Ferdinand and Aben Comixa, in which the latter, as vizier and agent of Boabdil, though without any license of authority from him, made a sale of his territory, and the patrimonial property of the princesses, for eighty thousand ducats of gold, and engaged that he should depart for Africa, taking care, at the same time, to make conditions highly advantageous for himself.†

This bargain being hastily concluded, Yusef Aben Comixa loaded the treasure upon mules, and departed for the Alpuxarras. Here, spreading the money before Boabdil: "Senior," said he, "I have observed that as long as you live here, you are exposed to constant peril. The Moors are rash and irritable; they may make some sudden insurrection, elevate your standard as a pretext, and thus overwhelm you and your friends with utter ruin. I have observed also that you pine away with grief, being continually reminded in this country that you were once its sovereign, but never more must hope to reign. I have put an end to these evils. Your territory is sold— behold the price of it. With this gold you may buy far greater possessions in Africa, where you may live in honor and security."

When Boabdil heard these words, he burst into a sudden transport of rage, and drawing his scimetar, would have sacrificed the officious Yusef on the spot, had not the attendants interfered, and hurried the vizier from his presence.‡

The rage of Boabdil gradually subsided; he saw that he had been duped and betrayed; but he knew the spirit of Ferdinand too well to hope that he would retract the bargain, however illegitimately effected. He contented

*Letter of the sovereigns to Hernando de Zafra, from Barcelona. Feb. 1493.
†Alcantara, Hist. Granad. iv. c. 18.
‡Marmol. Rebel. l. 1, c. 22.

himself, therefore, with obtaining certain advantageous modifications, and then prepared to bid a final adieu to his late kingdom and his native land.

It took some months to make the necessary arrangements; or rather his departure was delayed by a severe domestic affliction. Morayma, his gentle and affectionate wife, worn out by agitations and alarms, was gradually sinking into the grave, a prey to devouring melancholy. Her death took place toward the end of August. Hernando de Zafra apprised king Ferdinand of the event as one propitious to his purposes; removing an obstacle to the embarkation, which was now fixed for the month of September. Zafra was instructed to accompany the exiles until he saw them landed on the African coast.

The embarkation, however, did not take place until some time in the month of October. A caracca had been prepared at the port of Adra for Boabdil and his immediate family and friends. Another caracca and two galliots received a number of faithful adherents, amounting, it is said to 1130, who followed their prince into exile.

A crowd of his former subjects witnessed his embarkation. As the sails were unfurled and swelled to the breeze, and the vessel bearing Boabdil parted from the land, the spectators would fain have given him a farewell cheering; but the humbled state of their once proud sovereign forced itself upon their minds, and the ominous surname of his youth rose involuntarily to their tongues: "Farewell, Boabdil! Allah preserve thee, *El Zogoybi!*" burst spontaneously from their lips. The unlucky appellation sank into the heart of the expatriated monarch, and tears dimmed his eyes as the snowy summits of the mountains of Granada gradually faded from his view.

He was received with welcome at the court of his relative Muley Ahmed, caliph of Fez, the same who had treated El Zagal with such cruelty in his exile. For thirty-four years he resided in this court, treated with great consideration, and built a palace or alcazar, at Fez, in which, it is said, he endeavored to emulate the beauties and delights of the Alhambra.

The last we find recorded of him is in the year 1536, when he followed the caliph to the field to repel the invasion of two brothers of the famous line of the Xerifes, who at the head of Berber troops had taken the city of Morocco and threatened Fez. The armies came in sight of each other on the banks of the Gaudal Hawit or river of slaves, at the ford of Balcuba. The river was deep, the banks were high and broken; and the ford could only be passed in single file; for three days the armies remained firing at each other across the stream, neither venturing to attempt the dangerous ford. At length the caliph divided his army into three battalions, the command of the first he gave to his brother-in-law, and to Aliatar, son of the old alcayde of Loxa; another division he commanded himself, and the third, composed of his best marksmen, he put under the command of his son the prince of Fez, and Boabil, now a gray-haired veteran. The last mentioned column took the lead, dashed boldly across the ford, scrambled up the opposite bank, and attempted to keep the enemy employed until the other battalions should have time to cross. The rebel army, however, attacked them with such fury, that the son of the king of Fez and several of the bravest alcaydes were slain upon the spot; multitudes were driven back into the river, which was already crowded with passing troops. A dreadful confusion took place; the horse trampled upon the foot; the enemy pressed on them with fearful slaughter; those who escaped the sword perished by the stream; the river was choked by the dead bodies of men and horses, and by the scattered baggage of the army. In this scene of horrible carnage fell Boabdil, truly called El Zogoybi, or the unlucky;—an instance, says the ancient chronicler, of the scornful caprice of fortune, dying in defence of the kingdom of another, after wanting spirit to die in defence of his own.*

The aspersion of the chronicler is more caustic than correct. Boabdil never showed a want of courage in the defence of Granada; but he wanted firmness and decision; he was beset from the first by perplexities, and ultimately, by the artifices of Ferdinand and the treachery of those in whom he most confided.†

ZORAYA, THE STAR OF THE MORNING.

Notwithstanding the deadly rivalship of this youthful sultana, with Ayxa la Horra, the virtuous mother of Boabdil, and the disasters to which her ambitious intrigues gave rise, the placable spirit of Boabdil bore her no lasting enmity. After the death of his father, he treated her with respect and kindness, and evinced a brotherly feeling towards her sons Cad and Nazar. In the capitulations for the surrender of Granada he took care of her interests, and the possessions which he obtained for her were in his neighborhood, in the valleys of the Alpuxarras. Zoraya, however, under the influence of queen Isabella, returned to the Christian faith, the religion of her infancy, and resumed her Spanish name of Isabella. Her two sons Cad and Nazar were baptized under the names of Don Fernando and Don Juan de Granada, and were permitted to take the titles of Infantas or princes. They intermarried with noble Spanish families, and the dukes of Granada, resident in Valladolid, are descendants of Don Juan (once Nazar), and preserve to the present day the blazon of their royal ancestor Muley Abul Hassan, and his motto, Le Galib ile Alá, God alone is conqueror.

*Marmol. Descrip. de Africa, p. 1, l. 2, c. 40. Idem, Hist. Reb. de los Moros, lib. 1, c. 21.

†In revising this account of the ultimate fortunes of Boabdil, the author has availed himself of facts recently brought out in Alcantara's history of Granada; which throw strong lights on certain parts of the subject hitherto covered with obscurity.

FATE OF ABEN COMIXA.

An ancient chronicle which has long remained in manuscript, but has been published of late years in the collection of Spanish historical documents,* informs us of the subsequent fortunes of the perfidious Aben Comixa. Discarded and despised by Boabdil for his treachery, he repaired to the Spanish court, and obtained favor in the eyes of the devout queen Isabella by embracing the Christian religion, being baptized under her auspices, with the name of Don Juan de Granada. He even carried his zeal for his newly adopted creed so far as to become a Franciscan friar. By degrees his affected piety grew cool, and the friar's garb became irksome. Taking occasion of the sailing of some Venetian galleys from Almeria, he threw off his religious habit, embarked on board of one of them and crossed to Africa, where he landed in the dress of a Spanish cavalier.

In a private interview with Abderraman, the Moorish king of Bujia, he related his whole history, and declared that he had always been and still was at heart a true Mahometan. Such skill had he in inspiring confidence that the Moorish king took him into favor and appointed him governor of Algiers. While enjoying his new dignity, a Spanish squadron of four galleys under the celebrated count Pedro de Navarro, anchored in the harbor, in 1509. Aben Comixa paid the squadron a visit of ceremony in his capacity of governor; gave the count repeated fetes, and in secret conversations with him laid open all the affairs of the king of Bujia, and offered if the count should return with sufficient force, to deliver the city into his hands and aid him in conquering the whole territory. The count hastened back to Spain and made known the proposed treachery to the Cardinal Ximenes, then prime minister of Spain. In the following month of January he was sent with thirty vessels, and four thousand soldiers to achieve the enterprise. The expedition of Navarro was successful. He made himself master of Bujia, and seized in triumph on the royal palace, but he found there the base Aben Comixa weltering in his blood and expiring under numerous wounds. His treachery had been discovered, and the vengeance of the king of Bujia had closed his perfidious career.

DEATH OF THE MARQUES OF CADIZ.

*Padilla, Cronica de Felipe el Hermosa, cap. 18, y. 19, as cited by Alcantara.

APPENDIX B
RECONSTRUCTED CHAPTERS 34, 35

This appendix faithfully reproduces the scribal reconstruction included in the Murray manuscript of the two chapters whose duplicate copies both went to America. The inconsistently applied custom of using an opening quotation mark at the beginning of every line within a quotation has been ignored, as it has been throughout the Twayne edition; all other punctuation is maintained. Irving left no indication on these manuscript pages that he read them after the scribe had written them.

A few days cleared up the mystery and brought tidings of their steeds led in triumph into the gates of Granada and their bleeding heads, borne at the saddle bows of the warriors of El Zagal. Their fellow knights who formed a part of the garrison were struck with horror at the dismal story and panted to revenge their death. Their number however was too much reduced by this loss, to take the field for the Vega swarmed with the troops of El Zagal. They could not even venture forth to forage for provisions, and the defeat of the Count de Cabra having interrupted their customary supplies, they were reduced to such extremity that they had to kill several of their horses for food.

Don Gutiere de Padilla, Clavero of Calatrava,* the commander of the fortress, was pondering one day over the gloomy state of affairs, when a Moor was brought before him who had applied at the gate for an audience. He bore a budget and appeared to be one of those itinerant merchants who wandered about the country in those days, hanging on the skirts of armies, to purchase the spoils of the soldiery, and who would pretend to sell amulets, trinkets and perfumes, but would often draw forth from their wallets articles of great rarity and value: rich shawls, chains of gold, necklaces of pearls and diamonds and costly gems, the plunder of camps and cities. The Moor approached the Clavero with a mysterious look. "Senor" said he "I would speak with you alone, I have a precious jewel to dispose of." "I need no jewels" said the Clavero, abruptly, "take thy wares to the soldiery." "By the blood of him who died on the cross" exclaimed the Moor with earnest solemnity "do not turn a deaf ear to my offer, the jewel I have to sell would be to you of inestimable value, and you alone can be the purchaser."

The Clavero was moved by the earnestness of the Moor, and perceived that under the figurative language common to his countrymen, he concealed some meaning of importance. He made a sign therefore to his attendants to

*Clavero of Calatrava is he who bears the keys of the castle, convent and archives of the order. It is an office of great honour and distinction.

withdraw. The Moor looked after them until the door closed, then advancing cautiously: "What will you give me" said he, "if I deliver the fortress of Zalea into your hands?"

Zalea was a strong town about two leagues distant, which had long been a hostile and dangerous neighbour to Alhama; its warriors laying frequent ambuscades to surprize the Knights of Calatrava when out upon a forage, and to intercept and cut off their supplies and cavalgadas.

The Clavero looked with mingled surprize and distrust at this itinerant pedlar who thus offered to traffic for a warlike town. "Thou talkest," said he, "of selling me Zalea; what means hast thou of making good the sale." "I have a brother in the garrison," replied the Moor, who for a proper sum paid down will admit a body of troops by night into the Citadel."

"And for a sum of gold then" said the Clavero, regarding him with stern scrutiny, "thou art prepared to betray thy people and thy faith."

"I abjure them and their faith," replied the Moor, "my mother was a Castilian captive her people shall be my people and her religion my religion"

The cautious Clavero still distrusted the sincerity of this mongrel moor and pyebald Christian. "What assurance" continued he "have I that thou wilt deal more truly with me, than with the Alcayde of the fortress thou wouldst betray? To me thou hast no tie of fealty, to him thou owest thy allegiance."

"I owe him no allegiance!" cried the Moor, fire flashing from his eyes, "The Alcayde is a tyrant   a dog! He has robbed me of my merchandize, stripped me of my lawful booty, and ordered me the bastinado because I dared to complain. May the curse of God light upon me if I rest contented until I have ample vengeance."

"Enough," said the Clavero, "I will trust to thy vengeance even more than to thy Christianity."

Don Gutiere now summoned a council of his principal Kinghts; they were all eager for the enterprize as a mode of revenging the death of their companions, and wiping off the stigma cast upon their order by the late defeat. Spies were sent to reconnoitre Zalea, and to communicate with the brother of the Moor; the sum to be paid as a recompense was adjusted and every arrangement made for the enterprize.

On the appointed night a party of Cavaliers set out under guidance of the Moor. When they came near to Zalea their leader bound the hands of the guide behind his back, and pledged his knightly word to strike him dead on the least sign of treachery, he then bade him lead the way. It was midnight when they arrived in silence under the walls of the citadel. At a low signal a ladder of ropes was let down. Gutiere Muñoz and Pedro de Alvanado were the first to ascend, followed by half a dozen others. They surprized the guard, cut them down, threw them over the wall, and gained possession of a tower. The alarm was given the whole citadel was in confusion, but already the Knights of Calatrava were in every part. They called each other to remember their brethren massacred in the valley of the Vega and their bloody heads born in triumph to Granada. They fought with sanguinary fury; most of the half armed and bewildered garrison were put to the sword, the rest were taken prisoners, in an hour they were masters of the citadel, and the town submitted of course. They found the magazines stored with all kinds of provisions with which they loaded an immense train of beasts of burden, for the relief of the famishing garrison of Alhama.

Thus did the gallant Knights of Calatrava gain the strong town of Zalea with scarcely any loss, and atone for the inglorious defeat sustained by their companions. Large reinforcements and supplies from the sovereigns arriving soon after, strengthened them in their own fortress and enabled them to keep possession of their new conquest. This gallant affair took place about the same time as the capture of Cambil and Alahar; and these two achievements gave a prosperous termination to the chequered events of this important year Ferdinand and Isabella retired for the winter to Alcalá de Henares where the Queen on the 16th of December gave birth to the infanta Catherine afterwards spouse to Henry VIII of England.

CHAPTER 35
DEATH OF OLD MULEY ABEN HASSAN.

The personal exploits with which El Zagal had commenced his reign, in surprizing the Knights of Calatrava and defeating the Count de Cabra had given him a transient popularity, which he had promoted by feasts and tournaments and other public rejoicings in which the Moors delighted. Knowing however the uncertain nature of the people over whom he reigned, he feared some capricious revolution in favour of his deposed brother Muley Aben Hassan. That once fiery old monarch, was now blind and bedridden and lived in a kind of durance in the city of Almuneçar. He was treated however, with deference and attention, for the garrison had been originally appointed by himself. El Zagal, having now a little leisure during the interval of the campaigns, became suddenly solicitous about the death of his brother, and had him removed to Salobreña for the benefit of purer and more salubrious air.

The small town of Salobreña was situated on a lofty hill, that rose out of the centre of a beautiful and fertile valley on the Mediterranean coast. It was protected by a strong castle, built by the Moorish Kings as a place of deposit for their treasures. There also they sent such of their sons and brothers as might endanger the security of their reign. They lived here, prisoners at large, in a state of voluptuous re,pose under a serene sky, in a soft climate and luxuriant valley. The palace was adorned with fountains and delicious gardens and perfumed baths: A harem of beauties was at the command of the royal captives, and music and the dance beguiled the lagging hours.

Nothing was denied them but the liberty to depart, that alone was wanting to render the abode a perfect paradise.

Notwithstanding the extreme salubrity of the air, blankspace, and the attentions of the commander, who was devoted to El Zagal, and had been particularly charged by him to be careful of his brother, the old monarch had not been removed here many days before he expired. There was nothing surprizing in this event, for life with him had been long glimmering in the socket, but the measures immediately taken by El Zagal roused the suspicions of the public, with indecent haste he ordered that the treasures of the deceased should be packed upon mules and brought to Granada, where he took possession of them, to the exclusion of the children. The Sultana Zorayna and her two sons were imprisoned in the Alhambra in the tower of Comares, the same place where by her instigation the virtuous Ayxa la Horra and her son Boabdil had once been confined. There she had leisure to ruminate on the disappointment of all her schemes, perfidiously executed for the advancement of those sons who were her fellow prisoners. The corpse of old Muley Aben Hassan was also brought to Granada, not in state, like the remains of a once powerful sovereign, but transported ignominiously on a mule. It received no funeral honours, but was borne obscurely to the grave by two christian captives, and deposited in the royal Osario or charnel house.*

No sooner were the people well assured that old Muley Aben Hassan was dead and buried, than they all with one accord began to deplore his loss and extol his virtuous memory They admitted that he had been fierce and cruel, but then he had been brave; he had, to be sure pulled down this war upon their heads; but he likewise had been crushed by it. In a word he was dead; and his death atoned for every fault; for a King just deceased is generally either a hero or a saint. In proportion as they ceased to hate Muley Aben Hassan, they began to hate his brother El Zagal. The manner of the old King's death, the eagerness to seize upon his treasures, the scandalous neglect of his corpse and the imprisonment of his Sultana and children, all filled the public mind with dark suspicions, and the name of El Zagal was often coupled with the epithet of Fratricide, in the low murmurings of the people.

As the public must always have some leading person to like, as well as to hate, there began once more to be an inquiry after Boabdil el Chico. That unfortunate monarch was living at Cordova, under the shade of the cold friendship of Ferdinand who had ceased to regard him with much attention when he had ceased to be useful to his interests. No sooner, however, did the public favour once more incline towards him, than the kindness of the Catholic monarch immediately revived. He furnished him with money and

*Cura de los Palacios cap. 77. [The scribal text reads "Casa."]

means again to elevate his standard and create a division in the Moorish power. By this assistance Boabdil established the shadow of a court at Valez el Blanco a strong frontier town on the confines of Murcia where he remained, as it were, with one foot over the border and ready to draw that back at a moment's warning. His presence however gave new life to his faction in Granada. It is true, the more courtly and opulent inhabitants of the quarter of the Alhambra still rallied round the throne of El Zagal, as the great seat of power; but then the inhabitants of the Albaycin, the poorest part of the community, who had nothing to ask and nothing to lose, were almost unanimous in favour of the indigent Boabdil. So it is in this wonderful system of sublunary affairs; the rich befriend the rich, the powerful stand by the powerful, while the poor enjoy the sterile assistance of the poor; thus each one seeks his kind, the admirable order of all things in maintained and a universal harmony prevails.

SEGMENTS USED AS COPYTEXT

With the exceptions listed below, copytext for the Twayne *Granada* has been the scribal/holograph manuscript located at the John Murray Archive, 50 Albemarle Street, London. Copytext for segments in Twayne lines listed on the left are:

3.2–5.16 Introduction and first paragraph (revised for Murray after the first version had been sent in): holograph, Barrett Collection, Univ. of Virginia.

8.25–8.33 p. 16 (missing from Murray): holograph, Pierpont Morgan Library.

10.11–10.17 unnumbered p. following p. 23 (missing from Murray): holograph, Pierpont Morgan Library.

119.13–124.9 chapters 34, 35, pp. 481–496 (reconstructed by Irving when the first Murray manuscript was inadvertently sent to Philadelphia): Berg Collection, New York Public Library.

164.6–169.20 chapters 50, 51, and first half of 52, pp. 629-647 (missing from Murray): English first edition (London: J. Murray, 1829).

198.1–198.13 unnumbered p. following p. 737 (missing from Murray): holograph, Pierpont Morgan Library.

213.4–213.10 unnumbered p. following p. 793 (missing from Murray): holograph, Pierpont Morgan Library.